RECREATION AND LEISURE IN MODERN SOCIETY

SECOND EDITION

RECREATION AND LEISURE IN MODERN SOCIETY

SECOND EDITION

RICHARD KRAUS
Temple University

GOODYEAR PUBLISHING CO., INC.

Santa Monica, California

Library of Congress Cataloging in Publication Data

Kraus, Richard G
  Recreation and leisure in modern society.

  Bibliography: p.
  1. Recreation—United States. 2. Leisure—United
States. 3. Recreation—Canada. 4. Leisure—Canada.
I. Title.
GV51.K7 1978   790'.0973   77-20705
ISBN 0-87620-811-1

Y-8111-0

ISBN: 0-87620-811-1

Current Printing (last digit):

10 9 8 7 6 5 4 3 2

Cover and Text Design: Bruce Kortebein

Production Editor: Pam Tully

Permissions Supervisor: Stacey Maxwell

Printed in the United States of America

To Michael and Vera Kraus

PREFACE

This is the second edition of a book which first appeared in 1971, and which has been widely used as a foundations text in departments of professional preparation in recreation, parks, and leisure studies. Although other excellent books have dealt with such separate areas as the history of recreation, psychology of play, or sociology of leisure, this was the first attempt to deal with all of these topics in a single text—as well as to provide a comprehensive picture of the overall leisure service delivery system.

How does this edition of *Recreation and Leisure in Modern Society* differ from the first?

The book has been reorganized so that, although it includes the same major sections, they have been placed in a more logical sequence. More important, it has been brought fully up to date in dealing with the critical changes in modern society which affect recreation and leisure—such as economic trends, growing concerns about the environment and energy needs, the changing relationships between the cities and their surrounding suburban communities, and the fuller priority being given to such groups as the physically or mentally disabled, the aging, the economically disadvantaged, ethnic and racial minorities, and girls and women.

Throughout, the conviction expressed in the first edition that recreation must be perceived as a vital form of community service, as well as a critical aspect of national economic and social well-being, has been strengthened and reinforced. The responsibility of the developing recreation and parks profession to deal effectively with significant social problems and needs continues to be a major theme of this text.

An additional change is that *Recreation and Leisure in Modern Society* now incorporates much more information and analysis regarding Canadian development in recreation and parks. While slower to develop in the leisure field than the United States, Canada has made remarkable strides over the past fifteen years, in terms of federal, provincial, and municipal recreation programs, and today has a number of outstanding university and college curricula in this area.

Acknowledgement should be made of professionals and educators who assisted in the preparation of this edition.

Particularly in gathering fresh information on Canada, the following educators were extremely helpful: Elliott Avedon and David Ng of the University of Waterloo, William Theobald, formerly of Waterloo and now at Purdue University, and David W. Parker of Mount Royal College. William Knott of the Ministry of Culture and Recreation in Ontario, provided a wealth of useful materials. Denny Neider of the Canadian Parks/Recreation Association, and such provincial or municipal administrators or public relations officers as Emmett H. Smith and Rick Curtis of the Province of Alberta, O. Johanson of Winnipeg, J. Boddington of Edmonton, and Terri Smith of Vancouver, also were generous with their help. Cor

Westland of Recreation Canada responded kindly to repeated requests for assistance, and a number of therapeutic recreation specialists, including Terry W. Knight and James M. Montagnes of the Penetanguishene, Ontario, Mental Health Centre, and Al Sinclair of the Midwestern Regional Centre in Palmerston, Ontario provided useful insights.

In the United States, literally hundreds of professionals sent statistics, reports, manuals and other publications describing the recreation-related functions and accomplishments of their organizations. For example, in the armed forces, the following gave full assistance: Col. Thomas D. Byrne and Col. Robert E. Carrell of the U.S. Army; Col. E. J. Artnak of the Marine Corps; John E. Moler of the Air Force; and George C. Schaefer of the Navy. Many administrators of major outdoor recreation agencies were helpful, including John Needy of the Tennessee Valley Authority and John R. Vosburgh of the National Park Service. A number of state officials assisted, including especially Russell Porter of the California State Department of Parks and Recreation. Charles Pezoldt of Metro Dade County, Florida, Richard C. Trudeau of the East Bay Regional Park District in California, Bob Zicker of King County, Washington, Oka T. Hester of Greenboro, North Carolina, and Glen Lyles of Mountain View, California, are only a few whose help should be acknowledged.

Dozens of voluntary organizations also provided useful information, and thanks are given to James Butler of Little League Baseball, Jane Edginton of the Sierra Club, Kit Mahon of Girls Clubs of America, Marisa Guerin of the National CYO Federation, Dale M. Lonheim of American Youth Hostels, Ara P. Warren of Girl Scouts of U.S.A., and William B. DeCarlo of the National Industrial Recreation Association.

The author would be remiss if he did not also mention the help he received from other recreation and park educators—either in terms of direct assistance, or through their writings, many of which are cited in this text. Specifically, he wishes to name the following outstanding professors who have provided strong leadership in this field and whose ideas have influenced his writing: Thomas Stein and H. Douglas Sessoms of the University of North Carolina; Janet MacLean of the University of Indiana; Leslie Reid of Texas A and M; James F. Murphy of the California State University at San Jose; Gerry O'Morrow of Indiana State University and Fred Humphrey of the University of Maryland; John Nesbitt of the University of Iowa; and Fred Martin of the California State University at Sacramento. Other individuals who have provided leadership in recent years include: Geoffrey Godbey and Betty van der Smissen of Pennsylvania State University; John Neulinger of the City University of New York and Rick Crandall of the University of Illinois, who have contributed to the emerging field of the psychology of leisure; two leading researchers, Doris Berryman of New York University and Diana R. Dunn, now of Arizona State University; Carlton Van Doren of Texas A and M; Elsie McFarland of the University of Alberta and Richard Knapp of the University of North Carolina, leading historians of the recreation and park movement in Canada and the United States; Joseph J. Bannon of the University of Illinois; Jean Mundy of Florida State; Seymour Gold of the University of California at Davis; two specialists in therapeutic recreation at the University of Illinois, Carol A. Peterson and Scout Lee Gunn; and especially David E. Gray, of the University of California at Los Angeles, who has consistently provided a quality of innovative and analytical thought that has been of immense value to the recreation and park field.

In conclusion, the author suggests that it is the purpose of this book not only to inform and explain, but also to arouse and challenge the reader. In this effort, he hopes that he has written an interesting, readable, and provocative text that will stimulate others—both faculty members and students alike—to do their own research and thinking, and that will contribute to better understanding of this field of growing national concern and importance

RICHARD KRAUS
Temple University
January, 1978

CONTENTS

RECREATION AND LEISURE IN MODERN SOCIETY

SECOND EDITION

ONE

CONCEPTS
OF RECREATION,
PLAY,
AND LEISURE

RECREATION AND LEISURE TODAY: AN OVERVIEW

The terms *recreation* and *leisure* convey a kaleidoscope of images—people playing tennis, a potter at the wheel, children climbing a playground jungle gym, a community symphony orchestra in rehearsal, a family touring a national park—and a host of other enjoyable pastimes or hobbies.

Such brief images, however, give only a partial understanding of the role of recreation and leisure in modern society. Like the blind men and the elephant, we all tend to know only what we experience directly, and so we have widely different perceptions of this subject. For some, recreation means the network of public agencies that provide such facilities as parks, playgrounds, golf courses, and community centers to serve people young and old in modern cities and towns. For others, recreation is found in a senior center or Golden Age club, a sheltered workshop for the mentally retarded, or a hospital for physical rehabilitation. Others may view recreation in economic terms, seeing it through the eyes of the manufacturer of sports equipment, the travel agent, or the amusement park operator. Still others may think of recreation and leisure chiefly as the source of important human values, providing the opportunity for emotional release, creative satisfaction, social gatherings, and other experiences linked to deep personal fulfillment.

The possibilities are endless. Recreation and leisure are concepts that have fascinated mankind since the golden age of Athens; they have been condemned in some societies and highly valued in others. In modern society, recreation and leisure represent major forms of human activity and experience, as well as important areas of governmental responsibility and economic development.

This text seeks to provide a comprehensive understanding of the field of recreation and leisure for students and professionals, with three major emphases: (1) an analysis of the scholarly meaning of recreation and leisure, as seen from the perspectives of such social and behavioral sciences as history, sociology, psychology, and economics; (2) a clear picture of the scope of recreation and leisure today, in terms of organized programs, sponsors, leadership, funding, and professional organizations; and (3) a discussion of the goals and overall philosophical base of the recreation and leisure field in modern society, as well as the problems, issues and challenges that face its leaders.

Why is such a broad understanding of the field of recreation and leisure essential for those who are, or who seek to become, its administrators, supervisors, and leaders? Why is it necessary to have not only a wide range of information about the field, but also an in-depth comprehension of its scholarly implications and major trends and issues?

The reason is that any field of service that seeks to be a *profession*—an area of significant public service, staffed by highly trained and well-qualified individuals— must have practitioners with more than a nuts-and-bolts knowledge of how to conduct its activities. Many millions of Americans and Canadians are able to direct recreation activities and do so regularly—in their families, as Scout leaders or Little League coaches, as hospital volunteers, and in dozens of other familiar settings. What distinguishes them from the recreation *professional* is that the professional must meet high standards of specialized training, be affiliated with appropriate organizations, and have a rich understanding of the full range of recreational needs, programs, and results.

It is the purpose of this text to present such information, thus providing a solid foundation of the behavioral and social principles underlying recreation and leisure in contemporary society. Recreation has traditionally been viewed as activity carried on within one's free time, chiefly for relaxation and self-renewal for further work. Only in recent years has recreation been seen as a valuable aspect of personal growth, a significant social institution, and an important community asset.

Similarly, play has historically been regarded as an aimless or childish pursuit. Today, however, we recognize that play is an important means of learning—a key element in the development of children and youth, and a widely found aspect of group behavior in all animal and human societies. The concept of leisure has also received considerable attention from political scientists, sociologists, and economists in recent years, and many theories of leisure have been proposed. The concept of leisure presented in this book is simply that leisure is discretionary time—time we can spend as we choose.

Indeed, the idea of choice is critical to any examination of recreation, play, and leisure. Past centuries, dominated by highly moralistic codes of behavior and the Protestant work ethic, tended to denigrate leisure and play as idleness—or worse, as the devil's work. Today, they are widely accepted; proponents of recreation extoll its ability to meet critical human needs, help build community solidarity, maintain sound mental health, and prevent or minimize juvenile delinquency and other forms of social pathology. Yet it is important to understand that recreation, play, and leisure are not inherently good *or* evil: they may be boring, time killing, superficial, or even self-degrading and destructive. On the other hand, recreation and leisure do provide the opportunity for positive growth, creative self-discovery, and the enhancement of the quality of life for *all* people.

To understand this fully and to have a sound philosophy of the goals and values of recreation and leisure in modern life, it is essential to understand its past history—and to be aware of its social, economic, and psychological characteristics in today's society. Should recreation be regarded chiefly as an amenity, or should it be supported as a form of social therapy? What are the recreation needs of such special

3

populations as women and girls, the aging, the poor, racial minorities, and the disabled? How do the priorities of organized recreation vary according to the community served—urban, suburban, small town, or rural? What is the relationship between the role of government in recreation in the United States and Canada, and the activities of other recreation sponsors? Such questions are dealt with fully in this text.

To set the stage, it is important to recognize that only during the past several decades have recreation and leisure assumed major importance as social institutions, forms of public service, and economic enterprises. In earlier times, although there were widespread forms of play, the scarcity of leisure and the prevalence of work-oriented social attitudes prevented the mass of the population from taking part freely in a range of recreation pursuits.

Social Factors Supporting the Recreation Movement

Today recreation pervades almost every area of American life and involves tremendous energy, interest, and expenditure, both by participants and by those who sponsor recreation programs. What are the factors that led to the growth of the recreation movement, and to the establishment of government, voluntary, private, and commercial recreation services? The following passage describes them briefly; they are analyzed in fuller detail in later chapters.

The Growth of Leisure

In modern industrial society, leisure has grown markedly for most people. Thanks to advanced mechanical processes in factories, agriculture, and the service fields, the productive capacity of workers has increased dramatically. In effect, the workweek has been cut in half since the early days of the Industrial Revolution.

More holidays and longer vacations are now being granted to American and Canadian workers. With improved social security benefits and pension plans, average employees are assured fifteen or more years of full-time leisure following retirement. Taken altogether, these factors mean that we have been given a dramatic gift of free time to spend throughout our lives, in ways of our own choosing. One major research study has estimated that most adults have between twenty-five and fifty hours of unobligated time per week, and that younger and older persons have between fifty and seventy such hours per week.[1] With the exception of a small percentage of more heavily committed individuals (such as highly paid professionals and business executives), the average employed adult has far more hours of leisure per year than he has of paid work.

Increasing Affluence

Over the past several decades and particularly during the so-called soaring sixties (as some financial analysts called them), the Western world has witnessed a steady growth of national income, buying power, and total productivity. In the 1960s personal income in the United States climbed from $383 billion to $686 billion, and the gross national product almost doubled. Although the rate of growth slowed markedly during the 1970s—because of widespread inflation, unemployment, and a recession—today more and more people have substantial sums to spend on hobbies, entertainment, television sets, vacation travel, and a host of other leisure pursuits. Indeed, recreation spending today has been estimated as close to $200 billion per year in the United States (see chapter 5).

As a consequence, participation in recreation activities has increased tremendously in modern society. With the exception of such population groups as the aging, the poor, and the disabled, Americans and Canadians are now able to indulge their leisure wishes to a point never before possible.

Higher Level of Education

Research studies have determined that those with an advanced education tend to engage more widely and intensely in recreation. The Outdoor Recreation Resources Review Commission found that those with a college education engaged in a greater number of outdoor recreation activities, and on far more occasions per year, than those who held only high-school diplomas.

One of the effects of higher education is to expose the individual to a variety of ideas and experiences, inevitably broadening his leisure interests, promoting habits of varied recreation participation—in music, art, and literature, in travel, in sports and outdoor recreation, and in many kinds of community service. The increasingly high proportion of modern youth attending college (it has been estimated that currently about 55 percent of those who finish high school go to college) will continue to stimulate participation in a wide range of leisure pursuits.

Expanding Population

There has been a striking population growth in the Western world. In 1967, the population of the United States reached 200 million.

By 1976, the population was about 215 million. Similarly, the population of Canada, although much smaller, has continued to grow steadily—from 19 million in 1964 to almost 23 million in 1976. Although the fertility rate declined sharply in the 1970s, the population has nevertheless continued to expand, with clear implications for recreation. Great new numbers of people will require leisure activities, particularly older persons, who make up an increasingly high proportion of the population.

Urbanization and Suburbanization

One of the key factors in the early development of the recreation movement was the growth of America's factory cities. Millions of immigrants settled in urban areas during the nineteenth and early twentieth centuries, joining the great numbers of people who left rural areas to find work in the cities. As people huddled together in crowded slums without natural places for play or the traditional social customs of the countryside, it became obvious that leisure posed an important problem for industrial urban society.

5

So it was that the recreation movement in the United States and Canada got under way. It took the form of playgrounds for children, playfields for youth and adults, networks of parks throughout our cities, and the establishment of settlement houses, community centers, and "character-building" organizations for children and youth. Thus, urbanization resulted in a need for organized recreation service that was met by both public and voluntary agencies.

The most striking aspect of growth in metropolitan regions today is suburbanization. Great numbers of people (particularly in the United States) have moved out of the cities into large, new suburban settlements. In some cases the cities themselves have expanded to incorporate these suburbs, but in most they remain independent—exclusive from and in competition with their parent communities. Meanwhile, millions of the poor have moved into the central cities from impoverished rural areas, bringing with them the many problems of welfare, crime, housing, and education. This development has radically affected the provision of recreation and parks since in spite of limited budgets, the cities are being asked to serve populations with new recreation needs and interests.

Population Mobility

Another important factor contributing to the growth of the recreation movement has been the increased mobility of the population. When the automobile first became popular, it gave a major impetus to recreational participation. People left their homes in droves to seek amusement. They drove at night to theaters, movie houses, dance halls, bowling alleys, and nightclubs. They thronged in their Model T's and Model A's to the great new stadiums built during the 1920s to see professional baseball, college football, and championship boxing matches.

Travel in itself became a popular new pastime, resulting in the widespread development of state, provincial, and national parks, seashores, and recreation areas. Tourism—by train, car, boat, and plane—emerged as a major industry, tied to the development of major amusement complexes and to charter flights and tours arranged through industry, membership organizations, and even public recreation and park departments. Thus, the increasing mobility of the average family became a key aspect of modern recreation and leisure.

Advances in Modern Technology

Closely related to mobility in its action as a major stimulus to recreational participation is the development of modern technology. In addition to creating vast amounts of new leisure through greater employee productivity, technology has also removed much of the toil from our everyday lives by providing such labor-saving devices as dishwashers, power mowers, and snowblowers, and by introducing frozen foods and similar convenience items. Technology has made traditional pastimes more accessible through such innovations as artificial ice-skating rinks, snow-making machines, and ski lifts, and has made entirely new forms of play available to us, including skin diving and scuba diving, electronic games, and—most pervasive of all—home television entertainment.

6

The Cultural Explosion

A vital aspect of the recreation movement throughout the United States and Canada has been the so-called cultural explosion. Following World War II, there was a remarkable surge of interest in the graphic and plastic arts, in theater going, literature, music, and dance, and in museum attendance in both countries. The growth of music provides a dramatic example. In 1966, a survey conducted by the American Symphony Orchestra League indicated that since 1950 there had been an 85-percent increase in the number of persons playing musical instruments in the United States.[2] In terms of the number of orchestras, bands, dance bands, opera productions, and school-age instrumentalists, the growth rate was nearly five times that of the nation's population during the same period.

In Canada, there was similar growth on all levels, with considerable assistance provided by Canada Council on the national scene, and by numerous provincial cultural authorities. It should be noted, however, that the term *cultural explosion* refers to an essentially *amateur* and therefore recreational approach to the arts. This growth of interest has been marked by several factors, including the building of numerous community cultural centers, the sponsorship of expanded arts programs by many colleges and universities, and the increased aid given by government to individual artists and performing groups. Surveys carried out in the 1970s by Louis Harris and other leading research firms have indicated that public opinion has grown more and more favorable toward the arts, and that they are now viewed as an essential contribution to the quality of everyday life.[3]

The Expansion of Social Welfare

A striking aspect of government policy over the past several decades has been the expansion of social-welfare programs for population groups suffering from disability or deprivation. Instead of the callous disregard shown such special populations in past centuries, today there are concerted efforts to meet their human needs and, whenever possible, to help them find meaningful roles in society.

Within the recreation movement this trend was most strikingly illustrated by the growth of concern about retarded children and youth that began in the early 1960s under the administration of President Kennedy. The Kennedy Foundation joined forces with the Federal and state governments and a number of professional organizations in physical education and recreation to promote recreation services for the retarded. This coalition initiated research, supported demonstration projects and pilot programs, and helped prepare professional personnel.

During the middle 1960s, concern also began to grow about the plight of aging persons in the United States. Based on the recommendations of the earlier White House Conferences on Aging, the establishment of the Federal Administration on Aging through the Older Americans Act of 1965 gave a major impetus to recreation planning for the aging. Substantial assistance was given to the preparation of professional personnel to work with the aging, and to new multiservice programs throughout the nation meeting their needs.

This trend has given rise to a major area of professional service in recreation for special populations. Known originally as hospital recreation or recreation

7

therapy, today this field is widely identified as *therapeutic recreation service*. During its early period of development it was found almost exclusively in hospitals and other treatment institutions. Today, many programs for special populations are provided in the community itself, in day-care centers, sheltered workshops, special clubs, and similar settings.

Professional Development in Recreation and Parks

For several decades, recreation was a highly fragmented field of public service, its administrative functions housed in a variety of settings: park departments, recreation departments, school boards, departments of highways, public properties, and even welfare departments. Practitioners belonged to a variety of professional organizations, each with a different focus—one for professional recreation workers, another for lay groups, another for park managers, and yet another for therapeutic recreation specialists. The consequence of this fragmentation is that the public's perception of recreation has often been limited and unclear.

Within the past two decades, however, the recreation field has developed a much clearer and more visible image. Many public departments have merged park and recreation functions, thus strengthening and increasing their efficiency in this area of service. Stronger programs of registration, Civil Service screening procedures, and in some cases certification or licensing have resulted in a higher caliber of individuals entering the field. Several major national organizations joined together in the United States in 1965 to establish the National Recreation and Park Association; in Canada a similar body, the Canadian Parks/Recreation Association, has helped unify the recreation profession and promote its positive image. Another key factor has been the rapid growth of college and university curricula in recreation and parks; by the mid-1970s there were about 350 programs of professional preparation in the United States and Canada.

Public Attitudes toward Recreation

Until quite recently, Americans and Canadians tended to have a narrow and repressive view of recreation and leisure. The Puritan heritage in colonial New England strongly forbade many forms of play and recreation. While much of the opposition to such activities had been overcome by the time of the American Revolution, during the nineteenth-century industrial expansion Americans continued to regard work as the most important element in life, a belief reflected in popular morality and even in religious teaching.

With the growth of leisure and affluence for large sectors of the population have come a new acceptance and respect for recreation, both as a form of personal expression and as an area of public responsibility. This acceptance has been supported by voters in the most practical and meaningful way—through increased budgets for the expansion of park and recreation facilities and programs on all levels of government. This support is based on a growing public recognition that organized recreation accomplishes more than simply using up idle hours—it meets important social and personal needs in our society.

8

The Leisure-Service Delivery System Today

In examining the present scope of organized recreation service, it is important to recognize that it has four major components in modern society. These are:

1. *Government agencies*—Federal, state, and provincial agencies, and local departments of recreation and parks—that provide leisure services as a primary function, as well as hundreds of other agencies (such as those concerned with social service, education, special populations, and the armed forces) that offer or assist recreation programs as a secondary responsibility.

2. *Voluntary organizations*—nongovernmental, nonprofit agencies, both sectarian and nonsectarian, serving the public at large or selected elements of it with multiservice programs that often include a substantial element of recreational opportunity. Such organizations include national youth programs like the Boy Scouts and Girl Scouts, and the YMCA and YWCA.

3. *Private membership organizations,* such as golf, tennis, yacht, athletic, and country clubs, along with a wide range of service clubs and fraternal bodies, that provide recreational and social activities for their own members and in some cases assist community recreation needs as well.

4. *Commercial recreation enterprises,* including a great variety of privately owned, profit-oriented businesses, such as stadiums, ski centers, bowling alleys, nightclubs, movie houses, theaters, health spas, dancing schools, and amusement parks.

These four types of organizations tend to operate independently in most communities, offering a wide range of leisure services. In some cases, they are intended to meet significant community needs or to accomplish valuable social goals. In others, their sole aim is to satisfy the interests and wishes of their members, or to clear a substantial profit. Although there is considerable duplication of services in many areas—particularly in many metropolitan areas where side-by-side government agencies may offer similar facilities and programs without coordinated planning—in some regions there is a strong trend toward cooperative planning and even joint sponsorship arrangements among community departments.

As organized recreation service continues to expand, it must meet several important challenges. These are key issues and problems facing the recreation profession in the United States and Canada; they are outlined briefly in the remainder of this chapter, and discussed more fully in later sections of the text.

Challenges Facing the Recreation Movement

The Challenge of Increased Leisure

If past trends continue, we will move steadily toward an era in which there will be an overwhelming bulk of leisure for most of the population. Some social scientists have actually estimated that within a few decades we might approach the point where 2 percent of the nation's workers would be able to produce all the goods needed for the entire population.[4] On the face of it, this would appear immensely appealing. It would mean that for the first time in history the average man or woman would no longer be compelled to work long hours each day, but would be free to carry on pursuits that bring pleasure, creative fulfillment, relaxation, growth, and knowledge. With a considerably shortened workweek, more frequent holidays and vacations, and a longer period of retirement, the amount of discretionary time would expand tremendously.

However, the trend in employment in recent years has *not* been to give all classes of workers an equal proportion of increased leisure. Instead, the highly skilled professional or managerial worker continues to work long hours, while lower-level workers have shorter work schedules. Unless artificial restraints are exerted on industry and unions to keep people at work, it appears that there will be few jobs in the years to come for the least capable and most poorly educated people in our society. Those with marginal skills will probably have intermittent periods of employment or none at all. Labor economists assure us that the manual jobs that used to occupy such workers are rapidly disappearing.

How will such people live if there is no work for them to do? The welfare process, which removes pride and incentive, has been responsible for perpetuating the poverty cycle for large numbers of disadvantaged families. It would appear that some alternative solution—such as a guaranteed annual income, or government-sponsored employment—is inevitable as a replacement for welfare.

But even if economic support is supplied for this mass of individuals, how do we meet their need for the sense of satisfaction and self-worth that comes from work? If people no longer have work to fill substantial portions of their time and to provide them with a sense of making a contribution to society, what other commitments or outlets will they find? How can our society as a whole meet this challenge of ever-increasing leisure? Will we use it in empty, negative, ultimately demoralizing ways? Or will we discover ways to use leisure so that it makes life more fulfilling and rewarding, and contributes constructively to the physical, cultural, and intellectual well-being of the nation?

If great masses of people are unemployed, will they be able to *enjoy* their free time—and will the working portion of society feel that these people *deserve* leisure as such, and be willing to subsidize recreational opportunities for them? With the continued decline of the work ethic and of work itself, we will have to come to grips with the nonwork spheres of our lives and find fuller satisfaction and meaning in leisure as a rich opportunity for self-development, creative growth, continued education, and community service.

The Challenge of Education for Leisure

Far from being a strictly contemporary concern, the need to educate for leisure was recognized in a number of earlier societies. Even in ancient Athens (as a later chapter will show) the proper use of leisure was very much the concern of philosophers like Plato and Aristotle; education for the young Athenian citizen was heavily based on developing the arts of leisure for lifelong use.

In the United States, with the publication in 1918 of the National

Education Association's report *Cardinal Principles of Secondary Education,* there was formal recognition for the first time of the need to prepare people for the constructive and creative use of leisure.[5] The alternative—that without such education great masses of free time might be used in negative or socially pathological ways—was clearly seen. Through the decades that followed, however, few school or college educators have actually attempted to come to grips with leisure as a serious concern, or to deal effectively with it in their curricula. If education is to be concerned with the real lives of students, it must prepare them to use their time wisely and constructively. In addition to the total process of general education—with in-depth exposure to the arts, literature, science, social studies, and other areas clearly relevant to the creative use of leisure—there should be a direct concern with exploring the role of leisure in society and in one's own life.

This can no longer be seen as solely within the province of the formal educational structure—the established schools and colleges of the nation. Many other kinds of agencies educate people of all ages for leisure. Business and industrial concerns, the armed forces, religious organizations, and rehabilitative agencies all offer courses and special leisure programs for adults, in some cases specially designed to equip them to use their retirement fruitfully. Individualized or small-group leisure counseling is increasingly being provided for disabled individuals who are re-entering community life.

Realistically, however, only a small percentage of the population is being reached effectively by such programs of leisure education and counseling. Most people have had no systematic exposure to leisure education, and remain largely unaware of the potential value of leisure in their lives. How can the recreation profession promote such awareness nationwide? While the National Recreation and Park Association has mounted pilot programs in this direction, establishing this public awareness remains a critical challenge facing the recreation field today.

The Needs of Special Populations

A closely allied concern is the needs of those who have special emotional, mental, social, or physical disabilities. While a steady growth of concern about such populations has accompanied the development of therapeutic recreation service, great numbers of aging persons still remain isolated, without adequate recreational opportunity. The same is true of the mentally retarded, the orthopedically disabled, and the neurologically impaired. The strong movement to take the mentally ill out of custodial institutions and help them in community-based facilities in many cases has resulted in no recreational or activity therapy programs provided at all for such persons. Probably most severely deprived of all the groups with "enforced leisure" is the group of people confined to penal or correctional institutions, many of which lack any sort of organized recreation programs at all.

Less dramatic (but equally important) are the needs of other special populations who have been systematically underserved by public and voluntary recreation agencies. These include the economically disadvantaged in both urban and rural settings who lack the money to use private or commercial facilities as well as the mobility and knowledge to take advantage of available public resources. Other such populations include women and girls—who have historically received services inferior to those provided for males—and racial and ethnic minority groups. What is needed is a concerted effort to examine the programs and services available today, and to take positive steps to provide a fuller level of needed service to those groups with the greatest leisure needs.

Environmental and Energy-Related Needs

Closely linked to the growth of the recreation movement in the United States and Canada has been the effort in both countries to protect and reclaim the environment from thoughtless pollution and damage by industrial and residential development, indiscriminate strip mining, logging, the flooding of streams and lakes with chemicals and waste, and the destruction of wildlife breeding areas. A number of significant environmental programs have been initiated in the United States since the mid-1960s, with the Federal government helping the states to acquire massive amounts of land for outdoor-recreation purposes, as well as helping them with beautification, waste disposal, and air and water cleanup efforts.

Similar efforts have been made throughout Canada, but the battle is only beginning. Conservation efforts require a realistic determination of national values and priorities, particularly in those cases where industrial development and job opportunity for the residents of a region conflict directly with the need to protect and set aside natural resources that might otherwise be lost forever. This often involves a choice between short-range benefits and long-range losses. Even when land has been successfully set aside for national-, state-, or regional-park purposes, there is the question of how it should be used. Recreation itself can cause forest "slums" or lake or stream "cesspools," through the destruction of vegetation and wildlife, littering, and the poisoning of the natural environment. The increased use of off-road vehicles like motorcycles and snowmobiles is a vivid example of such abuse. What is needed is a clear differentiation of appropriate recreational uses (such as "high density," "general outdoor recreation," or "historic and cultural") and a classification system that protects natural and primitive areas from any form of destructive intrusion.

This problem is closely linked to the problem of energy conservation, which first appeared as a major worldwide issue with the oil shortage of the early 1970s. It seems clear that we can no longer live with values that permit both a ruthless pollution of the environment and wasteful and unnecessary uses of the world's limited and unrenewable resources. In many ways we have moved into a new "era of limits" affecting the way we live, work, and play. Waste recycling, smaller vehicles, the use of alternative heating systems, more healthful diets, and more exercise are all likely to result from this trend. Experts predict that travel patterns in particular will change sharply in response to this situation, accompanied by an increased use of nearby recreation and park facilities. People will tend to camp in one location rather than go on long vacations on the road. Mass transit may be used more and more for vacation travel, with a preference for airplane rather than automobile transportation. Thus, the continuing energy shortage will have a strong impact on national recreation patterns.[6]

Clearly, the process of developing programs and policies that will maintain a balance between human needs (both economic and recreational) and environmental and energy concerns is one of the most difficult challenges facing recreation-and-park professionals and planners today.

The Challenge of Planning

Implicit in the preceding sections has been the crucial need today for more effective concepts and models of recreation and park planning. In the past, urban land-use planning consisted of defining the major uses to which land should be put (based on existing resources and projected population and economic trends) and then zoning areas of the city for development, renewal, or other specified functions. Recreation-and-park planning was based on concepts of "neighborhood" and "community" (see chapter 15), and on standards for spaces and facilities which were widely accepted by professional organizations and government agencies.

Today it is recognized by many planning authorities that this traditional approach to planning needs radical rethinking. The assumption that all neighbor-hoods have similar needs and are to be served equally has worked neither in practice nor in theory. Because of rapid population shifts, changing patterns of living, and new kinds of urban problems, there is a need for more innovative and sophisticated city planning.

Complex metropolitan governmental structures—with overlapping school, township, municipality, and park districts—call for new levels of cooperation and coordinated planning. In many cases regional action has been initiated by a number of linked cities and states. Local government today is assisted by state and Federal authorities in open-space acquisition and resource development, and in a number of cases Federal, state, or provincial authorities have developed parks in or close to central cities.

The critical challenge, then, is to put in motion planning that will involve *all* appropriate levels of government and agencies in developing not only facilities, but operational systems to meet today's urgent community needs. Planning must involve more than space and facilities; it must deal with programs, personnel, and budgets, as well as such elements as transportation, law enforcement, and related social programs.

The Challenge of Fiscal Support

It has been pointed out that America's leisure resources and programs have expanded impressively in recent years. However, only about 5 percent of the total amount spent on recreation each year comes from the budgets of governmental or voluntary agencies; the rest is spent for commercial or private-membership activities.

This means that as a nation we are entirely willing to spend many billions of dollars on commercially purchased pleasure—including gambling, alcohol, and similar forms of amusement—but that we lend only grudging and limited support to programs that serve the public at large with constructive and creative leisure opportunities. In a period of growing inflation and increased demands upon government, recreation is obviously at a disadvantage when budgets are cut, since its importance must be measured against that of services critical for the survival of the population.

The problem has become more difficult in recent years, with more and more middle- and upper-class families meeting their leisure needs through private arrangements, such as pools, tennis courts, and other recreation facilities attached to condominiums and apartments. Such individuals tend to resist expansion or

13

added support for recreation and parks on the local level, unless they perceive this expansion as meeting their needs directly.

Many communities are placing increased reliance on special fees and charges to help pay the costs of operating programs or even to amortize the costs of developing facilities. Such charges tend to exclude from participation those at the lower end of the socioeconomic scale. The poor—who need public leisure opportunities the most—are served the least. Clawson and Knetsch have pointed out that

> In a great many American cities, park and playground acreage is more unevenly distributed than is personal income. The lowest income areas of the city have an even smaller share of recreation area than they have of personal income, while the highest income sections have relatively generous parks and recreation areas. . . . This situation is made still worse by the racial pattern of urban living. The low-income central city areas so deficient in recreation space are likely to be Negro; the suburban and outer city ring areas, generously supplied with recreation, are likely to be white. One of the great myths of the outdoor recreation field is that free public parks are a boon to "poor" people; actually it is the poor who frequently lack them. [7]

While other methods of funding might be explored, the real need is to provide a substantial degree of support for community recreation from regular tax funds. In *The Affluent Society,* John Kenneth Galbraith made the point that Americans in particular have been willing to spend huge sums *privately* to purchase expensive goods and services, but have been unwilling to spend enough of their incomes to support essential public services.[8] He suggests that many of our most serious social problems, particularly those of today's youth, stem from this reluctance to divert our financial resources as a nation from private spending to public spending. As we attempt to bridge the gap between the haves and the have-nots in our society and to meet the needs of those with enforced leisure but limited financial resources, we will have to meet the challenge of providing fuller fiscal support for organized community recreation services.

The Challenge of Professional Development

As recreation-and-park programs continue to expand as an area of significant public service throughout the United States and Canada, it will be essential to strengthen leadership, supervision, and administration in the field.

One important problem has been the failure of the recreation field to present a single clear image to the public. This is in part because the recreation movement has had diverse roots in the modern era, and in part because its practitioners have received training in a variety of specialized fields (or, too often, in none). It will therefore be necessary to define the preparation of recreation professionals more precisely, to indicate that it is an umbrellalike field covering many specializations, which nevertheless contains an important core of theoretical knowledge. This common core will strengthen higher education in recreation, parks, or leisure studies—as well as in the more specialized areas of preparation—giving the diverse branches of recreation a common identity. Clearly, this revision of education for the recreation field will have to be supported by a more effective system of curriculum accreditation than has existed over the past two decades (see chapter 12).

We must also improve personnel practices in the recreation and park field. We must develop ways to: recruit qualified candidates systematically; screen all professionals through state, national, or other systems of registration, certification, or upgraded civil service standards; and clarify the relationship of recreation to other important fields of community service. Particularly in the great cities and their surrounding metropolitan areas, it will become increasingly important to encourage minority-group members, the disadvantaged, women, and the disabled to enter the recreation field professionally—and to provide them with the opportunity for real career advancement.

The Challenge of the Cities

Without question, among the most serious social problems facing Americans today is the condition of the cities. Our giant urban complexes are in one sense the pride of our nation; they are the seat of business and industry, communications, culture, and higher education. At the same time, many of them are wracked by congestion, growing crime, slums, poverty, and other pathologies of body and spirit. The urban riots that took place during the 1960s were only one symbol of the discontent endemic in America's cities. Equally significant was the flight of millions of white middle-class families to the suburbs and the consequent socioeconomic and racial polarization of many metropolitan areas.

But it is clear that America's cities are not going to be abandoned. Many people who moved from the cities years ago have returned to them, finding them centers of excitement, vitality, and rich opportunity for living. Some of our widely shared stereotypes about cities have been dispelled; for example, a recent survey showed that mental health in urban centers is significantly *better* than in rural areas.[9] And it is clear that while the problems of the cities are great, so is the determination to solve them.

What is the role of recreation in this hoped-for transformation of the nation's great urban centers? It must be recognized that urban problems are not just abstract questions of the economy, housing, education, or crime; they involve the human spirit and the total quality of life available to urban residents. Planners and investors are coming to recognize that the city must be transformed into a pleasant and happy environment in which to live. In city after city in which slums have been replaced by new middle- or mixed-income developments, the provision of attractive and varied recreation facilities and programs has been recognized as one of the key elements in attracting and holding new residents.

The Challenge of Change

We are living in a world of rapid social and technological change. Inventions have transformed the means of production and the character of daily living, of travel, and of business. The computer-based economy, the tremendous proliferation of knowledge, shifting lifestyles, and the impact of energy shortages all affect our lives radically.

Beyond the obvious physical and economic changes have been even more striking spiritual and moral changes. Many of the rules and values long accepted in society no longer hold. What was first described as the "beat" and then the "hippie" movement represented far more than a comparatively small segment of American youth's "tuning out" by seeking sexual freedom and a hedonistic way of life. Today a substantial number of young people—not only in the United States and Canada but throughout the world—are challenging old values and seeking to establish a new, franker, and freer kind of society. Family structure is far less stable and secure today than in the past, and both parental and religious authority have been sharply undermined.

Minorities of every kind—racial, ethnic, economic, sexual, and minorities of age—today seek a fuller role in community life, and a stronger voice in their own affairs. It will be the task of today's and tomorrow's recreation-and-park professionals to meet such demands creatively, with innovative and meaningful responses. Among the trends identified for the years immediately ahead are expanded interest in physical fitness, hobbies, the arts, community service, adult education, and outdoor recreation—with a strong emphasis on activities involving active participation and creative self-discovery, rather than on passive forms of entertainment.[10]

It is predicted that in the anticipated "era of limits" lifestyles will become more economical, with living space shrinking, more family members working part time or interchanging traditional roles, more rehabilitation of older homes, greater emphasis on healthful diet and activity, and greater use of low-energy-cost forms of mass or personal transportation. Within this context recreation and leisure are bound to be influenced by, and to play an important role in, the adjustment to new conditions and needs. How effective the field will be will depend in large part on its professional leaders. Their ability to develop creative solutions to new social problems and to enlist the support of community residents and agencies for their programs will be critical in the years ahead.

Recreation and park professionals obviously see themselves in a variety of roles. Some regard their mission as essentially to provide needed facilities and services in a "nuts-and-bolts" operation. They see their work as a matter of practical logistics, as any civil servant or businessman manufacturing a product might do. Such individuals do not see themselves as civic leaders or as people who shape community life significantly; instead, they are people who meet a concrete need in the most efficient and practical way possible.

On the other hand, many recreation-and-park professionals do regard themselves as people with a "mission." They feel their task is to impart a new vision of creative and holistic leisure to the public at large. They see recreation as a means of dealing with critical social needs and problems—of serving the disabled, preventing delinquency, improving intergroup relations, and building community unity. For them, recreation is a significant tool for bringing about constructive social change.

Still other professionals—particularly college educators and researchers—tend to see recreation and leisure in scholarly and somewhat abstract terms. In their eyes, the study of the sociological and psychological aspects of leisure and play represents the heart of professional concern.

Some educators and practitioners regard recreation and leisure as a scientifically based field with roots in engineering and management science. Such individuals make heavy use of systems approaches to planning, developing complicated models and processes for decision making.

In contrast, many professional and lay leaders have a highly environmen-

16

talist viewpoint, placing natural and aesthetic values uppermost in their thinking. Others have extremely vague, theoretical, or idealistic views of the nature of recreation and its potential. Some are grandiose in their claims for recreation and leisure, while many others are modest to the point of being apologetic for the field.

A Stance for Professionals

Given this wide range of personal orientations and ambitions, what is an appropriate stance for recreation-and-park professionals in the years ahead? Despite charges that they sometimes seek to be "all things to all people," it would seem that perhaps this is what leisure practitioners *must* be.

In their work they must deal with land, people, machines, budgets, and governmental processes. They must be concerned with human goals, frailties, and moral and spiritual values. They must balance rehabilitative needs with economic necessity, engineering principles with social problems, scholarship with reality. They must be hardheaded businessmen and businesswomen at the same time that they are community organizers, propagandists, preachers, teachers, therapists, planners, and scholars. They must be both modest and realistic in their claims, and ambitious in their vision of what recreation can provide in community life.

To accomplish this general task, it is essential that recreation-and-park practitioners have a comprehensive historical and contemporary understanding of their field—its traditions, theories, and specializations. If they are to be effective spokesmen for recreation as a vital form of community service, they must be thoroughly familiar with its goals and objectives, patterns of sponsorship and programming, and research findings. It is the purpose of this text to provide this in-depth understanding of the field.

Chapter One

1. *The Challenge of Leisure: A Southern California Case Study* (Claremont: Southern California Research Council, Pomona College, 1967), p. 17.
2. "Concert Music U.S.A., 1966," *Music Journal,* February 1966, p. 94.
3. "Survey Reveals Positive Attitude Toward Arts," *Parks and Recreation,* June 1974, p. 6.
4. Richard Bellman, quoted in Edward T. Chase, "Four Days Shalt Thou Labor," *New York Times Magazine,* 20 September 1964, p. 28.
5. *Cardinal Principles of Secondary Education: Report of the Commission on the Reorganization of Secondary Education of the National Education Association,* Bureau of Education Bulletin no. 35 (Washington, D.C.: Department of the Interior, 1918).
6. See "Research Notes" in *Canada Tourism News,* May 1975, p. 3.
7. Marion Clawson and Jack L. Knetsch, *Econmics of Outdoor Recreation* (Baltimore: Johns Hopkins Press, 1960), p. 151.
8. John Kenneth Galbraith, *The Affluent Society* (Boston: Houghton Mifflin, 1958), pp. 256–57.
9. "Mentally, the Urban Life Beats the Rural," *New York Times,* 8 May 1977, p. E-7.
10. "How Americans Pursue Happiness," *U.S. News and World Report,* 23 May 1977, pp. 60–76.

PLAY, RECREATION, AND LEISURE: A CONCEPTUAL ANALYSIS

An examination of the broad field of recreation and leisure in modern society reveals that the terms *recreation* and *leisure* themselves are often used ambiguously; they need to be clearly defined, along with a closely related term— *play.*

There are several major theories of leisure, each with widely varying implications for the role and significance of leisure in contemporary life. Recreation may be viewed simply as a means of restoring people for renewed work through relaxing and pleasurable activity, or it may be defined as a separate and highly meaningful form of human activity. Play is often thought of as a trivial and childish activity; yet it has been described by psychologists and anthropologists as a critical aspect of human development, and as an activity found in all human societies. It therefore becomes necessary for us to explore the conceptual meaning of each of these terms.

A variety of scholarly disciplines contributes to our understanding of the recreation and leisure field. Today recreation and leisure represent multidisciplinary areas of learning and professional practice. Philosophers, psychologists, and sociologists may all study patterns of leisure behavior—but so too may economists, political scientists, or even geographers, historians, anthropologists, and folklorists. Each of these areas of scholarship is reflected in the pages that follow.

The Meaning of Play

For centuries, the term play has been used as a synonym for recreation. Indeed, in the United States and Canada what began with children's playgrounds and after-school programs gradually evolved into today's recreation movement, covering a much broader span of ages and interests. Exactly what *is* the meaning of play? *Is* it identical with recreation?

The word *play* is derived from the Anglo-Saxon *plega,* meaning a game or sport, skirmish, fight, or battle. This is related to the Latin *plaga,* meaning a blow, stroke, or thrust. It is illustrated in the idea of striking or stroking an instrument or playing a game by striking a ball. Other languages have words derived from a common root (such as the German *spielen* and the Dutch *spelen)* whose meanings include the playing of games, sports, and musical instruments.

The most common understanding of play is that it consists of enjoyable activities that we engage in for their own sake, in a free and spontaneous way. Mitchell defined play as "self-expression for its own sake."[1]

Play is traditionally thought of as a child's activity, in contrast to recreation, which is usually described as an adult activity. De Grazia expresses this view, saying:

> Play is what children do, frolic and sport. . . . Adults play too, though their games are less muscular and more intricate. Play has a special relation to leisure. . . . When adults play, as they do, of course, they play for recreation.[2]

Kaplan reinforces this view, suggesting that the term play is used in one of two senses:

> (a) a light, informal, make-believe action, such as the play of children;
> (b) a more formal, stylized, intense and even serious presentation of some aspect of life on a "stage."[3]

It is an oversimplification, however, to think of play as just frolic and sport, or as light, informal, make-believe activity. Throughout history, the phenomenon of play has been a serious concern of philosophers and educators; from the time of ancient Greece, they have written of its value in raising children (see chapter 6). The first serious attempts to define play and to formulate theories that would clarify its essential purpose occurred in the nineteenth and early twentieth centuries. Six theories of play gained prominence in Europe and America at this time.

Early Theories of Play

Surplus-Energy Theory

The English philosopher Herbert Spencer, in his mid-nineteenth-century work *Principles of Psychology,* advanced the view that play was primarily motivated by the need to burn up excess energy. He was influenced by the earlier writing of Friedrich von Schiller, who had suggested that when animals or birds were fully fed and had no other survival needs, they vented their exuberant energy in a variety of aimless and pleasurable forms of play. Schiller thus saw play as essentially purposeless. Spencer extended this theory, adding two components: the elements of imitation and a physiological explanation of play. Based on the observation of animals, he pointed out that play . . . is very commonly simulation of the types of activities which an organ carries on when it is being forced to exercise processes conducive to life. . . . so with the kitten running after a cotton-ball, making it roll and catching it, crouching as though in ambush and then leaping on it, we see that the whole sport is a dramatization of the pursuit of prey . . . an ideal satisfaction for the destructive instincts in the absence of real satisfaction for them.[4]

Spencer saw play among children as representing the dramatization of adult activities; the sport of boys, such as chasing, wrestling, and taking one another prisoner, involved "predatory instincts." Even the games of skill practiced by adults were seen as involving the same motivation—satisfaction in getting the better of an antagonist. He wrote:

This love of conquest, so dominant in all creatures because it is so correlative of success in the struggle for existence, gets satisfaction from a victory at chess in the absence of ruder victories.[5]

Spencer conceptualized play as the underlying basis for a number of other human activities; indeed, he described it as the origin of all art. He also attempted to develop a scientific explanation for play, based on the organism's inner need to use bodily organs which are "over-rested and under-worked." He felt that in animals who were lower on the evolutionary scale the occasion for play arose less frequently, since energies were more constantly expended in survival activities; among the higher animals, time and strength were not always depleted in providing for immediate needs.

While Spencer's physiological theories lack credibility today, many would still subscribe to his view of play as an outlet for surplus energy. The weakness of his position is that it explains only one form of play, the play of children.

Recreation Theory

Another early theory of play, regarded by many as the converse of the Schiller-Spencer view, was developed by Moritz Lazarus, professor of philosophy at Berlin University. He suggested that rather than serving to *burn up* excess energy, play provides a way of *conserving* or *restoring* it. In other words, when one is exhausted through toil, play recharges one's energy for renewed work.

Lazarus distinguished between physical and mental energy, pointing out that when the brain is "tired" (provided that it is not overtired), a change of activity, particularly in the form of physical exercise, will restore one's nervous energy. To illustrate, the desk worker who plays tennis after a long day's work simultaneously discharges surplus physical energy and restores mental energy. This theory was directed primarily at adults, who were seen as requiring recreation in order to be restored for further work. Lazarus felt that children were most inclined to play when they had an excess of physical and mental energy, and thus did not really use play for recreative purposes.

This theory was influential in developing popular attitudes favoring play, particularly for adults. For centuries, play was regarded as a frivolity and a waste of time; some even saw it as evil when compared to work. However, when play was

20

defined as a means of restoring the worker for renewed labor, it became justifiable. In today's society, it is no longer necessary to support play because of its recreative value; instead, it is seen as important for its own sake. Nonetheless, many modern men and women still regard play as a reward for work, and as a means of recharging their physical or psychic batteries for further work.

Instinct-Practice Theory

A more elaborate explanation of play was put forward by Karl Groos, a professor of philosophy at Basel, who wrote two major texts—one in 1896 on the play of animals and another in 1899 on the play of humans.

His theory was heavily based on the Darwinian theory of natural selection. Groos conjectured that play helped animals in the struggle for survival by enabling them to practice and perfect the skills they would need in adult life. He concluded that the more adaptable and intelligent a species was, the more it needed a period of protected infancy and childhood for essential learning to take place. Thus among humans there was a lengthy early period during which children engaged in varied activities to perfect skills before they really needed them.

Groos saw play as assuming the role of a single, generalized instinct. In practice, it took four major forms: (1) fighting play, including contests, hunting play, and mental and physical competition; (2) love play and courtship activities; (3) imitative or dramatic play; and (4) social play. While it was necessary to distinguish between play and work, he conceded that work might include an element of play:

> Even the most serious work may include a certain playfulness. . . . when pleasure in the activity as such, as well as its practical aim, becomes a motive power. . . . And it can hardly be doubted that this is the highest and noblest form of work.[6]

Groos's major contribution was in assigning a serious biological purpose to activities otherwise seen as aimless. The concept that play represents an important technique through which the young of various cultures are educated to carry out the tasks and functions of adulthood was highly significant, and influenced many modern educators. While the observations of both ethologists and anthropologists in recent years have strongly supported his theory, it is obvious that it has important deficiencies as a total explanation of play. It applies chiefly to the play of children and does not explain play by adults, who have already mastered essential life skills. In addition, Groos's theory ignores other important motivations for play, such as the urge for pleasure, emotional release or creative expression, and the influence of the environment in directing play into culturally approved or directed forms.

Catharsis Theory

The catharsis theory was based on the view that play—particularly competitive, active play—serves as a safety valve for the expression of bottled-up emotions. Among the ancient Greeks, Aristotle saw the drama as a means of purging oneself of hostile or aggressive emotions; by vicarious sharing in the staged experience, the onlooker purified himself of harmful feelings. A number of early twentieth-century writers expanded this theory. Carr, an American psychologist, wrote:

> Catharsis . . . implies the idea of purging or draining of that energy which has *anti-social possibilities*. . . . The value of football, boxing, and other physical contests in relieving the pugnacious tendencies of boys is readily apparent as examples. Without the numberless well-organized set forms of play possessed by society which give a harmless outlet to the mischievous and unapplied energy of the young the task of the teacher and parent would be appalling.[7]

Others, like G. T. W. Patrick, gave a physiological interpretation to the cathartic process, seeing its value as primarily in a restoration of disturbed balance in the organism. Patrick pointed out that strong emotions such as fear or anger cause a whole series of internal changes to take place in the organism (such as increased blood sugar or adrenalin) to prepare it for strenuous responses demanded to meet the threatening situation. Patrick suggests that although such emotions often occur in modern society, with the body preparing itself for violent action, the physical means of discharging tension and hostility are usually not available. It is the specific cathartic function of play—especially of active games and sports—to use up such energies and help the body restore itself to a balanced state once again.

Coupled with the surplus-energy concept, the catharsis theory suggested a vital necessity for active play to help children and youth burn up excess energy and provide a socially acceptable channel for aggressive or hostile emotions and drives. Among other modern social scientists, Konrad Lorenz has written extensively on aggression, and points out that it was probably in ritualized fighting that sport had its origin. He concludes that the major value of sport today lies in providing a healthy safety valve for dangerous forms of aggression.[8]

While this concept is an important one today, it too offers a narrow view of play. It deals only with active and competitive activities, ignoring other forms of play. It ignores motivations for sport other than the need to express hostility. And finally, it does not face the reality that sport—rather than draining or discharging aggression harmlessly—may even arouse and excite it.

Recapitulation Theory

A widely discussed theory of play at the turn of the twentieth century was the so-called recapitulation theory advanced by G. Stanley Hall, a prominent American professor of psychology and pedagogy. Hall's dual interest in evolutionary theory and education led him to study children's behavior with scientific rigor; for the first time a serious scientist concerned himself with the kinds of dolls children preferred and their building sand castles.

The recapitulation theory was based on the idea that children were a link in the evolutionary chain from animal to man, experiencing the history of the human race in their play activities throughout childhood and adolescence. Hall wrote:

> The past holds the key to all play activities. None survives unless based on purely hereditary momentum. The view of Groos that play is practice for future adult activities is very partial, superficial and perverse.[9]

Through play, children were thought to be re-enacting the lives of their caveman ancestors, engaging in activities—like fishing, canoeing, hunting, or camping—that were vital to the species eons ago. Play was seen as "the purest expression of heredity. . . . not doing things to be useful later on, but . . . rehearsing racial history." Hall developed a "culture-epoch" analogy that showed how children traveled in their play through successive periods of human history, such as the *animal* stage, the *savage* stage, the *nomad* stage, and ultimately the *tribal* stage of development. To each of these he attached typical forms of children's play found at each stage of maturation.

Hall's theory was obviously more applicable to a primitive, preindustrial society in which village customs were handed down faithfully and in which many games and sports replicated earlier customs and traditions than to a modern, urban culture heavily dependent on newly developed technological games, toys, and entertainment.

Relaxation Theory

The American psychologist G. T. W. Patrick extended his physiological theory of recreation by asserting that it was essential for man's healthy functioning in modern society that he find active outlets in play. According to Patrick, the stress and strain of modern life put humans under excessive tension, resulting in a higher incidence of mental illness:

> There is a marked decline in the power of American workers to withstand the strain of modern life. They wear out sooner than they did a few years ago. The chances of death after reaching the prime of life have increased because of . . . the breaking-down of the heart, arteries, kidneys, and of the nervous and digestive system. [10]

This trend, he speculated, was due to the tension and nervous fatigue caused by industrial, urban life. Patrick also believed that modern man was forced to constantly repress the impulse to revert to primitive kinds of behavior as natural releases for emotion. As a consequence of this inhibition he saw a growing demand for rest and relaxation through such artificial means as narcotic drugs, tobacco, and alcohol. It was Patrick's view that mankind needs healthy forms of physical and emotional activity to compensate for these added strains and tensions and for his inability to use traditional activities as outlets for emotion. Thus, play was seen as having the critical function of providing relaxation in modern life.

Patrick was one of the first authorities to differentiate clearly between the play of children and that of adults. He saw the former not as a means of relaxation but as a significant element in social growth and a release for instinctive drives. In contrast, the play of adults was chiefly valuable as a form of relaxation, to compensate for the stress of modern life.

Each of the traditional theories of play just summarized has some degree of merit, although none of them would withstand rigorous analysis today or provide a total explanation of the significance of play in modern society. Indeed, it is questionable whether any single definition, theory, or concept could possibly encompass all forms of play.

23

Twentieth-Century Concepts of Play

During the first three decades of the twentieth century a number of psychologists and educators examined play, particularly as a developmental and learning experience for children. Kilpatrick and Dewey wrote of its value in education, and Lee and Gulick explored its role in community life (see chapter 8). As the play movement developed and courses in play leadership began to be offered in American colleges, it became necessary to formulate a broader and more widely applicable theory of play.

Self-Expression Theory

Two leading physical educators, Elmer Mitchell and Bernard Mason, attempted to develop a more convincing explanation of play than had yet been provided. In their text *The Theory of Play,* they saw play primarily as a result of the drive for self-expression. Man was perceived as an active, dynamic creature with a need to find outlets for his energies, to use his abilities, and to express his personality. The specific types of activity that he engages in were, according to Mitchell and Mason, influenced by such factors as his physiological and anatomical structure, his physical-fitness level, his environment, and his family and social background.

In addition to these elements, the "self-expression" theory also suggested that certain "universal" wishes of man were influential in shaping play attitudes and habits. These included: (1) the wish for new experience; (2) the wish for participation in a group enterprise; (3) the wish for security; (4) the wish for response and recognition from others; and (5) the wish for the aesthetic.

Mitchell and Mason's analysis avoided the pitfalls of earlier theories by explaining the varied forms play takes among different individuals of all ages. Because it incorporated a variety of motivations and psychological theories that had gained influence in the early part of the twentieth century, their theory of play was accepted by many educators and recreation professionals in the United States and Canada.[11]

As the recreation field grew in importance, a number of leading social and behavioral scientists began to examine play empirically, and to formulate theories of play which related it to broader analyses of social behavior and structure.

Anthropological Analysis of Play

A number of modern anthropologists have studied play in primitive societies, seeing it as a revealing and significant aspect of daily life. One authority, Edward Norbeck, points out that human play should not be regarded simply as childish behavior, or as a form of trivial or lighthearted amusement. Play, defined as "voluntary, pleasurable behavior that is separated in time from other activities and that has a quality of make-believe," is found among many living creatures and throughout the entire class of mammals. However, of all forms of life, Norbeck says, man is the "supreme player."

People of every age and in a wide range of occupations engage in such activities as sports and games; dancing, singing, comedy, drama, art, and music; and hobbies. Norbeck points out that human play typically occurs at times of religious celebration, shifts in work, and changes in social status. Play behavior is commonly found at rites of birth, coming of age, marriage, and death and burial—indeed, all the important social events of mankind tend to be incorporated into social observances that include a rich element of play. Norbeck concludes that play is both a biological and a sociocultural phenomenon; he feels that it has significance in many areas, often in those involving important social problems. He writes:

> Play is universal human behavior. It is therefore presumably vital to human existence. Societies regard and handle play differently. Some provide it a place of honor and put it to social use. Other societies, notably our own in recent centuries, have held play in dishonor, a course of action that has borne positive results in monumental economic achievements but that, at the same time, has presented us with a train of social problems. [12]

Other anthropologists have documented the role of playlike activities in primitive societies. Bronislaw Malinowski describes the use of varied rituals in the communal lives of primitive tribes as a unique blending of both practical and mystical beliefs and customs, intended to deal with forces of nature that cannot otherwise be combated or controlled. Such rituals are kept strictly apart from work:

> Every magical ceremony has its distinctive name, its appropriate time, and its place in the scheme of work, and it stands out of the ordinary course of activities. . . . Work is always tabooed on such occasions, many of which are uniquely playlike. [13]

Food is frequently a part of ceremonies of a religious character, at harvest celebrations, seasonal feasts, or the return of successful hunters or fishermen. Ceremonies at birth, rites of initiation, and acts of mourning and commemoration for the dead are all collectively celebrated, and often involve feasting. Malinowski points out that there are many occurrences of collective play in areas of life not dominated by religion. He writes:

> Collective work in the gardens, as I have seen it in Melanesia, when men became carried away with emulation and zest for work, singing rhythmic songs, uttering shouts of joy and slogans of competitive challenge, is full of this "collective effervescence." . . . A battle, a sailing regatta, one of the big tribal gatherings for trading purposes, a . . . corroboree, a village brawl, are all from the social as well as from the psychological point of view, essentially examples of crowd effervescence. [14]

Another anthropologist, Felix Keesing, describes a number of the key functions of play within primitive cultures. These include the following: (1) pleasurable, or hedonistic, effects; (2) relaxing, or energy-restorative, functions; (3) "integrative" effects, which develop stability and cohesion among both individuals and groups in the society; (4) therapeutic or sublimative functions, which channel off conflicts, aggressions, and hostilities; (5) creative opportunities for innovation and self-expression; (6) communicative functions, which assist learning and habit formation among both children and adults; and (7) symbolic values, in expressing cultural values and beliefs. [15]

Keesing observes that in some cases the same activity may readily be adapted to new uses and needs, while retained in its original form for traditional purposes. The ceremonies of American Indians are frequently used in one form for tourist exhibitions and in another quite different form as part of traditional religious practice.

Ultimately, Keesing suggests, traditional play practices are most likely to persist when they have a continuing functional relation to social structure, child rearing, religion, or other behaviors linked to important social needs and values. The playlike aspects of tribal behavior are remarkably open to innovation and cross-cultural transfer; they provide important opportunities for the analysis of a tribe's social and cultural change and development.

Psychological Analysis of Play

During the past several decades, a number of leading psychologists and psychiatrists have written extensively on play as a significant aspect of human behavior. One modern psychologist, Lawrence K. Frank, has pointed out that play is now regarded as an important developmental experience for children both psychologically and emotionally. Frank writes:

> Play, as we are beginning to understand, is the way the child learns what no one can teach him. It is the way he explores and orients himself to the actual world of space and time, of things, animals, structures, and people. Through play he learns to live in our symbolic world of meaning and values, of progressive striving for deferred goals, at the same time exploring and experimenting and learning in his own individual way. Through play the child practices and rehearses endlessly the complicated and subtle patterns of human living and communication which he must master if he is to become a participating adult in our social life.[16]

Jerome Bruner, a leading authority on cognitive growth and the educational process and past president of the American Psychological Association, reinforces this view, pointing out that even apparently casual play expressions are structured and governed by rules, and contribute significantly to childhood learning. He states:

> We have come a long way since Piaget's brilliant observation that play helps the child assimilate experience to his personal schema of the world, and more research on play is under way. We now know that play is serious business, indeed, the principal business of childhood. It is the vehicle of improvisation and combination, the first carrier of rule systems through which a world of cultural restraint replaces the operation of childish impulse.[17]

In addition to personality development and cognitive growth, play is also closely linked to psychoanalytical theory. A number of Sigmund Freud's major theories, including the "pleasure principle," were highly relevant to understanding play, and Freud's followers were influential in using play as a medium of treatment through the development of play-therapy techniques. Erik Erikson, for example, sees play as

26

a function of the ego, an attempt to bring into synchronization the
bodily and social processes of which one is a part . . . the emphasis [being
placed] on the ego's need to master the various areas of life.[18]

Erikson describes play as a way of testing fate and causality and a means of
breaking away from sharply defined social reality and the confinement of time and
space. In working with disturbed children, Erikson has supported the use of play
therapy as a form of creative expression and a means of gaining security. He
comments that "to play it out" is the most natural self-healing measure childhood
affords.

M. J. Ellis suggests that from a psychological perspective play should not be
thought of as a single kind of activity. Instead, the key element in understanding and
conceptualizing play lies in the motivation for carrying it on (*why* one plays), and the
style of participation (*how* one plays). Thus, it is easier to deal with the concept of
"playful" as an adverb than of "play" as a noun. In considering the various theories
of play that have been advanced over the past several decades, Ellis suggests that two
in particular provide convincing explanations for a major portion of play involvement. The *competence-effectance* theory is based on the observation that a great
deal of play consists of exploration; a primary purpose of such play is to demonstrate
competence, and to master the environment. A second theory that has gained much
support recently is the *stimulus-arousal* theory, which views the need for excitement, risk, and challenge as key motivation for play.[19]

Sociological Analysis of Play

The bulk of the sociological investigation of play consists of studies that examine the
relationship between patterns of leisure activity and such variables as social class,
age, sex, residence, occupational status, and similar factors.

The French sociologist Roger Caillois has examined the play experience
itself by classifying games characteristic of various cultures and identifying their
apparent functions and values. Caillois has established four major types of play and
game activity: *agon, alea, mimicry,* and *ilinx*.[20]

Agon refers to activities that are competitive and in which the equality of
the participants' chances of winning is artificially created. Winners are determined
through such qualities as speed, endurance, strength, memory, skills, and ingenuity.
Agonistic games may be played by individuals or teams; they presuppose sustained
attention, training and discipline, perseverance, limits, and rules. Clearly, most
modern games and sports, including many card and table games involving skill, are
examples of agon.

Alea includes those games or contests over whose outcome the contestant
has no control; winning is the result of fate rather than the skill of the player. Games
of dice, roulette, baccarat, and lotteries are examples of alea.

Mimicry is based on the acceptance of illusions or imaginary universes. It
includes a class of games in which the common element is that the subject makes
believe or makes others believe that he is someone other than himself. For children,
Caillois writes,

> the aim is to imitate adults. . . . This explains the success of the toy
> weapons and miniatures which copy the tools, engines, arms and

27

machines used by adults. The little girl plays her mother's role as cook, laundress and ironer. The boy makes believe he is a soldier, musketeer, policeman, pirate, cowboy, Martian, etc.[21]

Clearly, this analysis reflects a pattern of sex stereotyping in children's play that has been sharply challenged in recent years. On the adult level, mimicry is found in theatrical presentations or games involving simulation and role playing. Caillois sees a strong relationship between agon and mimicry in contests such as boxing or wrestling, football, tennis, or polo games, which are

> intrinsic spectacles, with costumes, solemn overtures, appropriate liturgy and regulated procedures. . . . In a word, these are dramas whose vicissitudes keep the public breathless, and lead to denouements which exalt some and depress others. The nature of these spectacles remains that of an *agon,* but their outward aspect is of an exhibition.[22]

Ilinx consists of play activities based on the pursuit of vertigo or dizziness. Historically, ilinx was found in primitive religious dances or other rituals that induced the trancelike state necessary for worship. Today it may be seen in children's games that lead to dizziness by whirling rapidly, and in the use of swings and seesaws. Among adults, ilinx may be achieved through certain dances involving rapid turns or through such amusement park rides as the whip or loop-the-loop.

In Caillois's view, the entire universe of play is based on these categories. They may overlap to some degree when activities include elements of more than one style. Some gambling activities, like betting on horse races or roulette, have elements of agon in that the bettor may carefully research his betting choices or use a betting system. On the other hand, they represent alea in that ultimately the player has no control over the outcome of the play activity.

Caillois also suggests two extremes of style that characterize play and games. The first of these, which he calls *paidia,* involves exuberance, freedom, and uncontrolled and spontaneous gaiety. The second, *ludus,* is characterized by rules and conventions, and represents calculated and contrived activity. Each of the four forms of play may be conducted at either extreme of *paidia* or *ludus,* or at some point on a continuum between the two. Caillois's analysis provides a rich historical perspective on play activity, showing how many play artifacts and activities—such as masks, kites, tops, and balls, as well as songs, games, and dances—are the cultural residue of past "magical" beliefs and rites that have lost their original potency and are now played as a matter of tradition and custom. He suggests also that the drives underlying primitive behavior still strongly influence modern man.

The Play Element in Culture

Another influential theory of play was advanced by the Dutch social historian Johan Huizinga, in his provocative work *Homo Ludens.*[23]

Huizinga advances the thesis that play pervades all of life. He sees it as having certain characteristics. It is a voluntary activity, marked by freedom and never imposed by physical necessity or moral duty. It stands outside the realm of satisfying physiological needs and appetites. It is separate from ordinary life both in its location and its duration, being "played out" within special time periods and in such special places as the arena, the card table, the stage, and the tennis court. Play is controlled, says Huizinga, by special sets of rules, and it demands absolute order. It is also marked by uncertainty and tension. Finally, it is not concerned with good or evil, although it has its own ethical value in that its rules must be obeyed.

In Huizinga's view, play reveals itself chiefly in two kinds of activity—contests *for* something and representations *of* something. He regards it as an important civilizing influence in human society, and cites as an example the society of ancient Greece, which was permeated with play forms. He traces historically the origins of many social institutions as ritualized forms of play activity. For example, the element of play was initially dominant in the evolution of judicial processes. Law consisted of a pure contest between competing individuals or groups. It was not a matter of being right or wrong; instead, trials were conducted through the use of oracles, contests of chance that determined one's fate, trials of strength or resistance to torture, or verbal contests. Huizinga suggests that the same principle applies to many other cultural institutions:

> . . . in myth and ritual the great instinctive forces of civilized life have their origin: law and order, commerce and profit, craft and art, poetry, wisdom and science. All are rooted in the primeval soil of play.[24]

Although in modern society we have tended to regard play as nonserious, even frivolous, it may obviously be carried on for stakes that are as important as life or death. High-risk sports such as hang-gliding or extremely violent spectator sports are the most obvious example of this. Indeed, Huizinga points out that war itself developed historically as a kind of game. The elements of competing national armies (teams), stratagems and deception, elaborate codes for prisoners, hostages, and noncombatants, permissible weapons, and honorable behavior all support the idea of war as a game on a giant scale. Until recently, armies went off to fight in a spirit of national celebration. Even today in some primitive cultures warfare is practiced as a game and carried on under strict limitations rather than in a serious attempt to wipe out or actually conquer one's opponents. The origins of much modern play are inextricably bound up with warfare. Many sports, for example, once represented military skills. Hunting, horsemanship, archery, fencing, and shooting are recreational activities once essential to warfare.

One may observe Huizinga's thesis at work in other important social institutions. The stock market or "investment game" is an obvious form of gambling—and recognized by many stock counselors as such. Beyond this, the conduct of much actual business—including the development of new technology, advertising strategy, personnel "raids," and even the pervasive practice of company spying—suggests that business is often approached as an exciting game. Competitions for the best salesmen, testimonial dinners, references to the sales or management group as our "team" (sports terminology has become widespread both in business and in politics), and the common practice in both Europe and America of hiring athletes as employees so they can participate in sports contests with competing companies are further evidence of this phenomenon.

The modern industrial leader (as revealed in a recent study of 250 top executives in leading American companies) likes to take calculated risks and is fascinated by new techniques. This person views his own career in terms of options and possibilities, as if it were a huge game. His character may reveal a number of contradictions. He may be at once cooperative and competitive; detached and

29

playful but also compulsively driven to succeed; a team player or a hopeful superstar; a team leader or a rebel against bureaucratic regulations; a "jungle-fighter" or a loyal company man. Maccoby writes:

> Unlike other business types, he is energized to compete not because he wants to build an empire, not for riches, but rather for fame, glory, the exhilaration of running his team and of gaining victories. His main goal is to be known as a winner, and his deepest fear is to be labeled a loser.[25]

Huizinga concludes that within contemporary civilization, play is slowly declining. In sports, for example, games have been raised "to such a pitch of technical organization and scientific thoroughness that the real play spirit is threatened with extinction." It has become too serious a business. He suggests that in many other areas of life—such as warfare, contemporary politics, and international law—the old play rules are no longer respected, and that culture therefore suffers.

Finally, Huizinga identifies the essential elements of play—"its tension, its mirth, and its fun." He suggests that the *fun* of playing resists all analysis, all logical interpretation. It does not imply fun in the sense of amusement or laughter, but rather the sense of deep absorption, uncertainty, anticipation, and finally *freedom* that in his view characterizes all real play.

Huizinga's major contribution was that he was the first respected scholar to give serious attention to play as an intrinsic element of such fundamental social institutions as war, law, religion, and politics. His work, coupled with the findings of such scholars as Caillois, Norbeck, Keesing, and Malinowski, makes it apparent that play has an important role in all cultural practice. Human beings at all stages of societal development take part in assemblies, wear uniforms, have feasts and testimonial dinners, march and sing, and enjoy spectacles and displays—not as light or trivial forms of amusement, but because they all share fundamental needs for such group involvement.

Play Defined

In the first edition of this text, the author wrote:

> *Play* customarily is . . . regarded as an activity carried on within leisure for purposes of pleasure and self-expression. It tends to be active and to be carried on in a spirit of competition, exploration, or make-believe. Customarily, play is regarded as a child's activity, although an adult may also engage in play and under some circumstances may find play in his work.[26]

Recognizing the complexity of play, a number of points should be added to this definition:

1. Play is a universally found form of human and animal behavior, particularly among mammals and the order of primates. It apparently stems from a basic instinctive drive, although obviously much play behavior is culturally induced or learned activity.

30

2. Play is generally regarded as voluntary, pleasurable, and nonserious. However, it often involves intense commitment, discomfort or physical risk, time, and expense, and may meet significant personal or societal needs.

3. Play covers a wide range of behavior. It may consist of casual, informal exploration, or of unstructured "fooling around" among the participants. On the other hand, it may include participation in highly structured activities, such as games and sports, music, art, drama, dance, and community rituals.

4. When carried on by children, play is generally regarded as being future oriented, since it is part of the process of acculturation and teaches significant skills useful in later life. Among adults, play is usually thought of as meeting the need to relax, gain release or outlets for other personal drives, find pleasure, and enrich one's creative development.

5. Although their forms vary considerably, certain types of play appear to be found in all cultures. These include competition, gambling, mimicry, and play activities that, in Caillois's terms, alter one's state of consciousness.

6. Among humans, there is considerable evidence that play is, or has been, fundamentally linked to important social functions, such as law, religion, warfare, art, and business. Similarly, in many societies play helps in achieving communication, and a sense of unity, as well as in defining and expressing values, carrying out therapeutic and educational functions, and channeling aggression in nondestructive ways.

Generally, play is viewed as a positive form of human experience or behavior. However, play may also have some less desirable connotations. To some, play may be suspect because it tends to divert children or adults from the "real" business of life. Being a "playboy" or "playgirl" in modern society may arouse an air of disapproval as well as envy, since it implies being uninvolved and irresponsible. To "play" at an activity while others work seriously is equally reprehensible. Moreover, Neale points out that the concept of play often has negative implications for human relationships:

> To play with another is considered as an attempt to deceive and curry favor. To play around with others of the same sex can mean making sport of them. To play around with members of the opposite sex can refer to dalliance and promiscuity. The term "play" does have positive connotations such as freedom and pleasure, but it is clear that our society is quite ambivalent about them. Any culture oriented toward work will find play to be incomprehensible and dangerous.[27]

Given this background, how does the term *play* relate to the concept of *recreation?* As indicated earlier, play and recreation are *not* the same, although they are often thought of interchangeably and obviously have a good deal in common.

The Meaning of Recreation

Historically, the term "recreation" stems from the Latin word *recreatio,* meaning that which refreshes or restores. In its traditional sense, recreation has been regarded as a period of light and restful activity, voluntarily chosen, which restores one for heavy, obligatory activity, or work. This view is essentially the same as the "recreation theory of play" described earlier. Even in the modern era, this point of view is often expressed. De Grazia wrote:

> *Recreation* is activity that rests men from work, often by giving them a change (distraction, diversion), and restores (re-creates) them for work. When adults play—as they do, of course, with persons, things and symbols—they play for recreation. Like the Romans, our own conception of leisure is mainly recreative.[28]

This point of view lacks acceptability today for two reasons. First, as most work in modern society becomes less demanding, many people are becoming more fully engaged, both physically and mentally, in their recreation than in their work; thus the notion that recreation should be light and relaxing is far too limiting. Second, the idea that recreation is primarily intended to restore one for work has no meaning for such groups as aging persons who have *no* work, but who certainly need recreation to make their lives meaningful.

Contemporary Definitions

Most modern definitions of recreation fit into one of three categories: (1) recreation has been seen as an activity carried on under certain conditions or with certain motivations; (2) recreation has been viewed as a process or state of being—something that happens within the person while engaging in certain kinds of activity with a given set of expectations; and (3) recreation has been perceived as a social institution, a body of knowledge, or a professional field.

Most definitions, particularly those advanced by authors within the field, have regarded recreation as a form of activity or experience. Thus, the Neumeyers write of recreation as:

> any activity pursued during leisure, either individual or collective, that is free and pleasureful, having its own immediate appeal, not impelled by a delayed reward beyond itself or by any immediate necessity.[29]

A second definition, offered by Hutchinson, includes the element of social acceptability:

> Recreation is a worthwhile, socially accepted leisure experience that provides immediate and inherent satisfaction to the individual who voluntarily participates in an activity.[30]

32

Other definitions offered over the past three decades have included the following elements:

1. Recreation is widely regarded as *activity* (including physical, mental, social, or emotional involvement) as contrasted with sheer *idleness* or complete *rest*.

2. Recreation may include an extremely wide range of activities, such as sports, games, crafts, performing arts, fine arts, music, dramatics, travel, hobbies, and social activities. They may be engaged in individually or in groups, and may involve single or episodic participation, or sustained and frequent involvement throughout one's lifetime.

3. The choice of activity or involvement is voluntary, free of compulsion or obligation.

4. Recreation is prompted by internal motivation and the desire to achieve personal satisfaction, rather than by extrinsic goals or rewards.

5. Recreation is heavily dependent on a state of mind or attitude; it is not so much *what* one does as the reason for doing it, and the way the individual *feels* about the activity, that makes it recreation.

6. Although the primary motivation for recreational participation is personal enjoyment, it usually results in intellectual, physical, and social growth. It is usually stressed that when recreation is provided as part of a community service program, it must meet appropriate standards of morality and provide healthy and constructive experience.

Recreation as Activity

One might logically challenge a number of these statements. First, although recreation *is* widely regarded as activity rather than complete idleness or rest, it may range from the most physically challenging pursuits to those with much milder demands. Watching television, listening to a symphony orchestra, reading a book, or playing chess are all forms of recreation.

In a more critical vein, some authorities have suggested that we should not think of recreation as activity *at all*. Gray and Greben suggest that this is a false perception of recreation, and suggest instead that recreation should be seen as a "peak experience in self-satisfaction" that comes from successful participation in any sort of personal enterprise. They write:

> Recreation is an emotional condition within an individual human being that flows from a feeling of well-being and self-satisfaction. It is characterized by feelings of mastery, achievement, exhilaration, acceptance, success, personal worth, and pleasure. It reinforces a positive self-image. Recreation is a response to aesthetic experience, achievement of personal goals, or positive feedback from others. It is independent of activity, leisure, or social acceptance.[31]

33

Avedon supports this position, commenting that many activities, including those with survival or utilitarian value, may have recreational value for participants. This is so, he suggests, because the values we ascribe to any activity are not inherent within the activity, but stem from our own thinking and past experience. Based on this idea, he describes recreation as

> . . . an internal psychic phenomenon, and . . . a different, individualized experience for each of us. That which we collectively label "recreation" is the result of a social convention, and is really only an approximation, because the experience is different for each of us.[32]

While the arguments just cited are persuasive, it is difficult to conceptualize recreation as an emotional condition or a rather complex psychic phenomenon, if one's professional responsibility is to provide a recreation program for large numbers of people that will meet their varied leisure needs and interests. Essentially, then, recreation should be regarded as involvement in certain types of experiences that will yield the personal benefits of pleasure, a sense of accomplishment and mastery, and creative expression.

Voluntary Participation

With respect to recreation's being voluntary, it should be recognized that free choice does not always operate in such matters. One's opportunity to select recreation activities is often limited by a lack of choice. In many cases, a real degree of compulsion or pressure is exerted to get people to participate. In treatment centers, for example, patients are often strongly urged to take part in certain activities. According to current thinking, if patients are *forced* to take part against their will, these activities should not be regarded as recreation in the true sense. If, however, though compelled to take part at the outset, the patients come to enjoy the activities and to take part willingly, these activities might then rapidly become recreation.

Motivations for Participation

Many current definitions of recreation stress that it should be conducted chiefly for personal enjoyment or pleasure. Often it is stressed that satisfaction should be *immediate*. This raises some obvious questions. Many worthwhile pastimes take a long time to master before they yield the fullest degree of satisfaction. Some complex activities may cause frustration and even mental anguish—as in the case of the golf addict who is desperately unhappy because of poor putting or driving. In such cases it is not so much that the participant receives immediate pleasure as that he is absorbed and challenged by the activity; his pleasure will probably grow as his skill improves.

What of the view that recreation must be carried on for its own sake, and without extrinsic goals or purposes? It is essential to recognize that human beings *are* usually goal-oriented, purposeful creatures. When they engage in recreational activity, they frequently do so for reasons that go beyond personal enjoyment or satisfaction. These may include the need to make friends, keep fit, release tension, gain prestige or status, and develop creative potential. There are many reasons for recreational involvement that transcend the search for diversion alone, and the *best* recreation activities are those which do meet significant and varied personal needs.

Social Desirability

Although some definitions of recreation do not include the element of social desirability, this must be a key aspect of any definition of recreation when it is a form of public or voluntary agency service. A view of recreation that sees it only as activity conducted in one's leisure time for fun might include a wide range of harmful or self-destructive pursuits. Compulsive gambling, abuse of narcotic drugs, or promiscuous sexual activity could all be thought of as recreation. Jensen presents the opposite view—that recreation must be wholesome to the individual and to society, and must serve to recreate him physically, psychologically, spiritually, or mentally. He writes:

> In order to qualify as recreation, an activity must do something desirable to a participant. It must enrich him and add joy and satisfaction to an otherwise routine day. Recreation should be clearly distinguished from amusement, time-filling, or low-quality participation. [33]

Whether or not one accepts this position, it is important to recognize that all publicly financed programs *must* have significant goals and objectives to deserve and obtain support. It therefore becomes necessary to make an important distinction. Recreation, as such, may not imply social acceptability or a set of socially oriented goals or values. When, however, it is provided as a form of community-based service, supported by taxes or voluntary contributions, it *must* be attuned to prevalent social values and *must* be aimed at achieving desirable and constructive results.

Forms of Involvement

Recreation encompasses a wide range of possible behaviors and satisfactions. These may be categorized by types of activity, such as: games and sports; music, drama, and dance; arts and crafts; and outdoor recreation. Recreational behaviors can also be grouped according to the essential physical or psychological character of the participation. Murphy and Williams suggest a wide range of behaviors, as follows:

> *Socializing behaviors:* activities such as dancing, dating, going to parties, or visiting friends, in which people relate to one another in informal and unstereotyped ways.

> *Associative behaviors:* activities in which people group together because of common interests such as car clubs, stamp-, coin-, or gem-collecting groups, or similar hobbies.

> *Competitive behaviors:* activities including all the popular sports and games, but also competition in the performing arts, or in outdoor

activities in which individuals compete against the environment or even against their own limitations.

Risk-taking behaviors: an increasingly popular form of participation, in which the stakes are often physical injury or possible death.

Exploratory behaviors: in a sense, all recreation involves some degree of exploration; in this context, it refers to such activities as travel and sightseeing, hiking, scuba diving, spelunking, and other pursuits that open up new environments to the participant.

Vicarious experience: much modern recreation consists of reading, watching television or motion pictures, viewing the art works of others, listening to music, or attending spectator sports events.

Sensory stimulation: behaviors which center about hedonism and the stimulation of the senses as a primary concern include drinking, drug use, sexual activity, and such visual experiences as light shows and rock concerts, which may blend different kinds of stimuli.

Physical expression: many activities, such as running, swimming, dancing, and yoga, may involve physical expression without emphasizing competition against others.[34]

Ideally all such activities, when pursued for pleasure or other significant personal values, should be viewed as recreation. However, often they are not. For example, a leading author, Thomas Kando, suggests that intellectual pursuits should not really be thought of as forms of recreation:

> . . . recreation . . . frequently refers to sports and outdoor activities and almost never refers to activities that are intellectually strenuous. . . . Unlike the leisure ideal, recreation . . . describes activities that are generally not edifying . . . [35]

This is an unfortunately narrow point of view, both in its theoretical base and its practical implications. There is no reason why intellectual, artistic, or other culturally significant activities should *not* be considered legitimate forms of recreational participation. Many public recreation-and-park departments provide extensive courses, workshops, and performance series in the arts. Often they sponsor or cosponsor ballet, opera, or other musical organizations and events, and numerous recreation agencies operate arts centers. Clearly, such pursuits belong within the domain of recreation.

Recreation as a Social Institution

Recreation is usually thought of as a form of *personal* involvement or experience carried on for pleasure. It might also, however, include many forms of service activities in which individuals do volunteer work in community agencies, serve on community boards, or assist in other civic enterprises as a form of recreational participation. Beyond this view of it as personal involvement, Avedon points out that some authorities regard recreation as a social institution in its own right, representing a form of collective behavior within specific social structures. He writes:

> . . . as in the case of other social institutions, recreation has form, structure, traditions, patterns of operation and association, systems of communication, and a number of other fixed societal aspects. . . .

> [it has] a formal relationship pattern sanctioned by society, a form and structure that arises and persists because of a definite felt need of the members of society, as in the case of education and [the] hospital system.[36]

Once chiefly the responsibility of the family, the church, or other local social bodies, recreation has now become the responsibility of a number of major agencies in our modern, industrial society. These may include public, voluntary, or commercial organizations that operate parks, beaches, zoos, aquariums, stadiums, or sports facilities. Recreational activities may also be provided by organizations such as hospitals, schools, correctional institutions, and branches of the armed forces—organizations which have other primary functions but provide recreation as a secondary form of service. Such organizations today spend and earn many billions of dollars each year, and employ hundreds of thousands of professional workers. Clearly, then, recreation has emerged as a significant social institution, complete with its own national and international organizations and an extensive network of programs of professional preparation in colleges and universities.

Recreation Defined

Based on this analysis, recreation may be defined as follows:

> *Recreation* consists of activities or experiences carried on within leisure, usually chosen voluntarily by the participant—either because of satisfaction, pleasure, or creative enrichment derived, or because he perceives certain personal or social values to be gained from them. It may also be perceived as the process of participation, or as the emotional state derived from involvement.

> When carried on as part of organized community or voluntary-agency programs, recreation must be designed to meet constructive and socially acceptable goals of the individual participant, the group, and society at large. Finally, recreation must be recognized as a social institution with its own values and traditions, structures and organizations, and professional groups and skilled practitioners.

The Meaning of Leisure

The statement is frequently made that one of the most crucial challenges of the present day is the need to come to grips with the "new leisure." What exactly *is* leisure?

Etymologically, the English word *leisure* seems to be derived from the Latin *licere,* meaning "to be permitted" or "to be free." From *licere* came the French *loisir,* meaning "free time," and such English words as *license* (meaning originally immunity from public obligation) and *liberty*. These words are all related; they suggest free choice and the absence of compulsion.

The early Greek word *scole* or *skole* meant "leisure." It led to the Latin *scola* and the English *school* or *scholar*—thus implying a close connection between leisure and education. The word *scole* also referred to places where scholarly discussions were held. One such place was a grove next to the temple of Apollo Lykos, which became known as the *lyceum*. From this came the French *lycée*, meaning "school"—again implying a bond between leisure and education.

From a conceptual point of view, "leisure" has at least four widely found meanings: (1) the "classical" view of leisure, as exemplified in the writings of de Grazia and Pieper; (2) the view of leisure as a function of social class; (3) the concept of leisure as activity carried on in free time; and (4) the concept of leisure as free time.

The Classical View of Leisure

Aristotle regarded leisure as "a state of being in which activity is performed for its own sake." It was sharply contrasted with work or purposeful action, involving instead such pursuits as art, political debate, philosophical discussion, and learning in general. The Athenians saw work as ignoble; to them it was boring and monotonous. A common Greek word for work is *ascholia,* meaning the absence of leisure. Thus, as Kando points out, Greek civilization

> defined work as a function [namely the absence] of leisure, whereas we do the exact opposite, defining leisure as nonwork.[37]

For the Athenians particularly, leisure was seen as the highest value of life, and work as the lowest. Since the upper classes were not required to work, they were free to engage in intellectual, cultural, and artistic activity. Leisure represented an ideal state of freedom, and the opportunity for spiritual and intellectual enlightenment. Within modern philosophies of leisure that have descended from this classical Athenian view, leisure is still seen as occurring only in time that is not devoted to work. However, it is far more than just a temporary release from work used to restore one for more work. Instead, according to Pieper,

> leisure does not exist for the sake of work—however much strength it may give a man to work; the point of leisure is not to be a restorative, a pick-me-up, whether mental or physical. . . . Leisure, like contemplation, is of a higher order than the active life. . . . [it involves] the capacity to soar in active celebration, to overstep the boundaries of the workaday world and reach out to superhuman, life-giving existential forces that refresh and renew us before we turn back to our daily work.[38]

Pieper goes on to say that leisure does not represent mere idleness; indeed, this is the very opposite of leisure. And De Grazia stresses the view that free time is not necessarily leisure; anybody can have free time, but not everybody can have leisure. "It is an ideal, a state of being, a condition of man, which few desire and fewer achieve."[39] Both authors agree that leisure involves a spiritual and mental attitude, a state of inward calm, contemplation, serenity, and openness.

How meaningful is this classical view of leisure today? It has two drawbacks. First, it is linked to the idea of an aristocratic class structure based on the availability of slave labor. When Aristotle wrote in his *Treatise on Politics* that "it is of course generally understood that in a well-ordered state, the citizens should have leisure and not have to provide for their daily needs," he meant that leisure was given to a comparatively few patricians and made possible through the strenuous labor of the many.

In modern society, leisure cannot be a privilege reserved for the few; instead, it is widely available to all. It must exist side by side with work that is respected in our society, and it should have a meaningful relationship to work. Moreover, the classical view of leisure imposes an extremely narrow definition on this concept. De Grazia specifically rejects the modern concept of recreation, seeing it as an inappropriate use of leisure. Recreation, he says, is purposeful and intended to restore one for further work; therefore, it cannot be considered part of leisure. He suggests also that the tendency of modern Americans to fill their free time with chores, hobbies, trivial pursuits, and various community-service projects means that they have no real leisure.

This view of leisure sees it essentially as a privilege reserved for the fortunate few, rather than as an opportunity for all. Great masses of people are interested today in such free-time pursuits as hobbies, sports, and the arts. To suggest that none of these can be a legitimate use of leisure—but rather that leisure must be a contemplative, rather mystical state of being—is to limit the concept so greatly that it becomes meaningless for most people today.

Leisure as a Symbol of Social Class

The view of leisure as closely related to social class stemmed from the work of Thorstein Veblen, a leading American sociologist of the late nineteenth century. Veblen showed how, throughout history, ruling classes emerged that identified themselves sharply through the possession and use of leisure. In his major work, *The Theory of the Leisure Class,* he pointed out that in Europe—during the feudal and Renaissance periods and finally during the industrial age—the possession and visible use of leisure became the hallmark of the upper class.

Veblen attacked the "idle rich"; he saw leisure as a total way of life for the privileged class, regarding them as exploiters who lived on the toil of others. He coined the phrase "conspicuous consumption" to describe their way of life throughout history:

> The . . . gentleman of leisure . . . consumes freely and of the best, in food, drink, narcotics, shelter, services, ornaments, apparel, weapons and accoutrement. . . . He must cultivate his tastes . . . he becomes a connoisseur . . . and the demands made upon the gentleman in this direction therefore tend to change his life of leisure into a more or less arduous application to the business of . . . conspicuous leisure and conspicuous consumption.[40]

To maintain their status, Veblen wrote, members of the leisure class—from the feudal nobleman to the self-made millionaire industrialist—had to give valuable presents and expensive feasts and entertainments to impress society. Chiefly through Veblen's influence, the concept of the leisure class came into being. His analysis is not as applicable to contemporary life as it was to the time when it was written, since the working classes today tend to have far *more* free time than industrial managers, business executives, and professionals. Veblen's contempt for leisure as belonging only to "the idle rich" no longer applies with full force, both because of this greater working-class leisure and because of the involvement of the present generation of our most wealthy and influential families (such as the Rockefellers, Harrimans, and Kennedys) in finance and public life. Thus, with the exception of a small group of "jet setters," the class he criticized no longer exists.

Leisure as a Form of Activity

A third influential concept of leisure is that it is nonwork activity in which people engage during their free time. For example, the International Study Group on Leisure and Social Sciences states that

> leisure consists of a number of occupations in which the individual may indulge of his own free will—either to rest, to amuse himself, to add to his knowledge and improve his skills disinterestedly and to increase his voluntary participation in the life of the community after discharging his professional, family and social duties.[41]

Similarly, a leading French sociologist, Joffre Dumazedier, defines leisure in these terms:

> Leisure is activity—apart from the obligations of work, family and society—to which the individual turns at will, for either relaxation, diversion, or broadening his knowledge and his spontaneous social participation, the free exercise of his creative capacity.[42]

An American sociologist, Bennett Berger, supports this concept by pointing out that the sociology of leisure during the 1950s and 1960s consisted of "little more than a reporting of survey data on what selected samples of individuals do with the time in which they are not working, and the correlation of these data with conventional demographic variables."[43]

Other sociologists who have defined leisure as activity have examined it in relation to work roles and to the degree of constraint or obligation affecting the choice of activity. For example, Kelly suggests a typology in which three types of leisure activity appear: (1) *unconditional leisure*—activity independent of work influence and freely chosen, as an end in itself; (2) *coordinated leisure*—activity which is similar to work in form or content (such as a work activity carried on at home as a hobby), but not required by the job; and (3) *complementary leisure*—activity which is independent of work in its form and content, but in which the need to take part in the activity is influenced by one's work—as in the case of a businessman who takes part in the work of community organizations because he is *expected* to.[44]

Leisure as Unobligated Time

The most common approach to leisure, and the one used in this text, is to regard it as nonobligated or discretionary time. In a number of sociological references, this concept of leisure is clearly stated. The *Dictionary of Sociology* offers the following definition:

> Leisure is the free time after the practical necessities of life have been attended to. . . . Conceptions of leisure vary from the arithmetic one of time devoted to work, sleep, and other necessities, subtracted from 24 hours—which gives the surplus time—to the general notion of leisure as the time which one uses as he pleases. [45]

This view of leisure sees it essentially as time which is free from work or from such work-related responsibilities as travel, study, or social involvements based on work. It also excludes time devoted to essential life-maintenance activities, such as sleep, eating, or personal care. Its most important characteristic is that it lacks a sense of obligation or compulsion.

"Semi-Leisure"

Dumazedier comments that if leisure is governed in part by commercial, utilitarian, or ideological concerns or purposes, it is no longer wholly leisure. He suggests that activities in which there is a degree of such obligation or purpose be regarded as "semi-leisure." Semi-leisure occurs when the world of work and of primary obligations partially overlaps with the world of leisure. [46]

For example, some uses of free time that are not clearly work nor paid for as work may contribute to success at work. A person may read books or articles related to his work, attend evening classes that contribute to his work competence, invite guests to a party because of work associations, or join a country club because of its value in establishing business contacts or promoting sales. Within community life, those nonwork occupations which have a degree of obligation about them—such as serving on a school board or as an unpaid member of a town council—may also be viewed as part of a person's civic responsibility. In terms of time, energy, or degree of commitment, it would be difficult to distinguish such activities from work.

Another shadow area lies in those uses of time which are normally part of maintenance and therefore not regarded as recreation, such as eating, sleeping, and performing household responsibilities. Eating often becomes a leisurely and pleasurable experience, as in the case of a country picnic or a gourmet meal at a fine restaurant. Such activities as gardening or do-it-yourself projects may also involve creative interests, and be cheerfully carried out and enjoyed as hobbies beyond their significance as forms of necessary home maintenance.

Even the notion of free choice in leisure is somewhat questionable. One's choice of leisure activities may be influenced by community values and expectations, or by the knowledge that certain uses of leisure may prove advantageous. Very few actions are completely disinterested or free of compulsion; often, as one continues to engage in an activity, one begins to perceive it as a source of social approval or of other rewards.

The strict view of leisure as time that lacks *any* obligation or compulsion is

41

also suspect. If one chooses to raise dogs as a hobby or to play an instrument in an orchestra, one begins to assume a system of routines, schedules, and commitments to others. De Grazia suggests that none of these semi-leisure activities should be regarded as true leisure. He points out that the approximately eight hours left over each day after work and sleep are typically devoted to such activities as

> shopping, grooming, chores, transportation, voting, making love, helping children with homework, reading the newspaper, getting the roof repaired, trying to locate the doctor, going to church, visiting relatives, and so on. Do all these activities rightly belong to free time?[47]

A somewhat more generous view of leisure than De Grazia's would suggest that many of these activities—such as going to church, making love, reading the newspaper, or visiting relatives—might indeed be construed both as uses of free time and as leisure activity. The most important element in making such a determination would be whether the individual in question has a reasonable degree of free choice, and whether he *perceives* the time as leisure.

Values in Leisure

The question is frequently asked, "Is leisure simply free time, or *must* it be spent in a certain way?" Miller and Robinson, for example, define leisure as "the complex of self-fulfilling and self-enriching values achieved by the individual as he uses leisure time in self-chosen activities that recreate him."[48] The implication is that free time becomes leisure only when it is spent in the deliberate pursuit of significant and worthwhile experiences. Lee writes, for example, that

> leisure is the occasion for the development of broader and deeper perspective, and for renewing the body, mind and spirit. . . . Leisure provides the occasion for learning and freedom for growth and expression, for rest and restoration, for rediscovering life in its entirety.[49]

If one accepts the premise that only free time spent in desirable or self-enriching ways is really leisure, a philosophical question arises. Is there some universally acceptable set of values that can be used to determine what is a desirable use of free time? Is it what the individual regards as desirable for himself or herself? Many individuals engage in activities which society as a whole regards as harmful or antisocial, such as the use of illegal narcotics, criminal gambling activity, or adulterous sexual involvement. It is probable that many who enjoy such pursuits would vigorously defend their right to carry them on and would argue that—in their view—these activities are self-enriching and self-fulfilling.

Clearly, the task of determining which activities *are* desirable becomes extremely difficult if one relies only on the judgment of participants. It is equally difficult if one attempts to use as criteria the rules established by society. These vary according to region and such other factors as religious affiliation. In some states "wet" and "dry" counties exist side by side; a person may drink hard liquor at a bar in one community, be obliged to bring his bottle in a brown paper bag to a restaurant in another, and may not be permitted to drink at all in a third. One may bet on horse races at a parimutuel window with complete legality, but not be permitted to drive half a mile away and make the same bet through a bookmaker.

This inconsistency is illustrated in a recent news article on so-called victimless crimes:

> In Connecticut, it is legal to bet on jai alai and dog races, but not on tennis matches or track meets. It is all right in New Jersey to purchase a three-digit "number" from the state's computerized "Pick-It," but not from a runner on the street. Casino gambling will be permitted soon in Atlantic City, but nowhere else in New Jersey. Las Vegas-type betting became legal in New York City last week, but only for religious and charitable organizations. New Yorkers may drink at home at any hour, but not at a neighborhood tavern from four to eight o'clock in the morning. In New York State, certain sexual activity is legally permissible for married couples but illegal for unmarried people.[50]

All this demonstrates that it is extremely difficult to classify leisure solely as time spent in the pursuit of desirable and socially constructive values. It would be more realistic to conclude that leisure represents *all* free time and that it provides the basis for freedom of choice. Within it, one may engage in a wide range of activities—including some which are negative and destructive and others which are positive, self-enhancing, and constructive for the community as a whole.

Dependence on Work

A final question is whether work must exist for leisure to exist. Since leisure is traditionally seen as time free from work, how can one conceive of leisure without work? Dumazedier has said, "Leisure in the modern sense presupposes work." According to the Protestant ethic, both leisure and recreative activity could be justified only if they helped to restore one for work. If one did not work, one was not entitled to leisure and by definition did not have any.

If this premise is accepted, one might then ask, "Who does not work?" The answer would include several classes of people—the very rich, young children, retired persons, unemployed people, people in prisons, and the ill and handicapped. Obviously, leisure should not be a serious problem for very rich people; they have both the potential free time and the resources to do as they wish with it. Older persons, although they no longer work, once did; the leisure they now have comes as a complement to their earlier work. They view leisure in their retirement as something they have earned, as a reward for the efforts of their working years. Similarly, young children may use their free time in play, as preparation for adult work. In the context of a lifetime, both the old and the young thus *deserve* leisure.

But what about the very poor person who cannot find work—or the severely handicapped individual who will probably never be able to work?

The position that such people have no leisure and that therefore society need not be concerned about what they do with their free time is sheer nonsense. It is still free time—and it may be used productively to provide pleasure and constructive self-enrichment, or negatively, in passive self-destructive ways. Society's unwillingness to accept leisure as a *right* of the unemployed person, and to supply recreation facilities and programs for the poor, has led to serious recreational deprivation and urban unrest.

Holistic Concept of Leisure

The sharp contrast between work and leisure has become blurred in recent years. Once viewed by proponents of the Protestant work ethic as solely the means to restore man for work, leisure is now often thought of as the richer, more significant aspect of existence, while the interest and significance of work have declined. Max Kaplan suggests that the earlier views of leisure either as an end in itself (the classical view, which sees leisure as a celebration of life) or as the means to an end (leisure as recreation for renewed work, or as a form of social control or therapy) are now being fused in a *holistic* concept of leisure. Far more than simply free time or a listing of recreational activities, leisure must be viewed as a central element in culture, with deep and intricate ties to the larger questions of work, family, and politics.[51]

Murphy accepts the holistic view, writing of leisure

> as a construct, a full range of possible forms of self-expression which may occur during work or leisure. . . . this perspective eliminates the dichotomy drawn between work and leisure, which has been a formidable barrier in the path to enjoyment of leisure opportunities for many people. According to the holistic concept . . . the meaning of work and leisure are inextricably related to each other.[52]

Leisure Defined

In conclusion, leisure may be defined as follows:

> Leisure is that portion of an individual's time which is not devoted to work or work-connected responsibilities or to other forms of maintenance activity and which therefore may be regarded as discretionary or unobligated time.

> Leisure implies freedom of choice, and must be seen as available to all, whether they work or not. Leisure is customarily used in a variety of ways, either to meet one's personal needs for self-enrichment, relaxation, or pleasure, or to contribute to society's well-being.

Given this definition, how does leisure relate to the concepts of recreation and play? Obviously, it affords an opportunity for them both. The bulk of our leisure in modern society is filled with a variety of recreational pastimes, although it may also be used for such activities as continuing education, religion, or voluntary community service.

In turn, it should be understood that although play and recreation tend to overlap, they are not identical processes. Play, as described in this chapter, represents

44

not so much an activity as a form of behavior—marked stylistically by teasing, competition, exploration, or make-believe. Play can occur during work or leisure, whereas recreation can occur only during leisure. Recreation is seen as a form of human activity and experience that, although often playful in manner, is not always so—as in the case of such recreational pursuits as traveling, going to museums, reading, and other cultural and intellectual activities. One might conceptualize a model with play at one end of a spectrum and leisure at the other; where they join, recreation occurs. As a final distinction, recreation is generally thought of as goal-oriented and constructive activity, particularly when it is community sponsored. Play, on the other hand, covers a wide range of possibilities—from the most richly creative and self-enhancing behavior to the most negative and self-destructive.

Following this initial interpretation of play, recreation, and leisure, the chapters that follow provide a psychological, sociological, and economic analysis of the recreation field.

Chapter Two

1. Allen V. Sapora and Elmer D. Mitchell, *The Theory of Play and Recreation* (New York: Ronald, 1961), pp. 114–15.

2. Sebastian de Grazia, *Of Time, Work and Leisure* (New York: Doubleday-Anchor, 1962), p. 233.

3. Max Kaplan, *Leisure in America: A Social Inquiry* (New York: Wiley, 1960), p. 20.

4. Herbert Spencer, quoted in Harvey C. Lehman and Paul A. Witty, *The Psychology of Play Activities* (New York: A.S. Barnes, 1927), p. 13.

5. Ibid., p. 14.

6. Karl Groos, *The Play of Man* (New York: Appleton-Century, 1901), p. 400.

7. Harvey A. Carr, "The Survival Values of Play," quoted in Lehman and Witty, *The Psychology of Play*, p. 19.

8. Konrad Lorenz, *On Aggression* (New York: Harcourt, Brace and World, 1963).

9. G. Stanley Hall, *Youth* (New York: Appleton-Century, 1920).

10. George T. W. Patrick, *The Psychology of Relaxation* (Boston: Houghton Mifflin, 1916), p. 13.

11. The original source of this theory was W. P. Bowen and Elmer D. Mitchell, *The Theory of Organized Play* (New York: A.S. Barnes, 1923). Bernard Mason contributed to its development. Now see Sapora and Mitchell, *Theory of Play*, pp. 90–103.

12. Edward Norbeck, "Man at Play," in *Play: A Natural History Magazine Special Supplement*, December 1971, p. 53.

13. Bronislaw Malinowski, *Magic, Science and Religion* (New York: Doubleday-Anchor, 1955), p. 29.

14. Ibid., p. 42.

15. Felix M. Keesing, "Recreative Behavior and Culture Change," *Papers of the Fifth Congress of Anthropological and Ethnological Sciences*, 1956, pp. 130–31.

16. Lawrence K. Frank, quoted in Ruth E. Hartley and Robert M. Goldenson, *The Complete Book of Children's Play* (New York: Thomas Y. Crowell, 1963), p. 43.

17. Jerome S. Bruner, "Child Development: Play Is Serious Business," *Psychology Today*, January 1975, p. 83.

18. Erik Erikson, *Childhood and Society* (New York: Norton, 1950), p. 184.

19. M. J. Ellis, *Why People Play* (Englewood Cliffs, N.J.: Prentice-Hall, 1973), pp. 80–111.

20. Roger Caillois, *Man, Play and Games* (London: Thames and Hudson, 1961).

21. Ibid., p. 21.

22. Ibid., p. 22.

23. Johan Huizinga, *Homo Ludens: A Study of the Play Element in Culture* (Boston: Beacon Pr., 1944, 1960).

24. Ibid., p. 5.

25. Michael Maccoby, *The Gamesman: The New Corporate Leaders* (New York: Simon and Schuster, 1977), p. 100.

26. Richard Kraus, *Recreation and Leisure in Modern Society* (New York: Appleton-Century-Crofts, 1971), p. 266.

27. Robert E. Neale, *In Praise of Play* (New York: Harper and Row, 1969), p. 12.

28. De Grazia, *Of Time, Work and Leisure,* p. 233.

29. Martin H. Neumeyer and Esther Neumeyer, *Leisure and Recreation* (New York: Ronald, 1958), p. 22.

30. John Hutchinson, *Principles of Recreation* (New York: Ronald, 1951), P. 2.

31. David E. Gray and Seymour Greben, "Future Perspectives," *Parks and Recreation,* July 1974, p. 49.

32. Elliott M. Avedon, *Therapeutic Recreation Service: An Applied Behavioral Science Approach* (Englewood Cliffs, N.J.: Prentice-Hall, 1974), p. 46.

33. Clayne R. Jensen, *Outdoor Recreation in America* (Minneapolis: Burgess, 1973), p. 8.

34. James F. Murphy et al., *Leisure Service Delivery System: A Modern Perspective* (Philadelphia: Lea and Febiger, 1973), pp. 73–76.

35. Thomas M. Kando, *Leisure and Popular Culture in Transition* (St. Louis: Mosby, 1975), p. 28.

36. Avedon, *Therapeutic Recreation,* p. 47.

37. Kando, *Leisure and Popular Culture,* p. 23.

38. Josef Pieper, *Leisure, the Basis of Culture* (New York: Mentor-Omega, 1952, 1963), p. 43.

39. De Grazia, *Of Time, Work and Leisure,* p. 5.

40. Thorstein Veblen, *The Theory of the Leisure Class* (New York: Viking Pr., 1899, 1918), p. 73.

41. Isobel Cosgrove and Richard Jackson, *The Geography of Recreation and Leisure* (London: Hutchinson University Library, 1972), p. 13.

42. Joffre Dumazedier, *Toward a Society of Leisure* (New York: Free Pr., 1962, 1967), pp. 16–17.

43. Bennett Berger, "The Sociology of Leisure: Some Suggestions," in Erwin O. Smigel, ed., *Work and Leisure: A Contemporary Social Problem* (New Haven, Conn.: Coll. & U. Pr., 1963), p. 28.

44. John R. Kelly, "Work and Leisure: A Simplified Paradigm," *Journal of Leisure Research* 4 (1972): 50–62.

45. See Neumeyer and Neumeyer, *Leisure and Recreation,* p. 19.

46. Dumazedier, *Society of Leisure,* p. 250.

47. De Grazia, *Of Time, Work and Leisure,* p. 59.

48. Norman Miller and Duane Robinson, *The Leisure Age* (Belmont, Calif.: Wadsworth Pub., 1963), p. 6.

49. Robert Lee, *Religion and Leisure in America* (Nashville: Abingdon, 1964), p. 34.

50. Tom Goldstein, "Rethinking 'Victimless' Crimes," *New York Times,* 6 February 1977, p. E-5.

51. Max Kaplan, *Leisure: Theory and Policy* (New York: Wiley, 1975).

52. James F. Murphy, "The Future of Time, Work and Leisure," *Parks and Recreation,* November 1973, p. 26.

3

PSYCHOLOGICAL ASPECTS OF PLAY

This chapter examines the phenomenon of play from the perspective of the behavioral scientist. It is essentially concerned with three major aspects of play: (1) the role of play in *personality development;* (2) the function of play in the *learning process;* and (3) the relationship of play and recreation to *mental health,* as seen by leading modern psychiatrists and psychoanalysts.

The essential point of this chapter is that play has become widely recognized as a significant aspect of human development and behavior. Although professionals have been aware of its importance for centuries, the Western world's moralistic disapproval of play has prevented the full recognition of its benefits until fairly recently. During the early decades of the twentieth century, play was regarded by many authorities as an experience of dubious worth. For example, the 1914–15 edition of *Infant Care,* the official publication of the United States Children's Bureau, represented the infant as "a creature of strong and dangerous impulses":

> Playing with the baby was regarded as dangerous; it produced unwholesome pleasure and ruined a baby's nerves: "The rule that parents should not play with the baby may seem hard, but it is no doubt a safe one. . . . The dangerousness of play is related to that of the ever-present sensual pleasures which must constantly be guarded against."[1]

Gradually, however, in the decades that followed the same publication came to regard play as natural and desirable, and it recommended that mothers play with their children. By the 1940s Ruth Strang, a leading child-guidance authority, wrote, "The play life of a child is an index of his social maturity, and reveals his personality more clearly than any other activity."[2] Similarly, two widely read child psychologists, Gesell and Ilg, stated that "deeply absorbing play seems to be essential for full mental growth."[3]

47

The Role of Play in Personality Development

Psychologists examined the role of play at each stage of life, beginning with infancy and moving through the preschool period, middle and late childhood, and adolescence. They identified the first form of play in infancy as "sense-pleasure" play, in which the baby discovers and relishes moving, exploring his own body, and experiencing such environmental stimuli as sounds, flavors, and tactile sensations. During later infancy, children begin to explore "skill-play," exercising their capacity for action. Early in the toddler period, young children take part in "dramatic play," using toy dolls and animals to re-enact scenes from everyday life and act out functional relationships and roles. Erik Erikson describes this total process of development in the following terms:

> The child's play begins with, and centers in, his own body. It begins before we notice it as play, and it consists first in the exploration by repetition of sensual perceptions, of kinesthetic sensations, and of vocalizations. . . . Next, the child plays with . . . available persons and things . . . with the small world of manageable toys.[4]

The content of individual play often proves to be the young child's way of reliving difficult experiences and achieving a sense of control over them. The child learns that he is capable of dealing effectively with the outside world. Many play experiences provide an opportunity for what Bruno Bettelheim calls "self-regulation." He points out that many children's activities have important psychological significance, as in games of "not flinching . . . holding one's breath . . . not crying out . . . conquering a sense of revulsion, and so on."[5]

Often the child's purpose is to test dangers or dispel fears of the unknown in what may appear to him to be a chaotic and dangerous world. Bettelheim suggests that as simple a game as "peek-a-boo" symbolically means to the child that even if he is temporarily out of her sight, his mother will not abandon him but will look for him and find him; thus, he gains confidence and learns that he need not always be under her careful protection. Similarly, in activities centering around the use of swings, slides, and merry-go-rounds or being swung around or tossed in the air and then caught by a parent, the child deliberately seeks giddiness and danger, in order to be sure that the feat can be mastered and the danger will pass. Other forms of children's play that involve fear and risk—such as a game of "hide-and-seek" involving dark hiding places—symbolize the child's leaving his secure home and being able to return to it safely.

Thus play provides a medium through which children can develop inner psychological strengths and methods of self-control. Play also offers an ideal channel for social maturation.

Social Development through Play

Children normally begin to play when only a few weeks old, by appreciating the attention of others with cooing and smiling and, when ready, reaching out and touching them. Before long, the child is rhythmically pulling, pushing, or hitting the bars of his crib, or manipulating rattles and other playthings. By the age of five or six months, many children can take part in simple gesture games like "patty-cake," and their play becomes increasingly imitative.

In terms of social structure, Millar points out that children typically move through several stages: (1) solitary play, carried on without others nearby; (2) parallel play, in which children play side by side without meaningful interplay; (3) associative play, in which children share a common game or group enterprise, but concentrate on their own individual efforts rather than group activity; and (4) cooperative play, beginning at the age of about three, in which children actually join together in games, informal dramatics, or constructive projects. By the age of six or seven children tend to be involved in loosely organized play groups, leading to much more tightly structured and organized groups in the so-called gang age between eight and twelve.[6]

Throughout this process, the child's personality is developing. Youngsters learn how to cooperate and to compete, to quarrel and to make up, to gain and to lose friends, to obey and to disobey rules. Taking turns, respecting others' property rights, accepting group values—all these are important elements in the play experience of children.

The play activities themselves become increasingly sustained and complex as children grow older. Dramatic play during the first two or three years is episodic and incomplete, but by the time they are in kindergarten, children are able to act out more elaborate roles and scenarios in cooperation with others. At first games are extremely simple and improvised, with an emphasis on rudimentary physical skills and rules; later, they become much more structured.

Effect of Rich Play Experience

The environment of play gradually expands from the crib to the playpen to the entire room, and ultimately to the backyard, the playground, and the street. The child explores the air, the water, the ground; he climbs, he kicks, he runs, he wades and swims. Throughout all this, he practices language and manipulatory skills; he finds out about gravity, velocity, the weight and strength of objects and tools and their uses, and about how various forms of behavior elicit different responses from others. All this is essential for the fullest possible self-development.

Playfulness appears to be closely linked to creative and inventive thinking among children. Bruner cites one study in which three- to five-year-olds were encouraged to play with a specially designed "supertoy" that permitted a wide variety of possible uses; the children were then rated on their degree of inventiveness, as "nonexplorers, explorers, and inventive explorers." Four years later, the experimenter rated the children on a number of personality tests, including one for creativity:

> The more inventive and exploratory the children had been in their previous play with the supertoy, the higher their originality scores were four years later. In general, the nonexploring boys viewed themselves as unadventurous and inactive, and their parents and teachers felt they lacked curiosity. The nonexploratory and unplayful girls turned out to

be rather unforthcoming in social interactions, as well as more tense than their more playful comrades.[7]

In another longitudinal study of people who had been studied as children, Bruner reports that those subjects who "had the most interesting and fulfilling lives were ones who had managed to keep a sense of playfulness at the center of things."

The Role of Play in Adolescent Development

Psychologists who have done extensive research with teen-agers in areas related to play and recreation have been primarily concerned with their social and emotional growth.

It has been found that the teen-ager's self-image is closely related to participation in extracurricular activities. A study of over five thousand high-school students of varying social, religious, and national backgrounds revealed that those with a high degree of self-esteem tended to take part actively in sports teams, musical organizations, publications, outdoor recreation, and social activities. Those with a low degree of self-esteem were much less involved.

Obviously, extracurricular or other group recreational experiences can offer youth an opportunity for satisfying involvement with others, and provide a sense of acceptance and security that contributes to psychological well-being. Jersild found that the most popular teen-agers were those who had the spontaneity and willingness to enter games and similar activities. Liveliness, cheerfulness, gaiety, and the ability to suggest or initiate group projects and social events were found to be important elements in being accepted by one's peers. It was also found that athletic prowess in particular is related to such factors as a youth's willingness to rub elbows with others, his aggressiveness, and his ability to enter easily and freely into social contacts:

> There is perhaps no single department of the high school that offers greater opportunity than the physical education department for studying the individual student, his style of life, his potentialities for being spontaneous and free, his hesitancies and lack of self-confidence, his need to vanquish, or his need at all costs to avoid defeat or to avoid a contest in which he might look awkward.[8]

A number of recent studies (summarized later in this text) have examined: (1) the relationship between success in athletics and positive self-concept, outgoingness, and self-confidence; (2) the relationship between early parental influence and encouragement of children and later sports participation; and (3) correlations between specific personality traits and patterns of leisure participation.

Contribution to Career Development

Another important value of recreation in teen-age life is that it leads to a development of interests, some of which have important carry-over values for later life.

During the 1920s and 1930s extracurricular activities were seen as having important utilitarian values in opening a pathway to occupational involvement, by helping the individual understand his own interests and capabilities and begin to make intelligent choices for the future. This function was stressed during the Depression, when avocational interests and aptitudes were used as a means of providing career guidance. Many counselors working with unemployed young people found it necessary to provide them with guidance in the constructive use of leisure. In addition, since many of these young people lacked obvious vocational skills and experience, counselors examined their hobbies and other recreational pursuits to diagnose potential job aptitudes.

The Exploratory-Drive Theory and Its Offshoots

A number of psychologists interested in personality development have advanced a theory of self-concept formation based on the "exploratory drive." Their view is that both animals and human beings are motivated to seek as well as to avoid or reduce stimulation. Jordaan writes:

> A good deal is known about the ways in which hunger, thirst, sex, pain and the fear of punishment motivate the behavior of animals; much less is known about the behavior of animals when these drives are not present and about the other sources of motivation which might influence and direct their behavior. Some investigators . . . have postulated the existence of an exploratory drive and concluded that animals and humans are motivated to seek, as well as to avoid or reduce stimulation . . . with motives . . . which can be described by such names as manipulation, exploration, curiosity, and play.[9]

It is suggested that certain kinds of situations lead to exploratory urges—including both circumstances in which there are few stimuli (often characterized by boredom) and others which provoke risk-taking, self-inflicted stress, and a deliberate search for thrills and excitement. Obviously, exploratory activity may encompass a wide variety of pursuits, such as writing, music, acting, art, homemaking, or science activities. As with extracurricular activities, exploratory activities may be extremely valuable in promoting positive self-concepts and in helping individuals make sound career-development choices.

Exploratory-drive theory has also inspired two contemporary theories of play, both closely related to personality development. More and more, it is believed that play is a form of arousal-seeking behavior. As Jordaan pointed out earlier, instead of being used to *reduce* drives or tension, or to create a state of calm or relaxation, its purpose is frequently to *stimulate* the individual, to provide excitement and challenge. Play may become a form of information seeking, of testing an environment, or of seeking novelty, surprise, ambiguity, laughter, or release. Ellis points out that as such activity occurs the participant "is continually and actively involved in the process of interaction with the environment" and is receiving a constant flow of information. As he investigates the environment or manipulates its elements, he seeks to control or master it, gaining—if he is successful—a feeling of personal competence and mastery. This motivation for play has come to be known as the "competence-effectance" drive, and underlies much play activity.[10]

A closely related drive is the basis of the "stimulus-arousal" theory of play.

It suggests that a key motivation for play is the need to seek novelty, excitement, physical challenge, and risk—that rather than be content with the safe and familiar, many individuals seek the excitement of the unknown or dangerous. Examples of such play are obvious, including an incredible range of games, sports, contests, and stunts, some of them chosen simply for their uniqueness. An article in *Time* magazine chronicles the range of varied activities sought out by adventurous record seekers:

> Some venturesome souls achieve fame by scaling the world's highest peaks or plumbing the oceans' deepest bottoms. Their feats faithfully find their way into the *Guinness Book of World Records,* as do the odysseys of marathon smoke-ring blowers, balloonists, goldfish swallowers, grape eaters, yo-yo spinners, Scrabble players, prune devourers, face slappers, Pogo-stick jumpers, leapfroggers, barrel jumpers, needle threaders and record breakers in 10,000 other *Record*-worthy categories.[11]

Often the search for excitement and challenge involves taking considerable physical risks. Hang-gliding, a relatively new sport, claimed at least seventy-five lives in the three years following its inception on Southern California's sand dunes. White-water canoeing can be equally dangerous: Georgia's Chattooga River, one of the world's most dangerous streams, saw nineteen drownings over a similar period. Yet increasing numbers of hobbyists are avidly seeking out such sports:

> They are a growing breed, entrusting their fate to the whim of swirling air currents, churning water, hidden depths, or unyielding cliffs. They may be nature lovers or daredevil show-offs, action-starved office workers or middle-aged housewives. But America's thousands of gliders, white-water paddlers, rock climbers and divers share a zest for life—enhanced by the real and chilling possibility of injury or death.[12]

A leading psychiatrist, Dr. Edward Stainbrook of the University of Southern California, gives his explanation of this trend:

> So much of life has become sedentary, inhibiting action; thrill-seeking expresses an almost desperate need for assertive mastery of something.[13]

Such examples of popular play give support to the concept of play as arousal-seeking behavior. Erik Erikson suggests that play, within such a context, represents an attempt to "hallucinate ego mastery." In this sense, work represents reality, or the sober responsibilities of life, while play represents unreality—the opportunity to step out from the defined limits surrounding our everyday existence.

The Role of Play in the Learning Process

A second major aspect of play, as viewed by psychologists, is its contribution to the learning process. As discussed in the previous chapter, Karl Groos's instinct-practice theory conceptualized play as a form of childhood preparation for adulthood. A number of psychologists who investigated child behavior during the early decades of the twentieth century concluded that play was essential to develop a child's initiative, resourcefulness, and originality. Educational experiences, it was believed, should be presented so that the child would pursue them voluntarily as a form of play; the child would give them a time, place, and order of his own, engaging in them freely, with full absorption, and without the need for punishments or rewards. Considerable use was made of playlike projects and approaches to learning during the so-called progressive education period in the United States.

One leading educational experimenter at this time was Maria Montessori. She was an Italian educator whose innovations in preschool education in the slums of Rome early in the twentieth century produced remarkable effects. The Montessori method was based on intense observation of young children and on developing techniques of teaching that made use of so-called didactic materials—various objects, tools, rods, blocks, boxes containing bells, multicolored tablets, and child-sized furniture. While Montessori did not regard what she was doing with children as "play" (she avoided the use of this word entirely, instead referring to it as "work"), the activities themselves and the way they were conducted were extremely playlike. The child was not told what and how he was to learn; instead, he worked at his own pace and rhythm, in a spontaneous process of exploration, skill development, and cognitive growth.

In spite of Montessori's work, there was comparatively little systematic analysis of the play method in education during the first decades of the twentieth century; what was done was usually supported by enthusiastic sloganeering rather than by objective evaluation. Gradually the progressive emphasis died out, particularly in the 1950s when, after the Russian Sputnik, critics demanded increased rigor and academic emphasis in American schools. The extensive use of play equipment such as toys, blocks, paints, and tools and of activities such as cutting and pasting, singing, and storytelling that had characterized early childhood education was replaced by much more structured, formal learning experiences in kindergarten and the early primary grades. In some experimental Head Start programs during the 1960s the play-oriented nursery-school approach was abandoned entirely, and replaced by drill-like reading, arithmetic, and other cognitive-development activities.

In spite of this trend, some authorities on elementary education have continued to press for more individualized, creative, and stimulating approaches to teaching and learning. Lois Murphy, Director of Developmental Research at the Menninger Foundation, comments that early-childhood education must nourish such cognitive functions as curiosity, reflectiveness, and problem solving, and that this can best be done in the following ways:

> Learning to be active, to make things for oneself, to clarify observation, to develop concepts of space, size and weight, are contributions of block-construction and work with plastic materials, such as clay or paints. . . . Cooking demonstrates measurements and effects of heat. Growth is observed in a garden. Information is extended by calendars, thermometers, heaters. Play telephones stimulate communication.[14]

In recent years, the unique contributions of play as an aspect of learning have been supported by research in several different areas: (1) investigations of primate play behavior by leading ethologists, in field settings; (2) the contributions of Jean Piaget, a leading authority on child development; and (3) an expanding body of information on the use of games as channels for teaching and learning.

Field Investigations of Play

Ethologists who have studied the behavior of primates in natural settings have concluded that play is a particularly important aspect of their development. Slow maturing monkeys and apes invest thousands of hours of activity and energy in chasing, wrestling, boxing, swinging through trees, manipulating objects, and playing what are clearly recognizable as games with their age-mates.

Suomi describes the stages of play in the first years of primate life. Young (four- to eight-month-old) monkeys engage in two types of activity: rough-and-tumble play, best described as a "monkey wrestling match," and approach-avoidance play, similar to a game of tag, in which the animals rarely come into physical contact. It is primarily through such play that young monkeys learn to interact socially with other monkeys; dominance hierarchies are established which persist throughout adulthood. Aggression becomes a more pronounced part of behavior as monkeys grow older. Suomi suggests that there is definite survival value in aggression as long as it is socialized. Wild monkeys must learn to protect their troops from predators and other hostile monkeys. However, undirected and uncontrolled aggression might destroy their society; therefore, it becomes necessary to practice aggression in controlled intergroup situations:

> A major function of play is the development of control over the intensity and the target of aggressive behavior. Play very likely has a similar function for humans. One only has to watch a professional football game to be convinced.[15]

Play also represents an arena in which primates develop what appear to be sex-related patterns of behavior. At an early stage of life, young male monkeys differ sharply from females in their play. They are far more active and aggressive. In contrast,

> . . . few females get caught in rough-and-tumble play, and in approach-avoidance exchanges they are chased more than they pursue. A female infant rarely initiates a play bout with a male. Male monkeys, however, try to play with anybody and anything.[16]

Sexual elements—including mounting and pelvic thrusting—are seen in the play of primates, particularly among monkeys. Millar describes such activity as play which leads to the development of behavior patterns related to definite biological functions, such as feeding, fighting, and reproduction—without, however, accomplishing the actual purpose of the function. In other words, such play acts represent practice for later "real" behavior. Other play activities among primates involve investigating and exploring the environment, manipulating and experimenting with objects, and learning specific motor skills related to food gathering or survival.

The "practice" function of play has been illustrated even more vividly in anthropological studies of primitive societies. Leacock describes play among rural African tribes as clearly a rehearsal for adult responsibilities. In African societies, she writes, play

> entails technical as well as social practice, for boys and girls build and thatch small houses and make and use various tools and utensils

according to local practice. The boys make axes, knobkerries, spears, shields, slings, and bows and arrows, and may also build miniature cattle kraals. Girls make pottery for cooking real or imaginary food, clay or reed dolls, and perhaps mats or baskets of plaited grass.[17]

In many other ways, children gather knowledge of tribal customs and values or practice forms of adult behavior through play. In the Gikuyu tribe of Kenya, children learn through riddles and puzzles, or are told of their people's history through lullabies and stories. Read writes that in Malawi a typical amusement of Ngoni boys of five to seven was playing at law courts. They sat around in traditional style with different boys representing the "chief" and his "elders" the "plaintiffs" and "defendants" presenting their cases,

> . . . and the counselors conducting proceedings and cross-examining witnesses. In their high, squeaky voices the little boys imitated their fathers whom they had seen in the courts, and they gave judgments, imposing heavy penalties, and keeping order in the court with ferocious severity.[18]

Such examples show how among animals or in primitive human cultures play provides an important medium for learning. In modern, industrialized society the examples are less obvious. Nonetheless, there has been considerable investigation of play as a basic element in human development and cognitive growth.

Play in Cognitive Development

The leading psychologist over the past several decades in the field of child development has been Jean Piaget, professor at the University of Geneva and director of the *Institut Rousseau*. Piaget suggests that there are two processes basic to all mental development—*assimilation* and *accommodation*. Assimilation is the process of taking in, as in the case of receiving information in the form of visual or auditory stimuli. Accommodation is the process of adjusting to external circumstances and stimuli. Within Piaget's theory, play is specially related to assimilation, the process of mentally digesting new and different situations and experiences. Anything important that has happened is reproduced in play; it is a means of assimilating and consolidating the child's emotional experiences.[19]

Piaget regarded play primarily as repetition of an activity already mastered, rather than as an attempt to investigate or explore it further and develop a capability for dealing with it more effectively (which would be part of accommodation). Some psychologists have criticized Piaget's analysis of play as being severely limited; they feel his theory views play as only a "transient, infantile stage in the emergence of thought," lacking an originating or innovating role in the development of new concepts. In part, this is because Piaget regarded play and imitation as distinctly separate phenomena; while play was part of assimilation, imitation was part of accommodation. In contrast, most systematic observers of children's behavior regard imitative activity as a basic element of play.

Another leading authority on cognitive development has been Jerome Bruner, formerly director of Harvard University's Center for Cognitive Studies and now professor of psychology at Oxford. Bruner's analysis suggests that cognitive development in children has three broad stages. In the first, which he calls the "pre-operational" stage, the child's mental task consists chiefly of establishing relationships between experiences and their results, and of learning how to understand and represent the external world through symbols established through simple generalizations. The second stage, that of "concrete operations," involves the child's learning to gather data about the environment and to understand and be able to predict its operations within his own mind, rather than through trial and error. In the third stage, "formal operations," the child's ability becomes based on hypothetical propositions and understandings of relationships, rather than on immediate experiences and observation.[20]

Bruner stresses the need to establish the child's sense of autonomy as well as encourage his intense involvement if the fullest degree of learning is to occur. He urges that children be freed from the immediate controls of environmental rewards and punishments, the need to gain parental or teacher approval, and the need to avoid failure. Learning should be approached as the discovery of ideas, rather than as learning "about" something. In a recent article, Bruner summarized the results of a study of the effects of play on the problem-solving abilities of three- to five-year-olds. This study focused on a basic principle of learning—that in approaching complex tasks, too much motivation can interfere with learning by placing pressure on the learners and creating a state of anxiety and frustration:

> By deemphasizing the importance of the goal, play may serve to reduce excessive drive and thus enable young animals and children to learn more easily the skills they will need when they are older.[21]

In a comparison of play as a method of learning with several other techniques of instruction, Bruner found it to be highly effective. Beyond this, the experimenters were struck by the tenacity with which the children in the experimental group stuck to their task. Even when they had temporary failures they were able to persevere, "because they were able to resist frustration and the temptation to give up. They were playing."

Games and Games Theory

Games represent a particularly useful form of play-related learning activity. A number of anthropologists and psychologists have examined the relationship of games to child rearing in primitive societies; it has been found that games reflect the lifestyles and fundamental values of the tribes in which they are found.

For example, games of physical skill predominate in societies which stress achievement and success as important life goals. Strategic games that simulate war and combat are found chiefly in tribes with complicated social and political structures. Games of chance reflect tribal religious practices and beliefs. In one series of studies, Sutton-Smith and Gump explored the role of children's games in more advanced cultures. They concluded that games provided children with "action-based social relationships," giving them the opportunity to assume a variety of roles and status positions and providing gratification and psychological release.[22]

There has been a marked increase in the use of games specially devised to teach fundamental concepts, provide information, and encourage strategic behavior. James Coleman, a leading authority on adolescent development, has written on the value of playing games as a learning experience:

Recently, educators have begun devising games for high school and pre-high school students that simulate complex activities in a society. One of the ways that simulation and games were first combined was in war games. Many of the oldest parlor games (chess and checkers, for example) were developed as war simulations long ago, and today armies use games to develop logistic and strategic skills.

From war games developed the idea of management games, a simulation of management decision-making which is used in many business schools and firms to train future executives by putting them in situations they will confront in their jobs.[23]

Coleman and his associates at Johns Hopkins have developed a number of games that simulate aspects of society—a *Life Career Game*, a *Family Game*, a *Community Response Game*, and a *Consumer Game* (in which the players are consumers and department-store credit managers). Games developed in other settings have been used to help children learn simple scientific, mathematical, and linguistic concepts. One firm provides game kits and visual aids that use playlike approaches to teach number relationships and mathematical symbols; puzzle boxes and equation games are just two of these approaches. Other games deal with civics, government, history and political science, banking, international trade, geometry, and physics.

Games are particularly useful in shaping social attitudes. Recognizing that children today are overly exposed to values that stress competition and winning at all costs—often resulting in feelings of failure and rejection—T. D. Orlick of the University of Ottawa has experimented with games deliberately conceived to encourage mutual acceptance, cooperation, and positive forms of group interaction. It was found that cooperative social behavior could be significantly increased in groups of young children without a loss in motivation.[24] Similarly, a special Quaker Project on Community Conflict has used games to train schoolchildren in non-violent response techniques. Focusing on four central themes—cooperation, personal affirmation, communication, and conflict resolution—the games have been used successfully in several public-school systems in the United States.

The Role of Play in Psychoanalytical Theory

The dominant figure in the development of psychoanalytical theory was Sigmund Freud, whose contribution during the early twentieth century was immense. Many of Freud's fundamental concepts of personality development, as well as his exposition of psychological mechanisms, have profound implications for the understanding of play.

Freud's View of Play

Freud believed that the child brings into the world a somewhat unorganized mentality, called the *id,* which is dominated by powerful drives for self-preservation, the alleviation of hunger, and sexual expression (called *libido*)—all linked to the continuation of the species. As the child grows older, Freud suggested, a portion of

57

the id becomes transformed into the *ego,* which tries to govern the id when it behaves in socially disapproved ways. When sharp conflicts arise between the two (typically, the ego refuses to let the sexual impulses of the id express themselves freely), neurosis occurs. A third element, the *superego,* represents a modified or exaggerated part of the ego. It personifies all the prohibitions and strict rules of conduct imposed on the child by authority figures and may be perceived as a powerful conscience and sense of duty.

As the child moves from instinct-dominated infancy to socially adjusted adulthood, many conflicts and frustrations are dealt with or worked out through play. Play is constantly used to re-enact unpleasant experiences or frightening events, in order to gain control over them and dispel their effects. Millar writes:

> Exciting events, i.e. unpleasant tensions and conflicts, are repeated in phantasy or in play because repetition reduces the excitement which has been aroused. Play enables the child to master the disturbing event or situation by actively bringing it about, rather than by being a passive and helpless spectator.[25]

Children frequently use play symbolically, to express forbidden urges or frightening emotions in acceptable form. For example, plunging a doll in water or throwing it against a wall may relieve a jealous sibling's feeings—without hurting the newborn baby. It is believed that children often enjoy playing in dirt, sand, or water as acceptable substitutes for "soiling" or "wetting" themselves. Children who fear going to the doctor are likely to dose their dolls or toy animals with "medicine," or even to perform operations on them.

In the continuing attempt to resolve conflicts between the drives of the id and the controls exerted on them by the ego and the superego, a number of psychological mechanisms are employed. Freud described these as *sublimation, regression, compensation, repression,* and *identification.* Each may be directly related to play involvement.

Sublimation is the process through which sexual energies and aggressions are rechanneled into socially desirable activities. Artistic activities are often regarded as a form of sublimation for those who are not able or permitted to express sexual drives directly and must divert them into other, more culturally acceptable forms. In *regression,* the individual returns to behavior characteristic of his childhood, an easier and less demanding time. Play frequently provides an opportunity to engage in activities fixated at an early stage of development. *Compensation* occurs when an individual with certain limitations (possibly of a physical nature) that prevent his being successful within one sphere of activity pours his energies into another form of activity to achieve success and satisfaction. Play obviously provides many such compensatory outlets. *Repression* consists of an individual's refusing to face the cause of his tension and anxiety; play may offer a means of reducing the tension that has been repressed and therefore not relieved on a more fundamental level. A final mechanism, *identification,* may involve one's engaging in an activity because one identifies subconsciously with a person whom one loves or admires. Thus, a child may express this impulse by engaging in pursuits his parents enjoy.

A number of Freud's other theories had a significant impact on the concepts of play and recreation. He advanced the "pleasure principle," which suggests that man's basic desire is instinct gratification. Many of the substitute activities that occur because of lack of sexual gratification are thought to arise because of this urge.

In his later writings, Freud asserted that man was dominated by a "repetition compulsion," described earlier as the effort to repeat and master unpleasant events through play. Alderman comments:

> Generally speaking, Freud's view of play is as the projection of wishes and reenactment of conflicts and events in order to master their disturbing effects. He felt that play can reveal the inner life and the motivational structure of the individual.[26]

Freud also hypothesized that the so-called death instinct was a primary motivating factor in human behavior. Some of his followers have concluded that high-risk activities, such as sky diving, car racing, mountain climbing, and other extremely dangerous sports, represent the influence of the death wish. Such activities clearly have become a major preoccupation in modern life. There seems to be an inordinate fascination on the part of human beings—particularly males—with violent, dangerous, and even masochistic forms of play. Juvenile gangs that mug, rob, and kill largely for the fun of it; mountain climbers who scale the sheer, rock faces of cliffs, remaining pinned against their surfaces like crawling ants for several days without rest; snowmobilers who race over courses several hundred miles long in the frozen north, often at the cost of frostbite or worse—all these exemplify the fascination with risk and danger.

Freud's death-instinct theory is also apparent in riots, disturbances, and other forms of social conflict or ritual which, although serious in their purpose, also manifest distinct elements of play. The belief that one's hostile or aggressive drives may be harmlessly dispelled through sport or similar activity is highly questionable when one examines the frequent effects of sport. In Latin-American countries, Europe, and even the British Isles, major team sports such as rugby or soccer frequently end in pitched battles among the players, attacks upon officials, and even riots, with hundreds of spectators being injured or killed. The fans themselves are often stirred up to fever pitch, and it is now recognized that heart attacks represent a serious hazard at sports stadiums; in a recent year, several hundred spectators with heart disease died while watching sports. Nor are such forms of behavior limited to sports. As many as 180 celebrators died through violence in a recent year in Rio de Janeiro, while cavorting in the Brazilian Lenten Carnival. And pathological forms of play—such as playing "Russian Roulette," or playing "chicken" on the highway—are all too common, frequently resulting in fatal accidents.

Such examples of dangerous or violent forms of play appear to lend credence both to Freud's death-wish theory and to the "stimulus-arousal" theory of play described earlier. However, this may be an oversimplification. When George Willig, a young toy designer who enjoyed mountain climbing as a hobby, scaled the sheer face of the towering World Trade Center building in New York City before thousands of hypnotized onlookers, his accomplishment was hailed as a fantastic feat of courage. Willig commented afterwards that he resented hearing others suggest that mountain climbers have a death wish. "I don't have a death wish," he said. "I have a life wish, and when I climb, I really feel alive." Seen in this light, such daring feats seem better explained by the "stimulus-arousal" or "competence-effectance" theories of play described earlier than by Freud's death-wish theory.

Freud also saw hidden meaning in play involving wit and humor. Although many jokes or play expressions appear to be meaningless or nonsensical, he felt that they invariably contain double meanings and are used to mask or disguise an individual's real impulses and thoughts. What is too hostile, sexual, or painful to be openly expressed is often stated as a joke, making it less provocative. Humor is used to make a veiled attack on oneself or others and, when analyzed, is an important means of understanding behavior.

Freud's general view of play was that it served as a means of denying and repressing reality; many of the interpretations of play and recreation based on his theories are essentially negative. It must be recognized, however, that he spent most of his career working with severely neurotic patients, and that it was on the basis of his experience with this population that he developed his total theory of personality. It is not surprising that play and recreation from this vantage point seem replete with negative and self-destructive elements. It is important to stress that play may also serve a number of highly positive psychological functions—as an ego-rewarding activity, a means of obtaining security within group situations, a form of reality testing, and a constructive outlet for varied emotional drives and creative impulses.

Play Therapy

The most direct application of Freud's theories of play came about through the development of play therapy as a treatment technique for emotionally disturbed children. This approach, developed by Melanie Klein and other followers of Freud, involved a variety of methods. Usually the therapist sought to establish a permissive and free setting, and a trusting, warm relationship with the child under treatment. Play itself was used to let the child spontaneously "play out" his problems, through the symbolic use of dolls, toys, or other equipment, and provided the medium through which the therapist could observe and understand the child. Axline wrote that play therapy

> . . . may be described as an opportunity that is offered to the child to experience growth under the most favorable conditions. Since play is his natural medium for self-expression, the child is given the opportunity to play out his accumulated feelings of tension, frustration, insecurity, aggression, fear, bewilderment, confusion.[27]

Relationship of Play and Mental Health

A number of contemporary psychiatrists and psychoanalysts have supported the position that there is a strong relationship between play, recreation, and leisure values on the one hand, and emotional well-being on the other.

Karl Menninger, for example, pioneered the use of play and recreation in the treatment of the mentally ill, in the conviction that a well-rounded play life is essential to maintaining a healthy emotional balance. Menninger suggests that play provides the opportunity for many "miniature victories" that compensate for the injuries inflicted by the daily wear and tear of life. Under his direction, a study carried out at the famous Menninger Sanitarium in Topeka, Kansas, compared the hobby interests of a number of seriously ill patients with those of a group of relatively well-adjusted patients. It was found that the well-adjusted patients pursued nearly twice as many hobbies as the patients who were seriously ill.

Menninger concluded that in his work with psychiatric patients, he consistently found them deficient in the capacity for play, and unable to develop balanced recreational interests and skills.[28]

Alexander Reid Martin, a highly regarded psychiatrist who served for twelve years as chairman of the American Psychiatric Association's Committee on Leisure Time and Its Uses, has written extensively on the problem of leisure in relation to mental health today. Martin has found that the Protestant work ethic and the overemphasis on work values in our society have made it extremely difficult for many people to use their leisure in self-fulfilling and satisfying ways. Within his professional practice, he has found many highly successful individuals who can justify themselves only through work, and who feel intensely guilty about play. Often they suffer from what Martin calls "week-end neurosis," and it is not uncommon for them to have severe psychological upsets while on vacation.

The real need, Martin suggests, is for individuals to become more autonomous and to develop a set of inner values and resources that will help them use their leisure in confident and enjoyable ways. Society today provides a host of what Martin calls "external resources" for leisure, resulting in

> . . . the present overdependence upon television, movies, travelling, motorboating, games, spectator sports, rock festivals, etc. Excessive use of such external resources accounts for the present billion-dollar leisure-time market. . . . in other words, we have to continue to provide these external substitutes until we can clearly identify and eradicate those factors in our work culture that impair our inner resources.[29]

Even in communities that have a wealth of recreation facilities and agencies, Martin comments, young people often feel that there is "nothing to do," and fall back upon vandalism, drug taking, or other antisocial forms of play. What is critically needed, he concludes, is a fuller understanding of the meaning of leisure in our society, and a stronger effort to build those inner resources that will see play and recreation as worthy forms of personal expression.

Another leading psychiatrist, Erich Fromm, in his book *The Sane Society* suggests that people today suffer from a lack of autonomy and self-direction in leisure and recreation, as in other aspects of their lives. As consumers, they are manipulated and sold products they do not really need or understand. Marketing techniques in the twentieth century have created a receptive orientation, in which the aim is to "drink in," to have something new all the time, to be a passive, alienated recipient of leisure goods that are thrust upon one. Fromm writes of the consumer:

> He does not participate actively, he wants to "take in" all there is to be had, and to have as much as possible of pleasure, culture and what not. Actually, he is not free to enjoy "his" leisure; his leisure-time consumption is determined by industry, as are the commodities he buys; his taste is manipulated, he wants to see and to hear what he is conditioned to want to see and to hear; entertainment is an industry like any other, the customer is made to buy fun as he is made to buy dresses and shoes. The value of the fun is determined by its success on the market, not by anything which could be measured in human terms.[30]

Fromm describes modern man as having a "push-button" mentality; his heavy dependence on mechanical devices excludes the possibility of real relationships or meaningful experiences. The tourist who is constantly occupied with taking pictures sees nothing at all, and does nothing except through the intermediary of the camera. When he returns home, "the outcome of his 'pleasure' trip is a collection of snapshots, which are the substitute for an experience which he could have had, but did not have."[31]

Self-Actualization through Play

Closely linked to this position are the views of Abraham Maslow, who stresses the need for individuals to develop to their fullest degree of independence and creative potential. Maslow developed a convincing theory of human motivation, as part of which he identified a number of important human needs, arranging them in a hierarchy of priority. As each of the basic needs is met in turn, humans are able to move ahead to meet more advanced needs and drives. Maslow's theory included the following levels of need:

> *Physiological needs:* food, rest, exercise, shelter, protection from the elements, and other basic survival needs

> *Safety needs:* self-protection needs on a secondary level—protection against danger, threats, or other forms of deprivation

> *Social needs:* needs for group associations, acceptance by one's fellows, giving and receiving affection and friendship

> *Ego needs:* needs for enhanced status, a sense of achievement, self-esteem, confidence, and recognition by others

> *Self-actualization needs:* needs for being creative, and realizing one's maximum potential in a variety of life spheres[32]

Obviously, play and recreation can be important elements in satisfying at least the three highest levels of need in Maslow's hierarchy. As does Fromm, Maslow stresses the need for individuals to be more spontaneous and creative, and to see meaningful values in a variety of expressive experiences—including both work *and* play.

New Directions in Play Research

The writings of Menninger, Martin, Fromm, and Maslow, although based in part on their clinical experiences, also represent their own philosophical views, and are therefore to some degree subjective. In contrast, psychologists today are contributing to a growing body of empirical research in play and leisure.

The Psychology of Leisure

Within the past several years, an increasing number of psychologists have studied the motivation, values, attitudes, and perceptions of leisure involvement. Neulinger and Crandall point out that much of this new research emphasis has come about because we are no longer satisfied to *name* the activities that people engage in; we now want to know what they *mean* to participants.

Especially as a humanistic and "holistic" approach to leisure becomes more fully accepted, psychological analysis of play activities will contribute to our understanding in this field. Neulinger and Crandall write:

> A psychological definition of leisure . . . emphasizing self-development and fulfillment through freely chosen, meaningful activities, makes leisure particularly relevant and valuable for those sections of our society that are presently underprivileged in one way or another.[33]

A number of studies in the 1970s have begun to explore such theoretical questions as the relationship between play and leisure activities and personality; the influence of parental values and early play experiences on later leisure choices; and varied dimensions of leisure participation. Spreitzer and Snyder, for example, have examined the affective meanings attached to leisure participation, and have concluded that when work does not permit self-actualization and self-expression, leisure tends to take on an important compensatory meaning as a form of self-definition.[34] Similarly, Neulinger and Breit found that persons who lack strong job satisfaction and commitment are more likely to identify themselves through their leisure than those satisfied in their work, although work tends to be the more powerful means of self-actualization for most people today.[35]

Howard examined the relationship between several types of leisure involvement and a number of important personality traits. He found, for example, that individuals who prefer *outdoor-nature* pastimes tend to be adventurous, forceful, and self-reliant, while those who score high on *sports* activities tend to be aggressive, incautious, spontaneous, and pleasure seeking.[36]

Such research is helping to bridge what was formerly a gap between the social and behavioral sciences in the study of play behavior and leisure attitudes and involvement. It seems probable that a key aspect of play behavior—the dynamics of group participation—will become an increasingly important subject for investigation by social psychologists, particularly in the field of sport psychology.

The Psychology of Sport

There has been relatively little empirical and systematic investigation of sport attitudes, motivations, and behavior in the United States and Canada until recently. However, interest in this field is growing, and Singer predicts that the myths, superstitions, and half-truths that have provided the basis for much instruction and coaching in sport will soon be replaced by a body of valid information gathered through rigorous experimental and observational methods. He writes:

> The American Psychological Association has identified a number of specialty areas as branches of psychology. The five areas most relevant to sport psychology [are] developmental, personality, learning and training, social, and psychometrics.[37]

Specifically, the following areas are appropriate for investigation: the identification of athletes with desirable psychological attributes; the understanding and treatment of younger athletes; the progression of athletes as quickly as possible from performance potential to performance realization; the motivation of athletes during the preseason, preevent, and event; effective development of team morale and favorable attitudes toward both competition and cooperation; understanding group dynamics and leadership; and understanding the psychological problems of individual athletes.

A number of studies reported in the *Research Quarterly* in the mid- and late 1970s illustrate the directions being taken by researchers in sport psychology. Morgan sums up several of these and the psychological concepts they support: (1) that athletes in various forms of sports have distinctly different personality structures, on the basis of psychological measurement of traits and characteristics; (2) that high-level performers in athletics are characterized by psychological profiles that generally distinguish them from lower-level performers; (3) that "emotional first aid," to deal with psychological needs and problems, should be regarded as being as important as physical first aid after competition; and (4) that there often is a lack of congruence between the conscious and unconscious motivations of athletes.[38] There have been numerous other studies—by O'Connor and Webb,[39] Ibrahim and Morrison,[40] and Martin and Myrick,[41] among others—of personality traits of athletes, self-actualization and self-concept among athletes, and other psychological aspects of sports participation.

Within these new areas of the psychology of sport and leisure, it is obvious that play and recreation are becoming increasingly important subjects for scientific investigation. This is equally true in the broad field of sociological research, as presented in the next chapter.

Chapter Three

1. Quoted in Eda J. LeShan, "The 'Perfect' Child," *New York Times Magazine*, 27 August 1967, p. 63.

2. Ruth Strang, *An Introduction to Child Study* (New York: Macmillan, 1951), p. 495.

3. Arnold Gesell and Frances Ilg, *The Child from Five to Ten* (New York: Harper, 1946), p. 360.

4. Erik Erikson, in Morris L. Haimowitz and Natalie R. Haimowitz, *Human Development: Selected Readings* (New York: Thomas Y. Crowell, 1960), p. 303.

5. Bruno Bettelheim, "What Children Learn from Play," *Parents' Magazine*, July 1964, pp. 4, 9–10, 102.

6. Susanna Millar, *The Psychology of Play* (Baltimore: Penguin, 1968), pp. 178–84.

7. Jerome S. Bruner, "Child Development: Play Is Serious Business," *Psychology Today*, January 1975, p. 83.

8. Arthur Jersild, *The Psychology of the Adolescent* (New York: Macmillan, 1963), p. 106–7.

9. Jean Jordaan, in Donald E. Super, Reuben Starishevsky, and Norman Matlin, *Career Development: Self-Concept Theory* (Princeton, N.J.: Coll. Ent. Exam., 1963), p. 42.

10. M. J. Ellis, *Why People Play* (Englewood Cliffs, N.J.: Prentice-Hall, 1973), pp. 80–111.

11. "Oddball Olympics," *Time*, 13 May 1974, p. 72.

12. Pete Axthelm, "The Thrill Seekers," *Reader's Digest*, November 1975, p. 217.

13. Ibid.

14. Lois Murphy, "Letter to the Editor," *New York Times Magazine*, 12 November 1967, p. 42.

15. Stephen J. Suomi and Harry F. Harlow, "Monkeys at Play," in *Play: A Natural History Magazine Special Supplement*, December 1971, p. 75.

16. Ibid., p. 73.

17. Eleanor Leacock, "At Play in African Villages," in *Play: A Natural History Magazine Special Supplement*, December 1971, p. 60.

18. Ibid., p. 61.

19. Millar, *Psychology of Play*, p. 55.

20. Jerome S. Bruner, *On Knowing: Essays for the Left Hand* (Cambridge, Mass.: Harvard U. Pr., 1962), pp. 34–36.

21. Jerome S. Bruner, "Child Development," p. 82.

22. Brian Sutton-Smith and Paul Gump, "Games and Status Experience," *Recreation,* April 1955, p. 172.

23. James S. Coleman, "Learning Through Games," *National Education Association Journal,* January 1967, p. 69.

24. T. D. Orlick, "Games of Acceptance and Psycho-Social Development," in Timothy Craig, ed., *The Humanistic and Mental Health Aspects of Sports, Exercise and Recreation* (Chicago: American Medical Association, 1975), pp. 60–65.

25. Millar, *Psychology of Play,* p. 29.

26. R. B. Alderman, *Psychological Behavior in Sport* (Philadelphia: Saunders, 1974), p. 35.

27. Virginia Axline, *Play Therapy: The Inner Dynamics of Childhood* (Boston: Houghton Mifflin, 1947), p. 16.

28. Karl Menninger, *Love Against Hate* (New York: Harcourt, Brace and World, 1942), p. 185.

29. Alexander Reid Martin, "Leisure and Our Inner Resources," *Parks and Recreation,* March 1975, p. 10a.

30. Erich Fromm, *The Sane Society* (New York: Fawcett Paperback, 1955), p. 124.

31. Ibid., p. 125.

32. Abraham H. Maslow, "A Theory of Human Motivation," *Psychological Review,* July 1943, pp. 370–96.

33. John Neulinger and Rick Crandall, "The Psychology of Leisure," *Journal of Leisure Research,* 3 August 1976, pp. 181–84.

34. Eldon E. Snyder and Elmer Spreitzer, "Work Orientation, Meaning of Leisure and Mental Health, *Journal of Leisure Research,* Summer 1974, pp. 207–19.

35. John Neulinger and Miranda Breit, "Attitude Dimensions of Leisure," *Journal of Leisure Research,* Summer 1969, pp. 255–61.

36. Dennis R. Howard, "Multivariate Relationships between Leisure Activities and Personality," *Research Quarterly,* May 1976, pp. 226–37.

37. Robert N. Singer, "Sport Psychology," *Journal of Physical Education and Recreation,* September 1976, p. 24.

38. William P. Morgan, "Selected Psychological Considerations in Sport," *Research Quarterly,* December 1974, pp. 374–89.

39. Kathleen A. O'Connor and James L. Webb, "Investigation of Personality Traits of College Female Athletes and Nonathletes," *Research Quarterly,* March 1976, pp. 203–10.

40. Hilmi Ibrahim and Nettie Morrison, "Self-Actualization and Self-Concept Among Athletes," *Research Quarterly,* March 1976, pp. 68–79.

41. Warren S. Martin and Fred L. Myrick, "Personality and Leisure Time Activities," *Research Quarterly,* May 1976, pp. 246–53.

THE SOCIOLOGY OF LEISURE

This chapter is concerned with the collective behavior of Americans and Canadians within the broad area of leisure and recreational participation. It examines leisure as a social phenomenon and a form of social interaction influenced by such variables as socioeconomic class, occupational prestige, lifestyle, disability, economic capability, and ethnic or racial affiliation. It is based on two key assumptions: (1) that leisure is an important institution in modern society, which both influences and is influenced by other institutions and trends; and (2) that the systematic sociological analysis of leisure and recreation is not only of scholarly value, but can contribute significantly to intelligent social planning to improve the quality of contemporary life.

While this chapter does not attempt to see modern leisure through the prism of any single sociological perspective or viewpoint, it does cite numerous examples of research by reputable sociologists—both those who have identified it as an area of primary concern, and those who have dealt with it as part of a larger issue.

Early Studies of Social Class and Leisure

One of the most familiar maxims in the professional literature of recreation service has been that all community residents should be provided with *equal* recreational opportunities. A number of early sociological investigations disclosed, however, that Americans differed significantly in their recreational interests, according to social class. The term *class* generally refers to the horizontal stratification of a population by such factors as family background, occupation, income, community status, group affiliation (race, religion or nationality), and education. Lloyd Warner, a leading sociologist, wrote:

> By class is meant two or more orders of people who are believed to be, and are, accordingly ranked by the members of the community, in socially superior and inferior positions. A class system also provides that children are born into the same status as their parents. A class society distributes rights and privileges, duties and obligations, unequally among its inferior and superior grades. A system of classes, unlike a system of castes, provides by its own values for movement up and down the social ladder . . . in technical terms, social mobility.[1]

A Pioneer Study of Suburban Leisure Patterns

One of the first studies of leisure was conducted by Lundberg, Komarovsky, and McInerney in 1934.[2] It involved an analysis of 2,460 individuals in Westchester County, New York, grouped under seven headings: labor, white collar, professional and executive, housewives, unemployed, high school students, and college students.

Lundberg and his associates reported that 90 percent or more of the leisure of all classes except students was divided among seven activities: eating, visiting with friends, reading, public entertainment, sports, listening to the radio, and motoring. Each group examined had characteristically different patterns of behavior. For example, housewives tended to spend the bulk of their free time on sociability, while men who had substantial amounts of leisure tended to spend it on visiting, reading, public entertainment, sports, and radio. Within each area of participation, there were also marked qualitative differences in leisure activity exhibited by the groups examined.

While this study provided only tentative generalizations about the varying uses of leisure by different population groups and did not specifically identify social class as a variable, it was unique in being a pioneer attempt to study the relationship of leisure to key sociological variables.

Social Class and Leisure Behavior

R. Clyde White carried out a systematic study of the relationship between social-class differences and the uses of leisure.[3] He investigated several census tracts in Cuyahoga County, Ohio, using a sampling of families that was representative of income, education, racial composition, occupation, and age distribution in the county's population as a whole. These families were grouped into four social classes: *upper-middle, lower-middle, upper-lower,* and *lower-lower.* White then studied the families' uses of leisure under nine major categories, and also examined the settings in which leisure activities were performed.

He found that the home was the most frequently used leisure setting, with commercial amusements a close second. There was much less involvement in community-provided facilities, such as parks, playgrounds, or Community Chest agencies. In general, the study found that the lower social classes made greater use of such facilities than the middle classes. Other distinctions were made between lower-

and middle-class uses of such leisure facilities as radios, phonographs, television, movies, theaters, and taverns. These distinctions grew sharper with age:

> It is clear that the tendency to choose leisure activities on the grounds of membership in a particular social class begins in adolescence and becomes more pronounced in maturity. . . . As people get older and settle into the ways of the class to which they belong, they choose leisure activities which are congenial to their class.[4]

To illustrate, junior-high-school youth of the upper-lower class had more leisure than those of the upper-middle class, devoting almost twice as much time to radio, television, movies, and sports as did their counterparts. Certain sex differences were also found; boys tended to be more involved in entertainment and sports, while girls had more remunerative work and home duties.

Leisure and Prestige Levels

A third major study of leisure patterns was reported in 1956, by Alfred C. Clarke.[5] Viewing leisure as an aspect of social stratification, he identified five groups of urban adult males along a continuum of occupational prestige. With this population, he explored two basic questions: (1) whether participation in specific activities was significantly linked to occupational-prestige levels, and (2) if such relationships were found, what kinds of preferences were displayed on each level.

Clarke found that men on the highest prestige level were most frequently involved in such activities as attending theaters, concerts, or motion pictures, visiting museums or art galleries, playing bridge, reading for pleasure, and doing community-service work. Men on the lowest prestige level were the most frequent participants in watching television, going to the zoo or to baseball games, spending time in taverns, fishing, playing with their children, driving their cars for pleasure, playing poker, and going to drive-in movies.

Clarke concluded that while differences in leisure behavior were clearly related to prestige levels, some of the class-connected expectations about leisure might be dying out. He called for new, rigorous research that would take into account such elements as economic, religious, and political affiliations.

Occupation and Leisure Behavior

Joel E. Gerstl explored the influence on leisure behavior of *different* occupations pursued by people of approximately the *same* prestige level.[6] He selected three upper-middle-class occupations for his analysis: the independent professional practitioner (dentist), the organization man in the corporate business world (advertising man), and the salaried intellectual (college professor).

Distinct differences were found, both in the amount of leisure time each group had and in the kinds of activities they enjoyed. Professors reported the longest workweeks (averaging fifty-six to sixty hours), with much work being done at home; advertising men averaged forty-five hours a week, with some of this done at home; and dentists averaged forty hours a week, with little work done at home. As for leisure choices, the subjects reported sports involvement as shown in table 4-1.

68

Table 4-1

Participation in Selected Sports by Occupation

Activity	Ad Men	Dentists	Professors
Golf	32	27	0
Hunting	7	18	1
Fishing	17	28	5
Bowling	8	4	0
Swimming	29	13	10
Boating-sailing	8	2	2
Hiking-walking	13	1	10
Skiing	10	0	3
Tennis	9	6	6
Other Activities	18	19	10
Total score	151	118	47

Source: Joel E. Gerstl, in Erwin O. Smigel, ed., *Work and Leisure* (New Haven, Conn.: College and University Press, 1963), p. 151.

Professors participated most in cultural activities, such as theater or concert attendance. Certain characteristics of each profession were seen to be relevant to recreational choices. The dentists' high level of interest in hunting and fishing suggests the need for change from a physically confining, delicate, and tension-filled job. The advertising men's high involvement in golf, swimming, boating, and tennis may well be linked to the need to do business on the green or in the clubhouse. Gerstl concluded that the contrasts among occupations within a single social stratum

> indicate that the crucial explanatory factor is that of the occupational milieu—consisting of the setting of the work situation, the nature of the work performed, and the norms derived from occupational reference groups.[7]

One might speculate that, rather than occupation's determining an individual's leisure pattern, certain personality traits affect his choice of both profession and leisure patterns and recreational interests.

Social Class as a Determinant of Leisure

In recent years, a number of sociologists have suggested that the traditional concept of social class is no longer useful in predicting leisure interests and attitudes. Max Kaplan commented that the concept of "class" was becoming less useful in the social sciences; inexpensive travel, the mass media, and widespread affluence have brought many forms of leisure within the reach of almost everyone. He concluded that in leisure activity, more than in any other area of American life, "social class" had become an outmoded concept.[8]

Similarly, the sociologist Nels Anderson stated that class lines have become less strictly drawn:

> All classes attend the same ball games, the same prize fights, the same night clubs, even the same opera. All listen to the radio and view the same television programs. All attend dances or go to the horse races. The difference is in money outlay; how much is spent for the fishing outfit, the automobile, the television set, the seat at the opera or the table at the night club.[9]

Certainly there has been a blurring of social-class stratification in modern society, a blurring reflected in leisure behavior. However, although relatively large numbers of people now have both leisure and a degree of affluence, it would be sheer nonsense to suggest that the pastimes of all levels of society are basically the same, that it is only a matter of where we sit at the opera. There continue to be two important distinctions in the choice of leisure activity that are closely related to social class—*cultural taste* and *opportunity*.

It is obvious that the so-called cultural explosion that followed World War II did not reach and involve all social classes equally. In a comprehensive study of the performing arts during the 1960s, Baumol and Bowen found that the audience for them was drawn from an extremely narrow segment of the national population, and was remarkably alike in makeup from city to city and from art form to art form. It consisted, they wrote,

> of persons who are extraordinarily well educated, whose incomes are very high, who are predominantly in the professions, and who are in their late youth or early middle age. Even if there has been a significant rise in the size of audiences in recent years, it has certainly not yet encompassed the general public. If the sociological base of the audience has in fact expanded, it must surely have been incredibly narrow before the boom got under way.[10]

Another key factor which influences patterns of leisure involvement today is economic. As the next chapter will clearly document, the vast expansion in recreational participation today is heavily dependent on financial capability.

Recreation for the Rich

An excellent way to illustrate the disparity that exists between those who have comfortable incomes and those who live at or below the poverty line is to examine the availability of recreational opportunity according to where one lives. Recreation has become an essential part of the packaging of housing for the well-to-do. For example, Starrett City, a huge apartment complex on 153 acres overlooking Jamaica Bay and Gateway National Seashore in New York City, offered the following recreational facilities in the late 1970s: a clubhouse—with meeting rooms, hobby and craft facilities, and an auditorium; a racquet and swim club—with nine all-weather, day-and-night courts and an Olympic-sized pool; football and baseball fields; basketball courts; children's playgrounds; bicycle paths; and various recreational programs with leadership for people of all ages.

While this may be an extreme example, many suburban developments,

70

particularly newer condomiums, also feature communally owned and operated recreation facilities. These often include swimming pools, tennis courts, clubhouses, and similar facilities. Many hundreds of private home developments today have their own golf courses, marinas and waterfronts, and sports complexes. As a vivid illustration, the Village of Oak Brook, a privately developed thirty-square-mile enclave west of Chicago that was built in the late 1960s, offered prospective purchasers an eight hundred-acre sports center, an eighteen-hundred-acre forest preserve, and

> a polo club and 12 polo fields, soccer fields, a private air strip that is the home of a glider soaring club, a golf course, a riding academy and riding trails with stables for 300 horses, skeet shooting, upland game-hunting areas and a fox-hunting preserve. . . . Inside the village limits also are another private golf club, a public course and a lake for canoeing, sailing and skating.[11]

There are many other examples of how the rich can meet their recreation needs in diversified and attractive ways. There are a number of community flying clubs, whose members join together for share-the-cost weekends or longer trips throughout the United States and occasionally to Europe and South America. When ski resorts become overcrowded, the solution of the very rich is to buy their own mountain and develop their own ski center, with members of private associations building their .own lodges and maintaining exclusive social communities around the center. Exclusive children's dancing classes are found in all large cities today. They are highly class oriented, with long waiting lists; some parents put their children's names on them at birth. Only the wealthy need apply.

The degree to which economic ability determines the use of leisure was illustrated in a study carried out by the Outdoor Recreation Resources Review Commission. The results shown in table 4-2 are based on an extensive sampling of the United States population over the age of twelve reported in 1962.

Table 4-2

Percentage of Population Taking Part in Specific Activities, Based on Income Levels

Family Income	Boating	Camping	Horseback Riding	Walking for Pleasure	Fishing
Under 1,500	4	3	2	19	24
1,500–2,999	0	4	3	28	21
3,000–4,499	19	6	4	32	28
4,500–5,999	24	8	6	36	32
6,000–7,999	28	10	7	37	32
8,000–9,999	33	13	7	37	31
10,000–14,999	41	18	11	37	39
15,000 and up	36	10	13	46	27

Source: *Outdoor Recreation for America: Report to the President and to Congress of the Outdoor Recreation Resources Review Commission*, Vol. 1 (Washington, D.C.: U.S. Government Printing Office, 1962), pp. 37–38.

It is obvious that high family incomes are closely correlated with participation in outdoor recreation. Even in those activities where the differences in the degree of participation among income levels are not great, it is likely that there will be a great difference in the *nature* of participation. The rich man goes fishing for salmon in Canada or for big-game fish from a cabin cruiser in the Caribbean; the poor man uses a hand line in a local pond or fishes from the banks of a semipolluted river near his home.

There continue to be marked differences in leisure participation based on certain social factors that, taken as a whole, unmistakably constitute social-class affiliation. The affluent, well-educated, suburban professional or business executive engages in a much greater variety of activities, and with greater frequency, than his less-educated, poorer, urban-dwelling counterpart. Anderson's conclusion that the poor attend the same nightclubs, operas, and horse races as the rich but simply buy cheaper seats is difficult to accept.

Recreation for the Poor

No major sociological study has focused specifically on the use of leisure by the poor, although a number of studies cutting across class lines have touched on this concern. During the Depression of the 1930s, the Welfare Council of New York City investigated three aspects of the lives of young people: employment, education, and leisure.[12] The report concluded that while there was abundant diversion in the city for those who could pay their own way, for the great mass of young people recreation had to come primarily through public provision—if it was to come at all. This was particularly true of youth in the lowest socioeconomic bracket.

In a landmark study of the impact of social class on adolescent life, *Elmtown's Youth,* August Hollingshead devoted two chapters to participation by teen-agers in both organized and unstructured leisure activities. Lower-class youth tended to be excluded from many clubs, youth organizations, and extracurricular school activities; they were financially unable to take part in many forms of commercial recreation, and sought out the less-approved forms of pleasure seeking. For them it was the search for pleasure, Hollingshead noted, that led to delinquency charges. He wrote:

> The nightly search for excitement by speeding, shooting firearms along the river roads, drinking, picking up girls, gambling, with now and again a fight, brings many of these young people face-to-face with the law. Pleasure-bent youths violate the mores, if not the law, almost every night. . . . In almost every one of these cases [delinquency convictions] the delinquent behavior is a concomitant of clique activity or sex play.[13]

In a more recent study, Herbert Gans analyzed a lower-class Italian-American population in Boston. Much of his report is concerned with the out-of-school, nonwork activity of teen-agers. Gans comments that West End adolescent peer-group life alternates between killing time and episodic searching for action.

> "Action" generates a state of quasi-hypnotic excitement which enables the individual to feel that he is in control, both of his own drives and of

the environment. Also, it allows him to forget that he is living in a routine-seeking world, where . . . adults make and enforce most of the rules. As previously noted, this state may be achieved through a card game, an athletic contest, a fight, a sexual adventure, or through an attack on the adult world (in the form of petty mischief, minor thefts, vandalism, etc.)[14]

Gans takes the position that much of the action-seeking behavior of lower-class youth is similar to that of middle-class adolescents. However, the lower-class teen-agers and young adults that he observed tended to meet on street corners, in tenement hallways, or in and around the small soda shops that dotted the neighborhood. Those who came under the influence of the church, the school, and the settlement house appeared to accept such influence as symbolic of a "routine-seeking" and upwardly mobile way of life. Thus, even in this relatively homogeneous population, the nature of each individual's leisure involvement symbolized his class aspiration.

Study of Leisure Values and Attitudes

Other more recent studies have continued to examine leisure participation in relation to socioeconomic variables. For example, in 1969 Rabel Burdge reported an examination of 1,635 adult residents of Allegheny County, Pennsylvania.[15] Subjects were divided into four groups on the basis of occupational prestige levels, with the highest class representing professionals and high-level management officials, and the lowest class consisting of unskilled workers.

As in the earlier investigation by Clarke, Burdge found that persons in the highest prestige classes participated in the greatest variety of leisure activities. Such outdoor recreation activities as water-skiing, snow skiing, and sailing were significantly associated with the highest prestige level. Other outdoor recreation activities like fishing, hunting, and bicycling involved subjects on the second-highest prestige level. Members on the lowest prestige level most frequently attended such spectator sports events as stock-car races, boxing, and wrestling matches. In analyzing his findings, Burdge commented that one of the ways "people prepare for entrance into a higher social class is to imitate the leisure behavior of that group." To illustrate, while Class I (highest-level) participants were most active in playing golf on golf courses, Class II subjects were more often involved in miniature golf or in using driving ranges.

Other sociological studies of leisure in the 1970s have tended to examine values and attitudes as a primary concern. Neulinger and Breit, for example, conducted a questionnaire study of 320 working adults, intended to explore the degree to which they defined themselves through leisure, as well as the extent to which work attitudes related to attitudes towards leisure. They succeeded in identifying seven key variables: (1) amount of work or vacation desired; (2) society's role in leisure planning; (3) self-definition through work or leisure; (4) amount of perceived leisure; (5) autonomous versus passive leisure pursuits; (6) affinity to leisure; and (7) importance of public approval. The researchers comment:

> We believe that we have identified . . . relatively independent dimensions in the leisure domain that are important in the characterization of a person's attitude toward leisure [which] should help us predict his reactions to issues of leisure and indicate whether leisure represents a blessing or a curse to him. It remains for further research to test these predictions.[16]

A number of studies have sought to determine the influence of childhood experience on leisure attitudes and behavior. Yoesting and Burkhead found that the frequency and range of childhood outdoor-recreation involvement had a significant effect on adult participation.[17] Kelly explored the process of socialization toward leisure by examining the origin of activities enjoyed during adulthood; he found that about half of these were first undertaken in childhood, primarily in the family setting, while the other half were begun during the adult years. There were distinct differences in the *kinds* of leisure involvement learned at different ages or in different settings.[18] Snyder and Spreitzer studied the nature of sports involvement, and found that it seemed to involve members of all demographic, social, and psychological characteristics. They concluded on the basis of their research that sports served to stimulate tension rather than to reduce it, and that the primary function of play in general was to provide an enjoyable disequilibrium and add novelty and excitement to life—not just as compensation for monotonous, unsatisfying work, but rather to heighten the enjoyment of all areas of everyday living.[19]

The continuing flow of research carried on by faculty members and advanced students in university curricula in the behavioral sciences and in recreation and leisure studies promises to provide a fuller understanding of attitudes, values, and motivation in the field of leisure.

Research in Special Populations

A number of significant studies have been conducted to examine the leisure patterns of special populations. For example, Sessoms and Oakley studied a group of hospitalized alcoholics in Butner, North Carolina, who were undergoing a month-long treatment program at an alcoholic rehabilitation center.[20] They found that, in comparison to a sample of adults studied as part of the Outdoor Recreation Resources Review Commission's research, these adult male alcoholics had an extremely limited pattern of active recreation involvement. They also found that there was a distinct pattern of drinking in connection with other leisure pursuits, and that some of these pursuits apparently encouraged drinking, while others inhibited it.

Babow and Simkin examined a random sample of 300 newly admitted male and female psychiatric patients at Napa State Hospital in California.[21] As in the Sessoms and Oakley study, they found a strikingly low level of leisure involvement, although they were not able to determine whether this was because of the unique characteristics of the patients themselves or because of a general lack of recreational opportunities prior to hospitalization.

Such studies promise to be useful both in determining the possible influence that disability may have on recreational participation and in suggesting the special benefits that may derive from certain forms of leisure activity.

74

Inventories of Leisure Participation

Studies of leisure involvement are today being conducted on national, state or provincial, and local levels. For the most part these surveys are inventories of recreational participation. They may record *all* forms of activity of a particular group, or concentrate on a major area of activity like outdoor recreation or on a specialized subarea like hunting and fishing. For example, the Canadian Outdoor Recreation Demand Study (CORDS), begun by Parks Canada in 1966, sought to measure patterns of recreation demand, population participation rates through household studies, park visitor statistics, various forms of tourism, and a number of similar concerns. Individual Canadian provinces have also carried out extensive analyses of recreational participation and tourism, and local municipalities have done extensive recreation surveys.

Analysis of Groups of Participants

In addition to studying patterns of involvement, researchers are now looking in depth at the kinds of groups that participate in given activities and sometimes contrasting different groups of participants.

Many researchers have examined water-based recreation through aggregate studies of the characteristics of participants, such as occupation, income, age, education, and place of residence. Field and O'Leary sought to determine the influence of social-grouping patterns on varied forms of water-based recreation.[22] Using a sample of 1,504 adult residents of western Washington, western Oregon, and northern California, they found distinct differences in the type of water recreation carried on by informants, based on social factors. Family groups tended primarily to visit beaches, swim, and boat. Friendship groups tended to engage more heavily in fishing, or to reflect other specialized interests. The implication of this study was that to comprehend leisure participation more clearly, it is necessary to look beyond the traditional demographic variables and examine the social systems that underly much participation.

In some cases, such studies may provide direct input to outdoor-recreation planning. For example, metropolitan Toronto planning officials were faced in the early 1970s with the need to develop a coherent conceptual scheme for the development of fifty miles of Lake Ontario shoreline.[23] There had been a great increase in boating within the area, climbing from 30,000 boats in use in 1967 to a predicted 100,000 by 1985. With congestion increasing on the roads to areas outside Toronto, it was anticipated that boating—with all its allied water-based recreational activities, like sailing, water-skiing, fishing, picnicking, swimming, and skin diving—would intensify greatly in the metropolitan area. It was known that there were essentially three patterns of boating involvement: *cottages* (many families had built vacation homes along waterfront areas); *marinas* (where people kept their boats in the water); and *boating ramps* (where people could take their boats on trailers, to move them in and out of the water). Rather than examine recreational boaters at the point of destination (which was the typical pattern of research in this field), the Toronto planners decided to study them at the point of origin. They did so through an extensive household study which explored (among other factors) profiles of types of owners, boat sizes and types, occupations and incomes of boaters, and preferences in such services as gas, supplies, snack bars, and mechanical assistance. The data gathered proved extremely helpful in making key planning decisions about the location and type of public-boating facilities proposed for metropolitan Toronto.

In some cases, subgroups of participants have been examined in detail. To illustrate, the domain of winter sports would appear to appeal to a relatively homogeneous population; yet Knopp and Tyger carried out a study of two populations—snowmobilers and cross-country skiers—that examined their attitudes towards environmental issues and policies. As might have been expected, the ski tourers, who engage in a self-propelled activity that is quiet, unobtrusive and harmless to nature, were much more committed to supporting controls designed to protect the natural environment than the snowmobile hobbyists were. The researchers drew the following conclusions:

> Fundamental differences in attitudes toward the environment and public land management may exist between participants in different forms of outdoor recreation. A recreation activity may become associated with a particular social grouping; thus the conflict may become increasingly polarized. . . . This study revealed a consistent and significant difference in attitudes between snowmobilers and ski tourers. These attitudes may be indications of larger cultural trends. . . . If so, recreation planners and area managers may do well to observe these cultural trends rather than base their predictions of future demand entirely on extrapolations from current participation rates.[24]

The Sociology of Sport

A number of specialized areas of leisure involvement have become the subject of sociological analysis. Sport in particular has become an important area for systematic social research. Kenyon and Loy point out that research in the sociology of sport is broadening and deepening, and that there is a growing spirit of scientific inquiry regarding the role and cultural significance of sport throughout the major nations of the world. They write:

> Sociologists and scientifically inclined physical educators are making searching studies of sport, often with the encouragement and financial backing of their governments. It is a reasonable assumption that the study of sport within the culture will experience a steady growth, now that international and national councils and committees, as well as university departments and individual scholars and scientists, have become alert to its significance.[25]

The social sciences in particular are concerned with the customs, traditions, value systems, and economic aspects of sport, along with its place in the cultural hierarchy.

Given the overwhelming preoccupation with sport in the United States, and the corruption of values that exists on many levels of sport, there is a need to better understand its place in the complex fabric of national and international society. How does sport affect, or how is it affected by, political forces, social and economic structures, religion, education, modern technology, and the arts? Kenyon and Loy point out that the framing of intelligent questions and the design and execution of sound research in the sociology of sport will contribute greatly to our dealing effectively with these issues and problems in modern society.

The Influence of Racial and Ethnic Identity

Another critical aspect of modern life is racial and ethnic affiliation and its influence upon leisure attitudes, opportunity, and participation. In the United States, this sociological question is best illustrated by our largest minority population, American blacks.

It should be pointed out that the words "disadvantaged" and "black" are often linked as though synonymous in the literature on recreation and leisure in the urban setting. It would appear that all blacks are poor, and vice versa. Clearly, this is *not* the case. Most people receiving welfare in America are white, and there are many middle-class and wealthy blacks. However, it is also true that blacks have represented a unique group in American society; they were brought to this continent as slaves, and have since been subjected to both legal and social discrimination and oppression in education, employment, housing, *and* recreation. Their participation in recreation must be seen in this light, and we must face the fact that when we examine the needs of disadvantaged persons in inner cities, we are primarily concerned with blacks—along with other racial or ethnic minorities, the elderly, and the disabled.

Leisure Activities of American Blacks

As long ago as the 1920s, Lehman and Witty examined children in elementary and junior and senior high schools and came to the conclusion that black children tended to participate much more actively in social forms of play than white children. They questioned whether this "excessive sociability" was desirable if it meant that other areas of development were being neglected—a question echoed today by those who decry the overwhelming interest in promoting such sports as basketball in the inner city, while ignoring other potential areas of development for its inhabitants. Lehman and Witty speculated about the psychological significance of play for black children, suggesting that it might serve as a form of compensation for areas of social deprivation or for lack of academic success.[26]

The Swedish sociologist Gunnar Myrdal, in *The American Dilemma,*[27] his landmark study of the American black, discussed the inadequate provision of recreation programs and services for blacks in American communities, as well as the patterns of segregation that were enforced by law in the southern and border states, and by social custom in the north (see also chapters 8 and 16). Documenting the inadequacy of facilities and supervised play programs in city after city, Myrdal reported that blacks everywhere expressed to him their concern about the "great damage" done to black youth by the lack of recreational facilities and programs. Myrdal found that it had been necessary for the urban black of the 1930s and early 1940s to find much of his recreation in his own social and athletic clubs, churches, and lodges—on a racially segregated basis, of course.

Another striking analysis of the leisure activities of American blacks was provided by E. Franklin Frazier in *Black Bourgeoisie*.[28] This controversial work described middle-class black society in America as involved in an intense struggle for status, in which the social activities of business and professional people represented both a means of differentiating them from the mass of poorer blacks and of compensating for their exclusion from white society.

Frazier believed that since prejudice made it so difficult for the American black to succeed in any area of life, he fictionalized his efforts; playing became the one activity he could take seriously. He indicted black middle-class society for what he saw as its excessive preoccupation with sports, gambling, and the numbers racket, and for its self-deceiving attempts to exaggerate its own social status. For many blacks, he wrote, "play" represented an escape from frustration; in a highly moralistic way, he condemned the "narcotizing" effects of alcohol, sex, and gambling on middle-class blacks.

Frazier concluded that the American "black bourgeoisie," despite their relative success, were still beset by feelings of insecurity and guilt—the "free and easy" life they seemed to lead was a mask for an unhappy existence. Long before the "black is beautiful" movement of the late 1960s, Frazier charged that many American blacks were ashamed of their racial origins, saw blackness as a reason for self-contempt (having internalized the prejudices of white Americans), and regarded Africans and African culture condescendingly. The prophetic nature of his writing is illustrated by the recent emphasis given to the development of Afro-American cultural programs by black organizations in the United States. Programs in "black studies," including African music, dance, and cultural history, were introduced in many such organizations, as well as in schools, colleges, and urban recreation programs following the urban riots of the sixties.

Other Research on Race and Leisure

A study of consumer expenditures conducted by the Wharton School of Finance in the early 1950s showed marked differences between black and white families in money spent on such items as admissions, radio, television, and musical instruments.[29] The 1962 Report of the Outdoor Recreation Resources Review Commission indicated that blacks engaged in outdoor-recreation activities far less frequently than whites.[30]

In 1967, Kraus studied participation in public recreation-and-park programs in selected urban and suburban communities in the New York metropolitan area, including New Jersey and Connecticut. He found that the involvement of black and white residents varied markedly in such activities as sports, cultural programs, and activities for specific age groups—although it was a limitation of his research that demographic characteristics, including income, could not be held constant for blacks and whites.[31]

Another study, reported by Short and Strodtbeck in 1965, examined the leisure behavior of several hundred black and white gang members in Chicago.[32] This report found distinctly different patterns of involvement on the basis of race. Black gang members tended to be more frequently involved in antisocial activities related to physical violence and heterosexual activity, including the fathering of illegitimate children. On the other hand, white gang members were reported to be more frequently involved in homosexual behavior, the use of alcohol and hard narcotics, gambling, auto theft, and a number of other delinquent acts.

There has apparently been a considerable reduction of interracial tension and prejudice in the United States since the 1960s, and American blacks are more fully accepted on all levels of economic and social life than in the past. However, it would be self-deluding to suggest that social exclusion and differences in the quality of recreation and leisure no longer exist. As a simple measure of the differences that apparently continue to exist between white and black Americans, a 1975 survey by the A. C. Nielsen Company found that nonwhite households spent 16 percent more time (over an hour a day) watching television than households in general. What accounts for this difference? Is it due to socioeconomic factors, the black lifestyle, or the exclusion of blacks from other forms of leisure opportunity?

The role of television as an attitude maker has had a considerable impact on race relations. The fact that blacks have been widely accepted as entertainers on network television in the United States has contributed to their positive image. The hostility and resistance that white Americans—particularly in the South—once showed towards popular black entertainers' being on television has greatly diminished. It is revealing that when *Roots,* the television series based on the Alex Haley novel recounting the fictionalized history of his family, became a striking hit in the winter of 1977, there was no significant resistance to it by Southern television stations and viewers, despite the harsh picture it painted of slavery and past race relations in the South.

Perhaps the key area of public entertainment and leisure activity in which American blacks have excelled has been college and professional team sports. Particularly in the most popular professional sports—baseball, football, and basketball—blacks have been the superstars of the 1960s and 1970s, especially in proportion to the number of blacks in the population. And yet, even given this overwhelming success and the millions of dollars earned by top black athletes, it is apparent that there are subtle forms of exclusion and prejudice that continue to operate in the sports world. In certain areas of sport, such as golf and tennis, there are almost no blacks on the lucrative professional circuits. Loy has demonstrated that black athletes are assigned to certain types of roles in sport and discouraged from other, more central roles, based on statistics of team membership.[33] And Edwards makes a strong case that prejudice continues to exist, and that black athletes are widely exploited for their skills in college sports—without true acceptance as human beings.[34]

Value Orientations and Leisure Attitudes of Mexican-Americans

A number of other studies have examined the influence of ethnic identity on leisure-related values and attitudes. Jackson carried out a study that contrasted the views of two ethnic populations (Anglo and Mexican-American) on two socioeconomic levels (school teachers and school custodians). The four groups represented were questioned about their value orientations towards individualism, future versus present time, mastery versus subjugation to nature, and a number of similar issues related to work and leisure. He reported the following:

> Mexican-American teachers were the most positively oriented toward vacation and free time. Anglo custodians expressed most affinity toward work.

> Both Mexican-American teachers and custodians found in leisure a

greater measure of self-definition than did Anglo teachers and custodians.

No group favored a strong role for society in leisure planning, but Mexican-American custodians preferred the least action.[35]

In general, Anglo teachers and custodians and Mexican-American teachers tended to identify with values generally associated with the dominant cultural tradition, while Mexican-American custodians subscribed to a different set of values. While such studies are somewhat theoretical, they have important implications for those concerned with the practical planning of recreation-delivery systems.

Influence of Sex on Leisure Attitudes and Roles

Another major factor in the sociology of leisure is sexual identification. It is worthy of note that many of the studies described earlier in this chapter dealt only with *men,* and their leisure values or involvements. Clearly, women were regarded as playing a less significant role than men within the work world—and therefore as less interesting subjects for leisure research. However, many references in the general sociological literature cast light on how the opportunities of women in recreation and leisure have been influenced by their social roles.

Sex Stereotyping in Leisure

From early childhood on in our society, play provides a medium for acculturation into what have been accepted as appropriate sex roles. Little girls have been accustomed to playing with dolls, cooking sets, and other household toys. Boys, on the other hand, play at being firemen, truck drivers, cowboys, or soldiers. Not only are the *kinds* of play different, but also the *status* levels. Girls are nurses, but boys are doctors. Girls are stewardesses, boys are pilots. Such make-believe play is a realistic representation of prevalent sex roles in adult society, but this is the very pattern that feminists—and indeed *all* concerned adults—seek to reverse. Sex-stereotyped play activities in early childhood represent a form of brainwashing and arbitrary limitation for *both* girls and boys.

Little boys who are forced to play at only "masculine" activities are also being deprived. For them to be creative, to enjoy artistic activities, to cook, to sew, or to engage in other expressive forms of play is seen as inappropriate. More and more parents and play leaders are trying to break through such stereotypes to open up children's play to a wider range of possibilities. It should be recognized that these are not uniquely American forms of discrimination against the female sex. In many other societies the kinds of recreational experiences regarded as suitable for girls and women are sharply circumscribed in comparison to those encouraged for boys and men.

Life in the Vaucluse

In a classic study of life in a rural French village in the region known as the Vaucluse, Wylie describes the kinds of pastimes engaged in by adolescents.[36] Teen-age girls are expected to go to school and to work hard; while they may go to a movie or dance once a week, or for a "promenade" on Sunday afternoons and holidays, their time is limited, and they must behave circumspectly. In contrast, teen-age boys might often play cards and drink late at night or go on sprees to bars and brothels in neighboring towns without incurring social disapproval. Men have a good deal of free time, which they spend in the cafés, drinking and playing *belote* (a popular card game), or taking part in *boules* (a form of bowling) or hunting. Their wives, however, have almost no free time, and must manage to infuse their daily tasks with a modicum of sociability:

> A woman's day of necessity is so full that she must contrive to combine her recreation with her work. She could finish her daily shopping in a fraction of the time it usually takes her, if she did not use her marketing tour as an opportunity for recreation. She stops to talk to friends she meets in the street . . . at Reynard's grocery . . . the bakery . . . and butcher shop the scene will be repeated.[37]

Other tasks, such as bringing crops to market or gathering mushrooms, also represent a "pleasant form of recreation." Often women invite friends in to have a cup of coffee in "work-and-talk" circles, in which they sew or knit while chatting. Thus work is entwined with recreation; however, more overt recreational opportunity is sharply limited for girls and women.

Male Bonding in Leisure

In part, such deprivation represents the desire of men in primitive societies to be together and to *exclude* women. The anthropologist Lionel Tiger makes a strong case that in cultures where men's toil is heavily physical and often risky—as in mining or fishing communities—they share a common bond of closeness and understanding, a bond reflected in male clubs, secret societies, lodges or fraternal orders, sports, and a variety of other social structures. Tiger describes a small Newfoundland community, Cat Harbour, a heavily male-dominated society:

> Only men can normally inherit property, or smoke or drink. . . . Men are seated first at meals and eat together—women and children eating afterward. Men are given the choicest and largest portions, and sit at the same table with a "stranger" or guest.[38]

Within such societies, women are not paid for their work, and are looked down on in many ways. Regarded as "polluting" the water, they are usually not permitted to go out in fishing boats. Indeed, Tiger points out that an elaborate antifemale symbolism is woven into the fabric of communal life; "strong boats are male, and older leaky ones are female." There is little tenderness or affection between males and females; love, even in sexual relations, is inhibited, and preadolescents are separated along sexual lines. Boys and men spend time together at sports and in drinking together at night; girls and women are sharply limited in their leisure, as in the Vaucluse.

81

Discrimination in Sport

Tiger's thesis of male bonding is presented most vividly in terms of sport. He suggests that sport behavior is functionally equivalent to the hunting pattern with which human males have been acculturated through many centuries of evolution. Male interest centers about violent team sports, and there has been until recently a widespread exclusion of women from major sports events or competitions. While it is understandable that women would have been excluded from those contact sports in which size and strength are critical, the widespread discrimination against women in sport clearly reflects a broader form of social prejudice, and a desire to maintain sport as a masculine domain.

For example, the anthropologist William Arens has identified football—with its emphasis on violent, aggressive play, team strategy, and division between the sexes—as a unique illustration of American attitudes. He suggests that football is a male preserve that symbolizes both the physical and cultural values of masculinity. It depends heavily on a degree of muscle power and speed possessed by relatively few males and probably no women. While women today can and do excel in a variety of other sports, they are totally excluded from traditional football. Arens gives an amusing example of how football as a "bastion of male supremacy" was symbolically invaded by women—and how men responded:

> In an informal game between females in a Long Island community, the husbands responded by appearing on the sidelines in women's clothes and wigs. The message was clear. If the women were going to act like men, then the men were going to transform themselves into women. These "rituals of rebellion" involving an inversion of sex roles have often been recorded by anthropologists.[39]

It is a curious paradox that within the militant, intensely *macho* atmosphere of football (evidenced in part by the exaggeratedly male uniform: enlarged head and shoulders, a narrow waist, and skintight pants accented by a metal codpiece), men are permitted by custom to engage in frequent gestures of physical affection. Arens writes, "Dressed in this manner, players can engage in hand holding, hugging and bottom patting that would be disapproved of in any other context, but which is accepted on the gridiron without a second thought."[40]

As pressures mount to reduce sex stereotyping in recreation and to provide women with a greater measure of leisure opportunity, the question arises: how will this affect traditional patterns of family life in modern society? A number of sociologists have carried out significant research on family play patterns and marital interaction within the sphere of leisure activity.

Family Leisure Patterns

Bell and Healey examined family leisure patterns within the broader framework of traditional and nontraditional family structure.[41] They began by defining three types of conjugal roles played by husbands and wives: (1) *joint roles,* meaning activities carried out by husbands and wives together, or by either mate at different times; (2) *complementary roles,* meaning roles that are different for husbands and wives, but fitted together to form a whole; and (3) *independent* or *segregated roles,* referring to those activities carried out by husbands or wives without relation to each other. These roles are then examined within the context of social networks and ranked according to the density or degree of "connectedness" that family members have with each other.

Based on this conceptual framework, Bell and Healey describe two types of marriages, which in turn result in different approaches to the use of leisure. In the *traditional* marriage, there is rigid sex-role separation, with wives and mothers concerned with domestic and maternal responsibilities, and husbands concerned with outside economic and leisure interests (the societies described by Wylie and Tiger clearly reflect this sort of marriage). Power relations in the traditional marriage are generally characterized by male dominance or paternalism, ranging from benevolent to repressive. Patterns of leisure for men and women are influenced by a fundamental sex-role segregation. Women's lives center about the home and domestic tasks; relationships not based on kinship or neighborhood association are strongly discouraged. In contrast,

> the world of the man is extra-domestic, and within this world are contained all his interests and pursuits. His major reference group is composed of male friends of either occupational, kin or neighbouring acquaintances . . . and he associates with these in the local working men's club or pub. Primary allegiance is to this peer group and all leisure activities are carried out within it. [42]

In contrast, the *nontraditional* marriage avoids rigid sex-role definitions and expectations. Husbands and wives have considerable personal autonomy, with the chief governing principle of behavior being that "persons should be free to express their individuality within the context of consideration for other family members." Typically, both husbands and wives work, and both have numerous shared interests as well as other separate leisure involvements, both inside and outside the home. Within this context, leisure becomes a significant means of defining one's personality and values, and an instrument for expressing affection, interdependence, and the mutuality of interests among all family members.

A number of other recent studies have examined the practical implications of leisure activity for marital interaction and cohesiveness.

Orthner studied a random sample of 223 husbands and 228 wives, examining the relationship between shared leisure activities and communication and task sharing in the marital relationship as a whole. He concluded that

> in general . . . the greater the frequency of interaction in the leisure activities selected by the respondents, the greater the shared communication in the marriage. [43]

It was also determined that the number of years a couple had been married was a significant variable; shared leisure activities were most indicative of open marital communication during the early years of marriage. Relationships among the types of leisure activities enjoyed, family task sharing, and the interactional scheme of the marriage were less clear.

A similar study by West and Merriam, carried out at St. Croix State Park in Minnesota, sought to measure the relationship between shared family outdoor recreation interests and family cohesiveness. [44] While moderate support was gained for the proposition that outdoor recreation helped to build and maintain positive family interaction, it was concluded that more effective research designs and measurement techniques would be needed to develop conclusive findings.

Changing Work Attitudes in American Society

Another important area of sociological investigation has been changing work attitudes and the implications of these changes for leisure education and the provision of leisure services. Historically, work has been seen as the cornerstone around which one's life is built. Dubin writes:

> It is a commonplace to note that work has long been considered a central life interest for adults in most societies, and certainly in the Western world. Indeed, the capitalist system itself is asserted to rest on the moral and religious justification that the Reformation gave to work.[45]

So strong was the glorification of work as the means of salvation that Max Weber described the Protestant world as being caught in an "iron cage" in which the accepted values were asceticism, restraint, productivity, and harder work for higher profits. The capitalist religion of work thus provided man in the industrialized Western world not only with financial reward but also with a sense of self-respect.

The ability to work has been seen by Freudian psychoanalysts as an integral part of mental health, and even today sociologists point out that depression and accompanying unemployment are traumatic, sometimes resulting in mental illness, alcoholism, and even suicide. Such attitudes are not unique to the Western world. In Soviet society the worker has actually been made a national hero, in order to promote production.

However, even beyond societal pressures, there have been other important motivations to work. Santayana suggested that there are three basic motivations for work: want (economic need), ambition (the drive for power), and the love of occupation (intrinsic satisfaction in one's craftsmanship).[46] Dumazedier points out that work is a unique human experience, since "it puts man in rapport with materials, with tools and also with other men. Through work he acquires social status."[47]

Decline of the Work Ethic

There is growing awareness, however, that the tradition of work's being at the moral and religious core of life is no longer widely accepted. Much work today is of a highly specialized, assembly-line nature; instead of being responsible for turning out an entire product (as was the case for the craftsman of an earlier time), the modern industrial worker rarely has a sense of meaningful involvement with his or her product.

Anderson commented on "declining worker interest in the job," writing that "it is generally recognized that most workers who sell their time seem to have little interest in the job or in the enterprise."[48] Dubin supports this view:

> The factory and factory work as sources of personal satisfaction, pride, satisfying human associations, perhaps even of pleasure in expressing

84

what Veblen called the "instinct of workmanship," seem clearly subordi-
nated in the American scene.[49]

By the early 1970s, there was considerable evidence that the work ethic no
longer held the respect it once had:

> In offices and factories, many Americans appear to reject the notion
> that "labor is good in itself." More and more executives retire while still
> in their 50s, dropping out of jobs in favor of a life of ease. People who
> work often take every opportunity to escape. In auto plants, for example,
> absenteeism has doubled since the early 1960s, to five percent of the
> work force; on Mondays and Fridays it commonly climbs to fifteen
> percent. In nearly every industry, employees are increasingly refusing
> overtime work. . . . Beyond that, an increasing number of Americans see
> no virtue in holding jobs that they consider menial or unpleasant.[50]

Indeed, historians have begun to suggest that labor never really did accept
the work ethic as classically defined. Herbert Gutman, in a recent history of the
working class in the United States, points out that there have been worker-factory
tensions marked by sabotage, arson, and rioting from the very beginning, and that
severe forms of discipline and regimentation were needed to keep the assembly lines
rolling.[51]

Even if it is no longer a source of emotional or social satisfaction or a means
of self-definition, is work still important? Obviously, it is needed for sustenance.
Beyond this, however, for many the job continues to fill what would otherwise be a
void in life; Reisman comments that the importance of work lies not so much in the
work itself as in simply having a job. It is the job and the "punctuations of life" that
having a job provides that are the essential psychological components of regular
employment.[52] In a society where most men and many women work, the job is like a
metronome, regulating the individual's routine of waking and sleeping, of time on
and time off. Berger poses the issue raised by changed attitudes toward work:

> As work loses its power to command the moral identifications and
> loyalties of men, as men look away from work to find moral experience,
> society loses an important source of normative integration. . . . In such
> a situation we may expect . . . the transfer of functions formerly
> performed by the institutions of work to the "leisure institutions," and
> this, it seems to me, is precisely the significance of the enormous increase
> in attention which the problem of leisure has received in recent years.[53]

Time magazine suggests that workers' expectations are much higher than in
the past; they do not reject work so much as they demand from it more than money.[54]
Instead of mind-numbing, dull, and repetitious toil, they want to be challenged
through a restructuring of the work experience. Increasingly, both in Europe and
America, experiments are being carried out in the transformation of work. Within
the automobile industry particularly, teams of workers have been permitted to
redesign their tasks to avoid repetition and monotony. Workers are being rotated in
their assignments, are being allowed greater flexibility in their schedules through a
system of "flex" or "sliding" time, and are being given a fuller measure of equality
and responsibility in many plants. There is evidence that such changed policies have
reduced absenteeism and accidents, while maintaining or even accelerating the rate
of production.

Contemporary Attitudes Toward Leisure

Entirely apart from our attitudes towards work, it is apparent that we need to develop a fuller appreciation and understanding of leisure, as well as the ability to use it in self-fulfilling and satisfying ways.

The use of leisure is to some extent a matter of one's total value system. There is considerable evidence (both in the United States and in Canada) that we have not yet developed a lifestyle that accepts leisure and applies to it a coherent and healthy set of values.

First there is the apparent inability to accept the freedom that leisure has to offer. It has been pointed out that many Americans suffer from "weekend neurosis"; nervous breakdowns, heart attacks, and many forms of acute psychosomatic illness are all too likely to occur during free time. Indeed, many adults tend to transfer to their leisure all the compulsive attitudes that characterize their work. They work at their play and surround themselves with a host of commitments and obligations that take away any possible sense of leisurely self-enrichment, relaxation, or creative self-development. As Walter Kerr has written in *The Decline of Pleasure:*

> We are all of us compelled to read for profit, party for contacts, lunch for contracts, bowl for unit, drive for mileage, gamble for charity, go out for the evening for the greater glory of the municipality, and stay home for the weekend to rebuild the house.[55]

Tyranny of the Clock

Unlike other cultures—such as those of Greece or Japan—that might be described as "time affluent," our culture is "time famished." Smith describes the Japanese attitude towards time as follows:

> The Japanese are not tyrannized by the clock, nor is there an emphasis on scheduling of activities. Both work and leisure-time activities tend to follow an unpredictable pattern. . . . Meals are not necessarily eaten on a schedule, and missing a meal is no great tragedy. The approach to appointments is notoriously casual, and . . . pre-arrangement of appointments is not considered essential, for it is expected that everyone's schedule is . . . flexible.[56]

Mead points out that Greeks "pass" the time; they do not "save," "accumulate," or "use" it. Peasants do not watch the clock; they get up at sunrise to go to the fields, and they return at sundown. Greeks find it distasteful to organize their activities strictly by the clock. At church, people are not impatient waiting for services to begin, and the church fills up gradually. Mead writes:

> When Greeks who follow their traditional ways invite, they say, not "Come at seven o'clock," but "Come and see us." To arrive to dinner on time is an insult, as if you came just for the food. You come to dinner, and the dinner eventually appears.[57]

86

In contrast, Linder points out, in Western industrialized society we are dominated by calendars, schedules, wristwatches, and time clocks. Both at work and in our family and social lives we adhere strictly to time commitments, and abhor a lack of punctuality in others. Linder describes life in a wealthy Canadian suburb, Crestwood Heights:

> In Crestwood Heights time seems almost the paramount dimension of existence. . . . His wife has her own activities outside the home which are carefully scheduled. . . . The children have their school—which demands punctuality—scheduled appointments with dentists and dancing teacher, and numerous social activities. Home life is indeed often hectic . . . and the resultant schedules are so demanding that the parents feel themselves constantly impelled to inculcate the virtues of punctuality and regularity in themselves and the child, at meal hour, departures for picnics, and such occasions.[58]

This regimentation so evident in our Western lifestyle results in leisure's losing much of its spontaneity and freedom. Beyond this, many authors feel that we have tended to overvalue the "consumption" of leisure activities and products, and to undervalue the process of taking part in meaningful leisure activity. We purchase sports cars, phonograph recordings, vacation homes—or we attend the opera, the theater, the sports event, or the concert—without ever savoring their meaning or enjoying enriching personal experiences through them. For example, Linder writes that it has become increasingly popular for married couples to hold large cocktail parties devoted to the "simultaneous consumption of food and people." Efforts to economize one's time in this way, he suggests, lead in due course to having many casual acquaintances and no close friends:

> The environment of the typical consumer is a dense jumble of things: a house and a summer cottage; cars and a boat; TV, radio, and a record player; records, books, newspapers, and magazines; clothes and sports clothes; tennis racket, badminton racket, squash racket, and table tennis racket; footballs, beach balls, and golf balls; basement, attic, and closets, and all they contain. It is the total time spent in using all these things that increases; simultaneously, however, the time allocated to each of them individually is declining.[59]

Without question, there is a growing need to clarify our expectations of leisure and the values we hope to achieve from it, both as individuals and as a society. The French sociologist Dumazedier writes:

> Leisure is more and more conceived for its own sake, to satisfy new personality needs at whatever cultural level. Everywhere a dwindling of work values and a development of leisure values has been observed, especially among the young. . . .
>
> Any overall policy aimed at enhancing the *quality of life* by a new allocation of time and space ought to begin by reassessing the implications of leisure for all areas of social and personal life. It is these facts which prompted me to speak of the possible advent of a leisure civilization. This civilization is not a golden age starting tomorrow. It is

87

a set of new social and cultural problems which, to be solved *tomorrow,* must be seriously considered *today.*[60]

As Kaplan writes, "One's leisure, in the end, is his choice of life. . . . Leisure, ultimately, is an opportunity to master time—and ourselves."[61]

Chapter Four

1. W. Lloyd Warner and Paul S. Lunt, *The Social Life of a Modern Community* (New Haven, Conn.: Yale U. Pr., 1941), p. 82.

2. George Lundberg, Mirra Komarovsky, and Mary Alice McInerney, "The Amounts and Uses of Leisure," in Eric Larrabee and Rolf Meyersohn, eds., *Mass Leisure* (Glencoe, Ill.: Free Pr., 1958), pp. 193–98.

3. R. Clyde White, "Social Class Differences in the Uses of Leisure," in Larrabee and Meyersohn, *Mass Leisure,* pp. 198–205.

4. Ibid., p. 204.

5. Alfred C. Clarke, "Leisure and Occupational Prestige," in Larrabee and Meyersohn, *Mass Leisure,* pp. 205–14.

6. Joel E. Gerstl, "Leisure, Taste and Occupational Milieu," in Edwin O. Smigel, ed., *Work and Leisure: A Contemporary Social Problem* (New Haven, Conn.: Coll. and U. Pr., 1963), pp. 146–67.

8. Max Kaplan, *Leisure in America: A Social Inquiry* (New York: Wiley, 1960), p. 92.

9. Nels Anderson, *Work and Leisure* (New York: Free Pr., 1961), p. 34.

10. William J. Baumol and William G. Bowen, *Performing Arts: The Economic Dilemma* (New York: Twentieth Fund, 1966), p. 46.

11. William Robbins, "Houses in a Suburb of Chicago Offering Originality at a Price," *New York Times,* 9 January 1966, p. R-1.

12. See Nettie P. McGill and Ellen N. Matthews, *The Youth of New York City* (New York: Macmillan, 1940).

13. August B. Hollingshead, *Elmtown's Youth: The Impact of Social Class for Adolescents* (New York: Wiley, 1949, 1961), p. 410.

14. Herbert J. Gans, *The Urban Villagers: Group and Class in the Life of Italian-Americans* (New York: Free Pr., 1962), p. 65.

15. Rabel J. Burdge, "Levels of Occupational Prestige and Leisure Activity," *Journal of Leisure Research,* Summer 1969, pp. 262–74.

16. John Neulinger and Miranda Breit, "Attitude Dimensions of Leisure," *Journal of Leisure Research,* Summer 1969, pp. 255–61. See also their replication study in the *Journal of Leisure Research,* Spring 1971, pp. 108–15.

17. Dean R. Yoesting and Dan L. Burkhead, "Significance of Childhood Recreation Experience on Adult Leisure Behavior: An Exploratory Analysis," *Research Quarterly,* Winter 1973, pp. 25–35.

18. John R. Kelly, "Socialization Toward Leisure: A Developmental Approach," *Journal of Leisure Research,* Summer 1974, pp. 181–93.

19. Eldon E. Snyder and Elmer Spreitzer, "Orientations Toward Work and Leisure as Predictors of Sports Involvement," *Research Quarterly,* December 1974, pp. 398–406.

20. H. Douglas Sessoms and Sidney R. Oakley, "Recreation, Leisure and the Alcoholic," *Journal of Leisure Research,* Winter 1969, pp. 21–31. See also Paul M. Sheridan, "Therapeutic Recreation and the Alcoholic," *Therapeutic Recreation Journal,* 1st quarter 1974, pp. 14–17.

21. Irvin Babow and Sol Simkin, "The Leisure Activities and Social Participation of Mental Patients Prior to Hospitalization," *Therapeutic Recreation Journal,* 4th quarter 1971, pp. 161–68.

22. Donald R. Field and Joseph T. O'Leary, "Social Groups as a Basis for Assessing Participation in Selected Water Activities," *Journal of Leisure Research,* Spring 1973, pp. 16–25.

23. John Weakley, "The Participation, Spatial Distribution, and Consumption Patterns of Boaters Residing in Metropolitan Toronto," *Recreation Review,* November 1971, pp. 6–21.

24. Timothy B. Knopp and John D. Tyger, "A Study of Conflict in Recreational Land Use: Snowmobiling vs. Ski-Touring," *Journal of Leisure Research,* Summer 1973, pp. 6–17.

25. John W. Loy, Jr., and Gerald S. Kenyon, *Sport, Culture, and Society* (New York: Macmillan, 1969), p. 14.

26. Harvey C. Lehman and Paul A. Witty, *The Psychology of Play Activities* (New York: A.S. Barnes, 1927), p. 161.

27. Gunnar Myrdal, *The American Dilemma* (New York: Harper and Row, 1944, 1962), pp. 346–47, 1274–75.

28. E. Franklin Frazier, *Black Bourgeoisie* (New York: Collier, 1957, 1962).

29. Cited in Kaplan, *Leisure in America,* pp. 95–97.

30. *Outdoor Recreation for America: Report to the President and to Congress of the Outdoor Recreation Resources Review Commission* (Washington, D.C.: U.S. Government Printing Office, 1962), 1:37–38.

31. Richard Kraus, *Public Recreation and the Negro* (New York: Center for Urban Education, 1968), pp. 36–53.

32. James F. Short, Jr., and Fred L. Strodtbeck, *Group Process and Gang Delinquency* (Chicago: U. of Chicago Pr., 1965), pp. 36–53.

33. John W. Loy, Jr., "A Case for the Sociology of Sport," in Larry Neal, ed., *Leisure Today: Selected Readings* (Washington, D.C.: American Association for Leisure and Recreation, 1975), pp. 50–52.

34. Harry Edwards, *The Revolt of the Black Athlete* (New York: Free Pr., 1969).

35. Royal G. Jackson, "A Preliminary Bicultural Study of Value Orientations and Leisure Attitudes," *Journal of Leisure Research,* Fall 1973, pp. 10–21.

36. Lawrence Wylie, *Village in the Vaucluse* (New York: Harper-Colophon, 1957, 1964), pp. 98–122.

37. Ibid., p. 268.

38. Lionel Tiger, *Men in Groups* (New York: Random, Vintage, 1969), p. 135.

39. William Arens, "An Anthropologist Looks at the Rituals of Football," *New York Times,* 16 November 1974.

40. Ibid.

41. Colin Bell and Patrick Healey, in Michael A. Smith, Stanley Parker, and Cyril S. Smith, eds., *Leisure and Society in Britain* (London: Allen Lane, 1973), pp. 160–65.

42. Ibid., p. 162.

43. Dennis K. Orthner, "Patterns of Leisure and Marital Interaction," *Journal of Leisure Research,* 1976, no. 2, pp. 98–111.

44. Patrick C. West and L. C. Merriam, Jr., "Outdoor Recreation and Family Cohesiveness," *Journal of Leisure Research,* 1970, no. 2, pp. 251–59.

45. Robert Dubin, "Industrial Workers' Worlds," in Larrabee and Meyersohn, *Mass Leisure,* p. 215.

46. See Anderson, *Work and Leisure,* p. 26.

47. Ibid.

48. Ibid., p. xiii.

49. Dubin, "Industrial Workers' Worlds," p. 220.

50. "Is the Work Ethic Going Out of Style?" *Time,* 30 October 1972, p. 96.

51. Herbert G. Gutman, *Work, Culture and Society in Industrializing America* (New York: Knopf, 1976).

52. David Reisman, "Leisure and Work in Post-Industrial Society," in Larrabee and Meyersohn, *Mass Leisure,* p. 370.

53. Bennett Berger, "The Sociology of Leisure: Some Suggestions," in Smigel, ed., *Work and Leisure: A Contemporary Social Problem,* p. 35.

54. "Is the Work Ethic Going Out of Style?" *Time,* 30 October 1972, pp. 96–97.

55. Walter Kerr, *The Decline of Pleasure* (New York: Simon and Schuster, 1965), p. 39.

56. Robert J. Smith, "Japan: The Later Years of Life and the Concept of Time," in Robert W. Kleemeier, ed., *Aging and Leisure* (New York: Oxford U. Pr., 1961), pp. 95–100.

57. Margaret Mead, *Cultural Patterns and Technical Change* (Paris: UNESCO, 1953), pp. 90–92.

58. Excerpted from J. R. Seeley, R. A. Sim, and E. W. Loosley, *Crestwood Heights* (New York: Wiley, 1963), pp. 63–74.

59. Staffan B. Linder, *The Harried Leisure Class* (New York: Columbia U. Pr., 1970), p. 90.

60. Joffre Dumazedier, *Sociology of Leisure* (Amsterdam: Elsevier, 1974), pp. 212–13.

61. Max Kaplan, *Leisure: Theory and Policy* (New York: Wiley, 1975), pp. 412–23.

5

THE ECONOMICS OF RECREATION AND LEISURE: ACTIVITIES AND EXPENDITURES

This chapter summarizes how much more discretionary time we have gained in the United States and Canada over the past several decades, and how this time has become available. It then proceeds to describe the major kinds of recreational activity carried on during leisure time. Estimates are made of the total amount of money spent each year on varied forms of recreation, and the impact of recreation on the economy is discussed.

While a number of examples of Canadian recreation-and-leisure patterns are cited, the primary focus is on developments in the United States. No attempt is made to analyze the full spectrum of leisure participation in the light of current economic theory. Instead, the major emphasis is on the relationship of recreation to the economic structure of modern society; the current uses of leisure; and the nature of spending for recreation.

Since the coming of the industrial age there have been essentially two opposing viewpoints on the meaning of leisure in the modern world. One group of social thinkers has seen the expansion of leisure as the basis for creating a great new era of individual and community cultural development. This viewpoint was expressed by A. Whitney Griswold, then president of Yale University:

> Now we stand on the threshold of an age that will bring leisure to all of us, more leisure than all the aristocracies of history, all the patrons of art, all the captains of industry and kings of enterprise ever had at their disposal. . . . What shall we do with this great opportunity? In the answers that we give to this question the fate of our American civilization will unfold.[1]

In contrast to this view, there has been widespread apprehension that leisure represents a great threat to American society. It was feared by many that the laboring classes would misuse their free time in riotous dissipation. During the first half of the nineteenth century, "the fourteen-hour day" and the "wholesome discipline of factory life" were defended by preachers and employers alike as a deterrent to drunken leisure among urban workers, a view not entirely rejected by organized labor itself.[2] There has been a constant fear that people would grow slothful and passive in their uses of free time, and would seek the cheapest and most tawdry amusements. Boredom, alienation, and the use of drugs, alcohol, and sex as time killers have all been seen as possible dangers of increased leisure.

What *are* the actual statistics on and dimensions of today's leisure? How *is* discretionary time used in American society? This chapter seeks to answer these questions.

The Availability of Leisure Today

As later chapters will show, the peak of free time in Europe was reached during the Middle Ages, when due to the great number of church-decreed holidays in European countries, there were more than 160 workless days per year. As religious authority declined in Europe and the Industrial Revolution accelerated, the workday increased to as many as thirteen or fourteen hours per day, six days a week. The number of holidays was radically slashed. During the early decades of the nineteenth century, work was at its height and leisure at a minimum. But progressive legislation and union contracts gradually reduced the length of the workweek in Europe and the United States.

The first eight-hour day was won by craft workers in the construction industry during the 1890s, and in the decades that followed union workers in the garment, railroad, and steel industries also gained an eight-hour day. The sharpest reduction of average weekly work hours occurred between 1900 and 1930, when they declined from 67 to 55 for farm workers and from 56 to 43 for those in industry. The passage of the Fair Labor Standards Act in 1938 set 40 hours a week as a desirable standard for most American industrial workers. During the 1940s and 1950s, many major industries and businesses adopted a 37.5- or 35-hour workweek as standard practice. In some labor contracts, even more striking workweek reductions were achieved. In 1962 the International Brotherhood of Electrical Workers in New York City achieved a pioneering contract that included a basic 25-hour workweek.

Such dramatic reductions in the workweek were made possible by mechanization and technological innovations in production that permitted a dramatic increase in production output per man-hour. However, the workweek did not continue to decline at such a rapid rate during the 1960s and 1970s. In the 1960s, weekly hours on the job remained high because of the current level of prosperity, with attractive premium payments for overtime. By the early 1970s, the average workweek was 37.6 hours, with much of the continuing growth of nonwork time coming from other factors, such as retirement, holidays, and vacations.

The Four-Day Week

Another important trend likely to have implications for the growth of leisure and the provision of recreation services in the years ahead is the emergence of the four-day workweek. Mobley and Hellreigel write:

91

A few firms experimented with the four-day work-week during the mid-1960's, but in 1969 interest began to develop rapidly. . . . by 1971 estimates of the number of converted companies ranged from 125 to about 370. A recent study published by the American Management Association estimates the present rate of conversion is between 60 and 70 companies per month.[3]

It should be stressed that the four-day workweek does not bring an automatic reduction in working hours; instead, many companies that have adopted it have simply rescheduled work assignments on a four-day, ten-hours-a-day basis. Many union officials have resisted the four-day workweek for this reason, seeing it as a threat to the eight-hour day that unions fought to obtain. They also fear that it may simply encourage workers to "moonlight,"—to take second jobs—while other workers have none. A major breakthrough came in the fall of 1976, when the Ford Motor Company signed a contract with the United Automobile Workers Union that would give the workers twelve additional paid days off, besides regularly scheduled holidays, over the life of the contract—resulting in what labor experts described as a "toe in the door" leading to a four-day workweek in American industry.

In general, the reaction of workers to the four-day week has been favorable, with improved morale and in some cases a decline in absenteeism and sick leave. Mobley and Hellreigel comment that the implications of the shortened workweek are obvious: it will give families greater opportunity to use vacation homes or visit outdoor-recreation areas for extended weekends, and will also result in a need for new programming approaches by local recreation-and-park departments to meet the needs of residents with added free time during the week.

Holidays and Vacations

In their investigations of Middletown, U.S.A., the Lynds noted the rarity of time off from work during the latter years of the nineteenth century:

> "Vacations in 1890?" echoed one substantial citizen. "Why, the word wasn't in the dictionary!" "Executives of the 1890 period never took a vacation," said another man of a type common in Middletown thirty-five years ago, who used to announce proudly that they had "not missed a day's work in twenty years."[4]

By the 1920s, two-week summer vacations with pay had become increasingly common among middle-class families, but were still quite rare for working people. In 1940, only about one-quarter of all union members received annual vacations with pay; for most of these, the maximum vacation period was only one week. The average number of paid holidays was about two per year, although many workers received additional holidays without pay. Since World War II, paid holidays have greatly increased.

The four-week vacation for employees of long standing came into common practice during the mid-1960s. In the automobile industry, for example, it was granted as an automatic job benefit for employees with fifteen years of service. In a number of other industries, five-week vacations are automatic after twenty years of service. In the steel industry, collective bargaining has achieved thirteen-week vacations every five years for employees of long standing.

In addition, a substantial number of added holidays are being provided through new industry-union contracts and legislative action designed to provide extended weekends. In some industries, each employee is given a holiday on his or her birthday, taken as part of a three-day weekend. In 1968, Congress passed legislation creating four permanent three-day weekends by shifting Washington's Birthday, Memorial Day, Veteran's Day, and Columbus Day to specified Mondays. While the law was compulsory only for Federal employees, many other governmental and industrial agencies followed suit in observing these holidays.

It should be understood that the United States is not uniquely liberal in this respect; indeed, it lags behind a number of other industrial nations in providing vacation time. For example, all French workers—from office boys to factory foremen—are given four weeks' vacation starting with the first year of work, and many French workers take holidays of up to seven weeks a year. In Germany it has been estimated that the number of paid holiday and vacation days will rise to thirty-five per year by 1985.

The Effect of Retirement Policies

Another dramatic source of increased leisure has come about for older persons as a result of two factors—longer life spans and improved employee retirement programs and benefits. Industrial retirement pension plans and Social Security programs institutionalizing mandatory retirement at age sixty-five have resulted in a much higher percentage of older workers leaving their jobs than in the past.

Major union contracts of municipal employees are increasingly providing improved retirement benefits, and many union leaders have agreed to contracts permitting employers to retire high-salaried older workers in order to provide more jobs for younger workers. In 1940, only 70 out of 1,000 men who were sixty-four years of age retired from the labor force within a year. By 1960, the figure had jumped to 234, a fourfold increase over the twenty-year span. Another revealing change is that the proportion of men and women over sixty-five still working has dropped from 68 percent in 1890 to 22 percent in 1974. With life expectancy continuing to rise, substantial numbers of early retirees are now able to look forward to fifteen, twenty, or twenty-five years of nonwork life—a prospect that has both its rewards and its terrors.

It would be easy to conclude that leisure is indeed becoming a vast new resource, easily available to all. However, the actual availability of leisure is sharply differentiated by sex, social class, and occupation, among other factors. Indeed, a number of sociologists or economists have suggested that it has been greatly exaggerated—that we have far *less* real leisure than we think.

Who Really Has Leisure?

Of the various subgroups in our society, who really has leisure? A number of sociologists have concluded that women are at a disadvantage compared to men when it comes to leisure—working women because they are burdened with both paid and unpaid responsibilities, and nonworking women because their home labors are generally underestimated and undervalued, and because their daily lives are generally limited and less exciting than those of men. It should be recognized that women have moved with increasing numbers into the labor force. Juanita Kreps writes:

> With women, the changes have been . . . dramatic, touching all age groups. Beginning with wartime work in the early 1940's, their representation in the labor force has continued its sharp climb. Now, three and a half decades later, women's work profiles show a much steadier commitment to market jobs, particularly among educated women, with careers often uninterrupted by childbearing.[5]

A fourteen-nation study of 25,000 men and women carried out in the late 1960s by the International Social Council, an agency of UNESCO, revealed that working mothers had an average of only 2.8 hours of free time per day, compared with 4.1 for working fathers. Even the widespread assumption that homemaking is much simpler today than in the past—because labor-saving devices and products like dishwashers, electric vacuum cleaners, and frozen foods provide vast amounts of free time—has been disputed. In a recent issue of *Scientific American,* Vanek presented the striking statistic that in 1966 the average full-time housewife spent about 55 hours per week at household tasks, in comparison with 52 hours in 1924. It is conjectured that women spend more time shopping than in the past; that families have rising standards in household cleanliness and other domestic matters (because of pressure from television and the women's magazines); and, that the labor-saving gadgets themselves are so frequently inoperative and require so much time for repair, that they have not reduced the time spent at home chores as much as popularly thought.[6]

Another serious discrepancy in the availability of leisure affects many in the upper socioeconomic brackets, especially those employed as professionals or high-level business managers and executives. Once thought of as having *more* leisure, members of this social group actually have less discretionary time than white-collar or blue-collar workers. Wilensky writes:

> With economic growth the upper strata have probably lost leisure. Professionals, executives, officials and proprietors have long workweeks, year-round employment. Their longer vacations and shorter worklives [delayed entry and often earlier retirement] do not offset this edge in working hours. Although life-time leisure decreases with increased status, the picture is one of bunched, predictable leisure for elites whose worklives are shorter; and intermittent, unpredictable, unstable leisure for the masses, whose worklives are longer.[7]

Wilensky concludes that, considering both those occupations which *necessitate* long hours (proprietors, some young skilled workers, and foremen) and those in which men *choose* to work hard (professors, lawyers), there appears to be a slowly increasing minority of the male urban labor force working fifty-five hours a week or more.

De Grazia points out that in addition to these factors, those who hold executive or professional positions also tend to be community leaders, accepting numerous civic and charitable responsibilities that consume their time. Frequently they spend large amounts of time commuting from suburbs, traveling on business trips, or entertaining business associates. In contrast, those on the lower levels of employment tend to have leisure thrust upon them by union contracts, personnel policies, and guaranteed holidays and retirement plans.

The Leisure "Explosion"—Divergent Views

Some social scientists have concluded that the widely acclaimed growth in leisure has been exaggerated. Pointing out the extent to which people use their free time today in work-connected responsibilities, community involvement, and home chores, de Grazia concludes that "the great and touted gains in free time since the 1850's . . . are largely myth."[8]

Linder agrees, pointing out that the reduction in working hours has been accompanied by an increase in overtime work and multiple employment or "moonlighting." He argues that within our "time-famished" culture, the emphasis on getting and using consumer goods has, in effect, reduced the time available for really leisurely pursuits.

These arguments are obviously based on the classical view of leisure presented in chapter 2, which sees leisure as a way of life devoted to a celebration of self and to a contemplative existence that bars all forms of work or work-connected tasks. The time that members of the business or intellectual elite may give to voluntary roles as board members of community agencies is not necessarily time withdrawn from leisure. Indeed, it might be argued that such voluntarily undertaken service activities represent a higher and far more valuable use of free time than watching a baseball game on television or dozing in a hammock—which most individuals today would accept as *real* leisure.

Accepting leisure as discretionary time, one must conclude that it has grown tremendously in recent years for the bulk of the population in the United States and Canada. Many experts predict that it will continue to grow in a variety of ways.[9] The real problem is to help people learn to use this discretionary time in the most enjoyable and rewarding ways, and then to provide appropriate outlets for them.

Patterns of Leisure Availability and Use

As indicated earlier, leisure is available today in widely varying amounts and degrees. It is most often found in the evenings and on weekends for working people or those attending school. Major blocks of leisure come during special holidays during the year, which may provide several consecutive days of nonwork time, or during vacations, which may extend to several weeks of free time. There is bunching, too, in the amount of leisure available within one's lifetime: there is much free time for young children and the old, and much less for those in the middle years of life.

Southern California Analysis of Leisure

This study provides one of the most detailed analyses of leisure ever conducted in any region of the United States.[10] Covering fifteen counties with a population of 12.6 million, the report's conclusions were based on a large sampling of all ages and social classes. It determined that approximately 110 billion hours were available to all Southern California residents during the course of a year. These hours were used in the following ways:

Time Use for All Groups	Percent
Sleeping, eating, and personal care	47
Leisure	25
Work and related travel	12
Housework and child care	9
School and study	5
Other unpaid productive activities	2

Each of these categories varies greatly according to the age, sex, and social role of individual subjects. Thus, "school and study" were much higher than five percent for young people and much lower for aging persons. Employed Southern Californians were found to work about 40.5 hours each week for pay. If part-time employees were excluded from this group, however, it was found that the typical full-time employee worked about 46 hours a week. Most fully employed adults enjoyed fewer than 30 hours of leisure each week. This estimate is close to that of Dumazedier, who calculated that the average fully employed French worker had 2.5 hours of leisure on weekdays and 8 hours on weekend days, amounting to approximately 28.5 hours of leisure per week.

The Southern California Research Council summarized the way in which this free time appeared:

> Leisure is taken in bits and pieces. According to our time budget for Southern California, about one-third of all leisure hours is taken as daily leisure, in small pieces after school or work. About one-fourth is absorbed by family members in weekend leisure pursuits. Vacations and holidays are the settings for yet another one-sixth of the total. The remaining one-fourth is time spent "at leisure" by children too young for school, retired persons, the chronically unemployed and the institutional population.[11]

Obviously, many factors influence the nation's use of leisure in recreational activity. Two of the most important of these are population trends and affluence.

96

Population Trends in the United States

According to the "census clock" of the United States Department of Commerce, the United States population reached a total of 200 million on November 20, 1967. It took the country about four centuries after European settlement to reach its first 100 million in 1915; the next 100 million was achieved within only fifty-two years.

Of the 1967 total of 200 million, about 102 million were female and about 98 million male. Life expectancy for men climbed from 53.5 years in 1920 to over 66.5 in the late 1960s; for women, from 71 years to about 73.5 during the same period.

Farm population was reported in 1967 to be less than 6 percent of the total population, and steadily decreasing. During the 1950s and 1960s there was a spectacular population shift from rural to urban areas; since most such migrants tended to fall in the younger age brackets, this trend contributed to a higher birth rate in metropolitan areas, particularly in the inner-city slums. The prediction was made that unless the trend was halted, by the end of the century America's large cities would be predominantly populated by blacks and other racial-minority groups, while the surrounding suburbs would be almost exclusively white. It was also predicted that the population of the United States would continue to climb rapidly, reaching the 300-million mark by the year 2000.

How accurate were these predictions? What changes have taken place over the last decade?

The birth rate in the United States declined abruptly in the early 1970s. The fertility rate, according to Federal statistics, fell to 1.8 children per family, significantly below the "replacement level" of 2.1 children, and far below the 3.7 rate of the late 1950s. By 1976, it was apparent that the sudden decline in the birth rate was not a casual phenomenon. In consequence, there were 7.6 million fewer American children age thirteen and under than there were in 1970—even though there were more women of childbearing age.

Although population-trend predictions are risky, most American demographers believe that low fertility rates will continue because of the availability of effective contraception, liberalized abortion and divorce laws, the postponement of marriage, and the changing role of women. Reinhold writes that the full impact of the transition to an older society will be deferred because the ranks of "baby boom" children, born between 1947 and 1961, are now moving through young adulthood. Inevitably, however, if the low birth rate continues, the population of the United States will become increasingly elderly, with sharp implications for the broad field of social services:

> It seems safe to assume that a country dominated by the old will need less baby food, toys, teachers and maternity wards. Conversely, demand should rise for retirement homes, medical care, recreational facilities and entertainment suiting the tastes of the elderly.[12]

Serious questions have been raised about the impact of this population trend on society as a whole, with some social scientists expressing concern that American society may stagnate, becoming less creative and innovative and more conservative in its values and lifestyles.

Another significant trend in the United States has been the shifting of the majority of the country's population to the South and the West. In 1970, the South and the West had eight million fewer residents than the North. Six years later, in America's Bicentennial year, the Census Bureau reported that the nation now had a population

> of 214,659,000, up 1.63 million over 1975. Most of the growth was in the South and West, where the population reached 107,417,000, while the population in the North was 107,242,000.[13]

Clearly, this too represented an important long-term population trend that would seriously affect national policy in the field of recreation and leisure. Coupled with this trend has been evidence that more and more of the nation's largest metropolitan areas have been holding steady or declining in population over the past several years; people are leaving both the big cities and the suburbs to move to small towns and rural areas.

Affluence of the American Economy

During the 1960s in particular, the American economy expanded at a rapid rate. In 1968, records were set for industrial production, personal income, employment, retail sales, and capital outlays. During the five-year period between 1963 and 1968, unemployment declined from 5.7 percent of the labor force to 3.4 percent; the number of persons existing below minimum poverty levels declined by about 12.5 million; and the net financial assets of American families increased by $460 billion— over 50 percent. There was a prevailing optimism about the economy, reflected in *Time* magazine:

> In the past ten years, the growth of the American economy has far outstripped the comprehension of most individuals; even economists are at a loss for an abstract theory to explain it. But beyond dispute is the fact that never before has man transmuted energy and raw material into wealth at such a fantastic rate. With 7 percent of the global land mass and 6 percent of its population, the U.S. produces about one-third of the world's goods and services. . . . In 1968, the U.S. gross national product was twice that estimated for the Soviet Union, and the output of one American corporation, General Motors, was greater than the G.N.P.'s of all but 13 of the world's nations.[14]

However, the economy slowed sharply in the mid-1970s. Steady inflation, unemployment, and a business recession that reached a peak after the oil and gasoline shortages of 1973 and 1974 cut dramatically into the sense of economic well-being that had prevailed in the preceding decade. Although dollar income continued to expand, real buying power declined.

This serious recession affected governments on all levels, forcing them to freeze or cut back on their budgets at a time when operational expenses were continuing to mount because of inflation, the energy shortage, and expanded welfare and environmental programs. Many municipal governments teetered on the edge of bankruptcy, and school systems throughout the United States went on "austerity" budgets or in some cases were forced to temporarily shut down.

Although government and voluntary-agency recreation-and-park programs were clearly affected by these economic trends, public spending on recreation continued high. As the remainder of this chapter will show, spending on the purchase of leisure-connected products and services—including sports and camping equipment, travel, entertainment, and a host of recreational goods—reached new levels in the mid-1970s.

Total Spending on Leisure and Recreation

In 1972, *U.S. News and World Report* described the growth of spending on leisure and recreation in the United States as a "leisure boom" that had grown to phenomenal proportions, representing $105 billion dollars a year:

> The money Americans are now spending on spare-time activities exceeds national-defense costs. It is more than the outlay for construction of new homes. It surpasses the total of corporate profits. It is far larger than the aggregate income of U.S. farmers. It tops the over-all value of this country's exports. And estimates are that the dollar volume of leisure-time expenditures will more than double during the decade of the '70s.[15]

Impressive as this estimate was, it was considerably below other assessments of recreational spending during the same period. A leading brokerage firm, Merrill Lynch, Pierce, Fenner and Smith, described the leisure market in the late 1960s as rapidly approaching the $150-billion mark, and predicted that it would reach $250 billion by 1975.

Other financial authorities supported this view. The editors of *Forbes* magazine, a leading business publication, calculated in January, 1969, that the combined leisure and education market in the United States represented a total annual expenditure of $200 billion. Conservatively, the first edition of *this* text calculated annual consumer spending on recreation in the United States as $125.9 billion.[16]

Recent Estimates of Consumer Spending on Recreation

There is widespread agreement, based on a number of indexes, that spending on recreation and leisure in the United States has continued to climb steadily during the 1970s, despite the economic slump. The *Statistical Abstract of the United States* reported that consumer spending on recreation had risen to $60.5 billion in 1974, the most recent year that statistics were available at this writing (see table 5–1).

It should be noted, however, that this report includes only a portion of actual leisure spending. If one were to add domestic and foreign travel by tourists, or such forms of leisure expenditure in the mid-1970s as gambling, alcohol, and tobacco, the total would be much higher (see table 5–2).[17]

Table 5-1

Personal Consumption Expenditures for Recreation: 1950 to 1974 (stated in millions of dollars)

Type of Product or Service	1950	1960	1970	1974
Total Recreation Expenditures	11,147	17,855	40,999	60,544
Books and maps	674	1,139	2,356	3,049
Magazines, newspapers, sheet music	1,495	2,164	3,900	7,078
Nondurable toys and sport supplies	1,394	2,477	5,477	7,993
Wheel goods, durable toys, sports equipment, boats, pleasure aircraft	869	1,976	5,511	8,853
Radio and television receivers, records, musical instruments	2,421	3,003	8,885	13,270
Radio and television repair	283	774	1,079	1,408
Flowers, seed, and potted plants	457	703	2,134	3,276
Admissions to specified amusements (includes motion pictures, opera, theater, non-profit entertainment and spectator sports)	1,781	1,652	3,141	4,016
Clubs and fraternal organizations	462	728	1,197	1,432
Commercial participant amusements (includes billiard parlors, bowling alleys, dancing, riding, shooting, swimming places, amusement parks, etc.)	448	1,200	2,317	3,169
Parimutuel net receipts	239	539	1,144	1,614
Other (includes photo developing, collectors' acquisitions, pet costs, camp fees, etc.)	624	1,500	3,858	5,386

Source: U.S. Bureau of Economic Analysis, printed in Statistical Abstract of the United States, 1976

While a number of these figures represent estimated portions of total spending on any item, they are *conservative* estimates, based on reported governmental statistics or industry reports. It should be noted that the following items are *not* included: (1) spending on vacation properties or second homes, clearly a recreational item that amounts to billions of dollars each year; (2) spending on illegal gambling, estimated to be as high as *hundreds* of billions of dollars each year;

(3) pornography, which, if it can be considered recreation, represents spending of about $2 billion each year; and (4) a wide variety of general items, such as home swimming pools, barbecues, and leisure clothing, which cannot readily be estimated.

Table 5-2

Other Reported Recreation Expenditures (in billions of dollars)

Domestic vacation travel (portion of total travel assigned to "vacation" or "pleasure")	40.0
Foreign vacation travel	7.5
Alcohol	22.9
Tobacco and tobacco products	13.8
Legal gambling (includes gross parimutuel betting, casinos, lotteries, etc.)	19.0
Estimated expenditure on eating out for recreation	15.0
Total reported expenditures	118.2

Total Recreation Spending

Combining the two sums just presented yields an annual total of *$178.7 billion* for annual consumer spending in the United States—as indicated earlier, a *conservative* estimate. This sum does not include the amounts spent by governmental and voluntary agencies each year in providing recreation facilities and services, which may reasonably be estimated at $10 billion,[18] or the amounts spent by private industry in constructing manufacturing plants, resorts, stadiums, or other major capital investments to meet leisure needs. It seems likely that the correct figure for all leisure spending, if it were possible to gauge it correctly, would be well in excess of $200 billion.

Major Categories of Recreational Involvement

A number of studies have attempted to assess the total nature of leisure participation in the United States. One such analysis was done in 1960 by the Stanford Research Institute, based on data obtained from the Outdoor Recreation Resources Review Commission, Michigan State University, and the National Recreation Association. This report suggested that Americans tended to engage most often in easily accessible activities that do not require specialized equipment, elaborate organization, or supervision. Of the ten most frequently listed activities, several (rest, relaxation, watching television, visiting with friends and relatives, reading, studying) are normally carried on at home. Other major studies confirm the fact that the most popular activities are simple, inexpensive ones, like driving and walking for pleasure, swimming, or picnicking. On the other hand, strenuous, dangerous, or less-accessible activities—like water-skiing, mountain climbing, or canoeing—are much less frequently engaged in.

A number of major categories of participation are described in the following section. These include: (1) popular sports, including both participant and spectator activities; (2) outdoor recreation, including such activities as boating, hunting, fishing, and camping; (3) travel and tourism, including the development of new types of amusement complexes; (4) other forms of commercial entertainment and cultural activity; (5) various forms of recreation centered around real estate, including new residential communities and shopping centers; (6) gambling; (7) television; (8) technologically based activities; and (9) a variety of other miscellaneous hobbies.

Sports Participation Today

Without question, participation in sports represents a major leisure interest for the great mass of youth and adults today. Sports have become big business; they are moneymakers, sponsored by powerful commercial interests and promoted by advertising, public relations, television, radio, magazines, and newspapers.

On every age level there are characteristic forms of sports competition. Children and youth may participate in a variety of leagues operated by youth organizations, schools, or recreation departments. For children, the emphasis is on such team sports as baseball, basketball, and football. For adults, it shifts to involvement in golf, tennis, bowling, winter sports, and the like.

Surveys of Sports Participation

Which are the most popular participant sports? For a number of years, the Athletic Institute, a nonprofit organization concerned with the promotion of athletics, physical education, and recreation, conducted an annual survey that yielded statistics of national participation in major sports activities. The institute identified the most popular activities as bicycling, boating, volleyball, bowling, camping, fishing, softball, roller-skating, billiards, shooting sports, and golf.[19]

Another means of assessing the relative popularity of sports activities in the United States was through the yearbooks published by the National Recreation and Park Association, which gave detailed information about trends in sports facilities and programs provided by local (county and municipal) recreation-and-park departments. The most popular activities reported in the 1960s were: for *adults,* softball, swimming, tennis, basketball, volleyball, and picnicking; for *youth,* baseball, basketball, swimming, tennis, volleyball, and picnicking. Among the recreation-sponsored activities that doubled during the decade were such sports as bowling, regulation and touch football, golf, track and field, boating, horseback riding, synchronized swimming, and skiing.[20]

A comprehensive report was issued in 1974 by the A.C. Nielsen Company, a prominent market-research firm, based on an analysis of 2,000 survey households involving 6,375 persons across the United States.[21] It identified the most popular participant sports (including a number of outdoor-recreation activities, like camping and fishing) for children and adults of both sexes. While the study was geared to providing useful information to manufacturers, advertisers, and potential sports investors, it gave interesting insights into the influence of age and sex on the choice of activities. For example, it showed that while swimming was the most popular activity for all groups, it was far less attractive to adults than to children.

Table 5-3

Popularity of Participant Sports Based on A. C. Nielsen Survey

Activity	Number of Participants Reported
Swimming	107,191,000
Bicycling	65,613,000
Fishing	61,263,000
Camping	54,435,000
Bowling	38,218,000
Table Tennis	33,501,000
Pool and Billiards	32,920,000
Boating (other than sailing)	32,629,000
Softball	26,362,000
Ice Skating	24,874,000

Findings of the Nielsen Company survey for all age groups together are reported in table 5-3.

It should be noted that *none* of the major team sports except softball appear on this list. Basketball and baseball do, however, appear on the list of the ten favorite participation sports for boys and girls under the age of eighteen. Such sports find their greatest popularity among youth. The National Federation of State High School Associations, representing state athletic associations of the fifty states and the District of Columbia, reported in December, 1976, that 4.1 million boys and 1.65 million girls had participated in interscholastic sports in 1976. Strikingly, the increase in sports participation for girls (in comparison with the previous survey two years before) was almost *ten times as great* as for boys. Basketball continued to be the most popular sport. So-called lifetime sports, including tennis and golf, also enjoyed major increases in participation, as did soccer.

According to *U.S. News and World Report,* the ten fastest growing participant sports between 1973 and 1976 were tennis, skiing, jogging, snowmobiling, basketball, bowling, bicycling, pool/billiards, boating, and camping. Some activities increased in national participation by as much as 30 or 40 percent during this period.[22]

Clearly, participant sports make a major contribution to the national economy. In the early 1970s it was reported that four million skiers spent $1.3 billion a year on their sport, and twelve million golfers spent $3.0 billion a year, including club memberships and the cost of equipment. Other major sports activities and outdoor recreation pursuits reflect similar spending.

Spectator Sports

Without question, attending sports events in person or vicariously through television is a major leisure pursuit in the United States today. This is dramatically illustrated by the salaries paid to professional athletes today. In 1973, the *average* salary of players in the National Basketball Association was $90,000; in the National Hockey League, $40,000; and in major league baseball, $37,000. Many athletes today make $100,000 a year or more, with several earning several hundred thousand dollars a year.[23] All forms of professional sport have expanded their leagues and number of teams, with a rapid shifting of franchises to municipal or county governments that would subsidize hugh new stadiums or areas that would provide large new audiences of unjaded fans.

Equally important has been the need for advantageous locations for television broadcasting contracts. The major networks, with tremendous advertising revenues based in sports programs, have competed hotly for the right to broadcast games. The American Broadcasting Company paid $4.5 million to cover the 1968 Olympic Games in Mexico, while in 1977, the National Broadcasting Company agreed to pay the Soviet Olympic authorities up to $80 million to broadcast the 1980 Moscow games.

Sports have clearly become big business, and television has been a key factor in making them so. This trend has influenced the nature of college and even secondary school sports. While they are nominally amateur, many college teams can no longer be seriously regarded as a form of cocurricular or recreational activity. Instead they are a kind of training ground, or minor league, for highly skilled performers, most of whom have been recruited into colleges because of their sports ability.

This system of highly competitive and publicized secondary school and college sport is uniquely American; it is found in no other nation in the world and is essentially an expression of the fact that our approach to sport is heavily spectator oriented.

Attendance at major spectator events has been reported in the *Statistical Abstract* (see table 5-4).[24]

Although not reported in these surveys, the second most popular form of spectator sport (in terms of paid attendance) has been elsewhere reported as *automobile racing,* with paid attendance by forty million persons a year in 1968. In contrast to those attending horse-racing events (who come primarily to bet at parimutuel windows), auto racing fans come primarily because of the spectator appeal of the sport itself. Because automobile racing must necessarily cover large areas, the crowd is spread out, and huge numbers may watch at once:

Table 5-4
Statistics of Major Spectator Sports in U.S.

Activity	1950	1960	1970	1974
Racing (horse and greyhound), total attendance:	35,374,000	54,803,000	82,364,000	92,074,000
pari-mutuel turnover (in millions of dollars)	1,805	3,680	6,707	8,540
Football, college attendance	18,962,000	20,403,000	29,466,000	31,235,000
professional attendance	2,115,000	4,054,000	9,991,000	10,675,000
Baseball, major league attendance	17,659,000	20,261,000	29,000,000	30,254,000
Basketball, professional league attendance	NA	1,986,000	7,113,000	9,469,000

The Indianapolis 500 brings in perhaps 225,000 spectators. Daytona has gates of 100,000 and Riverside 80,000. Auto racing is even more popular abroad. One event alone, the Twenty-Four Hours of Le Mans, has had as many as 400,000 spectators. [25]

The huge crowds that attend auto racing events have been compared to those attending the Circus Maximus in ancient Rome. Few other sports are as dangerous to participants (and sometimes to the audience). While such hugh events are strictly professional, much stock-car racing and hot-rod competition (dragracing) is either semiprofessional or amateur. Car racing is a unique blend of technical appeal, hero worship, and the ever-present risk of sudden death.

Dwarfing the "live" attendance figures in professional and college sports are the figures of television attendance. Football in particular has become an immensely popular spectator sport for the home fan for several months each year, with whole weekends devoted to nonstop watching of college and professional football games; a single major "pro" game, the Super Bowl, is estimated to have as many as eighty million watchers. Other sports events of worldwide interest, such as heavyweight boxing matches and world soccer championships, have drawn television audiences in the hundreds of millions.

Outdoor Recreation Activities in the United States

Another major area of recreation participation is outdoor recreation. In 1965, the United States Bureau of Outdoor Recreation reported that the participation of individuals in outdoor recreation—including everything from hiking to surfing—had reached a total of 6.5 billion "occasions" (acts of participation by one person in a given activity) during the calendar year. The bureau predicted that there would be 10 billion such occasions in 1980 and 17 billion in the year 2000, based on a projection of current trends.

Outdoor recreation is somewhat difficult to define, since it ranges from basketball played on an outdoor court, swimming in an outdoor pool, or even concerts in outdoor amphitheatres, to such activities as mountain climbing, scuba diving, backpacking, snowmobiling and cross-country skiing that are clearly dependent on the natural environment and cannot be conducted indoors. Whatever definition one applies, it is clear that outdoor recreation—particularly travel and tourism—has a major economic impact in today's leisure world.

Boating as Recreation

Figures released in 1967 by the National Association of Engine and Boat Manufacturers and the Boating Industry Association indicated that there were a total of 8.2 million boats in the nation's pleasure-craft armada, with approximately 41.7 million persons taking part in boating with some frequency. Ten years later, in 1977, the number of boats in use had climbed to 10.1 million, with more than 50 million boating participants. In all, Americans were spending more than $5 billion a year on boating. [26]

Boating is a particularly important form of recreational activity because it provides the basis for many other pastimes: fishing, scuba diving, water-skiing, and

105

especially camping. It has been reported that of the total number of people who camp outdoors, well over 50 percent seek out lake or reservoir campsites, with a high percentage of campers owning outboard motors or boats. A recent trend in boating is the growing interest in canoeing; it has been estimated that 2.5 million Americans now canoe regularly, with their ranks increasing by up to 500,000 a year.

Fishing and Hunting

A major survey of hunting and fishing conducted in 1970 by the Bureau of Sport Fisheries and Wildlife of the United States Department of the Interior revealed that among those nine years old or older, almost fifty-five million persons fished, hunted, or both to some extent, spending seven hundred seventy million recreation days in these pursuits.[27]

Table 5-5

Statistics of Hunting and Fishing in 1970

	Fishermen	Hunters
Number of participants	33,158,000	14,336,000
Total money spent	$4,958,883,000	$2,142,648,000
Number of recreation days	706,187,000	203,689,000
Number of trips	576,210,000	176,201,000
Total miles traveled	29,482,799,000	9,284,953,000

As an example of the economic impact of these pursuits, fishermen and hunters paid over $230 million in Federal excise taxes and Federal and state license fees in 1970. Table 5-6 demonstrates the activities engaged in on the properties of just *one* Federal agency, the Forest Service of the United States Department of Agriculture, during a recent year.[28]

In addition to such traditional forms of outdoor recreation, one may point out that the exotic, high-risk forms of activity have been growing rapidly. Dunn and Gulbis write:

> Parachuting, mountain climbing, motorcycling, auto racing, white water canoeing, hotdogging, snowmobiling, and spelunking are among the risk recreation activities which have gained devotees during recent years. Between 1971 and 1973, the Southern California Hang Glider Association increased from 25 to 4,000 members; by 1975, an estimated 25,000 hang gliding buffs nationwide were trusting their fates to the whims of cliff and mountainside air currents. Hot-air balloon pilots, registered by the Balloon Federation of America increased from 5,000 to 15,000 between 1963 and 1973.[29]

Even such unusual activities have strong economic impact. For example, Dunn and Gulbis point out that these sports become the basis for new industries that design and manufacture equipment; publish guidebooks and magazines;

106

Table 5-6

Recreation Use of National Forests: Servicewide Summary, 1974

Activity		Visitor-Days[a]	Percent
Camping		51,543,500	26.7
Picnicking		6,933,200	3.6
Recreation Travel (Mechanized)		44,332,900	23.1
Automobile	37,385,200		
Scooter & Motorcycle	3,580,300		
Ice & Snowcraft	3,022,500		
Other	344,900		
Boating		5,790,100	3.1
Powerboats	3,679,000		
Self-Propelled Boats	2,110,800		
Games & Team Sports		747,800	.4
Water-Skiing & Other Water Sports		1,154,100	.6
Swimming & Scuba Diving		3,928,800	2.0
Winter Sports		8,377,800	4.3
Skiing	6,935,000		
Other	1,442,800		
Fishing		16,402,500	8.5
Hunting		14,422,800	7.5
Hiking & Mountain Climbing		8,514,300	4.4
Horseback Riding		2,815,100	1.5
Resort Use		3,934,200	2.0
Organization Camp Use		4,232,900	2.2
Recreation Residence Use		6,979,900	3.6
Gathering Forest Products		2,187,400	1.1
Nature Study		1,011,800	.5
Viewing Scenery, Sports & Environment		6,186,000	3.2
Visitor Information (Talks, etc.)		3,420,700	1.8
Servicewide Total:		192,915,800	100.0

[a]*Visitor-day* consists of a recreational use of land and water that aggregates twelve person-hours. May entail one person for twelve hours, twelve persons for one hour, or any equivalent combination, either continuous or intermittent.

support lobbying and professional standards; organize instruction, competition, and tours; and carry out a variety of other functions, many of them income producing.

A final important aspect of outdoor recreation is the organized camping movement. Today, some 10,500 resident camps are accredited by the American Camping Association, but these represent only a fraction of the number of camps serving millions of Americans young and old each year. In addition to the typical camp program, which operates on a fixed site, and offers a variety of outdoor-recreation, sports, social, and cultural activities, there are more and more camps in unique program areas, like special sports camps, camps for the overweight, trip-and-travel camps, and "arts" camps.

Travel and Tourism

Another major form of recreation involves vacation and weekend pleasure travel, including (1) foreign travel; (2) travel to a specific domestic destination, such as a major amusement complex or national park, with stops along the way; (3) short trips to vacation homes or camping areas; and (4) travel which mixes business with pleasure.

The motel industry has shifted its emphasis from providing places to stay while en route to a destination to developing places that have become places to stay in themselves. Major chains now emphasize recreation and entertainment facilities to encourage weekend vacations with package deals for couples and families. One motel chain executive commented:

> Swimming pools, air conditioning and room T.V. are just points of departure now. Some of our motels offer golf, horseback riding, tennis, boating, fishing, even duck hunting and skeet shooting.[30]

Many motels situated near large cities now offer vacation getaways. Travel that includes the use of such facilities may be part of a total vacation, a vacation in itself, or even part of a business trip. Similarly, eating, usually thought of as a maintenance activity, frequently becomes a form of leisure activity. It was reported in the mid-1960s that eating out had become one of the largest industries in the United States, with families in the upper-income brackets actually spending one-third of their food dollars for dining out. The boom in leisure spending and tourism has resulted in a dramatic growth in roadside restaurants, restaurants in airline and bus terminals, and restaurants in resorts and national parks.

Foreign travel has become an increasingly important part of this form of leisure activity. Cosgrove and Jackson point out that by 1966, international tourists were spending over $13 billion each year, an increase of 450 percent since 1950.[31] Godbey and Parker write:

> In some countries, international tourism is a much more important component of the economy than it is in the United States. In Canada, for instance, with one-tenth of the population of the United States, half as many international tourism dollars are generated; a sizable portion of the tourists are Americans. Spain, with a population of 33 million, had 24.1 million tourists visit in 1970, and will have an estimated 50 million per year by the end of the decade.[32]

Surprisingly, tourism has been able to withstand the protracted economic slump of the past several years. Kneeland reported that even during the deep recession of 1975 millions of Americans were indulging themselves at the nation's winter playgrounds as if there were no tomorrow:

> In record or near-record numbers, they are gambling in Las Vegas, swimming and soaking up the sun in Florida and Hawaii, frolicking on the rides at Southern California's Disneyland or testing the Colorado ski slopes.[33]

This readiness to spend freely on tourism is a worldwide phenomenon. All the industrialized nations of the world suffered from continued unemployment and rising inflation during the early and mid-1970s. Yet the Paris-based Club Méditer-ranée, which had operated 47 vacation villages in thirteen countries (including clubs in Europe, North Africa, the Near East, Tahiti and the Caribbean) in 1970, had expanded its operations to 75 resort villages by 1976. Its worldwide sales were an impressive $170 million in 1975, and the club's directors intend to expand to 300 to 400 villages worldwide by the year 2000.[34]

Major Entertainment Complexes

Closely linked to travel as a form of recreation has been the expansion of "fun centers" throughout the United states, like California's famous Disneyland. This major entertainment complex is the leading example of such business ventures. Built in 1955 at a cost of over $50 million, it covers 65 acres in Anaheim, California. Disneyland is a unique amalgam of the past and present, of fairyland fantasy and modern space science, and includes a massive, independently operated hotel complex. Accommodating as many as 60,000 persons at one time, by the mid-1960s Disneyland had attracted over forty-five million visitors, including many kings, queens, and heads of state—and this success had led to the construction of a second major Disney complex, Walt Disney World, at Lake Buena Vista, Florida. Crompton and Van Doren point out that Disney effectively resurrected a dying industry. The outdoor amusement park, once an important form of popular entertainment, had become a cultural anachronism. Disney's contribution, they write, was to emphasize cleanliness, courtesy, and safety, in marked contrast to the traditional amusement park.

> The theology of pleasure is reinforced by promotional messages. The theme park creates an atmosphere in which the visitor is likely to experience fantasy, glamour, escapism, prestige, and excitement. . . . Once inside the gate, the visitor is completely shut off from the outside world and immersed in an enjoyable recreational experience. . . . The theme parks' primary market is the family; theme parks keep a family involved and entertained for a whole day.[35]

Other entertainment entrepreneurs followed the Disney example, and by 1976 at least three dozen parks of similar scale had been built around the United States, including Disney World; Busch Gardens in Williamsburg, Virginia; Worlds of Fun in Kansas City; Six Flags Over Georgia in Atlanta; and Six Flags Over Texas, in Dallas. Some parks concentrate on a single theme, such as Opryland, U.S.A., in Nashville, and the Land of Oz, in North Carolina. Still others incorporate moving rides through settings based on literary, historical, or international themes; entertainment; and typical amusement park "thrill" rides like roller coasters and parachute jumps. Perhaps better than any other commercial attraction, the modern amusement park demonstrates the need to carefully analyze consumer leisure wishes, and to design attractions that respond to the changes in progress in our contemporary culture.

Another example of the widespread investment in recreational facilities has been the wave of stadium construction throughout the United States. These stadiums often host a variety of entertainment and business-exposition activities. A leading example is the Astrodome, in Houston, Texas. This marvel of modern technology, a fully enclosed structure that costs $37 million to build, attracts several million patrons a year. The temperature inside is always seventy-two degrees, and events are never rained out. Beautifully designed and decorated, the Astrodome is so huge that the eighteen-story Shamrock-Hilton Hotel could stand on second base and not touch its dome or walls. The stadium complex also includes a $26-million, 116-acre amusement park called Astroworld, a 12-acre Astrohall exhibition center, and a $16-million group of motor hotels. The major sports teams that play in the stadium are owned by the Astrodome's controlling corporation. In addition to professional and college baseball, football, and basketball, the Astrodome has scheduled major boxing events, racing, polo, bloodless "bullfights," Gaelic football, religious revivals, and the circus.

Throughout the United States and Canada, other cities and counties have built huge new stadiums, sometimes through syndicates of local investors, but often with financial help from the city or county itself. In a number of cases a municipality has built and owns a stadium, which it then rents out to major sports teams or for other leisure uses.

Recreation Related to Real Estate Investment

It is apparent that recreation has become closely interwoven with other elements of the total economic structure of modern communities. A typical example of this is the inclusion of commercially sponsored recreation attractions in suburban shopping centers. In response to the increasing reluctance of suburban dwellers to drive into the central cities, huge new regional shopping complexes today offer motion-picture houses, restaurants, bowling alleys (often with child-care facilities), theaters, and other leisure attractions. The shopping center, according to *U.S. News and World Report,* is replacing the city park and the corner drug store as "the core of 'community belonging' in America."

Shopping center managers have often planned recreational events to attract families. South Shore Plaza in the Boston suburb of Braintree has offered art shows, musical festivals, auto shows, and free jazz concerts to the public. Other shopping centers have provided community rooms to be used as coffee houses by area youth, or provided mall areas to be used free of charge by church, civic, and school groups for charity bazaars and fairs. However, many shopping centers have found that masses of "floating" teen-agers cause unforeseen problems. The manager of the South Hills mall, a huge enclosed center on the south side of Pittsburgh, commented:

> When we started to develop these malls, we thought they should be like the old Roman forums, where people could not only buy but be entertained and meet their friends. . . . But when they also come to loaf and use us as a place to hang out, we've had trouble. They've been pushing dope, loitering in the walkways, and using obscene language. We had no choice but to close that coffee house.[36]

Nonetheless, in some recently built regional shopping centers, there has been a deliberate attempt to see recreation as a prime item to be merchandised. Nicholls and Jones point out that tennis courts, ice- and roller-skating rinks, movie theaters, bowling alleys, swimming pools, miniature golf courses, and libraries are only some of the leisure facilities to be included in such centers. The latest trend, they suggest, has begun in suburban Chicago, where two large regional shopping centers are providing cultural as well as traditional amusement activities. Woodfield is currently the world's largest shopping center, with 240 stores and over 2.2 million square feet of climate-controlled space on three levels. In 1974

> a variety of internationally and locally famous dancers, bands, choral groups, musicians and actors performed in the Greek amphitheater built and designed to complement the shopping experience. The Chicago Symphony, for example, performed for approximately 50,000 shoppers at one performance that year.[37]

Old Chicago, the world's first combined amusement park and shopping center, opened thirty-five miles southwest of Chicago in 1975. This $40-million enclosed structure has 200 retail stores and eating establishments—in addition to a 300-seat theater featuring vaudeville acts, thirty-one other rides and attractions, and continuous daily entertainment of all sorts.

Recreation in Residential Developments

Recreational activities are offered by many condominium developments, apartment complexes, retirement communities, and other residential projects. The famous Sun City retirement community, in Arizona, had over 25,000 elderly residents in the mid-1970s, with the expectation of expanding to 50,000 by 1980. The community has six shopping centers, nine golf courses, and five recreation centers (one containing the state's largest indoor swimming pool), as well as an amphitheater, a stadium, two lakes, and the country's first synthetic-surfaced lawn-bowling green. Sun City residents also enjoy tennis, swimming, billiards, shuffleboard, arts and crafts shops, dances, lectures, concerts, bicycling, and weekly stage shows. In many such retirement communities, residents must pay special membership fees to use certain recreation facilities.

The vacation-home business has evolved into a huge and sometimes shady financial operation during the past two decades; in 1971, the Office of Interstate Land Sales of the United States Department of Housing and Urban Development estimated that over $4 billion was being spent annually in developing and purchasing lakeside recreational subdivisions. Other home developments—either of primary residences or vacation homes—have been clustered around golf courses, pool and tennis clubs, marinas or boating-access canals, and even air strips.

Thus, in shopping centers and residential developments, recreation clearly provides an important economic magnet.

The Growth of Cultural Activities

Another important area of leisure involvement in the United States and Canada has been centered around rapidly growing public interest and involvement in the arts. This cultural "explosion" has been evidenced by the building of cultural centers and museums, growth in spectator events and participation, and personal consumption related to all the arts.

To illustrate, there was a remarkable growth in all forms of musical activity in the United States after World War II. During the period from 1939 to 1965, the number of American symphony orchestras more than doubled—from about 600 to 1,401 (more than half the world's 2,000 orchestras). By the late 1960s, it was estimated that there were over 37 million amateur musicians in the United States, with more Americans attending symphony concerts than going to major- or minor-league football games. Similarly, a study conducted by Statistics Canada found that in 1972 more Canadians paid to go to the theater, opera, ballet, and concerts than paid admission prices for sports events.[38]

The bulk of this growth in participation and attendance has centered around *amateur* music, theater, dance, and art. For example, Kando points out that the phenomenal 1,200 percent increase in opera-producing companies over a twenty-eight-year period reflected almost exclusively the growth of amateur opera. While there is a vigorous commercial summer theater movement in the United States, the bulk of theater production is nonprofit (including 20,000 college, school, club, and church drama companies); the Broadway theater, which formerly was the center of serious drama, has declined steadily.[39] Indeed, Baumol and Bowen have pointed out that since 1929 American spending on the arts has declined in relative terms from 15¢ per $100 of disposable income to only 11¢.

During the 1970s sharply escalated costs of production obliged many major symphony orchestras, ballet and opera companies, and other cultural institutions (including museums and libraries) to curtail operations, raise fees, and even in some cases to close down. Kando points out that European countries have been far more vigorous in supporting the arts than the United States, in some cases taxing other forms of entertainment heavily to subsidize cultural activities.[40] While we have tended to view government support of the arts as a potential source of censorship or thought control, it should be noted that Federal funding through the National Endowment for the Arts rose from $2.5 million in the mid-1960s to an allocation of $82 million for 1976. Many states and provinces also offer strong programs of assistance to the arts and humanities (see chapter 9).

Within community-sponsored recreation programs, there has been a dramatic growth in the number of local recreation departments offering such activities as ballet, modern dance, community theater, painting, and sculpture. Hundreds of cities have also built special centers for the performing and graphic arts, including New York City's famous $142-million Lincoln Center for the Performing Arts and the Kennedy Center for the Performing Arts in Washington, D.C.

Spending on Gambling

In sharp contrast to the financial problems that have recently afflicted the major professional performing arts companies is the area of gambling. Historically a popular leisure activity in all societies, gambling today represents a phenomenal expenditure. It was noted earlier that *legal* gambling, including all forms of parimutuel betting, state-sponsored lotteries, and reported turnover in licensed casinos, represented a $19-billion-per-year industry. It has been estimated that *illegal* gambling involves about $30 billion a year (some authorities have made estimates as high as $500 billion a year, but this figure is generally rejected), with as much as $6 to $7 billion falling into the hands of organized crime. An increasing number of states, including Massachusetts, Delaware, Maryland, and Michigan, have developed weekly, computerized public lotteries to raise funds. As a dramatic example, in New York State lottery sales figures in 1976 totalled $1.5 billion. Some states also sponsor off-track betting parlors, and it seems likely that Nevada's successful legalization of gambling as a popular industry, controlled and taxed by state authorities, will spread increasingly to other states.

A recent survey commissioned by the National Gambling Commission concluded that six of every ten American adults participated in some form of gambling during 1974. Indeed, Gallup surveys have concluded that gambling is the "major American business," with card games (about which it is almost impossible to gather precise data) accounting for more than half the total money wagered.[41]

Given the definition of recreation suggested by authorities such as Clayne Jensen (see chapter 2), which stresses social value and positive moral character, some might challenge whether gambling should be regarded as recreation at all. However, there is little question that the majority of its participants regard it as an enjoyable and acceptable form of leisure activity. Other morally questionable forms of leisure involvement, such as drug use and drinking, represent major areas of spending by the public.

The key issue suggested here is whether as a nation we can permit such huge amounts of money to be spent on forms of play that in many cases are seriously harmful to personal or family well-being, while more positive and desirable forms of recreation are denied adequate financial support.

Television as Popular Leisure

Without question, the most significant influence on the use of leisure today has been television. By the late 1970s, television sets were being marketed in a variety of new forms, including a tiny British model with a two-inch screen weighing less than two pounds, and a giant set with a six-foot screen, selling for about $2,500. In 1977, the Music Corporation of America, a huge California-based entertainment conglomerate, began to market a "videodisc" system that would bring a full range of educational and entertainment programs on discs similar to long-playing records into the ordinary home, to be shown on special player systems attached to regular television sets.

A Nielsen survey published in 1975 reported that 97 percent of American homes have TV sets, with 41 percent having two or more sets. In the average American or Canadian household the TV set is turned on six hours a day, a figure surpassed only in Japan, where it is on over seven hours a day.

Television watching has obviously displaced other forms of leisure activity to a marked degree. Attendance at movie theaters declined from about 3.4 billion admissions in 1948 (the year television networks got under way) to about 1.1 billion a year in the late 1960s. It is clear that participation in many other forms of recreation must have dropped drastically because of television. Its appeal, of course, is that it is easily available (being safe at home in an age of "danger in the streets" constitutes a marked advantage) and requires no strain or effort on the part of the viewer—only that he or she stay awake and suffer through the many commercials that punctuate the actual entertainment. In addition, television offers every level of taste and entertainment; animated cartoons for young children, rock-and-roll shows for teenagers, situation comedies, talk shows, action and soap-opera dramas, and old movies.

Obviously, some television programs are excellent forms of cultural fare, particularly children's series like "Sesame Street." On the other hand, what is essentially negative about television—apart from its questionable level of taste and preoccupation with violence—is its essentially passive character. Instead of creatively expressing himself or being meaningfully involved with others, the television watcher becomes little more than a blotter soaking up sight and sound. In millions of homes throughout the country, exactly the same pictures appear on the screen (in fact, they appear later in many other countries as well in dubbed versions). This leveling of taste through the cumulative impact of the standardized media could only be achieved through modern technology. And it is technology that must be recognized as the most important modern influence on the use of leisure.

The Influence of Technology on Leisure

The appeal of television is due in large part to the technological ingenuity that underlies modern programming. Using small portable cameras that capture all sorts of sports events, such programs as "The Wide World of Sports" have telecast over 100 different types of contests in many different countries. In 1965, when a team of mountain climbers scaled the Matterhorn to celebrate the hundredth anniversary of the first climbing of the mountain, they were met on top by an ABC camera crew that had climbed up the day before. Television cameramen today film under water, and use instant replays, slow-motion closeups, split screens, and other newly devised techniques to ensure that the home watcher can see far more accurately and vividly than the fan who is actually on the scene.

Not only has technology given us more leisure; it is also shaping and changing our use of it. In addition to television, technology has created new forms of recreation and undoubtedly has others on the drawing board. Popular music today is heard chiefly not by listening to "live" musicians, but through taped cassettes, on car radios, and recordings played at home on stereo equipment. The most recent technological fad involves citizens'-band radios—it was estimated in 1976 that Americans had spent more than $1 billion in a single year to buy over 12 million C.B. rigs. These are widely used in trucks, recreation vehicles, automobiles, and homes, and while they have certain practical functions, they also are obviously recreational. C.B. radio broadcasters constitute an informal fraternity, with characteristic nicknames and jargon, clubs, newspapers, and magazines.[42]

Technology permits humans to alter their environments and to create new settings for play. The expanded ski industry is based on the ability of ski promoters to make artificial snow, extending the skiing season and making it feasible to build expensive winter-sports complexes far south of the regions that would normally sustain such sport. Artificial ice rinks, refrigerated toboggan chutes, and snowmobiles are technological innovations that have created new approaches to winter sports.

Mass-produced power boats, many made of plastic, are used for recreation in combination with other water-based pastimes (some also technologically based, like scuba diving). New processes have made it possible to build giant dams and reservoirs, and even to locate lakes in desert areas by using plastic undercoatings to prevent drainage into the subsoil. Many marinas in northern climates are now equipped with automatic bubbling mechanisms that prevent freezing, so boats may

114

remain safely in the water throughout the year. The year-round heating of pools in cooler climates and the invention of artificial surf (a Japanese innovation that creates five-foot breakers in large inland pools) are other examples of how technology can make swimming more comfortable and appealing throughout the year.

In 1976 a new aquatic vehicle was put on the market; a jet-propelled, unsinkable motorcycle that rides the waves on skis. Developed in Southern California, this $1,900 vehicle draws only three inches of water, and is powerful enough to tow a stunting water-skier—one more example of technology's creating new play opportunities.

On land, off-road vehicles have proliferated. Badaracco points out that fifteen years ago, off-road vehicles were virtually unknown. Today, more than seven million are operating in the United States:

> Almost 2½ million trailbikes and minibikes were sold in 1970. Snow-mobiles, which accounted for 259 sales in 1959, reached total sales of two million in 1973. All-terrain vehicles increased from 2,000 manufactured in 1967 to 18,000 in 1971. An estimated 200,000 dune buggies were in operation nationally in 1972.[43]

Flying has gained widespread popularity; several years ago, the Aircraft Owners and Pilots' Association reported that of 600,000 fliers in the United States, about 250,000 are private pilots who fly about 120,000 private aircraft. A substantial number of these are used primarily for family or individual recreation or, when owned by industrial firms, for combined business and leisure functions. In addition to flying for recreation, many hobbyists have taken up sky diving, ballooning, or gliding—all based on equipment developed through modern technology. At the same time that one appreciates the positive contributions that technology has made to our leisure lives, it is necessary to raise two serious questions about its effects.

Effects of Technological Play

First, while mechanically based forms of play both extend and supplant man's capabilities, they limit his personal participation. One might compare the slot-car racing fad of the 1960s (a pastime in which players sit at control boards in commercial centers, pressing a switch with one finger, while complicated little cars zoom around a maze of raceways) with the nature of the experience the participant might have while bicycling, running, or being involved in any other form of direct personal recreation. Today's comparable technological fad is electronic games—electronic hockey, target shooting, table tennis, and other competitive games played on TV screens through little hand-held "player control units." Such games, which became popular in the early 1970s, are widely found in hotels and motels, bars, amusement centers, and homes. The latest trend, Becker suggests, is computer game playing. Pointing out that large, centralized computer systems are within everyone's reach today (through remote terminal devices), he comments:

> People have devised games for computers almost as long as there have been computers. These games can take several forms. Many tend to mimic other games . . . [like] card and grid games which are easily adaptable to machines. Others tend to simulate life occurrences, giving them a recreational quality—lunar landings, auto races, target gliding,

and other activities involving speed, trajectory, and time have been adapted. Finally, programs designed to puzzle and challenge are also employed—geographic mazes and "hangman" [the word game] are a few examples.[44]

While such activities have a special appeal, they inhibit personal creativity and meaningful participation. Their depersonalized quality may be illustrated by the coin-operated driving game called "Death Race." Players behind the wheel try to run down humanoid figures on a television screen (to the outrage of the National Safety Council). The player who scores highest by hitting the dodging figures is an "expert driver."[45]

Another little discussed and potentially insidious form of technological play relates to sex. One of the more extreme examples of alienation and depersonalization in our society may be found in the tremendous growth of sex products (films, books, magazines, phonograph albums, and "action" devices) purchased, used, or viewed by both men and women. By providing vicarious or person-to-object involvement, such mechanical devices destroy the essential human quality of sex, substituting for it an alienated, withdrawn kind of involvement.

Economic Exclusion

A second concern stems from the fact that technologically based leisure is inevitably more expensive than traditional leisure activities. Numerous major corporations have moved into the leisure field, providing diversified products and services at a handsome profit. The Tandy Corporation, for example, grossed over $640 million in 1975 from a wide range of electronic products (C.B. radios, tape recorders, and stereo equipment); hobby and handicraft kits and supplies; vending machine operations; sports equipment; and varied goods and services. MCA (Music Corporation of America) grossed a comparable sum in the preceding year, from: service divisions that made feature films, television series, phonograph records, and video equipment; representation of top entertainers; operation of studio tours and facilities in Yosemite National Park; retail gift sales; and a host of leisure-connected goods.

It is obvious, then, that big business has definitely moved into the leisure field. Without question, it is today in a position to program the tastes of millions of American families—by creating products and services, advertising them heavily, giving them "status," and, in effect, dominating large chunks of contemporary leisure.

While this is understandable in a society committed to free enterprise, it also means limited leisure possibilities for those who cannot afford to pay their way. The entire question of recreational opportunity is closely linked to financial capability—particularly when *public* recreation and park departments, as well as *private* concerns, begin to charge substantial fees for participation. This poses serious questions about public policy in leisure service, which are discussed later in this text.

Other Forms of Nonaffiliated Play

In addition to expensive, technological forms of play, there are also many different nonaffiliated and essentially noncommercial activities that people carry on during their leisure time.

These activities include a wide range of hobbies, social activities, casual outdoor-recreation pursuits, learning activities, volunteer functions, and craft or artistic pursuits. In many cases they may be carried on without any sort of organizational sponsorship or assistance, and without buying any sort of product or equipment. Yet even such pastimes become commercial if they reveal any potential for making money.

Flea markets, garage sales, and handicraft swapping are prime examples. Originally a casual form of mixing business and pleasure—a way of cleaning out the attic or garage, or of buying inexpensive trinkets and gadgets—this extremely popular form of semileisure has turned into a highly organized and commercialized activity. Throughout the country hundreds of drive-in theaters sponsor large-scale flea markets, as do churches, voluntary agencies, and even some public recreation and park departments. Garage sales in some communities are operated by professional sales teams, particularly when families are selling homes and must sell substantial amounts of home furnishings. Attending such sales is an enjoyable form of leisure activity for many families, particularly on weekends.

Other activities that began in casual ways wind up as highly structured and commercialized pursuits. Square- and folk-dancing, initially forms of casual entertainment conducted in rural settings, have become advanced and complicated activities; beginners must take lengthy instructional courses, and then join established clubs. Magazines, amplifiers and loudspeaker systems, phonograph records and tapes, well-paid callers and teachers, and regional festivals and workshops are all part of the structure surrounding such hobbies today.

To the uninitiated, flying a kite would appear to be the ultimate self-directed, noncommercialized activity. Yet, this increasingly popular activity has spawned an International Kitefliers Association with thousands of members. This association sponsors numerous competitions and festivals, and participants buy kites from companies that produce expensive, aerodynamically designed models sold round the world. Horseshoe pitching, throwing darts, and shuffleboard are all activities that, although they may be approached on a casual, noncommercialized, individual basis, also involve organizations, the marketing of products, and large-scale competitions. Skateboarding is a prime example of a juvenile pastime which had a brief period of popularity, died out, and then was revived with new and better products, publicity, and organizations. Today the skateboarding "frenzy" is said to have thirty million enthusiasts—including many adults, professional teachers, and stunt experts—and has resulted in championship tournaments and commercially operated skateboarding centers. A recently revived skateboarding magazine quickly sold out its first edition of 100,000 copies!

Pet care, horseback riding, games, and toys all represent multibillion-dollar forms of leisure activity that contribute to the total economic impact of recreation in modern society.

Leisure Expenditure in Canada: An Overview

Many leisure activities popular in the United States are also pursued in Canada. A special report of the Canadian Imperial Bank of Commerce reviewed recreation trends during the 1960s and made predictions for the 1970s.[46]

It pointed out that the sale of recreation "durables" (radios, television sets, record players, pleasure boats, sporting and camping equipment, cameras, and similar items) was steadily increasing in proportion to total consumer expenditures. The money devoted to Canadian production of travel trailers and mobile homes, for example, grew from less than $15 million in 1962 to over $46 million in 1967. The total spending in Canada by Canadian and foreign tourists was estimated as at least $3 billion annually. Particularly in view of Canada's rich wilderness, aquatic, and camping resources, it was pointed out that outdoor recreation and winter sports represented important and growing areas of participation.

As in the United States, cultural programs in Canada in such areas as art, music, theater, and dance, have expanded rapidly. In 1952 Canada had 162 museums, art galleries, and similar institutions; by 1968, the number had increased to over 700. However, despite the contributions of the Canada Council and such enterprises and cultural centers as the Stratford Festival, the National Theatre School in Montreal, and the National Arts Centre in Ottawa, such cultural programs continue to require subsidy.

More recently, a number of major studies of travel, tourism, and vacation attitudes and trends have been carried out by the Canadian Government Office of Tourism. One report, published in April, 1975, indicated that 58 percent of all Canadian adults took vacations each year, amounting to 7.6 million vacation trips. Statistics Canada concluded that travel in Canada has continued to rise steadily and that it now represents a $7-billion industry.

Other popular pursuits in Canada include a wide range of home do-it-yourself hobbies, including gardening, construction, and building items from electronic kits. Adult education has become a major leisure pursuit, with enrollment in part-time and noncredit courses in Canadian colleges and universities growing by 80 percent during a five-year period in the 1960s.

Big Is Best (Economically Speaking)—Or Is It?

The prevailing attitude regarding the growth of recreational participation and expenditure has been favorable, particularly in respect to outdoor recreation, tourism, and travel. In general, cities, states, and regions have accepted the notion that "big is best." As the number of tourists has increased each year—along with their spending on food, gas and oil, and a variety of recreational services—states and provinces from Florida to British Columbia have gloried in this boon to their local economies. Forty-seven of the fifty American states, for example, report that tourism ranks among their top three industries.

In a number of cases, cities have sponsored major fairs or expositions that have enriched their image and provided a variety of facilities for continuing use by their own residents. The Seattle World's Fair, for example, left that city with outstanding cultural and sports facilities. Spokane's Expo '74 provided the opportunity to clean out a "skid-row" area of the city, and to develop new roads and outstanding recreation facilities. Montreal spent over $1.3 billion in construction for the 1976 Olympics, but much of this paid for sports facilities, stadiums, amphitheatres, and housing useful for the future.

Other cities regularly sponsor an annual event—such as Louisville's Kentucky Derby or the Indianapolis 500 racing car competition—that draws hundreds of thousands of visitors and provides a positive, colorful image for the city on a year-round basis. In Indianapolis, for example, the major automotive companies maintain year-round warehouses, testing and research centers, and a variety of other tours and events built on the popularity of the speedway competition. Other cities rely on the theater, nightclubs, art museums, and similar cultural facilities to stimulate tourist spending.

Apart from the large cities, many smaller communities are almost completely dependent on tourism for their livelihood. The tiny community of West Yellowstone, Montana, located in the most sparsely populated county in the forty-eight contiguous states, has only seven hundred residents. Yet it has forty souvenir shops and seventy-one motels in a twenty-four-block area, and exists chiefly to serve the 2.5 million tourists who visit Yellowstone National Park each year. Since the park (like many tourist regions) is very much a seasonal attraction, West Yellowstone has made strenuous efforts to extend the season—by building a convention center and a large indoor skating rink, and sponsoring dog-sled, snowshoeing, snowmobile, and even ice-fishing races and competitions.

When the voters of New Jersey approved the establishment of legal casino gambling in Atlantic City in November, 1976, it was seen by the city's residents as the basis for renewed prosperity for this somewhat run-down seashore resort. Land values shot up immediately and wheeler-dealers began to lay their plans for reaping the golden harvest that was to come.

How real are such expectations? How much of a boon is recreation to local economies?

Obviously, tourist spending in outdoor-recreation regions and in urban hotels, restaurants, nightclubs, and theaters provides a significant boost to local businesses and employment. A number of studies have clearly demonstrated the positive influence of recreational development on land values and the tax base, particularly around natural and man-made lakes and reservoirs. However, there is also evidence that the impact of the so-called multiplifier effect, which suggests that the initial expenditures by travelers and tourists are multiplied several times over through subsequent rounds of transactions within a region, is exaggerated.[47]

The initial premise—that recreation provides income, jobs, and support for local business—is sound. However, recreation facilities are not *always* successful ventures, as many a farmer who turned his back pasture into a golf course has found out. Frequently the projections of profit or income are faulty, and too often the potential negative effects of a recreation enterprise are not realistically assessed.

Risks and Deficits

A number of the most popular outdoor-recreation activities are subject to factors beyond the control of the individual entrepreneur. The ski industry, greatly expanded in the expectation of the joint arrival each fall of sufficient snow and swarms of eager skiers, has on occasion fallen victim to the fluctuations of weather and the effects of fuel and energy shortages. Such variables make outdoor-recreation enterprises risky at best.

Poor planning—or at least planning founded on faulty conceptual analysis—has also been responsible for the failure of several major amusement parks. Warner Brothers' $10-million Jungle Habitat—a huge nature preserve in New Jersey where giraffes, baboons, lions, and tigers ran free and cars drove through the grounds slowly, with their windows rolled up—appeared to be a real winner at the outset. Crowds were tremendous, lining up to wait for several hours to gain entrance to the park. Yet after a year or two, it became apparent that people were not coming back; Jungle Habitat did not have the diversified appeal to guarantee second and third visits. In the fall of 1976, it closed.

One of the wonders of the amusement world was the Super Dome, built at a cost of over $175 million by the state of Louisiana. Advertised as the largest enclosed sports arena in the world, this mammoth structure was opened in August, 1975, to widespread acclaim. Less than a year later, Louisiana sought to sell it; it had not attracted the sports teams, spectacles, and other program features that had been expected, and was running at a deficit. The Super Dome provides another example of faulty planning and projections, particularly in calculating the cost of running this huge facility, and the fees that had to be charged to cover this cost.

There are many such overly optimistic projections. Ellis and Knott provide a vivid example:

> . . . we offer the case of a decision on the part of the Metro Toronto government to invest $14 million for a special 3.5 mile ride through its new zoological park. A financial feasibility analysis made in 1973 showed that operating and capital costs could be recovered and a substantial profit realized, based on an attendance at the zoo in the 3,000,000 annual range. Whatever data used in the study were clearly inadequate (or . . . incompetently applied) for the actual 1975 attendance is under the 1,200,000 level. It is not now considered likely to rise above the 2,000,000 mark in future. Thus, the supposedly profitable investment will turn out to be a substantial loser, perhaps of over $1,000,000 per year, and the impact of this on the willingness or ability of Metro government to spend on other recreation facilities is incalculable.[48]

Recreation a Mixed Blessing

In addition to the impact of such poor planning on the development of recreation facilities, an entirely new factor has come into play. For several decades environmentalists have strongly opposed all development of state and national parks and wilderness areas. Along with such forms of commercialism as mining, logging, and building pipelines, recreation has been resisted—particularly the kind of recreation that would bring with it roads, buildings, and large numbers of vehicles. Pitched battles have been fought for years to resist such recreational enterprises, both public and private.

In addition to concern about protecting the environment, a number of states are now saying, "Keep out!" Oregon, for example, is discouraging new residents, on the basis that "we're too crowded already." We are no longer worshipping the idea of growth, increased business, and expanded national product uncritically. In some states, such as Minnesota, Michigan, and Wisconsin, there is a growing feeling that out-of-state tourists should be discouraged, in order to preserve nature areas and wildlife for resident campers, hunters, and fishermen. Just as the majority of small towns and suburban communities surrounding the larger cities today restrict their recreation and park facilities to their own residents, it seems probable that in the years ahead many states will no longer seek to attract tourists because of the revenues they bring, but instead will discourage and, if necessary, bar them.

Improved Recreation Planning Is a Must

One of the solutions to the problem of recreational overdevelopment is better planning research to determine the probable needs, uses, and impact of recreation projects under consideration.

New and more sophisticated techniques for quantifying specific supply-and-demand variables and relating them to the public's collective decision to engage in certain activities are being developed. Gravity-model calibration is being used to study the tourist-attraction patterns of specific recreational attractions or regions, as well as such variables as travel costs and alternatives, the influence of economic conditions, the proximity of major metropolitan populations, and the existence of competing attractions within a region.[49] Cluster analysis, which examines the related interests of groups of potential participants, helps to define the "activity packages" that will be most helpful in attracting large numbers of participants to given sites or complexes.[50] More sophisticated methods to measure or predict the ecological impact of alternative forms of recreation use on given environments are being developed.[51] Local planning studies are no longer being carried out solely on the basis of the traditional open-space standards or facilities-per-population guidelines used in the past. Instead, each county or regional study must assess potential receptivity or need for a particular facility in light of competing attractions; the opportunity for year-round multiple uses; economic factors involved in acquiring, constructing, and operating the facility; and, more important today than ever, the potential of the facility to justify itself economically by attracting and continuing to attract substantial revenues. The techniques used to plan private and commercial recreation enterprises are today also used to plan public ones, although the planning of public facilities may involve different political, philosophical, or practical factors.

In carrying out such planning, it must be recognized that trends in recreational interests and participation change rapidly in modern society. A study in the early 1970s revealed that only a tiny percentage of adult Americans engaged regularly in fitness-oriented activities; yet by the late 1970s there was a nationwide explosion of interest in aerobic activities, particularly jogging and running. Participation in bowling, which had enjoyed an immense popularity, declined rapidly several years ago, and economic reports in the late 1970s suggested that the interest in tennis, particularly in indoor centers, and the growth of "singles" developments had also peaked and was declining. Soccer, a sport widely viewed as too European for most Americans, began to boom at just this time. Clearly, the economic forecaster capable of predicting such abrupt changes in public interest would be a valuable member of the planning staff of any major corporation or public agency in the leisure field.

This chapter has demonstrated that recreation and leisure have become major economic forces serving varied needs, and heavily influenced by modern technology. It has become evident that unlimited recreation and park expansion is illusory, and that more sophisticated and intelligent planning techniques and policies must be used in developing recreation facilities and enterprises in the years ahead.

Chapter Five

1. A. Whitney Griswold, *Life*, 28 December 1959.

2. Harold L. Wilensky, "The Impact of Economic Growth on Free Time," in Erwin O. Smigel, ed., *Work and Leisure: A Contemporary Social Problem* (New Haven, Conn.: Coll. and U. Pr., 1963), p. 130.

3. Tony A. Mobley and Don Hellreigel, "The Four-Day Workweek," *Parks and Recreation,* November 1974, p. 16.

4. Robert S. Lynd and Helen M. Lynd, *Middletown* (New York: Harcourt, Brace, 1929), p. 261.

5. Juanita M. Kreps, "Sex, Age and Work," *New York Times,* 19 April 1976, p. 27.

6. Joann Vanek, "Time Spent in Housework," *Scientific American,* November 1974, p. 116.

7. Wilensky, "Impact of Economic Growth," p. 113.

8. Sebastian de Grazia, *Of Time, Work and Leisure* (New York: Doubleday-Anchor, Twentieth Century Fund, 1962), p. 79.

9. See Burt Nanus and Harvey Adelman, "Forecast for Leisure," *Journal of Health, Physical Education and Recreation,* January 1973, p. 61.

10. *The Challenge of Leisure: A Southern California Case Study* (Claremont: Southern California Research Council, Pomona College, 1967).

11. Ibid., p. 18.

12. Robert Reinhold, "New Population Trends Transforming U.S.," *New York Times,* 4 February 1977, p. 1.

13. *Annual U.S. Census Population Report* (Washington, D.C.: U.S. Department of Interior, 1977).

14. "What Is Holding Us Back?" *Time,* 24 January 1969, p. 24.

15. "Leisure Boom: Biggest Ever and Still Growing," *U.S. News and World Report,* 17 April 1972, p. 42.

16. For a detailed estimate of consumer spending on recreation in the late 1960s, see Richard Kraus, *Recreation and Leisure in Modern Society* (New York: Appleton-Century-Crofts, 1971) p. 317.

17. See *Statistical Abstracts of the United States* (Washington, D.C.: Bureau of the Census, 1976), pp. 215–16, 219, 396; Geoffrey Godbey and Stanley Parker, *Leisure Studies and Services: An Overview* (Philadelphia: Saunders, 1976), pp. 109–16; and *U.S. News and World Report,* 7 April 1972, pp. 43, 45.

18. For an earlier breakdown of nonconsumer spending on recreation by government and voluntary agencies, see Richard Kraus, "The Economics of Recreation Today," *Parks and Recreation,* June 1970, pp. 19–21, 51–53.

19. See the most recent issue of "Sports and Recreation Participation Survey," Athletic Institute, Chicago, 31 January 1967, and previous annual reports of *Athletic Institute Sportscope.*

20. *Recreation and Park Yearbook, 1966* (Washington, D.C.: National Recreation and Park Association, 1967), p. 53.

21. "Swimming Still Rated Top Participant Sport: Camping on Increase," *New York Times,* 24 March 1974, p. S–1.

22. "The Boom in Leisure—Where Americans Spend 160 Billions," *U.S. News and World Report,* 23 May 1977, p. 63.

23. Leonard Koppett, "In Pro Salaries, N.B.A. Is No. 1," *New York Times,* 11 March 1973, p. 4.

24. *Statistical Abstracts of the United States,* p. 219.

25. "U.S. Auto Racing," *New York Times,* 4 February 1968, p. 15–S.

26. "Boating: A Sport for the Masses," *New York Times,* 16 January 1977, p. 16–S.

27. *National Survey of Fishing and Hunting,* Bureau of Sports Fisheries and Wildlife, U.S. Department of the Interior, (Washington, D.C: 1970).

28. *Estimated National Forests Recreation Use,* Report of U.S. Forest Service for Calendar Year 1974, Department of Agriculture, (Washington, D.C.: 1975).

29. Diana R. Dunn and John M. Gulbis, "The Risk Revolution," *Parks and Recreation,* August 1976, p. 12.

30. Frank Litsky, "Motels Aren't Just for Sleeping Anymore," *New York Times,* 18 July 1966, p. 38.

31. Isobel Cosgrove and Richard Jackson, *The Geography of Recreation and Leisure* (London: Hutchinson University Library, 1972), p. 47.

32. Geoffrey Godbey and Stanley Parker, *Leisure Studies and Services: An Overview* (Philadelphia: Saunders, 1976), p. 110.

33. Douglas E. Kneeland, "Resort Business Booming Despite Economic Slump," *New York Times,* 10 March 1975, p. 1.

34. "Sun Spots," *Newsweek,* 5 January 1976, p. 44.

35. John L. Crompton and Carlton Van Doren, "Amusement Parks, Theme Parks, and Municipal Leisure Services: Contrasts in Adaptation to Cultural Change," *Journal of Physical Education and Recreation, Leisure Today,* October 1976, p. 45.

36. Seth S. King, "Supermarkets Hub of Suburbs," *New York Times,* 7 February 1971, p. 58.

37. Leland L. Nicholls and Robert S. Jones, "Leisure in the Modern Market Place," *Parks and Recreation,* December 1976, p. 98.

38. For a fuller review of Canadian development in the arts, see *Leisure Time in Perspective: Canadian Imperial Bank of Commerce Report* (Toronto: 1970).

39. Thomas M. Kando, *Leisure and Popular Culture in Transition* (St. Louis: Mosby, 1975), p. 113.

40. Thomas M. Kando, "Culture, Money and the Government," *Journal of Physical Education and Recreation, Leisure Today,* October 1976, p. 47.

41. "Gambling as Business and Sport," *Intellect,* November 1972, pp. 80–81.

42. Michael Harwood, "America With Its Ears On," *New York Times Magazine,* 25 April 1976, p. 28.

43. Robert J. Badaracco, "ORV's: Often Rough on Visitors," *Parks and Recreation,* September 1976, pp. 32–33.

44. Robert H. Becker, "The Future Is Now for Computer Games," *Parks and Recreation,* December 1976, p. 12.

45. " 'Death Race' Game Gains Favor, But Not with the Safety Council," *New York Times,* 28 December 1976, p. 12.

46. See *Leisure Time in Perspective.*

47. Hays B. Gamble, "Regional Economic Impacts from Outdoor Recreation," in Betty van der Smissen, ed., *Indicators of Change in the Recreation Environment: A National Research Symposium* (University Park, Penn.: Pennsylvania State University, 1975), pp. 221–42.

48. Jack B. Ellis and William B. Knott, "Determinants and Trends of Leisure in Canada," (Paper presented at Canadian Congress on Leisure Research, Laval University, October, 1975).

49. Bernard Malamud, "Gravity Model Calibration of Tourist Travel to Las Vegas," *Journal of Leisure Research,* Fall 1973, pp. 23–33.

50. Jay Beamon and Sandy Lindsay, "Practical Applications of Cluster Analysis," *Recreation Review,* August 1975, pp. 13–21.

51. For a detailed discussion of the environmental impact of outdoor recreation, see articles by Elwood L. Shafer, Carlton S. Van Doren, Robert Stottlemyer, and John W. Andresen in *Indicators of Change in the Recreation Environment—A National Research Symposium* (University Park, Penn.: Pennsylvania State University Press, 1975), pp. 327–99.

TWO

THE HISTORY
OF RECREATION
AND LEISURE

6

THE EARLY HISTORY OF RECREATION AND LEISURE

As one examines the role of recreation and leisure in modern society, it is helpful first to view it through the lens of historical perspective. Throughout the study of history, one must ask: What has been the nature of man's play? How much leisure has he had? Did the educational system of each period make use of play activities? How did philosophers and religious leaders regard leisure? This chapter seeks to answer such questions with respect to play in primitive societies, the pre-Christian era, the Dark and Middle Ages, the Renaissance, the Reformation, and finally the period immediately preceding the Industrial Revolution in Europe and America.

The Play of Primitive Man

A chronological study would begin by examining the play patterns of prehistoric man during the Paleolithic and Neolithic epochs. However, since knowledge of early cultures is limited, it is more profitable to examine the cultural patterns of primitive tribes of today or the fairly recent past that have been studied by direct observation.

Attitudes toward Work and Leisure

Primitive man does not make the clear distinction between work and leisure that we tend to make in modern society. Industrial man sets aside specific periods of time each day for work and other periods for rest and relaxation. Primitive man has no such precise separation; he tends to work only when work is available and necessary,

126

and often infuses his work with rites and customs that lend it variety and pleasure. Craven comments:

> To every member of the community falls his share of labor and of play, his opportunity for participation in the important rites and mysteries; the orientation of life is physiologically and socially toward long periods of leisurely work, interspersed with occasional periods of intensive efforts.[1]

In primitive society work tends to be varied and creative, rather than a specialized task demanding a narrow aspect of the worker's skill, as in modern industry. Work is often accompanied by ritual that is regarded as essential to the success of the planting or harvest or to the building or hunting expedition. The ritual may involve prayer, sacrifice, dance, or feasting, which thus become part of the world of work.

This tends to explain the function of primitive art, which developed as a by-product of necessity. In primitive tribes, tools, weapons, pottery, and other implements are made chiefly for utilitarian reasons, either for self-defense or to perform the work of the tribe. Usually, however, they are decorated or formed in stylized ways to provide magic identity, meaning, or power. Although the functional purpose of the decoration may ultimately be forgotten, both the decoration and the form of the object are retained as a matter of custom or because they are aesthetically pleasing. In more advanced societies, art then becomes a profession, and art is created for its own sake rather than for the utility of an object. It is important to recognize that in primitive settings the urge to create art is never a matter of pleasure alone, but is closely linked to practical functions.

Games and Sports

In primitive societies, play may have many sources. Popular juvenile or adult games are often vestiges of warfare—now practiced as a form of sport. Occasionally play activities depict historical events, transportation practices, or the use of household or farming implements. When an activity is no longer useful in its original form (such as archery for hunting or warfare), it may become a form of sport. Often, the origin is religious ritual. Throughout man's history, games have been a part of religious festivals or celebrations. McIntosh writes:

> The Tailteen Games in Ireland, wrestling among the Aztecs, the team game of Tlachtli played by Maya people in Central America, and ju-jitsu practiced by the Samurai Warriors of Japan, all had religious significance. In Britain, too, the early history of some games of football suggests that fertility rites were involved.[2]

In many primitive tribes there is a dualism, or division of the community into halves, each often marked by distinctive totems (usually a sacred bird or animal), that dictate a complicated system of obligations, taboos, and customs between the tribal halves. There tends to be a constant sequence of contests and rivalry between the two groups and, at the same time, a process of constant help and mutual assistance. Together, the two groups perform a series of precisely designed

127

ceremonies; often the games played as part of such ceremonies symbolize a continuing struggle between good and evil or life and death.

The game of *tlachtli,* which was widely practiced in Central America centuries ago, is an example of such a contest. *Tlachtli* courts were about 200 feet long and 30 feet wide, situated near temples. A stone ring was fixed about halfway up the wall at either end. The players struck a rubber ball with their knees or hips, the purpose being to drive it through one of the rings. Spence characterized its symbolic purpose in these words:

> The game of *tlachtli* probably symbolized the motions of some heavenly body, the sun or the moon. The ball with which it was played was represented in the Mexican manuscripts either as half-light and half-dark in color, or sometimes in four hues. . . . This dualistic myth assumes the character of an everlasting game of ball in which the fortunes of the universe are tossed, now into light, now into shadow, by the contending powers.[3]

Sometimes games of this type were so seriously regarded that the captains of losing teams were sacrificed following the contest. Indeed, sports were frequently a modified form of warfare, as were the lacrosse games of the North American Choctaw Indians. These contests often involved as many as a thousand young braves and continued many hours, resulting in numerous injuries and deaths. Such contests were a means not only of testing warriors in battlelike situations but also of keeping their fighting morale high.

Primitive tribes today often practice dangerous and painful sports. For example, at the Arctic Winter Games in recent years, Eskimo contestants have competed not only in such conventional sports as cross-country skiing, ice-hockey, or figure skating, but also in unusual games peculiar to their culture. These include contests like kicking a sealskin ball dangling from a pole, precision whip-flicking, and bouncing on a walrus hide. Other games include traditional forms of what could best be described as "self-torture" endurance contests, such as the "knuckle hop" (hopping a distance on toes and knuckles), "arm pulls," "finger pulls" and "ear pulls," all involving high levels of pain. One contestant explained:

> The traditional Eskimo life included lots of pain—hunger, cold, frozen ears. So indoors we would torture ourselves to get used to the pain.[4]

Probably the leading example of sport carried on as warfare—or vice versa—is found in the Willigiman-Wallalua and Wittaia tribes of New Guinea. Every week or so, these two neighboring mountain peoples, who have the same language, dress, and customs, arrange a formal battle at one of their traditional fighting grounds (see photographs in Plate 1). As described by anthropologists who have observed the tribes, these frays seem more like a dangerous field sport than true war:

> Each battle lasts but a single day, always stops before nightfall (because of the danger of ghosts) or if it begins to rain (no one wants to get his hair or ornaments wet). The men are very accurate with their weapons—they have all played war games since they were small boys—but they are equally adept at dodging, and hence are rarely hit by anything.[5]

In addition to formal, arranged contests, however, the two New Guinea tribes (who, despite their cultural similarities, regard each other with hatred), also practice sneak raids, during which they mercilessly slaughter men, women, and children. Victories are celebrated by *etais,* or victory dances, and are part of an unending cycle of fighting, death, mourning, and revenge. The fighting continues not for the usual reasons for waging war. The Willigiman-Wallalua and the Wittaia do not capture territory, goods or prisoners, nor do they ever really try to annihilate their enemies and thus end the warfare. They fight because they "enthusiastically enjoy it, because it is to them a vital function of the complete man, and because they feel they must satisfy the ghosts of slain companions."[6]

As indicated in chapter 3, the play life of children in primitive cultures includes many games, contests, and rituals which are clearly designed to prepare them for adult life. In American Indian societies, boys were not only trained to develop warrior skills, but also taught to survive unarmed and unclothed in the wilderness. Girls, through their play, were taught the household crafts expected of mature women. Through dancing, singing, and storytelling, both sexes learned of the history and religion of their cultures.

In some primitive societies, games and sports served more specialized or unique uses. Huizinga points out that ritualized verbal contests were often part of judicial proceedings among North American Indians and Eskimos. Among the rice farmers of the Ifugao country in the Philippines, wrestling was used to settle cases of disputed ricefield boundaries. Loy and Kenyon write:

> The reasoning behind this practice was that the ancestral spirits of the contestants knew which party was in the right, just where the true boundary was, and would see to it that he who was right would win. In spite of this expressed faith in supernatural intervention, the Ifugao were sufficiently practical to insist that the wrestlers be approximately evenly matched. Owners of adjacent fields could do the actual wrestling, or might choose champions to represent them.[7]

Village boundaries were determined several hundred years ago on Pukapuka, an atoll in the Northern Cook Islands, by having pairs of wrestlers compete along a provisional boundary. After seven days the struggle was ended, and the location of the wrestlers determined the final boundary between the villages—a vivid example of territoriality and the function of sport in primitive cultures.

As early human societies grew increasingly complex during the prehistoric era, they developed specialization of functions. Humans learned to domesticate plants and animals, which permitted them to shift from a nomadic existence based chiefly on hunting and food-gathering to a largely stationary way of life, based on grazing animals and planting crops. Kando writes:

> The size and density of human groups increased. Villages replaced bands and camps. Some energy could now be devoted to activities other than food getting. For the first time, some members, supported by a farming majority, could develop into full-time specialists as religious, medical, political, and crafts experts. The division of labor was thus under way.[8]

Ultimately, ruling classes developed, along with soldiers, craftsmen, peasants, and slaves. As fixed villages and cities came into being and large estates were

129

tilled (often with complex water storage and irrigation systems) and harvested by lower-class workers, upper-class societies gained increased power, wealth, and leisure. Thus in the landed aristocracy of the first civilizations that developed in the Middle East during the five millennia preceding the Christian era, we find for the first time in history a leisure class.

Recreation and Leisure in Pre-Christian Civilizations

Ancient Egypt

The Egyptian culture was a rich and diversified one; it achieved an advanced knowledge of astronomy, architecture, engineering, agriculture, and construction. The Egyptians had a varied class structure, with a powerful nobility, priesthood, and military class, and lesser classes of workers, artisans, peasants, and slaves. This civilization, which lasted from about 5,000 B.C. well into the Roman era, was richly recorded in paintings, statuary, and hieroglyphic records.

The ancient Egyptians led a colorful and pleasant life; it is said of them that their energies were directed to the arts of living and the arts of dying. They engaged in many sports as part of both education and recreation, including wrestling, gymnastic exercises, lifting and swinging weights, and ball games.[9] In general, athletics were performed chiefly by the lower classes and the soldiery; the upper classes were more sedentary and enjoyed being entertained. Bullfighting was a popular spectacle, and at least at its inception was religiously motivated. The Egyptians were known to have used fishing rods as early as 2,000 B.C. Huntsmen in Egypt comprised a distinct social class who either hunted by themselves or attended the nobles at the hunt.

Music, drama, and dance were forms of religious worship as well as social entertainment. The Egyptians had complex orchestras that included various stringed and percussive instruments. Groups of female performers were attached to temples, and the royal houses had troupes of entertainers who performed on sacred or social occasions. Slaves were often taught both dancing and music, and in the later dynasties developed into a class of professional performers who provided entertainment for the nobility at private dinner parties or in public squares of large cities.

The diversions of peasants and field laborers were few and inexpensive. They assembled in the "house of beer," which was probably the equivalent of modern bars or saloons, and apparently were much given to drunkenness. Egyptian children played with toy dolls, boats, marbles, tops, and balls. Such adult games as chess, checkers, backgammon, and other table games also originated during this period.

Following the Roman conquest, Egypt was much influenced by the Roman way of life. During this period of Roman rule, clubs and drinking societies became common. Sex for the first time became a marketable, commercial item; prostitutes (who had originally been "vestal virgins" performing what were regarded as religious rites in the temples) now provided a secular form of entertainment. Apparently prostitution was licensed by the state or municipality, which required prostitutes to pay taxes in order to work at their trade. In addition, there were many other forms of popular entertainment including both private and public festivals on imperial and religious holidays. Most large towns had theaters and regular mass athletic contests, and the Egyptians spent increasing sums for professional entertainment.

Thus we see among the ancient Egyptians a wide variety of recreational pursuits, at first largely reserved for the nobility and later becoming available to all classes. It is worth noting that even in this earliest period of recorded history, many forms of play related to gambling, drinking, and vice were apparently countenanced and controlled by the state.

Ancient Assyria and Babylonia

The land known as the "fertile crescent" between two great rivers, the Tigris and the Euphrates, was ruled by two powerful empires, Assyria in the north and Babylonia in the south. These kingdoms were in power for approximately 26 centuries, from about 2,900 B.C. until the invasion by Alexander the Great in 330 B.C. Like the ancient Egyptians, the Assyrians and Babylonians had many popular recreation activities, such as boxing, wrestling, archery, and a variety of table games. Music and dancing were a part of both religious practice and social entertainment. And, like the Egyptians, the Assyrians drank beer and palm wine; there were many tavernkeepers who catered to the public.

Royal Estates and Parks

Contenau writes, "We may sum up the leisure occupations of a king of Assyria as the harem, listening to music, dancing, sedentary games, and the giving of banquets for his nobles."[10] He was also devoted to hunting; the nobles of Assyria went lion hunting in chariots and on foot, using spears. The chase was a daily occupation, recorded for history in numerous reliefs, sculptures, and inscriptions. Ceram writes that as early as the ninth century B.C.

> the Assyrians had animal parks, "paradises," as they called them, precursors of our zoological gardens. Within their large confines were kept freely roaming lions and herds of gazelles. They arranged battues— that is, hunts, in which the animals were driven by beaters and hunted with nets.[11]

These early parks were primarily spectacular sites for royal hunting parties but also provided settings for feasts, assemblies, and royal gatherings. On the estates of other monarchs during the ninth and tenth centuries B.C. were vineyards, fishponds, and the famed hanging gardens of Babylon. Contenau writes:

> beside cultivating gardens for purely utilitarian purposes, the kings of Assyria enjoyed creating botanical gardens, containing collections of non-indigenous species—notably the plants and trees of the Amanus mountains. In much the same way, the Egyptian kings instructed their expeditions to collect and bring back the rarest species.[12]

Ancient Israel

Among the ancient Israelites music and dancing were performed for ritual purposes as well as for social activities and celebrations. The early Hebrews distinguished dances of a sacred or holy character from those which resembled pagan ceremonies.

131

For example, they condemned dancing around the golden calf as a form of idolatry which reflected the influence of the Egyptian religion (which worshiped the bull Apis as a major deity).

Thus the idea was established that recreation was related to morality. Some forms of play which had their origins in religious practice were ultimately condemned as immoral or pagan. The concept that a society might be strengthened or weakened through leisure and its uses was to be more fully developed by the Greeks and Romans, who believed it to be the state's responsibility to provide facilities for the use of leisure and, in time, to provide entertainment for the masses.

Recreation and Leisure in Ancient Greece

In the city-states of ancient Greece, particularly in Athens during the so-called Golden Age of Pericles from about 500 to 400 B.C., mankind reached a new peak of philosophical and cultural development. The Athenians took great interest in the arts, in learning, and in athletics. These pursuits were generally restricted to the wellborn, aristocratic noblemen, who had full rights of citizenship including voting and participation in affairs of state. Craftsmen, farmers, and tradespeople were also citizens, but had limited rights and less prestige. Labor was performed by slaves and foreigners, who outnumbered citizens by as much as two or three to one.

The amenities of life were generally restricted to the most wealthy and powerful citizens, who represented the Athenian ideal of the balanced man—a combined soldier, athlete, artist, statesman, and philosopher. This ideal was furthered through education and through the varied religious festivals, which occupied about seventy days of the year. The arts of music, poetry, theater, gymnastics, and athletic competition were combined in these sacred competitions. At least five such festivals—the Olympic, Pythian, Istmian, Nemean and Panathenaic games—were celebrated each year; the major contests were usually running, horse and chariot racing, wrestling and boxing, and discus-throwing.

Sports appear to have been part of daily life and to have occurred chiefly when there were mass gatherings of people such as the assembly of an army for war, or the wedding or funeral of some great chieftain. "For where people are gathered together, something must be done to entertain them, and the most natural form of entertainment is some form of competition."[13] There also were bardic or musical events, offering contests on the harp and flute, poetry, and theatrical presentations. The concept of sports and gymnastics was closely linked to art. Physical prowess was celebrated in sculpture and poetry, and strength and beauty were seen as gifts of the gods.

From earliest childhood, Athenian citizens engaged in varied athletic and cultural activities. Young children enjoyed toys, dolls, carts, skip ropes, kites, and seesaws. When boys reached the age of seven, they were enrolled in schools in which gymnastics and music were primary elements. They were intensively instructed in running and leaping, wrestling, throwing the javelin and discus, dancing (taught as a form of military drill), boxing, swimming, and ball games.

Greek Philosophy of Recreation and Leisure
The Athenian philosophers believed strongly in the unity of mind and body and in the strong relationship of all forms of human qualities and skills. They felt that play

132

activity was essential to the healthy growth of children, both physical and social. Thus, in Book 4 of Plato's *Republic,* Socrates says:

> our children from their earliest years must take part in all the more lawful forms of play, for if they are not surrounded with such an atmosphere they can never grow up to be well-conducted and virtuous citizens.[14]

Plato believed that education should be compulsory, and that it should provide natural modes of amusement for children between the ages of three and six. He suggested that classes should be held each day at village temples, with nurses ensuring that children behaved in an orderly and proper manner.

> Education should begin with the right direction of children's sports. The plays of childhood have a great deal to do with the maintenance or non-maintenance of laws.[15]

He also decried the fact that lawmakers tended to regard changes in children's games lightly:

> they fail to reflect that those children who innovate in their games grow up into men different from their fathers; and being thus different themselves they seek a different mode of life, and having sought this, they come to desire other institutions and laws.[16]

Music and dance were also essential for the full development of youth. Plato urged that all children, boys and girls alike, be instructed in the performing arts and tested with frequent contests. These arts were to be consecrated to the gods, since the gods themselves were musicians and dancers. Both gymnastics and music were directed toward a total cultivation of the body and the emotions as the foundation upon which to build a sound intellectual and physical life. Athenian men continued to engage in sports, games, and the arts throughout their lives; fit and active citizens were essential for maintaining national security. Such exercises were seen not as a grim discipline, however, but as a creative and enjoyable experience. Pericles wrote:

> We cultivate the mind without loss of manliness; whereas our adversaries from early youth are always undergoing laborious exercises which are to make them brave, we live at ease and yet are equally willing to face the perils which they face. We have our regular games to provide our weary spirits many relaxations from toil.[17]

The Athenian philosophers recognized the need for both leisure and recreation, although they regarded the two differently. Aristotle commented that it was necessary to work vigorously and to defend the state in order to secure leisure.

> Therefore, a city must be temperate and brave and able to endure; for truly, as the proverb says, "There is no leisure for slaves," and those who cannot face danger like men are the slaves of any invader.

133

He commented further on the distinction between leisure and amusement.

> Nature requires that we should be able, not only to work well, but to use leisure well; for, as I must repeat once again, the first principle of all action is leisure. Both are required, but leisure is better than occupation and its end; and therefore the question must be asked, what ought we to do when at leisure? . . . we should introduce amusements only at suitable times, and they should be our medicines, for the emotion which they create in the soul is a relaxation, and from the pleasure we obtain rest. But leisure of itself gives pleasure and happiness and enjoyment of life, which are experienced not by the busy man, but by those who have leisure.[18]

The Athenians regarded leisure as an opportunity for intellectual cultivation, including music, theater, poetry, and political and philosophical discussion (see chapter 2). Gymnastics and sports were seen as somewhat more purposeful, since they increased strength, fitness, and courage; regarded as an obligation to the state, they were performed by all citizens.

Changes in Greek Approach to Leisure

The ancient Greeks developed the art of town planning to a high level and customarily made extensive provisions for small parks and gardens, open-air theaters and gymnasiums, baths, exercise grounds, and stadiums. During the time of Plato, the gymnasium and the park were closely connected in beautiful natural settings, often including indoor halls, gardens, and buildings for musical performances. Early Athens had many public baths and some public parks, which later gave way to privately owned estates. Under the reign of Alexander the Great, larger hunting parks were developed by the aristocracy.

A gradual transition occurred in the Greek approach to leisure and play. At first, all citizens were expected to participate in sports and games, and the Olympic games were restricted to free-born Greeks only. Gradually, however, the religious and cultural functions of the Olympic games and other festivals were weakened by athletic specialization and commercialism. In time, sports and other forms of activity such as drama, singing, and dance, were performed only by highly skilled specialists (drawn from the lower classes, or even slaves) who trained or perfected their skills throughout the year to appear before huge crowds of admiring spectators. Chariot races became more popular, and hippodromes were built for audiences to watch professional drivers compete. As amateurs were replaced by professionals, interest in athletics as a popular pursuit for all citizens declined, and the strength of the state itself was weakened.

Recreation and Leisure in Ancient Rome

Like the Greek city-states, the Roman republic during its early development was a vigorous and manly state. The Roman citizen, although he belonged to a privileged class, was constantly ready to defend his society and fight in its wars. He willingly participated in sports and gymnastics which kept his body strong and his spirit courageous. Numerous games held in connection with worship of various Roman gods later developed into annual festivals. Such games were carefully supervised by the priesthood and supported by public funds, frequently at great cost. The most important of the Roman games were those that celebrated military trimphs, which were usually held in honor of the god Jupiter, the head of the Roman pantheon.

Like the early Greeks, young Roman children had toy carts, houses, dolls, hobbyhorses, stilts, and tops, and engaged in many sports and games. Young boys were taught various sports and exercises such as running and jumping, sword and spear play, wrestling, swimming, and horseback riding. The Romans, however, had a different philosophical concept of leisure from that of the Greeks. Although the Latin words for "leisure" and "business" are *otium* and *negotium,* suggesting the same view of leisure as a positive value in life and work as a negative element, Kando points out that the Roman society represented

> the first manifestation of the expansionist work society that culminates 2,000 years later in the industrial West. Empire building and bureaucratic organization are Rome's legacy to the world. They developed out of hard and frugal . . . work. . . . Leisure to the Romans meant primarily rest from work.[19]

The Romans tended to support play for utilitarian rather than aesthetic or spiritual reasons. In general, they valued sport chiefly because of its practical benefits. The great medical authority Galen said, "The best gymnastics is that which not only exercises the body but delights the spirit." The Romans were much less interested than the Athenians in varied forms of cultural activity. Although they had many performing companies, usually composed of Greek and southern Italian slaves, the Romans themselves did not actively participate in the theater. As for dance, after a brief period beginning at about 200 B.C. when it was fashionable for Roman patricians to dance, they began to disapprove of dance as a manly activity. Cicero wrote:

> no man, one may almost say, ever dances when sober, unless perhaps he be a madman; nor in solitude, nor in a moderate and sober party; dancing is the last companion of prolonged feasting, of luxurious situation, and of many refinements.[20]

Even more than the Greeks, the Romans were systematic planners and builders. Their towns generally included provisions for baths, open-air theaters, amphitheaters, forums for public assemblies, stadiums, and sometimes parks and gardens. They developed buildings for gymnastic sports, modeled after the Greek palaestra, including wrestling rooms, conversation areas for philosophers, and colonnades where games might be held in winter despite bad weather. Wealthier Romans often had private villas, many with large gardens and some with hunting preserves. The Romans were also the first to build floral greenhouses, using mica for windowpanes.

Social Changes and Mass Leisure

As the empire grew more powerful, the simple agricultural democracy of the early years, in which all Romans were citizens and free men, shifted to an urban life with sharply divided classes. There were four social levels: the *senators,* who were the richest, owning most of the land and power; the *curiales,* who owned twenty-five or more acres of land and were officeholders or tax collectors; the *plebs,* or free common

135

people, who owned small properties or were tradesmen or artisans; and the *coloni,* who were lower-class tenants of the land. As the society grew more wealthy and corrupt, with immense fortunes being made by the conquest of vast provinces throughout Europe, the middle-class curiales tended to disappear. Some rose to join the ranks of the senators, but a greater number joined the plebs.

The society became marked by the wealth and profiteering of businessmen and speculators, with the cooperation of the rulers and governing officials. In time, a huge urban population of plebs lived in semi-idleness, since most of the work was done by coloni and slaves brought to Rome by foreign conquests. Gradually it became necessary for the Roman emperors and senate to amuse and entertain the plebs; they did so with doles of grain and with public games—thus the slogan "bread and circuses."

As early as the reign of the Emperior Claudius in the first century A.D., there were 159 public holidays during the year, 93 of which were devoted to games at public expense, which included many new festivals in honor of national heroes, foreign victories, and other occasions. By A.D. 354, there were 200 public holidays each year, including 175 days of games. Even on working days, the labor began at daybreak and ended shortly after noon during much of the year.

As leisure increased and the necessity for military service and other forms of physical toil or effort declined for the Roman citizen, he began to do fewer and fewer things for himself. The normal practice was for him to be entertained or to follow a daily routine of exercise, bathing, and eating. The Roman baths became popular social and athletic clubs, but were not exclusive; gradually public baths were established throughout Rome. The huge Baths of Trajan included hot rooms, cold rooms, and a swimming bath, two palaestrae for general exercise, and a running track. Other buildings in this complex included a library, administrative offices, refreshment rooms, gymnasiums, and courts for ball games. By the fourth century A.D., there were over 856 baths in Rome which could accommodate over 60,000 people at once, either free of charge or for a nominal fee.

Roman citizens themselves were no longer as active in sports as they had once been. Increasingly, they sought to be amused and to entertain their guests with paid acrobats, musicians, dancers, and other artists. Athletes now performed as members of a specialized profession with unions, coaches, and training schools and with conditions of service accepted and approved by the emperor himself.

Corruption of Sport and Entertainment

Gradually, the traditional sports of running, throwing, and jumping shifted into an emphasis on human combat—first boxing and wrestling and then displays of cruelty in which gladiators fought to the death for the entertainment of mass audiences. By the time of the Emperor Tiberius (A.D. 14–37), competitive sport in the Roman Empire had become completely commercialized and debased. To maintain political popularity and placate the bored masses, the emperors and the senate provided great parades, circuses, and feasts. Fantastic sums were spent on sponsoring the games, often bankrupting both the public treasury and private fortunes. The Roman games featured chariot races and other equestrian events. Contests were fought to the death between gladiators in pairs or larger groups, using all sorts of weapons, on foot, on horseback, or in chariots. Even sea battles were fought in artificially constructed lakes in the Roman arenas. Imported wild beasts, such as tigers and elephants, were pitted against each other or against human antagonists. The scale of these bloody entertainments was tremendous. The Circus Maximus was said to have accommodated 385,000 spectators, and other amphitheaters held audiences that sometimes totaled half the adult populations of their cities. Often the taxes of entire provinces were expended on cruel spectacles.

Under the reign of Caligula and Nero, the persecution of Christians became particularly unrelenting. Both animals and humans were maimed and butchered in cruel and horrible ways. Spectacles were often lewd and obscene, leading to a mass debauchery, corruption, and perversion of human spirit. The term "Roman holiday" came to mean a wild and corrupt celebration. Tacitus wrote that many Christians

> were dressed in the skins of wild beasts, and exposed to be torn to pieces by dogs in the public games, that they were crucified, or condemned to be burnt; and at nightfall serve in place of lamps to light the darkness, Nero's own gardens being used for the purpose. [21]

Decline of Rome

For about seven centuries B.C., the Roman Empire had grown steadily. During the third and fourth centuries A.D., it declined and ultimately crumbled altogether under attack by pagan tribes from the north. Some historians have concluded that a major reason for the downfall of Rome was that it was unable to deal with mass leisure; its citizens grew physically weak and spiritually corrupt. Although they were great engineers and builders, soldiers and administrators, the ancient Romans did not have the coherent philosophy of life of the Athenians. When faced by the challenge of excess wealth, luxury, and time, they responded as a nation by yielding to corruption and losing the simple virtues that had made them strong as a nation.

Early Christian Era: The Dark and Middle Ages

Under attack by successive waves of northern European tribes, the Roman Empire finally collapsed. For a period of several centuries, Europe was overrun with warring tribes and shifting alliances. The organized power of Rome, which had built roads, extended commerce, and provided civil order, was at an end. Gradually the Catholic church emerged to provide a form of universal citizenship within Europe.

Having suffered under the brutal persecutions of the Romans, the early Christians condemned all that their pagan oppressors had stood for—especially their hedonistic way of life. Indeed, the early church fathers believed in a fanatical asceticism which in the Byzantine, or Eastern, Empire was marked by the Anchorite movement—the idea of salvation through masochistic self-deprivation.

Even in western Europe, early Catholic church leaders condemned Roman practices as displaying the essential depravity of human nature. In this setting, all forms of pleasure were seen as evil. H'Doubler points out that sharp distinctions were made between the "here" and the "hereafter," between good and evil, mind and body, spirituality and carnality:

> the paramount consideration of all living was to save the soul. Consequently, the body was looked upon as a hindrance. To exalt the soul, the body was ignored, punished, and bruised. Anything that expressed the livelier feelings of instinctive human nature or in any way suggested former pagan ways and ideals of living, was banished.[22]

Many aspects of Roman life were forbidden during the Dark and Middle Ages. The stadiums, amphitheaters, and baths that had characterized Roman life were destroyed. The Council of Elvira ruled that the rite of baptism could not be extended to those connected with the stage, and in A.D. 398, the Council of Carthage excommunicated those who attended the theater on holy days. The great spectacles and organized shows of imperial Rome were at an end; they were replaced by a new morality, which had its roots in the monasteries that were founded in the fourth through sixth centuries in Egypt and the Near East and later spread to Europe. The influential Benedictine order in particular insisted on the dignity of labor. Their rule read, "Idleness is the great enemy of the soul. Therefore, monks should always be occupied either in manual labor or in sacred readings."

Particularly in Ireland, France, the Low Countries, and Germany, monasteries were centers of learning and industry. With great zeal, monks cleared forests, reclaimed marshes, and cultivated barren plains. In an age of turbulence and warfare, monks became the symbol of stability; they helped to preserve Roman methods of agriculture, cattle raising, and fruit growing, and cultivated vast tracts of land throughout Europe. This was the emergence of what later came to be described as the Protestant work ethic—the idea that labor and toil were glorified, and that play and idleness were sinful.

It would be a mistake to assume that the Catholic church eliminated all forms of play. Many early Catholic religious practices were based on the rituals of earlier faiths. Priests built churches on existing shrines or temple sites, set Christian holy days according to the dates of pagan festivals, and used such elements of pagan worship as bells, candles, incense, singing and dancing. Douglas Kennedy writes that conversion to Christianity did not destroy the older forms of religious drama:

> In fact, some of the old ritual was adopted by the early Church and embodied in its own practices. The yearly cycle of Miracle and Morality dramas, which played such an important part in the conversion to Christianity of the ignorant and illiterate peasantry in England, owed much of their appeal to the familiar pagan material which was widely included in their presentation.[23]

Pastimes in the Middle Ages

Despite much church disapproval, many forms of play continued during the Middle Ages. Medieval society was marked by rigid class stratification; below the nobility and clergy were the peasants, divided into such ranks as freemen, villeins, serfs, and slaves. Peasants did not live on the lands they cultivated but in crude huts huddled together in small villages ranging from as few as fifty to as many as four hundred inhabitants.

Life in the Middle Ages, even for the feudal nobility, was crude and harsh. Manors and castles were little more than stone fortresses, crowded, dark, and damp. Knights were responsible for fighting in the service of their rulers; between wars, their favorite pastimes were hunting and hawking. Hunting was considered the loftiest pursuit to which the nobility could devote themselves. The French emperor Charlemagne, who lived during the latter part of the eighth century, was a great hunting enthusiast. Although most of his career was spent in waging war, he never missed an opportunity of hunting: so much so that it might be said that he rested himself by galloping through the forests. He was on those occasions not only followed by a large number of huntsmen and attendants of his household, but . . . by his wife and daughters . . . and surrounded by a numerous and elegant court who vied with each other in displaying their skill and courage in attacking the fiercest animals.[24]

Hunting skill was considered a virtue of medieval rulers and noblemen. The sport was thought helpful in keeping hunters from the sin of idleness (a vigorous, tiring sport, it was also believed to prevent sensual temptation). Hunting also served as a useful preparation for war. In a later era, the Italian Machiavelli pointed out that since the main concern of the Prince must be war, he must never cease thinking of it. In times of peace, thoughts of war should be directed to the sport of hunting:

he should be fond of hunting and thereby accustom his body to hardships, learning at the same time, the nature of topography, how mountains slope, how they are cut by valleys.[25]

The king himself designated certain royal forests for use by the nobility and appointed officers to enforce rigorous game laws in every forest and district. Clergymen were great hunting enthusiasts; bishops and abbots of the Middle Ages maintained numerous parks heavily stocked with game. In addition to hunting, hawking was extremely popular during the feudal period. The richest nobles throughout Europe maintained extensive falconry establishments to hunt small game and other birds. A well-trained falcon was highly valued, and hawking was considered a noble science.

Other pastimes during the Middle Ages were various types of games and gambling, music and dance, sports, and jousting. The games played in castles and medieval manors included early forms of chess, checkers, backgammon, and dice. Gambling was extremely popular, although forbidden by both ecclesiastical and royal authority. "Dice shall not be made in the kingdom," said one law in 1256, and "those who are discovered using them, and frequenting taverns and bad places, will be looked upon as suspicious characters." Other table games were forbidden from time to time; the Council of Paris in 1212 condemned even chess. "We strictly forbid," said Louis IX, "any person to play at dice, tables, or chess."[26]

As the chaos of the Dark Ages yielded to greater order and regularity, life became more stable. Travel in reasonable safety became possible, and by the eleventh century, commerce was becoming widespread. The custom of jousting emerged within the medieval courts, stemming from the tradition that only the nobility fought on horseback; common men fought on foot. Thus the term chivalry (from the French *cheval,* meaning horse) came into being. By the dawn of the twelfth century, the code of chivalry was developed, having originated in the profession of arms among feudal courtiers.

At the outset, tournaments were martial combat between great numbers of knights; violent and dangerous, they were often condemned by the church. Gradually the tournaments became more stylized and came to represent a form of war game. (The tournament was a contest between teams, and the joust was a trial of skill between two individual knights.) While there were different forms of attack, the purpose was to unhorse the opponent. An elaborate code of laws and regulations was drawn up for the combat; no one below the rank of an esquire was permitted to

139

engage in tournaments and jousting. McIntosh comments that the tournament, which in the thirteenth century was a serious form of military training for knights and their esquires, became a stylized and decorative pastime for the nobility of the fifteenth century.[27]

Games of the Common People

Meanwhile, what of the life of the peasantry during the Middle Ages? Hulme suggests that life was not all work for the lower classes. There were village feasts and sports, practical joking, throwing weights, cockfighting, bull-baiting, and other lively games. "Ball games and wrestling, in which men of one village were pitted against men of another, sometimes resulted in bloodshed."[28]

There was sometimes dancing on the green and, on holidays, miracle and morality plays (forms of popular religious drama and pageantry). However, peasants usually went to bed at dark, reading was a rare accomplishment, and there was much drinking and crude brawling. For peasants, hunting was more a means of obtaining food than a sport. Although the nobility usually rode through the hedges and trampled the fields of the peasantry, peasants were not allowed to defend their crops even against wild animals. If they were caught poaching, they were often maimed or hanged as punishment.

Typically, certain games were classified as rich men's sports and poor men's sports; sometimes the distinction was also made between urban and rural sports. As life in the Middle Ages became somewhat easier, an increasing number of pastimes emerged. Many modern sports were developed at this time in rudimentary form. A rough and ready form of football was played in England as a contest between the men of neighboring villages. Sir Thomas Elyot described the game as unfit for gentlemen: "foote-balle, wherein is nothing but beastlie furie and extreme violence, whereof proceedeth hurte, and consequently rancor and malice."[29]

Archery was popular and was encouraged by English kings during the fourteenth and fifteenth centuries because of its military value. Every Englishman was commanded to have a bow of his own height, and targets were set up in every town; inhabitants were required to shoot on all feast days or be fined. The famed writer Rabelais collected a list of 220 games played in France at this time, which included variations of tennis, billiards, skittles and shuttlecock.

Other types of entertainment became popular. People flocked to watch exhibitions of bear-baiting, bull-baiting, and even horse-baiting on village greens; these cruel shows were, in effect, throwbacks to the displays of the Roman era. Several places in London were set aside for such entertainments, and admission was charged. At other events the approach was more comic. At village feasts, wrestling matches between blindfolded contestants, fighting a fat goose with a stick, or attempting to seize a greased pig were burlesques of more serious combats. Fitzstephen, in describing London life in the twelfth century, wrote that each year on Shrove Tuesday, boys engaged in cockfighting in the morning and after dinner went into the fields to play ball. During the Easter holidays, water-jousting from boats on the Thames was organized and "upon the bridge, wharfs and houses by the river's side, stand great numbers to see and laugh there at."[30]

The people of the Middle Ages had an insatiable love of sightseeing and would travel great distances to see entertainments. There was no religious event, parish fair, municipal feast or military parade that did not bring together great crowds of people. When the kings of France assembled their principal retainers once or twice a year, they distributed food and liquor among the common people and provided military displays, court ceremonies, and entertainment by jugglers, tumblers and minstrels.

Growth of Holidays

The nobility of the Middle Ages generally had a great amount of leisure. Peasants usually worked as long as twelve hours a day; during the later Middle Ages and the Renaissance, the workday was extended to fourteen to eighteen hours for craftsmen and other city workers. However, hours were shorter during the winter months, and holidays were plentiful. The Catholic church had replaced the original Greek and Roman festival days with Christian holidays, and had made Sunday the day of rest. As increasing numbers of saints' days were added, members of craft guilds during the Middle Ages had as many as 170 days off (including Sundays, vacations, and special holidays) a year.

Recreation and Leisure in the Orient

Most accounts of recreation and leisure tend to deal only with its development in Europe and the Middle East. However, historians have noted the popularity of varied forms of sport and entertainment in ancient China and Japan. Gardiner writes that various combative sports, including boxing, wrestling, and football, were extremely popular in ancient China:

> An old Chinese writer, speaking of the town of Lin-tzu in the third century B.C., says, "There were none among its inhabitants who did not perform with the pipes or some string instrument, fight cocks, race dogs or play football."[31]

A detailed description of life in the city of Hangchow during the period of the Southern Sung Dynasty from A.D. 1227 to 1279 gives many examples of popular forms of recreation. At this time, Hangchow was the capital of China, the center of its economic and scholarly development, and the most wealthy city in the world. It was marked by an elaborate social structure, with an upper class composed of government officials, scholars, royalty and military officers, a merchant class of traders and businessmen, and a lower class of porters, laborers, servants and artisans.

According to Gernet, the people of Hangchow seem to have lived in an atmosphere of continuous feasting and entertainment, featuring jugglers, marionettes, Chinese shadow-plays, storytellers and acrobats. The wealthy surrounded themselves with a host of retainers who were maintained by the great families not as servants but because of their special skills:

> tutors, tellers of tales ancient and modern, chanters of poetry, zither players, chess players, horsemen, painters of orchids, literary men, copyists, bibliophiles. There were others who gave exhibitions of cockfighting or pigeon-fighting, who could imitate animal noises, train performing insects, pose amusing riddles, or who were experts in hanging paintings or arranging flowers for interior decoration . . .[32]

Hangchow was filled with places for social gatherings, such as gardens for pleasure outings, teahouses where rich people took music lessons, or boats on the lake where guests were entertained. The "pleasure grounds" were huge covered markets where lessons were given in dramatic art, singing and dance, and various types of theatrical displays were featured. In the city itself there were various literary, sporting and religious societies, including societies for football and polo, poetry and puppetry enthusiasts, archery and crossbow experts, and a host of other pastimes. Marco Polo wrote of prostitutes who seemed to have infiltrated everywhere in the capital:

> There was hardly a single public place, tavern, restaurant, hotel, market, pleasure ground, square or bridge where one did not encounter dozens of ladies of the town. A contemporary gives a list of the districts and addresses where low-class prostitutes were to be found in large numbers together. There were also brothels: "singing-girl houses" and taverns, which had for sign a bamboo shade over the light at the entrance. [33]

Gernet concluded that the incessant activity in the streets and markets of Hangchow and the pleasures, luxury and gaiety of the town must have made a vivid contrast with the general poverty of the countryside and the hard, monotonous and frugal life of the peasants.

The Renaissance Period

Historians generally view the first half of the Middle Ages (roughly from A.D. 400 to 1000) as the Dark Ages, and about the next 400 to 500 years as *le haut Moyen Age,* or high Middle Age. The Renaissance is said to have begun in Italy about A.D. 1350, in France about 1450, and in England about 1500. It marked a transition between the medieval world and the modern age.

As the major European nations stabilized during this period under more solidly established monarchies, power shifted from the church to the kings and their noblemen. There was an increase in urban manufacturing and trade and a growth of national states, along with a rising entrepreneurial class. In addition, there were new developments in science and philosophy and a rebirth of interest in the arts and literature of ancient Greece and Rome.

In Italy and France particularly, the nobility became patrons of great painters, sculptors, musicians, dancers, and dramatists. These artists were no longer dominated by the ideals and values of the Catholic church, but were free to serve secular goals. A great wave of music and literature swept through the courts of Europe, aided by the development of printing. Dance and theater became more complex and elaborate, and increasingly lavish entertainments and spectacles were presented in the courts of Italy and France.

People began to enjoy still more new forms of entertainment and amusement, which were often designated for one social class or another. Although Henry VIII tried to restrict tennis to noblemen and property owners, it became a popular sport among all classes in sixteenth century England; football was seen chiefly as a lower-class sport. In contrast, McIntosh points out that one of the most popular pastimes of the Italian nobility during the fourteenth and fifteenth centuries was football, known as *calcio.* Regulations in Florence stipulated that only those of high social class might play, such as "honorable soldiers, gentlemen, lords, and princes," and that "rapscallions, artificers, servants and low-born fellows" might not take part.

Similarly, Castiglione, an authority on the life of the Renaissance courtier, commended tennis and boating but criticized tumbling and rope-climbing as fit only for jugglers. The dance in particular was an important adjunct to court life in all of the palaces of the Renaissance. Queen Elizabeth of England was said to have selected her Lord Chancellor not because of his special knowledge in the law, but because he wore "green bows on his shoes and danced the Pavane to perfection." De Mille writes:

> All courtiers took a lesson every day and their dances were exact and rigidly schooled. They were simple in steps, gracious and pretty and very intricate, involving fancy floor patterns, separation from one another, and changing and lacing of arms. The emphasis was always on deportment and manner.[34]

As the Renaissance continued, music, dance, theater, and opera all became professionalized; throughout Europe, opera houses, theaters, and ballet companies were founded under royal sanction and subsidy. During the sixteenth and seventeenth centuries, the theater became particularly popular in England, where performances were in public squares and courtyards. Professional theaters were established in the 1570s and street theaters in the early 1600s. As more people entered the middle classes, the audience for such entertainments grew.

Play as Education

The Athenian philosophy which had supported play as an important form of education was revived during the Renaissance by such educators and writers as Vittorino von Feltre, Francois Rabelais, John Locke, and Michel de Montaigne. Von Feltre established a famous school in Mantua, Italy, in the early years of the fifteenth century, with a varied curriculum which gave much emphasis to games and play. Noting that the most zealous scholars were also the most eager to play, Vittorino encouraged contests in archery and ball games and regular exercises in riding, fencing, running, and jumping.

In early sixteenth century France, Rabelais advanced a number of revolutionary theories on education, emphasizing the need for physical exercises and games, as well as singing, dancing, modeling and painting, nature study and manual training. His account of the education of Gargantua describes play as an exercise for mind and body. The philosopher Montaigne later in the same century supported the concept of a unity of mind, body, and spirit, opposing the medieval ideal of a separation, or dualism, of mind and body. In *The Education of Children,* Montaigne wrote, "I would have his manner, behavior, and bearing cultivated at the same time with his mind. It is not the mind, it is not the body we are training; it is the man, and we must not divide him into two parts."[35]

Locke, an Englishman who lived from 1632 to 1704, was also concerned with play as a medium of learning. He recommended that children make their own playthings and felt that games could contribute significantly to character development, provided that they were properly supervised and directed. "All the plays and diversions of children," he wrote, "should be directed toward good and useful habits."

143

Locke distinguished between the play of children and recreation for older youth and adults. "Recreation," he said, "is not being idle . . . but easing the wearied part by change of business." He commented that a gentleman's serious employment should be "study: and when that demands relaxation and refreshment, it should be in some exercise of the body which unbends the body and confirms the strength and stamina."[36]

Another French philosopher, Rousseau (1712–1778), was also a great theorist of experimental education. His revolutionary text *Émile* advocated full freedom of physical activity, rather than constraint. Rousseau suggested that mankind should return to a state of nature marked by simplicity and freedom. He urged that children play freely in a variety of activities. Defending his theories, Rousseau wrote:

> You are troubled at seeing him [Émile] spend his early years in doing nothing. What! Is it nothing to be happy? Is it nothing to skip, to play, to run about all day long? Never in his life will he be so busy as now.[37]

He commented that Émile's work and play were alike to him; his plays were his "occupation." Rousseau also believed that play contributed to character training, and children should therefore be given activities that would satisfy their needs in each stage of their development. Sports and games were valuable in preventing idleness and anti-social activity. Rousseau was one of the first to suggest that sport be used for political and nationalistic ends. Asked to prepare a proposal on education for the reconstituted government of Poland, in 1773 he published *Considerations on the Government of Poland,* suggesting that games were to make children's "hearts glow and create a deep love for the fatherland and its laws." Further,

> the children should not be permitted to play separately according to their fancy, but encouraged to play all together in public; and the games should be conducted in such a way that there is always some common end to which all aspire to accustom them to common action and to stir up emulation . . . their games should always be played in public and shared by all. It is not merely a question of keeping them busy, or of cultivating a sound constitution and making them alert and graceful. The important thing is to get them accustomed from an early age to discipline, to equality and fraternity, to living under the eyes of their fellow citizens and seeking public approbation.[38]

Thus, there was increasing interest during the Renaissance in play, both as a form of popular entertainment and as a medium of education. It should not be assumed, however, that religious disapproval of play had died away completely; under the Protestant Reformation came even more severe attempts at repression.

Influence of the Protestant Reformation

The Reformation was a religious movement of the 1500s which resulted in the establishment of Protestantism. It was led chiefly by Martin Luther, a German monk, although other reformers including John Calvin in Switzerland and John Knox in Scotland were also influential. The Reformation was part of a broader stream which included economic, social, and political currents. In part it represented the influence of the growing middle classes, who allied with the nobility to wrest power from the church; rulers had gained power as nationalism spread and challenged the power of the church. After a series of civil wars, Catholicism remained the state religion in some nations; in others it was displaced, and in still others it existed side by side with new faiths.

The new Protestant sects tended to be more solemn and austere than the Catholic church. Calvin established an autocratic system of government in Geneva in 1541, directed by a group of Presbyters, morally upright men who controlled the social and cultural life of the community to the smallest detail. They ruthlessly suppressed heretics and burned dissenters at the stake.

Miller and Robinson describe the unbending Puritanism in Geneva.

"Purity of conduct" was insisted upon, which meant the forbidding of gambling, card playing, dancing, wearing of finery, singing of gay songs, feasting, drinking and the like. There were to be no more festivals, no more theaters, no more ribaldry, no more light and disrespectful poetry or display. Works of art and musical instruments were removed from the churches.[39]

Protestants in all countries made similar attempts to curtail public amusements, sports, the arts, and other pleasurable uses of leisure. Sports were identified with the luxury loving court, and the attempt to abolish them represented an attack on the monarchists by the new, hard working middle class.

Throughout Europe there was an aura of grim dedication to work and a determination to enforce old codes against play and idleness. A German schoolmaster named Franke wrote at the beginning of the eighteenth century:

Play must be forbidden in any and all of its forms. The children shall be instructed in this matter in such ways as to show them, through the presentation of religious principles, the wastefulness and folly of all play. They shall be led to see that play will distract their hearts and minds from God, the eternal good, and will work nothing but harm to their spiritual lives. Their true joy and hearty devotion should be given to their blessed and holy savior, and not to earthly things, for the reward of those who seek earthly things is tears and sorrow.[40]

The English Puritans waged a constant battle to limit or condemn sports and other forms of entertainment during the sixteenth and eighteenth century. Maintaining religious observation of the Sabbath was a particular issue. Although Sunday fairs and markets were prohibited by Henry VI, many Englishmen, having made an appearance at church, spent the rest of the day drinking in taverns, dancing, or enjoying other pastimes. "In the Sunday," wrote a much earlier moralist of Chaucer's time, "reigneth more lechery, gluttony . . . and other sins . . . than reigned all the week before."[41]

Under Henry VII, a document known as *The King's Book* stressed that Sunday should be spent in holy works and that those who spent it in "idleness, gluttony, riot or other vain or idle pastimes would be better occupied labouring in the field." This edict seemed to have little effect, however, and four years later, Thomas Cramer, Archbishop of Canterbury, complained that to sanctify the Sabbath was

145

not to pass over that day in lewd pastimes, in banquets, in dicing and carding, in dancing and bear-baiting, in bowling and shooting, in laughing and whoring, and in such-like beastly and filthy pleasures of the flesh; nor yet in bargaining, buying and selling . . . but to apply one's whole mind and body unto godly and spiritual exercises.[42]

Anglican clergy during the Elizabethan period bitterly attacked stage plays, church festival gatherings, dancing, gambling, bowling and other "devilish pastimes" like hawking and hunting, holding fairs and markets, and reading "lascivious and wanton books." However, people flocked to the theater, despite the admonition of clerics. One preacher complained that a "fylthye play" might call to itself a thousand spectators with one "blast of a trumpette," while "an hourse tolling of a Bell" would bring only a hundred to a sermon.

James I, however, recognized that the prohibition of harmless amusements like dancing, archery, and the decorating of maypoles caused public anger. In 1618 he issued a *Declaration on Lawful Sports,* in which he asked, "When shall the common people have leave to exercise, if not upon the Sundayes and holy daies, seeing they must apply their labour and win their living in all working daies?" Rebuking some "puritans and precise people" for punishing those who engaged in "lawful recreation and honest exercises" on Sundays and other holy days after the afternoon sermon, James stressed the military value of sport and the danger of an increase of drinking and other vices as substitute activities if sport were denied to people.

As for our good people's lawful recreation our pleasure likewise is, that after the end of divine service, our good people be not disturbed, letted or discouraged from any lawful recreation, such as dancing, either man or women, archery for men, leaping, vaulting or any such harmless recreation.[43]

During the Civil War and the Commonwealth period in England, there were increasingly strict laws to repress Sunday trade and pastimes. Fryer comments that by the closing decades of the eighteenth century, people in England were forced to take their Sunday pleasures by stealth:

The hallmark of the English Sunday was hypocrisy. Many who would not walk in the fields for pleasure, where their wickedness would be seen and commented on, did not scruple to drink all day in private alehouses. If one were rich enough, one could be more open about Sunday recreation—go in for coach racing, perhaps . . . or play cards in West End houses.[44]

Development of Parks and Recreation Areas

During the Middle Ages, the need to enclose cities within protective walls necessitated building within a compact area that left little space for public gardens or sports areas. As the walled city became difficult to defend after the invention of gunpowder and cannon, residents began to move out of the central city. Satellite communities developed around the city, usually with little definite planning.

As the Renaissance period began, European town planning became characterized by wide avenues, long approaches, handsome buildings, and similar monumental features. The nobility decorated their sizable estates with elaborate gardens, some of which were opened to public use, as in Italy at the end of the thirteenth century. There were walks and public squares, often decorated with statuary. In some cases, religious brotherhoods built clubhouses, gardens, and shooting stands for archery practice that were used by townspeople for recreation and amusement. Increasingly, cities were equipped with large public squares and courts where gatherings and entertainment might take place.

In seventeenth century France, other forms of space began to be provided for public use. Until this time, people relied on the use of meadows outside cities and towns for their sports activities. In crowded Paris, still constricted within its fifteenth century walls, the banks and bridges of the Seine were used frequently by the public at play. Responding to public demands for more open space in 1605, Henry IV had his planners design the Place Royale, an extensive plaza linked to a long promenade. In addition, other types of areas developed in seventeenth century Paris—green lawns along the ramparts of the river were useful for croquet and other popular sports, and alleys of trees were planted to create promenades where people might enjoy strolls during the evening.

Use of Private Estates

During the period from 1500 to the latter part of the eighteenth century, the European nobility developed increasingly lavish private grounds. These often included topiary work (trees and shrubbery clipped in fantastic shapes), aviaries, fishponds, summer houses, water displays, outdoor theaters, hunting grounds and menageries, and facilities for outdoor games. During this period, such famed gardens as the Tuileries and the Luxembourg in Paris and Versailles outside of Paris were established by the French royalty; similar gardens and private estates were found all over Europe.

Following the early Italian example, it became the custom to open these private parks and gardens to the public. At first they were opened only on special occasions or by caprice; some might be kept open for a time and then suddenly closed at the whim of the owner. In London the great parks were the property of the Crown, and in the eighteenth century they were completely given up to the use of the people. When Queen Caroline had a fancy to close Kensington Gardens, she asked her advisor, Lord Walpole, what it might cost to do so; he gave the significant reply, "Only three crowns."

Three major types of large parks came into existence during the late Renaissance. The first were royal hunting preserves or parks, some of which have become famous public parks today, such as the four thousand acre Prater in Vienna and the Tiergarten in Berlin. Second were the ornate and formal garden parks designed according to the so-called French style of landscape architecture. Third were the so-called English garden parks, which strove to produce naturalistic land-scape effects. This became the prevailing style in most European cities. Weir comments that although most of these magnificent park creations were designed and built for royalty, they became a rich heritage to later generations.

Apart from the development of large parks and gardens, what other recreative provisions were made for the public at large? In England, there were beginning efforts at city planning during the eighteenth century. Business and residential streets were paved and street names posted. Since it was believed that overcrowding led to disease (in the seventeenth century, London had suffered from recurrent attacks of the plague), an effort was made to convert open squares into

147

gardens and create more small parks. Deaths from contagious disease declined during each successive decade of the eighteenth century; this improvement was believed to have been due to increased cleanliness and ventilation within the city.

Growth of Popular Diversions in England

Great outdoor gardens were established to provide entertainment and relaxation. Vauxhall, a pleasure resort founded during the reign of Charles II, was a densely wooded park area with walks and bowers, lighting displays, water mills, fireworks, artificial caves and grottoes, entertainment, eating places and tea gardens. Supported chiefly by the growing class of merchants and tradesmen, the park's admission charge and distance from London helped to "exclude the rabble."

Other pleasure resorts open to the public during the eighteenth century featured music, singing, tea and coffee. They were considered helpful in raising moral standards; even the caustic critic Dr. Johnson declared, "I am a great friend to public amusements; for they keep people from vice."

Following the Restoration in England, Hyde Park and St. James Park became fashionable centers for promenading by the upper classes during the early afternoon. Varied amusements were held in the parks—wrestling matches, races, military displays, fireworks, and illuminations on special occasions. Aristocrats, merchants, and tradesmen all rode, drove carriages and strolled in the parks. Horse racing, lotteries, and other forms of gambling became the vogue.

Among the lower classes, tastes varied according to whether one lived in the country or city. Countrymen continued to engage vigorously in such sports as football, cricket, wrestling, or "cudgel playing," and to enjoy traditional country or Morris dancing and singing old folk songs. Many Londoners sought more exciting spectator events; animal baiting, cockfighting, and professional sports such as boxing became increasingly popular. Boxing became an enthusiasm of the well-to-do; servants were paired against one another while their masters laid wagers on the match.

Recreation in France

France provides another example of the growth of recreational opportunity during the Renaissance. For the wealthy in the eighteenth century, Paris was a "city of pleasure carried to a high pitch." They had the opportunity for leisurely play all week long—paying and receiving visits, dining, and passing evenings at gaming, at the theater, ballet, or opera, or at clubs. In contrast, the working classes had only Sundays and fête days, or holidays, for their amusements. La Croix points out, however, that these represented a third of the whole year; in addition to those holidays decreed by the state, the Catholic church had authorized or tolerated many other special celebrations. Many economists and men of affairs argued that the ecclesiastic authorities should be called upon to reduce the number. Voltaire wrote in 1756:

> Twenty fête days too many in the country condemn to inactivity and expose to dissipation twenty times a year ten millions of workingmen, each of whom would earn five pence a day, and this gives a total of 180

million livres . . . lost to the state in the course of a twelve-month. This painful fact is beyond all doubt.[45]

For the first time, one finds a concern about excessive leisure—both because of its economic effects upon industry and because of its supposed leading to "dissipation" among the lower classes. Within the larger cities in France, many places of commercial amusement sprang up. Cafes provided meeting places for the unoccupied to chat, read newspapers, play dominoes, chess, checkers, or billiards. The Marquis de Mirabeau is one of many who complained about the growing use of such establishments.

> The lower order of working men frequent the *guinguinettes,* licensed places of dissipation, which, it is rumored, the authorities tolerate because of the taxes levied on them. They all go home tipsy and are unfit for work the next day. Employers of labour will tell you that their men work half time on Saturday and on Monday sleep off the effects of their dissipation; they are not up to much on Tuesday, and if there should happen to be a saint's-day in the middle of the week they do not see anything of them the other four days.[46]

Taverns did not represent the sole leisure outlet of eighteenth century Parisians. There were many other opportunities for play; LaCroix comments that the upper classes still took part actively in fencing and riding, tennis, dice, cards and scandal, while the lower classes "had the monopoly of bowls, skittles, and archery."

People made frequent excursions to the country, where they enjoyed dancing in outdoor pavilions or sometimes bathing. In winter a great crowd would enjoy sliding on the ice of the frozen Seine. The chief amusement of Parisians of all classes and ages was the promenade, which the wealthy enjoyed every day and the lower classes on Sundays and holy days. For these, they visited the great parks, the Luxembourg and Tuileries Gardens, and others.

There were many public festivals on occasions of royal marriages, coronations or other times of celebration, when free wine and food were provided for the public and as many as a hundred illuminated boats cruised up and down the Seine as their bands played. Dancing continued through the year, with the lower classes visiting commercial dance halls or outdoor pavilions and the upper classes giving private balls for guests. The theater enjoyed a great vogue in eighteenth century Paris; many of the production expenses were paid by the Crown. Lower-class people were admitted inexpensively to the pit, while the upper class sat in more expensive boxes and loges. By the 1770s, all the chief cities in the provinces had theaters comparable to those in Paris, and there were many strolling companies that visited smaller towns.

Thus we see in France and England (presented here to illustrate the total European development during this period) widespread participation in varied forms of recreation by all classes. Throughout the late Middle Ages and Renaissance, authorities in both nations exerted pressures to control varied forms of public amusement which they regarded as immoral. Linked to this was the concern, expressed especially in France, that unlimited play and amusement (particularly drinking in taverns) was a threat to economic productivity and that the number of religious holidays had to be reduced for this reason. As a final trend, there was the development of both public and private places of amusement, and the emergence of

149

varied forms of commercialized entertainment which appealed to masses of people on all social levels.

This then was the status of recreation and leisure on the eve of the Industrial Revolution. Dramatic changes were soon to occur, both in the nations of Europe and in the new societies that were developing across the Atlantic.

Chapter Six

1. Ida Craven, "Leisure, According to the Encyclopedia of the Social Sciences," in Eric Larrabee and Rold Meyersohn, eds., *Mass Leisure* (Glencoe, Illinois: Free Press, 1958), p. 5.

2. P. C. McIntosh, *Sport in Society* (London: C.A. Watts, 1963), p. 4.

3. Lewis Spence, *Myth and Ritual in Dance, Game and Rhyme* (London: C.A. Watts, 1947), pp. 18–19.

4. "Anyone for Aqraorak?," *Time,* 27 March 1972.

5. "The Ancient World of a War-Torn Tribe," *Life,* 28 December 1972, p. 73.

6. Ibid.

7. John W. Loy, Jr., and Gerald S. Kenyon, *Sport, Culture, and Society* (New York: Macmillan, 1969), p. 92.

8. Thomas M. Kando, *Leisure and Popular Culture in Transition* (St. Louis: C. V. Mosby, 1975), p. 2.

9. E. Norman Gardiner, *Athletics of the Ancient World* (Oxford, England: Clarendon Press, 1930), pp. 3–8.

10. Georges Contenau, *Everyday Life in Babylon and Assyria* (London: Edward Arnold, 1954), pp. 132–33.

11. C. W. Ceram, *Gods, Graves and Scholars,* quoted in Charles E. Doell and Charles B. Fitzgerald, *A Brief History of Parks and Recreation in the United States* (Chicago: The Athletic Institute, 1954), p. 7.

12. Contenau, *Babylon and Assyria,* p. 109.

13. Gardiner, *Athletics of Ancient World,* p. 20.

14. Plato, *The Republic,* trans. Paul Shorey (Cambridge: Loeb Classical Library, Harvard Univ. Pr., 1930, 1953), p. 335.

15. Plato, *The Laws,* trans. R. G. Bury (Cambridge: Loeb Classical Library, Harvard Univ. Pr., 1926, 1961), p. 23.

16. Ibid., p. 37.

17. Pericles, quoted in Allen V. Sapora and Elmer D. Mitchell, *The Theory of Play and Recreation* (New York: Ronald, 1961), p. 18.

18. Aristotle, quoted in Robert Ulich, *History of Educational Thought* (New York: American Book, 1950), p. 17.

19. Kando, *Leisure and Popular Culture,* p. 23.

20. Quoted in Lincoln Kirstein, *Dance: A Short History of Classical Theatrical Dancing* (New York: G.P. Putnam, 1935), p. 7.

21. Quoted in Kirstein, *Dance: A Short History,* p. 57.

22. Margaret H'Doubler, *Dance: A Creative Art Experience* (New York: F. S. Crofts, 1940), p. 13.

23. Douglas Kennedy, *England's Dances* (London: G. Bell, 1950), pp. 31–32.

24. Paul La Croix, *France in the Middle Ages: Customs, Classes, Conditions* (New York: Frederick Ungar, 1963), p. 179.

25. Marcelle Thiébaux, "The Medieval Chase," *Speculum: A Journal of Medieval Studies,* 1967, p. 261.

26. La Croix, *France in Middle Ages,* p. 237.

27. McIntosh, *Sport in Society,* pp. 30–31.

28. Edward M. Hulme, *The Middle Ages* (New York: Holt, 1938), p. 604.

29. G. G. Coulton, *The Medieval Village* (Cambridge: Cambridge Univ. Pr., 1925), p. 93.

30. McIntosh, *Sport in Society,* p. 32.

31. Gardiner, *Athletics of Ancient World,* p. 15.

32. Jacques Gernet, *Daily Life in China on the Eve of the Mongol Invasion,* 1250–1276 (Stanford: Stanford Univ. Pr., 1962), p. 93.

33. Quoted in Gernet, *Daily Life in China,* p. 96.

34. Agnes de Mille, *The Book of the Dance* (New York: Golden Books, 1963), p. 63.

35. Quoted in Ulich, *History of Educational Thought,* p. 160.
36. Quoted in McIntosh, *Sport in Society,* p. 48.
37. Quoted in Walter Wood, *Children's Play and Its Place in Education* (London: Kegan Paul, Trench, Trubner, 1913), p. 48.
38. Quoted in McIntosh, *Sport in Society,* p. 54.
39. Norman P. Miller and Duane M. Robinson, *The Leisure Age* (Belmont, Calif.: Wadsworth, 1963), p. 66.
40. See Harvey C. Lehman and Paul A. Witty, *The Psychology of Play Activities* (New York: A.S. Barnes, 1927), p. 1.
41. See Peter Fryer, *Mrs. Grundy: Studies in English Prudery* (London: House and Maxwell, 1964), p. 90.
42. Ibid.
43. Quoted in McIntosh, *Sport in Society,* p. 43.
44. Fryer, *Mrs. Grundy,* p. 106.
45. Quoted in La Croix, *France in Middle Ages,* p. 346.
46. Quoted in La Croix, *France in Middle Ages,* p. 346.

7

RECREATION IN AMERICA: THE COLONIAL PERIOD AND NINETEENTH CENTURY

What was the history of recreation and leisure in the early American colonies? Tradition tells us that it was marked by stern Puritan repression of play in Calvinist New England, while in the middle-Atlantic and southern colonies, restrictions tended to be somewhat more relaxed after the settlers had established themselves on the new continent.

Those who settled the shores of North America brought with them both the pastimes and pleasures of their homelands and their attitudes of repression. Although there was a steady traffic between America and the British Isles of colonists, representatives of the Crown, fur traders, and other commercial travelers who carried newspapers, books, and other materials that imparted elements of culture, there was also a long and dangerous ocean journey that cut the colonists off from speedy communication or assistance.

The first need of the colonists was survival; they had to plant crops, clear forests, build shelters, and defend themselves against Indians. Over half the colonists who arrived on the Mayflower did not survive the first winter near Plymouth. In such a setting, work was necessary for survival; there was little time, money, or energy to support amusements or public entertainment. Without a royalty that had the wealth, leisure, and taste to patronize the arts, there was little opportunity for music, theater, or dance to flourish. But the most important hindrance to the development of recreation was the religious attitude.

Puritan Disapproval of Play

The Puritan settlers of New England came to the New World to establish a society based on a strict Calvinist interpretation of the Bible. Although the work ethic had not originated with the Puritans, they adopted it enthusiastically. In Woody's words, the early Christians had

> learned from Genesis: "in the sweat of thy face shalt thou eat bread, till thou return unto the ground." Work was conducive to piety. Manual tasks were idealized. Spinning, weaving, hoeing, carpentry, and like employments were urged by St. Jerome, St. Basil, Cassian and St. Benedict. . . . Leisure [idleness] was condemned: it hindered godliness; it was a snare of the devil. "Idle hands are the devil's workshop."[1]

Thus there were strict ordinances against gambling, drama, certain forms of music, and dancing—particularly dancing between men and women. Dancing in taverns and maypole dancing were especially condemned; Governor Endicott of the Massachusetts Bay Colony cut down the maypole at Merry Mount, grimly warning the revelers against this "pagan" practice. The theater was completely prohibited in several colonies during the seventeenth century. A number of New England colonies banned dice, cards, quoits, bowls, ninepins and similar pastimes in "house, yard or garden." There was especially strong enforcement of the Sabbath laws; Sunday work, travel, or recreation, even "unnecessary and unseasonable walking in the streets and fields," was prohibited.

Idleness was detested and work enforced. At Jamestown, Virginia, Sir Thomas Dale ruled that any tradesman who failed to work daily at his trade should be "condemned to the Galley" for three years. The Virginia Assembly decreed in 1619 that any person found idle should be bound over to compulsory work; it prohibited gambling, regulated drinking, and penalized excessively expensive attire. Other colonies established similar laws enforcing work; Morris points out:

> Not alone in the Puritan New England was idleness stigmatized as "the parent of all Vices," but throughout the length and breadth of the North Atlantic seaboard idleness was discountenanced. . . . Rhode Island classified together, "any Rougs, vagabonds, Sturdy beggards, masterless men, or other Notorious offenders whatsoever. . . . Colonial almanacs were studded with aphorisms on the sinfulness of being unemployed.[2]

Gradually, however, these stern restrictions declined in the southern colonies. There the upper classes had both wealth and leisure from their large estates and plantations, on which the labor was performed by indentured servants and slaves. Many of them had ties with the landed gentry in England, and they shared their tastes for aristocratic amusements. Dulles writes:

> Once the colony was firmly established, and the need for incessant work began to lessen, Virginians were more generally permitted to make the most of whatever opportunities for recreation their expanding life presented.[3]

Plantation Living in the South

Plantation life was marked by lavish entertainment and hospitality. Holidays, weddings, family reunions, and even funerals were observed by lavish feasting, dancing parties, and music. Hunting and fishing were especially popular, as was gambling. Card games of all types, lotteries, roulette tables, and dice were common. Carson writes:

> Gambling was not considered an evil in itself; it became a vice only when "inordinate" pursuit of the amusement led one to neglect his business or lose more money than he could afford. Professional gamesters were condemned for cheating if caught red-handed, but controlled "deceit" was only a mark of the skillful player. In Virginia, as in England, gaming was a gentleman's privilege, forbidden by law to those who were supposed to be working: apprentices, artificers, fishermen, husbandmen, laborers, mariners, servants of all kinds.[4]

Such "unlawful games" as bear-baiting, bull-baiting, bowling, cards, cock-fighting, quoits, dice, football, ninepins, and tennis were usually forbidden to working men, servants, apprentices, and students. Yet it is clear that they enjoyed these forbidden activities frequently. By the close of the eighteenth century, a French visitor, the Marquis de Chastellux, observed:

> The indolence and dissipation of the middling and lower classes of white inhabitants of Virginia, are such as to give pain to every reflecting mind. Horse racing, cock fighting, and boxing matches are standing amusements, for which they neglect all business.[5]

Horse racing became particularly popular, first in the South and then throughout the middle-Atlantic colonies. The theater too began in Virginia, where the first theater was erected in Williamsburg in 1716. By 1750 professional companies had begun to tour the colonies from New York to Savannah.

Restrictions in New England

In the northern colonies, Puritan magistrates attempted to maintain curbs on amusements long after the practical reasons for such prohibitions had disappeared. Early court records show many cases of young people being fined, confined to the stocks, or publicly whipped for such "violations" as walking in the streets and fields, gambling, dancing, or participating in other forms of "lascivious" behavior. Yet despite these restrictions, many forms of play continued. Earle writes of football being played by boys in Boston's streets and lanes, and points out that although playing cards (the "devil's picture-books") were intensely hated by the Puritans, they were abundantly imported from England and openly on sale.[6]

The lottery was introduced during the early 1700s and quickly gained the sanction and participation of the most esteemed citizens. Towns and states used lotteries to increase their revenue and to build canals, turnpikes, and bridges. This "acceptable" form of gambling helped to endow leading colleges and academies, and even Congregational, Baptist, and Episcopal churches had lotteries "for promoting public worship and the advancement of religion."

In the realm of sexual behavior, the practice of bundling was widely accepted. A fairly open invitation to premarital sexual activity, bundling permitted

154

engaged young couples to sleep together through the night, separated by a low wooden board. Despite the supposedly rigorous religious principles in New England, there is much evidence that

> among New Englanders of all social classes in the early part of the eighteenth century . . . fornication if followed by marriage, no matter how long delayed, was considered a venial sin, if sin at all.[7]

The Puritan magistrates in New England were especially strongly opposed to drinking; drunkards were subject to fine and imprisonment in the stocks, and sellers were forbidden to provide them with any liquor thereafter. A frequent drunkard, according to Earle, was punished by having a large *D* made of "Redd Cloth" hung around his neck or sewn on his clothing, and he lost the right to vote.[8] Yet by the early part of the eighteenth century, taverns were widely established throughout New England, providing places where gentlemen might "enjoy their bowl and bottle with satisfaction" and engage in billiards, cards, skittles, and other games. Drinking had become widespread throughout the colonies. Andrews writes:

> the colonists were heavy drinkers and . . . consumed liquors of every variety in enormous quantities on all important occasions—baptisms, weddings, funerals, barn raisings, church raisings, house raisings, ship launchings, ordinations . . . at meetings of commissions and committees, and in taverns, clubs, and private houses. In New England, a new officer was expected on training day to "wet his commission bountifully." Among the New England farmers beer, cider, cider brandy, and rum were the ordinary beverages. . . . Rum was distilled in all the leading New England towns, notably at Boston and Newport.[9]

Gradually, restrictions against play were relaxed in New England and elsewhere. Recreation was more acceptable when amusements could be attached to work, and thus country fairs and market days became occasions for merrymaking. Social gatherings with music, games and dancing were held in conjunction with work projects, such as house raisings, sheep shearing, log rolling, or corn-husking bees. Many social pastimes were linked to other civic occasions such as elections or training days for local militia. On training days in Boston, over a thousand men would gather on the Boston Common to drill and practise marksmanship, after which they celebrated at nearby taverns.

Even in the sports of the woods and waters, Puritans could find acceptable diversion, justified by necessity. The wolf, seen as the most hated and destructive of all wild animals, was a "proper prey." Countrymen caught wolves in pits, log pens, and traps, or on mackerel hooks dipped in tallow and baited by dead carcasses. Groups of hunters encircled wooded areas, beating the woods and swamps as they tightened the circle, driving the wolves before them. Often, the wolves were not killed outright. One contemporary writes

> that the inhuman sport of wolf-baiting was popular in New England, and he describes it thus: "A great mastiff held the Wolf. . . . Tying him to a stake we bated him with smaller doggs and had excellent sport, but his hinder legg being broken we soon knocked his brains out." Wolves also were dragged alive at a horse's tail, a sport equally cruel to both animals . . .[10]

As in England, fascination with such cruel spectacles was not limited to the torture of animals. Earle writes that diversion was furnished to the colonists by the punishment of criminals of all sorts. Offenders were not only whipped, set in the stocks, cage, or pillory, but were hung with "much parade before the eyes of the people, as a visible token of the punishment of evil living." Executions were especially widely publicized, and great crowds came to observe them. When a group of pirates were hanged in Boston in 1704, several hundred boats and canoes covered the river to watch the spectacle.

By the mid-1700s, the stern necessity of hard work for survival had lessened, and religious antagonism toward amusements had also declined. The Sunday laws continued in force in many settlements, however, and there was still a strong undercurrent of disapproval of play. Young John Adams, later to become president of the United States, wrote in his diary:

> Let no trifling diversion, or amusement . . .: no girl, no gun, no cards, no flutes, no violins, no dress, no tobacco, no laziness, decoy you from your books.[11]

Certain religious groups continued their firm opposition to all forms of play. The Methodist Episcopal church in the late eighteenth century revealed its distrust of idleness and the temptations of play in its statement of policy:

> We prohibit *play* in the strongest terms. . . . The students shall rise at five o-clock . . . summer and winter. . . . Their recreation shall be gardening, walking, riding, and bathing, without doors, and the carpenter's, joiner's, cabinet-maker's, or turner's business within doors. . . . The students shall be indulged with nothing which the world calls play. Let this rule be observed with the strictest nicety; for those who play when they are young, will play when they are old.[12]

During the time of national emergency preceding the impending Revolutionary War, the Continental Congress attempted to curtail the amusements of the colonial aristocracy. One of the articles of the "Association" of 1774 called upon the colonies to prohibit every "Species of Extravagance and Dissipation, especially all Horse Racing, and all Kinds of Gaming, Cock Fighting, Exhibitions of Shows, Plays and other expensive Diversions and Entertainment."

Why this drastic ban? Dulles speculates that it might have been an expression of disapproval of the way of life of the rich Southern planters by frugal, hard working New England delegates.[13] Many kinds of entertainment including theater, music, dance, and horse racing were prohibited during the period of the Revolution. After the war, however, these activities were revived and the social life and tavern pastimes of the people in both the North and the South became more widespread than ever before. Only in rural areas and on the growing frontier were people still isolated, and even there community gatherings, camp meetings, circuses, traveling lecturers, and fairs helped to provide a modicum of entertainment and social interchange.

With the beginning of the nineteenth century, an increasing number of Americans were living in cities and towns. Land was no longer unlimited, and the simple rural sports such as hunting and fishing that had been taken for granted were suddenly threatened. Conservation of land became an important concern.

Parks and Conservation in the Colonial Era

Compared with the nations of Europe, the early American colonies showed little concern for developing city parks. With land so plentiful around the isolated settlements along the eastern seaboard, there seemed to be little need for such planning. Even in the earliest colonies, however, particularly in New England, a number of towns and villages established "commons" or "greens," used chiefly for pasturing cattle and sheep, but also for military drill fields, market days, and fairs. Similar open areas were established in towns settled by the Spanish in the South and Southwest, in the form of plazas and large squares in the center of towns or adjacent to principal churches.

Beautiful village greens established during the Colonial period still exist throughout Massachusetts, Connecticut, Vermont, and New Hampshire. In the design of new cities, the colonists began to give attention to the need for preserving or establishing parks and open spaces. Among the first cities in which such plans were made were Philadelphia, Savannah, and Washington, D.C.

The description in a plan drafted for the city of Philadelphia in 1682 by William Penn's Surveyor-General reveals a conscious effort to provide public parks.

> The city, as the model shows, consists of a large Front-street on each river, and a High-street near the middle, from river to river, of one hundred feet broad, and a Broad-street, in the middle of the city from side to side, of the like breadth. In the center of the city, is a square of ten acres; at each angle to build houses for public affairs. There is also in each quarter of the city a square of eight acres, to be for the like used.[14]

The plans developed in 1773 by General James Oglethorpe for Savannah, the principal city of Georgia, made even more extensive provision for public open space and greenery. Oglethorpe spared many large forest trees when the site for the town was cleared, and his land-grant scheme permitted each freeholder, in addition to his own plot of land within the town, five rural acres for a garden and orchard. Besides the common and the public gardens covering ten acres of rolling land near the river, Savannah had twenty-four other small squares and open spaces, a remarkably generous allocation of parks for the colonial era in America.

When the new Federal city that was to become Washington was planned in 1791, Major L'Enfant envisioned a city with a number of majestic parks and pleasure gardens. His plan, developed with the aid of Jefferson and Washington, included fifteen squares (each to be developed by one of the fifteen states then in existence), boulevards, a "grand cascade," a President's Park, and other similar features. Some elements of the plan, however, were not carried out until a century later, and some not at all.

The majority of colonial communities made very limited provision for parks or open recreation areas. The Dutch colony of New Amsterdam (later to become New York) was typical; houses were built close together, facing extremely narrow streets. Only two open spaces were provided in the old part of the town—a small bowling green at the southern end, and an open field, which later became City Hall Park, in the northern end of the settlement.

Early Conservation Efforts

Almost from the earliest days of settlement, there was concern for the conservation of forests and open land. As early as 1626 in the Plymouth Colony, the cutting of trees without official consent was prohibited by law. The Massachusetts Bay Colony passed the Great Ponds Act in 1641, which set aside two thousand bodies of water, each over ten acres in size, for such public uses as "fishing and fowling." The courts supported this conservation of land for recreational usage. Pennsylvania law in 1681 required that for every five acres of forest land that were cleared, one was to be left untouched. Other laws prohibiting setting woods on fire or cutting certain types of trees were enacted long before the Revolution.

As early as the late seventeenth century, Massachusetts and Connecticut defined hunting seasons and established rules for hunting certain types of game. Although originally a means of obtaining food, hunting rapidly became a sport in the colonies. Andrews writes:

> The woods and waters offered endless opportunity in summer for fishing and in winter for such time-honored pursuits as hunting, fowling, trapping, and fishing through the ice. John Rowe of Boston was a famous and untiring fisherman; thousands of other enthusiasts played the part of colonial Isaak Waltons; and there was a fishing club on the Schuylkill as early as 1732.[15]

What appeared to be an inexhaustible supply of wildlife began to disappear with the advance of settlements and the destruction of the forests. Wildfowl in particular were ruthlessly hunted, especially in New England, and "so unlicensed had the destruction of the heath hen become in New York that in 1708 the province determined to protect its game by providing for a closed season."[16] Well before the American Revolution, the colonists had shown a concern for the establishment of parks and urban open spaces and for the conservation of forests and wildlife.

The Nineteenth Century: Industrial Revolution

The nineteenth century was a time of tremendous social change in both Europe and America. The Industrial Revolution extended from the late eighteenth through most of the nineteenth century.

Science and capital combined to increase production, as businessmen invested in the industrial expansion made possible by newly invented machines. Industry moved from home and the small workshop to new mills and factories with mechanical power. The invention of such devices as the spinning jenny, the water frame, the weaving machine, and the steam engine, all invented during the 1760s, drastically altered production methods and increased output.

Plate 1. Even today primitive New Guinea tribes practice warfare regularly as a form of violent team sport. Here, games of childhood are used to practice warlike skills; rival tribes skirmish on a hillside; and warriors dance to celebrate a victory.

Plate 2. Combative pastimes in other primitive societies: ancient Mayan art depicts sport carried on as a religious ritual in temple courtyards; King Shamba of the Congo is shown with the Mankala Board, a game popular in Africa and the Orient; and Brazilian Kalapalo Indians, who wrestle many hours each day, are shown.

Plate 3. Ancient forms of recreation: Persian noblemen of the 16th Century enjoying a polo match; Ajax and Achilles, heroes of Greek mythology, playing an early form of checkers; and the Egyptian Pharaoh Tutankhamen hunting lions.

Plate 4. During the Middle Ages and Renaissance, the court enjoyed jousting both as a form of amusement and training for warfare. One of the first vacation resorts in England was the King and Queen's Bath at Bath. European peasant recreation during this period, as portrayed by Breughel, was earthy and vigorous.

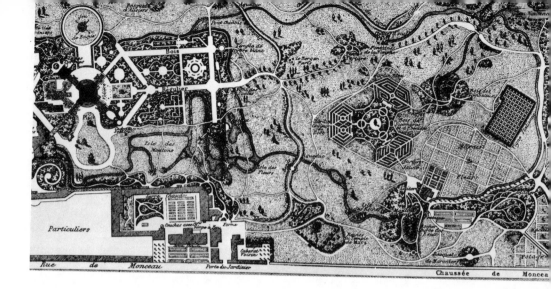

Plate 5. Popular recreation in 18th Century Paris included the use of handsome new parks and promenades, and such great public spectacles as this fireworks display on a bridge on the River Seine.

Plate 6. Nineteenth Century Americans enjoyed sport in many forms: a college boating regatta, ice skating on a frozen pond, and bowling.

Plate 7. In the mid-20th Century, youth life styles changed rapidly, as seen in a formal college prom (1950s), a poolside beer bust in a "singles" apartment complex (1960s), and a Louisiana rock concert along the Atchafalaya River (early 1970s).

Plate 8. Unusual fads and stunts were often keyed to the automobile and to highway travel. Teenagers risked their lives, playing "chicken" at high speed, while college students set records for cramming into a Volkswagen. Other students competed at pushing beds across the country.

The locomotive, the steamboat, and the telegraph, all invented during the early 1800s, gave rise to greater world trade, exploration, and colonization. Networks of canals, rapidly expanded railroad lines, the completion of the transatlantic cable, and the scientific study of navigation made possible a vast expansion of industry and created a totally new way of life.

Urbanization

Throughout the western world, there was a steady shift of the population from rural areas to urban centers. Because factory wages were usually higher than those in domestic industry or agriculture, great numbers of country people moved to the cities and new factory towns to work. Millions of European peasant families immigrated because of crop failures, expulsion from their land, religious or social discrimination, and political unrest. The American population increased rapidly. When Andrew Jackson became President in 1829, about 12.5 million people lived in the United States. By 1850 the total had reached 23 million, and a decade later America's population was 31 million. In the large cities, the proportion of foreign born was quite high; 45 percent of New York City's population in 1850 was foreign born, mostly Irish and German.

About 85 percent of the population in 1850 was still rural, living in areas of less than 2,500 population. However, as more and more people moved into factory towns and large cities along the eastern seaboard or around the Great Lakes, the United States became increasingly an urban civilization.

Expansion of Slums

Both rural and foreign immigrants moved into the congested tenement areas of growing cities, living in quarters that were inadequate for decent family life (often a family lived crowded in a single room), under unsanitary and unsafe conditions. The new urban slums were marked by congestion and disease; their residents were oppressed by low wages and recurrent unemployment and by monotonous and prolonged labor, including the use of young children in mills, mines and factories, and piecework tasks at home.

The Reduction of Leisure

The trend in manual occupations in Europe from the late Middle Ages to 1800 was toward longer working hours. With industrialization, the average working day in both France and England climbed from twelve hours with a two-hour rest in about 1700 to a fourteen- to eighteen-hour day in 1800. By 1850, the average workweek in French cities was about seventy hours. In addition, the number of holidays provided during the year was sharply reduced.

The peak of working hours appears to have been reached during the first half of the nineteenth century. Gradually, pressure by trade unions and industrial legislation improved the situation. In England, for example, factory acts during the first forty years of the nineteenth century removed the youngest children from factories and limited the working hours of others. The hours of labor were limited by law to ten per day in 1847; a nine-hour day was won by contract for most workers between 1869 and 1873. By 1919, the eight-hour day had been formally adopted in nearly all European countries.

The average industrial and agricultural workweek in the United States for the period between 1850 and 1960 is shown in Table 7-1, which illustrates the steady decline of work hours.

Table 7-1.

Changing Workweek in the United States, 1850–1960

Year	All Industries	Agriculture	Nonagricultural Industries
1850	69.7	72.0	65.7
1860	67.8	71.0	63.3
1870	65.3	70.0	60.0
1880	63.8	69.0	58.8
1890	61.7	68.0	57.1
1900	60.1	67.0	55.9
1910	54.9	65.0	50.3
1920	49.4	60.0	45.5
1930	45.7	55.0	43.2
1940	43.8	54.6	41.1
1950	39.9	47.2	38.8
1960	38.5	44.0	38.0

Source: Sebastian de Grazia, *Of Time, Work and Leisure* (New York: Doubleday-Anchor, Twentieth Century Fund, 1962), p. 419.

Development of the Protestant Work Ethic

The Puritan ideal, which glorified work and condemned leisure and play, became even stronger as a consequence of the Industrial Revolution. In part, it was seen as the way to religious salvation; in the United States, dedication to work became a hallmark of American life.

As industrialization became more widespread, there was a renewed emphasis on the importance of "honest toil" and a strong antagonism expressed against play. Religious leaders supported the twelve- or fourteen-hour workday as part of the "wholesome discipline of factory life."

Dubin comments that work ultimately became a basis for man's self-justification. "Indeed, the capitalist system itself is asserted to rest on the moral and religious justification that the Reformation gave to work."[17] Americans became more consciously dedicated to the Protestant work ethic than Europeans had ever been; their single-minded dedication to work was noted by many foreign visitors. One British visitor commented about the grim, business-minded American way of life:

> A Boston boy is a picture of prematurity. It can almost be said that every man is born middle-aged in every city in the Union. The principal business seems to be to grow old as fast as possible. The interval between their leaving school and commencing their business careers offers no

occupation to give either gracefulness or strength to body or mind. Athletic games and the bolder field sports being unknown . . . all that is left is chewing, smoking and drinking.[18]

Henry Adams, the noted American historian, agreed with this picture, commenting that Boston offered few "healthy resources for boys or men. . . . Sports as a pursuit was unknown." As a youth, he felt great guilt about occasional lapses into leisure activities such as fishing. Like all boys, he was constantly reminded that the worthwhile goals in life were success in industry and intellectual pursuits.

Not just in America, but throughout the Western world, life was seen as a sober business. The British philosopher and historian Thomas Carlyle expressed the spirit of his times in such statements as: "All work, even cotton-spinning, is noble; work is alone noble . . . a life of ease is not for any man, nor for any god," and "Even in the meanest sorts of labor, the whole soul of a man is composed into a kind of real harmony the instant he sets himself to work."[19] John Ruskin, the English critic, wrote, "Life without industry is guilt," and "When men are rightly occupied, their amusement grows out of their work."[20]

Work was considered the source of social and moral values, and therefore the proper concern of the church, which renewed its attack upon most forms of play. The church condemned many commercial amusements as "the door to all the sins of iniquity," and as late as 1844, Henry Ward Beecher, a leading minister of his time, savagely attacked the stage, the concert hall, and the circus, charging that anyone who pandered to the public taste for commercial entertainment was a moral assassin.

Despite these attitudes, many forms of play grew increasingly popular throughout the United States. City workers began to have free time and money to spend on various forms of recreation. In addition, a new middle class was emerging—a class that began to seek out varied forms of entertainment.

Growth of Popular Participation in Recreation

Dulles writes that despite a wave of religious revivals and attempts to repress play, the first half of the nineteenth century was a time of gradual expansion of popular amusements that have since played an increasingly important role in national life:

> The first half of the nineteenth century witnessed the growth of the theater as entertainment reaching out to all classes of people. It saw the beginnings of variety, minstrel shows, and the circus; the establishment of amusement parks, public dance-halls, concert saloons and beer-gardens; a revival of horse-racing and the rise of other popular sports. By the Civil War the nation was in the midst of these far-reaching changes in the recreational scene.[21]

The theater, which had been banned during the American Revolution, gradually gained favor in cities along the eastern seaboard and in major southern cities. Large theaters were built to accommodate audiences of as many as four thousand persons. Performances were usually by touring players who joined with local stock companies throughout the country, presenting "serious" drama as well as light-hearted entertainment which was later to become burlesque and vaudeville. By the 1830s about thirty traveling shows were regularly touring the country, some with menageries and bands of acrobats and jugglers. Ultimately they added riding and tumbling acts and developed into circuses.

Another popular form of stage entertainment, especially during the 1840s and 1850s (although they continued after the Civil War) were minstrel shows. Combining music, singing, dancing, and "blackface" comedy routines in which plantation blacks were caricatured by white performers in burnt-cork makeup, minstrels perpetrated a distorted image of blacks in American folklore.

Expansion of Sports Interests

A number of sports gained their first strong impetus during the early nineteenth century. Americans had enjoyed watching amateur wrestling matches, foot races, shooting events, and horse races during colonial days or along the frontier until professional promotion of sports events began in the early 1800s.

Professionalism in Sport

Crowds as large as forty and fifty thousand from all ranks of society attended highly publicized boating regattas, and five- and ten-mile races of professional runners during the 1820s. The first sports promoters were owners of resorts or of commercial transportation facilities such as stagecoach lines, ferries, and later, trolleys and railroads. These new sports impresarios made their profits from transportation fares and accommodations for spectators; later, they erected grandstands and charged admission.

Horse racing flourished; by mid-century both running and trotting races attracted crowds as large as one hundred thousand spectators. Foot racing was a highly professional sport, with match races for large purses and heavy wagers. Prize fighting also gained popularity as a professional contest. It began as a brutal, bare-knuckled sport, often prohibited by legal authorities, but by the time of the Civil War, gloves were used and rules established, and boxing exhibitions were becoming accepted.

Influence of the Civil War

Thus, by the time of the Civil War, interest in varied sports was widespread. Baseball was enjoyed as a casual diversion in the towns of New England through the early decades of the nineteenth century (in the form of "rounders" or "town-ball"), and amateur teams, often organized by occupation (merchants and clerks, or shipwrights and mechanics), were playing on the commons of large eastern cities by the mid-1850s.

The Civil War was a stimulus to recreational involvement for several reasons. One was the spreading of interests; men from different areas of the country learned each other's games and sports and took them home with them. Army camp life offered more free time than life at home, and there was no Puritanical influence to prevent certain forms of play.

162

Men on both sides of the great struggle engaged in a wide variety of recreational pursuits. Soldiers actively participated in combative sports (boxing and wrestling), cockfighting, fencing matches, boating and fishing, horseback riding, team sports, and other pursuits like tenpins, gymnastics, card playing, table games (checkers, chess, dominoes) and similar activities.

The Muscular Christianity Movement

Gradually, a number of leading mid-nineteenth century preachers began to argue that physical prowess and sanctity were compatible. Henry Ward Beecher drew a line between "harmful" amusements and those which contributed to well-being, saying, "Don't be tempted to give up a wholesome air-bath, a good walk, or a skate or ride every day (as) it will pay you back . . . by freshness, elasticity, and clearness of mind." For the first time, Americans took a hard look at themselves and were not pleased with what they saw. Oliver Wendell Holmes argued that widespread participation in sports would create a physically fit citizenry:

> I am satisfied that such a set of black-coated, stiff-jointed, soft-muscled, paste-complexioned youth as we can boast in our Atlantic cities never before sprang from the loins of Anglo-Saxon lineage. . . . We have a few good boatmen, no good horsemen that I hear of, nothing remarkable, I believe, in cricketing, and as for any great athletic feat performed by a gentleman in these latitudes, society would drop a man who ran around the common in five minutes.[22]

Athletic and outdoor activities gradually became more socially acceptable. Skating became a vogue in the 1850s, and rowing and sailing grew popular, especially for the upper social classes. The Muscular Christianity movement—so named because of the support given to it by leading church figures and because sports and physical activity were thought to build morality and good character—had its greatest influence in schools and colleges, which began to initiate programs of physical education and athletic competition. In addition, the newly founded Young Men's Christian Association based its program on active physical recreation.

In Europe since the late eighteenth century, sports had been seen as an important means of achieving physical fitness and national morale. J. F. Jahn envisioned a national sporting movement which would regenerate the German people after their crushing defeats in the Napoleonic Wars. During the early decades of the nineteenth century, Jahn's *turnen* (system of gymnastics) spread rapidly through Germany, where it had strong military and political support, and was soon adopted in other countries throughout Europe.

In England, the development of recreational sports was strongly influenced by social class. The British aristocracy greatly enjoyed golf and tennis in addition to such traditional field sports as hunting, shooting, and angling. Only the land-owning aristocracy were permitted to hunt on horseback; the game laws prohibited buying or selling game and as late as 1816 threatened heavy penalties for poachers. The lower ranks of society had a number of popular sports, including athletic competitions at country fairs such as a "mob" form of football.

Team sports gradually gained approval in the fashionable English public (actually private, or preparatory) schools. Earlier schoolmasters had opposed them because of their origins. McIntosh writes:

Headmasters were hostile to sport. Dr. Keats at Eton tried to prevent cricket against Harrow; the headmaster at Westminster tried to prevent rowing races with Eton, and Dr. Butler, headmaster of Shrewsbury, thought that football was "only fit for butcher boys."[23]

Despite lack of support, however, students organized their own interscholastic sports competitions. Gradually rugby football spread, then cricket and organized boating matches. In time, leading headmasters began to believe that sport improved discipline and contributed to "valuable social qualities and manly virtues." The headmaster of one school, who had referred to the "idle boys, I mean the boys who play cricket," was succeeded by one who said, "Give me a boy who is a cricketeer. I can make something of him." A number of leading clergymen gave support to sports; one spokesman, Charles Kingsley, summed up the argument in 1874:

> that games conduce, not merely to physical but to moral health; that in the playing fields boys acquire virtues which no books can give them; not merely daring and endurance, but, better still, temper, self-restraint, fairness, honour, unenvious approbation of another's success, and all that "give and take" of life which stand a man in such good stead when he goes forth into the world, and without which, indeed, his success is always maimed and partial.[24]

In America, colleges initiated their first competitive sports programs. In colonial New England, youthful students had engaged in many pastimes, some tolerated by college authorities and others prohibited. The first college clubs had been founded as early as 1717, and social clubs were in full swing by the 1780s and 1790s. By the early nineteenth century, most American colleges had more or less officially recognized clubs and social activities. The founding of social fraternities in the 1840s and the building of college gymnasiums in the 1860s added to the social life and physical recreation of students.

Intercollegiate sports competition in rowing, baseball, track, and football was organized. The first known intercollegiate football game was between Princeton and Rutgers in 1869; interest spread rapidly, and by the late 1880s, college games were attracting as many as forty thousand spectators. But it was baseball that drew the greatest public interest. The National Baseball League was formed during the 1870s, and the modern professional game and its system of major and minor leagues had begun. Baseball thrived also as an amateur sport for millions of persons in other settings: colleges, high schools, YMCAs, and community life.

Track and field events were widely promoted by amateur athletic clubs, some of which, like the New York Athletic Club, had many socially influential members who formed the Amateur Athletic Union and developed rules to govern much amateur sports competition. Gymnastic instruction and games were sponsored by the German *turnvereins,* the Czech *sokols,* and the YMCA, which had established some 260 large gymnasiums around the country by the 1880s and was a leader in sports activities. Other popular pastimes included croquet, archery, lawn tennis, and roller-skating, which became so popular that huge skating rinks were built to accommodate thousands of skaters and spectators. Women began to participate in such recreational pastimes, and also to enjoy gymnastics, dance and other athletics in school and college physical education programs. Bicycling was introduced in the 1870s, and within a few years hundreds of thousands of people had

164

become enthusiasts. During the last decades of the nineteenth century, there was a growing vogue for outdoor activities. Americans began to enjoy hiking and mountain climbing, fishing and hunting, camping in national forests and state parks, and nature photography.

Gradually, Puritan restraints decreased; although work was still valued as a moral virtue, recreation became more respectable. Church leaders of the 1880s and 1890s, recognizing that religion could no longer arbitrarily condemn all play, offered "sanctified amusement and recreation" as alternatives to undesirable play. Many churches made provisions for libraries, gymnasiums and assembly rooms. Dulles comments:

> Visitors from abroad in the 1890s were as much struck by the way Americans were now seeking out opportunities for play as those who had come to this country in the 1840s had been impressed by our apparent lack of interest in amusements.[25]

Growth of Commercial Amusements

Particularly in larger cities, new forms of commercial amusement sprang up or expanded rapidly. The theater in its various forms was more popular than ever. Dime museums, dance halls, shooting galleries, bowling alleys, billiard parlors, beer gardens, and saloons provided a new world of entertainment for pay. Added to these, many cities had "red light districts" where houses of prostitution flourished. Drinking, gambling, and commercial vice gradually became serious social problems, particularly when protected by a tacit alliance between criminal figures and big-city political machines.

Amusement parks grew up on the outskirts of cities and towns, often established by new rapid transit companies offering reduced-fare rides to the parks in gaily decorated trolley cars. Amusement parks featured such varied attractions as parachute jumps, open-air theaters, band concerts, professional bicycle races, freak shows, games of chance, and shooting galleries. Roller coasters, fun houses, and midget-car tracks also became popular.

The trend toward increased recreation was not unique to the United States. Dumazedier points out that it was during the mid-nineteenth century that Paris students organized the first clubs for athletic sports. Also established during this period were

> the French Stadium and the Racing Club of France and then the gymnastic societies. Coubertin, in 1864, organized the first sports meet in the great amphitheater of the Sorbonne; he also established teaching of sports and proposed the restoration of the Olympic games. Approximately at this time, youth movements were engendered among the bourgeoisie—in France, the Catholic Association of French youth . . . in England, the Boy Scouts.[26]

Commercial tourism also expanded rapidly abroad. The upper classes in England had been traveling to resort towns since the eighteenth century; with the addition of new holidays and a shorter workday in the mid-nineteenth century, great numbers of middle class families also began to enjoy outings to tourist areas in Britain. As in America, steamboat, coach, and railroad companies promoted such travel, sometimes building hotels and creating entirely new resorts in the countryside or at the seashore.

Concern about Leisure

For the first time, concern about the uses of leisure began to arise—less in terms of the sinfulness of play than the broader question of the potential role of leisure in modern society.

Intellectual and political leaders began to raise searching questions. The English author Lord Lytton commented, "The social civilization of a people is always and infallibly indicated by the intellectual character of its amusements." In 1876, Horace Greeley, a leading journalist, observed that although there were teachers for every art, science, and "elegy," there were no "professors of play." He asked, "Who will teach us incessant workers how to achieve leisure and enjoy it?" And in 1880, President James Garfield declared in a speech at Lake Chautauqua, "We may divide the whole struggle of the human race into two chapters: first, the fight to get leisure; and then the second fight of civilization—what shall we do with our leisure when we get it."

This new concern was an inevitable consequence of the Industrial Revolution. Americans now lived in greater numbers in large cities, where the traditional social activities of the past and the opportunity for casual, wholesome play were no longer available. They had increasing amounts of free time and could afford to pay for recreation. There was a need for organized recreation programs that would provide wholesome and enriching leisure experiences for all classes.

Beginning of the Recreation Movement

The term *recreation movement* is used here to describe those forms of leisure activity which are provided in an organized way by agencies of society, either governmental or voluntary, and which are intended to achieve desirable social outcomes. Four major streams of development had their roots in the nineteenth century: (1) the adult education movement; (2) the development of a network of national, state, and municipal parks; (3) the development of national voluntary organizations and of settlement houses; and (4) the playground movement in cities and towns.

The Adult Education Movement

During the early decades of the nineteenth century, there was considerable civic concern for improving intellectual cultivation and providing continuing education for adults. Again, this was found in other nations as well; in France, workers' societies determined to gain shorter workdays and more leisure time for adult study and cultural activities, and pressed vigorously for the development of popular lectures, adult education courses, and municipal libraries.

In the United States, this concern took the form of the so-called Lyceum movement, a national organization with over nine hundred local chapters. Its program consisted chiefly of lectures, readings, and other educational presentations

166

reflecting the view that all citizens should be educated in order to participate knowledgeably in affairs of government.

The Lyceum movement was widely promoted by such organizations as Chautauqua, which sponsored a leading summer camp program in upstate New York for adults and families, with varied cultural activities, sports, lectures, and other educational features, and which also sponsored a lecture circuit. While the professed purpose of Chautauqua was education, it actually provided substantial entertainment and amusement to its audiences. Even today, lecture series—often provided or sponsored by colleges or universities, civic groups, or women's clubs—are extremely popular activities in many cities and towns.

The Development of National, State, and Municipal Parks

Concern for preservation of the natural heritage of the United States in an era of increasing industrialization and despoilment of natural resources began during the first decades of the nineteenth century. The first major conservation action was in 1864, when Congress set aside the first extensive area of wilderness primarily for public recreational use, consisting of the Yosemite Valley and the Mariposa Grove of Big Trees in California, later to become a national park. The first designated national park was Yellowstone, founded in 1872. In the years that followed, other major unspoiled lands were added to the national park system, the national forests, and other land-management agencies (see chapter 9).

All such developments did not lend themselves immediately to an emphasis on recreation. The primary purpose of the national parks at the outset was to preserve the nation's natural heritage and wildlife. Brockman writes that the current interest in recreational use of national forest lands was not typical in the initial years of the forest conservation movement in the United States:

> Early foresters could not envisage the great public interest in the recreational values of the national forests . . . of the present day. . . . Consequently, although a few forestry leaders began calling attention to growing public interest in and use of national forests for outdoor recreation about 1910, official U.S. Forest Service recognition of recreation as a valid part of national forest management did not develop for more than a decade.[27]

As Federal park development continued, state authorities too became concerned with the preservation of their forest areas and wildlife. As early as 1867, Michigan and Wisconsin established fact-finding committees to expore the problem of forest conservation, followed shortly by Maine and other eastern states; within two decades, several states had established forestry commissions. Between 1864 and 1900, the first state parks were established, as well as a number of state forest preserves and historic parks. Because they are usually closer to large population centers, state parks tend to be more recreation oriented than national parks. Foss sums up their later development:

> State parks [today] . . . perform a very critical role in meeting recreational needs. Although in size they are only one-fifth of the acreage of the national parks, three times the number of people use them. The

167

reason is twofold: first, the state parks are close to metropolitan areas while the large national parks are distant from most large centers, being located mainly in the far West; second, the state parks, with few exceptions [have] picnic areas or campgrounds where tents can be pitched or where cabins can be rented.[28]

Municipal Park Development

America lagged behind Europe in the development of municipal parks, partly because it had no aristocracy which owned large cultivated estates, hunting grounds, and elaborate gardens that they could turn over to the public, as was the case in Europe. The first major park to be developed in an American city was Central Park in New York; its design and the philosophy on which it was based strongly influenced other large cities during the latter half of the nineteenth century.

There had long been a need for open space in New York. During the first three decades of the nineteenth century, plans were made for several open squares to total about 450 acres, but these were not carried out fully. By the early 1850s, the entire amount of public open space in all of Manhattan totaled only 117 acres. Pressure mounted among the citizens of the city for a major park that would provide relief from stone and concrete. The poet William Cullen Bryant wrote:

> Commerce is devouring inch by inch the coast of the island, and if we would rescue any part of it for health and recreation it must be done now. All large cities have their extensive public grounds and gardens, Madrid and Mexico [City] their Alamedas, London its Regent's Park, Paris its Champs Elysées, and Vienna its Prater.[29]

When the public will could no longer be denied, legislation was passed in 1856 to establish the park, and construction of the 843-acre site began in 1857. Central Park, designed by landscape architects Frederick Law Olmsted and Calvert Vaux, was completely man-made: "Every foot of the park's surface, every tree and bush, as well as every arch, roadway and walk, has been fixed where it is with a purpose." The dominant need was to provide, within the densely populated heart of an immense metropolis, "refreshment of the mind and nerves" for city dwellers through the provision of greenery and scenic vistas. The park was to be heavily wooded and to have the appearance of rural scenery, with roadways screened from the eyes of park users wherever possible. Recreational pursuits permitted in the park included walking, pleasure driving, ice skating in the winter, and boating—but not more organized or structured sports.

Before Central Park was built, people expressed concern about the behavior of those who would use it. The *New York Herald* declared in 1858 that it would be nothing but a "great bear-garden for the lower denizens of the city." Olmsted established strict rules for the park's use, however, saying, "A large part of the people of New York are ignorant of a park. . . . They will need to be trained to the proper use of it, to be restrained in the abuse of it." As executive head of the park, he hired a special police force to enforce an extensive code of regulations, including restrictions against walking on the grass, turning domestic animals loose, or damaging the landscape or wildlife in any way. Throughout its history, Central Park, like other great urban parks, has been the scene of constant battle between those who sought to keep it a quiet, secluded scenic area and those who wished to develop it more fully for active recreational uses.

168

In the decades that followed, other large city parks were developed—in 1883, Franklin Park in Boston, with 527 acres; in 1867, Fairmont Park in Philadelphia, with 2,816 acres, and numbers of others. Olmsted designed several of these himself; others were directly influenced by his work.

Establishment of Voluntary Organizations

During the nineteenth century, a number of voluntary organizations were established which played an important role in providing recreation services, chiefly for children and youth. One such body was the Young Men's Christian Association, founded in Boston in 1851, followed by the Young Women's Christian Association fifteen years later. At first, the Y provided fellowship between youth and adults chiefly for religious purposes. It gradually enlarged its program, however, to include gymnastics, sports and other group recreational and social activities.

These and other religious organizations, along with a host of youth-serving groups, were ultimately to provide a major segment of recreational opportunity for America's youth (see chapter 11).

Another type of voluntary agency which offered significant leisure programs was the settlement house, neighborhood centers established chiefly in the slum sections in the East and Midwest. Among the first were University Settlement, founded in New York City in 1886, and Hull House, founded in Chicago in 1889. Their staff sought to help poor people, particularly immigrants, adjust to modern urban life by providing services concerned with education, family life, and community improvement. Many of the early settlement house workers saw recreation as a major need; a pioneer social worker, Jane Addams, urged that recreation be provided as a safety valve for slum conditions, saying

> It is as if our cities had not yet developed a sense of responsibility to the life and the streets, and continually forget that recreation is stronger than vice and that recreation alone can stifle the lust for vice.[30]

Other leaders, in cooperation with such outspoken social reformers as Jacob Riis, Walter Vrooman, and Louise DeKoven Bowen, created a public awareness of the need for improved recreational opportunities in the cities. They welded public-spirited citizens, clergymen, educators, and newspaper editorial writers into a force that ultimately compelled action from civic officials and gave rise to the playground movement.

The Playground Movement

To understand the need for playgrounds in cities and towns, it is necessary to know what living conditions were like for poor people during the latter decades of the nineteenth century. The wave of urbanization which had begun earlier in the century had not reached its peak. The urban population more than doubled, from 14 to 30 million, between 1880 and 1900 alone. By the century's end, there were 28 cities with over 100,000 residents, chiefly because of the great waves of migration during the latter decades of the nineteenth century. A leading example was New York, where nearly five out of every six of the city's 1.5 million residents in 1891 lived in tenements. Social reformers of the period described these buildings as crowded, with

169

dark hallways and filthy cellars, and with inadequate cooking and bathroom facilities. In neighborhoods populated by poor immigrants, there was a tremendous amount of crime, gambling, gang violence, and prostitution.

Boston Sand Garden—A Beginning

Within the poor working-class districts, there were few safe places where children might play. The first such facility—and the one which is generally regarded as a landmark in the development of the recreation movement in the United States—was the Boston Sand Garden, established in 1885. A group of public-spirited citizens had a pile of sand placed in the rear of the Parmenter Street Chapel, in a working-class district. Young children of the neighborhood came to play in the sand with wooden shovels. Supervision was voluntary at first, but by 1887 when ten such centers were opened, women were employed to supervise the children. Two years later, the city of Boston began to contribute funds to support the sand gardens. So it was that citizens, on a voluntary basis, began to provide play opportunities for young children.

New York's First Playgrounds

In the country's largest city, Walter Vrooman, founder of the New York Society for Parks and Playgrounds, brought to the attention of the public that in 1890, there were three hundred and fifty thousand children without a single public playground they could call their own. Although the city now had almost six thousand acres of parkland, none of it was set aside for children.

Some reformers vehemently demanded parks and playgrounds as an escape from crowded, filthy tenement houses. One leading physician wrote, "Foul air prompts to vice and oxygen to virtue, as surely as the sunlight paints the flowers of our gardens." Speaking of slum children, he said,

> The varied opportunities of a park would educate him and his family in the enjoyment of open-air pleasures. Deprived of these, he and his are educated into the ways of disease and vice by the character of their surroundings.[31]

Other civic leaders pointed out that children whose parents worked lacked supervision and were permitted to grow up subject to varied temptations. Vrooman wrote that such children

> are driven from their crowded homes in the morning . . . are chased from the streets by the police when they attempt to play, and beaten with the broom handle of the janitor's wife when found in the hallway, or on the stairs. No wonder they learn to chew and smoke tobacco before they can read, and take a fiendish delight in breaking windows, in petty thievery, and in gambling their pennies.[32]

One businessman told Vrooman how his company had twice replaced all the windows in its buildings up to the fifth floor, only to have them broken again by neighborhood youth. He ended by saying, "We must give them a playground or throw them in the river."

Gradually, the pressure mounted. Two small model playgrounds were established in poor areas of the city in 1889 and 1891 by the newly formed New York

Society for Parks and Playgrounds, with support from private donors. A second new organization, the Outdoor Recreation League, opened a more ambitious playground called Seward Park, in June, 1893. League members raised substantial sums to pay for maintenance and leadership, and also for costs that might accrue to the city through accident damage suits, which had been a major fear of civic officials; however, the city government itself also assumed some of the financial responsibility for Seward Park.

In the years that followed, New York moved rapidly to develop a network of playgrounds that were administered and paid for completely by the city. All schools constructed after this time were required to have open-air playgrounds. In July, 1897, the first recreation piers were opened and became an immediate success; by 1902 there were seven such piers jutting out into the rivers surrounding Manhattan Island, providing new places to play and bathe.

Expansion of Playgrounds and Parks

By 1900, some fourteen cities had made provisions for supervised play facilities, and the playground movement was under full steam. Among the leading cities were Boston, Providence, Philadelphia, Pittsburgh, Baltimore, Chicago, Milwaukee, Cleveland, Denver, and Minneapolis. In each case, private initiative and financial support were prominent factors in getting the first playgrounds built and in convincing city governments to accept responsibility for providing play areas.

At the same time, municipal parks became increasingly well established throughout the United States. In addition to the urban parks mentioned earlier, the first metropolitan park system was established in Boston in 1892 and the first county park system in Essex County, New Jersey in 1895. In the West, San Francisco and Sacramento, California and Salt Lake City, Utah were among the first to incorporate large open spaces in town planning before 1900. The New England Association of Park Superintendents, predecessor of the American Institute of Park Executives, was established in 1898 to bring together park superintendents and promote their professional concerns.

Thus in the last decade of the nineteenth century, the playground and municipal park movements were receiving enthusiastic support. In time, these merged into a single recreation movement, concerned not only with the play needs of children, but leisure programs for all age groups.

To make this growth possible, however, a fuller rationale for the need for public recreation had to be developed. This was provided by a number of major pioneers of the public recreation movement—men like Clark Hetherington, Joseph Lee, and Luther Halsey Gulick—as well as by the theories of psychologists and educators regarding the value of play in human growth and development. This substantiation and the growth of the movement itself during the twentieth century are described in Chapter 8.

Chapter Seven

1. Thomas Woody, "Leisure in the Light of History," *Annals of the American Academy of Political and Social Science,* September 1957, pp. 5–6.

2. Richard B. Morris, *Government and Labor in Early America* (New York: Columbia Univ. Pr., 1947), pp. 4–6.

3. Foster Rhea Dulles, *A History of Recreation: America Learns to Play* (New York: Appleton-Century-Crofts, 1965), p. 5.

4. Jane Carson, *Colonial Virginians at Play* (Charlottesville: Univ. Pr. of Virginia, 1965), p. 53.

5. Quoted in Dulles, *History of Recreation,* p. 35.

6. Alice Morse Earle, *Customs and Fashions in Old New England* (Rutland, Vermont: Charles E. Tuttle, 1893, 1975), p. 239.

7. James Truslow Adams, *Provincial Society,* 1690-1763 (New York: Macmillan, 1927), p. 159.

8. Earle, *Customs and Fashions,* p. 166.

9. Charles McL. Andrews, *Colonial Folkways* (New Haven, Connecticut: Yale University Press, 1919), p. 104.

10. Earle, *Customs and Fashions,* p. 237.

11. Quoted in Dulles, *History of Recreation,* p. 44.

12. *The Doctrines and Discipline of the Methodist Episcopal Church in America* (Philadelphia: Parry Hall, 1792), p. 68.

13. Dulles, *History of Recreation,* p. 66.

14. Thomas Holme, quoted in Charles E. Doell and Charles B. Fitzgerald, *A Brief History of Parks and Recreation in the United States* (Chicago: The Athletic Institute, 1954), p. 24.

15. Andrews, *Colonial Folkways,* p. 113.

16. Ibid., p. 114.

17. Robert Dubin, "Industrial Workers' Worlds: A Study of the Central Life Interests of Industrial Workers," in *Work and Leisure: A Contemporary Social Problem,* Erwin O. Smigel, ed., (New Haven, Conn.: College and University Press, 1963), p. 54.

18. Guy Lewis, "The Muscular Christianity Movement," *Journal of Health, Physical Education and Recreation,* May 1966, p. 28.

19. Thomas Carlyle, *Past and Present* (Boston: Charles C. Little, 1843), Books 2 and 3.

20. John Ruskin, *Lectures in Art: The Relationship of Arts to Morals* (New York: Wiley, 1870) and "Sesame and Lilies," in *The Works of John Ruskin* (New York: Alden, 1885).

21. Dulles, *History of Recreation,* pp. 98–99.

22. Quoted in Lewis, "Muscular Christianity," p. 28.

23. P. C. McIntosh, *Sport in Society* (London: C.A. Watts, 1963), p. 65.

24. Quoted in McIntosh, *Sport in Society,* p. 77.

25. Dulles, *History of Recreation,* p. 203.

26. Joffre Dumazedier, *Toward a Society of Leisure* (New York: Free Press, 1967), p. 38.

27. C. Frank Brockman, *Recreational Use of Wild Lands* (New York: McGraw-Hill, 1959), pp. 67–70.

28. Philip O. Foss, *Recreation,* in Frank E. Smith, ed., *Conservation in the United States: A Documentary History* (New York: Chelsea House, 1971), p. 255.

29. Quoted in Henry Hope Reed and Sophia Duckworth, *Central Park: A History and a Guide* (New York: Clarkson N. Potter, 1967), p. 3.

30. Jane Addams, *The Playground,* March 1910, p. 24.

31. Thomas E. Will, "Public Parks and Playgrounds: A Symposium," *The Arena,* July 1894, pp. 276–77.

32. Walter Vrooman, "Playgrounds for Children," *The Arena,* July 1894, p. 286.

8

THE RECREATION AND PARKS MOVEMENT DURING THE TWENTIETH CENTURY

This chapter describes the development of recreation and parks as a form of municipal governmental service in the United States and Canada and the major trends and social influences which affected this movement during the twentieth century.

Growth of Public Recreation and Park Agencies

While no consistent effort was made to record the growth of municipal recreation and parks in the United States during the early decades of the century, some statistics are available which give a picture of its expansion. For example, in 1900 only 12 cities were reported to be providing for recreation through public funds. By 1906 there were 41, and by 1920, 465.

Between 1910 and 1920 the concept that city governments should assume responsibility for recreation programs and services became widely accepted. During the 1920s there was a considerable expansion of local facilities for recreation, including the use of school buildings. More and more states passed laws enabling local government to operate recreation programs, and between 1925 and 1935, the number of municipal recreation buildings quadrupled.

Park departments also expanded rapidly in the United States during this time. From 1892 to 1902, the number of cities possessing parks grew from 100 to 800, and by 1926, the figure was 1,680. Butler comments that during the 1920's

> the number and variety of recreation facilities increased by leaps and bounds. Playgrounds, golf courses, swimming pools, bathing beaches, picnic areas, winter sports facilities, and game fields were constructed in

173

unprecedented numbers. Municipal park acreage expanded during the latter half of the decade more than in any other period of equal length.[1]

Municipalities were discovering new ways of adding parks. Many acquired areas outside their city limits, while others required that new real estate subdivision plans include the dedication of space for recreation. Some cities acquired major park properties through gifts. The pattern that began to develop was to build a network of small, intensively used playgrounds throughout cities, particularly in neighborhoods of working-class families, and to create larger parks in outlying areas of the cities.

Chicago: A Leading Example

Of the major cities that initiated park systems at this early stage, Chicago was outstanding. It was one of the first cities to develop a network of neighborhood recreation parks, passing a $5 million bond issue in 1903 to acquire and develop recreation parks (ranging in size from 7 to 300 acres) in crowded neighborhoods in the southern part of the city. Ten of these parks, combining excellent outdoor sports facilities with field houses that included gymnasiums, clubrooms, shower and locker rooms, and branches of the public library, were opened in 1905. They set a new standard for American cities, particularly because the first convention sponsored by the new Playground Association of America was held in Chicago in 1907. President Theodore Roosevelt called the creation of the South Park playgrounds and centers "the most notable civic achievement of any American city," and Luther Gulick commented that

> Chicago, within a brief two-year period, set aside over $10 million for small parks and playgrounds, and since that time millions have been spent in developing, administering and enlarging the system. . . . All this is paid for by the city, not by private philanthropy. . . . The places have become recreation centers in the most promising sense. It is said that aldermen in Chicago lose all popularity with their constituents unless they secure playgrounds in their wards.[2]

Development of the Recreation Movement

An early historian of the recreation movement, Clarence Rainwater, outlined nine important transitions in the playground movement during this early period: (1) from provision for small children to services for all age groups, (2) from operation of facilities only during the summer to operation throughout the year, (3) from outdoor equipment and activities only to those which could be enjoyed year-round, (4) from an emphasis on serving only congested urban districts to serving both urban and rural communities, (5) from philanthropic support to public support and control, (6) from free play and casually organized events to directed play with leadership and carefully scheduled programs, (7) from a simple to a complex range of activities, including manual, physical, aesthetic, social, and civic projects, (8) from the provision of facilities to the definition of standards for the use of leisure time, and (9) from the satisfaction of individual interests to meeting group and community needs.[3]

174

As the field developed during the first three decades of the twentieth century, several persons emerged as spokesmen for play and recreation.

Joseph Lee

Perhaps the most influential pioneer of the recreation movement, Joseph Lee was a lawyer and philanthropist who came from a wealthy New England family. Born in 1862, he took part in a survey of play opportunities conducted by the Family Welfare Society of Boston in 1882. Shocked to see boys arrested for playing in the streets, he organized a playground for them in an open lot, which he helped to supervise. In 1898, Lee helped to create a model playground on Columbus Avenue in Boston that included a play area for small children, a boys' section, a sport field, and individual gardens.

Lee's influence expanded; he was in great demand as a speaker and writer on playgrounds and served as vice-president for public recreation of the American Civic Association. President of the Playground Association of America for 27 years, he was also president and leading lecturer of the National Recreation School, a one-year program for carefully selected college graduates, and in many other ways contributed to the developing playground and recreation movement.

Lee's view of play was idealistic and purposeful. In *Play in Education,* he outlined a set of major play instincts which he believed all children shared, and which governed the specific nature of play activities. He believed that play forms had to be taught, and required capable leadership. Lee did not make a sharp distinction between work and play, but saw them as closely related expressions of the impulse to achieve, to explore, to excel, to master. "True work is the highest form of play; but it is always the play element in work that is the most important."[4] Lee stressed that play was not carried on in pursuit of pleasure; indeed, in somewhat Puritanical fashion, he condemned such a motive:

> Pleasure results from play . . . but it is not the play motive. It is extraneous, a by-product; it does not in any way account for the play attitude or the direction of the play instincts. In play, the motive of the act is the doing of it. . . . The man who goes out to have a good time is usually disappointed. The one who goes out to play the game, and does play it for all it is worth, is never wholly so.[5]

Lee stressed that play might involve pain, sacrifice, and fatigue, and for these reasons, it helped to "drill" the child in the service of ideals and a dedicated way of life. His moralistic view of play was illustrated in his reference to recreation as a means of combatting "excessive youth preoccupation with sex."

Among other concepts Lee strongly promoted was that of the important role of the neighborhood unit in community life; he saw this as a survival from the "ancestral heritage" of village life and urged that community activities such as sports, festivals, and the arts become the responsibility of the neighborhood. Lee saw play as an important factor in reducing social pathology, not by specifically preventing juvenile delinquency, but by generally contributing to positive values.

Lee constantly fought for recognition of the need to use leisure constructively in modern society.

175

The problem of civilization is the problem of leisure. For those to whom leisure is denied, to whom loss of expression in industry is not made up in art of play, civilization is of doubtful benefit. [6]

Luther Halsey Gulick

Another leading figure in the recreation movement was Luther Halsey Gulick. A physician by training, he developed a special interest in physical education and recreation; he also had a strong religious orientation, as did many early play leaders. Beginning in 1887, Dr. Gulick headed the first summer school of "special training for gymnasium instructors" at the School for Christian Workers (now Springfield College) in Massachusetts. He was extremely active in the YMCAs in Canada and the United States, was first president of the Camp Fire Girls, and was instrumental in the establishment of the Playground Association of America in 1906. Gulick lectured extensively on the significance of play and recreation and taught a course in the psychology of play as early as 1899. He vigorously promoted expanded recreation programs for girls and women.

Like Lee, Gulick was profoundly concerned with the nature of play, recreation, and work. He distinguished play from recreation; play was an attitude or motivation for involvement, while recreation was important for its relaxing and energy-restoring functions. He defined play as "doing that which we want to do, without reference primarily to any ulterior end, but simply for the joy of the process." But, he went on to say, play is not less serious than work:

> The boy who is playing football with intensity needs recreation as much as does the inventor who is working intensely at his invention. Play can be more exhausting than work, because one can play much harder than one can work. No one would dream of pushing a boy in school as hard as he pushes himself in a football game. If there is any difference of intensity between play and work, the difference is in favor of play. Play is the result of desire; for that reason it is often carried on with more vigor than work.[7]

Gulick described recreation as different in character; for the adult, it meant relaxation, in sharp contrast to the child's outpouring of energy in play. He accepted the view that recreation's primary value was rest or relaxation to restore adults for further work; play, on the other hand, was more dynamic, demanding, and creative, and covered a wider range of involvements.

Gulick also pressed forcefully for recognition of the important role of recreation and leisure in contemporary life. He believed that the bulk of modern crime, as well as antisocial or "degenerative" behavior throughout all history, resulted from "wrong play and recreation." He urged that recreation be recognized as a nationwide concern, pointing out that huge sums of money were spent each year on commercially sponsored activities, when what was needed was fuller support of community-sponsored programs.

Attitudes of Educators toward Play

Gradually, a climate developed in American education which regarded play as a significant element in learning. A number of psychologists, including Carl Seashore,

William McDougall and John Watson, stressed the importance of play in the process of social development. Watson wrote:

> In short, play is the principal instrument of growth. It is safe to conclude that, without play, there would be no normal adult cognitive life; without play, no healthful development of affective life; without play, no full development of the power of the will.[8]

John Dewey, the leading American philosopher of the early twentieth century, was immensely influential in the development of modern educational practices. His view of education was that it was most effective when based on activity that challenged all one's faculties, physical, creative, and intellectual; one learned by doing. Dewey believed that the most meaningful learning activity was based on freedom of choice, deliberate and self-planned (rather than random or dictated) involvement, and activity which involved mental initiative and intellectual self-reliance.

Dewey saw work and play as closely related, highly motivated, and creative activities:

> Play and work cannot . . . be distinguished from one another according to the presence or absence of direct interest in what one is doing. A child engaged in making something with tools, say, a boat, may be just as immediately interested in what he is doing as if he were sailing the boat. He is not doing what he does for the mere sake of an external result—the boat—nor for the mere sake of sailing it later . . . his interest is free. He has a play-motive; his activity is essentially artistic in principle. What differentiates it from more spontaneous play is an *intellectual* quality.[9]

Dewey held that children should be introduced through play to the idea and the experience of more formal work and that they should move gradually from projects that yield immediate satisfaction to those that offer deferred satisfactions and require more careful planning and analysis. He made his support of play clear in the following passage:

> The idea that the need [for play] can be suppressed, is absolutely fallacious, and the Puritan tradition which disallows the need has entailed an enormous crop of evils. If education does not afford opportunity for wholesome recreation . . . the suppressed instincts find all sorts of illicit outlets. . . . Education has no more serious responsibility than making adequate provision for enjoyment of recreative leisure; not only for the fact of immediate health but still more, if possible, for the fact of its lasting effect upon habits of mind.[10]

Thus, throughout the first three decades of the twentieth century, a number of educators, psychologists and philosophers developed a body of theory and practice that gave strong support to the need for play both in education and as a form of community service. As a consequence, public opinion encouraged the expansion of organized playground and public recreation programs in American communities.

The play movement gradually became thought of as the "recreation movement," and began to embrace many other agencies and forms of service rather than simply playgrounds for children. A close working relationship with public school systems developed, and the movement spread from large cities to suburban and small-town settings. The construction of recreation facilities became a government function, with substantial support from tax funds. Whereas originally playgrounds were the major type of facility, recreation centers and other types of facilities were developed. Leadership shifted from volunteer or part-time supervisors to full-time, paid leaders and administrators, who came to regard themselves as specialists within a unique field of public service.

Social Factors Influencing the Recreation Movement

During the first several decades of the twentieth century, several major social factors influenced the shape of the recreation movement in the United States.

1. *Modern Science and Technology.* Major developments in industrial technology and production made life increasingly easy for working people. The amount of manual labor was reduced, as were working hours. Holidays, vacations, automatic retirement policies, and longer life spans as a result of increased medical knowledge all contributed to improved conditions.

2. *Continued Urbanization.* As increased numbers of people moved from rural to urban settings or immigrated to the cities, and as life patterns were altered by an industrial economy, the need for publicly sponsored recreation facilities, programs, and leadership grew more severe.

3. *Changing Nature of Work.* As work became increasingly specialized and mechanical in assembly-line factories, it lost personal meaning for many employees. Agreement was widespread that recreation and leisure could fulfill the need for personal satisfaction in industrial society.

4. *New Concepts of Recreation.* The religious objections to play that had persisted throughout the nineteenth century in some sections of the country declined still further. Many churches accepted increasing responsibility for their congregations' leisure and recreation.

5. *Growth of Transportation.* Technology and increased affluence made it possible for people to travel widely in their leisure. Public transit lines, the growing popularity of automobiles, and the expansion of good roads meant that Americans could travel on vacations or visit nightclubs, summer resorts, baseball stadiums and many other forms of entertainment which became popular during the 1920s.

6. *Role of the Schools.* Especially during the 1920s and 1930s, America's public schools provided many forms of community education. They sponsored youth and adult recreation programs and cooperated with other agencies by providing buildings or other needed physical facilities for play. In addition, schools accepted— nominally at least—the responsibility of "educating for leisure."

7. *Expansion of Commercial Recreation Opportunity.* For the first time, recreation became a major industry in its own right. During the 1920s, the growth of radio and motion pictures, bowling alleys, swimming pools, sports leagues and stadiums, and other commercially promoted pastimes were part of the total expansion of play as an important element in the economy.

8. *Need for Conservation.* Public-spirited citizens supported legislation and government programs to protect the natural environment by maintaining open spaces and setting aside forest preserves and sanctuaries in and around densely populated urban areas.

The Rationale for Organized Recreation

The justification for expanded municipal recreation programs formulated during the first three decades of the twentieth century was largely that recreation was necessary both to enrich the quality of life, and to prevent social pathology. President Herbert Hoover, addressing a White House Conference on Child Health and Protection in Washington in 1930 summed up this rationale:

> In the last half century we have herded 50 million more human beings into towns and cities where the whole setting is new to the race. . . . Perhaps the widest range of difficulties with which we are dealing in the betterment of children grows out of this crowding into cities. Problems of sanitation and public health loom in every direction. Delinquency increases with congestion. Overcrowding produces disease and contagion. The child's natural play space is taken from him. . . . Architectural wizardry and artistic skills are transforming cities into wonderlands of beauty, but we must also preserve in them for our children the yet more beautiful art of living.[11]

To some degree, the support for public recreation was based on the fear that without public programs and facilities adult leisure would be used unwisely. Many industrial leaders and civic officials believed that the growth of leisure for the working classes represented a dangerous trend; when unemployment increased they expressed concern about what idle men would do with their time. Similarly, when the eight-hour workday laws first came under discussion, temperance societies prepared for increased drunkenness, and social reformers held international conferences on the worker's spare time and ways to use it constructively.

The major concern, however, was for children and youth in the large cities and their need for healthful and safe places to play. Indeed, much "juvenile delinquency" arose from children being arrested for playing on city streets. Gulick wrote:

> Playing baseball on the streets of New York is forbidden by a city ordinance. Yet every day during the spring a large proportion of the boys brought before the judge of Children's Court are there for the crime of playing ball. The black-robed judge questions them from behind a high desk; a big policeman stands near to give testimony. The boys are in the position of lawbreakers, yet most of them are decent, respectable boys, frequently very young and much frightened.[12]

The lack of suitable play opportunities as a cause of juvenile crime was noted by many authorities during this period. One English writer commented that when left to the resources of the street, boys inevitably got into trouble, to be "birched in a police court" and to stand a "lively chance of becoming a criminal."

The belief that the best solution to juvenile delinquency was to provide play facilities for city children was widely shared by educators and law enforcement officials. A Philadelphia judge commented:

> The public playground is the greatest deterrent of juvenile delinquency and lawlessness among children. It stands for body and character

179

building, and produces better children, homes, morals and citizens. On the score of public economy alone, the playground is a necessity.[13]

Some authorities during this period reported reduced rates of juvenile delinquency in slum areas where playgrounds had been established. A probation officer of the juvenile court in Milwaukee described "a very noticeable dropping off of boys coming before the court" and a disappearance of "dangerous gangs," concluding that playgrounds and social centers were "saviors" for American youth. Typically, the judge of the juvenile department of the Orange County Court in Anaheim, California, noted that after

> the opening of supervised playgrounds in the public park in the summer of 1924, juvenile delinquency decreased. During the first six months of 1925, it was 70 percent less than for the same period in 1924.[14]

Although later studies were to question the validity of such statements, little doubt was expressed about the delinquency prevention value of recreation at this time. A closely related concern was that of safety. One survey by a major insurance company in 1930 revealed that in a single year there were 65,811 accidents to children playing in city streets, of which 2,310 were fatal. Most of these accidents occurred near the child's home; it was concluded that while better safety education and greater care by both children and motorists would be helpful, the better solution was adequate play spaces and leadership.

Commercial Amusements

In city after city around the country, there was also considerable concern about the growth of commercial amusements, which had become a lucrative business enterprise. Counts pointed out that prior to the rise of industrial civilization, recreation had been almost completely a function of the family and the neighborhood. As cities grew, however, neighborhoods changed and families lost their self-sufficiency.

> Business enterprise was quick to grasp the opportunity for material gain presented by the breakdown. . . . Commercial recreation has provided for the American people a bewildering variety of cheap forms of amusement; dance halls, houses of prostitution, speakeasies, pool and billiard rooms, vaudeville performances, burlesque shows, amusement parks, and many others. . . . And as the appetites of the population became jaded, thrill was added to thrill and sensation to sensation. That the consequent program of recreation was unsuited to the deeper cultural and spiritual needs of the people became clearly apparent.[15]

In such major cities as Milwaukee, Detroit, Kansas City, and San Francisco, extensive recreation surveys scrutinized the nature of commercial amusements, the extent and kind of their patronage, and their character. A survey of Detroit found 297 poolrooms, 16 billiard rooms, 36 bowling alleys, and 5 shooting galleries, the majority of which catered to boys and young men; many served liquor, allowed gambling, and were hangouts for criminals.

There was much concern about movies and stage performances, with frequent charges that they were immoral and led to the sexual "corruption" of youth. A study of vice in Philadelphia found that many places of entertainment were closely linked to the underworld:

> Many public dance halls, moving picture shows, and other amusement centers are breeding-places of vice—the rendezvous of men who entrap girls and of girls who solicit men. . . . The proprietors of these places are known to abet these vicious practices and, in many cases, to derive large revenue from them.[16]

A high percentage of privately operated dance halls had attached saloons which were freely patronized by young girls. Dancing seemed to be only a secondary consideration. Pickups occurred regularly, often of young girls who had come to cities from farms and small towns with a presumed degree of innocence; so-called "white slavers" plied their trade with little interference. Dance halls were often attached to disreputable rooming houses. Reformers, social workers, educators, and religious leaders shared the conviction that commercial recreation was directed to the lowest possible level and represented a degradation rather than an enhancement of the human spirit.

The same studies that examined commercial amusements also surveyed the socially approved forms of recreation. They found that in many large cities the schools were closed in the evenings and throughout the summer, that libraries closed at night and on weekends, that churches closed for the summer, and that publicly provided forms of recreation were at a minimum. Jane Addams concluded that the city had "turned over the provision for public recreation to the most evil-minded and the most unscrupulous members of the community."[17]

Gradually, pressure mounted for more effective controls of places of public amusement. In city after city, permits were required for operating dance halls, pool parlors, bowling alleys, and places for sale of liquor. The admission of minors, the prevention of gambling, the enforcement of closing hours, and the regulations concerning proper ventilation and sanitation were all more rigidly specified and enforced. Ultimately, with stronger regulation, the concern about commercial amusement and its effect on youth declined.

Fear of "Spectatoritis"

A new fear emerged that Americans were moving away from traditional, active ways of using their leisure to pursuits in which they were passive spectators. Edwards commented that instead of the "wholesome love of play," Americans now had a love of being "played upon." It had become wholly outdated to make one's "own fun."

> The professional entertainer holds sway in every field from which he is not rigidly excluded, every field in which the rights of the amateur are not vigorously asserted. . . . A social disease has been spreading broadcast among us. . . . The disease of *spectatoritis* is abroad in the land.[18]

Many shared Edwards' view of the "fan," whom he described as a "flabby creature symbolic of a multitude, a parasite upon the play of others, the least athletic of all men, never playing himself at anything, a spectacle hunter, not a sportsman." There was fear that with growing professionalism, America was moving toward a jaded sensationalism that would ultimately lead to the "Roman amphitheater and the Spanish bull-fight."

In the total effort to enrich leisure as a creative source of personal and social enrichment, several forces played a key part. These included: (1) the development of settlement houses and community centers; (2) the establishment of voluntary organizations which provided leisure services; (3) the founding of the Playground Association of America; and (4) the acceptance by the American educational system of the responsibility for educating for leisure and providing organized recreation services.

Settlement Houses and Community Centers

From the very beginning, the directors of the settlement houses and community centers that were established in larger cities during the 1880s and 1890s were vitally interested in play and recreation. Jane Addams, one of the pioneers in this field, was deeply concerned with the need to provide varied forms of play in urban slums, and spoke widely on the theme of "recreation and social morality." She was responsible for opening the first independent playground in Chicago, in a vacant lot adjoining Hull House, equipping it with swings, seesaws, slides, and sand bins. At Hull House, music, dance and drama were all part of the total program. The settlement house movement expanded rapidly during the first decades of the twentieth century. Well into the 1930s, these agencies regarded the provision of recreation services as one of their primary functions.

Growth of Voluntary Organizations

A closely related phenomenon was the growth of youth-serving organizations providing extensive recreation programs. Many of these agencies were nationally organized movements or federations; others were established on an independent, local basis. The National Association of Boys' Clubs was founded in 1906, the Boy Scouts and the Camp Fire Girls in 1910, and the Girl Scouts in 1912. Major civic clubs and community service groups such as the Rotary Club, Kiwanis, and the Lions Club were also founded between 1910 and 1917.

By the end of the 1920s, these organizations had become widely established in American life and were serving substantial numbers of young people. One of every seven boys in the appropriate age group in the United States was a Scout. The YMCA and YWCA had over 1.5 million members in 1926. Although these and many similar organizations were meeting important recreational and social needs of American youth and adults, it was apparent that a strong national voice was needed to provide leadership to the growing recreation movement in America.

Playground Association of America

In the early 1900s, a number of leading recreation directors called for a major conference to promote public awareness and effective practices in the field of leisure services. Under the leadership of Luther Halsey Gulick, representatives of park, recreation, and school boards throughout the United States met in Washington, D.C. in April, 1906. Unanimously agreed upon the need for a national organization, the conference members drew up a constitution and selected Gulick as the first president of the Playground Association of America. The organization had President Roosevelt's strong support.

The Playground Association was intended to develop informational and promotional services to assist people of all ages in using leisure time constructively. With assistance from the Russell Sage Foundation, the organization began to publish *The Playground,* a monthly magazine. Field workers traveled from city to city, meeting with public officials and citizens' groups and helping in the development of playgrounds and recreation programs. In order to promote professional training, the association developed *The Normal Course in Play,* a curriculum plan of courses on play leadership on several levels. In keeping with its broadening emphasis, the organization changed its name in 1911 to the Playground and Recreation Association of America, and in 1926, to the National Recreation Association.

Role of the Schools

As indicated earlier, school boards in a number of large cities had begun to operate after school and vacation play programs as early as the 1890s. Playground programs were initiated in Rochester, New York in 1907, Milwaukee, Wisconsin in 1911, and Los Angeles, California in 1914. These pioneering efforts were strongly supported by the National Education Association, which recommended that public school buildings be used for community recreation and social activities. The report of the fiftieth annual meeting of the NEA in 1912 included a number of major presentations concerned with the school's role in leisure programming. For example, one statement pointed out that

> much of the millions of dollars invested in our school systems is wasted owing to the fact that, outside of school, children form wrong habits due to unwholesome play conditions, and develop traits of character which make much of their school training useless. . . . [Today] many communities are trying to find out and to plan systematically for their recreational needs.[19]

In addition to playgrounds, other facilities of schools that could be useful for recreational purposes were assembly rooms and gymnasiums, swimming pools, music and arts rooms, and outdoor areas for sports and gardening. Increasingly, these were used for play activities. Education for the "worthy use of leisure" became one of the major objectives of modern education, as stated in the famous bulletin, "Cardinal Principles of Secondary Education," issued by the Commission on the Reorganization of Secondary School Education of the National Education Association:

> Aside from the immediate discharge of these specific duties [home membership, vocation, and citizenship], every individual should have a margin of time for the cultivation of personal and social interests. This leisure, if worthily used, will recreate his powers and enlarge and enrich

life, thereby making him better able to meet his responsibilities. The unworthy use of leisure impairs health, disrupts home life, lessens vocational efficiency and destroys civic-mindedness. . . . In view of these considerations, education for the worthy use of leisure is of increasing importance as an objective.[20]

Thousands of school systems between 1910 and 1930 established extensive programs of extracurricular activities, particularly in the areas of sports, publications, hobbies, social- and academic-related subject fields. The number of such programs almost tripled in secondary schools during this period. In many other school systems, actual programs of community recreation for all age groups were sponsored, or facilities made available to other public community agencies.

World War I

The nation's rapid mobilization during World War I revealed that communities adjacent to army and navy stations and training camps needed more adequate programs of recreation. The Council of National Defense and the War Department Commission on Training Camp Activities asked the Playground and Recreation Association to assist in the creation of a national organization to provide special wartime community recreation programs. The association quickly established the War Camp Community Service, which utilized the recreation resources of several hundred communities near military camps, providing wholesome recreation activities both for military personnel and civilians.

After the war, community recreation programs expanded. Butler writes:

> The people who saw during the war what community singing, pageants, athletic meets, and neighborhood parties could mean in community life insisted that means be devised for continuing them. . . . Social, civic, and religious agencies had acquired common interest in community recreation and a sense of responsibility for providing it.[21]

A new agency, Community Service, Incorporated, was established in 1919 to replace the War Camp Community Service, for the purpose of developing an expanded peacetime community recreation effort. Many community memorial buildings in honor of the war dead were established by voluntary efforts; community centers, particularly for youth, were set in motion.

Growth of Public Recreation during the 1920s

The decade following World War I was marked by increased leisure, affluence, and public involvement in recreational activities of all types. Established during this period were the National Park Service in 1916, which emphasized Federal support of outdoor recreation, the National Conference on State Parks in 1922, and the

American Association of Zoological Parks and Aquariums in 1924. Gradually, park administrators began to give active recreation a higher priority in park design and operation.

This trend was promoted by a National Conference on Outdoor Recreation, called by President Calvin Coolidge in May, 1924, and attended by several hundred representatives of 128 national organizations. One of their recommendations was that the American Institute of Park Executives and the Playground and Recreation Association jointly create a handbook on parks; in response, L. H. Weir wrote the two-volume *Manual on Parks*. In 1926, the National Recreation School for graduate training in recreation was established. It continued until 1935, under the sponsorship of the National Recreation Association, graduating a total of three hundred students, many of whom became leading administrators in cities throughout the United States.

By the end of the 1920s, a solid base had been provided for organized park and recreation services. The Federal government had become involved in the provision of outdoor recreation, and states had begun to expand their park systems sharply. There was now full awareness that varied recreation opportunities were needed for all ages and social classes. In 1928, May and Petgen wrote:

> Underlying the whole recreation movement, commercial and noncommercial, is the enormous productivity of American industry which has reduced the average work day and yielded a wage that allows the working man increased spending power for the good things of life. In other words the industrial revolution has democratized recreation in the United States. Working people own not only home but cars, radios, pianos and victrolas, and have a surplus of leisure and energy with which to enjoy these facilities. . . .

> The trend in the United States is to public control and direction of recreation. . . . The organized recreation movement has taken up good activities formerly enjoyed only by the rich and made them available to the general public through tax-supported recreation systems.[22]

The Depression of the 1930s

The Great Depression of the 1930s resulted in mass unemployment and involuntary idleness for American workers. By the end of 1932, an estimated 15 million people, nearly one-third of the labor force, were unemployed.

Municipal recreation departments found themselves in a difficult position. Although attendance in park and recreation programs mounted considerably, tax revenues declined and it became necessary to cut budgets sharply. Many cities, unable to pay their employees, issued scrip; others laid off thousands of workers. In order to meet the increased demand for recreation by unemployed adults or young people who had little money to spend on commercial amusements, recreation administrators attempted to reduce capital development, close down the least used facilities, and rely heavily on the use of volunteers. An additional problem was that the psychological state of those who were unemployed impaired their enjoyment of leisure:

Although many unemployed citizens used public recreation facilities more than before, the work ethic was still far from dead, even among the jobless. Given their enforced idleness, such people could hardly be expected to approach free time with the same healthy attitude as those regularly employed.[23]

In their efforts to meet this challenge, municipal recreation and park authorities received tremendous assistance from the Federal government.

Federal Recreation Projects

The Federal government soon instituted a number of emergency work programs related to recreation. Knapp points out that the Federal Emergency Relief Administration, established early in 1933, financed construction of recreation facilities such as parks and swimming pools and hired recreation leaders from relief rolls. A second agency, the Civil Works Administration, was given the task of finding jobs for four million people in thirty days! Among other tasks, this agency built or improved thirty-five hundred playgrounds and athletic fields in a few months.

Throughout the 1930s, such efforts continued. At one time, about forty-nine thousand persons were employed by the Recreation Division of the Works Progress Administration, and as late as 1940, sixty thousand out-of-school youth between the ages of eighteen and twenty-four were employed in National Youth Administration projects providing leisure services. The Works Progress Administration provided leadership for varied recreation activities in local communities, including direct operation of fifteen thousand community centers, and assistance to eight thousand more. Supervision was provided for parks, playgrounds, athletic fields, beaches, and swimming pools. Community social events were organized, and classes formed in dance, crafts, drama, music, and social studies. Knapp writes:

> Recreation under WPA auspices was . . . immensely popular at the local level. In the first year operations similar to normal community recreation functioned not only in many of the 1,159 cities with permanent public recreation programs but in 1,045 additional towns where the WPA provided the only organized recreation.[24]

By 1939, an estimated five million people, excluding spectators, were participating in the programs of the WPA's Recreational Division each week. Many of the employees of this program later found permanent employment in local recreation agencies.

Another major emphasis was on cultural programs. The Federal Art Project operated many community art centers, with a total attendance of 2.5 million in a single year. The Federal Music Project, which sponsored thousands of musical performances, had over a hundred Federal symphony and concert orchestras, and over one hundred and sixty thousand in its classes. The Federal Theater Project, with some one hundred companies operating in twenty states, gave a monthly average of twenty-eight hundred performances, reaching millions of Americans who had not previously been exposed to the creative arts. Altogether, the Federal arts programs gave employment to over thirty thousand writers, artists, musicians, dancers, actors, and directors.

Both the National Youth Administration and the Civilian Conservation Corps carried out numerous work projects involving the construction of recreational facilities. During the five years from 1932 to 1937, the Federal government spent an estimated $1.5 billion developing camps, buildings, picnic grounds, trails, swimming pools, and other facilities. The Civilian Conservation Corps helped to establish state park systems in a number of states that had no organized park programs before 1933. A vast quantity of work was done in national and state forests, much of it with recreational value. National Youth Administration workers constructed many buildings that had recreational uses, such as libraries, museums and art galleries.

According to Knapp, WPA projects spanned the entire nation, and built or improved 12,700 playgrounds, 8,500 gymnasiums or recreation buildings, 750 swimming pools, 1,000 ice skating rinks, and 64 ski jumps.[25]

Special Programs for Youth

In the large cities of the nation, "cellar clubs" emerged. These were youth-organized social and recreational groups, which sprang up spontaneously, often based on ethnic and racial ties. The clubs met in vacant stores, cellars, or building lofts, where young people were free of adult supervision and interference. The memberships of cellar clubs were between twenty and one hundred boys and young men, usually ranging in age from about sixteen to well past twenty-five. In New York City alone, there were six thousand such clubs by 1940.

The Federal government was much concerned with this trend. In large cities, federations of clubs were formed which established rules for behavior and operation. Settlement houses worked with club members, and the Youth Service Division of the WPA assigned many youth leaders to work with unaffiliated cellar clubs, seeking to end much of the petty racketeering and other forms of delinquency of club members and to help them achieve the status of youth agencies. Youth leaders employed by the WPA in this program were the forerunners of the street-club workers who emerged in large cities during the 1940s and 1950s to work with street gangs.

In addition, a number of cities established "play street" programs. Although such operations, which set aside streets for play in congested areas (by blocking off traffic and providing equipment and leadership), had been in existence for some years, they received a new emphasis during the depression. A number of cities set up experimental play street programs in the early 1930s, using Federal work relief funds to provide staff.

New Awareness of Leisure Needs

Although devastating in other ways, the depression had a generally positive effect on recreation. Instead of simply channeling billions of dollars into direct relief, as in the European "dole" system, the Federal government provided meaningful work for Americans. The lives of millions of people in thousands of communities were enriched. Great numbers of indoor facilities were built and outdoor recreation areas constructed and improved.

Another important effect of the depression was to stimulate the concern of the American people about the problems of leisure and recreation opportunity. A major investigation of the needs of young people conducted by the American Youth Commission during the 1930s identified recreation and leisure as among the most pressing needs. Field studies in a number of states revealed serious lack of recreational opportunities for all young people, but especially for blacks, girls, and rural youth.

The American Association for the Study of Group Work studied the overall problem and in 1939 published an important report, *Leisure, a National Issue.* Written by Eduard Lindeman, a leading social work administrator who had played a key role in government during the Depression, the report stated that the "leisure of the American people constitutes a central and crucial problem of social policy." Leisure was no longer only for the elite classes of society, it was available to all social classes. Lindeman believed that the relation of leisure to social policy was clearly evident in those totalitarian European states which during the 1920s and 1930s had embraced leisure as an integral part of their programs:

> In Germany, the latest and most extreme of these new autocracies, leisure is organized primarily for the purpose of propaganda, of sustaining an attitude of loyalty toward the state, and of keeping the time of the people . . . fully occupied in . . . mass activities. Recreation in totalitarian nations is merely another form of subservience to the state, a planned form of action which follows the usual pattern of regimentation.[26]

Lindeman urged that in the American democracy, recreation should meet the true needs of the people. Pointing out that American workers were gaining a vast "national reservoir" of leisure which would be estimated at 390 billion hours per year, he suggested that the "new leisure" should be characterized by free choice and a minimum of restraint. He urged, however, that if it were not to become "idleness, waste, or opportunity for sheer mischief," it was essential that an environment provide means for expression of free choices in positive ways.

Lindeman urged the development of a national plan for leisure and stressed the need for professional, trained leaders if the quality of leisure was to be enhanced:

> I have no doubt that a distinct profession of recreation leadership is now coming into being. Indeed, it is my expectation that this newer occupation will enlist recruits at an accelerated rate of speed and that within the next quarter century there will be a demand for at least one hundred thousand trained recreation professionals. Some of these will be concerned with problems of administration and planning; others will work in research; others will be engaged in developing newer forms of facilities; some will be supervisors, recreation teachers and trained specialists.[27]

Before Lindeman's urgent recommendations for formulating national policy in leisure could be acted upon, however, the nation underwent another major crisis even more sustained and dangerous to its existence than the Great Depression—World War II.

The Effects of World War II

This great conflagration, in which the United States became fully involved in December, 1941, compelled the immediate mobilization of every aspect of national life: education, manpower, industry, and a variety of social services and programs.

The Special Services Division of the U.S. Army provided recreation facilities and programs on military bases throughout the world, making use of approximately twelve thousand officers, several times that many enlisted men, and large numbers of volunteers. About fifteen hundred officers were involved in the Welfare and Recreation Section of the Bureau of Naval Personnel, and expanded programs were offered by the Recreation Service of the Marine Corps. These departments were assisted by the United Service Organizations, formed in 1941, consisting of the joint military effort of six agencies: the Jewish Welfare Board, the Salvation Army, Catholic Community Services, YMCA, YWCA, and the National Travelers Aid. The United Service Organizations functioned in the continental United States and outside of camps, in clubs, hostels, and lounges throughout the western hemisphere. Through USO Camp Shows, Incorporated, it provided professional entertainment for troops overseas and in many Veterans Administration Hospitals. The American National Red Cross established approximately 750 clubs in wartime theaters of operations throughout the world, along with about 250 mobile entertainment units, staffed by over 4,000 leaders. Its military hospitals overseas and in the United States involved over 1,500 recreation workers as well.

In American communities, many programs had to be curtailed during World War II because of manpower shortage and travel restrictions. However, recreation and park departments instituted special new programs to assist the war effort, including victory gardens, learn-to-swim programs, salvage drives, and many teen-canteen programs. Youth-serving agencies collected scrap metal and paper, made equipment and supplies for military recreation centers, and sold war bonds. The National Recreation Association established a new field service to help communities near military bases and training camps organize special programs for members of the armed forces.

Many municipal directors extended their facilities and services to local war plants and changed their schedules to provide programs around the clock. Because of the rapid increase of industrial recreation programs, the National Industrial Recreation Association was formed in 1941 to assist in such efforts. Also, the Federal Security Agency's Office of Community War Services established a new Recreation Division to assist programs on the community level. This division helped to set up three hundred new community programs throughout the country, including numerous child care and recreation centers, many of which continued after the war as tax-supported community recreation programs.

By the end of World War II, great numbers of servicemen and servicewomen had participated in varied recreation programs and services and thus had learned a new appreciation of this field of community service. Many people had been trained and had gained experience in recreation programs, and were ready to return to civilian life as professionals in this field.

Postwar Developments: The 1950s and 1960s

Following World War II, there was a marked increase in the number of municipal park and recreation departments in the United States and indeed in all forms of leisure participation throughout the nation. Trends and events affecting organized recreation service in the 1950s and 1960s included the following:

1. *National Concern with Physical Fitness.* Particularly during the 1950s, there was an emphasis on the need to develop and maintain the physical fitness of youth and adults. Comparative studies, including the Kraus-Weber tests, which showed that American youth were less fit than the youth of other nations, led schools to strengthen their programs of physical education. Many public recreation departments expanded programs involving fitness classes, conditioning, jogging, and sports for all ages.

2. *Programs for the Disabled.* A second area of increased emphasis was the provision of special services for the physically and mentally disabled. Various agencies of government concerned with rehabilitation were strengthened to meet the needs of disabled citizens, especially large numbers of returning veterans who sought to be reintegrated into community life.

The Federal government sharply increased its aid to special education. In recreation, this took the form of new services to aid retarded children, youth, and adults. Beginning in the mid-1960s, there was greatly increased emphasis on developing social and recreational programs for aging persons in both institutional and community settings. Overall, the specialized field of what came to be known as *therapeutic recreation service* expanded steadily in this period.

3. *Outdoor Recreation and Park Development.* Probably this was the largest single development of the postwar period, both in terms of popular participation and the expanding role of government on all levels. The report of the Outdoor Recreation Resources Review Commission in 1962 made the following major recommendations for: (1) a national outdoor recreation policy; (2) guidelines for the management of outdoor recreation resources; (3) expansion of programs to meet recreation needs and to preserve and protect the natural environment; (4) establishment of a Bureau of Outdoor Recreation in the Department of the Interior; and (5) Federal legislation to enact a grants-in-aid program to states for open space acquisition, beautification, and outdoor recreation development.

The Land and Water Conservation Fund program provided increased Federal support for conservation and open-space programs. By the end of the decade, approximately eighty agencies, commissions and other Federal bodies were involved in over three hundred separate outdoor recreation-related programs, including substantial assistance to states and cities in developing new resources and cleaning up the environment.

4. *Increased Federal Assistance to Recreation.* In addition to outdoor recreation grants, the Federal government began to provide fuller assistance to state and local agencies, to colleges and universities, and to other organizations in the recreation and park field. A number of agencies in the Department of Health, Education and Welfare and in the Department of Housing and Urban Development

developed funding programs to aid population groups in special need, through help in facilities construction and planning.

5. *Involvement in the Arts.* Following World War II (and in part because of the stimulus to the arts given during the depression), the United States embarked on a marked expansion of cultural centers, museums, and art centers, encouraged by the assistance of the Federal government through the Arts and Humanities Act of 1965 and by the establishment of various state arts councils.

6. *Growth of Commercial Recreation.* As outlined in chapter 5, a unique aspect of recreation in the United States during the post-World War II period was the tremendous growth of private and commercial recreation sponsors. Country clubs and yacht clubs, swimming, tennis and golf clubs, privately operated campgrounds and ski centers, and commercially owned amusement parks and similar facilities attracted over 1.8 billion visitors per year. This trend posed a potential threat to the spread of public recreation. In Knapp's words:

> Even though abundance could generate tax dollars for additional support of municipal recreation, increased wealth frequently meant that many citizens merely bought more televisions and personal recreation equipment while simply ignoring public recreation. . . . [suggesting] that municipal organized recreation in an affluent America might become more a social service to the poor, the old, and the very young than an institution enjoyed by all.[28]

7. *Unification of Recreation and Parks Movements.* During the 1950s and 1960s, the close cooperation between recreation and the fields of physical education, education, and social work that had characterized the earlier period of history declined. Although recreation continued to be linked with physical education in many university departments of professional preparation, its orientation now moved in the direction of parks management. There was a merger of the recreation and parks movement on all levels, illustrated in the joint departments that now provided municipal recreation services in most communities, and by the merger of five separate organizations into the National Recreation and Park Association in 1966 (see chapter 12).

8. *Concern with the Poor and with Minority Groups.* A major challenge to recreation arose as a consequence of the growing urban crisis of the mid-1960s, stemming from increased awareness of the needs of disadvantaged citizens and especially members of minority groups. Murphy writes that when great numbers of blacks migrated to the northern urban communities after World War I,

> for the first time blacks were brought into contact and competition with whites on a large scale, involving employment, education, housing, and recreation. The expanding concern for race relations necessitated a change in the provision of public recreation service, resulting in a specialized attempt to meet the leisure needs of black citizens through the Bureau of Colored Work of the Playground and Recreation Association of America [which] provided consultation services aimed at assisting racially segregated community recreation programs until World War II.[29]

Although the organized recreation movement had been concerned with the needs of minorities since the 1920s, recreation programs serving blacks were generally segregated and tended to provide inferior facilities and services. In the mid-1960s, based on civil rights legislation and under the sharp impact of growing black militancy, municipal recreation authorities developed "crash" efforts to improve services to the disadvantaged. Although substantial Federal assistance was given to this drive, it was clear at the decade's end that the challenge of providing services to the poor and to minority groups had not yet been solved.

9. *New Challenges.* Another challenge was created by the youth rebellion of the 1960s. Young people developed new kinds of recreation for themselves, often completely discarding traditional moral values as outmoded shibboleths. They were "doing their own thing," taking drugs in growing numbers and affirming new, permissive attitudes towards sexual behavior.

As young people sought new kinds of experiences and personal relationships, many of the traditional forms of recreation seemed no longer as relevant. The youth rebellion subsided in the 1970s, but it had made its mark, and a number of other special groups in the population such as women, the aging, and homosexuals were determinedly expressing their right to equal treatment. With the pressure of increasingly severe social crises in the cities, austerity budgets, and shifting responsibilities of government, it became more and more necessary for those responsible for recreation services to develop new, innovative approaches to program planning and to increase the level of financial support.

Beyond this, it was apparent that the rationale for service—in effect, the basic philosophy upon which recreation programs were to be developed—had to be revised to meet the needs of a new technological age and the ideals of a changing society. This new approach to leisure is described more fully elsewhere in this text (see Chap. 16). More specific examples of trends in programs and services on all levels of government and in voluntary, private and commercial agencies, are given in chapters 9 through 11.

Recreation and Park Development in Canada

The history of recreation and park development in Canada paralleled in many ways that of the United States, although there were certain distinct differences, both in timing and emphasis. Obviously, there are certain major differences between the counties, with respect to geography and climate, ethnic makeup, and cultural tradition. Leslie Bella, a Canadian recreation educator, writes of her country's

> bilingualism and multiculturalism, our curious constitutional bondage to Britain; our Northern climate, and our native peoples; our national parks, sparse population and resource-based industries; and our acceptance of government involvement in many areas—from "Medicare" and "Opportunities for Youth" to the Canadian Broadcasting System.[30]

Harold Brain, Commissioner of Parks and Recreation in Sault Sainte Marie, in a survey of the development of recreation and leisure in the province of Ontario points out that one of the characteristics of this region was its extremely low population until fairly recently. Only along the southern border has there been substantial industrial and urban development; northern Ontario, in contrast, was dotted with small towns and villages, as a result of mining and forest industries. He points out also that at the turn of the century, over 80 percent of Ontario residents were Canadian-born, indicating that the province had passed its pioneering era. While minority groups such as Germans, French Canadians, and Italians have comprised ethnic enclaves with distinct cultural traditions and leisure pursuits, over the past few decades these separate national groups have tended to merge into an assimilated society: "the ethnic groups are becoming more like each other, resulting in a trend toward a common denominator—a Canadian way of life."[31]

Brain notes a sharp decline in the strong British influence that caused the popularity of such sports as cricket and maintained a rigid social stratification in clubs and other leisure associations. Today the dominant activities are Canadian (hockey, curling, etc.), and such activities as sailing, golfing, skiing and horseback riding are open to all—dependent only on the ability to pay. Within the realm of leisure, social status has been replaced by economic capability.

While this survey gives a revealing overview of one province, what of the overall history of recreation and parks in Canada? Elsie M. McFarland has made a detailed analysis of this development and documented the various stages with considerable insight.[32]

History of Parks and Recreation

McFarland states that public recreation was slow to develop in Canada's larger cities, but with a dramatic growth in population and trend toward urbanization following World War II, there was a major growth of local public recreation authorities. Canadian federal and provincial governments have shared responsibility with local governments for the financing and construction of numerous parks, centers, and other facilities, along with assisting in special programs and projects.

How did federal and provincial concern with parks and recreation begin in Canada? Local self-government was slow to develop; the four provinces of Ontario, Quebec, Nova Scotia, and New Brunswick made the bulk of municipal decisions until well into the middle of the nineteenth century. Only in the 1840s and 1850s did the larger Canadian communities receive their charters for self-government. Nonetheless, a number of major municipal parks were established at an early time—considerably before they were established in the United States.

For example, the extensive Halifax Common was granted to public officers of the town of Halifax in 1763 by the Lieutenant Governor of Nova Scotia. Gore Park, in the city of Hamilton, was used as a park for several decades before becoming official city property in 1852. Public squares were established in Montreal as early as 1821; by the 1860s, there were thirteen such open spaces, and the city was considering purchasing what was to become Montreal's landmark park, Mount Royal Park. During the period of the 1880s and 1890s, other cities purchased and developed major municipal parks, such as Stanley Park in Vancouver, Victoria Park in London, and Rockwood Park in Saint John.

As in the United States, the philosophy of the early park planners was to provide scenic, secluded and natural open spaces and to exclude sports, entertainment, or other recreational activities that might encroach on their vision of what a park should be. First Ontario, then Manitoba and other provinces in the 1880s passed public park acts which empowered municipalities to establish parks and set standards for acquisition and management. Following this, a number of communities established boards of park commissioners and developed networks of large and small parks, in some cases with their own taxing power.

McFarland points out that supervised playgrounds in Canada developed for similar reasons as in the United States—to meet the needs of poor families in urban slums with a high incidence of crime, disease, and drunkenness. And, as in the neighboring country, private citizens promoted the need for playgrounds; the National Council of Women passed a resolution in May, 1901 urging the development of vacation schools and playgrounds. Progress was slower than in the United States, but by 1914 playground associations or commissions had been formed in nine cities—chiefly due to the pressure of women's councils. In Halifax, Saint John, Montreal, Toronto, and Hamilton, playgrounds were established under such leadership and gradually were taken over by school authorities or by municipal park boards; other cities such as Ottawa, Winnipeg, Vancouver, and Regina soon followed suit. They gradually expanded their efforts, hiring full-time playground supervisors and providing diversified program activities, with particular emphasis on sports. McFarland comments:

> There is ample evidence that the playground movement in Canada was part of the same movement that was spreading across the United States. Canadian leaders received much of their inspiration from United States' leaders and took an active part in United States' conferences.[33]

In contrast, a rather unique Canadian development in the sponsorship of municipal recreation came about through emerging community associations and service clubs. Especially in the western provinces in such cities as Vancouver, Edmonton, and Saskatoon, citizens' organizations concerned with civic development, the schools, or promoting athletics or cultural activities, merged into community leagues. These leagues vigorously promoted the development of playgrounds, swimming pools, community centers, and similar recreation facilities. In some cases, they took direct sponsorship for developing and managing community centers.

Following World War II, considerable encouragement was given to the development of community centers as a form of war memorial by the National Department of National Health and Welfare, through the National Council on Physical Fitness and related provincial government agencies. The function of such centers was described by the Honorable Brooke Claxton, Minister of National Health and Welfare:

> I think one of the ways in which we can gain a new sense of cultural and social purpose after the war is through community centres. They will provide in each city and town a meeting place where all citizens can make their contribution to our social life, to art, to music, drama and sport.[34]

In some cases, local citizens shared responsibility with municipal government authorities for fund raising and policy setting, according to prescribed formulas. Clearly such arrangements ensured that the programs provided would reflect neighborhood values and meet significant community needs, and helped to guarantee a high level of citizen interest and support.

Federal and Provincial Roles

Increasingly, the federal and provincial governments began to take an interest in community recreation. During the depression of the 1930s, first British Columbia, then Alberta and Saskatchewan sponsored, through their provincial departments of education, special sports and physical recreation programs to serve the needs of unemployed young people and adults.

In 1943, the National Physical Fitness Act established a council responsible for working with the provinces and disbursing funds to promote varied forms of physical activity as well as art, music, theater and other cultural and social programs. McFarland points out that the National Physical Fitness Council did much to assist municipal recreation by preparing and distributing films, reports, and pamphlets on recreation, offering scholarships for postgraduate study in physical education and recreation, and initiating diploma courses to train recreation personnel in small towns and rural areas. During the late 1940s, nine of Canada's ten provinces signed agreements with the federal government to cooperate under the act; Quebec declined federal assistance because of its concern about federal interference in education and its wish to maintain provincial autonomy.

Of the Canadian provinces, Quebec was the last to develop publicly sponsored recreation and parks. This reluctance was apparently due to its French and Catholic tradition, in which religious authorities played a strong role in sponsoring local playgrounds and centers (known as *oeuvre des terrains de jeux,* or O.T.J.'s). For several decades, the Catholic church administered most public recreation, through diocesan federations in the larger, primarily French-speaking cities. In the 1960s, Quebec was the only Canadian province without an official department responsible for leisure programs and policies, and it was not until 1968 that the provincial legislature established a Commission of Youth, Recreation, and Sport. Indeed, only in the late 1970s was a Department of Tourism, Recreation, and Parks approved by the assembly. On a local level, however, a number of excellent municipal recreation and parks departments as well as several college programs in recreation and leisure have been developed in Quebec.

During the late 1940s, a number of cities, such as Ottawa, Hamilton, and Peterborough, Ontario, established independent recreation committees or commissions and appointed full-time directors of recreation. Rapidly during the 1950s, the somewhat narrow concern with sponsoring playgrounds for children broadened to the total communitywide approach toward providing varied leisure services under the heading of recreation.

In British Columbia, for example, a new Community Programmes Branch was established in 1953 to assist local school boards and municipalities in providing recreation through organized night schools. Ontario, Alberta, and Saskatchewan followed with similar grants. Some provinces established training programs for local leaders, or sent field workers to small rural communities to promote the concept of active recreation—often encouraging them to establish sports leagues, operate community centers, or provide adult classes in both recreational and educational subjects. A chronology of this process appears in *Recreation Review,* which describes the experiences of field workers of the Community Programmes Branch of Ontario— and of the kind of resistance they often met. One of the original staff members recalled:

> I remember one time in a certain village in Northwestern Ontario when we 'phoned the manager of a nearby mine and said we're from the Provincial Government and we'd like to listen to your notion of how your community should develop and our chief resources are in the field of recreation. And he said, "Hell man, we don't need any more recreation, we've got fourteen prostitutes and seven bootleggers now. We don't really need you fellows." But I saw the time pass when that man took square dance courses and became leader of a very active square dance group in the mining community.[35]

Provincial grants were assigned to local recreation committees, to assist them in sponsoring programs; these grew rapidly through the 1950s. Various rural community organizations, such as agricultural societies, women's institutes, 4-H Clubs, Junior Farmers, and other bodies (many assisted by the Provincial Department of Agriculture) were drawn into their programs. The province's role was one of assisting, stimulating, enabling and promoting—but not providing direct services. Gradually, provinces such as British Columbia and Alberta discontinued their grants to citizens' groups and lent support instead to local government agencies.

The expansion of public concern about recreation led to plans to prepare professional leaders in this field. Initially, there were no Canadian degree programs in this field, and Canadians who sought advanced degrees in recreation attended universities in the United States. The province of Nova Scotia took a first step in 1946 with an eight-month course to prepare returned military personnel for work in community recreation. Two early attempts to establish degree programs met with little support and were discontinued. The Ontario Community Programmes Branch initiated a three-year in-service training program for municipal recreation directors in 1951; when the program was discontinued in 1963, over three hundred persons had received interim or permanent certificates.

In the early and middle 1960s, the University of British Columbia and the University of Alberta initiated four-year degree programs in recreation. Other colleges, particularly in Ontario, soon offered two-year diploma courses in recreation, with the University of Waterloo and the University of Ottawa following with four-year curricula. By the end of the 1960s, professional preparation in recreation and parks was well established in both two- and four-year Canadian colleges (see chapter 12). Professional development in Canada was also promoted by the work of the Parks and Recreation Association of Canada, which was founded in 1945. The association conducted surveys, published magazines, and held annual national conventions, much like its United States counterpart, the National Recreation Association. In 1967, it joined with the Canadian Association for Health, Physical Education, and Recreation, the city of Montreal, the French-speaking *Association Canadienne des Centres de Loisirs,* and the Canadian Welfare Council, to sponsor the first Canadian symposium on recreation. Two years later, the organization changed its name to Canadian Parks/Recreation Association.

As in the United States, park and recreation authorities in Canada merged into single governmental units, particularly during the 1960s. Often special legislation by provincial governments was necessary to dissolve local governmental bodies established under previous legislation and to permit setting up new, unified governmental units including both parks and recreation. In some communities parks and recreation continue to operate side by side as separate departments, and in others, either a park or a recreation department carries the full responsibility, sometimes in cooperation with the schools.

In summing up the situation at the end of the 1960s, McFarland concluded that much progress had been made in public recreation in Canada in recent years. Recreation was now recognized to the extent that universities were offering degree programs in it, and federal grants had given sufficient assistance to municipalities to permit them to offer competitive salaries to recreation professionals.

> Young people have been further encouraged to enter the recreation field because of federal and provincial scholarships and bursaries. Canada Council grants and scholarships have improved the cultural life of many communities and have enabled many young artists to advance their area of competence and return to offer leadership in their province. The growth of provincial and national recreation associations, although slow, gives promise for the establishment of professional standards, for a unified recreation voice.[36]

McFarland noted that critical challenges remained: (1) to assess realistically the need and appropriate focus for professional preparation in recreation and develop some measure of cohesion among the various colleges and universities in this field; (2) to better coordinate the efforts of municipal recreation authorities and to encourage them to move more vigorously into program areas not heavily supported by federal and provincial grants; and (3) to ensure that citizen participation on all levels in recreation planning and programming continued.

A national conference on leisure at Montmorency, Quebec in 1969, issued several major recommendations calling for: (1) a clarification of values of leisure in Canadian society, to involve not only the providers of recreation, but also the consumers; (2) national goals and interdepartmental planning and legislation to insure environmental resource protection and appropriate development of facilities and open spaces in both urban and rural settings; (3) a strengthened program of education for leisure, as well as improvement of research efforts in this field; and (4) the development of strategies for effective programs of cooperation, involving major federal, provincial, and local agencies, as well as voluntary and nongovernmental organizations.[37] At the heart of all the Montmorency Conference's recommendations was the desire to develop coherent and intelligent leisure policies applicable to the Canadian context, rather than to continue to develop without planning or to be excessively influenced by patterns of professional development in other nations.

Additional details of Canadian recreation and park programs and services during the 1970s are provided in the chapters that follow.

Recreation on the International Scene

The concluding section of this chapter examines the recent development of recreation in a number of European and Asian nations, as well as certain major aspects of international recreation activity. In Europe, recreation has not developed as an independent field of professional service to the extent that it has in the United States and Canada. However, in some respects European nations have achieved a higher level of sports participation for the masses of people and have promoted the arts more vigorously than in North America.

The general pattern in European nations has been to view leisure as a national or federal responsibility, as a means of promoting ideology and serving important national goals. This first became evident during the period prior to World War II, when such nations as Italy, Germany, and Russia used recreation as a means of social and political indoctrination of children, youth, and adults, through organized programs of sports and cultural activities.

The democratic states of Europe, such as England and France, approached recreation during this period either through national ministries of labor that assisted programs serving working people and their families, or through departments of education. Most actual program sponsorship was through voluntary organizations; Weir wrote in the 1930s:

> In European countries labor unions, churches, political groups or parties ... recognized in leisure or recreation a powerful instrument for the promotion of their particular social, economic, religious, or political theories, aims and purposes.[38]

In general, there was a greater concern with the leisure needs of adults than with those of children. Owing to close-knit family life in most European nations, the view was widely accepted that the place for children, outside of school, was the home (except for dictatorships which established powerful youth organizations for purposes of indoctrination). In most European countries, park planning was well developed early in the twentieth century. Many cities, by the early 1930s, had extensive provisions for parks and other outdoor recreation spaces. Typically, both the state and the large cities owned extensive acreage of parkland and forest areas, all open to the public for recreation. Major sports and gymnastic organizations, with strong government support, developed networks of sports arenas, playfields, and stadiums. Following is an overview of recreation and park policies and programs in several European and eastern nations.

Great Britain

As described earlier, parks and various forms of public entertainment were well established in England by the end of the eighteenth century. There was little concern with the needs of the working classes, however, until the Saturday half-holiday created additional leisure for the building trades, clerks, and manual workers, and led to increased interest in developing sports clubs and district sports leagues. Churches acted as sponsors for many football and cricket clubs during the 1870s, some of which later became independent professional teams. Gradually, concern about the use of leisure spread in Great Britain. Prime Minister Benjamin Disraeli said in an 1872 speech, "Increased means and increased leisure are the two civilizers of man,"—but many authorities worried about how leisure would be spent.

During the decade beginning in 1880, a system of loans granted by the national government through the Ministry of Health helped local officials establish playing fields. Play centers in settlement houses and working boys' clubs were established in the 1880s; soon there was a Federation of Working Boys' Clubs in London with over one hundred clubs and thousands of young members.

The National Playing Fields Association was formed in 1925 to promote sports and outdoor recreation facilities throughout Great Britain. Other organizations and societies were developed in this period to promote nonsports activities such as public gardens associations, drama leagues, and music and folklore societies.

In 1935, a Central Council of Recreative Physical Training was established, and two years later Parliament passed a bill giving financial support to local school and community sports programs. During World War II the Central Council of Recreative Physical Training was changed to the Central Council of Physical Recreation, which has been among the leading organizations to promote sports and other active leisure pursuits in Great Britain. It directly sponsors many activities, assists other organizations, and offers training courses in a wide range of physical activities. The Central Council operates varied facilities known as National Recreation Centers for leadership training. It is regarded as a voluntary organization, although about half its income comes from grants made by the British Ministry of Education; the rest is from donations and fees.

During the 1950s there was much concern in Great Britain about the role of sport in society. The Wolfenden Committee on Sport was established in October, 1957, to examine the total development of games, sports, and outdoor activities in the United Kingdom. Its report, issued in 1960, contained many valuable recommendations directed to the government, local authorities, youth, and sports organizations. The committee considered sport to be self-justified, although it recognized that sport also contributed to positive character development and health. With respect to juvenile delinquency, the report stated:

> The causes of criminal behavior are complex, and we are not suggesting that it would disappear if there were more tennis courts or running tracks; nor are we concerned to press for wider provision of opportunities just on the ground that it would reduce the incidence of those various forms of anti-social activities which are lumped together as "juvenile delinquency." At the same time, it is a reasonable assumption that if more young people had opportunities for playing games fewer of them would develop criminal habits.[39]

Assignment of responsibility to local government for developing parks and sports facilities was strengthened in 1959 by the Recreation Grounds Act, which provided assistance loans through the Minister of Housing and Local Government. The 1968 Countryside Bill ensured that national expenditure for parks and outdoor recreation would be much greater than in the past, and local authorities would assume more responsibility.

Youth Services in Britain

In Great Britain, youth services have been promoted for a number of decades by the National Association of Youth Clubs, a federation incorporating over thirty-five local associations of youth clubs in England and affiliated clubs in Scotland, Wales, and Northern Ireland. This organization promotes youth service organizations by providing training for leaders, consultation, publications, and research. The National Association of Youth Clubs and its member groups receive assistance from the

Ministry of Education's Youth Service Development Council and from many local educational authorities.

Youth club programs include such activities as:

> hobbies and construction projects; self-improvement activities, social activities, trip programming, sporting activities, including skiing, sailing, surfing and canoeing, and gliding; camping; birdwatching; boat racing; service projects in community programs; fund-raising, providing services to the handicapped and to hospitals; artistic and cultural activities.[40]

Some authorities have suggested that instead of being operated by voluntary and religious agencies, youth clubs should be a state service, operated through central or local authorities. In Great Britain, this approach has been strongly resisted.

> In a free and open society such as ours, a wholly state organized youth venture tends to be an anathema because people remember and are still disturbed by the fascist youth organizations which emerged in the 1930's. . . . A state youth organization . . . with dangers of political manipulation is unlikely in this country. The demand is for variety, freedom of form in organization and development, a mixture of organizations and a real partnership between the state . . . and voluntary movements.[41]

Although many special programs of higher education have been developed in Great Britain for youth leaders and park and recreation managers, this field has not yet developed as a recognized area of professional service as fully as it has in the United States and Canada.

Soviet Union

The Soviet Union is the leading example today of a major nation (actually a federation of republics, regions and national districts) with centralized economic planning and social management. Every aspect of Soviet life, including recreation and leisure, is regarded as part of a collective scheme to build national morale, improve health, and increase productivity. The concept of leisure within the Soviet Union has been closely linked to the promotion of "socialist discipline" and the development of community solidarity and a common morality. Whetten has commented:

> leisure activities are vitally important in a controlled society. Unless leisure time is carefully regulated, the "sense of sacrifice" which the worker is taught on the job could desert him in the hours he is away from it. . . . Realization of the state's ultimate goal thus depends, at least in part, on its success in controlling leisure time.[42]

The early Soviet concept of leisure was that it should be used by workers to "rest and gather strength for new labors and successes." Such use of leisure became a social responsibility as well as a constitutional right. Thus, the Russians developed an elaborate system of rest homes and vacation resorts for workers in coastal regions like Yalta, with the emphasis on nourishing diets, casual bathing, sunning, and rest— but not vigorous recreation. Beginning in the 1920s, the Soviet Union established a system of day-care centers for children, along with after-school, open-air programs, and summer camps. A comprehensive youth movement under state control includes ages from seven to twenty-five; games and athletics are an important part of the program. Indoctrination in the ideas of the Soviet state occurs on each level, through constant campaigns, drives, and parades, and a paramilitary approach to organization and membership. There are thousands of Pioneer Youth Palaces, or centers, which enjoy spacious quarters in the former palaces of Czarist royalty or in more recently built structures. For adults, there are ample clubs and societies; Whetten writes:

> Every effort is made to fill leisure time during the working year with as many culturally and educationally rewarding activities as possible. Local groups, such as hobby clubs, apartment-house councils, civil-defense units, the factory . . . study group, and the Konsomol or party cell, are organized and supported by the government. . . . Though the individual is not forced to join specific organizations, social pressure is strong enough to bring nonconformists to heel.[43]

Park Planning and Development

During the 1930s, Weir reported that Soviet social planning included extensive provision of parks, playgrounds, sports fields, stadiums, swimming centers and winter-sports facilities. Russian planners developed parks of "culture and rest," a type of general park controlled by special municipal authorities that offered all sorts of recreation and cultural opportunities for adults and children. Weir described the famous 731-acre Moscow Park of Culture and Rest, which opened in 1929, as a "cross between an American amusement park and a large landscape park," including Ferris wheels, parachute towers, and similar equipment, as well as areas for games, sports, dancing, reading, concert and theater performances, and numerous places for quiet enjoyment of nature.

Cultural Activity

The Soviet Union offers a tremendous amount of state-sponsored activity in the arts, including legitimate theater, opera, ballet, concerts, and circuses, as well as many schools to train performers. Bowers comments that in the large cities such as Leningrad and Moscow, there are far more facilities for cultural entertainment than in other cities of the world. For example, the Bolshoi Ballet in Moscow, which invariably plays to packed houses, receives a large annual grant from the state of millions of rubles, and employs nearly three thousand people, including artists, stagehands, scene builders, administrators and musicians.[44]

Sport in the Soviet Union

The Russians view physical education and sport as essential means of developing national strength, unity, and prestige. Physical education is a required and respected subject for all students. When their working day ends, millions of industrial and office workers, students, engineers and collective farmers crowd the nation's gymnasiums and stadiums. Each republic has hundreds of sports events, presentations, and holidays throughout the year. McLendon has written:

from early years through adulthood, millions compete . . . for badges
signifying athletic achievement. All participants are provided with
facilities, trainers, coaches, and—more important—opportunities for
organized competition and awards for recognition.[45]

This program is supported by thousands of juvenile sports clubs and special
schools, and vast numbers of organizations which promote training and competition
in over forty-six different sports on district, province, republic, and federal levels.
Hendricks writes that in the most recent five-year plan, begun in 1971, huge sums

have been allocated for building sports facilities and worker resorts.
Included are 120 major stadiums, 10 sports palaces, 120 huge swimming
pools, and numerous resorts for both summer and winter vacations.[46]

The spontaneous organization of sports groups without Party permission
and control (through the U.S.S.R. Union of Sports Societies and Organizations) is
forbidden, and all sports societies and groups are formed according to prescribed
statutes. Sport is considered an important means of impressing Soviet superiority
upon the rest of the world and inflating the U.S.S.R.'s prestige.

By systematically organizing sport exchanges with nations from all over
the world, the U.S.S.R. has won valuable beachheads of influence which
have been exploited to create a positive image of the Soviet Union . . . as
Soviet technicians are welcome in various parts of the world, so are
Soviet coaches.[47]

Leisure Trends Today

Increasingly, as the Russian people gain a fuller measure of affluence and leisure
(workers today typically have a thirty-five hour workweek, with numerous added
holidays), leisure is seen as a potential threat to the Soviet Union. Government
officials are concerned about the invasion of Western "decadence," in the form of
"immoral" entertainment, and conduct frequent drives against "shirkers" in industry and against the invasion of rock-and-roll dancing, foreign films and publications,
and modern art.

A leading sociologist, G. S. Petrosian, warned that free time must not lead
to idleness: "It is the time devoted to study, the raising of [occupational] qualifications, self-education and self-development." *Pravda* expressed the national view
clearly:

To care about the cultural recreation of the people is above all to ensure
the conditions making it possible for the working people to spend their
free time in such a way as to raise their general cultural and professional
level to improve [themselves] physically and aesthetically.[48]

Despite such warnings and the concern of the Soviet government, difficulties in promoting productive use of leisure persist. Alcoholism is a serious problem;
idling, the pursuit of "diversionist" or "bourgeois" activities, and even the increase of
television, now widely available to the Russian people, are all problems which
threaten the Soviet ideal of a vigorous and meaningful leisure life and which the

state is attempting to solve by new and stronger laws and other forms of social coercion.

Germany

During the twentieth century, the provision of recreation facilities and programs in Germany fell into three distinct periods: up to and including the 1920s, the era of Nazi domination, and the post-World War II period.

Germany was one of the first countries to develop a strong gymnastics and physical education movement, and had established many parks and other recreation facilities, including extensive playgrounds, during the nineteenth century. The Central Committee for Popular and Juvenile Games conducted national programs promoting sports and games during and after World War I. Immediately before and after World War I, cities developed planning standards for parks and open space, with minimum requirements for children's play areas and general recommendations for gymnasiums, aquatic centers, and other sports facilities. During the 1920s and early 1930s, German park planners created extraordinary amounts of open space in the form of parks and forests radiating from the densely populated central cities or in green belts surrounding urban areas.

Sports activities were based on a flourishing workers' sports movement, with thousands of adolescents participating in games and with strong voluntary organizations providing organized instruction, leagues, and facilities. Military training was forbidden following Germany's defeat in World War I, and much of the increased sports activity was undoubtedly used as a substitute. Drill fields were converted into athletic fields to maintain physical fitness and high morale. An estimated 5 million adults aged fifteen and over belonged to sports organizations.

The Nazi Era

When the National Socialist Party came to power in Germany, it assumed direct control of all physical education, sports, and recreation. As in the Soviet Union, the government used youth and adult clubs and societies as a form of propaganda and social control. The Hitler Youth Organization systematically organized the out-of-school activities for both boys and girls from six to eighteen, including sports and games, camping, hiking, first aid and hygiene, and other cultural pursuits. The goal was to promote National Socialist ideals, patriotic fervor, and physical vigor and strength.

For example, the program of the *Bund Deutscher Mädel,* the organization serving girls and young women, included gymnastics, handicrafts, folklore, foreign affairs discussions, games and music, and health services. Activities like hosteling and camping took on new meaning. Baldur von Schirach, leader of the *Hitler Jugend* (Hitler Youth Organization), stated:

> Everywhere now new youth hostels of the National Socialist type have come into being. . . . If German youth today takes hikes, it does not do so with a false and gushing sentimentality intoxicated with Nature, but even here it subordinates its action to a political purpose. . . . Through the youth hostel movement, even the poorest children . . . are given a chance to know the homeland for which they may be called upon to stake their lives.[49]

After World War II

Immediately after the war, under Allied occupation, funds were allocated for the rebuilding of recreational facilities and the operation of new youth centers in Germany. Many bombed-out sections of cities became sites for parks, green belts, sports facilities, and stadiums. Sports clubs again became extremely active; by the late 1960s, West Germany had about 35,000 clubs with a total membership of 7.4 million, and 41 percent of all male youths were active in organized sports.

Each particular sport is governed by an autonomous federal sport association; in addition, there are numerous state and regional sport societies and unions, coordinated by a national sports advisory council, which also works with trade unions, churches, and employers. Other cultural, social, and recreation activities are promoted by the *Bundesjugendring* (Federal Youth Ring). As in Great Britain, these national bodies are nongovernmental, although they receive financial assistance from the federal government.

Local governments give considerable support to the performing arts. Both states and municipalities provide subsidies to West Germany's 135 theaters and opera houses. In the cities, school authorities sponsor playgrounds and community centers. Thus the pattern of recreation in West Germany has shifted heavily to sponsorship by voluntary organizations and educational authorities, largely free from political or social indoctrination. In East Germany, by contrast, the approach is very much like that in the Soviet Union; sport is heavily subsidized and controlled, with a single-minded emphasis on bringing prestige to the nation through international sports victories. An intensive program of identifying gifted young athletes at an early age and providing them with outstanding coaching and a totally committed system of development resulted in this small nation of only 17 million citizens winning 90 medals at the 1976 Olympic Games in Moscow—more than any other country except the Soviet Union.

Recreation in Other European Countries

The Scandinavian countries are noted for their highly developed networks of social programs, including extensive services for aging and disabled persons. Denmark, Norway, and Sweden all have extensively developed park and playground facilities and programs, frequently in cooperation with local sports or gymnastic societies which sometimes have direct responsibility for programs.

Many Belgian organizations, particularly the Roman Catholic Church and major industrial firms, promote strong recreation programs. Publicly supported *Maisons des Loisirs* (Leisure Institutes) are sponsored in cities and towns, providing various forms of social, cultural, and educational enrichment. A unique venture in both Belgium and Holland provides leisure education for young workers between the ages of sixteen and eighteen, who attend *levenscholen* (Centers of Education for Life) during working hours, without loss of pay. These centers provide education for lifelong learning, aimed at the social, cultural and character formation of young workers, including courses

> arranged mostly around handicrafts, sports, and outdoor life, as well as an introduction to the technology of the mass media. . . . They deal with the real questions and interests of the young: recreation, leisure . . . and courses that deal with problems of life.[50]

204

In France, recreation sponsorship has been primarily in the hands of varied forms of voluntary management—industrial firms and unions, both Catholic and Protestant churches, and political movements, all of which operate youth and adult clubs. Since the early 1960s, the federal government has been especially concerned with problems of leisure and has greatly expanded parks, sports grounds, and other recreation facilities. France also provides extensive social services, such as clubs for senior citizens or day-care centers; many of these have strong recreation components.

In Israel, the bulk of public recreation is provided by the Sports and Physical Education Authority in the Ministry of Education and Culture. Since the establishment of the Zionist movement, Jewish nationalists have stressed the need for a "muscular Jewry" to enable a people who have traditionally been intellectuals, professionals, and craftsmen to survive in the harsh Palestinian desert. The *Maccabi* Sport Organization, the *Hapoel* Association, and similar athletic groups have strongly promoted international Jewish sports participation and competition. Since emphasis in Israel is strongly on maintaining the physical vigor and involvement of all the people, mass sports and popular community activities and events, rather than spectator programs, are heavily stressed.

The pattern of recreation development in these countries differs from American practice in several respects. The major thrust in most countries is through sports associations that promote various forms of physical recreation, usually with government financial assistance. In other areas of leisure such as cultural arts, substantial grants are given to private groups by national or municipal governments. Social services are highly developed, including many innovative programs for the disabled or other special populations.

Recreation Development in Eastern Nations

Recreation and Leisure in Japan

Since the 1920s, Japan has shown a major interest in Western sports such as baseball, hockey, basketball, boxing, track and field, and swimming. Prior to World War II, Japan displayed considerable interest in the organized recreation movement, founding a National Recreation Association based on the American model. Since World War II Japan has changed markedly from a nationalistic and autocratic government to a democratic society. Its expanding economy has created a higher standard of living for the Japanese people than anywhere else in the Orient, along with greatly increased leisure.

A Sports Promotion Law was enacted in 1961 to assist preparation for the approaching 1964 Tokyo Olympics, establishing guiding principles for sports development and giving both local and national government agencies the responsibility for developing sports facilities and leadership. Participation in various sports is widespread, leading to national competitions each year for the Emperor's and Empress's Cups. The Japan Amateur Sport Association and the National Ministry of Education assist in organizing these competitions.

In addition to this strong sports emphasis, there is a tremendous amount of popular recreation interest in Japan, much of it modeled after pastimes and programs in the United States. The development of express trains has encouraged millions of Japanese families to travel for fun; they enjoy visiting national historic sites and shrines, as well as varied recreational centers. Many privately operated recreation centers include huge ski complexes (some of which now use plastic slopes flowing with water for year-round skiing), several-tiered driving ranges, and other facilities described in *Life* magazine:

> In Japan, golf courses, beaches and ski slopes are packed beyond belief . . . newly affluent, they have leisure their fathers never knew and a restless vigor that demands outlet . . . Whatever the sport, the Japanese attack it with a fearsome determination to be *dai-ichi*—the very best. . . .
>
> Skating rinks have to stay open almost all night to handle the crowds. Skiers have to get to the railroad station six hours before train time to be sure of a place. . . . High school baseball teams pull 60,000 to their championship games. More than 250,000 climbed Mt. Fuji this year, leaving tons of debris on the sacred slopes. But the most ambitious project is privately owned Yomiuriland, a $20 million complex spread over 1,000 acres on the outskirts of Tokyo.
>
> Yomiuriland, though inspired by Disneyland, emphasizes sports instead of amusements. Besides its Olympic-size snowless ski jump, it has easier slopes for beginners, a 120-foot parachute jump, two golf courses . . . a chain of stocked fish ponds—and its own monorail to carry visitors from sport to sport.[51]

With all these innovations, the Japanese people still continue many of their traditional leisure pursuits linked to folk art, dance, theater, ceremony, and ritual, along with such combative activities as *Sumo, Kendo,* and *Judo.* A final important aspect of Japanese recreation is the important influence of industrial sponsorship; many large firms are extremely paternalistic, providing many services—including sports, cultural, and social activities—to their employees.

Recreation in Other Eastern Nations

In other Asian nations, characterized by problems of overpopulation and poverty, recreation and leisure are not so fully developed. In India and Pakistan, for example, although the national governments have taken beginning steps toward establishing varied recreation facilities and programs, the bulk of service is still provided by private or voluntary organizations such as the YMCA or Scouts. Large cities like Bombay and Calcutta have begun to develop stadiums and other sports facilities, and the Indian government plans to provide sport and recreation centers, along with libraries and cultural centers, in towns and villages throughout the country. *Balkan-ji-Bara,* the All-India Children's Organization, promotes programs for children and youth, and an Indian Recreation Association has been formed, with federal assistance, to promote recreation programs and train leadership.

Communist China

In Communist China, the pattern is similar to that in Soviet Russia; all forms of recreational activity—particularly the arts—are used to promote national propaganda and social control. This vast land of over 700 million people has made striking progress in sports over the past two decades. A Swedish writer commented in 1966:

> The restless giant behind the Bamboo Curtain is flexing its muscles in a dramatic sports renaissance . . . to challenge the United States and the Soviet Union for worldwide athletic supremacy.
>
> The government has subsidized the entire project, spending billions of dollars for schools, facilities, stadiums, training and equipment. And China has become sports-minded, with 65 million athletes, huge crowds jamming the big new arenas for athletic events [admission free] and a widespread eagerness for physical fitness.[52]

Both in the development of huge new stadiums and arenas and in the promotion of such sports as track and field, swimming, weight lifting, speed skating, and table tennis, Communist China strove to become a leading competitive nation, seeing sport as a means of attaining international prestige. During the early and middle 1970s, however, its emphasis changed, and since then sport has been used as a medium for friendly international exchange, with many American and European teams and other visitors traveling throughout Communist China. Competition has been de-emphasized in national sports events; emphasis is instead given to team play, sportsmanship, and development of national unity through sport. Nonetheless, socialist goals are frequently reiterated as the basis of all sports. Throwing the hand grenade is an official Chinese event included in national fitness requirements and competition on all levels for school children. And on all levels—in factories, communes, schools, and other centers—sports are seen as an integral aspect of patriotic determination and commitment.

Australia and New Zealand

Recreation has made rapid strides in recent years in these two relatively industrialized and technologically advanced nations, both with small populations and a high standard of living. In Australia, recreation has been closely attached to sports and physical education programs, with schools providing varied gymnastics, games, and sports. Community-based programs are sponsored by independent sports clubs and municipal authorities; other cultural and social activities are conducted by churches, community centers, and hospitals. Recently, parks development has accelerated under federal encouragement, and Australia now has a vigorous program of park and recreation professional development.

New Zealand, with a smaller population and a fine natural environment, has been slower to develop municipal park and recreation programs than Australia. Youth organizations are assisted by Youth Activities Officers based in the Department of Internal Affairs, and the Physical Education Branch of the National Education Ministry provides Adventure Camps for school children. New Zealand has outstanding national parks which serve both her own people and visiting tourists. A high level of employment and considerable leisure allow New Zealanders to pursue a host of hobbies and interests: music and the arts, boat building and sailing, many clubs, sports (especially rugby), horse racing with government-operated betting offices, and beer drinking, chiefly in hotels owned by the brewing companies. Ramsay comments that New Zealanders are proud of their beautiful country and take full advantage of its leisure opportunities—to the point that work values have lessened and high rates of absenteeism have resulted.

> Several million work days are sacrificed each year. . . . Staff records show that there is an extraordinary rise in incidents of "illness" after pay day, after long weekends, and during rugby tours.[53]

World Leisure and Recreation Association

A final important aspect of twentieth century recreation and park development has been the focus on international exchange and cooperative efforts in solving problems of leisure and promoting effective recreation and park programs throughout the world. The leading organization in this field is the World Leisure and Recreation Association, which was founded in 1952 at the National Recreation Congress in Philadelphia.

Known at the time as the International Recreation Association, the organization was headed by Director General Thomas E. Rivers, a highly experienced worker in the field of international exchange, with board members and officers representing England, India, Germany, the Philippines, Egypt, Japan, and Latin America. Its essential purpose has been to: (1) provide a central clearing house for the exchange of information and experiences among recreation officials throughout the world; (2) assist countries in establishing central recreation service agencies, programs, facilities, and leadership training; and (3) promote a world recreation movement designed to enrich the human spirit through the wholesome use of leisure. It has worked closely with the United Nations and its affiliated agencies, has provided services to over ninety nations, and has organized numerous exchange programs and published bulletins and pamphlets on international recreation development. In 1964, it sponsored a World Recreation Congress in Osaka and Kyoto, which was attended by five hundred delegates from thirty-two countries.

The work of the association has been widely acclaimed; in recognition of its work with the United Nations, U Thant, former U.N. Secretary-General, commented, "You are helping to create a climate where peace can flourish."[54]

A recent achievement of the renamed World Leisure and Recreation Association was to successfully promote international awareness of recreation and leisure as a significant area of societal concern at the U.N.-sponsored global Conference on Human Settlements, held in 1976 in Vancouver, Canada. This meeting, called HABITAT, was attended by some 2,000 delegates from 135 countries and more than 5,000 other concerned individuals from nongovernmental organizations attending a parallel conference, who gave strong support to recreation and leisure as a vital aspect of improving the quality of life of the world's peoples. A major recommendation approved by the official delegates expresses this conviction.

> As our cities continue to grow, there is an increasingly important basic human need to be provided for, in physical, mental and spiritual benefits to be derived from leisure and recreation. Leisure well used in constructive recreation is basic to the self-fulfillment and life enrichment of the individual, strengthening the social stability of human settlements,

both urban and rural, through the family, the community and the nation. Providing opportunities for pursuit of leisure and recreation, both physical and spiritual, in human settlements, improves the quality of life, and the provision of open space and facilities for leisure should be a concern of high priority.

National governments should co-ordinate and co-operate with the efforts of local and regional authorities and organizations in the planning, development and implementation of leisure and recreational facilities and programmes, for the physical, mental, and spiritual benefit of the people.[55]

This clear statement of belief on the part of leading government officials from many nations reflects the present acceptance of recreation and leisure as important national concerns throughout the world.

Chapter Eight

1. George D. Butler, *Introduction to Community Recreation* (New York: McGraw-Hill, 1976), p. 78.

2. Luther H. Gulick, *A Philosophy of Play* (New York: Scribner, 1920), p. 7.

3. Cited in Martin H. Neumeyer and Esther Neumeyer, *Leisure and Recreation* (New York: Ronald, 1958), p. 73.

4. Joseph Lee, *Play in Education* (New York: Macmillan, 1915, 1929), p. 38.

5. Ibid., p. 255.

6. Ibid., p. 476.

7. Gulick, *Philosophy of Play,* p. 125.

8. John B. Watson, *Psychology from the Standpoint of a Behaviorist* (Philadelphia: J.B. Lippincott, 1924), pp. 439–40.

9. John Dewey, "Interest and Effort in Education," in *Intelligence in the Modern World,* ed. Joseph Ratner (New York: Modern Library, Random House, 1939), p. 611.

10. John Dewey, *Democracy and Education* (New York: Macmillan, 1921), p. 241.

11. Quoted in James E. Rogers, "The Child and Play," *Report on White House Conference on Child Health and Protection,* 1932, p. 27.

12. Gulick, *Philosophy of Play,* p. 3.

13. Walter Wood, *Children's Play and Its Place in Education* (London: Kegan Paul, Trench, Trubner, 1913), p. 197.

14. Rogers, *Child and Play,* p. 36.

15. George Counts, "Social Foundations of Education," Report of the Commission on the Social Studies, 1934, p. 300.

16. Richard H. Edwards, *Popular Amusements* (New York: Association Press, 1915), p. 18.

17. Jane Addams, *The Spirit of Youth and the City Streets,* quoted in Edwards, *Popular Amusements,* p. 18.

18. Edwards, *Popular Amusements,* p. 134.

19. "Journal of Proceedings and Addresses of the Fiftieth Annual Meeting of the National Education Association," July 1912, pp. 233–34.

20. *Cardinal Principles of Secondary Education: Report of the Commission on the Reorganization of Secondary Education of the National Education Association,* Bureau of Education Bulletin No. 35 (Washington, D.C.: Department of the Interior, 1918), p. 10.

21. Butler, *Introduction to Community Recreation,* pps. 76–77.

22. Herbert L. May and Dorothy Petgen, *Leisure and Its Uses* (New York: A. S. Barnes, 1928), p. 258.

23. Richard F. Knapp, "Play for America: The New Deal and the NRA," *Parks and Recreation,* July 1973, p. 23.

24. Ibid.

25. Ibid., p. 42.

26. Eduard C. Lindeman, *Leisure: A National Issue* (New York: American Association for the Study of Group Work, 1939), p. 11.

27. Ibid.

28. Richard F. Knapp, "Play for America: A Trial Balance," *Parks and Recreation,* January 1974, p. 54.

29. James F. Murphy, *Recreation and Leisure Service: A Humanistic Perspective* (Dubuque, Iowa: Wm.C. Brown, 1975), p. 44.

30. Leslie Bella, *Recreation Canada,* 6, No. 33 (1975), 17.

31. Harold A. Brain, "The Dawning Age of Leisure," (unpublished paper, Sault Ste. Marie, Canada), n.d.

32. Elsie M. McFarland, *The Development of Public Recreation in Canada* (Vanier City, Ontario: Canadian Parks/Recreation Association, 1970), p. 1.

33. Ibid., p. 37.

34. Quoted in McFarland, *Public Recreation in Canada,* p. 45.

35. Gail Pogue and Bryce Taylor, "History of Provincial Government Service of the Youth and Recreation Branch," *Recreation Review,* March 1973, p. IV.

36. McFarland, *Public Recreation in Canada,* p. 77.

37. "Leisure in Canada," Report of Montmorency Conference on Leisure, Montmorency, Quebec, 1969.

38. Lebert H. Weir, *Europe at Play: A Study of Recreation and Leisure Time Activity* (New York: A.S. Barnes, 1937), p. 12.

39. P.C. McIntosh, *Sport in Society* (London: C. A. Watts, 1963), p. 114.

40. "Annual Report, National Association of Youth Clubs of Great Britain, 1967–1968," pp. 8–11.

41. Harold Haywood, *A Role for Voluntary Youth Work* (London: National Association of Youth Clubs, June 1968), p. 2.

42. Lawrence Whetten, "Leisure in the Soviet Union," *Recreation,* February 1961, p. 91.

43. Ibid., p. 92.

44. Faubion Bowers, *Broadway, U.S.S.R.: Ballet, Theater and Entertainment in Russia Today* (New York: Thomas Nelson, 1959), p. 13.

45. John B. McLendon, Jr., "The Soviet Union's Program of Physical Culture and Sports," *Journal of Health, Physical Education and Recreation,* April 1962, pp. 28–29.

46. Jon A. Hendricks, "Leisure in the Soviet Union: An Impressionistic Account," *Journal of Leisure Research,* Fall 1973, p. 55.

47. Henry W. Morton, *Soviet Sport* (New York: Collier Books, 1963), pp. 17–18.

48. Quoted in "Modern Living: Discovering the Weekend in Russia," *Time,* 9 May 1969, p. 73.

49. Quoted in George L. Mosse, *Nazi Culture* (New York: Grosset and Dunlap, 1966), p. 296.

50. Guido Deraeck and Livin Bollaert, "Education Permanente of Young Workers in Leisure Time and on the Job," *Journal of Physical Education and Recreation Leisure Today,* October 1976, p. 14.

51. "Frantic Lunge into Sport," *Life,* 11 September 1964, pp. 34–35.

52. Wolf Lyberg, "Communist China Bidding for Athletic Supremacy," *New York Times,* 16 January 1966.

53. Richard L. Ramsay, "New Zealand: Leisure as a Priority," *Journal of Physical Education and Recreation, Leisure Today,* October 1976, p. 12.

54. Quoted in C. Lynn Vendien and John E. Nixon, *The World Today in Health, Physical Education and Recreation* (Englewood Cliffs, N.J.: Prentice-Hall, 1968), p. 76.

55. "Leisure and Recreation Become World Priorities," *Parks and Recreation,* September 1976, p. 6.

THREE

THE RECREATION MOVEMENT TODAY

ROLE OF FEDERAL, STATE, AND PROVINCIAL GOVERNMENTS

This chapter is concerned with the role of the Federal, state, and provincial governments in the United States and Canada, with respect to recreation and parks.

Federal recreation functions in both countries have developed without a systematic plan. No single agency or authority has been responsible for determining appropriate goals or coordinating the work of all departments. For the most part, national government functions in recreation evolved as secondary outcomes of other programs. To illustrate, the initial purpose of the Tennessee Valley Authority in the Appalachian mountain region of the United States was to provide badly needed flood and erosion controls and inexpensive sources of electric power for rural regions. It soon became apparent that the great TVA lakes and reservoirs had the potential for providing enjoyable recreation for millions of campers and boating enthusiasts. Leisure activities rapidly became a major industry within the Appalachian region and contributed substantially to the economies of the states and communities involved. In many other government programs having to do with land, water, and wildlife maintenance or development, recreation use has become an increasingly important concern.

Functions of American Federal Government in Recreation

This section will examine the varied functions of the Federal government in recreation in the United States. Later sections will examine the functions of the

Canadian federal government and the state and provincial governments in both countries.

1. *Direct Management of Outdoor Recreation Resources.* The Federal government in the United States, through such agencies as the National Park Service or Bureau of Land Management, owns and operates a vast network of parks, forests, lakes and reservoirs, seashores, and other facilities which are extensively used for outdoor recreation.

2. *Conservation and Resource Reclamation.* Closely related to the preceding function, the government reclaims natural resources which have been destroyed, damaged, or threatened, and promotes programs related to conservation, wildlife, and antipollution controls.

3. *Assistance to Open-Space and Park Development Programs.* Chiefly with funding authorized by the 1965 Land and Water Fund Conservation Act, the Federal government has provided hundreds of millions of dollars in matching grants to states and localities to promote open-space development. Also, through direct aid to municipalities carrying out housing and urban development projects, the Federal government has subsidized the development of local parks, playgrounds, and centers.

4. *Direct Programs of Recreation Participation.* The government operates a number of direct programs of recreation service in Veterans Administration Hospitals and other Federal institutions, and in the armed forces on bases throughout the world.

5. *Advisory and Financial Assistance.* The Federal government provides varied forms of assistance to states, localities, and other public or voluntary community agencies. For example, many community programs serving economically and socially disadvantaged populations have been assisted by the Departments of Housing and Urban Development; Health, Education, and Welfare; and Labor, among others.

6. *Aid to Professional Education.* The government—particularly bureaus within the Department of Health, Education, and Welfare—has provided training grants for professional education in recreation in colleges and universities throughout the United States. These have been specially directed at meeting the needs of the physically or mentally disabled, and the aging.

7. *Promotion of Recreation as an Economic Function.* The Federal government has been active in promoting tourism, providing aid to rural residents in developing recreation enterprises, and assisting Indian tribes in establishing recreational and tourist facilities on their reservations. Such agencies as the Bureau of the Census and the Coast Guard also provide needed information for travel, boating, and similar pastimes. In 1973, Federal involvement in outdoor recreation alone had expanded to the point that

> over 80 agencies, commissions, committees, and councils were engaged in over 300 separate outdoor recreation-related programs. These programs range from management of parklands to general advisory functions and include programs for technical and financial assistance, planning, research, resource use regulation, and coordination.[1]

The scope of outdoor recreation involvement is illustrated in Table 9–1 and in the descriptions of the major Federal outdoor recreation-related agencies that follow.

Table 9-1

Acreage Operated by Federal Agencies in the United States with
Recreation Functions (1972)[2]

Agency	Acres
National Park Service	24,560,635
Forest Service	187,074,194
Bureau of Sport Fisheries and Wildlife	27,990,458
Bureau of Land Management	473,994,848
Bureau of Reclamation	7,584,737
Department of Defense	
Army, Navy, and Air Force	22,955,783
Army Corps of Engineers	10,612,013
Tennessee Valley Authority	910,687
Total	755,683,355

Source: General Services Administration (1973), supplemented by reports from Federal land managing agencies.

National Park Service

The National Park Service has the responsibility for protecting and maintaining all national parks and monuments, battlefield parks and sites, national memorials, military parks, the National Capital parks, and certain national cemeteries so that they may yield the maximum benefit and service to the American people.

The concept of providing outdoor recreation resources has become so strongly accepted within the National Park Service that it now provides tent, cabin, and hotel accommodations, bridle and hiking trails, marinas and boat docks, museums, and picnic facilities for public use. In many parks, it offers an interpretive nature program through conducted walks, tours, museums and other displays, lectures, and campfire programs. The Park Service does not allow hunting or commercial fishing, cutting of timber, or exploitation of other natural resources; its emphasis is strongly conservationist.

Most of the property administered by the National Park Service in its early years was west of the Mississippi, but particularly in recent decades, it has added major seashore parks and other areas elsewhere in the country and closer to urban centers. For example, East Coast sites now include the Fire Island National Seashore on Long Island, Acadia National Park in Maine, Assateague National Seashore on the Maryland coast, Cape Hatteras National Seashore in North Carolina, and Gateway East, in the New York–New Jersey harbor area.

Today the National Park Service has 309 different parks, including 186 historical sites, 77 natural areas, and 46 recreational facilities. The 38 major national parks comprise the chief recreational attractions, and the overall system attracts an increasing flow of visitors, reported in the mid-1970s as 217 million a year. Its rapid increase in recreational use has raised some key questions about the fundamental mission of the National Park Service, particularly with respect to its effort to meet *urban* recreation needs:

> Some defenders of the National Park Service argue that there is an inherent conflict between urban recreation and the objectives for environmental and historic preservation that have typified the Park Service's primary mission since 1916. Other Park Service defenders are equally persuaded that the only way to strengthen, and perhaps to avoid the loss of, a broad citizen constituency for the national park systems is to bring the system closer to where people live and work.[3]

The problem is made even more severe by the combination of overcrowding and reduced staffs, budget trims, and increasing thefts and vandalism in the national parks. In the summer of 1976, the number of visitors increased by up to 70 percent over the previous year in such major parks as Yosemite, Yellowstone, and Grand Teton. An obvious problem within all Federal outdoor recreation programs is the need to provide sufficient budgetary support to meet the growing public demands for facilities and programs.

National Forest Service

The second important Federal agency with a major responsibility for administering extensive preserves of wilderness for public recreation use is the National Forest Service within the Department of Agriculture. In contrast with the Park Service, the Forest Service is responsible not for scenic monuments and historical or geological treasures, but for huge areas of forests and grasslands. Rather than the National Park Service's single-use concept of preservation and public enjoyment of natural areas, the Forest Service accepts the multiple-use concept of Federally owned land under its control; mining, grazing, lumbering, and hunting are all permitted in national forests.

The Forest Service in 1974 was operating 197 million acres of publicly owned land in approximately 154 national forests, 19 national grasslands, and various small land utilization projects, chiefly within the western states. Over 190 million recreation visitor-days were recorded in 1974—a dramatic increase over 45.7 million visitor-days in 1955, and 156.5 million in 1968. Use of the forests extends from primitive exploration of wilderness areas by horse, by canoe, or on foot, to tent and trailer camping or accommodations at concession-owned hotels and lodges.

U.S. Army Corps of Engineers

The Corps of Engineers of the U.S. Department of the Army is responsible for the improvement and maintenance of rivers and other waterways to facilitate navigation and flood control. It constructs reservoirs, protects and improves beaches and harbors, and administers over 11 million acres of Federally owned land and water impoundments. This includes 390 major reservoirs and lakes; the majority of these are managed by the Corps, and the remainder are managed by state and local agencies under lease. Over two-thirds of the Corps' man-made lakes and reservoirs are located within fifty miles of Standard Metropolitan Statistical Areas (roughly defined as urban, or containing at least one city of fifty thousand or more residents).

Army Corps of Engineers recreation sites are heavily used by the public for boating, camping, hunting and fishing. Based on the Water Project Recreation Act of 1965, recreation and fish and wildlife development are regarded as equal in priority to other uses for which Federal water resource projects may be initiated. Visitor-days at Army Corps of Engineers sites have increased dramatically from 63 million in 1955 to 350 million in 1974. The Corps often leases shorelines along its reservoirs to commercial concessionaires or makes them available for private citizens and organizations to build camps and summer homes.

Bureau of Land Management

Established in 1946, the Bureau of Land Management has jurisdiction over federally owned public lands which have not been incorporated into specific national forests, parks, or other recreation areas. In all, it has exclusive responsibility for about 451 million acres of land (more than half of it in Alaska), under a system of multiple use that includes sustained yield, environmental quality protection, and recreation. These national resource lands contain some of America's most spectacular desert, mountain, and canyon scenery, used for float trips, hiking, off-road vehicle activity, picnicking, and other recreational pursuits. Recreational use of the national resource lands climbed from 9 million visitor-days in 1964 to 55 million in 1974, and is expected to reach 80 million by 1980.

Bureau of Indian Affairs

This agency exists primarily to provide service to American Indian tribes in such areas as health, education, economic development, and land management. It operates under civilian control in the Department of the Interior. Indian-owned properties today include about 58 million acres with over 5,500 lakes. The various tribes develop and manage recreational facilities such as campgrounds, museums, restaurants, and hunting and fishing areas, and provide guides and "packaged" hunting parties. As of the late 1960s, over 10 million visitors a year used Indian-owned land for recreation. In some areas, Indian arts and crafts products are sold in native-operated stores, and costumed ceremonial performances are presented as tourist attractions.

Bureau of Reclamation

Housed within the Department of the Interior, this agency is responsible for water resource development, chiefly in western states. Although its original purpose was to promote irrigation and electric power, it has accepted recreation as a function since 1936. The policy of the Bureau of Reclamation is to transfer reservoir areas wherever possible to other Federal agencies; often these become classified as National Recreation Areas and are assigned to the National Park Service for operation. The emphasis is on active recreation use such as boating, camping, hiking, hunting, and fishing rather than sightseeing. By the late 1960s, Bureau of Reclamation properties covered over 4.5 million acres of land and 1.5 million surface acres of water. Visitor attendance climbed from 6 million in 1950 to an estimated 56 million in 1972.

216

Tennessee Valley Authority

Although the purpose of the Tennessee Valley Authority when created by Congress in 1933 was to develop the Tennessee River for flood control, navigation, and electric power, its reservoirs have become increasingly valuable as recreation resources in Kentucky, North Carolina, Tennessee, and other southern and border states. The TVA itself does not operate recreation facilities, but makes land available to other public agencies or private groups for development.

The value of parks, camps, marinas, and other recreation facilities and equipment that have been placed on the shores of TVA reservoirs and lakes was estimated in 1974 at $482 million. Visitor-days were reported in 1968 at 44.3 million, and in 1974 at 61.9 million.

Fish and Wildlife Service

Housed in the Department of the Interior, the Fish and Wildlife Service has a direct responsibility to protect fish and wildlife on Federal properties throughout the United States. It administers laws for the protection and propagation of birds, mammals, reptiles, and amphibians, carries out research studies, conducts wildlife conservation education, enforces Federal game laws, and cooperates with state fish and game agencies in the control of injurious or destructive birds, animals, and fish.

The Fish and Wildlife Service consists of two separate bureaus: the Bureau of Commercial Fisheries and the Bureau of Sports Fisheries and Wildlife. In 1962, Congress declared recreation to be an appropriate "secondary purpose" of the National Wildlife Refuge system, and in 1966 it passed the Endangered Species Preservation Act; both acts have given strong support to the wildlife conservation program of the Bureau of Sports Fisheries and Wildlife. Today the refuge system operates about 370 nature preserves totaling 32 million acres.

The Bureau of Outdoor Recreation

The establishment of the Bureau of Outdoor Recreation in the Department of the Interior in 1962 was a major step toward the unification and promotion of Federal programs concerned with open space, natural resources, and outdoor recreation. The recommendations of the Outdoor Recreation Resources Review Commission to President John F. Kennedy stressed the need for fuller attention to major priorities in the area of natural resources and outdoor recreation. The commission urged the creation of a bureau that could provide leadership, coordinate programs and services, and stimulate state and local governments throughout the United States to promote open-space and outdoor recreation resource development.

The Bureau of Outdoor Recreation administers the Land and Water Conservation Fund, providing matching grants to states and municipalities for acquisition and development of outdoor recreation areas. It has become a leader in national land-use planning, through its administration of these funds and through its review of SCORPs (Statewide Comprehensive Outdoor Recreation Plans). Another specific responsibility of the bureau is to coordinate the National Wild and Scenic Rivers System and the National Trails System.

In addition, the Bureau of Outdoor Recreation conducts major studies of

217

national outdoor recreation needs and assists in the coordination of all Federal outdoor recreation programs, reviewing budgets and evaluating and monitoring programs in sixteen different agencies. It also is responsible for conveying Federal surplus property to state and local governments for public park and recreation use, and provides broad-based technical assistance to recreation suppliers and users.

Land and Water Conservation Fund Program

This fund was created to provide urgently needed public outdoor recreation areas and facilities. It was enacted into law by Congress in 1965 to assist states, local governments, and other federal agencies in their outdoor recreation and open-space programs. Funding is derived mainly from admission and user fees at Federal recreation areas, net proceeds from the sale of surplus Federal property, and the Federal tax on motorboat fuels. Of the total amount (projected at the outset to be about $160 million per year), 40 percent is made available to Federal agencies and 60 percent to states and territories as grants-in-aid on a 50 percent matching basis for planning, acquisition, or development projects. The emphasis is on acquisition rather than development, and on sites for direct recreation use rather than historic sites or museums.

Appropriations to states and territories from 1965 through the fiscal year 1974 exceeded $1 billion. The overall budget of the Land and Water Conservation Fund was authorized in 1975 at $300 million a year, with plans to raise it to $900 million within three years.

Federal Programs for Outdoor Recreation

A number of other Federal agencies have responsibilities related to outdoor recreation, particularly with respect to financial assistance.

The Agricultural Stabilization and Conservation Service has assisted many farmers in developing ponds and reservoirs on private land and stocking them with fish. The Farmers Home Administration gives credit and management advice to rural organizations and farmers in developing recreation facilities. The Soil Conservation Service has aided thousands of landowners in establishing one or more income-producing recreation areas.

The Department of Agriculture also assists rural residents to establish private recreation enterprises. Its Federal Extension Service aids community recreation planning in rural areas and advises states on outdoor recreation development, working in many states through extension agents at land-grant agricultural colleges.

In the Department of Commerce, the Bureau of the Census furnishes population statistics and projections needed for recreation planning, including trends in recreation demand and participation. The Business and Defense Services Administration provides useful publications, guides, and special studies for operators of resorts, restaurants, ski centers, and other recreation facilities and for manufacturers of recreation equipment. The Economic Development Administration researches the economic effects of recreation development on business in local communities, and provides grants and loans for public works. The Coast and Geodetic Survey Nautical Charting program provides charts and related information about tides, currents, and weather for safe navigation by boating enthusiasts.

Finally, in the area of economic development, the U.S. Travel Service promotes the nation's tourist attractions and facilities in varied ways.

The Office of the President has been active in the establishment of commissions and advisory bodies relating to open space and beautification. It has expanded the National Wilderness Preservation System, established a Clean Rivers Demonstration Program and a national system of hiking trails, and initiated numerous other Federal efforts to improve the natural environment, including sponsorship of numerous conferences on conservation and the establishment of a Council on Recreation and Natural Beauty.

A review of the total Federal role in outdoor recreation and park development reveals a tremendous growth of interest and support among the various departments and agencies involved, resulting in greatly increased recreation opportunities for the public at large and social and economic benefits to the regions involved. Despite these improvements, the success of Federal programs has been limited by the government's failure to provide adequate funding support to Federal operation of parks and other outdoor recreation facilities, and the failure to give strong, centralized leadership recognizing total national needs in the leisure field.

Other Federal Programs Related to Recreation

Another sphere of substantial Federal activity in the United States has been to meet the needs of urban populations, the poor, and the physically or mentally disabled. A variety of such socially oriented programs has been provided during the past two decades.

Programs under Health, Education, and Welfare

Since its establishment in 1867, the U.S. Office of Education has been concerned with recreation as part of the total spectrum of education and community service for children and youth.

Several recent acts of Congress have promoted the work of educational agencies in community-oriented programs, adult education, and informal social education, several of which have had implications for the support of recreation as a school-connected service. For example, Title I of the Higher Education Act of 1965 provided grants to states enabling colleges and universities to strengthen programs to solve community problems related to land-use and open-space planning. The Elementary and Secondary Education Act of 1965 provided grants for supplemental educational centers and services, in-service training programs, and institutions, which included camping, cultural, physical education and recreation, and other special programs to serve the physically and mentally handicapped. The Supplemental Education Centers and Services, under Title III of this act, authorized outdoor education and recreation projects such as nature centers, teacher training, museums, and field trips. The Community Schools Act of 1975 authorized several million dollars a year to support varied community education projects, including recreation.

The Office of Education has also supported several projects to adapt facilities and develop recreation programs for chronically ill or disabled children and youth. Through its Bureau for Handicapped Children and Youth, the Office of

219

Education has funded training programs in recreation in a number of colleges throughout the United States.

Administration on Aging

Authorized by the Older Americans Act of 1965, this Federal agency promotes comprehensive programs for aging persons, providing grants for training professional personnel, and demonstration projects intended to prepare professionals to work with older people. It also gathers information on new or expanded programs and services for the aging, and supports research projects in this field. Among the various local programs which have received funding under Title III of this act, as amended in 1969 and 1973, are: (1) continuing education services; (2) counseling services; (3) health-related services; (4) out-reach services for homebound or isolated aging persons; (5) referral services; (6) preventive services, to help older people avoid institutionalization; (7) legal services; (8) employment services; and (9) recreation services. Several years after the inception of these programs, participation by elderly persons was reported to be more than three times higher in recreation programs than in any other form of service provided under Title III.

Children's Bureau

This agency, created in 1912, is specifically concerned with the welfare of children and youth—especially in migrant families and among the physically and mentally disabled, the institutionalized, and the socially deviant. It has published guides and handbooks related to recreation and has worked through states and a variety of national organizations to promote improved services for young people. A major function of the Children's Bureau is to sponsor White House Conferences on Children and Youth every ten years, which consider recreational needs as an important concern.

Public Health Service

Through the Bureau of State Services, the Public Health Service provides technical assistance for the improvement of environmental, sanitation, and safety aspects of recreation facilities and programs. The Public Health Service has also awarded grants to the National Recreation and Park Association for the training of leaders to work with the ill, the disabled, and particularly the mentally retarded, in community settings. The National Institute of Mental Health, a branch of the Public Health Service, assists research into the cause, prevention, and treatment of mental illness, including recreation-related projects. The Public Health Service also sponsors a number of direct recreation programs at institutions such as the Federal leprosarium at Carville, Louisiana and St. Elizabeth's Hospital in Washington, D.C.

Rehabilitation Services Administration

This major agency in the Department of Health, Education, and Welfare administers the Federal law authorizing vocational rehabilitation programs designed to help the physically and mentally disabled gain employment and lead fuller lives. It assists state rehabilitation programs and has been responsible for varied special projects in the areas of research, demonstration, and training. Beginning in the 1960s, several college departments training therapeutic recreation specialists received curriculum development and scholarship grants from the Vocational Services Administration, which is now part of the Rehabilitation Services Administration.

In later legislation, such as the Education for All Handicapped Children Act of 1975 (PL–94–142), the Federal government has upheld its recognition of

220

recreation as a significant area of service for special populations. For example, the Federal Register of February, 1975 published changes in the regulation and guidelines for programs for the education of the handicapped, in which the U.S. Office of Education affirmed the need to recognize "physical education and recreation [as] an integral part of programs for the education of handicapped children."[4]

Thus the various agencies and bureaus operating under the umbrella of the Department of Health, Education, and Welfare in the United States have given some degree of support to recreation as a needed service, although this support must be characterized as minimal and inconsistent. Existing programs under HEW have fallen short of meeting the real needs of the handicapped and other special populations.

Recreation Functions Related to Housing and Urban Development

The Federal government has had an extensive record of promoting slum clearance and assisting housing programs in America's cities, with the provision of recreation areas and facilities in housing projects one of the components. As early as World War II, the Public Housing Administration of the Housing and Home Finance Agency helped provide recreation facilities in low-rent housing developments.

The Housing Act of 1961 provided grants to state and local governments for the acquisition of open-space lands in urban areas for park, recreation, conservation, scenic, or historic purposes. Administered by the Urban Renewal Administration, this act was the first major effort by the Federal government to promote open-space development in urban areas; it resulted in the acquisition of over 197,000 acres of land to meet outdoor recreation needs of urban residents.

The Federal Department of Housing and Urban Development was established in 1965, with responsibility for a wide range of Federally assisted programs including urban renewal and planning, public housing, mass transit, and open space. With funding of $7.5 billion for a four-year period, HUD was empowered to provide up to 50 percent of the cost of land acquisition, development, and beautification. Section 705 of the act, known as "the small parks program," authorized grants for the demolition of slums to create urban open spaces, and the Urban Beautification and Improvement Program supported numerous projects aimed specifically toward beautifying cities.

During the 1960s, the Demonstration Cities and Metropolitan Development Act and the Neighborhood Facilities Program provided substantial matching funds to help develop parks, playgrounds, youth centers, and similar facilities. These programs stressed the coordination of Federal, state, and local agencies. A special aspect of the Federal housing effort was the Model Cities Program, which provided extensive planning and development grants in depressed urban areas.

Federal Antipoverty Programs

The so-called Federal "war on poverty" initiated during the 1960s under the Johnson Administration gave considerable support to the provision of recreation services for economically disadvantaged urban populations. Its major impetus came from the Economic Opportunity Act of 1964, which created the Office of Economic Opportunity to coordinate all antipoverty programs on the Federal level. Among the major programs sponsored by OEO were the following:

Job Corps

This was a program established to provide training in vocational and basic academic subjects for out-of-work, out-of-school, young men and women between the ages of sixteen and twenty-one. It was a residential program which operated in over one hundred settings throughout the United States, both urban and rural. Recreation was an important aspect of the Job Corps training program, and also served as the basis for a number of Job Corps' projects—particularly those involving conservation efforts.

VISTA (Volunteers in Service to America)

This was a much smaller part of the antipoverty program, viewed by many as a domestic Peace Corps. VISTA assigned several thousand workers—chiefly young college graduates—to work in poverty areas including rural slums, impoverished villages, and Indian reservations. The role of VISTA volunteers in many cases included providing local recreation programs, community beautification projects, or recreation enterprise as money-making ventures.

Neighborhood Youth Corps

This was established under the Economic Opportunity Act as a work training program for unemployed young people, chiefly in the cities, but also in some suburban or rural poverty areas. Subcontractors (those employing youth on Neighborhood Youth Corps projects, receiving government funding for their salaries) were either governmental or voluntary nonprofit agencies. Many youths were assigned to work during the summers in recreation and park departments, schools, hospitals, or community centers, often with direct recreation leadership responsibilities.

Community Action Programs

These consisted of a considerable number of separate projects in local communities, sponsored by a variety of governmental, voluntary, or "indigenous" groups (referring to newly developed bodies of poor people themselves) organized on a neighborhood or community basis. During several summers in the 1960s, the OEO gave substantial grants to Community Action Programs—particularly in urban slums—to meet the recreation needs of poor people, and to provide an emergency form of employment and activity. With growing racial friction in the large cities and frequent summer outbursts, recreation was increasingly viewed as a useful safety valve for "ghetto" neighborhoods. The rationale of supporting summer youth programs, most of which had a substantial recreation element, was described as follows by the director of the Community Action Programs:

> Summer youth programs are intended to provide jobs, additional steps in preparation for work, educational upgrading, recreation, cultural enrichment, improved physical well-being, leadership training, and constructive community impact. Ideally, any summer program should offer each participant active experiences in a number of areas. It is anticipated that the impact of summer programs on the participants will be to increase their self-respect, self-direction, practical skills, community awareness and interests, as well as their capacity to work and play with others.[5]

In their later stages, Community Action Programs stressed "maximum feasible participation" by local residents in planning, organizing, and controlling their own programs. Many local organizations were formed for this purpose, often composed entirely of members of one particular minority or ethnic group. Some of these organizations used community centers built with funding assistance by HUD or Model Cities as their primary facility.

Beginning in 1969, most of these programs were sharply reduced; some were terminated, and others were transferred to other agencies. However, the Neighborhood Youth Corps continued to provide summer work programs for young people, along with other special youth programs sponsored by the Federal Departments of Agriculture, Interior, Transportation, and Labor. To illustrate, during the 1970s, the Department of Agriculture provided food grants for summer vacation programs for children and youth. The Department of Transportation helped fund programs to bus children from urban slums to recreation programs in outlying parks. The Recreation Support Program, sponsored by the Department of Labor, assisted many urban recreation departments in providing summer youth programs. As late as 1976, the Community Services Administration had the responsibility of monitoring over $300 million in grants to almost 900 local Community Action agencies.

Two other specially funded Federal programs relevant to recreation were CETA and LEAA. CETA (Comprehensive Employment and Training Act of 1973) was established to provide job training and employment opportunities for the poor and unemployed. Many thousands of CETA workers have been assigned by cities and other agencies to recreation and park jobs (in some cases, employees who were laid off for budgetary reasons were rehired as CETA workers). LEAA (Law Enforcement Assistance Act) is concerned with the total spectrum of crime prevention; its specially funded projects have included antidelinquency programs and assisting in improvement of correctional agencies. Recreation has been a significant component of these projects.

Recreation and the Armed Forces

Another major recreation function of the Federal government has been provision of facilities and programs for the armed forces, both in the continental United States and abroad.

For many years it has been the official policy of the Department of Defense to provide a well-rounded "morale, welfare, and recreational program" for the physical, social, and mental well-being of its personnel. During World War I, Special Services Divisions were established to provide social and recreational programs, to sustain favorable morale, curb homesickness and boredom, minimize fatigue, and reduce A.W.O.L. (absent without leave) and V.D. (venereal disease) rates. At the time of World War II, these special service programs were widely expanded, receiving considerable assistance from such civilian-supported agencies as the United Service Organization and the American Red Cross.

Each branch of the armed forces has its own pattern of recreation sponsorship and administration. The most diversified and strongly supported programs are within the Army and the Air Force.

U.S. Army Recreation

The U.S. Army Recreation Service Program, which is directed by the Office of the Adjutant General, was reported in 1976 to have approximately 9,000 full-time employees at some 375 installations worldwide (see Table 9–2).

To illustrate the scope of this program, the seven core programs listed above involved nearly 125.1 million participants at a total cost of $100.7 million.

Table 9-2

Recreation Facilities and Participation in U.S. Army for Fiscal Year 1975[6]

Core Program	Number and Type of Facilities	Participants
Arts and Crafts	550 facilities, including skill development centers, auto crafts shops, wood shops, and photo labs	6.8 million
Dependent Youth Activities	171 multipurpose centers	13.6 million
Library	328 libraries, 987 field collections	22.2 million
Music and Theater	298 facilities, including theater workshops, music centers, and unit entertainment centers	3.5 million
Outdoor Recreation	2,000 facilities, including Army Travel Camps, picnic areas, riding stables, marinas, and beaches	7.1 million
Recreation Centers	214 multipurpose centers	25.4 million
Sports	1,500 facilities, including gymnasiums, field houses, swimming pools, and playing fields	46.5 million

U.S. Air Force Recreation

The Special Services Program in the U.S. Air Force includes the following major elements: sports, motion pictures, social recreation programs, entertainment, arts and crafts, flying clubs, youth activities, recreation member clubs in special interest areas, outdoor recreation, open messes, libraries, supply and support services, child care, golf, and bowling.

> There are about 210 Air Force bases worldwide that have full-time manpower to conduct recreation programs. In round figures, there are 2,100 military and 6,100 civilians assigned to these programs. . . . In 1974, the total operating expense for the major recreation activities was $83.8 million. The total revenue generated by these activities to defray a portion of the expense was $36.1 million.[7]

With increasingly tight Federal budget controls, the Air Force has made a strong effort to keep operating costs level and to obtain sufficient income from activities such as bowling and golf to defray personnel costs (about 4,200 civilian employees are paid from nonappropriated funds).

U.S. Marine Corps

Recreation programs in the Marine Corps are operated by the Morale Support Activities Branch of the Personnel Services Division, and include a wide range of general activities such as bowling, camping, child care, hobby shops, libraries, motion pictures, social recreation, youth activities, and sports competition on several levels. In fiscal 1975, this overall program involved 1,705 full-time military and civilian employees and 759 part-time workers. In addition to appropriated funds expended that year, 43 separate recreation facilities operating aboard Marine Corps commands supplied $16.6 million of nonappropriated funds to support recreation activities.

The Marine Corps traditionally places a strong emphasis on physical fitness in its recreation programs and has developed many outstanding recreation facilities. For example, during the Vietnam War, the fifty thousand-man Third Marine Amphibious Force near Da Nang used

> a massive recreation complex [including] an Olympic swimming pool, a miniature golf course, a twenty-lane bowling alley, amphitheater, archery range, tennis courts, and a thousand-seat indoor theater . . . [elsewhere were] a beer garden and seashore cafe [and an] outdoor movie theater.[8]

U.S. Navy

In the Navy, recreation is provided by the Recreation and Physical Fitness Branch of the Bureau of Naval Personnel. There is no standard structure or recommended organization of Special Services within the Navy, and funds are derived largely from Navy Exchange sales. Most naval installations ashore have gymnasiums, golf courses, swimming pools, hobby shops, athletic fields, and movie theaters. Some Naval bases provide outstanding recreation facilities and staff. The Great Lakes Naval Training Center on Lake Michigan, for example, serves 34,000 people, with 38 full-time and 55 part-time civilian employees, and 64 military personnel attached to Special Services. The center operates an extensive sports program, with such facilities as a $2 million Bowlarium, an eighteen-hole golf course, a well-equipped gymnasium with thirty-two thousand square feet of floor space, eleven tennis courts, handball courts, and numerous other areas—many built with the assistance of a central recreation fund derived primarily from Navy Exchange fees.

Other facilities include three motion picture theaters on the base, indoor and outdoor swimming facilities, an indoor roller rink, two billiard parlors, a large library, social center, child care center, and varied well-equipped hobby shops. The recreation staff also sponsors an extensive sailing program, summer camp for children, organized tours, and low-cost ticket services for cultural and sports events in Chicago.[9] Shipboard services in the Navy are obviously much more limited, but many ships have facilities for physical fitness activities, hobby shops, lounges, and similar areas.

In addition to such programs attached to individual services, the armed forces promote an extensive range of competitive sports programs. Through interservice competition in such sports as basketball, boxing, wrestling, track and field, and softball, All-Service teams are selected; Armed Forces teams are then chosen to represent the United States in international competition. In recent years, military athletes have competed against forty-eight other nations in competitions throughout the world, sponsored by the *Conseil International du Sport Militaire.*

A special recreation service consists of recreation sites and family campgrounds sponsored by the individual branches of the armed forces, which include ski areas, camping, boating, hunting, and similar facilities. Through interservice agreements, these facilities are available to members of all military departments.

Veterans Administration Hospitals

A related aspect of Federal recreation service consists of programs provided within military and veterans' hospitals. In VA hospitals throughout the United States, recreation is provided (1) to improve and maintain patient morale; (2) to aid in the total rehabilitation process; and (3) to facilitate the patient's adjustment to the hospital and aid in his or her return to community life. Recreation programs are administered by the Physical Medicine and Rehabilitation Service of the Department of Medicine and Surgery of the Veterans Administration in about 170 hospitals serving approximately half a million patients each year.

Support of the Arts

A final important area of Federal interest in recreation in the United States is concern with the growing public interest in the arts and a wide range of cultural activities. President Johnson launched the National Endowment for the Arts in 1966 with an initial Federal contribution of $2.5 million. The amount has been regularly increased, and in 1976, the Federal government budgeted $86 million per year to support the arts. The National Endowment for the Arts and its advisory National Council provide grants to help individuals and nonprofit, tax-exempt organizations continue work in the arts, dance, literature, music, and theater.

Aid has been given not only to established arts organizations, but also to unconventional and innovative arts programs in communities throughout the United States. A special "expansion arts" category of funding has assisted coordinated arts programs and other unique community efforts, including programs for inner city areas, prisons, and other special settings.

Another example of Federal concern with the arts is the establishment of Wolf Trap Farm Park for the Performing Arts, an exciting new National Park Service facility in the rolling hills of northern Virginia, just a few miles from Washington, D.C. Programs at this cultural center have included world famous ballet companies, concerts, symphonies, and similar attractions, with thousands of tickets provided free to children and youth in the Washington area, often through schools or community organizations.[10]

Overview of Federal Recreation Programs

As this chapter has demonstrated, the Federal government in the United States is involved in a wide range of recreation programs. Sometimes, these programs take strange forms. For example, in 1975, to insure that the new FBI headquarters in Washington would be an even more successful tourist attraction than the old building—which had half a million visitors a year—the G-men visited Florida's Walt Disney World for first-hand advice

> on designing the tour route in the massive new building. Along with the traditional visits to the FBI crime laboratory and firing range, the new tour will offer an added attraction—an alcove fitted out with J. Edgar Hoover's own desk and chair, plus other mementos of the late director.[11]

Recreation, even when provided by government, must meet the competition, and so when U.S. Army officials at Fort Hood, Texas sought to "beef up" the attraction of their officers' and enlisted men's clubs, they decided to obtain the services of "go-go" dancers. The manager of the clubs felt that it would be desirable to go through competitive bidding, looked up "go-go dancer" in the contract coding manual, and when he found no such listing, created a code: X–KAKF–48–75–B–I–ICS–0012.

> An announcement was duly published in the Commerce Department's Business Daily, and bids were solicited from 27 purveyors of talent, such as talent agencies . . . to hire two dancers for a maximum of about $45,000 a year.[12]

Apart from such unusual examples, it is obvious that the Federal effort in recreation has developed very successfully in several important directions. However, the following problem areas must be identified:

1. *Support of Urban Programs.* The strongest Federal emphasis by far has been upon the development of outdoor recreation resources and facilities. Clearly a much fuller effort is needed to support and improve people oriented services, particularly in the great metropolitan areas where most of the population lives. In part, this effort has been made through the development of such outstanding new recreation areas as Gateway East (New York–New Jersey) and Gateway West (San Francisco). Nonetheless, it is clear that the preponderance of Land and Water Conservation Fund grants to the states have been used for the development of recreation facilities in suburban and rural areas. A study by the Center for Growth Alternatives, *Recreation in the Cities: Who Gains from Federal Aid?,* shows clearly that only

> a handful of the 26 major cities received substantial LWCF grants, and seven received no money at all. . . . Affluent suburban counties and municipalities have been big winners, as is the case in many federal grant programs.[13]

Beyond this, Federal funding has gone almost exclusively to the acquisition of property and to the development of facilities—without concern for operation of the programs. Typically, in many housing projects with playgrounds and community centers constructed with Federal assistance, there are no funds for program operation; without Federal aid, many economically depressed cities are unable to finance recreation programs.

The nature of Federal funding to the states and municipalities has undergone sharp change in recent years. Under the "new federalism," as outlined in the General Revenue Sharing process (formally authorized under the State and Local Fiscal Assistance Act of 1972), there was a shift from the *categorical grant* approach of previous years, which had required prior Federal approval of projects and careful supervision of performance. Instead, the *block grant* approach during the mid-1970s which involves less Federal control, and the *general revenue sharing* approach, under which funds are automatically distributed according to a population and fiscal formula, allow much greater latitude in local determination of how funds are used. It was reported in 1975 that recreation and cultural programs accounted for only 5 percent of general revenue sharing funds; most assistance went to public safety, education, transportation, and general government. In many cases, this approach has failed to meet the most critical recreation needs of low-income urban populations.

Although it is unrealistic to expect the Federal government to accompany all open-space or facility development grants with funding for current operations, it certainly could, through training, research, subsidies or matching grants, help to upgrade the level of program administration and leadership in many areas where facilities have been provided, and where there is a dearth of competent personnel. Another approach would be to coordinate facilities grants with grants provided by other Federal agencies that could help to provide leadership and maintenance costs. For example, the U.S. Department of Housing and Urban Development (HUD) and the Bureau of Outdoor Recreation signed an agreement in 1976 to coordinate planning activities within and between Federal and state levels of government. If extended to coordinated funding, this sort of joint planning could increase the benefits of facilities grants.

2. *Strengthened Federal Coordination.* A second important area of concern is the role of the Bureau of Outdoor Recreation. Although the BOR has been assigned the task of coordinating outdoor recreation, it has lacked sufficient authority and independence to accomplish joint planning and coordination among all government agencies operating in this field—much less those concerned with other aspects of recreation. To a great degree, the question of America's recreation needs and priorities has been treated as a political football. For example, one of Interior Secretary Walter Hickel's last acts before resigning was to conduct a major study of America's outdoor recreation needs and priorities which, in the form of a huge volume, *The Recreation Imperative,*[14] was presented to President Nixon. This document gave a detailed analysis of the country's critical needs and made a number of major recommendations for dealing with them seriously. It was shelved by the President, and in its place, a much more superficial and glossy report, *A Legacy for America,* was submitted to Congress.[15] Only after Senator Henry Jackson, chairman of the Senate Interior Committee, demanded that *The Recreation Imperative,* which gave a high priority to urban needs and urged a fuller level of expenditure, be released, was it printed for public distribution—four years later.

Many who are concerned with the development of recreation and leisure in the United States suggest the creation of a Federal agency, preferably on the cabinet level, with jurisdiction over *all* recreation programs and governmental operations (including those related to health, education, and welfare, housing and urban development, and other social concerns). Such a department would provide greatly needed national leadership and direction, and would lead to Federal recognition of the growing importance of leisure as a national concern and stronger support for professional development in this field.

228

Functions of Canadian Federal Government in Recreation

Many responsibilities concerning federal recreation programs and services are the same in Canada as in the United States. There are certain distinct differences—some of them stemming from the fact that Canada has a much smaller population, crowded within a much more narrow geographic belt along the lower portion of the country, and others stemming from the fact that the federal government in Canada generally has assumed a much stronger role in support of varied forms of community programs.

In a detailed analysis of the role of federal and provincial responsibilities for leisure services in two Canadian provinces, Burton and Kyllo point out that sixty-four federal departments and agencies assist in the provision of leisure services. Some have a major, direct involvement, such as the Department of Indian and Northern Affairs in national parks, or the Department of National Health and Welfare in amateur sport; others play a much more indirect role. Burton and Kyllo report that

> the nature of [federal] departmental and agency involvement also varies significantly from one to another. Some are involved only in research and policy development; some in coordination; some in the delivery of programs; and some in all of these activities. Some departments and agencies act only in a supportive role to others, while some are initiators and others are engaged in regulation and control. Some departments and agencies have a national orientation, while others are regionally or locally oriented.[16]

Federal Functions in Outdoor Recreation

The major Federal agency concerned with preservation of significant natural and cultural resources for the benefit and enjoyment of Canadians is Parks Canada, part of the Conservation Program of the Department of Indian and Northern Affairs. This agency has three major branches: (1) National Parks, (2) National Historic Parks and Sites, and (3) Policy, Planning, and Research. The National Parks Branch has developed, and is responsible for operating, twenty-eight major parks totalling over fifty thousand square miles. Its policy is to preserve significant scenic, geological, geographical, and biological resources for present and future generations. In addition, Parks Canada is responsible for operating or managing National Marine Parks, National Landmarks, National Wild Rivers, National Historical Trails, and National Parkways, as part of a total system.

Much of the actual design, construction and maintenance of recreation resources, including harbors, wharfs, marinas, rinks, landscaped parks, and highways and their adjacent facilities, is done by the Canadian Department of Public Works, which is the most extensive developer of land and buildings in Canada. The Canadian Government Office of Tourism in the Ministry of Industry, Trade, and Commerce promotes tourism through surveys, brochures, and general assistance in the growth of the travel industry in Canada.

Programs Related to the Arts and Culture

The Canada Council, in the Department of the Secretary of State, provides financial assistance and advisory services for the arts, humanities, and social sciences. Working with the assistance of advisory panels, the Council awards grants and fellowships in various areas of artistic and cultural activity. It helps to support individual professional artists in music, opera, dance, theater, visual arts, and literature, and also provides grants to artistic organizations. It also maintains a collection of Canadian art works, through the Canada Council Art Bank, and recently established an office to promote tours of performing artists in Canada and of Canadian artists abroad.

Through the Canadian Broadcasting Corporation, the Canadian Film Development Corporation, the National Arts Centre Corporation (which sponsors the National Arts Centre for the Performing Arts in Ottawa), and the National Film Board, the federal government directly sponsors considerable cultural activity.

Programs in Physical Fitness and Sport

The Department of National Health and Welfare has the major responsibility for promoting the mental and physical health of all Canadians.

The department's Fitness and Amateur Sport Branch promotes fitness, physical recreation, and amateur sport on all levels. It is divided into two sections: (1) Sport Canada, which provides direct support to national sport governing bodies, helps to stage national and international competition, assists in the development of outstanding sport facilities, subsidizes research and training of coaches, and even assists student athletes with grants-in-aid; and (2) Recreation Canada, a decentralized operation which provides grants to the provinces to promote physical recreation on a mass participation basis through program development, consultation, demonstration projects, conferences, and publications.

These two organizations have wide-ranging effects. Recreation Canada encourages fitness by offering employee fitness programs, by providing information, consultation, and research assistance, and by sponsoring major conferences. Sport Canada offers films, instructional aids, a sports caravan, and numerous other forms of help; it also operates the Administrative Centre for Sport and Recreation in Ottawa, which houses thirty-seven national sport and recreation organizations and provides administrative services for an additional twenty-five.

Services for Special Populations

No single Federal department in Canada has a major responsibility for providing recreation or related services for special populations, or for promoting therapeutic recreation as a rehabilitative discipline or social service. However, a number of different federal agencies have made contributions in this area. Recreation Canada, for example, has funded nationwide research studies intended to determine the present status of therapeutic recreation services in various provinces and communities. The Local Initiatives Program of the Department of Manpower and Immigration has provided funds to support community-based social programs which would in turn create local employment opportunities; many of these projects involve recreation services and meet the needs of special populations, including the handicapped.

The Canada Assistance Plan in the Department of National Health and Welfare provides funding to the provinces to help subsidize children's and youth programs, day care programs, special care institutions, and similar efforts, many of which include recreation. New Horizons, in the same department, assists aging and retired persons with projects designed to benefit themselves and their communities. A number of other agencies also deal with institutional services.

Professional Development in Recreation

The Canadian Parks/Recreation Association is the largest special interest group in Canada concerned with promoting recreation and leisure; its membership of approximately three thousand persons as of the mid-1970s consists chiefly of recreation and park professionals. It seeks to stimulate and advance the recreation and park movement in Canada in a variety of ways (see chapter 12). Approximately 80 percent of the operation budget of CPRA is derived from federal grants, most through the Department of National Health and Welfare and the Ministry of State for Urban Affairs.

Other departments have given significant assistance to professional development in Canada. The Department of Indian Affairs and Northern Development, for example, has awarded a number of National Parks Service scholarships for graduate studies in park and outdoor recreation departments or related fields such as regional planning, resource development, or ecological sciences. Other departments, particularly those concerned with travel and tourism, have provided extensive support for research to professional recreation organizations or college and university educators.

Other Federal Functions

Numerous other federal agencies in Canada provide or assist leisure services in one form or another. As in the United States, the Department of National Defence provides excellent recreation facilities and programs for members of the armed forces and their families. Armed forces lands also provide settings for much hunting and fishing. Military personnel and equipment are frequently used in displays, cultural and social events, and major sporting events both within Canada and abroad. Other departments contribute to environmental development and protection, economic programs, and cultural activities related to recreation.

In conclusion, the federal government in Canada provides extensive assistance to meeting recreation needs, both through its own programs and by helping to support the efforts of provincial or local government, or citizens' organizations in areas of special interest.

Canada gives more direct financial aid to sports and recreation organizations than the United States, where programs such as the President's Council on Physical Fitness and Sports have received a minimum of funding and have been mainly public relations campaigns. Cosgrove and Jackson comment that Americans led in the field of outdoor recreation planning until recently, but Canadian federal authorities have put forward more rigorous proposals for land-use zoning in federal and provincial parks, and have certainly given strong support to detailed analysis of travel, tourism, and outdoor recreation generally.[17]

To gain a fuller understanding of governmental functions related to recreation ai d leisure in both countries, it is necessary to examine the role of state and provincial governments in the United States and in Canada.

Functions of American State Governments in Recreation

The role of state governments in recreation and parks has generally rested upon the Tenth Amendment to the Constitution, which states, "The powers not delegated to the United States by the Constitution, nor prohibited by it to the States, are reserved to the States respectively, or to the people." This amendment, commonly referred to as the "states' rights amendment," is regarded as the source of state powers in such areas as public education, welfare, and health services. Under this mandate, each state considered it appropriate to provide recreation facilities and services to meet the needs of its citizens, within the following eight areas of concern.

1. *Enabling Legislation.* The power to establish public recreation and park programs is generally granted to municipal governments by constitutional, statutory, or charter provisions granted by the state legislature. Although local governing bodies have certain assumed powers in this area, through the principle of "police powers" or the "general welfare" clause in the Federal Constitution, specific legal authority is needed for them to acquire properties, employ personnel, or impose taxes to support recreation.

In almost all states today, county, municipal, or school authorities are authorized to operate facilities and provide programs. Enabling legislation may range from rather simple authorizations to fully detailed codes, including such elements as the method of acquiring and developing properties, financial recreation and park programs, and establishing public boards, commissions, and special districts.

2. *Outdoor Recreation Resources and Programs.* Each state government today operates a network of parks and other outdoor recreation resources. Between 1960 and 1970, states passed bond issues totalling nearly $2.8 billion for outdoor recreation land acquisition and facility development, and it was reported in the early 1970s that states managed almost 42 million acres of land for outdoor recreation purposes. The rate of participation and state spending has gone up steadily over the past two decades (see Table 9–3).

Although states have continued to spend heavily for outdoor recreation programs, with the annual rate of expenditure reported in 1973 as almost $614 million, the rate of growth has slowed. In some states, budgets have been frozen, and extreme shortages of personnel and equipment threaten a continued deterioration of overcrowded parks. Other states have increased user fees to provide funds for state park expansion programs. More and more states are using special taxes on motorboat fuel or funds derived from registrations and licenses for outdoor recreation to support their park and recreation programs. Many states are now using comput-

Table 9-3

Growth of State Recreation and Park Programs[18]

	1955	1960	1967	1970
Total attendance in recreation and parks	232 million	263 million	391 million	482 million
Total expenditure for capital and operating budgets	$87 million	$152 million	$295 million	$386 million

erized analyses of demand and use to plan their facilities development more efficiently, or use computerized campsite reservation systems to maximize use and income from state parks. As discussed in chapter 5, some states have begun to discourage tourism as a means of protecting their park systems and water resources against over-use and pollution.

3. *Promotion of Conservation and Open Space.* In addition to major funding programs which most states have implemented to acquire new acreage for their own park systems, state governments have also aided municipalities by coordinating and reviewing their applications for grants under the Land and Water Conservation Fund program, and providing matching funds, as described earlier.

Beyond the immediate task of acquiring open spaces or preventing pollution, states have other conservation functions: they manage wildlife resources, establish policies or laws governing hunting and fishing, plant trees and bird cover, and present intensive conservation education programs to children and youth, hunters, fishermen, and boating enthusiasts.

4. *Assistance to Local Governments.* State park and recreation agencies have assisted local authorities in a variety of ways; they provide consultants, do research studies, call conferences, and promote the work of recreation agencies on the local level.

Up to now, most state parks have been located in wooded or mountainous regions, usually at a considerable distance from metropolitan areas and therefore inaccessible to most city dwellers, particularly the poor and minority group members. Some states, however, have begun to acquire and develop parkland close to or actually within the boundaries of their most crowded cities, in order to provide needed services to urban populations. More and more, states are developing special programs of environmental education or initiating busing programs to state parks, to serve low-income urban residents.

California offers an excellent example. In addition to maintaining an extensive statewide system of 240 units of all sorts comprising over one million acres, the state has assigned $90 million of a recently passed $250 million bond issue to cities, counties, and districts, as 100 percent grants. Recognizing the special problems of metropolitan Los Angeles, the state park and recreation department established Malibu Lagoon State Beach as an intensive use area near the metropolitan area. California also acquired 310 acres for a new park in the Santa Monica Mountains, within the city of Los Angeles, and doubled the size of Mount Tamalpais State Park with the purchase of 2,150 acres in the San Francisco Bay region.

Another useful example is New York, where the legislature created a new State Park Commission for the city of New York in 1967. A leading accomplishment of this commission is the opening of New York's first state park in a city—Roberto Clemente State Park on the banks of the Harlem River in New York City. An urban park, Roberto Clemente obviously does not have extensive forest areas; instead, it offers a huge swimming pool, bathhouse, picnic area, games area, indoor gymnasium and large community center:

> The park is buzzing with activity from morning until late evening, 12 months of the year. Musical and theatrical performances, art displays, and athletic contests keep both participants and spectators occupied. And through the summer months it is the departure point for bus loads of youngsters, senior citizens, and neighborhood residents to state parks in the Palisades, Taconic and Long Island regions.[19]

5. *Recreation Sponsorship in Other Settings.* Another important function of state governments is to provide direct recreation services within the institutions or agencies it sponsors, such as mental hospitals, special schools for the mentally retarded, and penal or correctional institutions. Although statistics as to the scope of such programs are limited, it is apparent that this is a growing area of state involvement in recreation.

6. *Promotion of Professional Advancement.* While states promote effective leadership and administrative practices in recreation and parks by developing personnel standards and providing conferences and research support, their major contribution lies in the professional preparation of recreation practitioners in state colleges and universities. Of the colleges and universities in the United States with professional recreation and park curricula, a substantial majority are part of state university systems.

7. *Development and Enforcement of Standards.* As indicated earlier, states also have the function of screening personnel by establishing standards and hiring procedures, or by requiring Civil Service examinations, certification, or personnel registration programs in recreation and parks (see chapter 12).

Many states also have developed standards related to health and safety practices in camping and similar settings. State departments enforce safety codes, promote facilities standards, ensure that recreation resources can accommodate the physically handicapped, regulate or prohibit certain types of commercial amusements, and in some cases perform regular inspections of camps, swimming pools, resorts, or voluntary or proprietary institutions such as nursing homes and health-related facilities.

8. *Promotion of Recreation as Economic Asset.* A final important function of state governments is to promote all aspects of leisure involvement that support economic development. Those states whose climates are suited to retirement and year-round recreation or vacation travel (such as Florida, Arizona, or California) promote all sorts of events, facilities, and colorful regional recreational opportunities that will draw tourists. Other states with scenic views, forests, lakes, ocean front or winter sports areas describe themselves as "vacation lands" and actively promote such tourist attractions.

Tourism represents a multifaceted economic asset. Tourists and visitors to a particular site or event spend substantial sums for food, gift items, equipment, entertainment, and lodging; this money benefits various levels of the local economy and provides substantial employment. Most states sponsor and encourage festivals, tournaments, displays, and other programs to attract tourists.

Table 9-4

New York State Aid to the Arts, 1974

Museums	$2,866,057	Presenting Organizations (Management and Promotion)	$1,077,290
Music	2,549,495		
		Community Projects in Visual Arts	686,363
Art Service Organizations (Local Councils)	1,670,025		
		TV/Media	587,000
Theater	1,522,955		
		Film	499,000
Special Programs for Minority Groups	1,422,850		
		Literature	330,525
Dance	1,401,200	Architecture and Environment	328,400

Total: $14,941,160 (excluding $58,840 for miscellaneous statewide aid)

Source: New York State Council on the Arts.

Other State Functions

Typically, in many metropolitan areas there are overlapping and competitive county, municipal, and special district recreation and park agencies. States can make an important contribution in helping to coordinate such programs, particularly with respect to meeting the needs of inner-city residents, who are often unable to use recreation areas in the surrounding suburban communities.

It is becoming increasingly clear that we can no longer afford to allow strictly local responsibility for recreation resource development or land and water conservation. Just as no single municipality can clean up a polluted stream which flows throughout a state, so in the broad field of urban planning, recreation resource development, and conservation, problems *must* be approached on a statewide or even a regional basis. In such planning—as in many other aspects of Federal relationships with local communities—the state acts as a catalyst for action and as a vital link between national and local governments.

A final expanding function in many states is to provide support for the arts, through state arts councils that distribute funds to nonprofit organizations and performing groups in various areas of cultural activity. An example of one state's assistance to the arts in the mid-1970s is shown in Table 9-4.

Functions of Canadian Provincial Governments in Recreation

Although parks and open spaces have existed in Canada since colonial times, Burton and Kyllo point out that it was not until the 1930s that provincial park development got under way, and not until after World War II that recreation programming became a serious concern of both senior levels of government.[20]

235

Nature of Functions

Burton and Kyllo analyze provincial responsibility for recreation under several major headings: outdoor activities, sports and physical recreation, arts and culture, social activities, and tourism and travel. Within each such category, the government may have differing levels of responsibility: (1) *primary,* in which a department or agency is required to provide a given service; (2) *secondary,* in which an agency is specifically permitted, although not required, to provide a service; and (3) *tertiary,* in which an agency performs a recreation function because it is related to another primary responsibility.

During the past two decades, Canadian government functions in recreation, according to Burton and Kyllo, have gone through a series of phases

> in response to perceived or presumed needs of particular kinds. Thus, the theme for senior government activities during the 1950's was *physical fitness.* In the early and mid-1960's, it was *youth.* At the end of the 1960's and into the 1970's, it was cultural and *multicultural expression.* Now in the mid-1970's, there are two themes: *multicultural expression* continues, but together with a revived *physical fitness* thrust.[21]

To illustrate the policies and programs that provinces have developed in these areas, a number of examples are provided in the following section. These are drawn chiefly from Ontario and Alberta, but with some programs cited from other provinces.

Park and Outdoor Recreation Resource Development

By the 1960s, all Canadian provinces had embarked on a program of open-space and provincial park development, with the primary purpose to develop wilderness or natural parks permitting traditional forms of outdoor recreation such as hunting, fishing, camping and boating. In the 1970s, concern about the needs of municipalities increased. Provincial governments responded to this in two ways: (1) by establishing major provincial parks close to urban communities and readily accessible to their populations; and (2) by providing grants-in-aid programs to assist municipalities in developing needed recreation facilities.

As an example of the former, the Alberta Department of Recreation, Parks, and Wildlife established two major urban parks in the mid-1970s: Fish Creek Park in the city of Calgary, a thousand-acre facility with plans for expansion to three thousand acres, and Capital City Recreation Park, a unique resource estimated to cost $35 million, situated within the valley of the North Saskatchewan River, in Edmonton. Various Alberta government departments, including Lands and Forests; Environment; and Culture, Youth and Recreation, have been drawn into planning Capital City Park; with new water control structures on the river, the park will provide significant recreation opportunities for all within the Edmonton metropolitan area.[22]

Other provinces have established extensive grants programs to help municipalities acquire and develop recreation facilities. The province of Nova Scotia, for example, has a Capital Grant program which assists municipalities or community groups in constructing recreation and cultural centers, sports facilities, parks, playgrounds, and other outdoor recreation sites. In Ontario, the Community Recreation Centres Act makes grants available to municipalities for building or renovating community recreation centers (defined in the Community Recreation Centres Act of 1974 as including community halls, playing fields, tennis courts, swimming pools, snow skiing facilities, skating rinks and arenas, fitness trails, gymnasiums, and cultural centers). Communities may receive 50 percent matching grants ranging as high as $75,000. The Alberta Development Act of March, 1975, authorized a total of $200 million for cultural and recreation facility development throughout the province during the period from 1975 to 1984.

Sports and Physical Fitness Programs

These programs have received major emphasis from all provincial governments during the past two decades. For example, to aid in the construction of sports facilities, the Recreation and Sports Services Division of the Department of Rehabilitation and Recreation in Newfoundland and Labrador performs the following functions:

1. It grants financial aid to recreation agencies, ranging from municipal departments to amateur sports organizations.

2. It provides consultant and promotional services to local communities and sports and recreation organizations involved in any aspect of recreation.

3. It initiates research and planning efforts to meet provincial recreation needs.

4. It provides professional guidance to varied organizations in facilities development and program services, including the following:

   a. maintains liaison with amateur sport-governing bodies

   b. sponsors sports training, clinics, workshops, and seminars

   c. operates training centers in two cities

   d. sponsors provincial participation in Canada Games, Arctic Games, and Newfoundland Games

   e. maintains liaison with and assists the provincial park and recreation association

   f. provides films, printed materials, travel assistance, and other forms of aid to over forty provincial sports organizations

Other provincial agencies carry out similar functions. One of the most active provinces in this regard is Alberta, which has an extensive Coaching Development Program leading to three levels of certification, sponsored by the Sports and Fitness Branch of the Department of Recreation, Parks, and Wildlife.

Cultural Programs

Burton and Kyllo write:

> The provinces, too, have become involved in the provision of cultural services. . . . Support for the arts, expanded heritage programs, cultural facility development, multi-cultural interaction and cultural exchange are now also accepted provincial activities.[23]

Usually as these responsibilities become more fully accepted, provincial agencies are restructured to assume them. In Ontario, for example, a new Ministry of Culture and Recreation was established in 1975, with four major program responsibilities: (1) heritage conservation, (2) multicultural development and public libraries, (3) arts support, and (4) sports and fitness. Varied forms of assistance have been given to community arts organizations in music, drama and dance, along with grants to individuals and performing groups; libraries, museums, and other cultural institutions have also received assistance. Alberta and other provinces have made major efforts to preserve the cultural heritage of the region by protecting historic sites, areas of archaeological interest, provincial archives, and other documents or artifacts of provincial history.

There are numerous other examples of provincial programs in sponsoring and promoting recreation and leisure services, particularly in the areas of youth service, often as part of the work of the provincial ministry or department of education. Another growing emphasis has been concern with the physically and mentally disabled. As a single example, the Recreation to Special Services Branch in Alberta offers

> consultative services, information, Provincial, Area and Regional Workshops, and financial assistance to various clientele to facilitate greater recreational opportunities for the mentally and physically disabled, preschool and school age children, senior citizens and those in correctional systems, while making the public aware of the existence and needs of these individuals and groups.[24]

The Federal Local Initiatives Program has also allocated millions of dollars to the provinces, to assist recreation projects for the special populations of the aged, the mentally retarded, and the physically handicapped. In a recent fiscal year, Quebec received the greatest amount of funding under this program, with Ontario second.

In summing up their analysis of provincial recreation programs in Canada, Burton and Kyllo comment that the multiplicity of agencies and departments with leisure functions has led not to the duplication of efforts, but to organizations working at cross-purposes with each other. What is needed, they conclude—either through single centralized departments of recreation and leisure, or through provincial coordinating committees or councils—is more logical structuring of services and more efficient performance planning by federal departments, for maximum benefit of the public. The first National Conference of Provincial Recreation Ministers in Halifax, Nova Scotia in 1974 was an initial attempt to define the objectives of recreation as an important form of public service throughout all provinces.

This chapter has described in detail the recreation-related programs and services of Federal, state, and provincial governments in the United States and Canada. A second major aspect of government responsibility—the functions of local government—is analyzed in chapter 10.

Chapter Nine

1. *Outdoor Recreation: A Legacy for America* (Washington, D.C.: Bureau of Outdoor Recreation, U.S. Department of Interior, 1973), p. 73.

2. Ibid., p. 52.

3. "Editorial: The Urban Park Dilemma," *Parks and Recreation,* July 1975, p. 17.

4. For a summary of the impact of PL–94–142, see *AAHPER Update,* March 1977, pp. 1, 8.

5. Theodore M. Berry, "Memorandum by Director of Community Action Programs to Selected Community Agencies," (Washington, D.C.: Office of Economic Opportunity, May 8, 1967) p. 2.

6. Report from Col. Robert J. Carrell, Director, Recreation Services, Office of the Adjutant General, Department of the Army, January, 1976.

7. Report from John E. Moler, Directorate of Morale, Welfare and Recreation, U.S. Air Force, February, 1976.

8. Donald V. Joyce, "Recreation with the Marines in Viet Nam," *Parks and Recreation,* October 1966, p. 842.

9. Lt.Jg. Carol Couvaris, USNA, "Recreation for 30,000 Sailors," *Recreation Management,* November 1975, pp. 10–13.

10. Sidney G. Lutzin, "At Last . . . , Culture Comes to the National Parks," *Parks and Recreation,* March 1972, pp. 22–25.

11. "Periscope: FBI-Land, U.S.A., and Miss X-KAKF," *Newsweek,* 9 June 1972, p. 15.

12. Ibid.

13. "Washington Scene," *Parks and Recreation,* November 1975, pp. 12–13.

14. *The Recreation Imperative: A Nationwide Outdoor Recreation Plan* (Washington, D.C.: Senate Committee on Interior and Insular Affairs, Senator Henry Jackson, Chairman, June, 1974).

15. *A Legacy for America.*

16. Thomas L. Burton and Leo T. Kyllo, "Federal-Provincial Responsibilities for Leisure Services in Alberta and Ontario," Reports Funded by Provincial Governments of Alberta and Ontario, 2 (November 1974):5.

17. Isobel Cosgrove and Richard Jackson, *The Geography of Recreation and Leisure* (London: Hutchinson Univ. Library, 1972), pp. 77–78.

18. See *Recreation and Park Yearbooks,* 1961 and 1966 (Washington, D.C.: National Recreation and Park Association); *1967 State Park Statistics* (Washington, D.C.: National Conference on State Parks, June, 1968); and *Parks and Recreation,* November 1971, p. 45.

19. "New York State Parks," *Conservationist,* New York State Department of Environmental Conservation, August, 1976, p. 2.

20. Burton and Kyllo, "Federal-Provincial Responsibilities."

21. Ibid. 1(Vol. I):15.

22. *Capital City Recreation Park, (Province of Alberta, Environmental Planning Division, 1974).*

23. Burton and Kyllo, "Federal-Provincial Responsibilities 1(Vol. I):14

24. *Recreation Services to Special Groups Branch: Structure, Services, Policies and Regulations.* Province of Alberta, April, 1975, p. 5,1.

10

THE ROLE OF COUNTY

AND LOCAL

GOVERNMENTS

The preceding chapter described the contributions of Federal, state, and provincial governments in providing recreation and park facilities and programs. However, the major responsibility for sponsoring leisure opportunities for the bulk of the population in the United States and Canada belongs to local government on two levels: (1) county, township, or special park districts, and (2) local political subdivisions, consisting of cities, villages, or other municipal government agencies.

Local government functions in recreation and parks have grown steadily during the past three decades (see chapter 8). For example, in 1972, local governments in the United States spent almost $2 billion to purchase land, develop facilities, and operate outdoor recreation programs. Although comparable statistics have not been gathered for local recreation and parks in Canada, growth there also has been steady in scope and spending since World War II, as described in chapter 8.

County and Special Park District Programs

An intermediate stage between state and local government agencies, county recreation and park departments today provide large-scale or regional facilities and resources to meet outdoor recreation needs that other units of local government cannot adequately meet. County recreation departments often provide services for special populations; that is, programs for the aging or disabled, as well as services for all residents of the county, such as programs in the fine and performing arts. Counties may also assist local government through: (1) consultation services and planning specialists; (2) presentation of major events such as tournaments, drama festivals, or art exhibits, which motivate local groups and participants; and (3) promotion of professional development through conferences and training sessions.

Table 10-1

County Recreation and Park Operations in the United States

	1960	1966
Number of county park and recreation agencies	290	358
Number of park and recreation areas	2,610	4,149
Total number of employed professionals	7,990	11,912
Total acreage	430,707	691,042
Total expenditures (in millions)	$95.5	$195.7

Source: *Recreation and Park Yearbook, 1966* (Washington, D.C.: National Recreation and Park Association, 1967), p. 59, and *Recreation and Park Yearbook, 1961,* pp. 28–31.

Current Status of County Programs

During the early decades of the twentieth century in the United States, the major areas of county responsibility were usually such general functions as the administration of the law through the recording of legal documents, enforcement of the law by county sheriffs, maintenance of county roads, and operation of charitable and correctional institutions. Since World War II, the rapid expansion of suburban communities around the major cities of the country has given many county governments new influence and power. Counties have become a base for coordinating and funneling numerous Federal grants-in-aid programs. County park and recreation departments have expanded significantly; Table 10-1 illustrates their growth in the 1960s.

Examples of County Recreation and Park Development

Excellent examples of county recreation and park development in the United States are Dade County, Florida; King County, Washington; and Nassau County, New York.

Dade County, Florida

The Metropolitan Dade County Park and Recreation Department operates an outstanding network of sixteen major parks, beaches, gardens, auditoriums, and camping areas, as well as five golf courses and three large tennis centers. It offers four miles of sandy ocean beaches, atoll pools in Biscayne Bay, and five marinas offering wet and dry docks. In all, Dade County has eight thousand acres of carefully planned and developed park and recreation facilities serving more than eighteen million visitors and residents each year. Vizcaya, a unique seventy-room Italian villa built by a prominent industrialist and now owned by the county, serves as a magnificent museum and garden attraction. The Crandon Park Zoo, Dade County Auditorium, and other special facilities are unique elements in this recreation oriented metropolitan area, which depends heavily on its $3 billion annual income from tourists.

241

In addition to such facilities, the Metro Dade Park and Recreation Department also operates many special programs for all ages. It sponsors extensive summer playground and day camp activities, biking trails, gardens and nature walks, and a wide variety of classes and events for adults. Through directories and brochures the county also helps to promote a wide variety of recreational opportunities such as youth activities, physical fitness programs, and senior citizen clubs.

King County, Washington

The King County, Washington, Parks Division (a unit in the County Department of Planning and Community Development) is an example of how county recreation and park departments have expanded to meet growing urban and suburban needs during the past three decades. This impressive system, which includes the city of Seattle, was established in 1949, at which time it included 20 parks on 236 acres.

Thanks to passage of a large park-bond issue in 1968, King County embarked on an extensive land acquisition and park development program, involving the expenditure of $48 million by 1976. Today it operates 5,070 acres of land, including neighborhood, community, urban, saltwater, freshwater, and regional parks and nature areas ranging in size from one-quarter acre to nearly 500 acres. King County has sixteen pools, twelve beaches, six large community centers, two stadiums, and extensive sport, equestrian, biking, picnic, and boating facilities. The programs operated by the King County Parks Division include unsupervised informal play, tournaments, leagues, and instruction in a variety of sports, extensive arts activities, and special programs for the mentally and physically handicapped. King County has cooperative arrangements with several large school districts which provide for construction of major sports areas and outdoor facilities by the schools and maintenance and operation of programs by the county.

Nassau County, New York

Nassau County, adjacent to New York City on Long Island, was a comparative latecomer in park development; it was not until 1945 that Salisbury Park, the first park in Nassau County, was established. But like other suburban areas, Nassau County grew rapidly, from a population of 406,748 in 1940 to over 1.3 million in 1960, with the number of one-family homes increasing fivefold during this period. Within the five years prior to 1966, park holdings of the Nassau County park and recreation system doubled, and funds set aside for park development during the six years following 1966 totaled $73 million. A 1977 department report included the following summary of facilities, programs, personnel and expenditures:

> The Nassau County Department of Recreation and Parks maintains and operates about 5,700 acres of parklands, preserves, museum areas, and other specialized recreation facilities. These include 16 major active parks, including the 940-acre Eisenhower Park, which boasts three 18-hole golf courses, sprawling picnic areas, ballfields, a restaurant, amphitheatre, tennis courts, playgrounds, lake, golf driving range, jogging course, puppet theatre, bicycle paths, and other facilities.

Many parks contain swimming pool complexes, and four parks operate 9-hole golf courses. Park programs run the gamut from tennis tournaments to cultural events, and from fishing contests to arts and crafts. The county also operates two major indoor ice rinks, two artificial outdoor rinks, and a dozen natural ice skating ponds.

During the course of the year, the department sponsors many championship sporting events in such areas as wrestling, track and field, basketball, baseball and ice-skating. The Nassau County Marathon, which attracts runners from throughout the county, is now second only to the famous Boston Marathon.

In the works is a projected new 67-acre sports and recreation complex to be known as Mitchel Field. When completed, it will give the young athletes of Nassau County an unprecedented capacity to train and compete in Olympic-style events and at the same time provide a wide-ranging year-round recreation program for the general public.

The department operates an historical museum, two natural history museums, an arboretum, and miles of nature trails and preserve areas. The Old Bethpage village restoration, authentic to the last detail, depicts a typical rural Long Island village before the Civil War.

For pleasure boaters, there are numerous docking facilities and launching ramps. There is a fleet of 15 mobile recreation units which travel into local neighborhoods with activities such as puppet shows, roller skating, fashion training, music and sports. Numerous free programs are provided for senior citizens and the handicapped.[1]

As an example of the size of some outstanding county recreation and park systems, the Nassau County Department of Recreation and Parks employed a full-time professional staff of 1,250 in 1977, supplemented by 1,000 part-time and seasonal employees. Its programs and facilities attract more than 10 million visitors each year, and generate yearly revenue of about $3 million. The department's yearly operating budget in 1977 was above the $19 million mark, with additional capital expenditures ranging between $5 million and $10 million annually.

Regional and Special Park Districts

Many states have legislative provisions for regional and special park districts, usually in metropolitan areas, which often encompass several separate counties and municipalities.

East Bay Regional Park District

This special district in Oakland, California includes two large counties, Contra Costa and Alameda, in the Oakland region. Created in 1934, the East Bay district is one of the most progressive park agencies in the United States. With the help of a $53 million bond issue approved in 1973 and a new master plan for the acquisition and development of new parklands, the district today possesses over 41,000 acres in magnificent, scenic hills and mountains, bay beaches, lakes, streams and meadows, in 36 different parks, serving a population of 1.7 million.

The master plan, approved after lengthy hearings and careful review of goals and priorities by two large citizens' advisory committees, led to the acquisition of major new facilities, amounting to 15,700 acres at a cost of $15.1 million, since 1973. Today, surrounding a heavily urbanized and industrialized harbor area, the park district provides a wealth of regional trails and preserves, parks, wilderness, and shorelines, making possible swimming, boating, camping, hiking, nature study, and a host of other nature-oriented pursuits. Visitor days to the district's various parks have increased from fewer than a million in 1962 to 7.5 million in 1973, and a high of 10 million visitor-days in 1976. The district has also received over $7 million from HUD and the Land and Water Conservation Fund to assist its development program. General manager Richard Trudeau proudly comments:

> Probably no metropolitan region in the country is blessed with a greater variety of scenic and geographical attractions than the San Francisco Bay Area. Likewise, there may be no other region so environmentally oriented and directed, with a citizenry so alert and avant-garde in its thinking as this area of northern California.[2]

Creative fund raising, outstanding public and community relations, solicitation of citizens' suggestions, involvement of all social, ethnic, and economic classes, and environmental education are keynotes of the development of the East Bay Regional Park District and of its planning for the decades ahead.

Such vigorous programs of land acquisition as those just described are essential to obtain and protect land while it is still available and before prices increase to prohibitive levels. Many counties have enacted laws requiring home developers to set aside community recreation areas. One such example is Anne Arundel County, Maryland, which since 1957 has required all developers to allocate five percent of the land to be developed for park areas. Some county governments are establishing permanently protected green belts to halt the tide of construction. Strengthened zoning policies and more flexible building codes to permit cluster zoning of homes with larger and more concentrated open spaces are also helpful.

Municipal Recreation and Park Agencies

Municipal government is the term generally used to describe the local political unit of government such as the village, town, or city that is responsible for providing the bulk of direct community service such as street maintenance, police and fire protection, and education. Most areas depend on municipal government to provide many important recreation and park facilities and program opportunities, in addition to those provided by voluntary, private, and commercial agencies. Butler has suggested the following reasons for the growth of municipal recreation and park programs:

244

1. Municipal government offers many individuals their primary or only opportunity for wholesome recreational involvement, particularly among poorer people in large cities.

2. Only through government can adequate lands be acquired for playgrounds, parks, and other outdoor recreation areas.

3. Municipal recreation is "democratic and inclusive"; it serves all ages, races, and creeds, and places the burden of support upon the entire community.

4. Municipal recreation is comparatively inexpensive, when compared with private expenditure for recreation; yet, by spreading the cost of development over the entire population, it can provide a full range of facilities and services.

5. Local government gives permanency to recreation, assuring both continuity and the ability to respond to changing population needs.

6. The job is too large for any private agency, whereas the city, with its powers of land acquisition and taxation, can provide inexpensive communitywide non-profit services to meet total population needs.

7. Recreation plays an important role in the local economy, helping to stabilize property values and reduce social pathology, thus making communities more attractive for industries seeking new locations or families seeking new homes.

8. People demand public recreation and are willing to be taxed for it, as evidenced by steady growth of programs, passage of referendums and bond issues, and overall support of recreation through the years.[3]

The overall growth of local recreation and park programs during the period after World War II is illustrated in Table 10–2.

Table 10-2

Growth of Local Recreation and Parks Agencies

	1950	1960	1965
Total number of park and recreation agencies reported	2,277	2,968	3,142
Personnel:			
Total full- and part-time paid leadership	58,029	99,696	119,515
Full-time year-round	6,784	9,216	19,208
Volunteer	104,589	277,072	494,407
Total acreage in parks and recreation areas	644,000	1,015,461	1,496,378
Playgrounds under leadership	14,747	20,107	24,298
Buildings of all types	9,617	16,970	22,527
Total expenditures (in millions)	$269	$567	$905

Source: *Recreation and Park Yearbook, 1966* (Washington, D.C.: National Recreation and Park Association, 1967), pp. 41, 44–58, and *Recreation and Park Yearbook, 1961*, pp. 27–46.

The *Statistical Abstract of the United States* reported that in local communities average recreation and park spending had risen from four dollars per capita in 1960 to nine dollars per capita in 1970, and to fourteen dollars in 1974.

Functions of Municipal Recreation and Park Agencies

The responsibilities of municipal recreation and park departments fall under several major headings:

1. *Direct Provision of Recreation Opportunities.* Municipal departments acquire, develop, and maintain facilities needed for recreational participation, and provide skilled leadership to meet the needs of various age groups and individuals within the community.

2. *Coordination of Other Programs.* They provide in-service training and advisory services for other private, voluntary, or therapeutic agencies in the community, and help them coordinate their efforts to avoid duplication and overlap.

3. *Cooperate with Other Governmental Agencies.* They work closely with other branches of local government, and with Federal, state, and county authorities to develop long-range planning, effective programs of land acquisition, and, when feasible, joint programs of direct service.

Administrative Structure of Public Departments

During the early years of public recreation in the United States, the structure of administrative agencies and the assignment of recreation responsibility varied from area to area. Until World War II, most communities had separate recreation departments or separate park departments with recreation functions, or two such agencies existing side by side. During the 1950s and 1960s, however, the two fields merged: (1) many existing separate recreation and park departments joined forces in single administrative structures, and (2) the majority of the new departments created during this period were organized as joint recreation and park agencies.

In many of the large cities throughout the United States today, it is common for more than one public agency to have recreation and park functions. In addition to recreation and park departments and to public school systems, which have played an important role in the delivery of leisure services in many cities, the following types of departments or agencies also provide recreation services.

Police Departments

The police often operate youth service bureaus or precinct councils which assist in the operation of recreation centers, play streets, and sports leagues. They may also assign workers from other agencies to contact and work with unaffiliated youth.

246

Welfare Departments or Public Social Service Agencies

In some large cities, social service departments operate day-care centers for children of working parents, after school recreation and study centers for children of school age, multiservice centers for aging persons, or similar facilities.

Youth Boards

Youth boards, commissions, or bureaus are concerned with reducing the school dropout rate, providing educational tutoring and vocational assistance, counseling "problem" youth, and working constructively with antisocial gangs and individuals. Frequently, one of their major program elements is to provide teen-age recreation centers and activities.

Health and Hospital Departments

In some larger cities, municipal hospitals, like their state sponsored counterparts, provide therapeutic recreation programs. Particularly in psychiatric care, they may also sponsor out-patient clinics, after-care centers, "halfway houses," or other satellite programs in the community.

Housing Departments

Public housing projects built with Federal assistance often have playgrounds and community centers as part of their overall facilities. Services may include sponsoring tenants' clubs, day camps, senior centers, and youth programs. Many such programs are operated by outside agencies under special contracts to provide recreation activities.

Cultural Departments

Finally, in many cities, such publicly sponsored cultural agencies as libraries and museums offer a variety of leisure services, such as classes and special events, which answer educational as well as recreational needs of all age groups.

When several such agencies exist within a large metropolitan community, close cooperation is essential. Planning and organization of services and programs may include any of the following: (1) joint use of facilities, (2) exchange and joint training of personnel, (3) determination of community needs and planning for total recreation development, (4) promotion and public relations efforts, and (5) joint projects and research. In many cities, such cooperation involves contractual agreements for shared use of facilities, the assignment of program responsibilities, or even a portion of budgetary support.

Programs of Municipal Recreation Departments

Municipal programs fall into several major categories of activity: games and sports, aquatics, outdoor and nature oriented programs, arts and crafts, performing arts, special services, social programs, hobby groups, and other playground and community center activities.[4]

In addition, public recreation and park departments often sponsor large-scale special events such as holiday celebrations, festival programs, art and hobby shows, and sports tournaments. Many communities provide numerous formal instructional classes for youth and adults in various areas of recreation or self-development activities. Beyond this, most public departments offer an extremely broad range of opportunities for self-directed recreation, including the use of picnic areas, lakes, bicycling and riding trails, and other types of sports facilities or social centers.

Public recreation and park departments also assist other community agencies to organize, publicize, and schedule activities. Frequently, sports programs for children and youth, such as Little League baseball or Biddy basketball, are cosponsored by public departments and associations of interested parents who undertake much of the actual management of the activity, including coaching, fund raising, and scheduling. Similarly, many cultural programs, such as Civic Opera or Little Theater associations, are affiliated with and receive assistance from public recreation departments.

Profiles of Municipal Departments

Several departments are described here in fairly complete detail; others are summarized according to their unique aspects or special administrative approaches.

Omaha, Nebraska

Omaha has a well-established Department of Parks, Recreation, and Public Property, which operates a major auditorium and stadium complex, extensive boating facilities, and other unusual physical facilities. In the late 1960s, it undertook a major program of physical expansion, acquiring several large new parks. A $2.65-million bond issue was passed to finance a three-year expansion program, including a fifty-meter swimming pool, an artificial ice skating rink, a garden center, a lighted softball complex, and improvements to about one hundred areas throughout the city. Another major park and recreation bond issue of $7.56 million was approved in 1974 to include the development of new community centers, libraries, pools and athletic facilities, and the improvement of existing facilities.

Like other cities described in this chapter, Omaha conducts a highly diversified recreation program, deriving substantial fees from marinas, day camps, golf courses, instructional sports activities, permits and concessions, an outstanding indoor tennis complex, operation of a trap and skeet shooting center, and other facilities. These sources provided revenue of $2.18 million in 1975, when the total annual budget was $6.30 million. Omaha demonstrates how a city can operate large-scale recreation and park facilities which meet varied community needs. As an example, the municipally owned Civic Auditorium is almost completely booked during the course of the year with entertainment, conventions, sports events, and fairs; these events attract 1.25 million spectators and participants, contribute to the city's economy, and earn over $175,000 net profit annually. Omaha's recreation department also operates a fine stadium used for the College Baseball World Series, minor league baseball, and numerous other events each year.

Greensboro, North Carolina

Greensboro is an example of a smaller city that has given excellent support to recreation and park services. Operating under the council-manager form of government through a charter enacted by the North Carolina General Assembly, Greensboro's Parks and Recreation Commission consists of members appointed by the council and the mayor. Until 1973, recreation and parks were supported by a special property tax and individual bond issues for acquisition and development of facilities. Since 1974 when a change in state law made recreation and parks a mandated function of local government, recreation and park budgets have been a part of the city's general fund. Substantial additional funds have been derived from revenue sharing, state and Federal grants, and numerous contributions from industries, civic clubs, and other interested groups.

Greensboro is program oriented, offering an extremely wide range of recreation activities in six major divisions: Performing Arts, Special Populations, Special Activities, Playgrounds and Pools, Youth (High School Division), Community Centers, and Athletics. The program for special populations has been a pioneer in its field. Among other services, this division operates a day camp for varied special populations, reserving six weeks during the summer for school-aged mentally retarded children, and one week each for the pre-school retarded, cerebral palsy children, diabetic teenagers, senior citizens, and the blind.

The Youth Division sponsors a Greensboro Youth Council, an elected body of 150 senior high school students that operates 35 different programs for teenagers, including special events, youth employment services, radio and television shows, and numerous other projects. In addition, the Special Activities Division operates a Roving Leader Program to provide guidance and assistance to problem youth in the community. For an indication of the continued growth of Greensboro's public recreation and park operation, see Table 10–3.

Table 10-3

Greensboro, N.C. Parks and Recreation Department: Personnel and Participation

	1967	1975
Number of permanent department personnel	52	144
Number of temporary or seasonal personnel	125	350
Number of individuals registered in programs	39,000	90,612
Number of units of participation (in millions)	1.5	3.1

Source: *Annual Reports of Greensboro Parks and Recreation Department for 1967 and 1975.*

Vancouver, British Columbia

As indicated earlier, many Canadian municipalities have made outstanding progress in developing highly professional recreation and park programs over the past three decades. One of the best of these is the city of Vancouver, blessed with an unusual and beautiful physical setting along the Pacific Coast. Vancouver's park and recreation program operates under the direction of an elected Board of Parks and Recreation, with close links to the City Council, School Board, Resource Board, public libraries, aquariums, botanical gardens, and other civic organizations.

Despite continuing inflation, Vancouver has given high priority to developing and maintaining an extensive network of parks, beaches, pools, golf courses, conservatories, ice rinks, community centers, and an outstanding community zoo in famed Stanley Park. Overall financial operations of recreation and parks in Vancouver have grown steadily through the years, as shown in Table 10–5.

Table 10-5

Parks and Recreation Budgets in Vancouver, Canada

	1965	1975
Maintenance and operation of parks, including supervision of playgrounds, community centers, beaches, etc. (city tax appropriation)	$2,161,396	$8,780,419
Income operations, refreshment booths, tea rooms, boat rental, marina fees, etc., and capital expenditure from profits	$1,653,417	$3,026,230
Local improvement bylaws for recreation facilities construction	$113,310	None
Citywide capital funds for purchase and development of parks and facilities	$653,064	$4,693,148
Accounts receivable, miscellaneous projects for other authorities, etc.	$700,564	$2,008,709
Total expenditures and revenues	$5,281,751	$18,508,506

Source: *Annual Reports of Vancouver Parks and Recreation Department for 1965 and 1975.*

In addition to its facilities, Vancouver operates a wide range of recreation program activities, including tennis clinics and a junior tennis program, intensive sports and fitness programs, winter skiing activities, aquatics, special programs for the aging and the disabled, environmental education, guidance for "problem" youth, "bicycle Sundays," summer sports camp, and numerous community centers operated in cooperation with neighborhood associations. To illustrate the volume of participation in many activities, in 1975 there were 3.62 million separate units of participation in beach, indoor, and outdoor pool swimming, 355,830 visits to the city's conservatory (Vancouver emphasizes outstanding horticultural displays and historical sites), and over 390,000 rounds of golf played on the city's public courses. An efficiently managed operation, Vancouver's Board of Parks and Recreation carefully analyzes costs, personnel assignments, participation, and trends in public interest and involvement. A highly skilled planning and development team does the conceptual analysis and justification for new park and recreation facilities, receiving extensive citizen input in all planning decisions.

Philadelphia, Pennsylvania

Philadelphia is an excellent example of a large city which, despite severe problems of urban blight and poverty compounded by racial conflict in recent years, has moved ahead aggressively under the strong direction of a leading department administrator, the veteran Robert W. Crawford. Even when budgets were frozen in the mid-1970s, the Philadelphia Recreation Department presented intensified and imaginative new programs to meet human and social needs most economically and efficiently.

In Philadelphia, recreation functions are filled by three tax-supported agencies: the Department of Recreation, the Board of Public Education, and the Fairmount Park Commission. When the Philadelphia City Charter was inaugurated in 1951, it made provision for a Recreation Coordination Board to promote cooperation among these agencies. The Recreation Department works closely with the schools, using many school facilities as part of a full-scale interchange of swimming pools, gymnasiums, and outdoor sports facilities between the two city departments. Both agencies also work closely with the Fairmount Park Commission, using its various sites throughout the city and participating in joint planning of capital construction projects. The Recreation Department also provides recreation leadership at a number of different housing projects throughout the city, and works closely with such groups as the Philadelphia Society for Crippled Children and Adults, the Cerebral Palsy Association, the Pennsylvania Association for the Blind, and the Health and Welfare Council.

Special attention is given to working with "Youth-in-Conflict" gangs, and attempting to reduce problems such as delinquency, gang fighting, drinking, narcotics use, and vandalism. The Department of Recreation employs a corps of detached youth workers, who maintain close contact with such agencies as the Gang Control branch of the Police Narcotics Squad, the Crime Prevention Association, and the Police Athletic League.

The Philadelphia Recreation Department has developed many special services to provide programs in disadvantaged areas, particularly in minority-group neighborhoods. These have included summer job programs, expanded play-street operations, family camping programs, neighborhood teen canteens, college-directed "motivation" programs, summer science projects and arts classes in junior and senior high schools. Despite the reduced level of Federal funding for such programs, Philadelphia Recreation Department receives substantial grants from the Federal Office of Community Service Administration, the U.S. Department of Agriculture, the Department of Transportation, Model Cities, and Neighborhood Youth Corps to support such ventures.

However, the Philadelphia Department of Recreation is in no sense a limited "social welfare" operation. It operates a tremendous range of sports, cultural and other programs, as well as extensive facilities, including Veterans' Stadium, Kennedy Stadium, and Robin Hood Dell, which serve the public at large. In fiscal year 1976, its operating budget was $21 million, and its capital budget totaled $36.8 million.

Other Cities

Other cities throughout the United States and Canada offer interesting examples of unique recreation program emphasis or administrative structures.

251

Kansas City, Missouri

Kansas City provides a full range of facilities and program services, but is particularly noteworthy for its programs which serve special populations. It operates camping programs for disabled children who suffer from diabetes, cardiac problems, cerebral palsy, retardation, and epilepsy. The sessions are from several to ten days, and are offered through cooperation with voluntary organizations in Kansas City that serve disabled children, and that have joined together to form a Greater Kansas City Council on Recreation for the Handicapped. Older citizens in Kansas City are also served by a special summer camping program, and by Golden Age Clubs located in thirteen different locations throughout the city. These clubs, which are operated by the department both in its own centers and in churches, provide many special events, trips, service projects, publications, and other activities for aging persons.

Portland, Oregon

In Portland, the Recreation Division within the larger Bureau of Parks and Public Recreation relies heavily on affiliated civic organizations to sustain and conduct many cultural and artistic programs. Such organizations as the Civic Contemporary Dance Theater, a Junior Museum, Community Music Center, Portland Parks Art Center, Portland Actors Company, Little Loom House (weaving), Ballet Workshop, Teen-Age Theater Workshop, Portland Opera Association and other performing groups sponsor many cultural activities.

Since 1940, the Recreation Division has had an agreement with the Portland public school system for interchange use of facilities. When the failure of a school bond issue in 1967 compelled the school board to impose a fee system for use of school facilities, the question of payment by one city department to another arose. It was found that the schools used Park Bureau facilities for classes, playground activities, and competitive sport for 32,000 hours a week, while the Recreation Division used school gymnasiums and auditoriums for 26,000 hours a week. Recognizing the mutual benefit of this arrangement, the park and recreation department and the schools agreed to continue to exchange facilities by means of a permit system, charging fees only for special or unusual uses.

Long Beach, California

Long Beach is of special interest because of its administrative structure. Established in 1929 under what has been known as the Long Beach Coordinated Recreation Plan, the city's Recreation Commission has the following working arrangement: (1) "public recreation" is viewed as provision of varied programs and leisure settings for all age groups; (2) the program is supervised by a Recreation Commission of nine members, including the City Manager, Superintendent of Schools, a member of the City Council, and a member of the Board of Education; (3) the Director of Health and Physical Education in the city school system is also director of the total playground and public recreation department; (4) he is assisted by an Associate Director, who has a major responsibility for recreation, and who is also responsible to the City Manager; (5) the City Manager must approve all hiring in recreation; (6) funding is based primarily on a special recreation property tax, with the school contributing about one quarter of the Recreation Commission's total annual budget.

Long Beach is also noteworthy because of its outstanding aquatic program, which includes a wide range of activities: instruction; recreational, competitive, and synchronized swimming; water safety; diving; youth and adult sailing; water polo; boating; water skiing; and canoeing. Long Beach operates a huge Marine Stadium which hosts many aquatic shows and other special water events. The Belmont Plaza Olympic Pool, completed in 1968 for Olympic tryouts, continues to serve the community by providing aquatic programs. This huge building (five stories high, 240 feet long, and 150 feet wide) has a million-gallon eight-lane pool with an underwater television and sound system, the most modern electronic scoring and timing equipment, seating for 2,700 spectators and other facilities for community recreational aquatics.

Other Program Trends

In addition to the programs just described, there are many other general program trends in municipal and county recreation and park departments.

Expanded Activity in the Arts

More and more cities have established popular art centers or performing arts buildings for popular programs in the fine and performing arts. Communities with such programs include Phoenix, Arizona; Atlanta, Georgia; Nashville, Tennessee; and Richmond, Virginia.

> The Phoenix Parks and Recreation Division has affiliated itself with an active core of arts groups, including the Arizona Ballet Theatre, the Arizona Young Audiences, the Southwest Ensemble Theatre, the Strumming Amigos, and the Valley Opera. It also offers an extensive array of arts and crafts classes and sponsors the enormously successful People's Pops Concerts. . . .

> Atlanta's ambitious arts and crafts program offers a wide spectrum of courses in areas like pottery, sculpture, jewelry making, weaving, painting, picture framing, photography, woodcarving, leathercraft, silk screen, batik, quilting, stained glass, rug braiding, and china painting, in three arts and crafts centers with six full-time specialists and many part-time instructors. . . .

> Nashville's Metro Board of Parks and Recreation has converted an outmoded swimming pool complex into the Centennial Art Center, serving hundreds of participants in day and night classes, with four regular staff members and special workshops by artists from college and university faculties in the Nashville area.

> Richmond's Department of Recreation and Parks serves as an "impresario" for area arts programs and events, helping many cultural

groups get under way, working closely with the Federated Arts Council of Richmond, and sponsoring many major performing arts events.[5]

Cosponsorship by Local Industry

An important recent trend has been the development of special programs with the financial assistance of local businesses or industrial concerns. During the anti-poverty programs of the 1960s, large businesses contributed money to youth employment programs, sports tournaments, or entertainment series in many cities. Frequently, television stations, newspapers, automobile dealers, banks or insurance companies take responsibility for one major tournament or large-scale sports effort, which they help to publicize. Beer and soft drink companies often promote park concerts by outstanding individual or group performers. The Chase Manhattan Bank in New York sponsors the Chase Volunteers for Community Action, a special program through which an average of 300 Chase volunteers each year work with community groups, including recreation programs and events for the disabled or economically disadvantaged. IBM has given several hundred employees full or partial leaves of absence over the past several years to work with civic organizations and promote youth activities. The Miller Brewing Company has been extremely active in developing and carrying out environmental projects, combatting litter and conserving natural resources. The Miller distributor in Little Rock, Arkansas has sponsored an annual "Shoreline Arkansas River Clean-up," with the help of the Scouts and Army Corps of Engineers, and hundreds of volunteers.[6]

In other cases, major companies in cooperation with local departments jointly sponsor recreational events that promote their products. For example, the Wham-O Corporation, manufacturer of various innovative games and play equipment, conducts the National Hula Hoop Contest and the World Jr. Frisbee Contest, in cooperation with hundreds of local communities (over 725 in 1976); it provides contest kits, prizes, and other materials for local, state, and regional competitions, and free transportation, food, and lodging for the final competitions. Similarly, Kids' Dog Shows, cosponsored by the National Recreation and Park Association and the Ken-L Ration dog food company, offers a free, prepackaged Kids' Dog Show Kit including a planning guide, banners, posters, pennants, ribbons, badges, rating forms, and pet care booklets. Over one million contestants participated in locally sponsored dog shows using this service in 1975 and 1976. The Pepsi Cola Company sponsors the popular Hot-Shot Contest, a basketball shooting contest for youngsters, and the Ford Motor Company's Punt, Pass, and Kick contest has involved millions of contestants, with full coverage of the finals on nationwide television.

Alert municipal recreation and park departments take full advantage of these "tie-in" opportunities to operate special programs at a minimal cost, not only because of the free services involved, but also because of the assistance in planning and the opportunity to be part of a large-scale, highly publicized competition.

Joint Programming

This type of united effort, according to Dunn and Phillips,

> can be dubbed *synergetic programming,* or the process of combining the unique resources of more than one agency to produce leisure

services which could not be carried out successfully by one agency acting alone.[7]

A recent survey of over one hundred cities found that all but one municipal recreation and park department conducted joint programs with other agencies and organizations; more than half the respondents had ten or more "synergetic" programs during the year. They worked closely with voluntary agencies, schools and colleges, service clubs, and business and industry to promote sport, cultural, and other types of events and projects. The close cooperation of local government agencies is becoming more frequent on a broader administrative level. For example, NOR-WEST is a regional program in northern Westchester County, New York, which was formed to meet the special recreation needs of handicapped children and adults; four neighboring communities jointly fund this cooperative effort.[8] In another interesting example, the city of Mountain View, California works closely with the city of Los Altos and the joint Mountain View-Los Altos Union High School District, to schedule and promote a large-scale adult school during the academic year. This program includes hundreds of day and evening classes in both educational and recreational interests. The Mountain View Parks and Recreation Department also works closely with the Palo Alto area YMCA in cosponsoring several classes, particularly in the areas of fitness and motor skills.

Community School Programs

An increasing number of communities have moved vigorously toward developing community-school programs, seeking to make the schools the center of neighborhood life by providing educational, recreational, cultural, and social programs and services to meet the needs and interests of all residents. The premise of this approach, which has received continued support from the Charles Mott Foundation and recent Federal assistance in the United States, is that the public schools have an obligation to work closely with community groups to provide more services to the community than they have in the past. Decker writes:

> Community schools are open both days and evenings year-round and become a place where people, children as well as adults, go both to learn and to enjoy themselves. Lifelong learning and enrichment opportunities for all ages are provided in the school facility, but are not confined to the building itself. The school allies itself with the city, its busy streets and factories, its assembly lines, laboratories, shops, agencies, and organizations.[9]

Today, some 464 different school districts with several thousand school buildings are operating community school programs throughout the United States, and legislation has been passed in six states—Florida, Maryland, Michigan, Minnesota, Utah, and Washington—to operate and fund community education programs on a shared basis. The expectation is that all of the twenty thousand school districts throughout the United States will eventually be involved in one form or another of community education. Hovis suggests that an essential component of community education is that it provides the basis for a coordinated community recreation system, in which the various agencies providing leisure services in the community

255

form a coalition for sharing information, determining community recreation priorities, and developing plans for action.[10]

Mobile Recreation

Another important program trend in many communities has been the development of mobile recreation units consisting of such traveling programs as skatemobiles, mobile teen centers, sportsmobiles, show wagons, mobile puppet theaters, zoo mobiles, mobile libraries or film units, and a host of other readily portable programs. Such mobile units have been in use in rural communities for decades; they received a major impetus in many larger cities during the 1960s, when it became apparent that residents of urban slums were inadequately served by existing recreation facilities and programs. Portable programs were devised to bring sports, cultural activities, science, hobbies and other forms of entertainment into the neighborhoods, often on a schedule by which a given neighborhood might have a wide variety of special programs brought to its doorstep each week.

Although mobile recreation programs are firmly established in hundreds of cities throughout the United States and Canada, the concept is often applied in a much too limited way. Wallach points out that although mobile programs offer a highly flexible and cost-effective way to diversify leisure opportunities in geographically scattered settings, most municipal recreation and park departments design them to serve only children, the "normal" population, and summer programs. To overcome these limitations, Wallach urges that mobile recreation be designed to meet the needs of nursing homes, hospitals, and correctional institutions, and that they be provided for all age groups, in rural as well as urban settings.[11]

Probably the major challenge to recreation and park agencies in local communities in the United States and Canada today is the need for adequate financial support. In an era when several large cities have wavered on the brink of bankruptcy, school systems have pared their programs to survive on austerity budgets, and funding for libraries, hospitals, and other agencies has been cut to the bone, it has been difficult to protect recreation and park budgets against severe slashes.

Within this framework, recreation and park administrators in the United States and Canada must work vigorously in cooperation with directors of other voluntary, private, and commercial agencies to build public support for enriched and well-supported recreation services. It is essential that the public understand that recreation is not an amenity or diversion, but a significant form of community service. To provide a basis for this understanding, the final section of this text presents an exposition of the human and social values of recreation services and the planning approaches that will help the recreation field meet the critical challenges it faces.

Chapter Ten

1. *Program Report*, Nassau County, New York, Department of Recreation and Parks, February, 1977.
2. Richard C. Trudeau, "Life Begins at Forty," *Parks and Recreation*, November 1974, p. 3a.
3. George D. Butler, *Introduction to Community Recreation* (New York: McGraw-Hill, 1976), pp. 58–62.

4. For a fuller analysis of program activities, see Richard G. Kraus and Joseph E. Curtis, *Creative Administration in Recreation and Parks* (St. Louis: C. V. Mosby, 1977), pp. 111–154.

5. "Look at What They're Doing in . . . ," *Parks and Recreation,* June, 1974, pp. 46–52. See also Charles E. Fowler, "Arts in Parks: A Growing American Phenomenon," *High Fidelity / Musical America,* December 1974, pp. MA–11–13.

6. "Industry's Role," *Parks and Recreation,* December 1975, pp. 37–38.

7. Diana R. Dunn and Lamarr A. Phillips, "Synergetic Programming or 2 + 2 = 5," *Parks and Recreation,* March 1975, p. 24.

8. See Richard Kraus, *Therapeutic Recreation Service: Principles and Practices* (Philadelphia: W. B. Saunders, 1978), Ch. 11.

9. Larry E. Decker, "Community Education: Purpose, Function, Growth, Potential," *Journal of Physical Education and Recreation, Leisure Today,* April 1974, p. 7.

10. Watson B. Hovis, "Community Education: Supply and Demand Information Evaluation," *Journal of Health, Physical Education and Recreation,* April 1974, pp. 16–19.

11. For a summary of the conference on mobile recreation at which Wallach spoke, see Barbara K. Keller, "Recreation on the Move," *Parks and Recreation,* May 1974, pp. 29–30, 63.

11

RECREATION IN OTHER SETTINGS: VOLUNTARY, PRIVATE, AND COMMERCIAL

The previous two chapters described recreation programs provided by government. Although public departments are generally thought of as the chief source of leisure opportunity in modern society, a major portion of recreation in the typical community is provided by other types of agencies: voluntary, private, and commercial.

1. *Voluntary Agencies*. Nongovernmental, nonprofit organizations, voluntary agencies which have been established in the United States and Canada to meet important social needs—including recreation. Operating costs are usually derived from contributions, fees, charges, and membership dues, although many such agencies also share in United Fund, Community Chest, or similar charitable fundraising efforts, and many receive substantial support from public funds for special programs.

2. *Private Membership Organizations*. Private clubs are usually nonprofit organizations, although they may also be structured as businesses. They include boating, golf, tennis, or country clubs that operate their own facilities, and maintain a carefully selected membership, governed by elected officers. Usually self-sustaining, private clubs rely on internally generated income from initiation dues, annual fees, or other charges, rather than on tax funds or contributions.

3. *Commercial Recreation Enterprises*. The third major source of nongovernmental recreation opportunity is business sponsored programs, which include all sorts of commercial establishments such as privately owned and operated bowling alleys, swimming pools, golf driving ranges, movies, theaters, ice rinks, race tracks, sports stadiums, night clubs, bars, and a variety of schools, special classes, health spas, resorts, tourism-related businesses, and similar ventures.

Recreational opportunity must be seen as a huge interlocking system, involving both public and nonpublic sponsors. For example, the boating enthusiast may readily become involved with four different types of sponsors: (1) *commercial:* he purchases his boat and equipment from commercial manufacturers or dealers; (2) *voluntary:* he may be a member of the Power Squadron, a nonprofit group which offers courses to prospective boat owners in navigation or seamanship; (3) *private:* he may join a private boating club, and use its marina and clubhouse facilities; and (4) *government:* he will almost certainly make extensive use of publicly owned lakes, reservoirs, and waterways.

This chapter provides a detailed analysis of the three types of nongovernmental agencies, primarily through examples drawn from the United States, with a limited number of Canadian illustrations.

Voluntary Agencies in the Leisure Field

Community organizations which are described as "voluntary" usually have the following characteristics:

1. Usually established to meet significant social needs through organized citizen cooperation, community organizations represent the voluntary wishes and expressed needs of neighborhood residents. Thus, they are voluntary in *origin.*

2. Governing boards of directors or trustees are usually public-spirited citizens who accept such responsibilities as a form of social obligation. Thus, *membership* and *administrative control* are voluntary.

3. For *funding,* voluntary agencies usually rely on public contributions, either directly to the agency itself, or through a share of "community chest" fund raising. Contributed funds are usually supplemented by membership fees and charges for participation. In recent years, many voluntary organizations have also undertaken special projects for which they receive government funding.

4. *Leadership* of voluntary agencies is partly professional and partly voluntary. Management is usually by directors and supervisors professionally trained in social work, recreation, or education. At other levels, leadership is by nonprofessionals, part-time or seasonal personnel, and volunteers.

Voluntary agencies regard recreation as part of their total spectrum of service, rather than as their major function. Recreation is generally seen as a means of achieving improved social welfare goals, building character among youth, reducing social pathology, enriching educational experience, strengthening community unity, and similar objectives.

Types of Voluntary Agencies

This chapter will describe the following types of voluntary agencies: (1) youth-serving organizations; (2) religious social agencies; (3) settlement houses and community centers; (4) antipoverty organizations; (5) special-interest organizations; (6) agencies serving special populations; and (7) professional organizations serving the recreation and park field.

Youth-Serving Organizations

Nationally structured organizations which function directly through local branches or chapters, youth-serving groups have broad goals related to social development and good citizenship and operate extensive programs of recreational activity. Leading examples are the Boy and Girl Scouts and the Boys' and Girls' Clubs of America. There are hundreds of such organizations, many of them junior affiliates of adult organizations, and others independent and operated on a purely local level. Sponsorship is by such varied bodies as civic and fraternal organizations, labor unions, veterans' organizations and clubs, rural and farm organizations, and business clubs.

The Boy Scouts of America

Founded in the United States in 1910, the Boy Scouts is a powerful and widespread organization. In the United States alone, it has about 4.3 million members in 430 local councils; it is also part of a worldwide scouting movement involving over 100 other countries. Including the 1.5 million adults involved in Boy Scouting as leaders, the movement today comprises close to 6 million members; well over 35 million boys have been members of the Boy Scouts of America since its founding.

The primary purpose of scouting is the development of desirable traits of character and good citizenship, achieved through three levels of age related membership: Cub Scouts, Boy Scouts, and Explorer Scouts. The program emphasizes mental and physical fitness, vocational and social development, and the enrichment of youth hobbies and prevocational interests, relying heavily on outdoor adventure and scouting skills and on community service activities. The Boy Scout Advancement Program requires members to achieve mastery of specified skills.

About 50 percent of local Scout units are sponsored by religious agencies, although membership is not usually restricted to a single denomination. The organization firmly supports religious and spiritual values, however, and there have been cases of denial of membership to young applicants who demonstrated objection to the religious emphasis. Although the Scouts employ over 3,000 professional Scout executives and regional staff members, the bulk of actual Scout leadership is provided by parents and other interested adult volunteers.

The Boy Scouts have been widely regarded as a middle-class organization in American society, and as a small-town or suburban rather than a big-city phenomenon. However, beginning in the mid-1960s, the Scouts became more active in inner city, minority-group neighborhoods. In May, 1968 the Boy Scouts of America announced a nationwide campaign of expansion in city slums and impoverished rural areas, to attract greater numbers of black and Latin American youth. The original Scouting program focus on outdoor adventure and skills has been broadened to include urban activities. Today, along with camping and outdoor activities, Scouts may earn badges in urban conservation and cleanup or block renewal. In Chicago's inner city, they may learn to treat rat bites, repair broken steps, and read city maps—along with learning which snakes are poisonous, why the compass points north, and how to build a fire. Some areas have obtained grants from Model Cities or other Federal agencies to support such programs. The rapid shifts in the 1970s in social values that once supported traditional Scouting have caused some decline in Scouting's overall appeal. Nonetheless, an estimated one of four eligible American boys still recites the solemn Boy Scout oath ". . . to keep myself physically strong, mentally awake, and morally straight."

Girl Scouts of the U.S.A.

The leading voluntary organization serving girls in the United States is the Girl Scouts of the U.S.A., a national movement for girls between seven and seventeen. The Girl Scouts provides a sequential program of activities centered around the arts, the home, and the outdoors, with emphasis on character and citizenship development community service, international understanding, health, and safety.

Founded in 1912, the Girl Scouts today have approximately 3.5 million members in 355 councils. Membership is in four age groups, Brownies, Juniors, Cadettes and Seniors, which undertake successively difficult projects; Seniors, for example, may take on responsibilities in hospitals, museums, child care, or environmental programs. Like the Boy Scouts, Girl Scouts today conduct special programs for the poor, the physically handicapped, emotionally disturbed, mentally retarded, and similar populations.

While continuing to support its original purpose to inspire girls "with the highest ideals of character, conduct, patriotism and service," Girl Scouting recently changed the basic laws that provide the ethical basis for its movement:

> Original laws that said, for example, "A Girl Scout is a friend to animals," and "A Girl Scout is thrifty," now say "I will do my best to use resources wisely" and "to protect and improve the world around me." A law that said, "A Girl Scout is clean in thought, word and deed," now says that a Scout will do her best "to show respect for myself and others through my words and actions."[1]

While the national Girl Scout organization has taken no stand on the women's liberation movement, self-worth and self-realization have become increasingly important goals, and proficiency badges today stress important life skills for girls and young women.

Boys' Clubs of America

Another important youth-service organization is the Boys' Clubs of America. Founded in 1906, and now serving nine hundred thousand boys, this organization has almost a thousand building centers, chiefly in slum areas of cities. Programs are primarily recreational, offering sports and games, arts and crafts, social activities, and camping, but also include services in remedial education, work training, job placement, and guidance. The national goals and objectives of the Boys' Clubs include the following: citizenship education and leadership development; health, fitness, and preparation for leisure; educational-vocational motivation; intergroup understanding and value development; and enrichment of both family and community life.

Boys' Clubs provide many examples of unique services. The Syracuse Boys' Club provides guidance and recreation programs for boys confined in the county jail. The "junior deputies" program of the Atlanta club is designed to familiarize boys

261

with the methods police employ to prevent crime. The Chicago club provides basic education and prevocational training and job orientation programs in the clerical, automotive, and food-service occupations for out-of-school older boys. Other centers have comprehensive programs in creative activities like drama or writing, group therapy sessions for disturbed youth, and many other special projects. Although the Boys' Clubs depend primarily on voluntary financial support, in recent years about half of all clubs have received some form of government aid.

Girls' Clubs of America

The Girls' Clubs of America, founded in 1945, is the only federation providing daily programs for girls, usually in facilities owned by the organization itself. There are over 230 separate clubs throughout the country, serving over 180,000 girls from six to eighteen. One-third of all Girls' Club members have minority-group backgrounds (black, Oriental, Indian, or with Spanish surnames), and 68 percent of the clubs are situated in low-income areas and public housing projects. A high percentage of Girls' Clubs report serious problems of neighborhood delinquency and child abuse or neglect among their members. As a consequence, they are extremely active in delinquency prevention, counseling, job training and placement, and other social programs. Many Girls' Clubs members are on probation or in nearby correctional institutions.

The national Girls' Clubs movement seeks to be a significant force within the feminist movement. An active member of the Women's Action Alliance, it participated in formulating the U. S. National Women's Agenda. Representatives of the Girls' Clubs of America speak out for the rights and needs of girls in the public media, in forums, policy-making conferences, meetings of funding organizations, and at Federal hearings on youth problems. Its message is:

> Girls' needs are important. When they are unmet—as they have been—the symptoms of drug addiction, school dropout, personality problems, vocational disorientation, and premature parenthood among girls rise alarmingly. GCA is working hard to make sure that girls . . . receive equal attention with boys in national, state, and local planning for programs and services: equal funding, equally qualified staff, equal life opportunity, equal responsibility.[2]

It is a significant commentary that girls' organizations are not as well supported by funding agencies as boys' organizations. For example, in the mid-1970s, the average United Way allocation per member in Girls' Clubs was $13.50, while the allocation per member in Boys' Clubs was $22.00. In 1972 and 1973, foundation grants to boys' organizations totalled $14 million; in the same period girls' organizations received $3 million in foundation grants. Despite this second-class treatment in funding, Girls' Clubs programs and facilities have expanded rapidly in recent years. Recreation is an important aspect of the programs of Girls' Clubs, with special emphasis on competitive sports leagues and service to handicapped girls in integrated settings.

Other Nonsectarian Youth Programs

There are many other nonsectarian youth-serving organizations in the United States and Canada. Several examples follow.

Camp Fire Girls

Founded in 1910 and now serving over half a million members, Camp Fire Girls is primarily concerned with character building through a program of outdoor recreation, community service, and educational activities. The four age-level divisions, Bluebirds, Camp Fire Girls, Junior Hi, and Horizon Club, undertake various projects in career planning, community service, personal development and camping.

Police Athletic League

In over one hundred communities throughout the nation, law enforcement agencies sponsor Police Athletic Leagues. Operating chiefly in poverty areas, the programs rely primarily on civilian staffing and voluntary contributions for support, although they may receive technical assistance from officers on special assignment from cooperative municipal police departments. Police Athletic Leagues typically provide extensive recreation programming, indoor centers, and summer play streets, with strong emphasis on sports and games, creative arts, drum and bugle corps, and remedial education. Many leagues also maintain placement, counseling, and job-training programs, and assist youth who have dropped out of school.

4-H Clubs

Founded as self-improvement groups of rural young people around the turn of the century, 4-H clubs receive funding from various levels of government and assistance from county agricultural agents and land-grant college extension services. The primary purpose of the organization today is to promote better living in agricultural and rural areas, although there are clubs in many metropolitan regions as well. Over two million boys and girls are involved in 4-H Club programs, which include agricultural education, projects and competitions, home arts activities, conservation, and community service, and a strong program of recreation that includes trips and hikes, social programs, camping, and cultural activities.

Religious Social Agencies

Among the most active voluntary organizations meeting leisure needs in America today are agencies affiliated with major religious denominations. Recreation programs are provided by local churches or synagogues, and by youth or adult organizations affiliated with religious denominations. Typical activites provided by individual churches or synagogues include: (1) camping and outdoor conferences or institutes, which include recreation; (2) day camps, play schools, or summer Bible schools; (3) year-round recreation activities for families, including picnics, outings, bazaars, covered-dish suppers, carnivals, and other social programs; (4) programs in the fine and performing arts, sometimes based on religious themes; (5) fellowship groups for various age levels; (6) discussion clubs dealing with both religious and general subject matter; (7) senior citizens clubs and special programs for the handicapped; and (8) sports activities, including bowling and basketball leagues, or other structured or unstructured participation.

Almost all religious agencies today provide some such programs. One of the most active denominations in the leisure field is the Southern Baptist Convention, a powerful and growing religious body.

Today, such denominations as the Southern Baptists operate hundreds of well-equipped gymnasiums and recreation centers, with extensive

263

programs of sports and creative and cultural activities . . . for all age levels. Church leaders seek to stress moral purpose and spiritual meaning as they are embodied in leisure activity. They seek to promote a more holistic view of life—life not divided into separate spheres of work and play, but providing in all its aspects the opportunity for personal enrichment and spiritual growth.[3]

As a single example of church activities, the Second-Ponce de Leon Baptist Church in Atlanta

> has a professionally trained music director and several choirs. A huge sports and recreation program for the young includes bus and back-packing trips across the nation and a full-time counselor trained in psychology to help people with personal problems.[4]

Many other churches have similar programs.

National Youth Organizations
On a broader level, such organizations as the Young Men's Christian Association, the Young Women's Christian Association, the Catholic Youth Organization, and the Young Men's and Young Women's Hebrew Associations provide a network of facilities and programs with highly diversified recreation, education, and youth service activities.

YMCA and YWCA
Voluntary organizations affiliated with Protestantism in general, rather than with any single denomination, the Ys are devoted to the promotion of religious ideals of living, and view themselves as worldwide fellowships "dedicated to the enrichment of life through the development of Christian character and a Christian society." The actual membership of the Ys is multireligious and multiracial, however, as evidenced in a description of the organization in Canada today:

> The Y is a movement involving persons of all ages, creeds, colour and economic status in the task of providing opportunities for individual growth and community development. The Y in Canada consists of two independent National Voluntary Organizations, each with affiliated local associations. Local YM-YWCA's affiliate with both the National Council of YMCA's and the YWCA of Canada. Both organizations serve both sexes but the YWCA places a strong emphasis on the development of women. As a movement concerned with the total well-being of individuals and the quality of life in communities, the program of local Y's is designed to provide . . . opportunities for personal growth and for common action around social issues. Each local Y reflects the values, needs and resources of its own community.[5]

The membership pattern in the United States is similar. One out of four members of the YMCA is a girl or woman, and a 1960s study showed that the religious affiliation of Y members was 75.2 percent Protestant, 18.9 percent Roman Catholic, and 3.3 percent Jewish. In the United States, racial discrimination was formally banned by the National Council of YMCAs in the 1960s, and by the early

264

1970s, almost all Ys, in both the North and the South, had integrated membership rolls and facilities.

The Y has assumed a major responsibility for meeting public recreation needs in many American and Canadian communities. In smaller cities and towns, it frequently provides the best facilities for indoor aquatics, sports and games, physical fitness, social and cultural programs, and also the most effective organization and leadership. Both organizations have grown steadily in recent years; the YMCA expanded from 5.5 million members in 1965 to 8.8 million in 1975. Although the Y has voiced a strong commitment to urban needs, of the 130 branches developed between 1965 and 1975, almost all were built in suburbs. The YMCAs budget of $349 million in 1975 was derived from a variety of sources: membership fees, corporate and business contributions to the United Way, fund-raising drives, and government and foundation funds.

The image and program focus of both the YMCA and YWCA have changed sharply in recent years. For generations of Americans, the YMCA meant a leisurely swim in a heated pool, a brisk game of basketball, or a week at summer camp. However,

> without discarding its physical education programs, the "Y" has over the last decade adopted new goals, shifting from its old role as a "service station" for Christian youth to one as an active advocate of such social causes as racial tolerance, improved health care and better juvenile justice.[6]

Other trends in the YMCA have included: (a) participation of women in all activities, including competitive sports, fitness programs, and aquatics; (b) disappearance of most Bible study or worship activities, although the underlying principles remain Christian; (c) reflection of ethnic interests and intercultural activities; and (d) other programs designed to strengthen family life, improve health care, and promote world peace.

Similarly, the Young Women's Christian Association today is concerned with world fellowship, public affairs, community service, education, vocational development, and interracial understanding. Most YWCAs offer a broad range of classes in all sorts of physical activities, sports and dance skills, aquatics, fine and performing arts, hobbies, business skills, personal enrichment, and crafts, in addition to clubs for various age levels.

The YWCA has sought to change its image from a traditional, predominantly white, conservative organization to one more directly concerned with important social needs and problems. This new attitude is illustrated by the list of courses, clinics, and workshops offered by many YWs today: Assertiveness Training for Women, Career Development, Personal Finance, Living Single, The Marriage Contract, Sexual Consciousness-Raising, Focus: Women Over Forty, Survival in the City, Women's Self-Expression Workshop, Know Your Body, and The Divorce Experience.[7]

Both the YM and YWCA frequently work closely with other organizations in joint programs. In one large Canadian city, the YMCA collaborated with a private development company to provide a highly successful range of recreation and educational programs in a large apartment complex of eight thousand residents. In another interesting program, the YWCA has provided both an in-facility activity program and an after-care program in the Westchester County Women's Correctional Facility in New York State, with funding by the state and the Law Enforcement Assistance Administration.

Catholic Youth Organization

The leading Catholic organization concerned with providing spiritual, social, and recreational services for young people in the United States is the Catholic Youth Organization.

CYO originated in the early 1930s, when a number of dioceses under the leadership of Bishop Sheil of Chicago were experimenting with varied forms of youth organizations; it was officially established as a national organization in 1951, as a component of the National Council of Catholic Youth. Today, the National CYO Federation has a national office in Washington, D.C., as well as many citywide or diocesan offices. The parish, however, is the core of the Catholic Youth Organization, which depends heavily on the leadership of the parish priest and the services of adult volunteers from the neighborhood for direction and assistance.

Within its religious context, CYO is clearly recognized as a leisure program, meeting its goals through projects and activities operated through local clubs. The following statement illustrates the CYO's view of recreation as a means of rejecting negative or antisocial forms of leisure.

> The most vulnerable period in the lives of our young people are the leisure-time hours when they are on their own, away from the positive influences of family, school and church. The values and standards of these significant institutions can then be challenged by the growing impulse for self-assertion and the natural instincts of pleasure-seeking and self-indulgence. This sensitive situation encompasses nearly half the lifetime of the pre-teen and teen-ager and it is the mission of the Catholic Youth Organization to "move in" on these idle hours to an extension of the family, church and school with recreation, spiritual, apostolic, social and cultural programming that will give the youngster attractive alternatives to the appealing excitement of the "offbeat" activities that are the root of delinquency.[8]

This general purpose is again expressed in the same report: "Since 1936, the New York C.Y.O. has been in the thick of the struggle to prevent and overcome juvenile delinquency." The goals of the CYO, however, like those of other religious organizations that work with youth, are directly related to spiritual values. Through participation in the program, Catholic youth become involved in retreats, workshops, religious education, and service programs that strengthen and enrich their faith. The social program also serves to attract and involve young people in center activities, thus helping the priest maintain meaningful contact with the young people in his parish.

Sports are highly regarded not only as a means of attracting young people to CYO programs, but also as a way to impart desirable spiritual values. The coach is considered an important educator and transmitter of Christian values.

> Sports, well understood and practiced . . . contributes to the development of the whole person because it demands generous effort, careful self-control, mastery of self and respect for others, complete commitment and team spirit . . . these values contribute to the building up of

tomorrow's well-ordered society which we have characterized as the 'civilization of love.'[9]

The wide range of CYO services is illustrated by the following recreational facilities and programs offered in New York City in a recent year: 6 community centers, 4 settlement houses, 4 summer camps, an extensive Sea Cadet Corps, 17 antidelinquency recreation projects, 195 Teen-Age Leadership Clubs, nearly 600 Boy and Girl Scout Troops, 45 summer day camps, 36 young adult clubs, a Physical Fitness Council, a Young People's Symphony and Music Program, as well as recreation programs and swimming classes for mentally retarded and physically handicapped children. Many such programs are sponsored directly by the Catholic Youth Organization through its own centers (administered and financed by diocesan headquarters); while others are operated under the direction of parish priests.

Young Men's and Young Women's Hebrew Association

Like the YM and YWCA, the Jewish Y's do not regard themselves primarily as recreation agencies, but rather as community organizations devoted to social service, with a strong Jewish cultural component. Specifically, the YM and YWHA has defined its community role in the following way:

1. To meet the leisure-time social, cultural and recreational needs of its membership, embracing both sexes and all age groups.

2. To stimulate individual growth and personality development by encouraging interest and capacity for group and community participation.

3. To teach leadership responsibility and democratic process through group participation.

4. To provide certain limited guidance services, including individual counseling, in preparation for referral to specialized services when indicated.

5. To encourage citizenship education and responsibility among its members and, as a social welfare agency, to participate in community-wide programs of social betterment.[10]

The YM and YWHA identifies social group work as its major professional discipline, although it also draws upon qualified staff members from other specialized fields. A typical YM-YWHA or Jewish community center in a large metropolitan area serves as many as three or four thousand members of all ages. Program activities include a nursery school, an after-school and summer camp program for children, as well as a wide range of social, athletic and cultural activities for all age groups. Activities for teen-age youth include special programs designed to strengthen their sense of affiliation with Judaism.

The focus of the Jewish Ys has been the two broad areas of sports and physical fitness activities and cultural arts. In its 1977 report following a large-scale study of the health, physical education, and recreation programs, the Jewish Welfare Board urged that programs be restructured with a clear identification of goals, and that high priority be given to lifetime sports and fitness activities, carried on under medical guidance, and carefully designed to develop and maintain cardiovascular capacity, motor function, and general health and strength. The organization developed guidelines regarding competition in Y sports programs, and more effective rehabilitative programs for the handicapped and for those who have suffered accidents or cardiovascular episodes.[11]

The cultural activities of many Ys and Jewish Community Centers include extensive programs in the performing arts, the graphic and plastic arts, poetry, and other creative pursuits. One of the leading examples of a creative arts program is the Usdan Center, an outstanding 250-acre woodland campus for music, art, dance, theater arts, and recreation, affiliated with the major YM-YWHAs and Jewish centers in the New York Metropolitan area. Situated on Long Island, this unusual facility offers an outstanding professional staff, leading guest performers, and all levels of participation in the arts in an intensive summer camp experience. The Usdan Center has superb new contemporary buildings, developed with the assistance of the Henry Kaufmann Foundation, and also receives assistance from the New York State Council on the Arts.

Settlement Houses and Community Centers

Another type of voluntary agency which provides extensive recreational services is the settlement house. Founded in the United States in the late nineteenth and early twentieth century (see chapter 7), settlement houses are generally regarded as social work agencies, and draw their administrative personnel from that field. Their varied goals include education, counseling, health services, cultural enrichment, and recreation.

The Bronx River Neighborhood House in New York City is an example of a settlement house established in the post-World War II period to meet pressing urban needs in a rapidly changing community. It began in Bronx River Houses, a low-income project, and then expanded to include several other operations within a larger district known by city planners as Soundview-Bruckner, an area of four square miles with a population of over one hundred thousand. This district is a study in contrasts, including both run-down tenements marked by social pathology, and middle-income private housing of stable and responsible families.

The Bronx River Neighborhood Center, with the assistance of various Federal, state, and city agencies, operates three centers of its own, plus special programs in public schools, churches, and the community rooms of three middle-income projects. Activities include social and recreation services designed to serve all age groups. The center operates playgrounds, nursery programs, social clubs, classes, teams, lounges, councils, work projects, day camps, and special services for the disabled and aging.

Approximately 250 such settlement houses operate in disadvantaged areas of major cities of the United States today. In the past, settlement houses were governed primarily by wealthy board members who did not live in the neighborhoods served, and who assisted in private fund-raising efforts for their support. Today, the board members or trustees of settlement houses include many poor and minority-group members who live in the neighborhoods served and who represent the views of local residents. Funding is now derived from both private and government sources; in a recent year, Bronx River Neighborhood Houses received as much as 90 percent of its budget from government sources. Such extensive government funding tends to reduce the independence of such voluntary agencies in their policy making and to make them, in effect, semigovernmental agencies.

Other Organizations Serving the Disadvantaged

Closely linked in purpose to settlement houses, but with a somewhat more restricted focus and a lesser emphasis on social work leadership, are the many voluntary agencies which concentrate on meeting the needs of the poor—particularly children and youth—in urban slums. Two examples of such agencies in New York City are presented here; there are similar examples in other large cities.

The Fresh Air Fund
This agency was founded in 1877 with the intention of giving deprived city tenement children vacations in country settings. In the early years, these children were chiefly of immigrant families; today they come mostly from nonwhite populations of blighted urban neighborhoods. Supported by voluntary contributions, the Fresh Air Fund operates its own network of seven camps on the three thousand-acre Sharpe Reservation, where thousands of city children each summer enjoy country living, natural science activities, and remedial education. A "Friendly Town" program places many other children in private homes throughout a twelve-state Eastern seaboard area from Maine to Virginia.

The Children's Aid Society
Another leading example of voluntary organizations which serve disadvantaged children and youth, the Children's Aid Society was founded in 1853 as a nonsectarian agency to provide care for the "orphaned and destitute children who roamed the streets of nineteenth-century New York, by operating lodging houses and industrial schools and placing children in the West." Today, its variety of services include child care, foster home placement, free hot lunches, a visiting nurse and school nurse service, an adoption service, a dental clinic, and a free day nursery. The Children's Aid Society provides a comprehensive work, health, education, and recreation program, including extensive camping opportunities, in seven large centers in deprived areas of New York City.

Other Antipoverty Organizations

It was part of the philosophy of the antipoverty program of the 1960s that one important means of helping slum residents overcome poverty and its accompanying social pathologies was to give them power to plan and run their own social action programs. The program assisted in the establishment of antipoverty agencies in many large cities in the United States, controlled largely by the poor and their representatives. Their functions ranged from housing and legal assistance, political action, remedial education, and vocational training, to recreation, day camps, and cultural programs.

These indigenous antipoverty organizations received a major portion of their funding from the Federal Office of Economic Opportunity, and were expected to promote the economic advancement and job capability of ghetto youth. However, OEO and other Federal agencies also supported many clearly recreational activities, some of which provided jobs in areas such as acting, dance, arts and crafts, karate, film-making, photography and other cultural activities. Many programs gave special attention to Afro-American, Chicano, and Puerto Rican history and cultural traditions.

Special-Interest Organizations

Another major type of voluntary agency, special-interest organizations promote activities and public support for a particular type of recreation, rather than providing direct programs for the public. Such agencies are usually nationally organized, with full-time professional staff members who conduct promotional efforts through the mass media, pressing for favorable legislation and public support.

Special-interest organizations are often found in athletics, where they are concerned with the promotion of a specific sport such as tennis, golf, or basketball, or with the overall governance of amateur sport. These groups are often financially supported by business persons who have a stake in the activity's success, such as manufacturers of bowling, billiards, or boating equipment. Other special-interest groups represent popular interest in the cultural arts, through civic opera or regional ballet companies. Hobbies such as bridge, chess, rock collecting, and antiquing are also represented by such organizations. There are literally hundreds of such groups today; as soon as any activity gains the popularity to command public interest, adherents or promoters form an organization to represent it.

Following are examples of special-interest organizations operating within the field of conservation and outdoor recreation.

Sierra Club

Founded in 1892 and headed during its first two decades by the famous naturalist John Muir, the Sierra Club has sought to make Americans aware "of what we have lost and can lose during 200 years of continuing exploitation of our resources for commodity purposes and failure to realize their value for scenic, scientific and aesthetic purposes."[12] In recent years, the Sierra Club has become known for its battles to protect major natural resources threatened by commercial exploitation. However, its activities are not restricted to conservation; it is also the nation's largest skiing and hiking club, operating a major network of ski lodges and "river runners," numerous wilderness outings, and ecological group projects. Since 1959, the Sierra Club has become a major publisher of books on conservation and natural resources. Its membership has grown from about 7,000 in the mid-1950s, to over 144,000 in the mid-1970s.

Appalachian Mountain Club

This organization has a regional focus; its purpose when founded in 1876 was to "explore the mountains of New England and adjacent regions . . . for scientific and artistic purposes, and . . . to cultivate an interest in geographical studies." Since its inception, it has explored and mapped many of the wildest and most scenic areas in Massachusetts, New Hampshire, and Maine, in addition to promoting such sports as skiing, snowshoeing, mountain climbing, and canoeing.

Although practical conservation remains a primary concern of the club, it has also acquired various camp properties, published guides and maps, and maintained hundreds of miles of trails and a network of huts and shelters throughout the White Mountains for use by its members. It promotes programs of instruction and leadership training in such activities as snowshoeing, skiing, smooth and white-water canoeing, and rock climbing.

American Youth Hostels

This nonprofit membership organization gained much of its impetus from the European hostel movement which became popular during the early part of the

270

twentieth century, and which sought to promote educational and recreation travel and outdoor activities. AYH maintains centers providing simple overnight accommodations in scenic, historical, and cultural areas. Hostelers are expected to travel under their own steam; bicycling is a primary mode of travel, although other forms of transportation may be used to get to the starting point of a trip.

In the United States, there are thirty-one local AYH councils which sponsor varied adventure trips and excursions for young people, and give leadership training in ski-touring, camping, snowshoeing, sailing, canoeing, and similar activities. In addition, the American Youth Hostel helps Scouts, Ys, schools and other organizations to initiate their own hosteling programs. Many municipal recreation and park departments have also made hosteling available to the youth and families of their communities.

Other organizations promote different forms of outdoor recreation. For example, the National Campers and Hikers Association, the largest international family camping organization in North America, promotes varied forms of camping and hiking, works with other organizations, and supports natural resource conservation activities.

Voluntary Organization Promoting Boating

Boating and related aquatic activities are supported by a variety of voluntary organizations. The Boy and Girl Scouts, Camp Fire Girls, and many other youth agencies sponsor programs in swimming, life-saving, and boating safety. The American Red Cross Safety Service promotes and teaches life-saving, water safety, and first aid. Through its National Aquatic Schools, the Red Cross certifies teachers of swimming, life-saving, first aid, and small-craft handling.

Other voluntary boating organizations include: (1) the U.S. Coast Guard Auxiliary, an organization of volunteer boating enthusiasts who work closely with the U.S. Coast Guard in providing education in seamanship, safety, and small-boat handling, and conduct examinations of pleasure craft; (2) the U.S. Power Squadron, a volunteer organization whose members offer courses in piloting, navigation, and small-boat handling, and which cooperates in the enforcement of boating laws; and (3) the Outboard Boating Club of America, which provides similar services for this type of craft.

Community Councils

Other special-interest organizations are concerned with promoting open space and park programs in urban settings. One such example, in New York City, is the Parks Council. Founded in 1962, this nonprofit organization is

> dedicated to promoting the widespread adoption of imaginative, safe and practical playground design, the preservation and expansion of park land and the formulation of novel, fulfilling and substantial recreation programs.[13]

Supported by over forty affiliated community groups, the Council (1) testifies at city budget hearings; (2) sponsors tours of city parks and playgrounds; (3) sponsors vest-pocket parks and assists neighborhood and block associations in developing their own facilities or rehabilitating run-down areas; (4) promotes green belt development and opposes encroachment on existing open space and park land; (5) studies park maintenance and presses for improved operations; (6) examines

271

facilities in other cities, to develop innovative practices for New York; and (7) promotes public awareness of outdoor recreation and environmental needs. In numerous other cities, similar citizens' councils or planning bodies of a voluntary nature promote environmental action or assist recreation and youth services generally.

Voluntary Organizations Serving the Ill and Disabled

Another important category of voluntary organizations in American communities today is concerned with meeting the needs of individuals who have special limitations. Organizations like the American Cerebral Palsy Association and the National Association for Retarded Children have pressed vigorously to provide special recreation services for the disabled. Local chapters of these organizations have encouraged municipal recreation and park departments to expand their programs to include the disabled, urging the adoption of facilities standards to overcome the physical and environmental barriers which prevent the participation of the handicapped. Such voluntary organizations have established after-care centers, such as social clubs or halfway houses, to provide counseling, vocational, and social programs for discharged mental patients. Similar organizations serving the blind, deaf, and other disabled persons operate throughout the United States and Canada.

Private Organizations Providing Recreation Programs

A major portion of recreational opportunity today is provided by private membership organizations. Within the broad field of sport and outdoor recreation, there are many organizations which provide facilities or instruction related to skiing, tennis, golf, boating, and hunting or fishing. Such clubs frequently exist as independent, incorporated bodies, owning their own facilities, with policy set by elected officers and boards, and with the actual work of maintenance, instruction, and supervision carried out by paid employees.

A major characteristic of many such organizations is their social exclusiveness; membership policies screen out certain prospective members for reasons relating to their expected compatibility with current members. Many country clubs, golf clubs, and tennis clubs discriminate against members of certain races or religions, although application of their policies is often arbitrary and contradictory. For example, in suburban Washington, black members of the diplomatic corps are permitted to join the exclusive Chevy Chase Country Club, but black American residents of the area—even the black mayor of the nation's capital—are not. Similarly, the black commodore of the Jamaican Yacht Club holds an honorary membership in the Biscayne Yacht Club, Miami's oldest social club, although the club refuses to allow local Jews and blacks as members. Delaney comments:

> The two elegant private clubs are not unlike many of their counterparts across the country, from New York to California. A check of clubs in several metropolitan areas, including New York, Chicago, Philadelphia, Boston, Washington, Atlanta and Los Angeles, found that while some changes have occurred in recent years, discrimination in some of the most prominent and exclusive clubs remains policy and practice.[14]

It is important to recognize that although the ostensible function of such private organizations is to provide sociability as well as specific forms of leisure activity, the clubs also provide a setting in which the most powerful members of American communities meet regularly to discuss business or political matters, and often reach informal decisions or plans for action. Those who are barred from membership in such clubs are thus excluded also from this behind-the-scenes, establishment-based process of influence and power.

The recreation facilities of private membership clubs are usually of a higher quality than those offered by public or voluntary agencies. A private golf club, for example, is usually less crowded and more attractively designed and carefully maintained than public courses; it is also considerably more expensive.

Membership in fraternal orders and clubs has increased in recent years. In the early 1970s, the Loyal Order of Moose had a membership of over 1.1 million; the membership of the Benevolent and Protective Order of Elks rose to 1.5 million. Other fraternal groups such as the Eagles, Lions, and Masons, have huge memberships, with the total number amounting to several million. Such organizations, in addition to their religious and civic functions, provide a substantial amount of recreation for their members and families. Fraternal groups also tend to be discriminatory (see page 9) in their membership policies. Service clubs like the Kiwanis or Rotary Club tend to be more open to members and to give higher priority to public service projects, including recreation and other programs for the disabled.

Residence-Connected Clubs

Another form of restricted recreation program is based on real estate ownership. As shown in Chapter 5, many real estate developers recognize that one of the key selling points in home development projects is the provision of attractive recreational facilities. Thus, tennis courts, golf courses, swimming pools, health spas, and similar recreation facilities are frequently provided for the residents of apartment buildings, condominiums, or one-family home developments where residents may be families, "singles," or retired persons. It is important to recognize that only those who can afford to purchase or rent such residences are able to use these facilities. Because these people fill most of their leisure needs through private programs in membership-restricted settings, they are therefore less likely to support public facilities and programs.

In addition to the types of private groups just described, many cities have membership organizations which are less exclusive. In many large cities, there are clubs of European ethnic groups such as those of Ukrainian, Czech, Hungarian, or Greek descent. Most have their own clubhouse, frequently including sports and social facilities; some are attached to a church of the appropriate denomination. Much of the social life of such private groups revolves around traditional folk customs, including dancing, music, games, holiday events, picnics, and similar events. There are also many less exclusive country clubs on the fringes of large cities, which provide swimming, handball, or tennis, areas for card playing, and similar opportunities. Annual charges are considerably less than in the more exclusive clubs described earlier, and usually any community resident who wishes to join is welcome.

273

Commercial Recreation Programs

By far the largest amount of recreational participation in the United States and Canada today is offered by commercial enterprises. Such opportunities may be classified in various ways:

1. *Facilities and Areas for Self-Directed Activity.* Golf courses, swimming pools, ski centers, ice rinks, bars and taverns, bowling alleys, billiard parlors, riding stables, fish and game preserves, driving ranges, campgrounds, and boat marinas are examples of such profit oriented businesses. In each of these, the individual is more or less active in providing his or her own recreation.

2. *Enterprises Providing Entertainment.* Here the consumer is entertained in a generally passive way; this category includes theaters, indoor and outdoor movies, concert halls, nightclubs with floor shows, commercial sports stadiums, circuses, amusement parks, race tracks, carnivals, and similar enterprises.

3. *Enterprises Providing Instructional Services.* This category includes special schools, studios, or health centers that give instruction in music, dancing, the arts, physical fitness (including judo, karate, and other forms of self-defense), riding schools, and similar commercially operated instructional centers.

4. *Manufacturers and Suppliers of Recreational Equipment.* Many of the recreational activities pursued in the home or in the neighborhood do not require special facilities or instruction, but do involve the purchase of special equipment or materials. Thus, musical equipment (phonograph records and players, tape recorders, instruments and sheet music), toys, games, gardening equipment, books, magazines, radio and television sets, special clothing for play, barbecue equipment, and a host of other products all represent commercial recreation enterprise.

5. *Travel and Tourism.* As shown in Chapter 5, this is perhaps the largest area of commercial recreation enterprise; it includes the operation of motels, hotels, commercial campgrounds, amusement complexes and theme parks, as well as the management of tours, cruises, airline charters, and similar ventures.

All of these forms of activities, facilities, equipment, and services make possible a vast amount of leisure participation by people of all ages. Often the leisure opportunities provided by commercial sponsors are in direct competition with those offered by public and voluntary agencies, and unless the business manager is able to offer a clearly superior service, he may not be able to survive the competition. In many cases, however, the arrangement is a cooperative one, as when a public recreation and park department obtains the use of a commercial bowling alley or ice skating rink at a reduced rate for special classes, or a privately owned riding stable operates in a public park through a concession arrangement.

Employee Recreation Programs

A final category of recreation sponsorship involves the role of business and industry in providing programs of employee recreation. Such programs fit none of the previous categories; they are obviously not governmental, although some government departments and agencies have employee recreation programs, nor are they voluntary recreation agencies, since they are usually organized by or in connection with profit-making organizations. They are most logically categorized as private recreation programs, since they serve specific membership groups, are not normally open to the public, and are nonprofit in nature.

Company-Sponsored Programs

Employee recreation—a term that is often used interchangeably with industrial recreation—began in the nineteenth century but did not expand rapidly until after World War II. The *Wall Street Journal* estimated in 1953 that expenditures by business and industry for employee recreation amounted to $800 million annually. In 1975, the *New York Times* reported that 50,000 private companies were spending $2 billion a year on recreation related programs. Over 800 of the largest corporations active in this field belong to the National Industrial Recreation Association, founded in 1941 to promote employee recreation programs.

Three major purposes may be cited which justify making recreation an important component in industrial personnel services:

1. *Improvement of Employer-Employee Relations.* At an earlier period in American industrial development, there was considerable friction between management and labor, often resulting in extended and violent strikes. A major purpose of industrial recreation programs at this time was to create favorable employer-employee relationships and to create a sense of loyalty among workers. Today, with relative peace in most industries, this is still a significant goal of employee recreation. The overall program tends to create a feeling of belonging and identification among employees; group participation among workers of various job levels contributes to improved worker morale, increased harmony, and an attitude of mutual cooperation.

2. *Promoting Employee Efficiency.* It is widely accepted that a constructive program of employee recreation improves worker performance. Personnel experts have found that when workers spend their free time at constructive recreational activities, absenteeism resulting from emotional tension or illness, excessive use of alcohol and similar causes is reduced. Recreation also helps to combat workers' fatigue and boredom, and thus reduces accident rates. More and more companies have introduced fitness programs, with carefully designed cardiovascular conditioning activities under medical supervision, to improve the health of their employees.

3. *Recruitment Appeal.* Another purpose of employee recreation programs is to assist firms seeking to recruit or retain employees. An attractive program of recreation that can meet the needs of both the employee and his or her family can be persuasive. When an industry is a considerable distance from communities with adequate recreation and park facilities and programs for public use, it becomes virtually necessary for the company itself to provide leisure opportunities.

Administrative Arrangements and Activities

Administrative arrangements for employee recreation are many and varied. In some cases, the management provides facilities and leadership and maintains complete control of the operation. In other organizations, company directors provide facilities, and an employee recreation association takes actual responsibility for running the program. Other companies use combinations of these approaches. Frequently, profits from canteens or plant vending machines provide financial support for the program in addition to that from moderate fees for participation or membership. Many activities—such as charter vacation flights—are completely self-supporting; others are fully or partly subsidized by the company.

Some industrial firms restrict participation in recreation activities to employees and their families, while others make them available to the surrounding community. Frank Flick, an industrialist who has taken a leading position in this field, stresses the obligation of private business to play a significant social role in the community:

> A major development of our time is the discovery of the power of the private, commercial sector to help solve a wide variety of community problems. We see increasing evidence that business can hire and train the hardcore unemployed, educate functional illiterates, help reduce the rate of high school dropouts, help save alcoholics, even help rehabilitate criminals. Now I believe that industry should show what it can do to help meet community needs in the areas of recreation and health.[15]

To illustrate some of the possibilities in this area, the Flick-Reedy Corporation has been one of the world's largest industrial sponsors of Boy Scouts. It has designed its main building for the recreation use of the entire community, with thousands of children and adults using its gymnasium, auditorium, or dining room for special banquets and events each year. Its indoor swimming pool serves not only employees and their families, but business guests as well—in addition to members of church groups, Boy and Girl Scouts, 4-H Clubs, Little League, other local athletic associations, and hundreds of handicapped children.

Employee recreation programs include a wide range of activities. The National Industrial Recreation Association estimates that employees of its member companies alone purchase $200 million worth of discount tickets and merchandise each year, for sporting events, amusement parks, theater and hotel packages, and varied forms of merchandise—all through employee associations. Many companies sponsor a wide range of classes and special courses, some designed for vocational or career development, others for cultural interest or self-development. Fitness, as indicated earlier, has become a major aspect of employee activity programs; in Canada, the federal government has given major support to the drive to increase cardiovascular and aerobic fitness programs in business settings.[16] The variety of opportunities and activities is endless:

> The Teletype Company, in Skokie, Illinois, has many sports leagues for men and women, in such sports as basketball, bowling, softball, horseshoes, golf, tennis, and similar activities, along with many tournaments and special events during the year.

> Some companies operate large-scale country clubs, golf courses, or even parks and camps for their employees. The Texas Instruments Corporation has a 66-acre property 15 miles from its Dallas office, primarily for its Rod and Gun Club, and also operates a 60-acre campsite 85 miles away.

> So many families attend the Lockheed Employees Recreation Association's Christmas party for children that it is necessary to rent nine theaters to show Walt Disney films.

> Such companies as Eastman Kodak, IBM or Martin-Marietta pay the way for their management personnel to take mountain-climbing, raft

trips, and grueling ten-day hikes, in an executive-enrichment program developed by Chicago's Outward Bound School; the Coors Company uses the same program to screen inner-city blacks, uneducated Indians, or ex-convicts, before hiring them.[17]

Another example of the concern of corporations for their employees' personal well-being is the program initiated in 1977 by the International Business Machines corporation. To help their retiring employees learn new hobbies or business skills, IBM set up a tuition assistance plan under which it would provide up to $2,500 over a five-year period to assist employees to take courses related to recreation or forms of self-employment. Recognizing that these newly retired individuals would live an average of 15 to 18 years after retirement (based on recent statistical reports that life expectancy for men aged sixty-five is eighty years, and for women, eighty-three), IBM agreed to allocate almost a million dollars a year to this program so that its former employees could spend their leisure time in active and stimulating ways.

Provision of recreational opportunities for employees is not unique to American companies; many European firms offer similar programs. As a single example, the Duhamel Textile Company at Harnes, in northern France, operates a handsome modern chalet near Grenoble, with an elaborate ski and winter-sports recreation center for employees who visit the chalet in groups of forty, for four-week stays throughout the winter months. To make this program possible, employees voluntarily work an extra half-hour a day without pay through the full year. When they are at the ski center, they sew from 7 to 10 a.m., ski until 4 p.m., and then work for three hours more. There are many variations of this program, as well as extensive sports leagues, cultural activities, and fitness plans, sponsored by other European companies.

Union-Sponsored Recreation Programs

A number of leading labor unions sponsor extensive recreation programs and promote community recreation activities.

One of the most active unions in this regard is the United Automobile Workers, which has a special department of recreation and leisure-time activities, and has actively promoted many programs in local chapters, as well as social action and legislation supporting open space and community recreation services.

Another active union is the International Ladies Garment Workers Union. The ILGWU operates a $10-million vacation resort for its members. Camp Unity, in Pennsylvania, has seventy-eight buildings including a million-dollar theater, a large administration building and dining room seating 1,100 guests, a health club, tennis courts, and a beach on a mile-long lake; its program features such cultural activities as adult education and discussion groups, forums, and classical music events. Still other unions have retirement planning seminars and clubs or centers for their retired members.

Goals and Professionalism

This chapter and the preceding two have described in detail the four major categories of agencies that provide recreational facilities and programs in the United States and Canada today: *public, voluntary, private,* and *commercial.* Any meaningful examination of a modern community will reveal the diversity of such organizations and the roles they play in meeting leisure needs. For example, an urban core area study of a primarily residential area in the city of Toronto, published in 1972 by the Canadian Parks/Recreation Association, revealed a considerable number of organizations and facilities of all types which contributed to leisure opportunities. These included: (a) private clubs, including veterans' groups, ethnic associations, and other membership organizations; (b) several churches, synagogues, and Ys; (c) public, private, and religious schools and training centers; (d) community houses, day care centers, small parks, and playgrounds; and (e) other facilities outside, but serving the study area.[18]

Do all such organizations share the same philosophies and goals? Both public and voluntary agencies exist primarily to meet the needs of the public at large. Governmental recreation and park departments obviously function under policies formulated either by major public officials, or by boards or commissions that represent the public interest. Although voluntary agencies may have more specialized purposes and more independence in policy making, they too have a strong sense of values and social purpose.

In contrast, private and commercial recreation enterprises do not generally have such altruistic purposes. Private organizations exist to meet the social and recreational wishes of their members, and commercial enterprises are concerned primarily with earning a profit. Such a statement does not imply condemnation of either type of agency. Many of them provide wholesome and enjoyable entertainment, or the opportunity for healthy and desirable sports, cultural activities, travel, or similar pursuits. Frequently, private service clubs and commercial concerns work closely with public and voluntary recreation departments, helping to promote or subsidize desirable community services.

In the past, public and voluntary agencies have generally been regarded as part of the recreation movement, while private and commercial organizations have not. The degree of an organization's involvement in the recreation movement is often judged by its affiliation or nonaffiliation with professional organizations, and by its attitude toward the use of professional personnel. Because public and voluntary agency staff members are part of a social movement, they are expected to have special education that equips them to operate as professionals; they are also usually members of national, regional, or local professional organizations.

This suggests that an extremely important element of organized recreation and park service today is the training, background, and qualifications of those who staff recreation and park departments and agencies. The following chapter examines this topic in detail, outlining the past development of professionalism in recreation and parks and its current status, problems, and trends.

Chapter Eleven

1. Leslie Martland, "Girl Scouting, 64 Years Old, Is Changing," *New York Times,* 8 March 1976, p. 29.

2. *Girls' Clubs of America: A National Force for Girls,* (New York: Girls' Clubs of America Annual Report and Brochure, 1975), p. 8.

3. See Richard Kraus, *Recreation Today: Program Planning and Leadership* (Santa Monica, California: Goodyear, 1977) pp. 10–11, 159–166.

4. "Southern Baptists' Rapid Expansion," *New York Times,* 8 May 1976, p. 50.

5. Peter Witt, "Survey of Programs for Handicapped in Y's in Canada," funded by Recreation Canada Directorate, 1973.

6. Kenneth A. Briggs, "YMCA Branches Stress Social Activism," *New York Times,* 23 November 1976, p. 1.

7. See annual brochure of offerings, Central Branch YWCA, New York City, 1976–1977, or the brochure of any large urban Y.

8. "Youth . . . Apostles to Youth," (Annual Report of Catholic Youth Organization, New York, 1967), p. 3.

9. *Guidelines for Diocesan/National CYO Coach's Federation* (Washington, D.C.: National CYO Federation, 1976), pp. 1–2.

10. Irving Brodsky, "The New Role of the Community Center," *Social Welfare Forum* (New York: Columbia Univ. Pr., 1964), p. 201.

11. *Health, Physical Education and Recreation Study Committee Report* (New York: National Jewish Welfare Board, 1977).

12. Lawrence E. Davies, "Sierra Club Maps Expansion," *New York Times,* 9 December 1967, p. 52.

13. "Annual Report of the Council for Parks and Playgrounds," New York, 1968.

14. Paul Delaney, "Discrimination Remains a Policy and a Practice at Many Clubs," *New York Times,* 13 September 1976, p. 29.

15. Frank Flick, "The Untapped Potential: Industrial Recreation" (Chicago: National Industrial Recreation Association, 1974), p. 14.

16. See "Employee Physical Fitness in Canada," Report of Conference Sponsored by Ministry of National Health and Welfare, Ottawa, December, 1974.

17. "Executives: Operation Outdoors," *Time.* 16 December 1974, p. 36.

18. Paul Wilkinson, ed., *Recreation in a Community: An Urban Core Area Study* (Vanier City, Ontario: Canadian Parks/Recreation Association, 1972).

PROFESSIONALISM IN

RECREATION AND PARKS

The previous chapters have outlined the growth of recreation programs in the United States and Canada. Accompanying this expansion, the career field of professional leadership in recreation and park agencies has also grown rapidly. In 1965, financial columnist Sylvia Porter stated:

> As we move toward the peak recreation season of the year, the soaring profits-and-paycheck importance of "fun" in the United States emerges with brilliant clarity. . . . Today's surge in travel, sports, vacation, etc., has become a major creator of jobs—going far beyond the familiar categories of camp counselors, lifeguard, park ranger and the like.
>
> Recreation, in sum, is becoming a big, booming, professional business— dazzling even the most optimistic projections of a few years ago—and it'll become bigger, boomier and more professional year after year.[1]

In the same year, the U. S. Department of Labor issued a special *Occupational Outlook Quarterly* which recognized recreation as a field of rapidly rising employment, identifying sixty different occupations in which professionally trained workers delivered leisure services. Other reports by the U. S. Bureau of Labor Statistics during the early 1970s predicted that recreation would be a field of growing employment in the decade ahead.

Types of Positions in Recreation

Statements about employment in recreation are sometimes misleading, because they usually include *all* persons employed in leisure services; the recreation and leisure services fields are actually two separate categories of employment.

1. *The Broad Field of Leisure Services.* This includes equipment sales and manufacturing, entertainment, the operation of resorts, nightclubs, cruise ships, bowling alleys, and a host of similar occupations. Those who work in such fields can hardly be regarded as recreation professionals—particularly when they are specialists in other professional fields, who simply happen to be employed in a leisure related enterprise.

2. *Specific Employment in Recreation Roles.* In the past, the term *recreation professional* implied that the individual was employed in a leadership, supervisory, administrative, or other specialist capacity in a public recreation and park department or in a nonprofit agency with recreation program functions. Today, the concept of the recreation professional is somewhat broader, and includes positions in commercial recreation when they involve planning, management, or other professional functions.

How many people are employed in leisure related occupations today?

Estimates during the early and mid-1960s suggested that there were between 10,000 and 35,000 full-time recreation workers in the United States. An analysis of employment in recreation in the United States conducted in 1968 under a grant from the Department of Health, Education, and Welfare concluded that there were approximately 1.4 million full- and part-time workers in recreation; converted to full-time equivalents, the total was 949,431 persons.[2] However, this report was based on questionable sampling procedures and projections, and should have been regarded as an umbrellalike estimate of employment in the overall recreation field rather than a precise tabulation of professionals.

More recently, the *Statistical Abstract of the United States* reported that there were 274,000 social and recreation workers in the United States—a more conservative and probably more accurate figure.[3] The most comprehensive attempt to identify recreation employees in public recreation and park departments was reported by Godbey and Henkel, in November, 1976.[4] Based on a study of municipal park and recreation agencies, county systems, special districts, and state park systems, Godbey and Henkel identified 43,013 employees in eighteen job categories—ranging from executives, superintendents, and division heads, to activity specialists, recreation program leaders, and aides. Again, this report is only partially useful in providing an estimate of employment in the recreation profession, because it dealt with a limited sample, both as to type and number of agencies.

Based on all available information, it would seem reasonable to estimate that between 200,000 and 250,000 individuals with a primary concern for the provision of recreation and park facilities and services are employed today in Federal, state, municipal, and voluntary nonprofit agencies throughout the United States. In addition, several times that number are probably employed in private and commercial recreation related positions.

It is the purpose of this chapter to examine recreation as an area of professional service, and to determine its strengths and weaknesses, as well as its present and future trends.

Characteristics of a Profession

Exactly what is a profession? A position paper of the Society of Park and Recreation Educators defined it as follows:

> A profession is a vocation whose practice is founded upon an understanding of the theoretical structure of some department of learning or science and upon the abilities accompanying such understanding. This understanding and these abilities are applied to the vital practical affairs of man. . . . The profession, serving the vital needs of man, considers its first ethical imperative to be altruistic service to the client.[5]

In another analysis, Paul Douglass suggests that a profession is a body of career practitioners who by specialized education and skills assume the responsibility and power needed to (1) certify the adequate preparation of personnel and (2) assure ethical performance in the course of duty within a field of service that is regarded as a public trust.[6] Obviously then, the mission of the field itself must be analyzed in determining whether the recreation field should be considered a form of public trust. A statement of the American Park and Recreation Society outlined the major responsibility of the recreation field:

> It includes, but is not limited to, service to the total citizenry for its enjoyment, health, and general well-being through the continuous provision and up-grading of areas, facilities, leadership, and programs that will enhance the leisure pursuits of all mankind. It includes areas and programs administered for recreation purposes by all levels of government; private, semi-private, and religious organizations, youth serving agencies; commercial establishments; as well as the leisure pursuits of families and individuals.
>
> It also includes the acquisition, conservation, preservation, and restoration of physical and natural resources. It includes the education of lay and professional individuals for the wise use of leisure by the collection and the dissemination of information to keep pace with the cultural and leisure needs of a changing society.[7]

Public Recognition of the Field

The rapid expansion of recreation and park service over the past two decades provides evidence of public awareness of the need for this field, and readiness to support programs in it. However, there is also evidence that people either do not recognize and understand the recreation field, or regard it in limited or stereotyped ways.

Recreation professionals are frequently confused with physical education teachers, partly because many of the early playground leaders or camp directors *were* physical educators. Most college programs of professional preparation in recreation began as part of departments or schools of health, physical education, and recreation, and many still have such affiliations. A second stream of development for recreation workers in the United States came from the social work field, and a third from park management. Given these diverse origins, it is not surprising that the identity and role of recreation professionals have been unclear for many members of the public. Another source of confusion is that recreation workers may have other titles, or be affiliated with agencies or institutions that do not regard themselves primarily as leisure oriented. For example, in many hospitals, recreation professionals are known as "activity therapists"; in school systems, recreation programs may be described as "community education"; in the armed forces, they are part of Special Services; and in industry, recreation is connected to personnel management.

Recreation professionals themselves have assumed such a wide variety of roles that no single image stands out. Sessoms comments that "we would like to be all things to all people: entertainers, promoters, counselors, psychiatrist aides, and social analysts." He writes:

> I am afraid the public sees us either as ex-athletes, or gregarious, fun-and-game leaders wearing short pants, knee socks, and an Alpine hat, calling for all to join in.[8]

Sessoms later suggested that one of the problems was that recreation was not perceived as an occupational field which required special preparation and long-term training, and that it was ranked only "average" as an income producer.[9] A recent position statement of the National Recreation and Park Association stressed the need to improve the image of the field. Keller comments:

> There are many factors the profession controls that could be altered to enhance its image. Among these are: defined body of knowledge; specific policies and standards for the delivery of services; a code of ethics; standards and criteria for academic criteria to train professionals; new leadership techniques that would include leisure education, leisure counseling, value clarification skills, etc.; the assumption of a basic responsibility for enhancing people's awareness, knowledge, attitudes, and skills with respect to the use of their leisure; the involvement of the people being serviced; and the creative use of the media to improve the visibility of the profession and its services.[10]

Identity of the Professional

Who is the recreation professional today, and what role does he or she play? In a community agency, such as a public recreation and park department, the recreation professional is usually a person holding a college degree in recreation or a closely related field, employed on a full-time, year-round basis.

Depending on the size and scope of the agency, the professional is likely to have responsibilities and skills related to the following functions: (1) planning, design, construction, and maintenance of facilities; (2) recruitment, hiring, training, supervising, and evaluating of personnel; (3) planning and supervision of program services; (4) budgetary development and fiscal management; (5) effective cooperation with boards, commissions, or civic associations; and (6) public relations.

In some settings, the recreation professional may direct a major program related to rehabilitative service, multiservice programming for aging persons, adult education and recreation, or cultural activities. He or she may also be involved, not

283

as a direct practitioner, but as a consultant, research specialist, planner, or in similar capacities. Thus, the task of recreation professionals has become more complex and demanding—and more deserving of recognition and status. Hartsoe has pointed out that such recognition has generally come to those occupational fields which have satisfied five essential criteria: having a "systematic body of theory," "professional authority" based on specialized professional preparation, "sanction of the community" enforced through admission standards for the field, a "regulative code of ethics," and a "professional culture" based on professional organizations, shared values, and traditions.[11]

Professional Preparation in Recreation and Park Service

Although specialized training in recreation and park administration was available as early as the 1920s, through a one-year graduate institute sponsored by the Playground and Recreation Association of America, it was not until the late 1930s that American colleges and universities began to develop curricula in this field of service. By 1950, approximately fifty colleges offered such programs, and for the next fifteen years this figure remained relatively stable.

In the mid-1960s, following the strong stimulus to the merged recreation and park movement by Federal and state programs of resource development and the steady expansion of municipal departments, college enrollments in recreation and park increased sharply; the number of curricula offered in the United States and Canada reached 345 in 1975. Of this number, 187 were community colleges with two-year programs designed to provide technical training for admission to the field on a leadership level, or to provide the basis for transfer to four-year college programs. Development of curricula in Canada was later than in the United States, but by the mid-1970s Canada had six senior college or university programs and fifteen two-year recreation curricula.

Efforts to Upgrade Curricula

One of many conferences to establish standards and curriculum guides in recreation during the 1950s and 1960s was sponsored in 1962 by the American Association for Health, Physical Education, and Recreation. The conference established guides for the development of both undergraduate and graduate recreation curricula, determining the course content of degree programs and appropriate areas of specialization.[12]

Another project intended to upgrade higher education in recreation and parks was undertaken by the Federation of National Professional Organizations for Recreation in 1963, with a threefold purpose: (1) to develop for the National Commission on Accrediting a statement supporting recreation as a significant field of public service and as a profession; (2) to develop standards and evaluative criteria for recreation education at both undergraduate and graduate levels; and (3) to raise funds to carry out the actual process of accreditation.

In 1965, the Recreation Education Accreditation Committee identified several appropriate areas of degree specialization, and proposed guides for approved practices as well as specific criteria by which college departments might be judged. This document was revised, based on several pilot accreditations, and published again in 1972 by the National Recreation and Park Association Board on Professional Education.[13] Refined and more specific curriculum guidelines were the basis for the actual accreditation process, which began in 1976 with the selection of certain college and university programs for pilot accreditation visitations.[14] By 1978, the accreditation process was well under way, with numerous leading colleges and universities submitting their credentials for approval.

An important element in the improvement of programs of professional preparation in recreation and parks is the clarification of appropriate goals and course content on the three major levels of instruction: *two-year, baccalaureate,* and *graduate.* The four-year baccalaureate program is the basic degree program to prepare practicing professionals in such areas as recreation program administration (including such specializations as municipal, voluntary agency, school, industrial, and therapeutic recreation), recreation and park administration, and recreation resources management. Clarification of the specific requirements for the baccalaureate degree and the two-year and graduate programs is necessary to avoid duplication and ensure that each level of instruction fulfills its appropriate objectives.

Community College Curricula

During the late 1960s and early 1970s, many community colleges began to offer associate degrees in recreation, a trend which reflected both the rapid increase of two-year colleges in American education, and the need to prepare individuals for direct leadership and program services. The community colleges recognized that most four-year programs focused on educating supervisors and administrators.

Despite considerable criticism of the quality of the curricula and the narrow academic focus of many community colleges, clearly they serve an important purpose in introducing many young people to college and providing an opportunity for continued education at higher levels. Godbey comments that they are particularly valuable in breaking down barriers between the college and community, offering new channels for continuing education, and serving low-income, minority group students.[15]

It is essential that community colleges design their recreation curricula with extreme care, choose well-qualified faculty members, and maintain full articulation with four-year colleges that may accept their graduates. In an effort to assist community college faculty in upgrading their curricula, the U. S. Office of Education published in 1969 a recommended two-year curriculum in recreation program leadership and a career education handbook to assist high school students considering recreation study at community colleges.[16] Specialized curriculum development in therapeutic recreation in community colleges has been the basis of a three-year project funded by the Bureau of Education for the Handicapped at the University of Illinois.

With respect to transfer of community college graduates to four-year college recreation and park curricula, California's Society of Park and Recreation Educators developed a model identifying appropriate roles, objectives, and guidelines for curriculum development and transfer of courses.[17] Without question, this will continue to be an area of major concern in the field of professional education.

Functions of Graduate Education

Although it is generally recognized that the four-year curriculum should provide a broad base of general education and the core of essential knowledge related to recreation as organized community service, the function of graduate programs is not so clearly understood. Some authorities have argued that the field of recreation and parks should develop a graduate degree program of professional specialization following an undergraduate program of general recreation study, but there seems to be little support of this position. Instead, graduate programs accept students from other disciplines as well as those whose major field of undergraduate study was recreation.

In general, authorities agree that master's degree work should require advanced work in recreation and park administration or other specialized areas of service, and a research sequence to establish competence in the field and develop the planning and evaluation capabilities of practitioners. The doctoral level should focus on specialization in an advanced area of study and on the further development of research, planning, or consultant skills.

Enriching Scholarly Content

A strong case has been made for the need to enrich scholarly content in recreation and park curricula. Reid points out that the growth of public interest in leisure, tourism, health needs, ecology, and similar concerns has led many other college and university departments to initiate course work, research, and publications in recreation related areas. Addressing college and university professors, Reid asks:

> How many departments on your campus (other than Recreation or Park Administration) have initiated recreation-related courses in the past five years? How many other departments are placing some of their graduates in recreation-related positions? How many have initiated recreation-related research projects within the past five years? How many scholarly papers on recreation topics have been produced and published by other disciplines?[18]

He argues that many faculty members in departments such as biology, sociology, economics, and political science have obtained grants and fellowships in the field of leisure and recreation research, and that recreation and park educators have not contributed sufficiently to the growth of scholarly content within their own field. In Reid's view, if allowed to continue, this trend would lead to the decline of recreation and park programs in colleges and universities. To reverse the trend, he suggests that recreation and park educators give greater priority to advanced research and publication and assume a more significant role in scholarly activities on their campuses.

Sessoms supports this view, but points out the growth of the body of literature and research journals within the recreation and park field. With the increase in the number of students and the expansion of higher education has come an increase in specialized courses, which are reflected in more advanced and sophisticated research and publications. He suggests that higher education in recreation and parks has drawn appropriately on knowledge and principles in other disciplines, but it nonetheless suffers from certain deficiencies.

> The most apparent literature need is the production of data-based writings. Recreators can no longer afford to rely on speculations about

286

the nature of the park and recreation service and its "ideal" program; there is a limit to these armchair antics. Performance must be measured against standards, concepts against reality, and output against objectives and efforts—hard data, not platitudes. A profession grows as it develops its methodology, its understanding of its uniqueness, and the techniques most appropriate for the implementation of its programs. The literature of the recreation and park profession is evidence of substantial growth in this direction.[19]

Reviewing Performance

As higher education in recreation and parks has expanded, colleges, universities, and professional organizations have recognized the need for critical evaluations of performances. Studies of the graduates of community college recreation curricula in the Canadian province of Ontario and of graduates of the recreation and parks department of the University of Illinois have provided useful information about placement trends and professional career opportunities, and have had strong implications about the colleges themselves. The Society of Park and Recreation Educators has conducted surveys polling its members on the issues facing college and university curricula in recreation and parks, and the kinds of services that might be provided to the field by professional organizations.

Gearing Enrollment to Needs of the Field

Still other studies have begun to examine the rapid expansion of recreation and park curricula in relation to decreased job opportunities in the field during the 1970s.

> The market for college-trained recreation and park personnel has not expanded in the 1970's to the extent predicted. At the same time, the number of degree programs and graduates in this field has grown markedly, creating a probable imbalance between supply and demand. While well-qualified and capable graduates are able to find positions, more marginal candidates are likely to have greater difficulty. There no longer is the "seller's market" for recreation personnel that existed during the 1950's and 1960's.[20]

While some have suggested limiting the number of new degree programs, others have argued that this would be unwise and impractical, except through the accreditation process. Instead, the market for preparing recreation and park personnel should be open and competitive. The colleges with the best faculty and curricula are likely to turn out highly qualified students who will be successful in the field, and thus will maintain favorable reputations and will prosper. Colleges with weaker programs may find their enrollments declining and in some cases may terminate their curricula in a realistic adjustment to the needs of the field.

Other Forms of Professional Education

It is important to recognize that not all professional education in recreation and parks is in formal degree programs of colleges and universities. Many agencies offer in-service education programs, and professional organizations have been active in providing special seminars, conferences, and training sessions for people currently working in the field.

To illustrate, the Boys' Clubs of America has a formal training program

287

which operates nationally, consisting of five phases: (1) new worker briefing and registration, (2) orientation seminars, (3) advanced program seminars, (4) management preparation programs, and (5) executive training programs.[21] Other voluntary organizations and recreation departments conduct similar programs. The Jewish Welfare Board has carefully studied its health, physical education, and recreation programs in community centers throughout the United States and Canada, and has established a special graduate program at Temple University in Philadelphia to prepare workers in Jewish centers.[22]

The National Recreation and Park Association has sponsored a series of one-week executive development programs for recreation and park administrators, in cooperation with the University of Indiana, the University of Georgia, Washington State University, and North Carolina State University. These continuing education programs deal with specialized administrative concerns, such as "revenue sources management," "park and recreation maintenance-management," or "law enforcement and participant safety." The National Recreation and Park Association has also cosponsored graduate internships with a number of municipal recreation and park departments, as a specialized form of continuing education.

These illustrations suggest that national organizations play a key role in higher education, as well as other aspects of professional development. The major professional organization in this field in the United States today is the National Recreation and Park Association.

The National Recreation and Park Association

In all professional fields in the United States, it is essential that practitioners be represented by strong, unified national organizations which: (1) regulate and set standards for professional development; (2) promote legislation for the advancement of the field; (3) develop programs of public information to improve understanding and support of the field; (4) sponsor conferences, publications, and field services to improve practices; and (5) press for higher standards of training, accreditation, and certification.

Because of the varied nature of professional service in recreation and parks, and the strong role played by citizens' groups and nonprofessional organizations, many different associations were established through the years to serve the field. Five of these (the National Recreation Association, American Institute of Park Executives, National Conference on State Parks, American Association of Zoological Parks and Aquariums, and American Recreation Society) merged into a single body in 1965, with Laurance S. Rockefeller as president.

Within a year or two, other groups, such as the National Association of Recreation Therapists and the Armed Forces Section of the American Recreation Society, merged their interests with the newly formed organization. This national body, the National Recreation and Park Association, is an independent, nonprofit organization intended to promote the development of the recreation and park movement and the conservation of natural and human resources in the United States.

The National Recreation and Park Association is directed by a Board of Trustees which meets several times each year to guide its major policies. Several separate branches carry out the work and serve to coalesce the special interests of members; these include the American Park and Recreation Society (formed by the joining of the American Institute of Park Executives and the American Recreation Society); the National Society for Park Resources (formerly the National Conference on State Parks); the Armed Forces Recreation Society; the National Therapeutic Recreation Society; the Society of Park and Recreation Educators; the National Student Recreation and Park Society; and commissioners and board members. The American Association of Zoological Parks and Aquariums was initially a branch of NRPA, but withdrew in 1972. During the mid-1970s, proposals were advanced to alter this branch structure to increase effectiveness.

As indicated, NRPA sponsors conferences and institutions, issues varied reports and publications, provides field services, conducts research, and promotes legislation. Examples of such efforts in a recent year included the following:

> Presenting testimony in Congress based on the results of an investigation into youth camp safety, asking for stronger federal action in this field

> Taking steps to safeguard the lives of millions of children and youth in the United States by developing playground equipment standards

> Fostering positive attitudes toward leisure by developing a model leisure education program for the public schools, through a major grant from the Lilly Endowment of Indianapolis, Indiana

> Publishing a biweekly newsletter, *Congressional Action Report,* to inform members of legislation or bills relating to public works job programs, Land and Water Conservation Fund amendments, Youth Conservation Corps proposals, revenue sharing, and federal surplus property legislation

> Alerting its membership and the public at large to critical issues in recreation and leisure—including problems of the economy and employment, environmental concerns, and recreation's role in dealing with changing lifestyles in society

> Developing recommendations for providing leisure-time activities for disabled children and youth, and developing post-master's degree internship programs for therapeutic recreation consultant personnel, both through grants from the U.S. Office of Education.[23]

Individual branches of the National Recreation and Park Association also sponsor extensive programs and projects related to their specialized concerns. In addition, NRPA's staff has carried out consultation and correspondence services with thousands of practitioners, board members, and organizations throughout the United States and in a number of foreign countries. As a single example, it offered an extensive program of sports instruction, reaching over 200,000 persons in 111 communities, through a grant from the Lifetime Sports Foundation.

NRPA has sought to maintain a single, unified identity for the overall field of recreation service, without permitting its primary concern for publicly sponsored outdoor recreation and open-space programs to overshadow other important professional areas, such as voluntary agencies, community school programs, or the needs of special populations.

Other Professional Organizations

Many other organizations sponsor programs supporting the recreation professional. A leading example is the American Alliance for Health, Physical Education, and Recreation, which includes several thousand members employed primarily by school systems and colleges, who have a specialized concern with school-sponsored recreation programs, education for leisure, the promotion of school camping and outdoor education, and adapted physical education and recreation programs for the disabled.

The branch of this association most directly concerned with these functions is the American Association for Leisure and Recreation which (1) works closely on accreditation with NRPA (through the American Association for Leisure and Recreation-National Recreation and Park Association Joint Accreditation Steering Committee); (2) promotes community education in cooperation with other organizations, with assistance from the Charles Mott Foundation; (3) publishes *Leisure Today,* an outstanding series of special issues of the *Journal of Physical Education and Recreation;* (4) assists in job placement of personnel and similar functions. It also provides an ongoing service to agencies concerned with physical education and recreation for the handicapped, through the Information and Research Utilization Center, which assists in the dissemination of research findings and literature retrieval.

Other organizations which make an important contribution to this field include: (1) the American Camping Association, which acts as a voice for the organized camping field; (2) the American College Personnel Association, which includes many individuals working in student resident halls, college unions, or other social programs for college students; (3) the National Association of Social Workers (Group Work Section); (4) the Amateur Athletic Union, which promotes and sets standards for a wide range of participant sports in the United States; (5) the National Intramural-Recreation Sports Association; and (6) the National Industrial Recreation Association.

The major Canadian organization in this field is the Canadian Parks/ Recreation Association, which has its national office in Ottawa, Ontario. Its major objectives are:

1. To acquaint Canadians with the significance of leisure in a changing society;

2. To assist in the development, organization, and promotion of the parks and recreation service delivery system in Canada;

3. To involve the membership in the development of national policies of significance to the parks and recreation movement in Canada; and

4. To promote effective planning, design and development of parks and recreation facilities in Canada.

As indicated earlier, the CPRA receives substantial support from the Canadian government. It has over two thousand members, publishes a bimonthly magazine, *Recreation Canada,* sponsors an annual conference, provides consultation and technical assistance to both government and nongovernment agencies in the leisure field, conducts open-space studies, and represents Canadian interests at international meetings.

290

Recruitment of Recreation and Park Professionals

Until recently, there was a shortage of qualified applicants in the recreation and park field. Sessoms, Twardzik, Saltzman, and others suggested the development of more effective recruitment methods and a more positive image, to attract qualified young people.[24] Several factors which contributed to the shortage of personnel included: (1) the fact that recreation was a new professional field, and many students, parents, teachers, and guidance counselors knew little about it; (2) recruitment had become a highly competitive process because of a general shortage of job applicants in many fields; and (3) the perceived status, work expectations, and salary of the recreation field detracted from its appeal.

As a consequence, there were national and regional efforts to promote recruitment, particularly into programs of professional preparation, which were seen as the logical point of entry into the field. Several high schools in Evanston, Illinois, Wilmington, Delaware, and other cities, initiated recreation leadership courses to help recruit future professionals.[25] Career days were scheduled, campaigns launched to familiarize guidance counselors with the field, and other strenuous efforts made to stimulate the flow of new professionals into recreation and park service.

However, since the rapid increase of specialized curricula in recreation and parks in colleges and universities throughout the United States and Canada, this situation has reversed. Instead of a few hundred graduates each year, there are now several thousand. And instead of a wide open job market, population and economic trends of the 1970s—coupled with budget freezes and job cutbacks in communities and voluntary agencies—have limited the number of employment opportunities in many regions.

As a consequence, the challenge today is no longer to encourage great numbers of new applicants to enter the recreation and park field. Instead, the profession hopes to strengthen the overall job market for recreation professionals by (a) identifying and creating new potential areas of employment for recreation graduates; (b) establishing new types of curricula which are more closely in touch with growing employment opportunities, changing job roles, and community expectations; and (c) improving the process of professional education and job placement, to ensure that qualified candidates find appropriate entry-level employment.

Strengthening the Job Market

Voluntary agencies hire many thousands of professional group leaders, specialists, and administrators each year. Although such agencies are probably more closely connected with recreation than with any other area of professional service and higher education, they often do not identify themselves as part of the recreation movement and tend to hire individuals from a wide variety of backgrounds. Professional recreation curricula should be designed to deal with the concerns of such agencies. A strong effort should be made to place field workers and student interns in voluntary agencies, and to involve the agencies in the work of professional organizations. Strengthening this relationship will increase the availability of jobs for qualified recreation and park professionals in voluntary agencies.

Establishing New Curricula

The most common focus in recreation and park curricula has been on the preparation of leaders, supervisors, and administrators in public recreation and park departments. Gradually, new needs have emerged—for preparing specialists in resource management, industrial recreation, voluntary agencies, therapeutic service, college unions, outdoor education, and similar concerns. Today it is essential to explore new directions for curriculum changes, both to meet emerging needs and to provide employment opportunities for the growing number of recreation and park graduates.

The most obvious of these new specializations is the broad field of commercial recreation. Many colleges and universities have already developed new curricula in this field, with particular emphasis on travel and tourism. Universities entering this field may be concerned both with the direct management of commercial recreation facilities and programs, and with higher levels of administrative responsibility, planning, consultant work, or research. Colleges are beginning to offer new degree programs or special short-term continuing education workshops in fields such as commercial sports administration and performing arts management.

Even within the more traditional areas of recreation and park higher education, new emphases and roles have been identified. Temple University, for example, has initiated the nation's first urban recreation curriculum to meet professional needs in highly urbanized areas.[26] It has also pioneered the development of a graduate curriculum in therapeutic recreation, under a grant from the Bureau of Education for the Handicapped of the U. S. Office of Education.

Improving Job Placement Processes

In addition to developing specialized curricula to meet emerging needs, colleges and professional organizations have sought to improve the placement process through which qualified candidates are directed to job opportunities. Many organizations have prepared career information booklets, to ensure that those entering the field are aware of job opportunities and are able to prepare for them effectively. The Youth and Recreation Branch of the Ontario Department of Education has prepared a brochure, *Have You Considered Recreation as a Career?,* which outlines career opportunities, salaries, working conditions, admission requirements, certification procedures, and similar information.

The National Recreation and Park Association publishes *Park and Recreation Opportunities,* a bulletin including detailed analysis of career fields in specialized groupings and comprehensive nationwide job listings, as part of its total placement service, EMPLOY (Effective Measures: Prepare for and Locate Opportunities Yourself).[27] The Society of Park and Recreation Educators has held large-scale seminars at national congresses, dealing with problems of career development and job placement. The American Alliance for Health, Physical Education, and Recreation publishes a 120-page paperback, *Recreation and Leisure Time Careers,* and its publication *UPDATE* contains a job listing service called *Job Exchange Program.* Thus, on every level, efforts are being made to attract qualified individuals to programs of professional preparation, to give them realistic experience in the field, and to familiarize them with job opportunities both in traditional and more innovative career areas.

Standards for Admission to the Recreation and Park Profession

Each of the recognized professions in modern society has undergone a process of development in which its training gradually became more specialized and standardized, with education assigned to colleges and universities, and with admission to professional practice governed by a legally constituted branch of state government (often a department of education) working in cooperation with professional societies.

Customarily an individual qualifies in fields such as medicine or accounting by first completing an approved graduate degree program and then taking examinations through state education departments, which are developed and administered with the assistance of professional associations. The qualification requirements of public recreation and park departments is generally less structured than in other professions. There is a growing consensus that some system of impartial selection and admission to the recreation field should be imposed to ensure a high level of performance by qualified practitioners.

Licensing and Certification

Often used interchangeably, these terms refer to the process of evaluating the credentials of persons in occupational or professional fields and giving them legal permission to practice. The term *licensing* governs the scope of professional practice, defining the specific services that may be provided, the populations served, or other conditions. Licensing applies not only to health related fields, but to such areas of employment as driving taxis or operating barber shops. In contrast, the term *certification* governs the use of a professional title, protecting the field and the public against unauthorized or untrained practitioners. Frequently, it is used synonymously with *registration*.

Licensing and certification procedures may be based on such elements as education, experience, performance on written and oral tests, and personal recommendations. Two states which developed certification procedures in the late 1960s were New Jersey and Georgia.

New Jersey passed a state law in 1966 establishing a Board of Recreation Examiners with the Department of Conservation and Economic Development. Appointed by the Governor with the advice and consent of the New Jersey Senate, the board is responsible for establishing and modifying qualifications for positions, administering examinations for the certification and registration of recreation supervisors, and conducting research and studies related to professional standards in recreation. Georgia passed similar legislation in 1968 implementing formal certification procedures for recreation and park professionals. In both states, "grandfather clauses" provided waivers of the new hiring standards for those already employed in the field.

Although certification appears to be a logical means of enforcing professional standards among those employed in recreation and park positions, it has not been widely adopted. Leavitt commented, after the Georgia system had been in effect for three years, that the day of statewide mandatory professional certification for recreators was "somewhere in the distant future,"[28] and a 1971 study of state

293

recreation and park society presidents indicated that they were not strongly in favor of certification of professional recreation personnel.[29]

Yale argues persuasively that certification based chiefly on holding a recreation degree would exclude people with degrees in other fields who could provide the profession with stimulation, thus promoting uniformity and inbreeding to a dangerous extent.[30]

Nonetheless, it is widely accepted that the lack of an effective means to screen out unqualified personnel and to provide recognition for professional training is a major hindrance to the development of professionalism in recreation and parks. Although certification has not thus far been widely adopted, registration procedures have been successfully implemented.

Registration in Recreation and Parks

Registration consists of a review of the credentials of applicants by state or national professional societies, which testify that the applicants have or have not met certain qualifications. New York State, for example, has a voluntary registration plan, with standards established by the New York State Recreation and Park Society for nine levels of responsibility. Administered by a Board of Examiners and representatives from various state departments and other recreation organizations, this plan has sought to define personnel standards for each job level, based on the duties and distinguishing features of the position, the knowledge and abilities required for the position, and the minimum education and experience required. However, because of the voluntary nature of the registration process, only a limited number of public and voluntary agencies have made registration a requisite to employment. California has a similar registration plan, with a Board of Recreation Personnel that establishes standards for administrators, supervisors, and leaders, and provides incentive pay in many communities for registered personnel. For a number of years, the Indiana Park and Recreation Association has operated a registration program for qualified professionals.

Thus, in various forms, different state societies have established registration standards and procedures, to identify qualified personnel. However, since such plans have been more or less voluntary rather than compulsory, they depend on the cooperation of appropriate state and municipal agencies to respect and enforce their requirements.

National Registration by NRPA

Recognizing the difficulty of maintaining standards through fifty different state plans, the National Recreation and Park Association has developed and implemented a process of national registration.[31] Based on guidelines in a model registration plan approved by the NRPA Board of Trustees in 1973, NRPA has reviewed and approved the plans of a number of state societies. Enforcement of this national procedure has been facilitated through NRPA's Personnel Referral Service, in which registered candidates are identified and favored in the job placement process.

The National Therapeutic Recreation Society has developed its own registration plan, defining five levels of professional practice: Therapeutic Recreation Assistant, Therapeutic Recreation Technician, Therapeutic Recreation Worker, Therapeutic Recreation Specialist, and Master Therapeutic Recreation Specialist. This plan, with carefully delineated combinations of education and professional experience as criteria for registration, has been well received; well over one thousand professionals were granted registration by the late 1970s. Although the plan has the weakness of being a voluntary form of qualification, it has served as a model for many state societies or state departments to develop their own system of qualifications.

Another element in all registration plans has been their tendency to place heavy stress on professional education and require that individuals hold degrees from "accredited" institutions. However, until the late 1970s, no institutions had been rigorously evaluated for accreditation in recreation and parks (see page 285), and thus many individuals were accepted who had received degrees in programs of questionable quality.

Some states have also established special registration processes in therapeutic recreation service. In California, special registration requirements for therapeutic recreation personnel were approved in 1970. Lawrence cites a position paper of the California Park and Recreation Society.

> This special registration was created to indicate to the medical profession the validity of recreation as a therapeutic tool, and to place therapeutic recreation on an equal . . . level with the other Allied Health Professionals (occupational, physical, speech therapy) available in a medical setting.[32]

California's rigorous requirements included a baccalaureate or graduate degree in therapeutic recreation, a minimum of four hundred hours of supervised field work, completion of a special introductory course in recreation for the ill and/or handicapped, substantial study in allied disciplines, and an examination by the California Board of Parks and Recreation Personnel. Although this registration process grants a certificate and is recognized by many employing agencies, it lacks the strength of a state law which would prohibit practice by other than certified personnel. Strenuous efforts have been made in California for state legislation formally certifying therapeutic recreators as allied health professionals. In May of 1976, the Therapeutic Section Board of the California Park and Recreation Society unanimously voted to endorse licensure. Lawrence writes that this act

> represented a realization that existing federal and state laws appear to favor licensed health professionals and that medical insurance and reimbursement through use of public funds tends more and more to cover those services offered to consumers by state certified or licensed professionals . . . I [quote] from the 1971 H.E.W. Report on Licensure and Related Health Personnel Credentialing: "Under present statutes and regulations, when a health profession is licensed by a state, federal health insurance programs typically link qualification for reimbursement to state licensure requirements."[33]

295

Civil Service Procedures in Recreation and Parks

In the majority of states and provinces today, Civil Service systems provide the procedures by which recreation and park personnel are selected and employed in both community and institutional settings.

A single example of how Civil Service operates may be found in Suffolk County, New York where Civil Service was established as a hiring process under the 1941 Fite Law, leaving the form of administration to local option. There are three alternatives: state administration, administration through a county personnel office, or county civil service commission. Several job titles and descriptions (each with its own set of requirements) have been established by the Suffolk County Civil Service Commission, including Superintendent, Supervisor, Leader, Specialist, and Town Park Supervisor. For each of these, specific eligibility requirements include: (1) residence requirements; (2) examinations, usually constructed and graded by the State Civil Service Commission and administered by the county; (3) specific educational or experience requirements for each title; and (4) other specific personal or skill requirements. Based on these, municipalities send a statement to the Civil Service Commission for the position they wish to fill. The Commission determines the correct title and sends a list of certified, eligible candidates; the municipality must select an appointee from one of the top three eligible candidates.

Examinations are classified into two types: "competitive," which applies to the majority of full-time, professional positions; and "noncompetitive," which test basic proficiency without comparison of scores of other examinees, for such positions as recreation specialist, lifeguard, and swimming, skiing, or craft instructor. Despite the fact that a major purpose of the Civil Service has been to protect public employment from political patronage, resistance to more stringent hiring standards in recreation and parks has been strong.

Evidence of the extent to which standards are still minimal and loosely enforced is found in the 1976 study of public personnel in the United States by Godbey and Henkel. Substantial numbers of superintendents, directors, division heads, and district supervisors of recreation and parks were found to lack bachelor's degrees in recreation or related fields. Even among recreation supervisors and center directors in five major categories, 42 percent had less than a bachelor's degree. In Canada, despite strong recent efforts to promote certification of personnel, a study in the early 1970s showed a low level of specialized academic training among employees in public recreation and park agencies—and in voluntary, nonprofit agencies and institutions, none of the personnel with bachelor's degrees had majored in recreation.[34]

The best hope for strengthening personnel standards in both the United States and Canada would appear to be: (1) to proceed with developing strong state registration and certification plans; (2) to develop a national registry similar to the NRPA listing of professionals registered under approved state plans; (3) to incorporate standards developed by state societies in Civil Service job requirements; and (4) to move ahead vigorously with the evaluation and accreditation of university recreation and park curricula, so that the higher education requirement will have more meaning.

Affirmative Action in Hiring Practices

Another area of concern to the recreation and park profession today is the need to provide fuller opportunity for professional placement and advancement to certain population groups—primarily women, racial or ethnic minorities, and the handicapped—which have been discriminated against in the past. The Code of Federal Regulations which enacts the provisions of Title VI of the 1964 Civil Rights Act in the United States stipulates that agencies or institutions receiving federal funding may not discriminate in the provision of service or in hiring practices on the basis of race, color, sex, or national origin. Increasing pressure has been exerted, based on this clause and also on Title IX of the Education Amendments Act of 1972, to eliminate discriminatory practices, particularly against girls and women, in the area of sports and physical education.

A number of studies have shown that women tend to receive fewer high-level administrative positions and are paid lower salaries than men in recreation and park departments throughout the United States.[35] Theobald carried out an exhaustive study documenting the same situation in Canada. In addition to a widespread disparity between the amount and range of recreation programs offered to girls and women and those offered to boys and men, he found:

> There were almost 2.5 males to each female full-time recreation staff member in the cities investigated. The higher the level of responsibility, the fewer the number of females. . . . Females on an average received $1,300 less than males when entering the recreation profession. . . . the male to female salary ratio increased in each salary level.[36]

In response to legal pressures and more forceful demands by women and women's organizations, many Federal, state, and local recreation and park departments and agencies have begun to hire women in key areas of responsibility in greater numbers than in the past. Several states have employed their first women park superintendents, more and more women interns have been employed in major park districts and authorities, and many women have been hired as park rangers and naturalists, as city recreation directors or superintendents, and in key roles by professional organizations.

Racial and ethnic factors have also been an important hiring concern, following studies showing that blacks, Spanish-Americans, and other racial minority groups have held considerably fewer positions in recreation and parks (particularly on higher levels of responsibility) than their numbers in the general population would suggest. One obvious reason for this in the past was that lower percentages of such minority group members attended college and took special degree programs in fields like recreation and parks. Godbey reported in 1970, based on a study of 137 college and university curricula, that minority racial and ethnic groups were considerably underrepresented at all levels of professional study, except for community college programs.[37]

Efforts were made during the early 1970s to correct this imbalance, through special conferences and recruiting programs to stimulate the admission of blacks and other minority group members to programs of preparation. By 1976, a comprehensive study of public recreation and park agencies in the United States enabled Godbey and Henkel to report:

> With regard to minority groups, the data contains some surprises. Blacks, for instance, are not underrepresented in terms of their percentage of all public recreation and park employees, although American Indians and Orientals would appear to be. For all minorities . . . there is a special need for making continuing forms of vocationally oriented educational opportunities available. Few minorities are employed in the upper-level administrative positions, where the bachelor's and master's degrees are becoming increasingly prerequisite.[38]

A final area of concern regarding employment opportunities for special populations is the need to employ the physically and mentally handicapped in public recreation and park departments. It is something of a contradiction that many departments have striven to provide recreation programs for the disabled, or to modify their facilities to permit access by the handicapped in recent years, but have not been willing to consider their employment. Some experimental ventures in this direction have proven successful; the Washington, D.C. Department of Recreation, for example, has hired as many as twenty disabled employees (including mentally retarded and emotionally disturbed, orthopedically handicapped, blind, and deaf persons in summer day camps or in community centers. With adequate orientation and supervision, these seasonal employees proved to be competent and responsible staff members.[39]

Changing Roles of Professionals

As described earlier, the field of recreation and park service has expanded over the past two decades; the number of employees in the field has increased, and programs of professional preparation have improved. Public acceptance is widespread, and the overall picture is positive. It is important to recognize, however, that modern society is changing rapidly, particularly in urban and metropolitan settings, and that changing lifestyles, values, forms of social organization, and economic or social problems compel all areas of public service to examine and clarify their roles and responsibilities. Public acceptance and governmental support of public services agencies depends upon their defining and accomplishing substantial and meaningful goals.

Within this context, the function of organized recreation services and of the recreation and park profession itself has changed radically in recent years. In 1968, Sessoms carefully analyzed the recreation profession, concluding that its development had been affected by the following societal trends: the growth of travel as a form of family activity and as a status symbol for all groups; the growth of privately organized clubs and associations, particularly in suburban areas and small towns, which diminished support for public recreation; and the growth of varied forms of commercial recreation activity, creating in many people a passive, consumer orientation toward leisure, characterized by apathy and lack of imagination.

Sessoms concluded that the profession had failed to conceptualize sufficiently its changing functions, and that it needed both a clear-cut sense of social purpose and a rationale for program development, in addition to an understanding of three fundamental roles that have emerged: (1) the *park-recreation manager's* role, with emphasis on administrative responsibility and resource management; (2) the *social-therapeutic* role, in which practitioners deal with significant social problems and special needs; and (3) the traditional *playground-community* center role, which has been radically altered in both urban and suburban settings.[40]

Frissell described the role of recreation professionals as extremely diverse:

> At one end of the recreation spectrum are the "activity-oriented" programs. Here we find the urban recreation programs—playgrounds, organized sports, arts and crafts and day camps. In addition are such specialties as hospital recreation, commercial recreation, and organized group camp programs. At the opposite end of the recreation spectrum we find the "resource-oriented" programs—visits to parks, monuments, historic sites, seashores, wild rivers, and lakeshores, administered by national and state park agencies.[41]

With respect to professional preparation, Frissell asked whether it was possible to develop a single recreation curriculum capable of producing "superprofessionals" capable of being all things to all people. Indeed, the trend of the 1970s has been to develop increasingly refined and specialized college curricula that reflect the specialized professional roles assumed by workers in the field today.

Another trend in most areas of professional recreation service has been the move away from direct leadership functions, and toward planning, enabling, and organizing roles. For example, David Parker, then assistant superintendent in the Youth and Recreation Branch of the Ontario, Canada, Department of Education, wrote in 1969:

> We no longer consider the recreation service of providing activity programs as the prime role or function of the recreation authority, be it school board or municipal government. . . . In many of the larger municipalities, the role of the municipal recreation department has become one of providing a coordinating, consulting, and communicating service, thus leaving the provision of programs and activities to the private agency, the voluntary groups, and the school boards.[42]

This change has been most evident in the therapeutic recreation field, originally conceived as an institutionally based service. Early recreation therapists were thought of solely as program directors and activity leaders. Today, they are described as social systems specialists, responsible for developing broad programs in both the institution and in the community at large. They act as leisure counselors, as consultants to groups serving the disabled, as planners and researchers, as advocates for the disabled, and as catalysts for community action. Even in their direct relationship with clients in a service setting, their roles are complex. Avedon wrote in 1973:

> Specialists in therapeutic recreation concern themselves primarily with the human situation rather than limiting concern to activity participation in circumscribed situations. . . . therapeutic recreation service [operates] on three levels—supportive, re-educative, reconstructive. As a

supportive modality, therapeutic recreation service aims to strengthen personality aspects that are not yet affected. As a re-educative modality, focus is upon enabling an individual to make maximal use of existing potentialities even though some limitation is present. As a reconstructive modality, service is tailored to an individual's condition and situation, and is usually part of an interprofessional effort.[43]

The roles of professionals in the community at large must also be redefined or reconsidered. For example, when separate recreation and park departments were merged in many American state, county, and municipal agencies, two sets of professional workers with distinctly different value systems, perceived tasks, and methodologies, were thrown together. Howell points out that a degree of friction and conflict between recreation and park personnel exists in many agencies, often involving snobbery, stereotyping, and sharp disagreements as to appropriate functions and powers. Howell describes the argument often heard between "program" and "resource" personnel:

> The belief that recreation is the "operating agency" within the profession, while parks is merely the "maintenance shop"—i.e., parks exists only to support recreation—is a concept as old as the first organization chart and just as outmoded. . . . Too often, recreation personnel have been heard to assert that without their programs, parks personnel would be out of a job. This is usually countered with historical piety that parks existed long before recreation programs and that without park sites, an outdoor recreation program would not exist.[44]

Howell concedes the partial truth of both positions, but points out that within the political and administration structure of modern city and county government, neither parks nor recreation can survive alone. This interdependence suggests the need for strong efforts on all levels to create a climate of understanding and common purpose and, where possible, to fuse both program and resource-management responsibilities into single position functions.

Growing Sophistication in Professional Approaches

Recreation and park professionals must become more sophisticated and skilled in their day-to-day operations. This critical need is perhaps best illustrated in the field of travel and tourism administration, an area closely linked to both commercial recreation management and to a growing number of positions within Federal, state, and city agencies. Knowledge of economic theory, transportation systems, governmental programs, policies, and regulating agencies, resort area management, international business strategies, marketing factors, taxation, accounting and budgeting techniques, consumer behavior, human relations in tourism and travel, environmental and cultural geography, and personnel management are all part of the expertise required in high-level tourism and travel administration. Modern technology is producing new forms of entertainment in amusement and theme parks and urban entertainment centers, which pose a strong challenge to public recreation professionals as planners, developers, and managers.

There is little question that the social trends and needs of the decades ahead will require many recreation and park professionals working in public, voluntary, and therapeutic agencies to have expertise comparable to that of sociologists, psychiatrists, and social workers. The recreation professional's task in the Federal antipoverty programs of the late 1960s extended far beyond the direct provision or administration of recreation services as traditionally conceived; recreation trained individuals were employed as consultants, researchers, directors of antipoverty training programs, and administrators of multiservice agencies. Today, the director of a community youth center or senior center may be responsible not only for hobby activities, sports, or social activities, but also for administering nutritional programs, legal services, counseling and guidance, family services, paramedical functions, and a variety of other agency responsibilities.

The recent emergence of these expanded roles implies the need for a fundamental knowledge of the behavioral and social sciences if recreation and park professionals are to make a significant contribution to modern society. The professional, if he or she is to be more than a routinely capable practitioner or administrator, must understand the relevance of the recreation and parks field to a society of rapid change and must ensure that the profession meets the needs imposed by the changes.

Chapter Twelve

1. Sylvia Porter, "The Business of Fun," *New York Post,* 14 May 1965.

2. Donald E. Hawkins (project director). *Supply Demand Study, Professional and Pre-Professional Recreation and Park Occupations* (Washington, D.C.: National Recreation and Park Association, March 1968).

3. See *1976 Statistical Abstract of the United States* (Washington, D.C.: Bureau of the Census, 1976), which lists on pp. 374–375, 113,000 male and 161,000 female full-time professional recreation and social workers. The same source lists on p. 284 the total number of government park and recreation employees on all levels as 218,000.

4. Geoffrey Godbey and Donald Henkel, "The Manpower Study: A Report," *Parks and Recreation,* November 1976, pp. 23–27, 39.

5. "Education for Leisure," Position Statement of Society of Park and Recreation Educators, cited in *Proceedings of the 1975 Dallas-SPRE Institute,* Don Weiskopf, ed. (Arlington, Virginia: National Recreation and Park Association, 1975), p. 18.

6. Paul Douglass, "The Profession of Recreation on the Threshold of the Aesthetic Age" (Address at National Recreation Congress, Minneapolis, October 1965).

7. "Education of Leaders for the Leisure Services Professions," in *1975 Dallas-SPRE Institute,* pp. 18–19.

8. H. Douglas Sessoms, "A Critical Look at the Recreation Movement," *Recreation for the Ill and Handicapped* (Washington, D.C.: National Association of Recreation Therapists, July 1965), pp. 11, 14.

9. H. Douglas Sessoms, "The Manpower Crises: As Others See Us," *Parks and Recreation,* January 1970, pp. 40–41.

10. "NRPA Position Statements: Professional Image," Barbara Keller, ed., *Parks and Recreation* January 1976, p. 58.

11. Charles E. Hartsoe, "Recreation . . . A Profession in Transition," *Parks and Recreation,* July 1973, p. 33.

12. *Professional Preparation in Health Education, Physical Education and Recreation Education* (Washington, D.C.: American Association for Health, Physical Education and Recreation, 1962), pp. 86–102.

13. *Standards and Evaluative Criteria* (Arlington, Virginia: NRPA Board on Professional Education, December 1972).

14. Ira G. Shapiro, "The Path to Accreditation," *Parks and Recreation,* January 1977, p. 29.

15. Geoffrey Godbey, "In Defense of Associate Degrees," *Parks and Recreation,* January 1972, pp. 97, 112.

16. Peter J. Verhoven and Dennis A. Vinton, *Career Education for Leisure Occupations* (Lexington, Ky: Univ. of Kentucky, December 1972).

17. See Norm Olson and Larry Williams, "A Practical Approach to Articulation," in *1975 Dallas-SPRE Institute*, pp. 45–50.

18. Leslie M. Reid, "SPRE Forum: Open Letter to Educators," *NRPA Communique*, May 1971, p. 4.

19. H. Douglas Sessoms, "Our Body of Knowledge: Myth or Reality?" *Parks and Recreation*, November 1975, pp. 31, 38.

20. Richard G. Kraus and Barbara J. Bates, *Recreation Leadership and Supervision: Guidelines for Professional Development* (Philadelphia: W. B. Saunders, 1975), p. 91.

21. For fuller description of National Orientation and Staff Development Program of Boys' Clubs of America, see Kraus and Bates, *Recreation Leadership and Supervision*, pp. 157–158.

22. See *HPER Bulletin* (Philadelphia: Temple University, November, 1976), p. 5.

23. "Editorial: Research—Building Block for Progress," *Parks and Recreation*, November 1975, p. 15.

24. Donald Saltzman, "Recruitment Reappraised," *Parks and Recreation*, June 1968, pp. 25–26; and Louis F. Twardzik, "How We Fail in Recruitment," *Recreation*, November 1964, p. 469.

25. John H. Jenny, "Working into Leisure Occupations," *Journal of Physical Education and Recreation*, September 1976, p. 23.

26. Ira G. Shapiro, "Nation's First Urban Curriculum," in *SPRE Forum, NRPA Communique*, July 1971, p. 28.

27. Donald Henkel, "Personnel Referral Service," *Parks and Recreation*, May 1974, p. 48; and Christine Badger, "EMPLOYing New Perspectives on Jobs," *Parks and Recreation*, August 1976, p. 23.

28. H. Douglas Leavitt, "Certification," *Parks and Recreation*, January 1971, p. 123.

29. D. Weston Stucky, "Certification and Accreditation: Beliefs and Attitudes of Professionals in the Fields of Parks and Recreation" (Thesis, Univ. of Northern Colorado, Greeley, Col., 1971).

30. David R. Yale, "Certification, A Mistake . . ." *Parks and Recreation*, February 1975, p. 36.

31. Patricia A. Delaney, "Presenting Our Professionals," *Parks and Recreation*, August 1976, p. 27.

32. Patricia J. Lawrence, "Position Statement of AB4428 to Include Recreation Therapists" (Legislative Recommendation to Certify Recreation Therapists, submitted to Therapeutic Recreation Section and Board of Directors, California Park and Recreation Society, 1976). p. 1.

33. Patricia J. Lawrence, "Certification: The Time is Now" (Report of Therapeutic Section to California Park and Recreation Society, 1976), p. 1.

34. Charles Griffith and David Ng, "Recreation Personnel in Ontario Non-Tax Supported Agencies and Institutions," *Recreation Review*, February 1972, pp. 16–17, 20.

35. Dona L. Kerr, "The Status of Women in Parks and Recreation," *Parks and Recreation*, April 1975, p. 38.

36. William F. Theobald, *The Female in Public Recreation: A Study of Participation and Administrative Attitudes* (Waterloo, Ontario: University of Waterloo Research Institute and Province of Ontario Ministry of Culture and Recreation, 1976), p. 33.

37. Geoffrey Godbey, "Disadvantaged-Minority Group Students in Park and Recreation Curricula," *SPRE Forum, NRPA Communique*, October 1970, p. 19.

38. Godbey and Henkel, "Manpower Study," p. 25.

39. For report of a national project in this area, see Diana R. Dunn, ed., *Guidelines for Action . . . Developing Opportunities for the Handicapped in Recreation, Parks, and Leisure Services* (Washington, D.C.: National Recreation and Park Association and U.S. Social and Rehabilitation Services Administration, 1971).

40. H. Douglas Sessoms, "Critical Look at Recreation," p. 13.

41. Sidney Frissell, "Educating Recreation Professionals," *Parks and Recreation*, April 1967, p. 30.

42. David Parker, Ontario Department of Education (Letter to author, October 21, 1969).

43. Elliott M. Avedon, *Therapeutic Recreation Service: An Applied Behavioral Science Approach* (Englewood Cliffs, New Jersey: Prentice-Hall, 1974), pp. 19, 24.

44. R. L. Howell, "Whose Side Are You On?" *Parks and Recreation*, February 1974, pp. 44, 53.

FOUR

GOALS, PROBLEMS, AND ISSUES IN RECREATION SERVICE

13

PERSONAL VALUES OF RECREATION

This text now examines the contributions of recreational activities to the growth and development of people as individuals and as members of family constellations. Major areas of human growth and development have been identified in various ways. Behavioral scientists use the terms *cognitive* (referring to mental or intellectual development), *affective* (relating to emotional or feeling states), and *psychomotor* (meaning the broad area of motor learning and performance).[1]

Because these terms are somewhat narrow in their applications, this chapter will use instead the more familiar headings of *physical, emotional, social,* and *mental* development, in examining the personal values of recreation. Obviously, these areas are all closely related; however, in order to focus more sharply on each specific aspect of recreation's contribution to personal well-being, they are discussed separately.

Physical Needs Served by Recreation Activities

Physical recreation activities such as games and sports, varied forms of dance, and even such moderate forms of exercise as walking and gardening have significant effects on physical health. The values of such activities obviously differ according to the age level and developmental needs of the participant. For children and youth, the major need is to promote healthy structural development and growth and the acquisition of physical skills. It is essential that children learn the importance of physical fitness and develop habits of participation in physical activities which will serve them in later life. Awareness of physical fitness is particularly important in an

304

age of electronic gadgets, labor-saving devices, and readily available transportation which save time and physical effort, but encourage a sedentary way of life.

The physical fitness of American children became a matter of serious national concern when the Kraus-Weber tests after World War II showed the fitness of American boys and girls to be much lower than that of children in other nations. Expanded programs of physical education and community sports for youth helped American school children improve markedly on selected measures of fitness. More recently, however, other research studies have shown that the physical fitness of American boys and girls has not improved over the last decade, and that adult participation in activity is extremely low.[2] Bucher reported in 1974 that 49 million American adults do not engage in exercise for physical fitness, and that only three out of every one hundred adults participate in organized fitness programs.[3]

A striking phenomenon occurred, however, in the late 1970s; an explosion of interest in such activities as running and jogging led millions of adults of all ages to join jogging clubs or to run individually, day and night, through city parks and along highways and suburban streets. Although more and more marathons and "mini-marathons" were established, the great majority of these new running enthusiasts were not competitive; they enjoyed running for its own sake, and sought primarily to improve their own performances. Underlying this growth of interest in aerobic exercise was a widely shared concern about adult cardiovascular fitness. It was recognized that "crash" training programs, while they may have impressive immediate effects, tend also to be temporary.

It is essential that physical activity programs be continued beyond the school years, and that they be enjoyable, so as to provide motivation for lifelong participation. This incentive can best be achieved through such individual or group recreational activities as walking, swimming, tennis, skiing, or bicycling, all of which can readily be continued through the adult years. Guidry comments that medical experts have testified to the proven benefits of regular exercise—better health, stronger muscles, greater endurance, and a general feeling of well-being and energy. He writes:

> Leading medical authorities, including the U. S. Public Health Service, agree that poor fitness is a primary American health problem and recommend regular vigorous exercise as an effective solution. The cost of poor fitness, human and pecuniary, is staggering. Billions are paid for lost workdays, lost production, medical expenses, and insurance benefits. Worse, thousands of productive lives are cut short by avoidable health problems.[4]

In adults, the need for regular physical exercise is directly related to maintaining health and minimizing physical degeneration. Obesity has become a major example of the need for regular exercise in modern life.

Control of Obesity

Scientists are generally agreed today that physical activity plays a major role in weight control. Obesity among American adults has grown steadily, and is now a serious health problem in this country. Per capita energy consumption has decreased as much as 10 percent over the past fifty years because of the use of automobiles and other mechanical devices and the popularity of television and spectator sports. Hein and Ryan comment:

> Comparison of the food intake and body weights of height-matched individuals grouped according to the amount of physical activity in their lives revealed that, in general, inactivity loomed more important in overweight than the amount of food consumed.[5]

Generally, physical inactivity appears to precede rather than follow the onset of obesity. Dr. Jean Mayer, a leading authority on nutrition at Harvard University, maintains that exercise is essential to the control of both obesity and circulatory illness and is particularly helpful to those of middle age and beyond to preserve youthful body contours and maintain the condition of the body.[6] A continuing program of moderate exercise helps each individual maintain the capacity to meet situations which pose sudden demands for heavy or prolonged physical activity such as the need to clear away snow, run for a bus, or swim ashore from an overturned boat.

Preserving Cardiovascular Fitness

Americans are known to have more coronary attacks than the people of any other nation; heart and circulatory system diseases claim nearly a million lives in this country each year. The continuing rise in the percentage of such deaths is believed to be partly caused by the fact that more people are escaping such illnesses as pneumonia or tuberculosis and living to the age when degenerative vascular disease becomes more of a threat. Doctors have also noted, however, an alarming increase of mortality from cardiovascular illness among comparatively young adults, especially males. Among the conditions contributing to coronary disease are obesity, emotional stress, cigarette smoking, poor diet, and the lack of suitable exercise. Exercise has recently been shown to be effective in the reduction of cholesterol levels, another important factor in heart disease.[7]

A healthful regimen of physical exercise helps to reduce obesity and emotional stress, and thus contributes significantly to the individual's resistance to heart attack. Studies have shown that the occupations in which the incidence of coronary disease is highest are those which involve the least physical exertion. A classic British medical research report compared bus drivers and conductors on London buses, and postal clerks and postmen (job situations in which one class of employee is physically active and the other less so). It was found that there was a much higher rate of heart disease among the inactive workers.[8]

Some medical practitioners have strongly supported fitness programs such as the Royal Canadian Air Force exercises. Other specialists have supported jogging as an ideal exercise for the cardiovascular and respiratory systems, especially for persons beyond age thirty-five who seldom exercise regularly. The appeal of jogging may be that it is less an exercise program than an enjoyable recreational activity, especially when group participation adds the element of social interaction.

Recently an increasing number of heart specialists have suggested running (rather than jogging) as an important conditioning exercise. A conference sponsored by the New York Academy of Sciences supported running particularly for middle-aged and older persons, and for patients who had recovered from heart attacks (under competent medical supervision, of course). A Canadian specialist, Dr. Terence Kavanagh, has been conducting a special coronary rehabilitation program in Toronto during the past several years. In response to the concern that a vigorous running program might *cause* heart attacks, he pointed out that patients involved in his program

> had a fatal recurrence rate of 1.4 percent a year. This compares with most studies that show a fatal recurrence rate for heart attack victims in the population-at-large of 6 to 12 percent. The rate of non-fatal recurrences among patients in the exercise program approximated 1.5 percent a year, comparing with a rate of from 7 to 13 percent in the population-at-large.[9]

Fitness Programs in Public Recreation and Park Departments

Many public recreation and park departments have initiated conditioning programs for men and women, and some have constructed special facilities for this purpose. The San Diego Parks and Recreation Department, for example, has developed an extensive system of physical fitness trails which utilize portable exercise facilities to supplement permanent structures; these are moved from park to park to meet differing demands. A "Fun Fitness Trail" in Vancouver, Canada has twenty-four standard exercise stations at various points along the trail, with distances between exercise stations carefully calculated to allow for the exertion required by each exercise.

Other public departments have developed programs in cooperation with community organizations or with Civil Service personnel groups, such as midday exercise and swim programs making use of aquatic centers at a normally slack time of day, and "Sunday Fun Days" in which participants at all levels of ability compete at different distances, and in which the goal is not to win, but to participate and gradually improve one's performance.

Fitness in Industrial Programs

A major approach to developing fitness in Europe is to provide exercise breaks during the working day for all employees; many companies in Scandinavia, Germany, Austria, and the Low Countries have developed extensive physical fitness activities. In the United States, several large companies like Exxon and IBM have developed similar programs. Many Canadian companies, with the encouragement of the Department of National Health and Welfare, have also established highly successful fitness programs. Canadians have recognized that a high proportion of their citizens fall below recognized fitness standards. A large-scale testing program in Saskatoon, Saskatchewan revealed that Canadians failed to meet recommended average values for aerobic power, based on a standardized bicycle ergometer exercise task.

> Only 14 to 21 percent of the women and 7 to 35 percent of the men fall into good or high fitness categories. Nearly 50 percent of every age group

307

except the 15- to 19-year-old males fail to reach even the lower limit of the suggested average fitness range.[10]

To improve this situation, the Fitness and Amateur Sport Branch of Recreation Canada has vigorously promoted increased participation in company fitness programs.

Programs of Voluntary Agencies

Many voluntary community agencies, such as the YMCA, YWCA and YM-YWHA, have strong physical fitness programs, many of which include a battery of tests by which specific goals are designed for each participant according to his age, sex, and present physical condition.

As an example of the benefits of such a program, four forty-eight-year-old men began a Y fitness program in Richmond, Virginia. At the start, two of the four smoked, and all were overweight. Actuarial charts indicated that if they continued in their present lifestyle, all four would be dead before the age of sixty. After six months in the program, the smokers had quit, all four had lost an average of twenty-six pounds, and their resting heart rates had dropped 16 points each. Insurance charts indicated that if the men maintained their fitness levels, they would live to an average age of eighty-five.[11]

Safety Aspects of Recreation

Another way in which recreation promotes personal health and physical fitness is by establishing sound safety practices, particularly in the area of juvenile sports. A Cincinnati orthopedist, Dr. Nicholas Giannestras, sums up the problem:

> Certain competitive sports, fostered by overzealous adults, be they parents, sponsors, coaches or officials of elementary schools, are now played with such overemphasis, that they have become a health hazard.[12]

Risks are created when youngsters are unequally matched with opponents of greater strength and ability, or receive inadequate medical supervision or improper coaching. Dr. Melvin Thornton, chairman of the American Medical Association's Committee on the Medical Aspects of Sports, has presented guidelines formulated by national authorities in this field, which suggest (1) proper physical conditioning of young participants, (2) safe conduct of the sport, (3) careful grouping of athletes, (4) good protective equipment, properly fitted, (5) proper assignment of responsibility among parents, sponsors, coaches, and school authorities, (6) well-maintained facilities, (7) adequate health appraisals, and (8) careful consideration of important educational and recreational values, and policies that keep competition within sensible limits.[13]

A related area of concern is the need for effective safety practices in other types of recreational activities. Many hobbies, for example, cause accidents and illnesses similar to modern industrial hazards. People who do their own car maintenance, building, woodwork, painting, or decorating risk physical harm through exposure to asbestos dust, potentially dangerous power equipment, commercial paint strippers, or epoxy resins. Overexposure to the noise of snowmobiles over a sustained period of time can cause hearing loss, and British sources blame premature deafness among teen-agers on the loud music of discotheques, where the noise level is much higher than industrial limits of ninety decibels over an eight-hour shift. Even children's toys can be dangerous, as shown by the Federal Consumer Product Safety Commission's having banned some fifteen hundred different toys which present a serious risk to children.

The point is that although recreation provides important benefits to health and fitness, it can also be the cause of harm unless efforts are made to provide safety education and supervision and to protect participants from hazards.

Emotional Values of Recreational Participation

The mental health benefits of recreational participation have been well documented in the medical literature. Dr. William Menninger has written:

> Mentally healthy people participate in some form of volitional activity to supplement their required daily work. . . . Their satisfaction from these activities meets deep-seated psychological demands, quite beyond the superficial rationalizations of enjoyment. . . . There is considerable scientific evidence that the healthy personality is one who not only plays, but who takes his play seriously. Furthermore, there is also evidence that the inability and unwillingness to play reveals an insecure or disordered aspect of personality.[14]

Dr. Paul Haun, another highly respected psychiatrist, wrote that the medical case for play was undisputed; in his view, play is an essential element of healthy life, and provides a natural rhythmic alternative to work. This concept has been widely accepted in treatment programs for the mentally ill. Haun described the use of recreation in the hospital environment as a "potent normalizer" that helps to dispel the fear of isolation and social rejection of hospitalized patients. Recreation can provide the patient with familiar social roles through which constructive interaction with others can occur:

> It offers a gratifyingly wide opportunity for instinctual discharge in socially acceptable channels. . . . Competently administered and skillfully presented, it encourages the timid, disarms the aggressive, motivates the lethargic, calms the restless, and diverts the melancholic. As a necessary part of a hospital environment, genuinely attuned to the needs of the sick, it merits our serious attention.[15]

A leading heart research specialist, Dr. Joseph B. Wolffe, formerly president of the American College of Sports Medicine and medical director of the Valley Forge Medical Center and Heart Hospital, found that a special patient activity program resulted in lessening drug requirements for various types of patients from 35 to 50 percent and actually shortened hospital stay by approximately 15 percent. The need for sedatives and tranquilizers for patients suffering from neurocirculatory asthenia was reduced by 35 percent among patients participating in the program. Wolffe concluded:

> Recreation is more than physical medicine. It helps to make the patient . . . a part of a social milieu in the hospital. . . . The recreator's evaluation of actions and attitudes helps to fill an important gap in the physician's appraisal of a patient's physical and mental status. Opportunities for recreational activities in a hospital setting help to minimize introspection, lessen anxieties and neuroses irrespective of the patient's physical and mental conditions.[16]

Such statements from medical practitioners recognizing recreation as a potent force in maintaining or improving mental health are supported by certain findings of mental health specialists in educational settings. Dr. James Jan-Tausch of the New Jersey State Department of Education found in a study of suicides among public school children in New Jersey during a three-year period that nonparticipation in school recreational and extracurricular activities was closely related to despondency, social isolation, and suicide attempts. He wrote:

> With very few exceptions, the suicides in this study were not members of a chorus, a team, a cast or a publication. The most significant factor related to suicide among school children was the relationship between the child and the people with whom he socialized. In every case of suicide, the child was described as having no close friends, with whom he might share confidences or from whom he received psychological support. This investigator is of the opinion that participation in extra-curricular activities is a good deterrent of suicide.[17]

A related study by L. H. Richardson, a consulting psychologist at the City University of New York, examined college students who had sought psychological counseling. Richardson found that the leisure-time activities of these students were significantly more passive than the activities of students who had not sought counseling. He concluded that active recreational participation was closely linked to maintaining emotional stability and well-being.[18] More recent studies of patients in psychiatric hospitals have revealed their past participation in leisure activities to be extremely low.[19]

Suicide and mental illness are extreme examples illustrating the importance of recreation in maintaining emotional well-being, but many millions of other persons who operate within a presumably normal range of behavior have problems relating to tension, boredom, frustration, and the ability to use their leisure in satisfying ways.

The condition of the "workaholic" who is committed to unremitting work and feels guilty about enjoying recreation and leisure may have more serious medical implications than are commonly realized. A team of cardiologists at the Mount Zion Hospital and Medical Center in San Francisco has concluded that much heart disease is caused by an emotional component which produces "Type-A behavior," described as follows:

310

The Type-A man [is] ambitious, competitive, impatient and aggressive; he is involved in an incessant struggle against time and/or other people. His sense of *time urgency* is perhaps his most predominant trait. Almost always punctual, he is greatly annoyed if kept waiting . . .

The Type-A man does not usually spare the time to indulge in hobbies; or when he does, he prefers competitive games or gambling . . . [he] generally strives frantically for things worth *having* (a beautiful home, a better job, a bigger bank balance) at the expense of things worth *being* (well-read, knowledgeable about art, appreciative of nature).[20]

Epidemiological studies led the San Francisco research team to conclude that lifestyle and the creative use of leisure can be more important than diet or exercise in preventing heart attacks.

Another important indication of the need to develop more creative satisfactions through recreation and leisure is the prevalence of emotional tension among millions of persons today—evidenced by their use of alcohol, tranquilizers, or other drugs. Widespread, excessive drug use that creates addiction or alcoholism presents a problem which extends beyond the individual and becomes a matter of social concern.

Recreation and leisure provide a variety of legal and healthful ways in which people can find release from tension and enjoy intense pleasure—through music, dance, or other arts, through sport, through outdoor recreation activities, or through experiences such as yoga or transcendental meditation.

Clearly, recreation can be a vital force in maintaining mental health and preventing illness. Parents, teachers, counselors, and youth leaders must recognize the importance of recreation in the guidance of the emotional and psychological development of children, youth, and adults. Recreation is a means of establishing and reinforcing positive and realistic self-concepts and of offering pleasure and a sense of personal creative accomplishment, all of which contribute to emotional well-being.

Social Values of Recreation

As indicated earlier, many adults today find their primary social contacts and important relationships not in their work lives, but in voluntary group associations during leisure hours. The primary value of recreation in this respect is that it provides an opportunity for people to overcome a sense of isolation by entering informal neighborhood associations, religious organizations, or other social groups which provide friendship, sociability, and common interests.

For children, such groups offer a realistic training ground for both cooperation and competition. The youngster who is part of a group in an after-school center, summer camp, or teen-age social club is testing his social role and preparing for involvement in the adult world. Through group participation he learns to interact with others, to accept group rules and wishes, and when necessary, to subordinate his own views or desires to those of the group. Sports are thought to play a particularly important role in character development, a view expressed by Dr. Frederick Hovde, president of Purdue University:

> College football breeds discipline and leadership. . . . Competitive team sports keep us strong and vigorous. . . . I find no convincing evidence that leadership can be taught. It is something that can only be learned by facing successfully its demand on the individual's total capability.[21]

One of the most important elements of sport is the rigorous training process which requires dedication not just to a sport, but to a way of life. A leading college long-distance runner describes running as a character-building experience in which the daily workouts become more enjoyable and valuable than the weekly competition:

> The essence of the enterprise lies in the daily workout. It is the workout that regulates the runner's whole life—his eating habits, his social schedule and his academic future . . . the distance runner enjoys the daily routine of workouts more than the weekly ordeal of competition. The lust for victory is too often overemphasized as the motive to run.[22]

Similar views have been expressed about college rowing, a sport in which the competitor is subject to tremendous physical demands and in which he engages almost anonymously, as part of a total team effort. College crew captains stress that rowing is sport for its own sake, with no "good deals, no glory, no money" to be gained. They comment:

> An oarsman must have a burning desire to excel, the ability to push oneself to the limits of human endurance and still maintain poise and concentration . . . it's a discipline, a way of life. One's whole attitude changes under the value of crew. . . . The unity of the boat, the fanaticism and religious ardor of oarsmen all contribute to the crew's growth.[23]

The claims that sport is a means of character development must be considered in the light of the settings in which games are played. The desirability of character traits such as the ability to play by the rules, evidence good sportsmanship, and win or lose gracefully represent essentially middle-class values. Lower-class youth often find it difficult to accept such values. Short and Strodtbeck suggest that gang athletics in urban slums tend to emphasize individual performance and to serve immediate rather than long-term goals. Adolescent gang members are often so completely committed to the idea of winning at all cost that

> the rules of the game seemed to have a tenuous hold on their loyalties. It was not unusual for them when stern adult supervision was absent to avoid defeat in a sport contest by precipitating a fight.[24]

Often, the gang itself is not cohesive enough to withstand the effects of defeat, and sports failures are thus demoralizing. Beyond this, some psychologists have challenged the basic concept that sports contribute to character development.

312

In a study of approximately fifteen thousand athletes, Ogilvie and Tutko found the following character traits in many successful athletes: (1) they have great need for achievement and tend to set high goals both for themselves and others; (2) they are highly organized, orderly, respectful of authority, and dominant; (3) they have a high level of capacity for trust, psychological endurance, self-control, low anxiety, and the ability to express aggression. At the same time, they also found numerous "problem" athletes who were hyperanxious, success-phobic, and injury and depression prone. Ogilvie and Tutko concluded:

> We found no empirical support for the tradition that sport builds character. Indeed, there is evidence that athletic competition limits growth in some areas. It seems that the personality of the ideal athlete is not the result of any molding process, but comes out of the ruthless selection process that occurs at all levels of sport. Athletic competition has no more beneficial effects than intense endeavor in any other field.[25]

One of the most frequently expressed justifications of sports as a form of social development is that it provides a medium through which children and youth learn to compete, thus supposedly equipping them to survive in a tough, "dog-eat-dog" adult world. Yet there is evidence that our national stress on competition and glorification of winning as an all-consuming goal has serious negative effects on character. Studies of cooperative and competitive behavior of American children have shown that ten-year-olds repeatedly failed to earn rewards for which they strove, because they were too highly competitive and were unable to assist others in problem-solving games that required cooperation. In other situations, overcompetitiveness caused children to sacrifice their own rewards in order to reduce the rewards of their peers. In contrast, ten-year-old children in rural Mexico found it easy to cooperate with each other and to win the prizes that eluded their American counterparts.[26]

Overorganized, overcompetitive sports frequently eliminate the spontaneity that should be present in children's play, and impose negative values on participation, such as the emphasis on the highly questionable value of winning at all costs. Lundquist writes:

> In competitive sport the opponent is the enemy and obstacle in the way of victory. . . . The continuous use of terminology such as the "long bomb," "war," and "blitz," the references of gaining territory and more yardage than your opponents, the whole relationship to combat is all too obvious.[27]

These observations raise serious questions about the effect of sport on social development.

Effect of Sports on Education and Social Mobility

One view of the effect of sports participation is that it is detrimental to educational attainment. Durso points out Coleman's statement in *The Adolescent Society* that athletic participation discourages emphasis on scholarship and diverts school resources and student energies from the goal of academic excellence. Too often, outstanding high school graduating seniors find it almost impossible to get academic scholarships, while star halfbacks who can barely read or write find dozens of coaches beating at their doors with attractive offers for full scholarships and more.[28]

On the other hand, sociological studies of midwestern high school boys have shown that on all social class levels, athletes performed on a higher level academically than nonathletes and were motivated toward attending college at a much higher rate. Almost five times as many nonathletes as athletes dropped out of high school.[29] Comparisons of students with similar intelligence quotients revealed that athletes did better academic work than nonathletes. In general, participation in student activity programs seems to be closely related to the school's holding power and to provide constructive outlets for students' social and psychological needs.[30] Student organizations serve as a means through which students are able to define their social status, and those who participate in cocurricular activities tend to be more successful academically than nonparticipants. Indeed, it has been found that leading business and industrial executives were extremely active participants in cocurricular activities while at school or college.

In a recent study of women executives in American businesses, social psychologists Margaret Henning and Anne Jardin concluded that one hindrance to women who aspired to top corporate positions was that they had never had the opportunity to play team sports. For many corporate men, business represents a long battle on a metaphorical gridiron, played according to the rules and values of active sports. The fact that most women had not had early team experiences that helped them to plan strategies, take risks, deal easily with victory or defeat, or play as part of a team created deficits which, in Henning and Jardin's view, handicapped them severely in climbing the corporate ladder.[31]

Investigators have also found that sport provides social mobility for many disadvantaged young people by offering a feasible means of realizing upward aspirations. Hodges comments that football "has functioned as a highly effective status elevator for thousands of boys from blue-collar ethnic backgrounds."[32]

Loy points out four important values of sports which can contribute to upward mobility: (1) early participation may develop skills which permit direct entry into professional sports; (2) sports participation may promote educational achievement by providing scholarships and strengthening the student's motivation to remain in school; (3) it may lead to occupational sponsorship or assistance or to the kinds of contacts that assist later career development; and (4) it may lead to the development of attitudes and behavior patterns valued in the larger occupational world.[33]

In community life as well, recreational involvement tends to be seen as an avenue to status and success. William F. Whyte, in a study of slum youth, found two social groupings. One group, which he called the "corner boys," was content to hang around on street corners; this group had low occupational and prestige goals. The other group, which he called the "college boys," was much more ambitious and upwardly mobile. Whyte found that the "college boys" realized that certain kinds of affiliations and social behavior would help them in getting ahead. Correctly perceiving the neighborhood settlement house as representative of middle-class, goal-oriented values, they tended to join and become active in its clubs and programs.[34]

314

Plate 10. Other facilities are based on innovative designs, as in these unusual "leisure pools," in Swindon, and Rotherham, England. The Nassau County, N.Y., Recreation and Park Department features an old New England farm in a village restoration and a scale model of a Mississippi riverboat, the *Bicentennial Belle.*

Plate 11. Mass participation in modern recreation often involves huge crowds—seen here competing in a national bridge tournament, a Hula Hoop contest, and an off-road motorcycle race.

Plate 12. Residents of Levittown, N.Y., have built a network of night-lighted swimming pools supported by their own dues, rather than public taxes. Outdoor recreation—particularly camping and boating—have become tremendously popular. Here, the two are combined on a TVA lake.

Plate 13. In contrast, summer play opportunities in urban slums are sharply limited. In a poor neighborhood, children have painted their own game areas on the pavement. Here, children wade in a curbside puddle, while adults play cards on the sidewalk.

Plate 14. New programs and facilities are provided for the ill and disabled. "Wheelchair basketball" pits paraplegic veterans against a team of nonhandicapped servicemen. A nature trail for the blind has been designed by the National Park Service. Mentally retarded and neurologically impaired children are entertained.

Plate 15. Many outdoor recreation enthusiasts today enjoy high-risk activities,
such as mountain climbing and skiing in
the national forests, or surfing off the
Florida coast.

Plate 16. The creative arts and recreation: prisoners work on art projects in a state penitentiary creative arts program. Senior citizen uses muscle on ambitious wood sculpture. Folk dance attracts participants of all ages as seen in this Country Dance and Song Society of America festival.

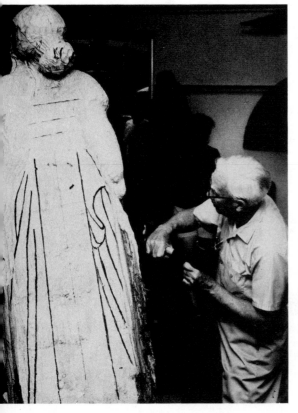

Intellectual Values of Recreation

In addition to improving motivation, physical recreation appears to promote more effective mental and cognitive performance. One writer states that

> the youngster who gets plenty of exercise . . . is more likely to do better academic work and be freer from tension than his passive, non-athletic roommate. . . . Participation in sports relaxes and challenges the student and enables him to concentrate more intensely. [35]

A study of West Point cadets revealed that academic failure occurred much more frequently (43.4 percent) in a group that was classified as "inferior" on physical performance tests than among students whose physical performance was "superior" (18.8 percent). Another study conducted at Phillips Academy in Andover, Massachusetts, demonstrated this linkage even more conclusively. The physical education department introduced an experimental morning physical activity program; it was found at the end of a testing period that those in the morning gymnasium classes had twice the number of honors and half the failures of those not in this special program. [36]

Such experts as Gesell, Jersild, and Piaget have found that children's earliest learnings are motor in nature, and form the foundation for subsequent learnings. Kephart states further that even in "pure thought" activities, the "muscular basis of behavior" provides an important foundation, and suggests that there is evidence that the efficiency of the higher thought processes can be no better than the basic motor abilities upon which they are based. [37]

In many other ways, recreational experience may contribute to the individual's cognitive development: as indicated in chapter 3, it promotes creative learning and self-expression for young children and stimulates conceptual growth. Such hobbies as reading, art, music, drama, nature study, and similar interests all make an important contribution to this growth. Recreation can be particularly important for the intellectual development of those who suffer from disability. A British study of physical activity programs for mentally retarded children showed that these programs improved not only the physical but also the mental performance of the subjects. [38] A three-year study of a remedial program for infants of underprivileged black families in Washington, D.C., conducted by the National Institute for Mental Health, found that over a twenty-one month period the subjects' average intelligence quotient climbed to 106, compared with 89 for a control group. While the program was described as "tutoring," the report indicated that

> since the children were too young for any formal schooling, the tutoring . . . consisted of play activities designed to stimulate mental and verbal capacity. [39]

Finally, a number of studies have shown that certain television programs have a markedly positive effect on childhood learning. "Sesame Street," for example, an extremely popular children's program sponsored by the Carnegie and Ford Foundations and the U. S. Office of Education, has reached many millions of young children each year. A test of its effect showed that pre-school children, particularly

315

those from poor families, who watched "Sesame Street" made gains in language, numerical, and reasoning skills that were two and one-half times as great as those made by comparable children who did not watch the program.[40]

In this and in many other ways, recreation contributes to the intellectual development as well as the physical, emotional, and social development of participants.

Recreation, Family Life, and the Needs of Major Age Groups

Any analysis of the personal values of recreational experience must necessarily examine the special needs of major age groups in the light of rapidly changing patterns of family life in modern society.

Family Life Today

The changed nature of family life throughout much of the United States and Canada has had profound implications for the upbringing of children. As increasing numbers of families have moved to suburban housing developments, much of the actual responsibility for raising children has shifted from the home to other settings. Urie Bronfenbrenner, a leading psychologist, points out that although parents still have the moral and legal responsibility for rearing children, they often lack the power or opportunity to do the job adequately. Parents tend to spend much less time with their children, and in many ways, children and youth have moved away from adult influence. Recent national studies suggest that many well-educated and affluent parents no longer adhere to traditional family values, and are unwilling to make sacrifices in their own lives for the sake of their children, another trend which reduces family "togetherness." Bronfenbrenner suggests that families today usually include only one or two adults, and functioning suburban neighborhoods have withered to a small circle of friends, chiefly accessible by automobile or telephone:

> Whereas the world in which the child lived before consisted of a diversity of people in a diversity of settings, now for millions of American children the neighborhood is nothing but row upon row of buildings inhabited by strangers.[41]

Many suburban housing developments today lack nearby stores, community services, institutions, and social structures; the way of life for many working adults is to come home, have a drink, eat dinner, mow the lawn, watch television, and sleep. Coleman points out that in modern society the natural processes of the family have been largely replaced by the formal structure of the school. Children no longer are helpful to families economically, and parents cannot help train them for a place in community life. Children are set apart in schools for ever longer periods of time; they tend to be grouped with other children who are much like themselves in age, social class, and even levels of ability. High school students in particular tend today to conduct their social lives entirely within their own groups, in

316

separate subcultures [which] exist right under the very noses of adults—subcultures with languages all their own, with special symbols, and most importantly, with value systems that may differ from adults.

> . . . the adolescent is dumped into a society of his peers, a society whose habitats are the halls and classrooms of the school, the teen-age canteen, the corner drugstore, the automobile, and numerous other gathering places.[42]

Within this society, subgroups are identified: the "straights" and "non-straights," the "jocks," the "freaks," and the "hoods." An Iowa high school senior comments:

> Groups are terribly demanding. You must conform to the unspoken demands of your group in any way they ask: appearance, attitudes and opinions. With drugs, smoking, sex, and alcohol rampaging even into junior high and grade school these days, pressures are incredibly hard on the teenager.[43]

Psychologists believe that the lack of meaningful contact between many parents and their children during leisure hours is a source of great difficulty. Bronfenbrenner points out that research on middle-class adolescents indicates that those children whose parents had been away from home for lengthy periods of time rated significantly lower on such traits as responsibility and leadership. It would seem then that the close and continuing contact between parents and their children offered by family recreation activities would be extremely important in the healthy personality development of children.

Recreation provides such opportunities in a variety of ways. Millions of families go camping each year, and spend relaxed weeks in a natural setting—boating, fishing, hiking and sight-seeing—often with other families whom they meet year after year at the same state parks or campgrounds. Many community organizations such as municipal recreation and park departments, Boy or Girl Scouts, and church groups sponsor special family events, which may involve social recreation, picnics and outings, swimming or sailing, hobby activities, camp weekends, or similar activities that promote family togetherness. Through such activities, many families strengthen important bonds of affection and communication.

Other families, however, do not seem to achieve this kind of relationship—either between parents and children, or between the parents themselves. Bronfenbrenner states that American children depend heavily on television to fill their leisure hours. Pointing out that television has been shown to have a marked effect on the attitudes and actions of observers, he asks:

> Is it any wonder that children, as they grow to adolescence, often turn out to be complete strangers to their dismayed parents? Why do an enormous number of young people from educated and middle-class families find it difficult or impossible to relate to anybody and therefore drop out?[44]

317

Effects of Television on Youth

S. I. Hayakawa, former president of San Francisco State University, suggested that television is a "powerful sorcerer" responsible for much of the alienation, rebellion, and deviant behavior of today's youth. Hayakawa's view was that because they often find parents, relatives, and teachers to be censorious or dull, children prefer the nondemanding world of television. Studies have shown that children may spend over twenty thousand hours in passive contemplation of the screen during their formative years; these hours are "stolen from the time needed to learn to relate to siblings, playmates, parents, grandparents, or strangers." Estimates according to the present levels of advertising and violence are that the average child, before reaching adulthood, will have been exposed to three hundred fifty thousand commercials and vicariously participated in eighteen thousand murders.[45] Studies have shown that intensive exposure to television stifles creative imagination and encourages a passive outlook toward life. It tends to perpetuate sex-role stereotypes, and in Hayakawa's view creates the illusion—even in its commercials—that there is an instant, simple solution to all problems rather than showing that in real life, patience, training, and hard work are necessary for success.

Beyond this, there is considerable evidence that television violence encourages violent and criminal behavior of youth. As early as 1969, the National Commission on the Causes and Prevention of Violence concluded that violence on television had to be reduced because it encouraged imitation and strengthened "a distorted, pathological view of society." Studies have repeatedly documented lowered inhibitions of aggressive behavior after exposure to violence on television, and there have been numerous examples of crimes committed shortly after similar crimes were shown on television.[46] Reports in the *Journal of the American Medical Association* and other authoritative sources conclude that the once popular "catharsis" theory that TV violence offers a healthy outlet for natural hostilities and aggressions does not hold up.[47] Indeed, a report of the Foundation for Child Development pointed out in 1977 that a majority of seven- to eleven-year-old children have serious fears of violence in the outside world—and that such fears are worse in heavy television watchers.[48] The implication of these findings is that other attractive and enjoyable recreational activities must be provided for youth, to prevent their becoming overdependent on an excessive amount of daily television viewing.

Other important values of recreational experience for younger children have been identified. Thomas Johnson, a child psychiatrist who has been an active consultant to major professional sports teams as well as to the national Little League organization, points out that competitive activities are essential to children's developing a realistic success expectancy. Commenting that sports are a normal and potentially beneficial part of each child's life, he suggests that they should include both unstructured and organized activities, and that they should help the child learn to deal with both winning and losing:

> All winning could be as harmful as all losing. There is value in a child's experiencing some frustration, tension and anxiety. Properly dosed, it promotes psychological growth. . . . The key to frustration's being helpful is that it not overwhelm the child so that he quits or ends up spinning his wheels with a hopeless feeling.[49]

Johnson points out that healthy children can accept the disappointment of losing, provided that they have a strong basic sense of self-worth, and that their parents and coaches support them, despite their losses or failures. More and more, parents and youth organizations are seeking ways to strengthen the positive values of sports competition, and minimize its dangers. In a junior hockey league program in Windsor, Ontario serving over thirty-six hundred boys annually, intensive efforts have been made to place greater emphasis on socialization and fun, to reduce excessively violent and aggressive play, and to enable players with wide ranges of skill to enjoy the game.[50] In the United States, a three-year study in elementary physical education funded by the U. S. Office of Education has sought to develop a more humanistic, creative, and child-centered approach to sport and movement education that would provide positive values for children served in today's school programs.[51] Such efforts obviously have important implications for recreation programs offered to children and youth in community settings.

Changing attitudes toward competition have resulted in the development of new games and sports that are less structured, less violent and aggressive, and more playlike and individualistic. Such games, with names like "infinity volleyball," "boffing," and "tweezli-wop" were created by sports figures affiliated with the New Games Foundation in California, and have been successfully introduced into many school and recreation programs.[52] The deemphasis of competition has also resulted in new types of sports facility designs. For example, most swimming pools have been designed in a strictly rectangular shape, in order to accommodate competitive swimming events. However, recognizing that the far greater use of pools is for recreation, innovative designers have created a number of recreational pools in British cities. These pools have nonrectangular shapes and such features as wave machines, slides, beach areas with gradients, learner areas, and lighting and plants that create a warm, relaxing, almost natural ambience for day and night swimming.[53]

Trends in Youth Values and Behavior

At the same time that we have permitted adolescents to become a distinct subculture in our society, glamorized by public adulation and spending power, they have also been frustrated by the lengthened period of required schooling before they can marry, hold a job, or assume a meaningful adult role. Much of the traditionally conceived rebellion of teen-agers arises from this frustration; they are challenging adult controls and seeking new forms of freedom and power, often according to a pleasure-oriented rationale that rejects traditional societal standards.

This rebellion reached its peak during the 1960s. High school and college students in the United States and Canada, as well as in other European nations, became engulfed in a wave of protest against the Vietnam war and social injustices. They demanded greater rights in school or college campus governance—and sometimes occupied administration buildings or campuses to achieve these rights.

With the cessation of the war, the granting of greater rights to students, and the relaxation of previous codes of behavior in many schools and colleges, the rebellion of the 1960s declined. By the early 1970s, students turned cool to political issues, campus activism died away, and personal pleasure seeking seemed to be the keynote of youth behavior. A large-scale study of youth by Daniel Yankelovich in 1974 indicated that the traditional values of morality, patriotism, and hard work had declined dramatically among both college and noncollege youth.

319

Sharply increasing numbers of both college and working-class youth want more sexual freedom. . . . Fewer of them objected to relations between consenting homosexuals on moral grounds and fewer think having an abortion is morally wrong, as compared with five years ago. . . .

The number of young workers who believed that religion was "a very important value" declined sharply. . . . Both students and workers indicated that they would welcome less emphasis on money . . . and fewer respondents believed that "hard work always pays off." Both young workers and college students felt that "self-expression" and "self-fulfillment" were important.[54]

Sexual Behavior of Youth

There is considerable evidence that premarital sexual activity has become increasingly accepted by youth. Studies have reported that the number of young Americans who are still virgins at the time they marry is rapidly declining and that American youth is "undergoing a revolution in its attitudes toward sex, life, and proper behavior." Although there are no conclusive reports of the incidence of sexual activity among youth, one indication of their changing mores comes from statistics on illegitimate births. One of about every eighteen babies born in the United States today is born to unmarried parents; this illegitimacy rate of approximately 5 percent is a considerable increase since 1940, when the rate was less than 1 percent. Although some of these unmarried mothers are adults, most are teen-agers. Medical authorities in Connecticut estimated that in a given year, the pregnancy rate among unmarried teen-age girls was equal to almost 17 percent of the teen-age female population.

Obviously, this trend reflects changes in sexual attitudes and morality in the overall society. Abortion has been legalized in many states, and birth control and family planning services are available nationwide. Pornography is subject to fewer legal controls, and is endemic throughout most cities and towns. Certain Protestant churches have relaxed their strictures against formerly unacceptable forms of sexual behavior, and it is widely recognized that a high proportion of Catholics refuse to accept the church's regulations on birth control and abortion. Homosexuality is no longer officially regarded as a form of mental illness, and bisexual lifestyles appear to be much more widely accepted. On college campuses, controls on the sexual behavior of students and faculty have been sharply reduced.

What are the implication of this trend for recreation and leisure? Many recreation professionals who work closely with young people—in community organizations, youth clubs, or in school or college residence programs—have observed a growing tendency to regard sex as a form of leisure activity or recreation. Godbey and Parker, for example, have written:

Sexual activity of many kinds is an important component of leisure activity. Although there is overwhelming evidence that sex-related activity constitutes an increasingly important use of leisure, sex is not often studied from the standpoint of leisure activity. Societal mores still prohibit its consideration as play or leisure activity.[55]

A professor of medical psychology at Johns Hopkins University, John Money, comments that a number of important societal factors have converged to support the consideration of a new ethic of recreational sex. Contemporary contraceptive methods, increased life span and changing attitudes about aging that extend sexual activity many years beyond the childbearing period, and the world population excess which compels many people to limit the childbearing rate are all factors that have encouraged many to abandon the view of sex as purely procreative in purpose. Money suggests that

> Youth . . . appears to be developing a new code of betrothal—a relationship of recreational sex that is not promiscuous but that also is not a permanent commitment to procreation.[56]

Pointing out that this change in beliefs and lifestyle is closely linked to other sex-coded roles of work, play, mores, and the law, he concludes that society needs research knowledge to help in formulating a new code of sexual ethics that will recognize its modern recreational character. The implications of this issue for recreation professionals are critical. The fact that sex may be pursued for "fun" purposes does not make it any less serious as a form of human activity. It must be recognized that in addition to the pleasure it provides, sex also fills an important need for human contact and meaningful relationships with others. Healthy sexual attitudes represent the other side of alienation or withdrawal. Unhealthy attitudes may represent exploitation, power seeking, thoughtless "machismo," or even violent aggression in forced rape. Increased sexual activity may lead to increased statistics of illegitimate pregnancy or venereal disease on a societal basis.

There has been some evidence that premarital intimacy may be linked with emotional problems. A University of Wisconsin study reported in the *Journal of the American Medical Association* revealed that a very high percentage of female students (86 percent) who had become psychiatric patients had engaged in premarital sexual intercourse, 72 percent of these with more than one person. The head psychiatrist concluded that "permissive sexual activity seems to be highly correlated with mental illness."[57] While this may not be a valid conclusion today, in view of the extremely permissive values that prevail throughout most of society, it suggests that for many emotionally disturbed young people today, sex represents an extremely difficult area of personal adjustment.

The recreation professional must realize that to the extent that other kinds of creative leisure experiences fail to meet the physical, emotional, and social needs of young people, they are likely to find sex increasingly attractive. Thus, if the recreation professional believes that premarital sex is undesirable or should be controlled—or if this is the view of the community or sponsoring agency—a rich and rewarding program of recreational activity will be a critical factor. Beyond this, in any program involving young people today, the recreation leader or supervisor *must* have a consistent code of values which he can communicate to them, and accurate information or referral sources with which to assist them when necessary.

Problems of Drug Abuse Today

Another important leisure-related aspect of youth behavior in recent years is the explosion of drug experimentation and abuse among many young people. The most frequent use is of such mood-altering drugs as marijuana, hashish, the amphetamines and barbiturates, and LSD and other hallucinogenics, and to a lesser degree such hard narcotics as heroin or cocaine. While estimates vary greatly, there is much evidence to suggest that a majority of students in schools and colleges are at least occasional users of marijuana or other drugs. During the early 1970s, for example, marijuana use more than doubled among 14- and 15-year-olds.[58]

What has caused this trend in modern youth's behavior? One important factor is that our society has become tremendously dependent on drugs, both as a form of medication and as tranquilizers. A 1976 report on the drug industry revealed that Americans spend $11 billion a year on prescription drugs and another $2.6 billion on over-the-counter pharmaceuticals. More than 75 million people regularly consume drugs—many of which have doubtful value or serious negative side effects.[59] Thus, the social climate is one which seems to condone drug use. For many young people drugs appear to have appeal both because they bring a feeling of euphoria, and because they provide an escape from reality. One college mental health authority suggested that "for people who are chronically unhappy, drugs bring some relief from a world without purpose." Corry wrote:

> Students themselves are not particularly articulate about why they take drugs. For kicks, they say, or because they are bored, or because drugs are easy to get or because drugs offer them deep personal insights. . . . They offer an illicit pleasure that is almost entirely without sanction in the adult world and they open an immense gap between parent and child.[60]

Some authorites have pointed out that drug use has existed throughout history and in many societies is an accepted and approved means of dealing with the drudgeries, pressures, or problems of everyday life. Godfrey Hochbaum wrote:

> Intoxicating beverages, tobacco, or similar substances, narcotics, and hallucinogens are only a few of these. . . . But in one form or another they have, with only few exceptions, always and everywhere been favored and widely used as a means to help people escape from or cope with the oppressive forces of reality. In fact, these means are in essence not very different from others to which all of us turn every day—going to a movie, reading a book, engaging in sports, or playing cards. All are means of escape, all help to relieve the constant daily stresses and strains on our minds and bodies.[61]

However, Hochbaum also pointed out that the reason society attempts to control the uses of such dependencies is that the benefits or pleasures which they yield are outweighed by the health hazards they create. Many young people (and increasing numbers of adults as well) dismiss these warnings and consider the use of drugs, particularly marijuana, primarily as a harmless form of recreation.

Many drug users argue that drugs are taken for reasons similar to those for drinking alcohol—and indeed, there is strong evidence that alcohol, despite its legal status and easy availability throughout most of the United States and Canada, represents a far greater social problem and health risk. There are an estimated ten million alcoholics in the United States today, and the Federal government alone spends over $160 million a year in alcoholism prevention and treatment programs. A 1977 Gallup Poll indicated that the number of families troubled by a drinking problem had risen by 50 percent since 1974, with the number of adult women drinkers in particular rising sharply.[62] Other recent studies have reported that as many as 28 percent of the nation's teen-agers are "problem" drinkers.

What do these trends imply for the field of recreation service? It seems clear that all such dependencies on externally induced mood alterations are closely linked to leisure attitudes and needs. Prevalent patterns of social behavior and entertainment promote drinking; television commercials and dramatic series convey the image that drinking is an essential ingredient in modern social life, and at everyday parties and get-togethers, beer, wine, and liquor have become an almost inescapable aspect of sociability. Many colleges now permit alcohol on campus, and some hospitals and nursing homes permit drinking under controlled circumstances, or even as a deliberate form of therapeutic treatment.

The history of "prohibition" in America suggests the impossibility of eliminating the use of alcohol as a form of pleasurable leisure activity. Instead, the problem is to curb its use among the very young and to encourage moderate rather than excessive use of alcohol. Research has shown that children brought up in totally abstinent households are more likely to become problem drinkers.

A study funded by the National Institute of Mental Health urged that (a) states consider lowering the drinking age limit, so that colleges could permit controlled drinking at campus social programs and thereby prevent students' driving to roadhouses and bars to drink; (b) that drinking among teen-agers be permitted at social and church gatherings under adult supervision; and (c) that parents and their children drink together on occasion, again in a restrained way.[63] While such recommendations fly in the face of many widely shared societal views, they are sustained by a number of strong, pragmatic arguments. The report also urged that social pressures to drink should be reduced and tolerance for abstinence be increased. People should be genuinely free to "take it or leave it."

Given the probability of continued change in public attitudes and societal customs or laws governing drinking and drug use, it seems clear that recreation professionals must have a full understanding of this problem and be prepared to deal constructively with it in their agencies. By offering the kinds of absorbing and challenging activities that provide deep personal staisfactions and social involvements, recreation leaders could thus lessen the need for other kinds of stimulants or ways of getting "high." They may also help to promote constructive and moderate use of alcohol or drugs, and to educate their clients in this area. Finally, in treatment centers for chronic alcoholics or drug addicts, recreation is a significant form of treatment service (see chapter 14).

Leisure Needs of Young Adults

A primary need of many young adults in modern society is to find social groups in which they can make friends and carry on the process of dating and courtship that will for many individuals ultimately lead to marriage. Particularly in cities and towns, where so many young adults seek employment after school or college, the environment tends to be anonymous and impersonal, offering limited opportunity for social interaction. Far too few public recreation departments or other voluntary, nonprofit organizations have recognized this need and made serious attempts to provide programs for young adults.

Growth of the Single Population

The lack of adequate recreation opportunity for single young adults has become increasingly evident during the past decade, as a consequence of the dramatic growth of the single population. The number of divorces per year in the United States has grown steadily; at the same time, there has been an increasing tendency toward older age at marriage. In 1975, for example, 40 percent of the women aged twenty to twenty-four were single, compared to only 28 percent in 1960; the number of unmarried men in the same age bracket rose from 53 to 60 percent over the same fifteen-year period. The Center for Health Statistics reported that the number of marriages each year in the United States has been declining steadily. The Census Bureau summed up the trend by reporting that American adults today are slower to marry and quicker to divorce than at any other time in history; the trend includes

> more young people staying single and maintaining their own households, more divorce and separation, more families headed by women and more children living with only one parent.[64]

In 1973, *Newsweek* reported that there were 48 million single adults in the United States. In the past, the term "single" usually meant a lonely person, a "loser" whose solitary status was, hopefully, a temporary inconvenience on the way to happy matrimony. Today, for many young people of both sexes, singlehood has become a happy ending in itself—or at least an enjoyably prolonged phase of postadolescence. While marriage is still the statistical norm, *Newsweek* commented that

> within just eight years, singlehood has emerged as an intensely ritualized—and newly respectable—style of American life.[65]

When the trend became obvious, a vast number of singles-only institutions sprang up to meet the needs of this newly recognized population with an estimated $40 billion annual spending power; apartment complexes, singles bars, weekends at resort hotels, "ex-married" clubs, and a variety of other organizations emerged, many of them using recreation as a product for sale, to help singles get together.

Clearly, recreation is an important need for this population. Within what many perceive as a smorgasbord of sexual opportunities, usually on a superficial and temporary level, many young adults seek other kinds of more meaningful relationships and group involvements—through volunteer service work, political club involvement, outdoor recreation clubs, or any of the wide variety of encounter groups or similar programs that have proliferated during the past decade.

Family Recreation

Despite the "singles" trend, the statistical norm for most adults in modern society continues to be a lifestyle which includes marriage. As young people shift to marriage and to raising a family, their social involvement tends to center around the neighborhood in which they live. The home itself becomes a center for parent and child activities, and married couples take part in recreation programs sponsored by religious agencies, civic and neighborhood associations, or P.T.A.s. As children move into organized community activities, parents begin to use their leisure time for volunteer service as adult leaders for Scout groups, volunteer teachers in coopera- tive nursery schools, Little League coaches and managers, or in similar ways.

Although the number of working mothers has increased in recent years, the majority of mothers of young children in modern families do not hold outside paid jobs. For them, many municipal recreation and park departments, YWCAs, or similar organizations, sponsor clubs, fitness programs, classes, or other types of recreational activities during the day while children are at school. In cities, social centers in housing projects or settlement houses often provide classes and similar activities during the day. Many community recreation departments or school adult education programs also provide evening classes in hobbies, sports, cultural activities or other forms of continuing education.

Through this age period, recreation should continue to provide relaxation, to help the family strengthen its ties, to encourage new interests, to expand social, cultural, and intellectual involvement—and, finally, to prepare adults for that period when the demands of earning a livelihood and raising a family will lessen, and leisure will become more available.

The Middle Years

The awareness of a changing lifestyle tends to occur first in married women who have not held paid jobs during their marriages. Once their children have become fairly independent, many mothers find that the demands posed by the home and family are much less pressing. They have increased available time as well as an increased need to find more fulfillment and meaning in life through new interests or challenges.

Many women find it necessary to decide at this time what they will do with the remainder of their lives. Some who worked or had specialized skills or professions before their marriages return to those fields. Others return to school or college to complete their education or earn an advanced degree. For many, increased leisure enables them to become involved in various community projects or causes. Some assume voluntary responsibilities in libraries, hospitals, mental health clinics, museums, or other community programs or institutions. Others hold positions on church or school boards, or in organizations such as the League of Women Voters. Other women at this stage of life do not choose to work or become involved in leadership service programs but instead join recreational, cultural or educational programs that enrich their lives and help them to develop their personalities and talents.

For both men and women during the middle decades of life, recreation should provide a transition to the coming years of maturity and aging. As earlier chapters have indicated, increasing numbers of Americans and Canadians cut their work ties sharply at retirement and are able to look forward to an extended period of comparatively healthy and independent living.

Recreation in Retirement

The abrupt ending of an active work life confronts retired individuals with a great bulk of free time. For some older persons, this is not an insurmountable problem; they are able to live independently and to maintain family ties and social contacts that keep them happy and involved. Many older persons who are financially able move to "leisure villages" or other types of retirement housing complexes where they can share a wide variety of recreational opportunities with others like themselves. Still others continue to live in their home communities, taking part in a normal range of community activities or enjoying the special programs of Senior Centers or Golden Age Clubs. For a great many retired persons, however, problems related to loneliness, boredom, and the lack of meaningful personal and creative involvement pose serious difficulties during retirement. Organized recreation services must continue to expand to fulfill the special needs of aging persons.

This chapter has dealt with the personal values of recreational experience to meet physical, emotional, social, and intellectual needs. It has also examined several of the special problems and needs that relate to family living and to each of the major age groups. Chapter 14 analyzes recreation's contribution to community life, particularly with respect to its broader social and economic functions.

Chapter Thirteen

1. Benjamin Bloom, ed., *Taxonomy of Educational Objectives, Handbook I, Cognitive Domain* (New York: McKay, 1956); and David Krathwohl et al, *Taxonomy of Educational Objectives, Handbook 2, Affective Domain* (New York: McKay, 1964).

2. Paul Hunsicker and Guy Reiff, "Youth Fitness Report: 1958, 1965, 1975," *Journal of Physical Education and Recreation,* January 1977, pp. 31–32.

3. Charles A. Bucher, "National Adult Physical Fitness Survey: Some Implications," *Journal of Physical Education and Recreation,* January 1974, p. 25.

4. Matthew Guidry, "Programming for Physical Fitness," *Parks and Recreation,* August 1976, p. 25.

5. Fred V. Hein and Allan G. Ryan, "Contribution of Physical Activity to Human Well-Being," *Research Quarterly,* May 1960, p. 267.

6. Jean Mayer, "The Best Diet Is Exercise," *New York Times Magazine,* 25 April 1965, p. 34.

7. For a recent discussion of the exercise explosion and the health values of activity, see "Keeping Fit: America Tries to Shape Up," *Newsweek,* 23 May 1977, pp. 78–86.

8. Henry L. Taylor, "The Mortality and Morbidity of Coronary Heart Disease of Men in Sedentary and Physically Active Operations," in Seward C. Staley, ed., *Exercise and Fitness* (Chicago: The Athletic Institute, 1960), pp. 20–39.

9. Bayard Webster, "Running is Debated as Benefit to Heart," *New York Times,* 28 October 1976, p. 20.

10. D. A. Bailey et al, "A Current View of Canadian Cardiorespiratory Fitness," *Canadian Medical Association Journal,* 6 July 1974, pp. 25–30.

11. Chris Olert, "YMCA Puts Heart in Fitness Program," Staten Island *Advance,* 17 October 1976.

12. Nicholas Giannestras, cited in Charles Mangel, "How Good Are Organized Sports for Your Child?" *Look,* 1 June 1971, p. 61.

13. Melvin Thornton, "Competitive Preadolescent Sports" in Timothy Craig, ed., *The Humanistic and Mental Health Aspects of Sports, Exercise and Recreation* (Chicago: American Medical Association, 1975), pp. 18–20.

14. William C. Menninger, "Recreation and Mental Health," *Recreation,* November 1948, p. 343.

15. Paul Haun, "The Place for Recreation in Mental Health," *Parks and Recreation,* November 1966, p. 906.

16. Joseph B. Wolffe, "Recreation as Prophylactic and Therapeutic Measure in Diseases of the Cardiovascular System," *Recreation in Treatment Centers* (American Recreation Society Hospital Section), September 1965, p. 30.

17. James Jan-Tausch, *Suicide of Children,* 1960–1963, Report of New Jersey State Department of Education, Trenton, 1964, p. 3.

18. L. H. Richardson, "Relationship of the Use of Leisure Time in High School to Effectiveness in College," *School Activities,* May 1962, pp. 262–64.

19. Irving Babow and Sol Simkin, "The Leisure Activities and Social Participation of Mental Patients Prior to Hospitalization," *Therapeutic Recreation Journal,* 4th quarter 1971, pp. 161–67.

20. Nancy Mayer, "Leisure—or a Coronary," *Travel and Leisure,* December–January 1972, p. 36.

21. Frederick Lawson Hovde, quoted in Miami *Herald,* 6 December 1967.

22. "Happiness for a Distance Runner," New York *Times,* 11 August 1968, p. 6-S.

23. William N. Wallace, "Why Row? College Captains Provide Answer," New York *Times,* 26 April 1964, p. S-7.

24. James F. Short, Jr., and Fred L. Strodtbeck, *Group Process and Gang Delinquency* (Chicago: University of Chicago Press, 1965), pp. 161, 244–46.

25. Bruce C. Ogilvie and Thomas A. Tutko, "If You Want to Build Character, Try Something Else," *Psychology Today,* October 1971, p. 61.

26. Linden L. Nelson and Spencer Kagan, "Competition: The Star-Spangled Scramble," *Psychology Today,* September 1972, pp. 53–56.

27. Al Lundquist, "Is It Just the Winning that Counts?" *Recreation Canada,* April 1973, p. 40.

28. Joseph Durso, *The Sports Factory: An Investigation into College Sports* (New York: New York *Times* and Quadrangle Press, 1975), pp. 18–46.

29. Walter E. Schafer and J. Michael Armer, "Athletes Are Not Inferior Students," *Trans-Action,* November 1968, pp. 61–62.

30. Percy V. Williams, "School Dropouts," *NEA Journal,* February 1963, pp. 10–12.

31. Robert M. Wald and Roy A. Doty, "The Top Executive—A First Hand Profile," *Harvard Business Review,* July–August 1954, p. 48.

32. Harold Hodges, *Social Stratification* (Cambridge: Schendkamn, 1964), p. 167.

33. John W. Loy, "The Study of Sport and Social Mobility" (Paper presented at Sociology of Sport Symposium, University of Wisconsin, November, 1968), pp. 14–15.

34. William F. Whyte, *Street Corner Society* (Chicago: University of Chicago Press, 1943, 1955), pp. 98–104, of 1955 edition.

35. Phyllis Lee Levin, "Putting Muscles into Marks," *New York Times Magazine,* 28 November 1965, p. 118.

36. Ibid., pp. 118, 125.

37. See Newell C. Kephart and Barbara C. Godfrey, *Movement Patterns and Motor Education* (New York: Appleton-Century-Crofts, 1969); and Newell C. Kephart, *The Slow Learner in the Classroom* (Columbus, Ohio: C. E. Merrill, 1971).

38. J. N. Oliver, "The Effect of Physical Conditioning Exercises and Activities on the Mental Characteristics of Educationally Sub-Normal Boys," *British Journal of Educational Psychology,* 28(1958):155-65.

39. John Leo, "I.Q.'s of Underprivileged Infants Raised Dramatically by Tutors," New York *Times,* 26 December 1968, p. 24.

40. William K. Stevens, "Tests Indicate TV Program Improves Children's Skills," New York *Times,* 28 January 1970, p. 22.

41. Urie Bronfenbrenner, "The Split-level American Family," *Saturday Review,* 7 October 1967, p. 60.

42. James E. Coleman, *The Adolescent Society: The Social Life of the Teen-Ager and Its Impact on Education* (New York: Free Press, 1962), p. 4.

43. Quoted in Jessie Dolch, "Teen Age Group Pressures In the 1970's," *Today's Education* (National Education Association), November–December, 1973, p. 41.

44. Bronfenbrenner, "Split-level American Family," p. 63.

45. A. C. Nielsen Survey, cited in *Newsweek,* 21 February 1977, p. 63.

46. Caryl Rivers, "TV Violence: Is It Creating Greater Violence in Real Life?" New York *Times,* 16 May 1976, p. E-8.

47. See "Kids and TV Violence" in *Changing Times,* March, 1976.

48. Richard Flaste, "Survey Finds That Most Children Are Happy at Home but Fear World," New York *Times,* 2 March 1977, p. A-12.

49. Thomas Johnson, "Developing A Realistic Success Expectancy in Young Athletes," in *Humanistic and Mental Health Aspects of Sports,* p. 69.

50. James H. Duthie and Richard Moriarty, "Retreading Sports Organizations," *Humanistic and Mental Health Aspects of Sports,* pp. 66–68.

51. Martha Owens, "Every Child A Winner," *Humanistic and Mental Health Aspects of Sports,* p. 58.

52. See "Editorial: The Competitive Question," *Parks and Recreation,* August 1975, p. 15; and Walt Anderson, "Don't Just Sit There," *Human Behavior,* January 1974, pp. 56–59.

53. Peter Sargent, "A Modern Approach to Leisure—Non-Competitive Pools," *Recreation Canada,* 34 (March 1976): pp. 7, 11–15.

54. Richard Severo, "Survey Finds Young U. S. Workers Increasingly Dissatisfied and Frustrated," New York *Times,* 22 May 1974, p. 45.

55. Geoffrey Godbey and Stanley Parker, *Leisure Studies and Services: An Overview* (Philadelphia: W. B. Saunders, 1976), p. 91.

56. John Money, "Recreational—and Procreational—Sex," New York *Times,* 13 September 1975, p. 23.

57. Quoted in Donald Janson, "Campus Sex Found Vexing Students," New York *Times,* 20 May 1967, pp. 1, 41.

58. Nancy Hicks, "Drug Use Called up Among Youths," New York *Times,* 2 October 1975.

59. *New York Magazine,* 23 August 1976, p. 48.

60. John Corry, "Drugs a Growing Campus Problem," New York *Times,* 21 March 1966, p. 27.

61. Godfrey M. Hochbaum, "How Can We Teach Adolescents About Smoking, Drinking and Drug Abuse?" *Journal of Health, Physical Education and Recreation,* October, 1968, pp. 34–35.

62. Gallup Poll cited in "Drinking Troubles More Families," New York *Times,* 13 February 1977, p. 35.

63. Reported in "A Little Family Cheer," *Time,* 23 October 1967, p. 92.

64. United Press International, 7 January 1976: "Census Finds Adults Wed Later, Divorce Sooner."

65. "Games Singles Play," *Newsweek,* 16 July 1973, p. 52.

14

SOCIAL FUNCTIONS OF COMMUNITY RECREATION

This chapter examines the role of organized recreation service in meeting important social needs, first with respect to the overall community and next in terms of population groups which have special disabilities or problems.

Goals of Community Recreation

The specific goals of community recreation are:

1. To enrich the quality of life in the community setting by providing pleasurable and constructive leisure opportunities for residents of all ages, backgrounds, and socioeconomic classes;

2. To contribute directly to the healthy physical, emotional, and social growth and development of participants through a varied range of recreational experiences and involvement;

3. To improve the physical environment and to make the community a more attractive place to live by providing a well-designed and carefully maintained network of parks and other green spaces, as well as lakes and beaches, natural areas, historic sites, zoos, and botanical gardens;

4. To prevent or minimize antisocial or destructive uses of leisure, such as delinquent gang behavior, drug abuse, or alcoholism, by providing appealing and challenging programs under leadership that offer young people desirable and enjoyable alternatives;

5. To meet the needs of special populations, such as the mentally retarded or physically disabled, either by the provision of sound recreation activities in residential treatment settings, or by guaranteeing access to recreation programs—on an integrated basis, where possible—in the community setting;

6. To strengthen neighborhood and community life by providing residents with the opportunity to work on special projects or programs in a volunteer service role, thus promoting civic pride and morale and neighborhood unity;

7. To improve intergroup relations among residents of different ethnic, religious, or social backgrounds, and to promote desirable human values, including respect for the dignity and worth of all people, as well as tolerance for diversity and varying lifestyles;

8. To help strengthen and maintain the economic health of communities by stimulating the growth of industry, providing cultural, sports, and other attractions that promote spending in the community, and enhancing residential development by keeping neighborhoods attractive and stable;

9. To promote community safety by offering activities such as aquatics and sports in supervised settings, controlling or limiting high risk activities such as drag-racing or skateboarding, and teaching safety principles in areas of outdoor recreation such as riflery or boating;

10. To provide vocational training and counseling and summer or part-time work opportunities for the socially and economically disadvantaged, particularly youth in urban slums;

11. To enrich cultural life by presenting courses and special events in the fine and performing arts: arts and crafts, painting and sculpture, music, drama, dance, and film making;

12. To provide a release for tension, aggression, or hostility in crowded urban settings, and to channel antisocial drives and impulses into constructive and socially acceptable activities;

13. To promote concern for nature by maintaining environmental education centers and sponsoring or cosponsoring ecological cleanup or other conservation-oriented projects;

14. To meet the needs of people for ritual, ceremony, and a periodic release from social constraints and scheduled work, through holidays, mass celebrations, and traditional community events.[1]

Each of these major goals of community recreation is discussed in the pages that follow.

Enriching the Quality of Community Life

Recreation's most obvious value, in the eyes of most participants, is that it provides the opportunity for *fun!* This term may mean different things to different people, but

330

it generally implies pleasure gained from sports and games, social activities, cultural or creative pursuits, or a host of other leisure involvements. Beyond this important goal, however, recreation contributes significantly to the quality of life in the modern community by offering the opportunity for meaningful contact and social relationships with others.

Particularly in the large city, residents often find life to be marked by a frantic pace, intense competitiveness, and a pervasive feeling of loneliness. The casual interpersonal relationships of the metropolis cause problems of isolation and unhappiness; often individuals find themselves in the lonely state of anomie. Obviously, people need more meaningful ways to make contact with each other in the modern metropolis, in direct, open, and friendly group situations. Beyond this, MacLean points out a new humanistic awareness in modern society, in which people are more concerned about self-actualization, identity, self-expression, and the opportunity for each person to reach his or her human potential.

> In a . . . hurried, noise-bombarded, harried, compacted, technological society, the opportunity for identity, positive self-image, social interaction, creative expression, and even the intellectual or physical stimuli to maintain physical and mental health may come in exciting leisure opportunities or not at all.[2]

In this way, as well as through the other social functions of recreation described later in this chapter, recreation contributes significantly to the overall quality of community life.

Contributing to Healthy Development of Participants

Chapter 13 analyzed the important values of recreation with respect to the healthy growth and development of participants. One such value which should be emphasized here is recreation's role in maintaining sound mental health. Although some social scientists have pointed out the lack of empirical evidence of the value of recreation in reducing or preventing mental illness, one such critic, Herbert Gans, conceded that satisfying leisure activity provides physical and emotional relaxation, reduction of fatigue, restoration of energy, and avoidance of activity with ill effects. Gans concluded:

> If satisfying leisure behavior as I have defined it is part of the good life, it would follow that it is a constituent part of mental health. Therefore, the recreation facilities which help to make leisure satisfying are necessary for the maintenance of mental health.[3]

To those who question the lack of valid evidence of this relationship, it must be stressed that such evidence is lacking in many other areas of community service as well. In fields such as individual or group psychotherapy, vocational training, or social welfare, specially funded research projects have failed to demonstrate clear-cut, positive outcomes of service. Yet it is generally accepted that such programs have significant value.

Making the Community an Attractive Place to Live

Our cities suffer from a variety of ills; one authority has written:

> It becomes increasingly obvious that the major challenge of our time is to make our cities livable. . . . Noise, congestion, polluted air, and traffic are the bane of urban, and, indeed, suburban existence. Green areas provide an antidote. As man cannot live by bread alone, so he needs to be surrounded by more than stone and concrete.[4]

We can no longer permit our cities to be congested by cars, poisoned by smog, cut off from natural vistas, and scarred by the random disposal of industrial debris, ugly signs, auto junkyards, decaying railroad yards and the scattering of slum tenements in commercial and industrial districts. It is essential to protect and grace rivers with trees, shaded walkways, boating facilities and cafes; to eliminate auto traffic in selected areas by creating pedestrian shopping plazas with sculpture, water displays, and sitting areas; to open up increased numbers of malls, playgrounds, and vest-pocket parks; and to provide opportunities for both active and passive uses of leisure for all ages.

The task is to create an urban environment in which people can live fully and happily, a process in which city planners, architects, engineers, and housing officials must all share the responsibility. But it is the recreation and park professional who is chiefly concerned with the need for parks, play areas, and other outdoor sites that will enhance the visual environment and provide useful settings for play. There are many ways to introduce natural beauty into the urban environment: green areas bordering parkways, small parks in the middle of business districts, and large open plazas in urban renewal or industrial complex areas all help to make communities more livable. Beyond this, the preservation of the great historic parks in many cities is essential; through judicious use recognizing the need to protect their often fragile ecology, they may serve as centers for community celebrations or mass events. Protecting existing natural areas and opening up waterfronts, which are scenes of great potential beauty in many cities, are also priorities.

Preventing Antisocial Uses of Leisure

As indicated in earlier chapters of this text, a traditionally important goal of local recreation and park departments in the United States and Canada has been to prevent or minimize antisocial or destructive uses of leisure such as juvenile delinquency and drug or alcohol abuse by providing leadership in appealing and challenging programs that offer young people attractive alternatives.

Since the early decades of the twentieth century, it has been widely accepted that vigorous group activities—particularly sports and games—are helpful in burning up the excess energy of youth, diverting their aggressive or antisocial drives, and keeping them off the streets and away from exposure to criminal influences.

Sociologists who began to examine the nature of youth gangs in large cities raised questions about the value of recreation as an antidelinquency measure. The researchers proposed more complex theories of juvenile delinquency, few of which identified the lack of recreation opportunity as a primary cause of deviant behavior. Nonetheless, most public and voluntary agencies that provide youth recreation programs continue to claim the reduction of juvenile delinquency as one of their primary contributions.

To determine the validity of this claim, it is necessary to define juvenile delinquency and to understand its causes. The concept itself is vague and ambiguous. Local jurisdictions vary widely in their definitions of delinquent acts, which may range from truancy, smoking, turning on water hydrants, or cursing, to more serious acts such as burglary, arson, or assault. Generally, juvenile delinquency is regarded as a form of deviant and antisocial behavior by youth, usually involving sustained or habitual defiance toward authority. In the late 1960s, the Task Force Report of the President's Commission on Law Enforcement and Administration of Justice described delinquency as the "single most pressing and threatening aspect of the crime problem in the United States," with one of every nine children being referred to juvenile courts before his eighteenth birthday. However, the report indicated that most juvenile infractions were in the area of property offenses:

> The public image of a vicious, violent juvenile population producing a seemingly steady increase in violent crime is not substantiated by the evidence available. . . . Violence appears neither as a dominant preoccupation of city gangs nor as a dominant form of criminal activity . . . even among those toughest of gang members.[5]

By the mid-1970s, this picture had changed. According to a major study carried out by the Center for Criminal Justice at the Harvard Law School, violence by youth gangs has grown steadily in such major cities of the United States as Detroit, Los Angeles, San Francisco, New York, and Chicago, with gang members increasingly attacking ordinary citizens. The report indicated that the "sophisticated weaponry in the gangs of the 1970s far surpasses anything known in the past" and that gang members often had automatic rifles, shotguns, and finely tooled pistols, rather than the crude zip-guns or bicycle chains of the past.[6] Another study in 1976, conducted under a grant from the Law Enforcement Assistance Association of the Federal government, indicated a sharp rise in schoolhouse crime, including a virtual reign of terror, frequent attacks on teachers, and widespread blackmailing or extortion of nongang members.[7]

Causes of Juvenile Delinquency

There are two schools of thought regarding the fundamental causes of juvenile delinquency, one that is primarily a psychological or psychogenic problem, and the other that its causes are sociological or cultural.

Psychological View

In the psychological view, delinquent behavior (referring not to occasional antisocial acts, but to habitual patterns of antisocial and criminal activity) is regarded basically as an attribute of the child's personality, rather than the social environment. Proponents of this position point out that even in high delinquency neighbor-

333

hoods, some children manage to maintain healthy social attitudes and live constructive lives. Healy and Bronner maintain that strong ties between parents and children can create stable and integrated personalities with socially positive values and the ability to resist the temptations of crime and antisocial gang affiliation.[8] Other investigators have developed psychological classifications of juvenile offenders which indicate that the more serious ones have relatively weak ego controls, are highly insecure, and have strong tendencies toward aggressive and hostile behavior.

The psychological approach assumes that juvenile delinquency is caused by early childhood experiences within the family; however, evidence indicates that later environmental factors have an important effect.

Sociological View

This position holds that juvenile delinquency today is a cultural problem whose real roots are in the society itself. Research has clearly shown that delinquency is highest in neighborhoods marked by slum housing, poor schools, broken or unstable homes, the lack of desirable adult models, and limited opportunity for social advancement. Proponents of this view reject the notion that juvenile delinquents are necessarily disturbed, and suggest instead that they deliberately reject established social values, obtaining reinforcement from peers within their immediate subculture which is stronger and more real than the overall culture.

Some sociologists, such as Cohen and Miller, suggest that the antisocial behavior of juvenile gangs represents hostility toward accepted middle-class values, and the substitution of typical lower-class values—respect for toughness, masculinity, and physical prowess, and a tendency to accept fate, rather than one's own actions as the determining factor in one's life.[9]

The idea that the frustrated aspirations of lower-class youth account for much gang behavior was developed most fully by Cloward and Ohlin. They established a typology of gangs, including the *fighting gang,* hostile and aggressive, deriving status from making war on the community and on other gangs; the *criminal gang,* involved in deviant behavior for financial gain through racketeering, theft, and the sale of illegal items; and the *retreatist gang,* which is involved with drugs, sex, and alcohol, and withdraws from actual conflict except when necessary for survival or to achieve an important objective.[10]

Role of Recreation

Each of these theories tends to ignore the role of recreation in the development of delinquent patterns of behavior even though a number of investigators through the years have identified play as one of the ways in which delinquency becomes established as a way of life. Tannenbaum located the beginning of the alienation of gang youth from societal controls and values in the random play activities of youngsters.

> In the very beginning, the definition of the situation by the young delinquent may be in the form of play, adventure, excitement, interest, mischief, fun. Breaking windows, annoying people . . . playing truant—all are forms of play, adventure, excitement.[11]

Cohen points out that much juvenile crime is committed "for the hell of it," entirely apart from considerations of gain or profit.

There is no accounting for the effort expended and the danger run in stealing things which are often discarded, destroyed or casually given away. . . . Unquestionably, most delinquents are from the more . . . "underprivileged" classes, and . . . many things are stolen because they are intrinsically valued. However . . . stealing is not merely an alternative means to the acquisition of objects otherwise difficult of attainment. Can we then account for this stealing by describing it as another form of recreation, play or sports?[12]

Similarly, Whyte's study of Boston lower-class youth quotes a leading gang member's description of fighting among gangs in his neighborhood: "There was a lot of mutual respect. . . . We didn't go out to kill them. We didn't want to hurt anybody. It was just fun."[13] Such explanations of the playlike nature of much juvenile gang activity are disputed by many sociologists. Block and Neiderhoff concluded that juvenile crime was almost invariably committed for utilitarian purposes and concrete gain. Short and Strodtbeck wrote:

Weapons and the intent of gang conflict are more lethal, and "kicks" more addicting. Theoretically, delinquency is seen as rooted less in community tradition and "fun," and more in frustration and protest or in the serious business of preparing for manhood as conceived by the gang members, including the "mysterious and powerful underworlds of organized crime."[14]

The sociological explanation that juvenile crime stems primarily from economic motives fails to recognize, however, that only a portion of today's delinquents are lower-class or minority-group urban youth; considerable amount of crime is committed by unaffiliated teen-agers, many of middle- and upper-class backgrounds in wealthier suburbs. Statistics in recent years indicate an increase in amateur shoplifting, auto theft, and vandalism. Thrill seeking and joy riding are primary reasons for car theft by juveniles, and vandalism is obviously motivated by reasons other than economic gain. In addition to such forms of delinquent behavior, many other acts reveal a search for excitement on the part of modern teen-agers. Drag-racing or pranks involving desperate risks (like playing "chicken" and risking head-on collisions on highways or in tunnels) are examples of such thrill seeking stunts.

Recreation's Role in Antidelinquency Programs

Youth programs which offer challenge and excitement might well fulfill the needs which motivate antisocial or criminal behavior of many youth. A research study of athletics in several midwestern high schools has demonstrated that only 7 percent of the boys who had participated for at least one full year in an interscholastic sport were apprehended for delinquent behavior, compared with 17 percent of non-athletes.[15] It seems likely that the excitement, the physical risk, the required strength, courage, and competitive elements of sport satisfy many of the impulses that among nonathletic teen-agers are channeled into delinquent activity.

Few studies have attempted to assess systematically the effect of organized recreation services on delinquency prone neighborhoods, chiefly because of the difficulty in isolating recreation as a factor when numerous other influences, both good and bad, are also at work. It is possible, however, to give some illustrations of its observed influence.

Effect of Recreation Programs

In New York City in the late 1950s and early 1960s, youth gang activity reached a new and virulent high. The rate of juvenile delinquency over a ten-year period was consistently twice as high in East Harlem as in the entire city. A major youth and adult center, the Wagner Center, was opened in this neighborhood by the Board of Education in January, 1959, with a new wing built adjacent to the school to provide needed recreation facilities. Of the thirty-five hundred members of the Wagner Youth and Adult Center, eighteen hundred were teen-agers. Through careful work with Italian, black, and Puerto Rican gang leaders, rules governing behavior in the center were developed, and a council was established to enforce them. Within a year, all eleven fighting gangs in East Harlem were disbanded, and no new gangs replaced them. Two hundred and fifty boys who had been gang members were now free of such affiliations, and the juvenile delinquency arrest rate in the area declined from 88.8 to 70 per 1,000 within a single year.[16]

One might question whether it was recreation as such that caused these results. Gans writes:

> It is true that playground programs or community center activities sometimes convert a delinquent into a pillar of the community. When this happens, however, I suspect that it is not due to the facility itself, but to the therapeutic talents of a leader who provides the delinquent with a surrogate father or brother; or to the existence of a group that offers him enough support to convince him that society is not always his enemy. This explains to me the success of the gang workers who have transformed fighting gangs into baseball teams. Although the surroundings in which this transformation often takes place may be recreational, this does not mean that recreation is a causal factor.[17]

Of course it is not the facility itself, or recreation as an abstract phenomenon, that helps to reduce delinquent behavior; however, recreation often attracts young gang members who would otherwise not attend centers or participate in programs or services that they perceived as efforts to change or improve them. When youth do participate in recreation programs, it becomes possible for adults to develop relationships with them, to assist them directly or refer them to other agencies or services, to help them enlarge their life perspectives and ultimately to become contributing and valuable members of society.

Many recreation departments, however, disclaim responsibility for working with problem youth. Often they bar gang members from their programs because they find them disruptive or because they discourage the participation of others. Similarly, many hard-core delinquents are unwilling to join public or voluntary agency programs because of the restraints they impose.

Those agencies that seek to attract and involve delinquent or potentially delinquent youth must adopt special methods. Youth workers are generally detached from organized programs and go out into the street, neighborhood hangouts, or other places where problem youth may be found. In Washington, D.C., where the Recreation Department has sponsored a Roving Leaders Program since 1956, street workers are responsible for several hundred young gang members and for many other youth who have sporadic associations with gangs. These roving leaders work closely with other community agencies to assist their clients with legal, vocational, family, or academic problems. Although recreation is not their primary concern, they help to organize trips, sports events, and other recreational involvements for gang youth.

New Concept of Recreation's Role

A thoughtful statement of recreation's role in working with problem youth was presented by Bertram Beck, executive director of the Henry Street Settlement in New York City. Beck suggests that the traditional view of recreation as nonpurposeful activity, sharply differentiated from work, is no longer meaningful for youth in urban slums, who are seeking to discover and assume adult roles. Simply "getting young people off the street" or "giving them something to burn up their energy" is not sufficient to meet their needs. Beck urges that work and play be combined to serve the total developmental goals of youth, and that recreational experiences be designed to help youth systematically explore their environment and develop the attitudes and competence that can help them get and keep jobs. The recreational system itself can provide jobs and training experiences for youth.

> The recreational system should be integrated with . . . educational, cultural, and community welfare facilities. The roots of organized recreation in child's play have been destroyed. It must now strive to mix work, learning, and play to serve both social ends and the purpose of self development. Only then can it be an effective instrument in socializing the young and preventing delinquency.[18]

A final aspect of the relationship between recreation and juvenile delinquency is the development of programs in custodial or correctional institutions for youth. Recreation in such institutions should be a means of keeping morale high, substituting constructive leisure interests and skills to supplant negative ones, building more positive social values, and helping participants develop favorable and constructive relationships with staff members. In institutions that serve emotionally disturbed youth, recreation is particularly important in rehabilitation. Disturbed youth who enter treatment centers are often unable to play. Redl and Wineman write:

> It is . . . important that the institution as a whole and every person in it are openly and explicitly accepting of children having "fun." . . . By their very definition, our hyperaggressive and extremely destructive children are in need of a good deal of program activity which involves the happy discharge of surplus aggression, diversion of destructiveness into excited large-muscle activity.[19]

Such activities provide informal situations in which children receive the affection and respect which helps them begin to form bonds of confidence and trust with adults. Gradually, disturbed and delinquent youth learn to exercise self-discipline, to gain a sense of their own autonomy, and to place trust in others; all these are purposes of recreation programs in such remedial settings.

Unfortunately, many correctional institutions for youth have only minimal recreation programs. They are extremely expensive to operate, costing in some states as much as $20,000 to $25,000 per child each year. The cost in one residential agency for young drug abusers was $45,000 per year, per client. Clearly, there would be a tremendous saving—in both human and financial terms—if youth services in the community itself were fully supported so that institutionalization of youth might become less necessary.

Needs of Special Populations: Therapeutic Recreation Service

Another critically important social function of organized recreation service in modern society is to meet the needs of special populations, through what has come to be known as therapeutic recreation service. Increasingly, recreation has gained recognition in the United States and Canada as a health-related service which has important implications for both the general population and for those who have physical, mental, or social disabilities. Luther Terry, former Surgeon General of the U. S. Public Health Service, confirms the value of recreation in this respect. He writes of health as

> the measure of man's capacity for coping with or adapting effectively to the physical, emotional, intellectual, social and economic demands of his environment. . . . Meaningful activity is important to health throughout the life span. In order to mature—physically, intellectually, emotionally and socially—a child must be exposed to appropriate stimuli. And so too must the adult if he is to remain at his peak. Today, people are increasingly involved in leisure activity. . . . More and more people have time on their hands. Moreover, the injudicious use of leisure time is a characteristic feature of both maladjusted teen-agers and adults, and of retired, elderly persons. Too often, because of ignorance, indifference, or inertia we are faced with the time-consuming and difficult task of reestablishing a human capacity which need never have been lost. Recreation has an important—and an increasing—role in rehabilitation.[20]

All people need diversified recreational opportunity. Those who suffer from disability, however, frequently find difficulty in meeting these needs in constructive and varied ways, partly because serious physical handicaps limit the potential range of participation. Much of the recreation deprivation of the disabled, however, is caused by society's failure to assist them to engage in activity to the full extent of their potential; many communities and organizations do not make the design adaptations that enable disabled persons to use recreational facilities fully. Some recreation and park agencies actually bar disabled persons from their programs, believing that the disabled would require specialized leadership which the agency could not afford. The stigma that society has attached to disability often causes administrators to fear that the presence of blind, retarded, or orthopedically handicapped participants would be distasteful to the public at large, who might then cease to use the facilities. Sometimes parents or relatives shelter the disabled excessively, and often the disabled person's lack of skill or fear of rejection by others may limit his recreational participation.

This picture has been rapidly changing. Increasingly, recreation profession-

338

als and others concerned with the needs of the disabled in modern society have fought to improve the opportunities open to them, in both institutional and community settings. Martin writes:

> As with other minority groups in our society, the disabled are becoming increasingly militant in their demands for conditions which enhance the potential for the satisfaction of basic human needs within a framework which emphasizes freedom of choice and individualization of leisure service design. The "take it or leave it" attitude which has characterized many administrative approaches to the provision of recreation and leisure services for the disabled in the past will become increasingly difficult to maintain in the future.[21]

Geddes supports this view, pointing to a wave of legislation that has compelled the schools in particular to provide enriched services for impaired children and youth, and that has led to increased programs of "mainstreaming," "normalization," and "deinstitutionalization." Parents, advocates for persons with handicapping conditions, and the disabled themselves have pressed for fuller opportunities in fields such as physical education and recreation.[22]

The effort to upgrade existing programs has been particularly evident in Canada. A national study of recreation services for the disabled, supported by Recreation Canada, and conducted by Peter Witt of the University of Ottawa, revealed burgeoning interest in improving recreation services for the handicapped at all levels. Witt found that such organizations as the Canadian Association for the Mentally Retarded, the Canadian Rehabilitation Council for the Disabled, and the Canadian Mental Health Association have all taken vigorous organizational, philosophical, or leadership steps in recent years to meet this growing need.

> At the Provincial and local levels, some of the affiliates of these organizations, chapters of the YM/YWCA and Municipal Departments of Recreation and/or Parks have begun to take the initiative for improving their recreation services for the handicapped. In addition, many of the institutions throughout Canada have begun to increase their recreational services.[23]

Recreation in Treatment Programs

A special function of recreation with respect to groups with disability is its use as a therapeutic or rehabilitative technique. Originally such services were provided primarily in hospitals, and the field itself was known as "hospital recreation"; more recently, the term "therapeutic recreation service" has become widely accepted, both by its own practitioners and by medical authorities. A publication of the National Center for Health Statistics of the Public Health Service defines the term:

> Therapeutic recreation is the specific use of recreational activity in the care, treatment and rehabilitation of ill, handicapped and aged persons with a directed program.[24]

339

Recreation is not usually a specific therapy on a one-to-one basis under medical prescription with the specific purpose of curing illness. The fact that many clients of therapeutic recreation are not ill, but rather disabled, means that they require recreation not as a form of treatment, but as an important service in their lives. The emphasis today is on recreation's role in facilitating healthy social interaction and creative experience, and making life more enjoyable and rewarding, thus contributing to rehabilitation in the broadest sense. This function has been broadly described by Dr. E. Mansell Pattison, in a passage dealing with therapeutic methods in psychiatric institutions:

> The thrust of milieu therapy is not to unlock specific psychodynamic conflicts, but rather to provide integrating, guiding, rehabilitating social experiences. This begins with those socializing activities that the most regressed patients can participate in, then on to social activities requiring more ego control and personal-relatedness, and finally to reality-oriented social functions that are part and parcel of every day living. Seen in this perspective, the adjunctive therapies are experiences in socialization and social interaction. The task of the adjunctive therapist is not that of individual therapist or extension thereof, but that of a social system specialist.[25]

This suggests that the primary purpose of recreation for the disabled, whether hospitalized or not, is to promote social integration and rehabilitation, to make life more rewarding, to prevent further disability, and to help patients or clients make the fullest possible use of their existing resources. Janet Pomeroy, who has directed an outstanding program for over twenty-five years in San Francisco with the severely multihandicapped, states that it is not possible to meet the leisure needs of the disabled without recognizing their other needs as well.

> The recreation agency is frequently the first and often the only agency with which the handicapped become involved. They bring with them a variety of problems and needs that are not the responsibility of recreation. However, recreation personnel can work closely with social agencies , in helping participants and their families to find the services they need. In turn, these agencies can provide valuable consultation services to the recreation staff, to the mutual benefit of the handicapped.[26]

This chapter now considers the specific functions of recreation with five special populations in both community and institutional settings: (1) the mentally retarded, (2) the mentally ill, (3) the physically handicapped, (4) the aging, and (5) the socially deviant.

Recreation Services for the Mentally Retarded

Mentally retarded persons are children and adults who are significantly impaired in their ability to learn and to adapt to the demands of society. The U. S. Department of Labor has estimated that about 125,000 retarded children are born each year, and that approximately 6 million Americans suffer from some degree of mental retardation. Some 30 million Americans, the families of the retarded, are closely affected by this problem.

It has been estimated that for every mentally retarded child enrolled in a special education class, there are four retarded children who are not receiving special aid. Play in particular, which should be a normal aspect of development, is often lacking in the lives of retarded children. Stein writes that

> mentally retarded boys and girls do not play spontaneously or innovate as normal children; they have to be taught to play whether the play be individual, parallel, or group. Many of the motor skills and abilities basic to play and recreation that most normal children learn from association and play with the gang on the block must be taught to the retarded.[27]

With the exception of a limited number of programs in state schools or similar institutions for the retarded, comparatively little attention was paid to the recreational and social needs of the retarded until the early 1960s. In 1962, the President's Panel on Mental Retardation urged that local communities, in cooperation with Federal and state agencies, expand services for this population. Many public departments and voluntary organizations have since initiated special programs for the retarded, often with assistance from the Joseph P. Kennedy Foundation, the National Association for Retarded Children, and the American Association for Health, Physical Education, and Recreation. Such programs are especially important because the majority of mentally retarded children and youth are not institutionalized, but live with their families.

Ramm writes:

> The retarded child living at home has little recreation opportunity. He may make friends with the children in his special class at school, but unlike the normal children who can play with their school chums in the neighborhood after school hours, retarded children are transported from their homes in different parts of town and have few friends in their own neighborhoods. A similar situation exists with mentally retarded adults who work in a centrally located sheltered workshop, or who do not work a' all. These people are victims of enforced leisure. They have a six-to-eight hour time block each weekday and more on weekends or holidays during which little or no activity is available to them. Many just sit and watch television.[28]

Many community-based programs are intended not only to provide pleasurable leisure activities for the retarded, but also to assist in their total development. Avedon described several of the specific goals of such programs: (1) to provide recreation education and information which help develop the individual's capacity for meeting his own leisure needs; (2) to use recreation to improve general health, minimize atypical appearance, and modify behavior to help retardates become more accepted in community settings; (3) to help individuals learn and practice useful recreational and social skills; (4) to counsel retarded youth and adults about recreational resources in the community, and arrange opportunities for involvement; (5) to act as a liaison between the community and the retarded individual and his family, to promote acceptance of the retarded in community programs and facilities;

341

and (6) to coordinate communitywide efforts to meet the overall needs of the retarded.[29]

A number of studies have explored the value of recreation and physical activity for the mentally retarded. Several research studies involving adapted physical education and recreation with the mentally retarded in Pennsylvania institutions have been successful in expanding their leisure interests,[30] reducing inappropriate or disruptive behavior,[31] and improving motor performance.[32] Community-based programs have also been successful in expanding the recreational participation, ability to persevere, and self-esteem of mentally retarded participants.[33] Such efforts are extremely important in improving the ability of retarded persons to live reasonably independent and satisfying lives in the community at large.

Recreation and the Mentally Ill

For the past several decades, recreation has been an accepted area of service in many mental hospitals throughout the United States and Canada. In some, it has been used primarily as a form of diversion to relieve boredom and improve patient morale; in others, it has been provided on the basis of medical prescription to help the patient in the resocialization process and the development of leisure skills and interests. A regional survey of recreation services in psychiatric hospitals during the early 1970s indicated the following major goals (Table 14-1).

Table 14-1.

Rank Order of Goals of Recreation in Psychiatric Hospitals[34]

1.	To help patients become involved in reality situations.
2.5	To help withdrawn patients become resocialized.
2.5	To provide emotional release and interests outside self.
4.	To improve the self-concept of patients.
5.	To create patient awareness of leisure needs, and improve motivation for participation.
6.5	To provide information useful for diagnosis or treatment.
6.5	To provide release for hostility and aggression.
8	To keep patient morale high.
9	To teach skills useful for leisure, after discharge from hospital.

Note: The second and third objectives were equally ranked, and are expressed as 2.5; the sixth and seventh objectives were equally ranked, and are expressed as 6.5.

Today, the provision of recreation services in programs serving the mentally ill has been radically altered by changing concepts and techniques of diagnosis and treatment. The modern concept of psychiatric care is based on the local community mental health center, which ties together such relevant psychiatric resources as out-patient clinics, day centers, halfway houses, in-patient services in general hospitals, and satellite programs operated by larger psychiatric hospitals.

New treatment methods—especially the use of tranquilizers and other powerful new drugs—have brought about these drastic changes and have created an approach to mental health care that stresses

342

a continuity of care from the point at which an illness is identified to the time when the former patient completely resumes his place in the community. The day is not far off when communities across the country will be prepared to offer a spectrum of services designed to support returned patients and also to prevent many persons from ever having to be hospitalized.[35]

In states such as Illinois and Massachusetts, the number of in-patients in mental hospitals has steadily declined, while the population of out-patient departments has increased tenfold. Emphasis is on voluntary admission and commitment, allowing patients to assume greater responsibility for their own management. Psychiatric patients are more frequently admitted to local general hospitals, rather than to large, distant psychiatric hospitals. A crucial aspect of such programs is the provision of community-based mental health centers with recreation and other related services that help patients make the transition from the hospital to the community.

Role of Leisure Counseling

An important element in assisting the patient's return to the community is the development of leisure counseling (often called "recreation" counseling). Individual and group discussion or counseling sessions are provided to meet the following objectives: (1) to assist patients to understand the role of leisure and recreation in their own lives, and to develop positive and constructive attitudes toward them; (2) to help them strengthen their existing interests and ties to family, friends, and community recreation programs; (3) to introduce them to new individuals and groups in the community; and (4) to mobilize community efforts to ease the transition of psychiatric patients back into community life, and help them become part of the mainstream of activity. Leisure counseling is not a highly theoretical process; McDowell points out that it is directly concerned with bringing about behavioral change, and may consist of both informal and highly formal or structured approaches.[36]

Gunn defines leisure counseling as a "helping" process which includes such stages as assessment of need and current status, determination of goals, program planning, referral, and evaluation. She writes that it may use

> specific verbal facilitation techniques to promote and increase self-awareness, awareness of leisure attitudes, values, and feelings, as well as the development of decision making and problem solving skills related to leisure participation with self, others, and environmental factors.[37]

Obviously, this approach is heavily dependent on the willingness and capability of community recreation departments and voluntary agencies to offer recreation programs in which the disabled and the mentally ill may participate. Haun commented on the artificial barrier that often prevents disabled persons—including the mentally ill—from taking part in community programs serving the so-called normal population:

> I have been in turn outraged, depressed and bewildered by . . . the baseless anxiety of municipal, county and state program directors at the

343

prospect of broadening their services to include, not just an arbitrarily chosen segment, but the entire residential population for which they do have responsibility. . . . I have been equally unsettled at the hesitancies and fears expressed by line personnel in playground work, in camping, physical education, and parks, at the prospect of developing programs for all comers.[38]

Haun suggests that recreation workers must learn to consider service to the disabled as a vital part of their total spectrum of activities. Even today, comparatively few public recreation and park departments have developed cooperative relationships with mental health centers to facilitate the transition of discharged or out-patients into their programs. It is an unfortunate commentary that in many states, although hospital populations have been reduced and community-based living facilities such as subsidized hotels or rooming houses have been established for psychiatric patients, the mental health department has often failed to provide these individuals with badly needed continuing rehabilitative programs, including recreation. Many states provide patients with medication, welfare payments, and a minimum of group psychotherapy, but do not provide other educational, vocational, or recreational services. In some communities, psychiatric patients are placed in "dumping ground" neighborhoods where they form a population of "floaters," unable to resume their former life styles, family responsibilities, or jobs, and bitterly resented by the permanent residents around them.

Recreation Service and the Physically Disabled

Another major segment of the population includes those with serious physical disability, such as amputees, paraplegics, the blind or partially sighted, and the deaf. According to a recent publication of the National Society for Park Resources, there are over 67 million Americans who have limiting conditions that require special consideration in the design of outdoor recreation facilities.[39] Too often, such individuals are prevented from enjoying a full range of satisfying leisure activity, not only by their actual impairment, but also by society's unwillingness to encourage or assist their participation and by poorly designed facilities that prevent or limit access and use by the disabled. According to the Bureau of Outdoor Recreation,

> great numbers of disabled persons are not receiving the benefit of our nation's recreation resources. The severity of their disabilities, architectural barriers, nonacceptance by society, and slowness of the recreation profession to adjust its programs and facilities to their needs all have contributed to a serious lack of opportunity.[40]

Widespread efforts are being made today to provide full access to recreation facilities for persons with limited mobility who require wheelchairs, crutches, or braces. The National Park Service and Forest Service have redesigned many parks, modifying steps, curbs, doors, and other points of access or convenience to permit use by the handicapped. Special boating and fishing ramps, wading and swimming pools, outdoor theaters, and cooking facilities have also been designed for this purpose. Trails for the blind, with Braille signs or tape-recorded messages at intervals provide access to natural settings. There are also specially designed nature trails for the deaf.

344

The overall goal of such efforts is to encourage "mainstreaming"—integrating the disabled into the general population of recreation participants. Gunn describes this process:

> Mainstreaming is both a process and a goal—the process of selecting methods of integrating people and programs that are as close to a typical way of doing things as possible, and the goal of enabling handicapped people to live and appear in ways which distinguish them as little as possible from the rest of society. The principles of mainstreaming do not mean that handicapped people will be made "normal" but that they will have every opportunity to fit into society and that society will accept them.[41]

Considerable progress has been made in designing special facilities to serve the disabled. A number of cities have designed special playgrounds or small parks for this purpose; associations and rehabilitation centers serving the physically disabled have also developed such facilities, particularly for children. Georgia, for example, has a state park designed solely for use by the disabled, situated within Fort Yargo State Park and built with partial funding from the Department of the Interior.

The first municipally sponsored recreation center specially planned, designed, and publicly financed for use by the mentally and physically handicapped, was constructed in 1976 in Washington, D.C. Sponsored by the District of Columbia's Recreation Department, this $2 million structure includes a swimming pool, auditorium-gymnasiums, arts and crafts shops, day-care centers, and an outdoor play and exploration area—all carefully designed for use by children and adults who are in wheelchairs, blind, or otherwise disabled. Such special facilities are intended not to separate the disabled from the general population, but to provide an environment in which they will learn recreational skills and gain confidence that will facilitate their moving into fully integrated situations.

In addition to constructing appropriate facilities, many voluntary agencies serving the blind, deaf, orthopedically disabled, or those with other physical impairments offer a wide range of special programs, which include trips and outings. More and more professional travel agencies have begun to charter flights to foreign countries for those who must use wheelchairs, crutches, or braces.

Sports Programs for the Physically Disabled

Too often, both the general public and recreation professionals have "tunnel vision" which prevents them from understanding the full potential of the physically disabled. Few people know, for example, that there are many blind skiers who, with a companion skiing close by and calling out directions, are able to schuss expertly down steep slopes! People are also likely to be dumbfounded at seeing a one-legged skier. These are only two examples of how the disabled have overcome their disabilities within a high risk sports activity.

Wheelchair sports in particular have become extremely popular, largely because of the stimulus provided when thousands of veterans of World War II returned home as single or double amputees or with paraplegia caused by spinal injuries. The National Wheelchair Athletic Association and the National Wheelchair Games, held annually in the United States, have enabled thousands of persons with serious disability to take part in wheelchair basketball, track and field events,

345

and numerous other forms of athletic competition. Since 1960, international wheelchair games, the "Paralympics," have been held annually at Stoke Mandeville, England, with special competitions held each fourth year immediately following the Olympics, in the Olympics' host city. In 1976 seventeen hundred handicapped athletes from seventy countries competed in a special Olympiad in Canada. Some of their accomplishments are amazing: a totally blind sprinter from Poland ran the 100 meters in 11.5 seconds, and a California paraplegic bench-pressed 562 pounds.[42]

In addition to these special sports programs for the disabled, many communities or other recreation agencies are making determined efforts to involve them in integrated programs as well. In many cases, disabled persons learn skills and confidence in special programs which assist them in entering other community facilities and programs.

Despite these growing efforts, however, some recreation agencies make no attempt to serve the disabled, or even actively bar them from participation. A recent study of camps in California showed, for example, that a majority of private and agency camps did not serve handicapped persons.[43] However, among the camps that did serve the disabled, the common practice (71 percent) was to provide integrated settings, an approach favored by the majority of respondents.

In an April, 1977, White House Conference on Handicapped Individuals, recreation programs for the disabled was one of the important opportunity areas dealt with in workshops and forums. National hearings on the recreation needs of handicapped persons were held in 1976, sponsored by the Architectural and Transportation Barriers Board, in cooperation with the U. S. Department of Interior, National Recreation and Park Association, and the President's Committee on Employment of the Handicapped. It seems clear that this social value of recreation and park programs will be increasingly important in the years ahead.

Recreation Services and the Aging

The aging population is clearly an important area of concern in American society today, and poses a major challenge for organized recreation service. In 1900 only 3.1 million, or one out of every twenty-five Americans, were over sixty-five. Thanks to modern medicine and lengthened life expectancy, in 1977, there were 23 million persons over sixty-five, more than one out of every ten. Predictions are that by the turn of the century over 30 million Americans will be over sixty-five, with about two-thirds of this number in the over-seventy-five age group that consumes the bulk of health, hospital, and nursing services.

We tend to oversimplify the concept of aging, and to assume that all older persons are very much alike. Far from this, they vary widely in economic, physical, and social status, and their ability to accept the changes thrust upon them by the process of aging. Service to older persons should therefore consider the following four major periods:

Preretirement

During the period between ages fifty and sixty-five, economic burdens related to child rearing, education, and home furnishing and improvement generally lessen.

During this period thoughtful preparation should be made for retirement; some countries, such as Sweden, have instituted plans to permit people to gradually decrease their working hours during the period from age sixty to seventy, by working part-time and collecting a partial retirement pension—thus easing the transition into retirement.

Postretirement

When work responsibilities are ended, many persons experience problems related to the increase of free time and sharp decrease in income. For many, the social contacts and sense of importance derived from work come to an end, and the need is to find new associations and commitments. Those who are financially well-off frequently enter retirement communities such as Rossmoor-Walnut Creek in California, Heritage Village in Connecticut, or Sun City, Arizona, which usually provide extensive facilities and organized programs. Rossmoor, for example, has some 160 clubs, ranging from groups that gather for bridge, pinochle, or square dancing, to philanthropic groups that make toys for mentally retarded children, or professional associations of former teachers or engineers.

> These clubs help to integrate newcomers into the community. They also help structure people's time, giving them some place to be or something to do at fixed hours and days. This can be particularly useful for men accustomed to going to an office, but it is also a boon for their wives. . . . Not only does it get the men out of their way, but it also helps preserve the distinction between male and female roles, which often gets blurred with retirement. A surprisingly large number of Rossmoor's clubs are designated as being for men only or for women only.[44]

Transitional Period

During the transitional period between the mid-seventies and mid-eighties, many persons experience a marked physical decline, become more socially isolated, and enter homes for the aged. Even though there is an inevitable loss of mobility and other physical capacities, however, major organic damage need not occur, and many older persons continue to function extremely well, both emotionally and socially.

Later Years

The remaining years of life tend to be marked by increasing disability, often with serious physical or intellectual incapacity. Although some older persons in their late eighties or nineties continue to be active participants in community life, the majority become increasingly dependent, and often enter treatment or custodial institutions.

For increasing numbers of older people in modern society, the years after sixty-five are a time of isolation and economic insecurity. John Gardner, formerly Secretary of Health, Education, and Welfare, commented for a Congressional committee on aging, "Our society is now designed to put most older people on the

347

shelf . . . to deal them out of the game." The isolation of the aging during the second half of the twentieth century has been accentuated by major changes in family structure. Most Americans no longer live in closely knit family groups. Married couples rarely continue to live with their parents, and even young single adults typically strike out on their own as soon as they are economically independent. Homes with three-generation extended families have vanished almost as completely as the horse and buggy. There are many communities in America in which there are almost no older persons, just as there are many sections of older cities in particular in which there are large numbers of elderly people—often living alone in residential hotels, institutions for aging persons, or S.R.O.s (single-room-occupancy units).

Many older persons today tend to withdraw from meaningful contact and involvement with others. One group of sociologists explained this phenomenon by a theory of disengagement, viewing withdrawal from social interaction as a normal process of aging. The "disengagement" theorists held that gradual withdrawal from meaningful human contacts and involvement was a necessary and inevitable process preceding death which the aging chose for themselves, and which others should accept. This theory has generally been rejected, and most authorities believe today that older people do not withdraw by choice, but because of a feeling of exclusion.

Effects of Aging

Many people tend to view the process of aging with fear and aversion, and to see older persons in stereotyped and inaccurate ways. For example, it is widely believed that aging is necessarily accompanied by a sharp decline in sexual interest and capability. Studies reveal, however, that substantial numbers of persons in their seventies and eighties are maintaining sexual relationships, both in and out of marriage.[45] Curiously, our Social Security laws penalize the widowed who remarry, by reducing Social Security benefits; for this reason, many retired persons live together but do not marry, to avoid having their retirement benefits cut.

The point is that the elderly retain human needs and appetites, and if they are to be physically and emotionally healthy, they must have a full range of opportunities which provide settings for friendship, social involvement, creative activity, and recreation. When denied these opportunities, many older persons tend to deteriorate psychologically and physically. The suicide rate for persons sixty-five and older is higher than for any other age group. Loneliness often leads to alcoholism among older persons; the death rate for alcohol related disorders among the elderly rose by over 50 percent during the 1950s and 1960s. Among aging persons with special disabilities, social isolation is even more pronounced. A conference on the aged blind, sponsored by the American Foundation for the Blind, concluded that social isolation was the most serious problem confronting the older visually handicapped individual.

Too often, aged persons are admitted to geriatric units in psychiatric hospitals (the aged occupy about a third of the beds in such hospitals) because they are unable to exist independently in the community, rather than because they are actually mentally ill. The existing disabilities of older persons are often aggravated when they are hospitalized or placed in nursing homes. It is possible to arrest this pattern and to counteract the feelings of rejection and isolation, insecurity, and loss of self-esteem that affect many older persons. Recent studies by graduate students at the Pennsylvania State University have shown that arts and crafts, games, and other purposeful group activities have had a positive effect on the socialization of aged mental patients, in both public and private psychiatric institutions. [46]

The most important challenge facing us today is to make the lives of aging persons in the community as rewarding and happy as possible, in order to prevent disability, withdrawal, and institutionalization. The U. S. Administration on Aging has assisted states and communities in developing programs for the aging, and has financed research in this field—much of it focusing on the role of leisure in the lives of older persons. A variety of specially funded programs have been developed, such as (1) the Foster Grandparent Program, which pays the elderly for supervising dependent and neglected youngsters; (2) the Retired Senior Volunteer Program (RSVP), which pays expenses for elderly persons involved in community service activity; and (3) the Senior Corps of Retired Executives (SCORE) which reimburses retired executives for expenses incurred in counseling small businesses.

Since the 1950s, recreation has been recognized as an important element in the lives of older persons. A report of the Special Senate Committee on Aging in 1977 revealed that poverty was steadily increasing among older Americans, particularly among minority group members. For the several million retired persons today living on incomes below the poverty level, provision of inexpensive recreational and social services by public and voluntary agencies is essential. Thousands of communities have developed Senior Centers and Golden Age Clubs in recent years, which often provide a full range of hobbies, social activities, special-interest groups, and the opportunity to take on responsibilities as officers, committee members, or in club service functions. To meet the needs of older persons most effectively, recreation cannot be isolated from other services, but must be integrated with health, nutritional, housing, legal, economic, and other forms of assistance. When considered as part of a multiservice approach, recreation has the unique characteristic of being attractive, interesting, and easy to enter; it is often regarded as a threshold or entry activity that attracts older persons to centers where they can then avail themselves of other special services and programs.

Programs which offer opportunities for community service, through which older people can help others, often provide the most meaningful activity for retired persons, from which they gain a deep sense of satisfaction and continuing worth. It is important to recognize that many people have an exaggerated sense of the problems of old age. A recent study of Louis Harris and Associates for the National Council on Aging suggests that the problems of older persons—except for health and fear of crime—are very much the same as those of younger people. A high proportion of older people see themselves as useful to their community, and are relatively satisfied with their lives. [47] Gray urges recreation professionals to reject the damaging stereotype of aging that is so widely shared, and to encourage continuing self-realization and growth through the entire life cycle, so that the elderly in our society continue to learn, to grow, and to enjoy their lives to the full extent of their potential. [48]

Programs for the Socially Deviant

A final important area of service with special populations involves the use of recreation in penal and correctional institutions or other rehabilitation centers for the socially deviant, such as those serving drug addicts or alcoholics. Many forward-looking administrators of correctional institutions or prisons have introduced varied programs of sports, arts and crafts, music and drama, or other special-interest activities. These programs serve both to improve morale within the institution and to equip discharged inmates to use their leisure constructively in community life. Unfortunately, most prison recreation programs are extremely limited. Hormachea writes:

> Correctional administrators pass the buck by placing the blame for inadequate recreation programs on the lack of funds and need for security. Manpower shortages are also cited. Lack of manpower plagues the whole correctional field; trained and qualified personnel are at a minimum. All too often, the task of recreation supervisor is given to an off-duty guard who played football in high school or displays some interest in sports or coaching. The therapeutic value of recreation is lost with these programs without purpose.[49]

Often, recreational programs in correctional and penal institutions—particularly smaller ones operated by county or municipal authorities—suffer from lack of adequate facilities for varied participation. A major reason for the poor recreation programs of correctional institutions is the basic attitude toward prison management held by administrators, legislators, and the public alike—that the primary purpose of prisons is to punish, rather than to reform and rehabilitate. As a consequence, too often, any institution that seeks to provide meaningful human services is seen as a "country club," and receives a budget that is painfully inadequate to support anything but custodial care. Fortunately, attitudes have improved in recent years, and many prisons have adopted more innovative approaches to rehabilitation, including efforts to eliminate brutality, provide more meaningful vocational programs and counseling services, arrange for furloughs so that inmates may visit their families or assume outside employment, returning to the prison at night. Some innovative state and Federal prisons in Massachusetts, Connecticut, and Texas have even experimented with minimum-security, coeducational programs, in an effort to help prisoners adjust to the outside world when they are released.

Alcoholism and drug addiction are patterns of socially deviant behavior that are closely linked to restricted and negative leisure attitudes and practices. Studies by Sessoms and others have shown that alcoholics have distinctly different patterns of social behavior and recreational interests from those of the normal population.[50] Other studies have shown alcoholics to be inhibited persons who have difficulty expressing themselves and finding release and enjoyment in socially approved ways. Sheridan points out, for example, that alcoholics typically describe the following "positive" effects of drinking: (1) it reduces anxiety, (2) it relieves social and/or inner tension, (3) it offers an escape from pressure and life problems, (4) it aids in relaxation and sleep, (5) it alleviates depression, and (6) it releases inhibitions.[51]

Deeply involving leisure pursuits—whether athletic, creative or social—can do much to relieve tension and anxiety of alcoholics and addicts, help them relax and unwind, and give them a new sense of self-worth. In both institutional and community-based programs serving such individuals, recreation is increasingly being provided as a rehabilitative or treatment service.

350

Strengthening Neighborhood and Community Life

One of the fundamental tenets of the pioneers of the recreation movement was that recreation helped to strengthen neighborhood and community life by giving individuals a sense of belonging and common purpose, helping to maintain social traditions and cultural ties, and enabling residents to join together cooperatively in volunteer service roles, thus promoting civic pride and morale and improving neighborhood life.

Involvement in recreation programs is often a means of developing a sense of identity and community acceptance. Vance Packard, who presented in *A Nation of Strangers* a convincing picture of Americans as highly mobile and rootless individuals, lacking an authentic sense of community "belonging," described a variety of ways in which new residents can become an "instant" part of community life. One way is through joining Newcomers Clubs, which sponsor gourmet dinners or dances, or family trips, excursions, or picnics; another is through membership in organizations like the YMCA, Scouts, or other leisure-related bodies, which provide a form of "instant plug-in" when one moves to a new community.[52]

In many cities, neighborhood councils or recreation committees help to guide the direction of local programs and centers, frequently providing volunteer leadership and funding as well. Particularly in urban areas which have suffered from budgetary cutbacks, groups of citizens have "adopted" parks and playgrounds, often providing volunteer leadership to clean and maintain such areas. Block associations may be formed to promote neighborhood programs for improved police protection and safety, better schools, or recreation projects of various types. Many communities sponsor neighborhood block parties or community festivals as a means of getting to know each other better and strengthening their feelings of unity, and also for fundraising purposes.

Improving Intergroup Relations

A closely allied goal is that of helping to improve intergroup relations among community residents of different racial, ethnic, or religious backgrounds by encouraging them to work together on commonly shared interests. Some communities have sponsored ethnic folk festivals presenting traditional music, dance, costumes, food, or other elements of cultural heritage, often with several different nationalities or ethnic groups participating. Certainly these festivals have done much to encourage good will, although no research has been carried out to determine their degree of effectiveness or to learn whether recreational events of this kind have a serious impact on the deeper forms of prejudice that exist in our society.

Strengthening Community Economic Well-Being

As described earlier, recreation has become a major source of business investment and income, and thus an essential element in the total national economy. A study for the Department of the Interior during the late 1960s reported that the 150 million visitor days spent in travel to the national parks each year resulted in a total expenditure of $6.35 billion.

On a regional level, New England is a leading example of the economic contribution of recreation. For years, this was an economically declining area; factories were closing and the population was moving to other regions of the United States. During the 1960s, however, New England had a strong economic recovery following the expansion of winter-sports facilities:

> Ski resorts are rising all over, especially in the northern tier. Building of the new lodges, motels and roads has had a major impact on the construction industry. . . .

> Vermont has the fanciest of the new ski resorts. Some offer such lures as heated outdoor swimming pools, sauna baths, ice skating, closed gondolas to take people up ski slopes . . . and cocktail lounges, night clubs and theaters.[53]

Like other forms of recreation, skiing has a multiplying effect. State officials estimate that for every dollar spent on skiing directly, winter visitors spend an additional four dollars for food, lodging, liquor, entertainment, gasoline, and other goods and services—and that this money is again "turned over" within the local economy.

On the municipal level, many major cities depend heavily upon conventions and tourism for economic support. Cities base their appeal on a variety of attractions, including culture and entertainment in the form of museums, symphonies, nightclubs, theaters, circuses and sports events. Many cities depend heavily on huge arenas or exhibition halls and auditoriums which house business, professional, hobby, or political conventions. The New York City Convention and Visitors Bureau announced in a recent year that the city had an annual total of 16.5 million visitors, including almost 3 million convention delegates and 1 million foreigners, who spent a total of $1.5 billion during their stay in the city.

Adequate provision for leisure is regarded as one of the hallmarks of healthy and sound communities. Typically, when regions or municipalities seek new business development or residential expansion, they stress their cultural, recreational, and educational resources. A former president of the National Association of Manufacturers stated that

> nothing is more important to the physical and emotional health of the men and women of industry than proper recreation activities. So important is this considered that few modern companies would consider locating a new plant or facility in a community without first surveying its recreation possibilities. Management knows that, in seeking competent and gifted personnel, its ability to attract and hold the men and women it wants often is decided by the little theatre, the park system, or the Little League.[54]

Generally, then, recreation is considered to be an important economic asset in bringing direct income and employment, helping to stabilize population, reduce turnover of employees in business, and attract new industries to American communities.

Promoting Community Safety

A little publicized but highly important value of community recreation is its function in promoting community safety, by providing leisure opportunities in safe and controlled environments. The most obvious example is swimming; if swimming in rivers, lakes, quarries, or the ocean were freely permitted and unsupervised, there undoubtedly would be thousands of additional fatalities each year. Recreation and park departments that provide careful supervision in pools or beachfronts make a major contribution to community safety.

Similarly, the supervision by public departments of organized sports leagues, ice skating, sledding, or other carefully directed activities helps to prevent many injuries and deaths. In addition, many departments offer courses in boating skills, riflery, camping, or even—in Vancouver—a driving skills program for young children which has a miniature-car facility complete with traffic lights, intersections, and police officers. Thus, an important social value of community sponsored recreation programs is that they help to reduce the rate of accidental injuries and death.

Providing Programs for the Disadvantaged

As chapter 10 has indicated, many cities, large and small, use recreation as a significant tool within the total spectrum of social services for the disadvantaged. Although America's economic development during the 1960s was unparalleled, many families continued to live in conditions of grinding poverty; the recession of the early and middle 1970s worsened the situation. A 1976 report revealed that 25.9 million persons lived in families that were below the federally defined poverty level of $5,500 for a nonfarm family of four; this represented 12 percent of the population, or nearly one out of every eight persons in the country. Poverty has been most severe for certain population groups, particularly the young, the old, and racial minorities. The Bureau of Labor Statistics reported in 1976 that the jobless rate for black teenagers was 40.3 percent, compared with 16.1 percent for whites of the same age.[55]

How effectively has organized recreation service met the needs of the poor and racial minority groups in American cities? To fully understand the present situation, it is necessary to look at the past.

Racial Segregation in American Life

Within the southern and border states, the first several decades of the twentieth century were marked by systematic racial segregation in the use of public park and recreation facilities. Blacks were excluded from playgrounds, public parks, swimming pools, and organized sports that were provided for white residents; any form of social or recreational contact between blacks and whites was rigidly prohibited by state laws and municipal ordinances. The recreation profession itself accepted this situation, and the National Recreation Association operated a special Bureau of Colored Work from 1919 until the early 1940s, which sought to expand recreation facilities and programs for blacks—on a racially segregated basis. In both the North and the South, public and voluntary recreation facilities for blacks were markedly inferior to those in white neighborhoods.

353

The pattern of segregated park and recreation programs and facilities began to break down after World War II, and was finally prohibited by Supreme Court decisions in 1963 disallowing segregation in municipally owned and operated facilities, and by the Civil Rights Act of 1964. Some communities resisted legal pressure by closing recreation and park facilities rather than permit interracial use; others transformed them into "privately owned" facilities for white members only. In many other cities, all formerly segregated recreation facilities were opened to black residents, with varying patterns of mixed use resulting.

In the 1960s the recreation profession began to take a special interest in meeting the needs of the poor—especially the nonwhite poor—in urban slums. This concern gained impetus when urban rioting erupted throughout the nation in 1964 and 1965 and brought the needs of inner city residents to the public's attention. Recognition that large numbers of unemployed teen-agers and young adults roamed the streets, out of work, bored, frustrated, and ready for violent action, led to a determination to use recreation to keep the summers "cool."

Recreation and park administrators began to develop expanded recreation programs in inner city neighborhoods, initiating sports clinics and tournaments, workshops in Afro-American arts, dance and theater, and busing programs to nearby parks. Portable pools and other mobile recreation units were rapidly built or purchased and trucked into disadvantaged neighborhoods.

The need for improved recreation facilities and programs was documented in the report of the National Commission on Civil Disorders to President Johnson in the spring of 1968. It showed that in city after city where serious riots had occurred, one of the angry complaints of ghetto residents had been the lack of adequate parks, swimming pools, recreation programs, and leadership. Indeed, poor recreation and parks were more frequently cited as a grievance by black residents in cities where serious riots had occurred than the discriminatory administration of justice, inadequate welfare programs, or poor municipal services.[56] In several cities where riots occurred, initial flare-ups arose from the inability of blacks to use certain recreation facilities (in Chicago, blacks could not enter public swimming pools in nearby white neighborhoods and were prevented from turning on water hydrants in their own streets during the hottest days of the summer).

In many summer programs, recreation came to be seen as a way in which community groups could work together for neighborhood improvement. The important role played by recreation in urban communities was stressed by a Federal official in the Department of Housing and Urban Development, who commented that political leaders in every city should realize

> that the recreation or parks department is one of the most important community links with the inner city, with the ghetto. . . .

> Few other agencies have the opportunity to work inside ghetto neighborhoods on a day-by-day and people-to-people basis. Few other city programs offer opportunity to direct participation in all phases of program development and execution by the neighborhood people themselves. In better ways than the police and schools, recreation programs can reach large numbers of people and bring city government face to face in friendship with individual families and people, bridging economic

354

barriers, ethnic differences, age differences and neighborhood bound-aries.[57]

Recreation was used as a form of job training or part-time summer work for young people. When the urban riots died out, the massive Federal support to the inner cities was sharply reduced, with the exception of some continuing programs described in chapter 10. In retrospect, many authorities would agree that leisure services must be recognized as an important area of community development, and not merely as a way to buy time and placate angry ghetto residents during the summer. It is also obvious that recreation in itself cannot possibly satisfy the frustrations that cause urban riots; this can be accomplished only by improving all areas of opportunity in the inner city, including education, housing, employment, and health.

Enriching Cultural Life

Another significant social value of recreation in the community is its programs in the fine and performing arts that enrich the cultural life of all residents. Traditionally, most public departments and voluntary agencies have sponsored arts and crafts as a regular aspect of playground or community center programs. Informal music participation, folk and square dancing, and classes in these activities have also typically been part of the community spectrum of activity.

In more and more communities, however, public departments have joined with special-interest associations to sponsor major cultural programs such as arts centers, symphony orchestras, ballet companies, or drama repertory groups. Surveys have indicated the high value the public places on artistic experience as a means of providing pleasure, the opportunity for creative release and expression, and as a critical dimension in human life.

Providing Release for Hostility and Aggression

Another important function of recreation in modern society is its potential for releasing violent and hostile drives in socially acceptable ways—essentially the "catharsis" theory described earlier. Over the past several years, concern about growing violence has increased throughout the world, but particularly in the United States, which ranks especially high among the industrial nations of the world in criminal violence. *Time* magazine commented that as a consequence of our past preoccupation with a folklore of violence, our bloody riots of earlier history, occasional multiple murders, overall homicide rate, and recent assassinations of major national figures,

> the rest of the world is ready to adjudge America as an excessively violent country in which brutal, irrational force can erupt any minute on a massive scale.[58]

The fact, of course, is that violence is a problem throughout the world. This propensity toward violence has existed throughout history; for the caveman, life was an incessant battle against the hostile Pleistocene environment, against other mammals for food, and against other humans for shelter, a water hole, or a hunting range. Violence was necessary and socially approved. Fischer writes:

> Success in battle was the basic status symbol. The best fighters were feted in victory celebrations, heaped with honors and plunder . . . the weak and timid, on the other hand, were scorned . . . and in many societies cowardice was punished by death. For nearly all of human history, then, the aggressive impulse—so deeply embedded in our genes— had no trouble in finding an outlet.[59]

In modern society, however, we have banned many socially approved outlets for pugnacity that were once available on the frontier or in rough-and-ready occupations. In a nation of city dwellers, the traditional testing ground of man against nature has all but disappeared. Life itself has become easier and safer, and warfare no longer provides a regular outlet for the primitive instinct for violence that it once did. We have shown remarkable ingenuity in inventing fashionable surrogates for violence, including such strenuous and risky sports as skiing, skin diving, surfing, mountain climbing, and sailing small boats in rough weather. These activities, however, are available chiefly to the well-to-do; they are too expensive for the poor and too remote from their lifestyle. Ultimately, Fischer concludes, many of the poor turn to crimes of violence, largely because of the need to vent aggressive impulses fanned by boredom, frustration, and anger.

Those who observed ghetto riots in America's cities during the summers of the 1960s understood that they were the expression of such frustration and anger. Yet there was also a curiously playlike aspect of these riots. Eyewitnesses reported that many of the riots had an air of holiday about them. In 1967, a policeman commented bitterly about Puerto Rican rioters in New York's East Harlem conflagration: "They're like kids. They get a big kick out of the riots. It's like a carnival to them." In Newark, New Jersey, during the tremendously destructive riot in the same year, marked by mass fighting and arson, Governor Hughes said that he had found the "holiday atmosphere" among the looters most repelling. A passing nun remarked, "They were doing it out of sport, you know, not maliciously. They were laughing like: 'Isn't this great fun, getting something for free.' "[60]

Even the element of racial antagonism was often surprisingly low-keyed. In Washington and Detroit, black and white spectators and looters mingled in apparent harmony, smiling and waving at white policemen and newsmen.[61] Although it is difficult to regard any experience involving arson, sniping, mass looting, and destruction as recreational in any true sense, it is worth noting that the riots served a need for excitement, release, and abandon.

The writings of Ardrey and Lorenz suggest that man has inherited violent and aggressive drives from his biological past, which must be controlled and used constructively. Bettelheim suggests two ways to minimize the dangers of violence: to curb it through education that provides understanding and mastery, and to provide acceptable outlets for it. He asks:

> What measures are we taking to help our children do a better job of mastering the disturbance of their communal life that comes from the instinct of aggression. . . . Children are supposed neither to hit, nor to swear at their playmates. They are supposed to refrain from destroying

their toys or other property. . . . But what outlets for violence *do* we provide for them?[62]

The challenge to the organized recreation movement, then, is to offer other types of experiences which will provide the same kinds of rewards or satisfactions as riots or other acts of violence, but without their devastating social consequences.

Promoting Concern for Nature

As shown in chapters 9 and 10, many recreation and park departments operate large-scale networks of parks, nature reserves, waterfront areas, and forests or other areas of open space. Recreation and park authorities often play a vital role in conservation. In some cities and towns, they have established nature museums or natural preserves for use by the schools, Scouts, Audubon Society or other ecologically concerned groups. Other recreation and park departments have taken the lead in planning and carrying out community cleanup programs, including the rehabilitation of run-down areas, recycling projects, or antipollution drives. Often recreation administrators help to mobilize public efforts in emergency situations, such as cleaning up beachfront oil spills.

New Haven is a single example of the way in which many departments today assume a leading role in conservation and environmental education.

> This city's park and recreation commission sponsors a 40-acre nature recreation center, which offers a laboratory for guided field trips, courses and workshops concerned with natural history, wildlife preservation, weather, astronomy, geology, and geography. Thousands of students on all grade levels . . . are served in a program jointly sponsored by the New Haven Park and Recreation Commission and the city's school board. Six ranger-naturalists teach courses in various aspects of nature and ecology, and are assisted by volunteers provided by the New Haven Nature Recreation Association. The center also provides field study opportunities and work periods for students at nearby Southern Connecticut State College. Plans are under way to expand this program by adding other nature centers and day camps, including a seashore center, to be concerned with marine biology and ecology.[63]

Meeting the Need for Ritual

A unique function of recreation in modern society is in meeting the needs of people for ritual. In past ages, people enjoyed a succession of year-round ceremonies and communal celebrations. Some of these still survive in modern communities in the form of fairs and carnivals, which combine historical displays, exhibitions of work products, and varied forms of entertainment, sports, and contests. Often, to acknowledge a national hero or a major national achievement, we celebrate with great tickertape parades. Major holidays, political events, and sports victories are also marked by celebrations and rituals. Even modern, industrialized man has a need for displays and rituals marked by music, parades, dancing, costumes, and huge cheering throngs. In the United States, Independence Day provides an occasion for such rituals; it remains an example of what John Adams called for in July, 1776:

> It ought to be commemorated as the day of deliverance, by solemn acts of devotion to God Almighty. It ought to be solemnized with pomp and parade, with shows, games and sports, guns, bells, bonfires and illuminations, from one end of this continent to the other, from this time forward, forever more.[64]

Even today, our presidential party nominating conventions are marked by ritualistic presentations of the colors, anthems, invocations, inspirational readings, presentation of badges and honors, and seemingly endless demonstrations in honor of the nominees:

> Balloons cascade from the ceiling. Sober men who earn their bread at the law, at the bank, at embalming, trot through the aisles in party hats, expressions of joy frozen rigidly on sweating faces, shouting and whooping like freshmen being hazed by the sophomores during hell week.[65]

The urge to participate in such displays is vividly demonstrated in college sports events. These events, particularly football, present spectacles of marching bands, drill teams, dancing choruses of elaborately costumed girls, banners, huge crowds with color-card displays, cannons booming, cheerleaders dressed in symbolic animal costumes, often huge parades before "bowl" games, bonfire pep rallies, and similar ceremonial aspects. Often, as in Latin American and certain European carnivals at the time of Lent, the emphasis seems to be on breaking down the distinctions of class and status, and temporarily abandoning the year-round code of seriousness, hard work, social restraints, and formality. It has been said that even a machine must have a little play if it is not to break down; the same axiom applies to people, both as individuals and as a society.

In general, the function of recreation within this final category of social value is to provide occasions and opportunities that extend beyond the purely utilitarian, providing the opportunity for enrichment of life, aesthetic involvement, personal and communal joy, release, and reward. All such experiences, whether they relate to the need for ritual and celebration, artistic achievement, or education, are part of the first function cited—that of enriching the total quality of life.

Although this chapter has focused primarily on the role of recreation in meeting the needs of groups with special problems, its most important function by far is to meet the needs of the public at large. The social values of recreation that have been outlined here are universal; they apply to all communities and groups in modern society.

Chapter Fourteen

1. Adapted from community recreation goals cited in Richard G. Kraus, *Recreation Today: Program Planning and Leadership* (Santa Monica, California: Goodyear, 1977), pp. 43–45.
2. Janet MacLean, "Leisure and the Quality of Life," in Timothy Craig, ed., *The Humanistic and Mental Health Aspects of Sports, Exercise and Recreation* (Chicago: American Medical Association, 1975), pp. 73–74.
3. Herbert J. Gans, "Outdoor Recreation and Mental Health," *Trends in American Living and*

Outdoor Recreation, Vol. 22 of the Report of the Outdoor Recreation Resources Review Commission (Washington, D.C.: U. S. Government Printing Office, 1962), p. 236.

4. Margaret Winters, "Green Areas Provide an Antidote," New York *Times,* 8 October 1967, p. D-27.

5. *Juvenile Delinquency and Youth Crime,* Task Force Report of the President's Commission on Law Enforcement and Administration of Justice (Washington, D.C.: U. S. Government Printing Office, 1967), p. 150.

6. Joseph B. Treaster, "Violence of Youth Crimes is Found at a New High," New York *Times,* 1 May 1976, p. 21.

7. "Crime and Vandalism Permeate Nation's Schools," *NEA Reporter,* February 1976, pp. 4–5.

8. William Healy and August Bronner, *New Light on Delinquency and Its Treatment* (New Haven: Yale University Press, 1936, 1957).

9. Albert K. Cohen, *Delinquent Boys: The Culture of the Gang* (Glencoe, Illinois: Free Press, 1955); and Walter B. Miller, "Lower Class Culture as a Generating Milieu of Gang Delinquency," *Journal of Social Issues,* 14 (1958):5–19.

10. Richard A. Cloward and Lloyd E. Ohlin, *Delinquency and Opportunity: A Theory of Delinquent Gangs* (New York: Free Press, 1960), pp. 20–30, 161–86.

11. Frank Tannenbaum, *Crime and the Community* (New York: Columbia University Press, 1938), pp. 17–20.

12. Cohen, *Delinquent Boys,* p. 26.

13. William F. Whyte, *Street Corner Society: The Social Structure of an Italian Slum* (Chicago: University of Chicago Press, 1955), p. 6.

14. James F. Short, Jr., and Fred L. Strodtbeck, *Group Process and Gang Delinquency* (Chicago: University of Chicago Press, 1965), p. 77.

15. Walter E. Schafer, "Interscholastic Athletes and Juvenile Delinquency" (Research paper presented at Symposium on Sociology of Sport, Madison, Wisconsin, November 1968).

16. As an example, see Roscoe C. Brown, Jr., *A Boys' Club and Delinquency,* Monograph No. 2., New York University Center for Community and Field Services, 1956, which assessed the impact of a new Boys' Club program on delinquency rates in selected districts of Louisville, Kentucky.

17. Herbert J. Gans, "Outdoor Recreation and Mental Health," p. 236.

18. Bertram J. Beck, "A Role for Recreation," in *Juvenile Delinquency and Youth Crime,* p. 404.

19. Fritz Redl and David Wineman, *Controls from Within: Techniques for the Treatment of the Aggressive Child* (Glencoe, Illinois: Free Press, 1952), p. 54.

20. Luther Terry, *Recreation in Treatment Centers* (American Recreation Society, Hospital Section), September, 1965, p. 3

21. Fred W. Martin, "A Philosophical Perspective on Leisure Service for the Disabled," *Journal of Physical Education and Recreation, Leisure Today,* May 1975, p. 27.

22. Dolores Geddes, "Physical Activity for Impaired, Disabled and Handicapped Individuals: What's Going On?" in *Humanistic and Mental Health Aspects of Sports,* pp. 103–107.

23. Peter A. Witt, *The Status of Recreation Services for the Handicapped* (Ottawa: Department of National Health and Welfare, 1974).

24. *Health Resource Statistics—1968* (Washington, D.C.: Public Health Service, 1968), p. 185.

25. E. Mansell Pattison, "The Relationships of the Adjunctive and Therapeutic Recreation Services to Community Mental Health Programs," *Therapeutic Recreation Journal,* 1st quarter 1969, pp. 19–20.

26. Janet Pomeroy, "Recreation Unlimited: An Approach to Community Recreation for the Handicapped," *Journal of Physical Education and Recreation,* May 1975, p. 31.

27. Julian U. Stein, "The Mentally Retarded Need Recreation," *Parks and Recreation,* July 1966, p. 574.

28. Joan Ramm, *Challenge: Recreation and Fitness for the Mentally Retarded,* American Association for Health, Physical Education and Recreation, September, 1966, p. 1.

29. Elliott M. Avedon, "Recreation's Responsibility and the Rehabilitation Process," *Journal of Rehabilitation,* January–February 1969, p. 29.

30. Karen Louise Hosty, "The Carry-over Effects of an Instructional Recreation Program on the Ability of Trainable Mentally Retarded Children to Use a Free Play Period," in Herberta Lundegren, ed., *Physical Education and Recreation for the Mentally Retarded* (State College, Pennsylvania: Pennsylvania State University, 1975), pp. 61–69.

31. Priscilla D. Fleming, "The Effect of Play Alternatives on a Specific Disruptive Behavior in

359

Hyperkinetic Trainable Mentally Retarded Children," in Lundegren, *Physical Education for Mentally Retarded*, pp. 70–82.

32. Renee F. Dorfman, "The Effects of the Frostig Move-Grow-Learn Program on the Sensory-Motor Skills of Trainable Mentally Retarded Children," in Lundegren, *Physical Education for Mentally Retarded*, pp. 83–89.

33. Janet A. Seaman, "Effects of Municipal Recreation on the Social Self-Esteem of the Mentally Retarded," *Therapeutic Recreation Journal*, 2nd quarter 1975, p. 75.

34. Richard Kraus, *Recreation and Related Therapies in Psychiatric Rehabilitation* (New York: Herbert Lehman College and City University of New York Research Foundation, 1972), p. 23.

35. Paul Douglass, "Community-Based Volunteers in Illinois Mental Health Therapy," *Parks and Recreation*, April 1967, p. 26.

36. Chester F. McDowell, Jr., "Leisure Counseling: Professional Considerations for Therapeutic Recreation," *Journal of Physical Education and Recreation, Leisure Today*, January 1976, pp. 26–27.

37. Scout Lee Gunn, "A Systems Approach to Leisure Counseling," *Journal of Physical Education and Recreation*, April 1977, p. 33.

38. Paul Haun, "The Place for Recreation in Mental Health," *Parks and Recreation*, December 1966, p. 974.

39. "Trends for the Handicapped," *Park-Practice Program*, published by National Society for Park Resources and National Park Service, July-August-September, 1974, p. 4.

40. *Outdoor Recreation Planning for the Handicapped* (Washington, D.C.: Bureau of Outdoor Recreation Technical Assistance Bulletin, 1967), p. 1.

41. Scout Lee Gunn, "Mainstreaming is a Two-Way Street . . ." *Journal of Physical Education and Recreation*, September 1976, p. 48.

42. *Newsletter of the Committee on Recreation and Leisure* (Washington, D.C.: President's Committee on Employment of the Handicapped, February–March, 1976), p. 1.

43. Susan C. Buchan, "Camping for the Handicapped in Selected Camps in California," *Therapeutic Recreation Journal*, 1st quarter 1975, pp. 38–41.

44. Sheila K. Johnson, "Growing Old Alone Together," *New York Times Magazine*, 11 November 1973, p. 40.

45. See "Romance and the Aged," *Time*, 4 June 1973, p. 48.

46. See reports of research by John Boudman and Jeannette Burdge in Herberta M. Lundegren, ed., *Penn State Studies on Recreation and the Aging* (State College, Pennsylvania: Pennsylvania State University, 1974), pp. 75–79, 61–66.

47. Louis Harris and Associates, *The Myth and Reality of Aging in America* (Washington, D.C.: The National Council on the Aging, 1975).

48. David E. Gray, "To Illuminate the Way," *Parks and Recreation*, October 1976, pp. 31–33.

49. Carroll R. Hormachea, "History and Philosophy of Treatment in Correctional Recreation," in Jerry D. Kelley, ed., *Expanding Horizons in Therapeutic Recreation II* (Champaign-Urbana, Illinois: University of Illinois, Office of Recreation and Park Resources, 1974), p. 100.

50. H. Douglas Sessoms and Sidney R. Oakley, "Recreation, Leisure and the Alcoholic," *Journal of Leisure Research*, Winter, 1969, pp. 21–31.

51. Paul M. Sheridan, "Therapeutic Recreation and the Alcoholic," *Therapeutic Recreation Journal*, 1st quarter 1976, p. 16.

52. Vance Packard, *A Nation of Strangers* (New York: David McKay, 1972), p. 156.

53. "New England's Big Comeback," *U. S. News and World Report*, 14 February 1966, p. 74.

54. Rudolf F. Bannow, "What Is Expected of Recreation by Management," *Recreation*, January 1960, p. 15.

55. Associated Press Dispatch, September 26, 1976, "2.5 Million Join Ranks of Poverty."

56. *Report of the National Advisory Commission on Civil Disorder* (New York: Bantam Books, 1968), pp. 7–8.

57. Dwight F. Rettie, "Areas and Facilities in the Inner City," *Proceedings. Congress for Recreation and Parks*. National Recreation and Park Association, October, 1968, p. 140.

58. "Violence in America," *Time*, 28 July 1967.

59. John Fischer, "Substitutes for Violence," *Harper's Magazine*, January 1966, p. 16.

60. For a number of eyewitness accounts of riots in major cities, see New York *Times*, 15 July 1967, pp. 10–11; 26 July 1967, pp. 18, 29; 7 April 1968, p. 62.

61. Tom Wicker, "Thousands Leave Washington as Bands of Negroes Loot Stores," New York *Times*, 6 April 1968, p. 23; and "Federal Troops Sent into Detroit," New York *Times*, 25 July 1967, p. 19.

62. Bruno Bettelheim, "Violence: A Neglected Mode of Behavior," *Annals of the American Academy of Political and Social Science*, March 1966, p. 51.

63. Richard Kraus, *Urban Parks and Recreation: Challenge of the 1970s* (New York: Community Council of Greater New York, 1972), pp. 38–39.

64. From a letter from John Adams to his wife, speaking of July 2, 1776, the day the Continental Congress passed a resolution calling for the independence of the American Colonies.

65. "That Time in the Nation . . .," New York *Times,* August 8, 1968, p. 24.

15

URBAN PLANNING FOR RECREATION AND PARKS

This chapter is concerned with the need to plan effectively to meet leisure and open space needs in modern cities and their surrounding suburbs. Nowhere in our society are the problems more acute than in our huge metropolitan centers. Their sudden emergence during the mid-1960s arose from the changed nature of the relationship between the central city and its outlying or satellite communities. The post-World War II "baby boom" was accompanied by a mass migration, chiefly of white middle-class families, from the central cities to the suburbs. At the same time, increasing numbers of poor people—many of them black or Spanish speaking, with limited educational and vocational skills—moved from rural regions, where they had been displaced by the consolidation of small farms into huge, mechanized agribusinesses, to run-down inner city neighborhoods.

Many businesses left the cities because of the difficulties of transportation tie-ups, growing taxes, and bureaucratic controls, thus shrinking the municipal tax base still further. The suburbanites who use the city generally do not pay an adequate share of its expenses for highways, utilities, cultural facilities, and police protection. With declining revenues and increasing costs, more and more cities are caught in a traumatic financial squeeze, and many are on the brink of bankruptcy.

In 1940, suburbs contained 27 million people, or two out of every ten Americans, and 19 million fewer than the cities. By the mid-1970s, more people were living in suburban communities (75.6 million) than in central cities (63.8 million). The nature of the suburbs themselves has changed sharply. They no longer offer the bucolic, hassle-free way of life they once promised; today many suburban communities are plagued by traffic jams, smog, industry and large-scale business and shopping developments, crime, and growing welfare rolls. Property taxes have climbed sharply in suburban school districts, and many schools are operating on austerity budgets.

Ideally, the problems of the central city and its surrounding suburbs should be handled through coordinated regional planning and integrated services—particularly in recreation and parks. This is not generally the case; in many metropolitan areas, the lack of organization borders on actual chaos. The National Commission on Urban Problems has reported that United States metropolitan areas are served by over twenty thousand separate local governments. The conglomeration of separate county, city, village, township, park, school district, and other public authorities surrounding many of our major cities makes effective action on important social problems extremely difficult.

Problems of Urban Recreation and Parks

Serious as the problems of suburban communities may be, it is within the central cities that recreation and park agencies face their most critical challenges. There is the obvious need to preserve and acquire more recreation and park areas, rather than permit the few remaining open areas in and around the cities to be swallowed up by urban sprawl. Linked to this is the need to maintain existing urban parks, recreation centers, playgrounds, and other facilities, and to carry out a large-scale program of rehabilitation of blighted areas.

A second important problem is the need to plan facilities and programs that effectively serve urban populations of varied ethnic, economic, and social backgrounds. Closely linked to both concerns is the need for adequate budgetary support for capital development and operation of parks and recreation. Based on an extensive study of leisure facilities and services in inner city, high density areas in twenty-five large American cities, Dunn writes:

> Glass and graffiti, broken equipment, and unmowed playgrounds may be familiar sights throughout many cities, not just in the ghettos. In some cities, recreation facilities are crumbling, staffs have been cut back, and services have been slashed.[1]

The average amount allocated for public recreation and park operating costs in the twenty-five cities studied was ten dollars per capita annually; Dunn concluded that this amount was woefully insufficient, and that many urban recreation and park systems were in critical financial condition. Her conclusions were supported by another national study by the Community Council of Greater New York, which documented the problems of budgetary cutbacks, personnel layoffs, vandalism, crime, and similar difficulties in many large American cities.[2]

The problems of recreation and parks departments stem partly from the overall budget difficulties which have forced many cities to close hospitals and day care centers, reduce the number of municipal employees, and shorten the hours of museums, libraries, and schools. However, it is also obvious that many cities give a lower priority to recreation and parks than to other public services. As far back as 1960, Higbee pointed out that enthusiasm for public parks had been superseded by other interests. Several decades ago, people of prominence in private and public affairs felt a social obligation to help make the city more healthful and attractive. Today, such persons satisfy their own leisure needs through private means, and

363

recreation and parks have gradually come to be seen as peripheral to other important purposes. Higbee wrote:

> The city fathers are too distressed by the agonies of welfare services, harassed by traffic pressures, and embarrassed by inadequate public schools to dwell on the more pleasant aspects of existence which parks and playgrounds represent. These facilities seem to be regarded as frills rather than as the absolute necessities which they really are.[3]

Since the once widely accepted view of recreation as a social amenity can no longer justify substantial public support in cities in crisis, careful planning is necessary today to ensure delivery of recreation as the vital community service it has become. It is also necessary to broaden the focus of urban planning for parks and recreation. Most planning efforts have stressed the acquisition of land and the development of facilities, particularly those programs developed with the assistance of the Federal government. There is considerable evidence, however, that the mere provision of play spaces—even if close at hand—does not guarantee satisfactory use. Systematic observations have shown many urban playgrounds and parks to be almost totally deserted, even at times when one would expect a high volume of use. Fear of crime and violence, vandalized or poorly maintained facilities, and the lack of attractive programs all account for a low level of use, particularly in inner city areas. Limited participation by the poor in outdoor recreation activities may also stem from their having different tastes, interests, and lifestyle. This suggests the need for urban recreation planners to explore perceptively the needs and interests of all urban residents and to analyze the city itself to determine what provision should be made for recreation.

Approaches to Urban Recreation and Park Planning

There are essentially three levels of planning in furnishing recreation and park facilities and services in modern communities: (1) total master planning that considers all aspects of community life, including residential and industrial development, housing, transportation, and recreation; (2) planning that concentrates on recreation and park resources, needs, and priorities as a separate concern (although it may be a unit in a total master plan); and (3) recreation and park planning dealing with a particular facility or the needs of a single neighborhood.

There is no single approach to urban planning, either in recreation and parks or in any other aspect of municipal development. Planners receive their training in a variety of disciplines, some in public administration, others in sociology, and still others in the fields of landscape architecture, engineering, law, or social work. Each planner is likely to apply the standards and values of the field in which he or she received professional training. For example, planners with a specialized background in economics tend to see recreation as part of a total ecosystem subject to the laws of supply and demand:

> Leisure activity can be viewed as a quasi-market system whose performance results from the interaction of demand and supply factors which

are subject to analysis. When costs are measured in terms of both money and time, and when transportation costs are specified as variables, it becomes possible to construct a model of the space economy of recreation activity which should become an important analytical perspective for the recreation planner in the future.[4]

In this framework, Wingo argues that if the consumer were able to cast his economic vote for the recreational services he prefers, it would then be possible to expand or reduce recreation activities (viewed as economic goods or products, some produced by the private market and others by public agencies) in response to the profitability signal. This approach would seem to exclude adequate recreation opportunities for the poor. Wingo suggests, however, that instead of offering the poor free but inferior services which they do not utilize, we should create popular activities and services which they will want—and then provide "a set of policies for rational subsidization of groups which would be priced out of the market by access costs or by the pricing mechanisms." Obviously, this solution would be dependent on society's willingness to subsidize more attractive and expensive leisure opportunities for the poor than it has been willing to do in the past.

Systems Planning

Systems analysis, a form of planning which became extremely popular with the introduction of the computer, is essentially an attempt to consider the functions and activities of any governmental or business organization within the structure of the total society. Each organization is a system of interrelated parts which influence each other, and the organization itself is part of a larger societal system. The systems approach, which seeks to develop conceptual models, identify alternative plans for action, and measure effectiveness of programs or problem solutions, tends to be most effective in large-scale organizations which have precisely determined goals and products or outcomes which are quantifiable. For these reasons, it has not been widely used in recreation and park planning, although it has received increasing attention in the field of therapeutic recreation service.[5]

Other Planning Approaches

Planners trained in architecture or landscape architecture tend to be primarily concerned with the visual effects of the urban environment and the need to create an aura of open space, beauty, pleasing design, and lovely vistas. The closely related conservationist approach gives major emphasis to the need to retain and protect open spaces, green belts, historic sites, and parks, and to resist using them for any purpose that might alter the natural environment.

Recreation and parks are frequently regarded as positive and attractive governmental functions and are subject to pressure for political reasons; this factor influences planning particularly in smaller, more affluent communities or suburban counties. Still other planners, especially those in larger cities, tend to be influenced by what might be called a social needs approach, which stresses opportunities and services designed to meet the needs of disadvantaged residents.

365

Traditional Approach to Urban Planning

The traditional approach is based on an imagined model of what the good community should be like. It assumes that each type of land use, such as light manufacturing, commercial development, residential development, education, or recreation and parks, may be seen in a logical kind of physical juxtaposition with all other uses. Physical placement is generally based on both the need for efficient access and convenient transportation between interdependent uses and on the desirability of keeping the least attractive uses away from those that are most attractive.

Certain diagrammatic approaches have been formulated to show how these varying land uses may be distributed in a master plan. One such approach consists of a concentric circle pattern, in which heavy industry is in the innermost sector of the city, surrounded by light manufacturing, lower-class housing, shopping areas, and sectors of middle- and upper-class housing, interspersed by rings of green space to provide insulation from the less desirable parts of the city.

The traditional approach has been based on two important elements: (1) the concept of self-contained, relatively homogeneous neighborhoods and communities and (2) the development of standards for recreation and park areas and facilities.

The Neighborhood Concept

A neighborhood is considered to be a section of a city or town offering a social and physical environment which meets such basic needs as education, shopping, churches, and centers for recreational or other social activities. Neighborhoods are of various sizes and shapes, but are often referred to in the planning literature as being about three-quarters of a mile to a mile square, and including about six thousand residents (about the population needed to support a single elementary school). Typical facilities which are generally recommended to meet neighborhood needs include the following:

1. *Neighborhood Play Lots.* The play lot is a small area of about twenty-five hundred to five thousand square feet set aside for the play of pre-school children, usually in crowded neighborhoods where yards are absent or unsuitable for play. The "tot lot" is often found in the center of a large housing project or as a smaller unit in a large playground or neighborhood park.

2. *Neighborhood Playgrounds.* The neighborhood playground is the major outdoor play center of a neighborhood. Primarily for children and youth between the ages of six and fifteen, it offers limited opportunities for older youth and adults. The playground usually includes an area with play equipment (swings, slides, etc.), a wading pool, a shaded quiet area with benches and a sandbox, areas for informal play, and other game areas. Many playgrounds also have a small building with storage space, lavatories, an office for the playground director, and sometimes indoor rooms which can be used for activities. Traditional planning usually recommends that playgrounds range in size from about 4.5 to 7.5 acres, and that they be located within a quarter-mile radius of each home in severely crowded neighborhoods and within a half-mile of each home in less densely populated areas.

3. *Neighborhood Parks.* Landscaped areas designed to provide attractive

366

open space and opportunity for passive recreation, neighborhood parks may range in size from very small areas up to thirty or more acres; they may be located independently or in conjunction with neighborhood playgrounds, playfields, or elementary schools.

The Community Concept

For planning purposes, a community is a larger residential area of a city, comparable in size to a high school district (as a neighborhood is comparable to an elementary school district). Communities are often composed of three to five neighborhoods, with populations ranging between twenty thousand and forty thousand residents, and extending for about two or three miles in diameter. The community is regarded as a natural grouping of neighborhoods and as a recognized area of the city. Community facilities generally include the following:

1. *Community Playfields.* Planners recommend that there be a community playfield within a half-mile to a mile of every home, depending on population density. Playfields frequently include a children's playground, fields for popular team sports, and multiple use hard-top courts. It is generally recommended that playfields offer at least one acre of space for each eight hundred of the total population served; thus, a community of sixteen thousand would have a twenty-acre playfield. Space standards also suggest that playfields should range between about twelve and thirty acres.

2. *Larger Community Parks.* The larger parks provide facilities for the following types of activities: family and group picnicking, day camping, horseback riding, boating, swimming, and fishing. They may also include golf courses, zoological gardens, athletic fields, ornamental gardens, athletic complexes, and winter-sports areas. Frequently, these parks also provide a setting for citywide community centers, museums, or libraries. Standards recommend at least one large community park with a minimum of one hundred acres for each forty thousand to fifty thousand persons.

Community planning guides also usually include recommendations for "reservations" (large tracts of land kept in a natural state), recreation centers that house auditoriums, gymnasiums, and other indoor facilities, and such other resources as swimming pools and beaches, stadiums, museums, nature trails, fairgrounds, and hunting and fishing areas.

Park and Recreation Space Standards

City planners have also developed guides for the minimum provision of park and outdoor recreation space, usually expressed in terms of the ratio of recreation acreage to the total population. The development of such standards has been described as follows:

> Quite early in the century, someone proposed that a municipality should provide ten acres of recreation space per thousand of the population. The actual origin of this standard is not known; however . . . because it was reasonable, and, no doubt, partly because of its simplicity, the figure

was widely accepted in this country, and is still the most accepted standard. It is generally applied only to recreation areas located within or immediately adjacent to the city, but not to outlying parks.[6]

Other countries also have planning standards, and some have made a more systematic attempt to justify them. In Great Britain, for example, the most widely respected space standard has been six acres of permanent playing space per one thousand population, excluding school playing fields, woodlands, ornamental gardens, golf courses, or other open spaces where the public may not take part in organized games or sports. Patmore indicates that this standard was developed by the National Playing Fields Association in 1925, based on a formula which assumed two hundred of every one thousand persons falling within the ten to forty age group would be dependent upon public facilities for games and sports.

> Their basic needs could be accommodated on a six-acre site, with just room for a senior football pitch, a junior football or hockey pitch, a cricket square, a three-rink bowling green, two tennis courts, a children's playground, and a pavilion.[7]

Various professional or regional planning bodies have accepted the principle of such standards and have proposed variations of them from time to time, based on changing needs or conditions. For example, the Committee on Park and Recreation Standards of the American Society of Planning Officials concluded in 1943 that the original standard was not practical for more densely populated cities, and that ten acres per two thousand persons should be set as a minimum in cities of over five hundred thousand, and ten acres per three thousand in cities of over one million. On the other hand, the International City Managers Association has consistently supported the formula of ten acres per one thousand persons as essential for a well-balanced recreation program.

In the mid-1960s, the National Recreation Association presented a revised formula of acreage standards, which included property owned both by local authorities and by nearby counties, park districts, and state agencies. The formula recommended that a minimum of twenty-five acres per one thousand residents be provided by local government authorities, and that sixty-five acres be provided by state government—a total of ninety acres. In addition to such population-ratio standards, other planning authorities have recommended that a minimum percentage of land of a community (typically 10 percent) be devoted to open space or recreation and park use. In some suburban counties, planning and zoning officials have conditioned the granting of building permits to home developers upon their setting aside such a percentage of land for recreation use by deeding the property to the local government.

Facilities Standards

Accompanying space standards, planning organizations have also recommended specific minimum requirements for recreation buildings, sports areas, or other special facilities, according to population totals. For example, planners have recommended a baseball diamond for every six thousand persons, a tennis court for every two thousand, and a gymnasium for every ten thousand.

Guides for Recreation and Park Planning

Traditionally, then, city planning for recreation and parks has been based on the concepts of "neighborhood" and "community," on the provision of specific types of facilities, and on the application of minimum space and facilities standards. In addition, several general guides have been developed by professional organizations and authors in this field, which provide a framework for effective planning.

1. Recreation and park systems should be established to meet total community leisure needs, and should provide equal recreational opportunity to all, as far as this is possible.

2. Planning should be based on a comprehensive and thorough evaluation of existing public, private, and commercial facilities and services, including the public schools, and should strive for the fullest possible coordination of these agencies.

3. Planning should reflect the needs and wishes of all citizens and should involve them in data-gathering and decision-making processes.

4. Each recreation center or park should be centrally located within the area it is to serve and should provide safe and convenient access for all residents. So far as possible, facilities should be equally distributed throughout the major areas of the city.

5. Each park or recreation facility should be designed individually to ensure its suitability for the specific population it is to serve.

6. Beauty and functional efficiency are equally important goals of planning, and convenience and economy of maintenance are important additional considerations.

7. It is essential to have a long-range plan for site acquisition, to ensure that properties within the path of urban development will be acquired while still available.

8. Efforts should be made to achieve space standards through acquisition in advance of anticipated needs, even if limited financial resources delay actual development of areas and facilities.

9. Properties acquired should be held in perpetuity (protected by law against diversion to other than park and recreation uses).

10. Public school buildings and grounds should be designed for the fullest community use, through reciprocal agreements and coordination between school and recreation and park authorities.

11. Recreation properties should be developed to permit the fullest possible use by different groups at appropriate times, on a year-round and round-the-clock basis.

12. It is the function of the recreation and park department to meet the community's needs for wholesome recreation rather than to act primarily as a land acquisition or development agency. Thus, planning should include not only land and facilities but also programs and administration.

Although these guides for recreation and park planning are generally constructive, the acreage and facilities standards approach, which is the basis of much actual planning, must be critically examined. More and more experts are coming to realize that these standards lack validity. Apart from the fact that they were arbitrarily devised, space and facilities standards have proven to be unrealistic, particularly for large cities. In 1955, a study of almost two hundred cities revealed that only 27 percent had achieved the basic minimum of ten acres per thousand of population.

The application of a uniform set of standards to all cities does not allow for differences in population makeup, availability of open space, recreational needs and interests, financial capability, mobility, topography, climate, and similar factors. The assumption that each neighborhood needs a uniform set of play lots, playgrounds, and small parks, or that it is possible to prescribe a given number of gymnasiums, bridle trails, or swimming pools simply on the basis of population totals, cannot be justified. Nonetheless, many planning studies continue to use the standards approach even today. The strength of the standards approach lies in its official support by respected planning and professional organizations and in its generally desirable level of provision of recreation space and facilities which may be adjusted to meet the needs and capabilities of specific communities.

The traditional approach is also meaningless in many newer suburban areas, which consist of large residential districts lacking central cores of governmental services. In some of the more extreme cases, schools, police and fire services, postal services, and sewers, sanitation, water, and highway services may all be provided by different jurisdictions. Such patterns are completely different from the traditional view of the community as a self-contained unit with a core of central services.

Criticism of Traditional Planning

Herbert Gans takes the position that much urban planning has been ineffective because it has been based on nineteenth-century ideals of efficiency, order, and beauty couched within a small-town framework of white, Protestant, middle-class values.[8] Assuming that the ideal city can be developed by providing an ideal physical environment, traditional planning has permitted architects and engineers to dominate the planning process and has assigned little importance to the social, economic, and political factors that influence human behavior. Gans urges that recreation and park planning decisions consider more carefully the real needs, lifestyles, and expressed desires of neighborhood residents.

Another authority, Jane Jacobs, has concluded that urban planning has often yielded low-income projects which segregate people by income, race, and even age, and deprive them of the vital sense of neighborhood "belonging" that should enrich community life.[9] She criticizes particularly the practice of continuing to build small parks and playgrounds based on outmoded concepts and models in our cities. The common reaction following outbursts of gang violence in large cities is to call for more parks and playgrounds. This proposed solution ignores the reality that street gangs in large cities often do their fighting in parks and playgrounds, and some of the highest urban delinquency rates have been recorded in the parklike belts around public housing projects.

Other planning authorities who have systematically examined the use of recreation and park facilities in American cities have found that many parks are no longer used by middle- or upper-class families and too often, in lower-class neighborhoods, have become hangouts for youth gangs and derelicts. Jacobs suggests that playgrounds and small parks be made more meaningful and attractive through the fuller provision of more varied and interesting kinds of activities. A careful choice of location would ensure easy access and increase the flow of people passing through and around them. "Demand goods" should be provided in the form of swimming, sports fields, fishing, boating, music, concerts, dancing, kite flying, model boat sailing, artificial skating rinks, and other kinds of attractive features that will encourage the involvement of people of all ages, through the day and evening.

New Planning Priorities

Entirely new approaches have emerged in the planning of recreation and park facilities in urban centers in recent years. One of the most interesting examples is the *social needs index* as a basis for determining planning priorities, formulated by the Community Council of Greater New York in a thorough analysis of recreation facilities, agencies, and leadership in the city's officially designated neighborhoods in the early 1960s.[10] The council analyzed the comparative need for service of each neighborhood, using three socioeconomic characteristics as criteria: (1) median family income, (2) juvenile delinquency rates, and (3) changing ethnic composition, which was linked to other needs for social service, such as housing or welfare assistance. An analysis of each neighborhood's recreation and park facilities, agencies, and services revealed that nine of the city's seventy-four neighborhoods contained over 53 percent of the total parkland in the city. In contrast, forty-five of the neighborhoods (particularly those in older and poorer areas) had only 10 percent of the park and recreation space. As a general pattern, the sixteen neighborhoods with the highest degree of socioeconomic need and community disorganization rated far below the city average of available public and voluntary agency group work and recreation resources and services. From a comparison of social need and presently available resources, the council developed a "needs index," to serve as the basis for establishing planning priorities.

As a follow-up, the City Planning Commission conducted a study that identified the areas of the city where social pathology and disorganization were highest, and assigned them three levels of priority for recreation and park development: (1) *major action areas,* where problems of poverty, deteriorated housing and crime were the worst and facilities and programs generally the poorest; (2) *preventive renewal areas,* densely crowded neighborhoods generally located in the path of outward migration from the major action areas; and (3) *sound areas,* in which social problems tended to be minimal and recreation opportunity relatively adequate. Compensatory approaches to allocating resources over a sixteen-year period were recommended to improve recreation opportunity in major action areas.[11]

Other planning approaches have focused less sharply on parks and playgrounds as such, and have been more concerned with the overall image of the city in modern life. One distinguished urban planner, Charles Abrams, stressed the need to provide a range of leisure resources and opportunities which make the city a visually attractive, interesting, and exciting place in which to live or visit.[12] Abrams points out that Americans vacationing in Europe visit the great cities of Paris, London, Amsterdam, and Rome—centers of culture, architecture and historical interest—but when vacationing in the United States, Americans usually travel through the countryside rather than to the cities.

Abrams reminds us that most American cities were blessed with good landscapes and waterscapes before becoming industrialized and polluted. Existing waterfronts, which too often are hidden behind highways or lined by unused wharves, should be utilized fully, providing attractions for sightseeing and casual recreation such as heliports and hydrofoil bases, marinas, seafood restaurants and fish markets, and other developments which encourage visitors. American cities should build, as many European cities have, recreational facilities like fishing piers, sunbathing areas, swimming barges and boating centers along their rivers; as water pollution decreases, these will become increasingly attractive.

Abrams urges that larger city parks become centers not only of natural beauty but of more active sports and other outdoor recreational activities that smaller areas cannot provide. Well-located chess centers, theater productions, concerts, dancing, and other planned evening recreational events would attract people to the parks and make them safer places to visit. For a much needed relief from steel and concrete facades, Abrams suggests that we vastly increase the number of trees, parks, and green spaces. Trees and shrubs are much more than "aesthetic props"; functional as well as beautiful, they provide ventilation and shade and absorb noise and dust.

City streets should be enhanced to provide places to stroll, sightsee, and bicycle. The character of such ethnic areas as Chinatown, Greenwich Village, Little Italy, and similar neighborhoods with outdoor markets, special celebrations and festivals, and other colorful customs should be protected. We need to encourage rather than discourage such enterprises as theaters, art galleries, bookstores, sidewalk cafes, cabarets, and coffee houses. Fuller municipal support should be given to opera and dance companies, folklore groups, and choral performing groups.

Equal to the need to attract visitors to the cities is the need to provide leisure opportunities for the urban residents themselves—places where young adults can meet socially under desirable circumstances, where mothers can bring their young children to play, where older people can find companionship and creative interests. The city should be ideally equipped to provide these opportunities; through well-planned use of its institutions, universities, special schools, libraries, museums, and other organizations, the large city is able to meet a much wider range of interests than suburban areas or small towns.

All of these suggestions provide important new ideas for urban planning. They must, however, be fitted into a total approach toward solving the problems and the city, which in turn must be based on a realistic understanding of current social trends and how they have affected the provision of recreation and parks in urban society. Seymour Gold has identified a number of these critical trends and factors, concluding that we have reached an "era of limits" as a consequence of the cost-revenue crisis affecting local governments. Limited help from Federal and state governments combined with high levels of inflation and unemployment make drastic cuts in municipal services inevitable.

> Small is beautiful, less is more. . . . we have reached the limits of unqualified growth and must make more rational use of existing resources. . . .

> Taxpayers . . . are not likely to approve bond issues or tax increases for local parks. They will develop a serious interest in the performance or effectiveness of leisure services to obtain the best value for their tax dollar. . . .

> The existing systems of recreation spaces will be all most communities can afford to maintain . . . which suggests making the best use of existing spaces that desperately need renewal.[13]

On the positive side, Gold suggests that "a new spirit of self-help, community involvement, and consciousness is emerging in many places. . . . Advocacy and pluralism are becoming expected dimensions of the planning and decision-making process." Government must begin to do things *with* people, rather than for them, and traditionally conceived recreation and park departments must merge their functions and capabilities with other community agencies and departments.

Based on such considerations, it is possible to identify a whole new set of guides for urban recreation and park planning. These are not intended as a replacement for the guidelines summarized earlier in this chapter, but rather as a broader statement about contemporary planning approaches in metropolitan centers.

Contemporary Guides for Urban Recreation and Park Planning

1. *Planning as a Total Community Concern.* Many urban recreation and park planning studies have examined only the physical aspects of recreation, and have further limited this focus to the parks, playgrounds, and other facilities operated by the public recreation and park department. To be truly effective, urban recreation and park planning today must deal with the total structure of leisure opportunity, including the facilities, programs, and services offered by public, voluntary, private and commercial agencies. Planners must consider recreation and parks as part of the total spectrum of social, educational, health, environmental, and transportation services. As a corollary, recreation and park planning must also be concerned with the needs of citizens on every socioeconomic level, of both sexes, and of all ages and ethnic backgrounds.

2. *Planning for Operational Effectiveness.* Traditional park and recreation planning has given primary emphasis to the acquisition and development of physical resources, such as parks, playgrounds and recreation centers. Today it is recognized that planning must also consider operational elements, such as the need for staffing, costs of maintenance, scheduling, and revenue potential of facilities. Particularly for people who lack mobility and easy access to recreation facilities that are at a distance from their homes, planning must deal with problems of transportation.

It is necessary to ask who will use specific facilities, at what times of the day, week, or year, what the costs of operation will be, and similar questions. When there are several agencies in the community that provide similar services, the planning process should consider recommendations for joint program operations or coordination and cooperation between agencies.

3. *Determination of Planning Priorities.* As indicated earlier in this chapter, uniform standards for recreation areas and facilities are no longer useful as the sole basis for making resource development decisions. Planners and municipal officials who continue to use uniform standards should recognize that they will be of greatest value when applied as general guidelines rather than as fixed or rigid standards. Particularly within large cities, planners must establish other ways of determining priorities for development of facilities.

One such approach has been suggested—the "needs index" method, which determines priorities based on the social needs of neighborhoods and the degree to which their existing facilities measure up to community standards.

Development of new classifications of recreation services and facilities will be necessary to identify program opportunities that will meet the needs of urban residents. Facility and use classification systems have been developed for Federal and state parks, ranging from primitive areas to high intensity recreation areas. However, urban planners have not thought in similar terms to meet the needs of inner city residents. Typically, when the National Park Service has established outdoor recreation areas in or near major urban centers, it has been difficult for their planners to conceptualize their roles and the range of facilities they should offer.

4. *Intergovernmental Planning an Essential.* Most planning efforts today are carried out within individual counties, municipalities, or townships. Meaningful urban planning must, however, begin to come to grips with the resources, capabilities, and problems of total metropolitan districts. A clear-cut assignment of responsibility for functions (such as the county or large park district providing major outdoor recreation resources or centralized programs in special interest activities, while the local city or village government meets daily needs and provides close-to-home recreation opportunities in playgrounds and community centers) is essential to effective planning. A key factor in this respect is the willingness of outlying communities to cooperate with central cities in the solution of jointly shared problems. It has become clear that suburbs cannot thrive while the cities they surround are decaying. Planning must help to point the way to effective, cooperative relationships between these two levels of government.

The Federal and state governments must also assume a more purposeful role in urban planning today. Since the inception of the Bureau of Outdoor Recreation and the Land and Water Conservation Fund, outdoor recreation plans (including detailed analyses of urban needs) have been developed in all fifty states. Federal and state authorities have established more and more large independent parks or recreation areas near urban centers. All this clearly suggests that meaningful planning to meet urban leisure needs requires the full participation of all levels of government.

A second important aspect of intergovernmental planning lies in the emergence of regional planning to meet metropolitan needs. Christian comments that "regionalism" has become an increasingly popular term in today's governmental vocabulary. With many park and recreation services widely accepted as regional in scope, and with a proliferation of organizations and agencies responsible for planning, review of grants, and implementation of major projects, there has been widespread debate among administrators and experts regarding issues of local control and accountability:

> Counties, special districts, and municipalities may all be involved with the planning, development, and operation of regional parks and recreation services. Recreation and parks in metropolitan areas cannot be viewed purely as local matters in the traditional sense. The old division of accountability or responsibility whereby local governments planned and developed their own park and recreation systems is no longer practical and functional in our highly structured and complex systems of urban government. Unfortunately, little agreement has evolved among the various local governments as to their proper roles . . . [14]

Christian describes several examples of cooperation between separate units of government, such as counties and municipalities, community and school agencies, and similar organizations, intended to define appropriate roles and help them share resources to maximize service delivery. Such approaches must be encouraged in metropolitan recreation and park planning.

5. *Meaningful Community Representation in Planning Process.* Urban planning today must provide opportunities for representation and involvement by all members of the community. During the 1960s, particularly in programs generated and funded by the Office of Economic Opportunity, the principle of "maximum feasible participation" in the planning and administration of community-based programs was established. Through the development of "community corporations," local "task forces" or "little City Halls," many cities have attempted to decentralize planning and decision making, and give local residents a voice in government action. Middle- and upper-class residents have usually been able to make their wishes known with respect to recreation and park needs in most communities. In recent years, poor people—particularly those who are black or Spanish-speaking—have demanded an equal share of policy-making and administrative roles in such programs.

What is a workable and constructive approach to meeting this challenge? Clearly, it cannot be to abandon decision-making and planning functions entirely to neighborhood groups. Decisions regarding what appears to be a local problem or demand can often be made only in the light of overall city policy or financial capability. In addition, it is often difficult to determine which one of several competing groups represents the real needs of the community. Nonetheless, it is essential that the planning process be made as responsive as possible to community residents. The variety of possible mechanisms include using interest inventories, forming local study committees, having residents represented on planning and policy-making boards, and submitting proposals or facilities designs to community organizations for their approval. Community residents should be consulted not after decisions are made but throughout the planning process.

6. *Sharper Focus on Disadvantaged Urban Areas.* Previous sections of this text have made it clear that if recreation and park service is to be a viable area of contemporary urban life, it must become more forceful in undertaking significant social problems, particularly with respect to serving disadvantaged and minority-group populations.

During the period of racial militance when rioting and looting were frequent throughout the inner cities of the United States, government concern was high, and substantial support was given to recreation programs in disadvantaged urban areas. Today, with such social turmoil at a low ebb, special Federal programs have been sharply reduced. Yet the problem has not disappeared. While great masses of society are able to spend lavishly to satisfy their leisure needs, the poor in both urban and rural areas have only the most limited and barren recreational opportunities. Yvonne Brathwaite Burke, Congressperson from California, comments that the average ghetto child never sees a national park; the masses who live in poverty never use a campsite or enjoy the streams, lakes, and trees at state recreation areas:

> A few blocks carved out of the city with park benches and swings and a little patch of grass is often the only way a park is envisaged by many. All too often these few blocks are characterized by gangs, muggings, and fear. Though thousands of Americans enjoy the recreation facilities of America, the ones who need it most do not.

375

Accessibility is the key word in describing minority concerns in the area of leisure and recreation. Far too often those who most need, but can least afford, recreation opportunities are denied access to available facilities and services.[15]

To provide equal access to the nation's recreation resources, Congressperson Burke concludes, it is necessary to examine the recreation needs of society, particularly in urban areas, and to begin comprehensive planning which involves recreation as an equal and separate component of the transportation, housing, education, and health systems needed in the immediate and distant future.

7. *Linkage of Recreation with Other Community Services.* It is essential that recreation and park planning be closely integrated with other areas of community service. Whenever feasible, facilities should be designed to house a multiplicity of functions. Community centers should be able to serve a variety of age groups with relevant programs: nonworking mothers and pre-school children during the day, children of working mothers in day-care centers, elementary school children after school, teen-agers and adults during the evenings, retired persons during the day. Centers should provide places where children may do homework and receive tutoring or participate in cultural enrichment programs. Job counseling, health and family guidance services, legal assistance, narcotics addiction programs, after-care programs for discharged mental patients, and sheltered workshops for retarded youth and adults are all part of the potential role of urban recreation centers. Centers may also provide a meeting place for local organizations, antipoverty agencies, and other community groups.

Recreation must be viewed—and planned for—as an important area of community need, a valuable supplement to other services, a means of having members of the community take on planning and leadership roles, and a "threshold" activity that attracts many participants to centers.

8. *Design of Areas and Facilities.* Improved design is an essential element of contemporary urban planning. Much of the past design of recreation and park facilities has been hidebound, based on standardized layouts appropriate only for stereotyped patterns of use. Entirely new approaches to the design of facilities are needed.

One example is the recent increased use of mobile and portable recreation units. Particularly during the summer months, many communities have made extensive use of mobile stages and theater units, arts and crafts and science wagons, skatemobiles and playgroundmobiles, and portable pools and play streets. As suggested earlier (see page 256), more effective planning would make use of mobile recreation units for all age groups, for the disabled as well as the healthy, for rural as well as urban areas, and in understaffed parks, playgrounds, or centers—as well as in the streets.

The design of playgrounds is another example of innovative facilities planning. Many cities have had playground revolutions in recent years. Designers have increasingly made use of new kinds of equipment for experimental and exploratory play by young children—free-form playhouses, animals, mounds, pyramids, tunnels, and climbing areas. Contemporary designers emphasize walls and separators that become play equipment in themselves and make imaginative use of benches and low walls to create sitting areas that are like outdoor rooms on different levels. Playgrounds today have become much more visually and aesthetically pleasing. Some playgrounds have been designed as centers for total neighborhood activity, providing both indoor and outdoor areas where teen-agers may hold social events and sports activities; where senior citizens may read, have discussions and parties, play chess and checkers, and listen to music; where families may hold parties and picnics; and where entire neighborhoods may have social events and community festivities. "Adventure" playgrounds have been designed to permit children to explore natural materials, build their own clubhouses or play equipment, and engage in creative forms of play.

In the slum areas of many cities, where open space is usually limited, there are often small parcels of land in the form of vacant lots or backyards, too often heaped with garbage and junk. Such areas may be reclaimed through the joint efforts of local community groups, block associations, and religious or social organizations, and designed as small "vest-pocket" parks or playgrounds. In planning such areas, full neighborhood participation is essential. Asner writes:

> We have set a pattern of self-help by requiring residents to *begin* the process by requesting their parks and by serving as partners in planning, construction, and maintenance. This is done to develop their initiative, resources and powers of decision-making. It is also done in self-defense. We know that residents feel a sense of proprietorship in something they ask for and help build. We also know they participate more if the facility is designed to meet valid needs which they pinpoint. The finished park produces a spirit of neighborhood solidarity and a close-at-hand focal point for getting together to plan community events, including additional neighborhood improvement.[16]

In addition to making design improvements, many crowded cities have become increasingly experimental in the use of space. Roof-top and high-rise recreation centers in congested areas, development of facilities in the space under elevated train tracks or highways, the use of air-supported structures for convertible year-round programs, and landfills using compacted garbage to build hills for skiing or other park areas are but a few of the possibilities for innovative planning of urban recreation facilities. Alert administrators will monitor the pulse of public recreation interests and will, when feasible, design new types of facilities to meet emerging needs. For example, the recreation department of Ocean City, Maryland recently built two small skateboard facilities to satisfy the growing interest of many young people who were skateboarding on public streets and sidewalks, causing frequent accidents.

> The total cost of the two facilities was approximately $28,000, about the cost of two tennis courts with lights. The maximum number of people that can use two tennis courts in one hour is eight. The recreation department has estimated that a minimum of 150 participants per hour use the small skateboard facility at peak times.[17]

Obviously, it would be a mistake to build new facilities to house every fad that might die out within a few weeks. However, alert departments will explore such possibilities carefully, and will closely integrate all facility design projects with the operational needs of the programs that are to go into them.

9. *Continued Emphasis on Open Space Acquisition.* Along with design and facilities improvements, urban planning must place a high priority on continuing to

acquire open space for recreation and park needs whenever it is possible to do so. Although the rehabilitation and operation of existing facilities are major concerns, it is equally important to develop new areas, particularly in the oldest and most crowded neighborhoods of cities.

The acquisition of open space must be within a framework of the total human, economic, and ecological needs of the community and region. Some properties should be preserved in their natural states—either because of their irreplaceable beauty and primitive quality, or because they are essential to wildlife. (Even within the boundaries of some modern cities, there are major flyways for wildfowl, breeding grounds, and similar areas that must be protected.) Planners must resist encroachment pressures that seek to take over parkland for other uses, particularly major parks that are outstanding examples of landscape design and civic beauty.

Beyond this, entirely new approaches to conserving natural areas must be explored. Tax deferral arrangements, leasing, use of marginal properties attached to highways, airports, or power generation sites, gifts, and dedication by subdividers all offer such possibilities. One outstanding recent acquisition was in Los Angeles, where the County Board of Supervisors accepted an open space easement for approximately 80 percent of Catalina Island, twenty-two miles off the Southern California coast, for fifty years. This unusual acquisition of over forty thousand acres of relatively untouched canyons, beaches, and wilderness areas was made possible through the transfer of title to a nonprofit foundation called the Santa Catalina Island Conservancy, allowing a tax reduction for the remainder of the property. Greben writes:

> Under the easement agreement, the conservancy is responsible for maintaining and controlling the area, while the county reserves the right to construct buildings and make recreational improvements, such as campsites, equestrian trails, museums, and similar facilities.[18]

Such innovative arrangements must be explored more fully in the future by all communities, both in the interest of preserving available lands and water areas for the future, and to provide badly needed recreation resources for urban populations of all types.

10. *Involvement of Recreation and Park Professionals in Planning.* Finally, if urban planning is to be most effective in this sphere, it must incorporate the professional judgment of recreation and park professionals. There is a crucial need to assign skilled planners to recreation departments, and similarly, a need to involve recreation and park professionals in work with planning specialists so that their special expertise contributes to the total planning process. Too often in municipal government, detailed plans for the design of recreation and park areas and facilities are seen by recreation professionals only after their completion. The Bureau of Outdoor Recreation reported in 1973 that

> only about half of all large city and county governments support ongoing recreation planning activities, and only 25 percent have planners assigned to this function on a full-time basis. However, 60 percent of the larger local governments surveyed have prepared or updated long-range, open-space-park-recreation plans in the last two years . . . generally [with] more emphasis on planning physical recreation resources

than on planning programs and recreation services or protecting locally significant natural resources.[19]

Obviously, the process of effective urban planning, evaluation, and research will be enhanced by increased participation of recreation and park professionals. Planning will also be more effective if it is approached on what Rettie calls a horizontal level. He describes how modern man constantly tries to impose vertical solutions on horizontal problems.

> In the United States, virtually all professional education is vertical; that is, knowledge is imparted on the basis of categorical subject matter. The landscape architect is taught landscape architecture. Period. The sanitary engineer is taught sanitary engineering. Period. The political scientist is taught political science. Period. And so on.[20]

But, Rettie continues, our most important contemporary problems are not easily solved by single disciplines. For example, the problems of cities cut horizontally across a great many disciplines—urban planning, architecture, transportation, recreation and parks, public health, public safety, energy shortages, and many others. Not until the necessity for an interdisciplinary approach is understood, and planners are equipped to apply horizontal solutions in these varied areas of concern, will our urban planning efforts be successful.

All meaningful planning must take into account the key social trends, problems, and issues that influence leisure behavior and government action. Chapter 16 analyzes these factors in detail, and draws implications for public policy and professional guidelines.

Chapter Fifteen

1 Diana R. Dunn, "Leisure Resources in America's Inner Cities," *Parks and Recreation,* March 1974, p. 56.

2 Richard Kraus, *Urban Parks and Recreation: Challenge of the 1970's* (New York: Community Council of Greater New York, 1972).

3 Edward Higbee, *The Squeeze* (New York: William Morrow, 1960), p. 235.

4 Lowden Wingo, Jr., "Recreation and Urban Development: A Policy Perspective," *Annals of the American Academy of Political and Social Science,* 1964, p. 129.

5 See for example Carol Peterson's application of systems analysis to therapeutic recreation in Elliott M. Avedon, *Therapeutic Recreation Service: An Applied Behavioral Science Approach* (Englewood Cliffs, N. J.: Prentice-Hall, 1974), pp. 128–55.

6 *Municipal Recreation Administration* (Chicago: International City Managers' Association, 1960), p. 66.

7 J. Allan Patmore, *Land and Leisure in England and Wales* (Rutherford, N. J.: Fairleigh Dickinson Press, 1971), p. 84.

8 Herbert J. Gans, "City Planning in America: A Sociological Analysis," in *People and Plans: Essays on Urban Problems and Solutions* (New York: Basic Books, 1968), pp. 58–61.

9 Jane Jacobs, *The Death and Life of Great American Cities* (New York: Random House, 1961).

10 *Comparative Recreation Needs and Services in New York Neighborhoods* (New York: Community Council of Greater New York, 1963).

11 Steven Reichstein and Neiland Douglas, *Recreation Facilities in New York City: A Method of Assigning Budgetary Priorities* (New York: Department of City Planning, 1968).

12 Charles Abrams, *The City Is the Frontier* (New York: Harper-Colophon Books, 1965, 1967), pp. 287–353 of 1967 edition.

13 Seymour M. Gold, ''The Fate of Urban Parks,'' *Parks and Recreation,* October 1976, pp. 13–14.

14 John W. Christian, ''In Partnership for the People,'' *Parks and Recreation,* October 1976, p. 25.

15 Yvonne Brathwaite Burke, ''Editorial: Accessibility Is the Key,'' *Parks and Recreation,* April 1975, p. 17.

16 Eve Asner, ''Vest Pocket Parks,'' *Parks and Recreation,* May 1968, p. 33.

17 Gary J. Arthur, ''The Ocean Bowl Story,'' *Parks and Recreation,* December 1976, p. 16.

18 Seymour Greben, ''An Island for the Future,'' *Parks and Recreation,* August 1976, p. 20.

19 *Outdoor Recreation: A Legacy for America* (Washington, D.C.: Bureau of Outdoor Recreation, U. S. Department of the Interior, 1973).

20 Dwight F. Rettie, ''A New Perspective on Leisure,'' *Parks and Recreation,* August 1974, p. 24.

CURRENT TRENDS, PROBLEMS, AND ISSUES IN RECREATION AND LEISURE

The remarkable growth of organized recreation service throughout the United States has been documented in earlier chapters of this text. Despite this growth, it is obvious that there are serious problems directly related to the role of the recreation and park profession in society. How are this field's major priorities to be determined? What yardsticks should be used in making decisions about facilities, programs, and population groups to be served? What solutions can be found for overcrowding, crime, and vandalism in our cities, for similar problems in many Federal and state parks, and for the pollution of the environment throughout the industrial world? What is the financial outlook for the support of public and voluntary leisure services—particularly in an era of economic stringency on all levels? In what ways can government provide more efficient and effective services within this field? How can professionals obtain fuller public recognition and support for program development in recreation and parks? These problems and issues are discussed throughout this chapter.

Social Role of Community Recreation Service

Probably the most important issue that must be faced today is the need to clarify the social role of community recreation service. At its inception, the recreation movement was reformist and socially purposeful. Its intentions were to combat the pathology of the slum, to prevent or reduce juvenile delinquency, to provide educational and cultural enrichment, and to use recreation as a means of strengthening community life and civic pride and unity. Gradually, as it merged with the parks movement, it moved into the development of such facilities as boating marinas, ski centers, golf courses, and sports and cultural complexes which tended to be supported by fee structures and to serve middle-class or well-to-do residents. Programs designed to meet the needs of disadvantaged populations or those with social or physical disability became more and more the concern of voluntary social agencies in the cities. David Gray described this process of change:

> The recreation movement was born with a social conscience. It grew up with the settlement house movement, the kindergarten movement and the youth movement that fostered the great youth agencies of the nation. Its earlier practitioners had a social welfare motivation in which the social ends of human development, curbing juvenile delinquency, informal education, cultural enrichment, health improvement and other objectives were central. Gradually the social welfare mission weakened and a philosophy which sees recreation as an end in itself was adopted; this is the common view in public recreation agencies throughout the country.[1]

Although recreation practitioners claimed important social benefits for recreation, they developed few programs that actually sought to accomplish these ends. Lip service was constantly paid to the ideal of equal leisure opportunity for all, but residents in affluent neighborhoods were far more successful in obtaining attractive parks and varied recreation services than the poor. Recreation was considered an ideal means of promoting group harmony; yet its practitioners made few efforts to bring about improved social relationships or integrated programs in racially mixed communities.

More recently, however, an increasing number of recreation and park professionals have begun to initiate socially purposeful programs. Especially in metropolitan areas, they have developed services for the physically and mentally disabled and for the aging. With the help of Federal grants, many have improved programs for the poor, for youth, or for other populations in special need. Yet, there remains the lack of a clear sense of social purposefulness and a sharply defined role in attempting to meet critical needs in modern life. More than any other spokespersons, Gray and Greben urged the recreation and park profession to pursue the following goals:

> To adopt a humanistic ethic as the central value system of the recreation movement.

> To develop and act on a social conscience that focuses park and recreation services on the great social problems of our time and develop programs designed to contribute to the amelioration of those problems.

> To develop a set of guidelines for programs that emphasize human welfare, human development, and social action.

> To establish common cause with the environmentalists and other social movements that embrace a value system similar to our own.

> To develop evaluation methods capable of measuring the contribution of

park and recreation experience to human welfare which can make us accountable for the human consequences of what we do.

To develop an effective interpretation program capable of articulating to a national and worldwide audience the meaning of park and recreation experience in human terms.[2]

Similar goals have also been expressed by Canadian recreation and park professionals, particularly in the Montmorency Conference on Leisure, which sought to extend and integrate government efforts in the leisure field, and bring about a new and enriched public awareness of the importance of recreation.[3]

If the expanded social role just described were fully accepted, it would force the abandonment of the idea that recreation is activity carried on for its own sake, without extrinsic goals or purposes. Those groups with the greatest need and the lowest capability for serving themselves independently would be given specially enriched services and facilities—in effect, a compensatory approach.

To make such expanded social goals a reality, it would be necessary to link recreation in a team effort with other social services, such as job training, remedial education and career-ladder projects, or multiservice centers and community improvement ventures. All this implies a totally new emphasis on recreation as a socially rehabilitative or therapeutic modality. It does not mean that recreation would no longer be concerned with providing pleasure to participants; this would continue to be a primary function. But "fun" would not be an end in itself.

It should be stressed that this point of view has not been widely accepted and carried out by professionals throughout the United States and Canada. Rejection of this view has been evidenced by the unwillingness of large numbers of delegates to National Recreation and Park Congresses to support strong statements of purpose that deal with social needs and important national priorities. One critic called the issues statements presented at the 1975 Dallas Congress passive and neutral, in their approach toward such issues as the economy, unemployment, environmental concerns, and recreation's role in society. He asked:

Does the statement that we have "respect for the diverse life-styles" mean that we respect the right of minority groups to use services and facilities to service their needs? Does it refer to our responsibility to respect the major social movements of our day such as the rights of America's women and elderly? Are we finally ready to take our place in the twentieth century and move beyond cards, bingo, and chess for our older Americans? Do the people of the Dallas Congress support a multiservice concept where our recreation centers provide the elderly with nutrition, outreach, transportation programs, preventative health, and counseling services?[4]

Similarly, he condemned the unwillingness of the Congress delegates, in floor votes, to support the special needs of urban Americans, despite severe shortages of parks and open spaces in many cities. Clearly, although many recreation and park professionals and educators accept the mission eloquently presented by Gray and Greben, many others are unwilling to accept this role, finding it irrelevant, inappropriate, or too expensive.

383

A Changing Framework of Leisure Values

We have traditionally assumed that recreation—and particularly community recreation service—must be socially desirable and constructive. Those who preach the doctrine of a new "leisure ethic" see recreation as a vital, socially liberating, and enriching kind of experience. Murphy, for example, writes of the "yearning" by youth to develop new lifestyles which will integrate work, leisure, and family life into a single, dynamic, meaningful life pattern. As this happens, and as the young "seek new kinds of sensory experience and personal relationships, many of the traditional forms of recreation opportunity no longer are as relevant as they have been in the past."[5]

This trend raises certain questions. If the changing lifestyles and leisure values of the young—or for that matter, the middle-aged or aging—come into conflict with the established values of society, or demand new kinds of services or recreational experiences, whose standard of social or moral desirability is to be used in recreation program planning? A corollary question is: if community recreation departments exclude many of the activities with the greatest appeal to large segments of the public, how will they be able to attract substantial numbers of participants?

The Basis of Moral Judgment

It is widely assumed that social desirability may be determined by a set of values which have been evolved by those who represent the "establishment" (opinion makers and responsible citizens, educators, ministers, civic officials, parents' groups, businesspersons, and other professionals concerned with community welfare).

Yet there is growing disagreement in our society on such matters, as well as increasing awareness of the gap between what we profess to be our social and moral values and what we practice. The Kinsey Report revealed that many of our most strongly accepted shibboleths regarding sexual behavior were secretly flouted by substantial proportions of the population. We have also had a highly ambivalent attitude toward gambling. On the one hand, gambling is generally regarded as morally questionable, or a social evil; on the other, it is widely used by state governments and even religious agencies as a means of obtaining revenue.

Our rejection of superimposed moral judgments and of attempts to govern leisure behavior in particular is illustrated by America's response to national Prohibition during the 1920s. It became a national pastime to defy and circumvent the law. A huge illicit liquor industry (manufacture, smuggling, and "speakeasies") was supported by the public and frequently operated hand in glove with elements of local government. Thus, in many ways, Americans have demonstrated that while they will pay lip service to official statements of what is desirable or morally worthwhile, in their private behavior they will operate quite differently. In recent years, resistance to traditional moral codes has become far more outspoken.

> The old taboos are dead or dying. A new, more permissive society is taking shape. Its outlines are etched most prominently in the arts—in the increasing nudity and frankness of today's films, in the blunt, often obscene language becoming endemic in American novels and plays . . . in freer fashions and franker advertising. And, behind this expanding

permissiveness in the arts stands a society in transition, a society that has lost its consensus on such crucial issues as premarital sex and clerical celibacy, marriage, birth control and sex education, a society that cannot agree on standards of conduct, language and manners, on what can be seen and heard.[6]

Accompanying these changes has been the proliferation of organized pornography in the form of films, "live shows," "adult" bookstores, massage parlors, "X-rated motels," and similar establishments. Prostitution has become increasingly open, and both Supreme Court decisions and a growing reluctance of law enforcement officials to prosecute "victimless" crimes have given a relatively free rein to the commercial exploitation of human sexuality.

Decline of Religious Influence

Accompanying and reinforcing such changes, there has been a decline in both the stability and the strength of many major religious institutions. In the Catholic Church, accepted practices such as the cloistered life for priests and nuns or the prohibition of birth control practices have been seriously challenged by the younger clergy and many Catholic laymen. The number of young Catholics entering seminaries has dropped steadily in recent years, and Catholic schools have undergone a severe threat from declining enrollments. Similar declines of religious authority are apparent in other major faiths. Studies reveal that many young Jews are rejecting Jewish education as irrelevant, and are demanding more meaningful religious practices. There is widespread agreement that organized religion—despite a slight upturn in attendance and religious interest in the mid-1970s—has lost much of its moral influence.

What many young people in particular seem to be seeking instead is a form of religious or spiritual involvement that provides a sense of revivalism, lay participation, and feelings of community based on mutual caring. The success of several Eastern faiths, such as Hare Krishna, the Mahararaj Ji communes, or the Rev. Sun Myung Moon's Unification Church, reflects this need. Similarly, the millions who have joined the "consciousness revolution," in such diverse forms of therapy or self-enrichment as Esalen, Synanon, Arica, Scientology, Bioenergetics or Transcendental Meditation, illustrate the human need for spiritual commitment or some form of faith that promises help in dealing with life's challenges.

Modern religious values are highly relevant to the question of leisure, because as shown in earlier chapters, our attitudes toward recreation and leisure in past societies were based on religious beliefs and influence. Beck points out that participation in leisure-time activities is more volitional and less easily controlled than many other areas of human behavior. He writes:

> The recreational system differs from other community systems because it abets and guides behavior that is natural and spontaneous to man. This is hardly true of the law enforcement system or the local welfare system. Recreation embraces all those actions that involve the pursuit of pleasure, and therefore aims to influence something that comes naturally to all people.

The definition of what kind of experience constitutes recreation is particular to the individual. One man's recreation is another man's work—or ennui. Therefore, a recreational system that seeks to use recreational activity to deter crime cannot superimpose any particular concept of what is and what is not pleasurable. It can only rule out of its orbit activities which, while pleasurable, are also criminal.[7]

This is a somewhat narrow view of the capability of organized recreation programs, since the program planners do have the ability to select and present only those forms of leisure activity which they regard as socially and morally desirable, and to ignore other forms of leisure activity. Other sponsors of leisure pursuits exist; a vast portion of organized crime in the United States is based on the satisfaction of varied forms of socially disapproved recreational interests. The most obvious of these relate to illegal gambling interests, control of organized prostitution and pornography enterprises, the bootlegging or sale of alcohol, operation of slot machines, and the distribution and sale of illegal narcotics.

The Role of Government

One might take the position that all these are clearly inadmissible forms of leisure activity, as far as sponsorship by government is concerned. Such a view would certainly be supported by the traditional philosophy of organized recreation service. Yet government often treads a narrow and shaky line between what is morally acceptable and upright and what could, under other forms of sponsorship, be regarded as criminal.

For example, since the time of the American Revolution, lotteries have been used from time to time to finance government projects in various states. During the 1960s, an increasing number of state governments began to sponsor parimutuel betting at racetracks and regular lotteries. By the mid-1970s, many states were operating O.T.B. shops (Off-Track Betting) and were holding large-scale, instant-payoff lotteries with lifetime income prizes running as high as a million dollars. State referendums were passed to permit cities like Atlantic City, New Jersey to offer legalized casino gambling to upgrade their local economies; immediately, dozens of other communities in financial crisis began to consider similar sources of revenue. In Nevada, not only is gambling legal, but prostitution has also been tolerated in fifteen of the state's seventeen counties. *Time* magazine commented that in many communities

> the brothel is practically an institution, like the corner drugstore and the county courthouse . . . grounds for civic pride. . . . One year, the town fathers of Wells noted that visitors seemed to be having trouble locating the red-light district, so they helpfully installed directional signs. . . . According to the Los Angeles *Times,* prostitution is one of the biggest industries in rural Nevada.[8]

Regulated by local government, prostitutes submit to regular health inspections, and their books are audited by tax agents. During the 1970s, a number of cities have tried to confine porno shops and movies to restricted sections of the downtown area, like Boston's "Combat Zone." Such forms of semiapproval, coupled with the fact that such attractions tend to be part of the drawing power of big cities for tourists, suggest that government tends to be a psychological, if not a financial partner, in such enterprises.

There are numerous other examples (including those states where liquor may be purchased only in state-owned retail outlets) of government, by tacit agreement or actual sponsorship, condoning varied forms of gambling, vice, and drinking. This approving attitude of governments reflects a general relaxation of legal controls over many leisure activities once prohibited or restricted. Many states have repealed or modified laws regarding adultery or homosexual activity; others have reduced penalties for marijuana possession and similar drug-related crimes, in what appears to be an accommodation to widely changing lifestyles.

Within this framework, how have public recreation agencies responded? Generally, they have been consistent to their traditional reformist philosophy. Some changes are beginning to occur; increasing numbers of recreation and park departments, for example, are operating clubs or other facilities which serve liquor as an accepted practice.

Some planners have challenged the appropriateness of public leisure agencies seeking to "impose" values on those they serve. Gans, for example, believes that it is inappropriate to use leisure as a means of achieving "nonleisure goals." He decries the tendency to provide recreational activities as a form of "societal therapy," and urges that leisure behavior be viewed as completely nonutilitarian and spontaneous. Carried to its logical extreme, this position would force public recreation agencies simply to give people whatever they wished—regardless of its social or moral desirability. With a freer hand, they could attract large crowds of participants and earn substantial sums with which to finance other programs. Why not have the recreation and park department (which, after all, is concerned with meeting people's needs during leisure) operate gambling halls with roulette, poker, and blackjack, with dollar machines for older folks, and nickel-and-dime machines for the kiddies? And how about nightclubs, saloons, strip joints, and even a few unobtrusive houses of prostitution? Carefully inspected and run with decorum, they might be called "health clubs." Or, if recreation agencies did not wish to run such operations directly, they might lease them to concessionaires or set up legal red-light districts and skim the cream off the profits through a heavy amusement tax.

Such suggestions might well mean that public agencies would be in full competition with commercial and private recreation; ultimately, they would have little justification for existing except as a money-making operation that helped to finance other areas of municipal government. Obviously, this is not a tenable or desirable position for recreation professionals to take.

Instead, they must come to the realization that what they do has serious moral importance. Gray and Greben point out that recreation constitutes a highly significant aspect of our modern social life:

> Recreation activities operate *within* the social environment and *form a part* of the social environment of the community and the nation. In many communities they are a conspicuous part of the pattern of social interaction. In areas where the neighborhood has lost its social interaction as an organizing device for human association, recreation activities are the primary arena beyond work and kinship. In communities with high rates of mobility, recreation may be more effective as a social nucleus than kinship.[9]

Gordon Dahl describes the radical shifts in our attitudes toward work and leisure in recent years. More and more theologians have discovered the creative and redemptive possibilities of play, and strong efforts are being made to reconsider personal and social values, and to develop a new moral economy of work, play, and worship. Dahl poses the important question whether American religion will nourish and fortify a leisure ethic as it has historically supported the work ethic.

> Or must Americans abandon their religious heritage in order to develop a "tradition of leisure?" We are well aware that the traditional morality has often stifled and subverted leisure, but can a leisure-oriented society survive without adequate moral values?[10]

Other religious leaders have joined forces to help people understand leisure and its effect on the physical, emotional, social, and spiritual dimensions of the individual and of society. In 1976, for example, a conference of theologians and lay delegates from around the world was held to deal with "The Gospel, Freedom, and Increasing Leisure." Sponsored by A Christian Ministry in the National Park, this meeting sought not simply to stimulate more church-sponsored recreation programs, but to help develop a meaningful leisure ethic.

Nor are church leaders alone in their search for new standards of morality and ethical purpose in leisure. Leading psychiatrists like Erich Fromm have pointed out that since World War II, we have created a superabundance of creature comforts, based on a consumption ethic that worships a seemingly endless flow of automobiles, air conditioners, pleasure boats, electric blankets, barbecue pits, and heated swimming pools. Yet at the same time, we have been internally destructive, in Fromm's view, producing cars with built-in obsolescence, killing thousands on the highways, polluting the environment, and subsidizing violence in the mass media, depicting human life as brutish and cheap. Fromm concludes that an excess of material things and material expansion has made Americans numb to many moral issues, and to the dangers of violence and dehumanization. He believes, however, that there is still a religious and humane tradition in America, which offers a democratic, ethical vision of the society, and seeks to accomplish good in the world.[11]

Accepting this position, it is obvious that a system of ethical values must be applied within the sphere of leisure activity. It can generally be accepted that it is the responsibility of public recreation and park agencies to provide programs that enrich personal enhancement and community growth, that respect the worth and integrity of each human being, that build physical, emotional, and social well-being, that stress active participation rather than spectatorship, and that draw people together rather than set them against each other.

But what scale of values should be used to determine which activities are desirable and which are not? In general, recreation and park directors must respect the views that are widely shared by the most responsible, influential, active, and socially minded members of their communities. Through elected or appointed boards, advisory committees, or neighborhood councils, directors test their own judgment of appropriate program goals and policies. Except in cases of extreme controversy or disagreement, it should be possible for them to find consensus in issues related to morality, social purpose, good taste, or similar concerns.

A second source of values stems from the philosophy of service formulated by recreation and park leaders throughout the nation, as expressed at national meetings, in the literature, and in regional conferences and workshops. Yet the right to make independent value judgments within one's sphere of expertise—even when in opposition to accepted community or professional beliefs—is a precious and important asset in any field. The recreation practitioner who seeks to invoke that right must, of course, be able to justify his or her position, in eloquent and persuasive terms, in order to gain community support.

Preserving and Improving the Natural Environment

Another major problem which faces recreation and park professionals today is the crucial need to preserve and rehabilitate our nation's land, water, and wildlife resources. It has become increasingly apparent that we have permitted great rivers and lakes to be polluted by waste, forests to be ruthlessly razed by lumbering interests, and wildlife to be ravaged by chemical poisons or thoughtless destruction of breeding and feeding grounds. Stewart Udall, as Secretary of Agriculture, commented that our national goals were oriented to the machine and full production, rather than to people and the quality of life:

> The Gross National Product is our Holy Grail; the economists and statisticians our keepers. Statistics concerning auto output, steel production, heavy construction, housing starts, freight-car loadings, have become the indices of the American advance. We have no environmental index, no census statistics to measure whether the country is more or less livable from year to year. A tranquility index, a cleanliness index, a privacy index, might have told us something about the condition of man.[12]

Greater and greater demands have been placed on our natural resource bank, with open space shrinking at an unprecedented rate. A million acres or more have been lost each year to development for residential or commercial uses. Of the original 127 million acres of wetlands and marshlands in the United States, crucial to many forms of wildlife, over 45 million *and has* have been destroyed by draining, filling, and dredging. As a single example, the most valuable estuary on the Pacific Coast is the San Francisco Bay complex, fed by the Sacramento and San Joaquin rivers—an eleven-hundred square-mile area of sloughs, channels, marshes, and farms that provides a huge ecosystem of plants, plankton, animals, fish, and birds. Great numbers of salmon, striped bass, shad, sturgeon, and other fish are spawned within this system, providing both game fishing and commercial opportunity for thousands along the Pacific Coast. This entire system has been threatened by a large-scale diversion of fresh water away from the delta by canals that are part of a massive irrigation scheme to supply Southern California with water, essentially a master plan designed to benefit a few large landholders with unwatered desert acreage.

As for pollution, probably the most dramatic example of our unwillingness to protect the natural environment has been the failure to construct adequate sewage and waste-treatment facilities by cities and states.[13] Widespread industrial pollution has made stagnant cesspools out of what were formerly sparkling lakes and rivers. Many other communities have poured huge amounts of raw, untreated sewage into rivers that were formerly pure-flowing streams, ideal for fishing and water sports. Information compiled by state and Federal biologists indicates that nearly thirteen thousand miles of streams and hundreds of natural lakes were poisoned by surface mining activities by the late 1960s.

Although a small band of determined conservationists had fought for years to prevent this steady deterioration of our national environment, it was not until the publication of Rachel Carson's *Silent Spring* in 1962 that the nation became aware of the dangers posed to wildlife by modern chemical poisons—especially the synthetic insecticides and herbicides that had been developed since World War II. Webster writes:

> *Silent Spring* is now credited by most environmentalists with being a consciousness-raising event that has resulted in a long-lasting environmental movement in the United States. This movement, concerned not with pesticides alone, encompasses a spectrum of interests ranging from air and soil pollution problems to radioactivity to urban affairs to aesthetics and the quality of life.[14]

At the same time, the recommendations of the Outdoor Recreation Resources Review Commission helped to promote a wave of environmental efforts by Federal, state, and municipal governments. The Federal Water Pollution Control Administration divided the nation into twenty major river basins and promoted regional sewage treatment programs in the areas. The Water Quality Act of 1965, the Clean Water Restoration Act of 1966, the Solid Waste Disposal Act of 1965, the Highway Beautification Act of 1965, and the Mining Reclamation Act of 1968 all committed the United States to a program of conservation and protection of its natural resources. By the mid-1970s, the U. S. Army Corps of Engineers, the Bureau of Reclamation, and the Federal Environmental Protection Agency were carrying out hundreds of facility planning and areawide waste treatment management studies, or assisting in the development of improved drainage systems or industrial waste control methods. Nonprofit organizations like the American Land Trust, the Nature Conservancy, and the Trust for Public Lands have taken over properties encompassing hundreds of thousands of acres—many of them donated by large corporations—for preservation or transfer to public agencies for recreation use. More and more cities have begun to convert their sewage into nutrient-laden sludge which is being returned to the environment in economically and ecologically sound ways, as a slow release fertilizer, instead of being discharged into rivers or the ocean. By 1976, Russell E. Train, chief of the U. S. Environmental Protection Agency, was able to say:

> With the help of the Bureau of Outdoor Recreation and the National Recreation and Park Association, the Environmental Protection Agency has launched a new initiative to assist state and local governments and civic groups in turning to public advantage the very large Federal program now underway to clean up our lakes and rivers. Existing national clean water legislation encourages Federal participation with state and local agencies aimed at capturing full public benefits—including open spaces and recreation opportunities—from the public investment wherever it exists along local waterways. We will need the expertise of the professional park and recreation community to translate

these opportunities into the enjoyment of new boating, fishing, hiking, and swimming experiences.[15]

Billions of dollars have been poured into cleaning up the Great Lakes, with hundreds of elaborate municipal and industrial facilities established to clean up fluid wastes before they reach the lakes. The U. S.-Canada International Joint Commission reported in 1976 that of the communities in the Great Lakes Basin, 94 percent on the Canadian side and 60 percent on the American side had developed adequate sewage treatment. Nonetheless, examinations of fish and aquatic plants show excessive levels of such persistent synthetic chemicals as the pesticides DDT and Mirex, and PCBs (poly-chlorinated biphenyls, suspected of having cancer-causing properties). It is now known that much of the contamination comes from the skies, in the form of rain and snow; this can be prevented only by removing the original sources of the pollution, which may be hundreds or thousands of miles away.[16]

It is obvious that despite the dramatic progress being made in combatting water pollution, it will take years of steady effort before the battle is won. Similarly, other antipollution programs such as the effort to recycle glass products, aluminum cans, or similar containers, or to reclaim the usable metal in obsolete cars, have been proceeding at a painfully slow rate.

In many cases, there has been strong resistance to environmental efforts. Typically, powerful commercial interests have resisted the establishment of new Federal and state parks. For example, the development of Redwood National Park in California was fought by spokesmen for the lumber industry, who claimed that the National Park Service's plan to preserve the giant redwood trees along that state's northern coast was "unnecessary, confiscatory, and economically depressing" and would threaten employment in the area. Such opposition continued even after a study by the National Geographic Society showed that 85 percent of the original redwood forests had been logged, that only 2.5 percent were protected in state parks, and that the remaining forests would disappear within thirty years if they were not protected. A similar battle has been waged between the giant oil companies that have been sinking offshore wells along the West Coast and conservationists who have fought to prevent further damage to wildlife and the total environment by escaping oil.

Numerous conservation organizations, including the Sierra Club, have mobilized to fight threats to the environment. They successfully defeated the proposal to construct a huge new jetport just north of Florida's million-and-a-half acre Everglades National Park. The jetport would have cut off the vital flow of water from the north and destroyed the intricate ecological system of the Everglades. The issues involved are not always easily decided. When the threat of damage to the environment is clear and overwhelming, resistance to destructive projects can readily be justified. However, a number of major dam projects during the late 1970s have been delayed or halted by conservationist efforts simply because they threatened a small number of fish or plants of a rare species.

For example, the long-planned Dickey-Lincoln hydroelectric dam, involving a massive $1.3 billion expenditure and extensive economic and social benefits for the state of Maine, was delayed in 1977 because it threatened the furbish lousewort, an obscure variety of snapdragon growing along the St. Johns River. Interior Department biologists, indicating their intention to place the lousewort on a protected listing under the Endangered Species Act (which would automatically halt the entire project) made clear that aside from its rarity, the plant had no special value.[17] Such rigid policies obviously are debatable.

391

Recreation as an Environmental Threat

Recreational use itself has been identified as a significant threat to the environment, and numerous outdoor recreation development projects have been resisted for this reason.

Much of the problem stems from sheer overcrowding and overuse. The nation's most frequently visited national park, the Great Smoky Mountain National Park in Tennessee, regularly has commuter-size traffic jams. There is insufficient space to accommodate the mass of campers and visitors during periods of peak demand; as a result, the physical ability of the land to support recreation use is severely strained, and hundreds of thousands of campers must be turned away from parks on busy weekends. One solution is to build additional access roads, and open up new camping and outdoor recreation areas. Yet conservationists strongly resist such approaches, arguing that further development would destroy the wilderness quality of this unspoiled preserve. A similar battle raged in 1969, when plans to develop Mineral King, an area of majestic twelve-thousand-foot peaks in California's Eastern Sierra Mountains, as a year-round vacation resort were announced by associates of the late Walt Disney. Angry environmentalists claimed that opening part of Sequoia National Park to road traffic for a $35 million year-round outdoor recreation complex expected ultimately to attract about 2.5 million visitors a year would despoil the natural glories of the region.

It has been shown that recreation is often seriously destructive to the natural environment. Many campgrounds suffer abuse to grass, exposed tree roots, eroded stream banks, and similar damage. Lake Powell, only five years after its construction in Glen Canyon in Arizona and Utah, was noticeably afflicted by pollution. Huge in size (186 miles long, with a jagged shoreline of 1,800 miles), Lake Powell received over 115,000 visitors a month in over 10,000 boats; the sheer accumulation of their sewage and garbage was ruining the giant lake.

Similarly, in large cities, conservationists have strongly resisted the use of natural areas for recreation, and fight to maintain parks as untouched areas of greenery. Inevitably, the use of great urban parks for recreation entails ecological costs. A free public concert in New York's Central Park attended by one hundred thirty-five thousand people left, in the words of Parks Commissioner August Heckscher, an "incredible sight." It took thirty garbage collectors and machines three days to clean up the residue of broken glass, cigarette butts, cans, gum wrappers, chicken bones, wine bottles, blankets, and newspapers, while conservationists angrily protested against the historic park's desecration.

Increasingly, steps have been taken to control the destructive effects of recreation and other uses of the natural environment. Some facilities that have already been built are being withdrawn. For example, the New York State Department of Environmental Conservation embarked on a process of removing all man-made structures—including docks, Jeep and truck trails, high elevation lean-tos, and even fire towers—from wilderness areas of the Adirondack Mountain Park, during the late 1970s. There has been a continuing review of the role of the major national parks in the United States; one major report urged that

> hotel-type accommodations, private automobiles and car-camping should be phased out of the national park units, and visitation limited to the physical, ecological and psychological carrying capacity of every unit.

392

The panel proposed the establishment of a dual system of "national wilderness parks" dedicated to preservation, and national recreation areas within a 50-mile radius of the 123 urban centers of more than 250,000 population.[18]

Simply stated, the problem is one of balancing recreation, park, and conservation needs and values against other legitimate public concerns. Often, economic interests come into play, as in the alliance of commercial fishermen with recreational fishermen in attempts to ban DDT during the late 1960s, when it was shown that this powerful pesticide threatened their livelihood. Sometimes, whole classes of recreationists come into conflict with each other, as in the case of off-road vehicle users in the nation's outdoor parks. Carrying capacity studies have revealed a major conflict between mechanized and nonmechanized recreationists—motorboaters and canoers, motorcyclists and campers or hikers, snowmobilers and cross-country skiers.[19]

When President Carter announced a plan to curb the use of off-road vehicles on environmentally sensitive public lands in 1977, a hornet's nest of protest was stirred up. Joining the users of snowmobiles, dune buggies and similar vehicles, major manufacturers of such equipment and other individuals with an economic stake in mechanized recreation joined in an angry protest against what was clearly a justifiable environmental action.

Long-Range Environmental Policies

Badly needed is a long-range planning effort that will deal constructively with the major issues and develop a framework for action that gets at the fundamental causes of pollution, rather than short-range, immediate problems. Within such a framework, it is entirely possible for economic, ecological and leisure-related interests to be harmoniously merged.

Energy considerations will be important in affecting planning for environmental protection. Less and less land will be wasted as more condominiums and townhouses are built, instead of single-family dwellings. Developers and local government planners will be expected to provide more immediately accessible open-space areas for outdoor recreation, to replace more distant sites. Eliminating automobile traffic throughout parks, promoting bicycling, hiking, and backpacking, planning conservation education programs, and developing other energy-saving approaches are likely both to benefit the environment and the cause of energy conservation. Beyond this, it seems clear that our national approach to conservation will have to be radically altered. At a recent wildlife conference convened by the Council on Environmental Quality, it was pointed out that in some forty years of Federal and state wildlife programming, more than 96 percent of expenditures have gone to protect the few dozen species of animals, birds and fish in which hunters and fishermen are interested.[20] To replace this approach, the council recommended that the goal be to establish and protect complete stable "ecosystems"—the varying complexes of interdependent animals and plants, on a far broader scale. Only in this way, it was argued, could humankind avoid the potential catastrophe resulting from thousands of years of exploiting and altering the earth's natural resources and relationships.

Serving the Disadvantaged: Women, Minorities, and the Disabled

Another major issue in contemporary leisure planning and recreation programming is the need to provide more adequate services for major segments of our national population that historically have been underserved in public and voluntary recreation programs. These include girls and women, ethnic minority populations (particularly when they are also economically disadvantaged), and the physically, emotionally, and socially disabled.

Girls and Women in Recreation

A pivotal principle of recreation programming is that all community residents should be given equal opportunity, regardless of sex, religion, ethnic, or socioeconomic background. Certainly this principle has not been consistently applied toward girls and women in public recreation programs. An earlier chapter dealt with the question of the equality of women in career opportunities, pointing out that they tend to be hired primarily on lower levels of departmental responsibility, and to be paid significantly less than male employees on comparable job levels. Discrimination against female employees in recreation and parks has been greatly reduced in recent years, and they are increasingly being employed on higher levels of responsibility, as described in chapter 12.

What has not been dealt with as constructively is the preferential treatment given to males in public recreation and park programs. Theobald comments that in Canadian municipal programs, the early recreation leaders, who tended to be female, provided well-rounded programs which included music, art, drama, crafts, storytelling and other social programs. As municipal departments assumed fuller responsibility for public recreation and male leaders replaced female ones, the program emphasis shifted strongly to physical activities and competition.[21] Heit and Malpass, in a study of program differentiation by sex for the Sports and Fitness Division of the Ontario Ministry of Culture and Recreation, concluded that boys and men had significantly more leisure opportunities than girls and women, reflected in the substantial inequity in the number of activities scheduled for boys compared to girls, the facilities provided, and the fact that girls were channeled into sex-stereotyped roles like choirs, cooking, theater arts, and cheerleading, rather than encouraged to take part in a full range of leisure pursuits.[22]

This pattern is apparent on all levels, both in the United States and in Canada. In part, it stems from an historical view of women as weak, inferior in skills, and socially lacking in the drive and confidence of men. Dulles wrote that in the nineteenth century, "an almost morbid prudery meant a more restricted life for women than in the 18th Century."

> If they had any leisure, the ladies took up embroidery, painting on glass, or china and waxwork. . . . But they kept indoors, and everything else including health was sacrificed to incredible standards of proper female decorum.[23]

In a 1953 publication of the National Recreation Association, the following comments suggested prevalent attitudes regarding girls and women in recreation programming:

It is usually more difficult to lead girls' groups than boys' groups. They need more personal attention, more help in getting started and more encouragement to keep going. Girls do not respond to highly organized competitive activities as well as boys do. They respond better to small group organization where individual interest is developed into individual achievement. Strange as it may seem, many girls need help in accepting with pride their role as women and an appreciation of the special responsibilities which will be theirs because they are women.[24]

A double standard of sexual morality meant that boys and men tended to be much freer with respect to the kinds of activities in which they could participate and the settings in which they could appear. Even a relatively innocuous activity like bicycling was assailed by the Women's Rescue League in Washington as an "immoral and physically destructive activity," and it was predicted that it would cause all women cyclists to become invalids. Gilbert and Williamson documented in 1973 the prejudice against females in sport in the United States:

There is no sharper example of discrimination today than that which operates against girls and women who take part in competitive sports, wish to take part, or might wish to if society did not scorn such endeavors. No matter what her age, education, race, talent, residence or riches, the female's right to play is severely restricted. The funds, facilities, coaching, rewards and honors allotted women are grossly inferior to those granted men. In many places absolutely no support is given to women's athletics, and females are barred by law, regulation, tradition or the hostility of males from sharing athletic resources and pleasures.[25]

Recently, a number of factors have increased sports opportunity for women dramatically. Title IX of the Education Amendments Act of 1972 was the basis for Federal guidelines that compelled schools and colleges to provide educational experiences on a nondiscriminatory basis, integrated where feasible, with a much higher level of support for activities for females. Such bastions of male-only participation as Little League were broken down in a number of states by court decisions, with girl athletes "cracking" formerly all-boy teams. In schools and colleges, female athletes have gained more support, and in some, have been accepted on formerly male teams.

The most vivid examples of female progress in sport has come in such professional women's sports as tennis or golf and in the great interest shown in Olympic events for women like gymnastics and swimming. It is entirely possible that the more meaningful impact, however, will be not so much in the acceptance of women as high-level competitive performers, with emphasis on power, dominance, and typically masculine styles of behavior, but rather that women may add elements to sport which place more emphasis on technique, style, and the application of humanistic rather than "win-at-all-costs" values to competition.

Modern society is in a state of transition in defining what appropriate masculine or feminine standards of behavior or social roles should be. Harris points out that such cultural definitions in sport have been extremely resistant to change.[26] Today, such changes are occurring rapidly, in part because of the feminist movement and the pressures it has exerted, and in part because of new scientific understanding

395

of the true physical capacity of women, with respect to body composition, strength development, gynecological considerations, and related factors.[27]

Clearly, a much fuller range of sports and other leisure programs must be provided for girls and women. Whether all activities should be provided equally and on an integrated basis, without any concern for possible sex differences, is questionable. Canadian recreation administrators, for example, tended to violently oppose the idea of girls and women playing in competitive hockey leagues. Particularly for younger children, segregation by sex can be important in development; Thomas Johnson, a leading child psychiatrist, points out significant values in providing some "islands of separation" between elementary school boys and girls. It is essential for children in the preadolescent years to gain a sense of what it means to be male or female; this is accomplished both by identification with the parent of the same sex, and with other children of the same sex.

> We usually find children of this age pulling away in some areas from the opposite sex and banding together in organizations and activities where they find a supportive sense of belonging from the group. It is a time when interest in all-boy or all-girl activities is high. Most children of this age are usually more comfortable in the company of their own sex. A primary value of organizations such as Campfire Girls, Scouts and Little League is that they provide opportunities for this grouping by sex. They help children get a sense of security through group strength and identification that prepares them for the later boy-girl relationships of adolescence.[28]

For this reason, Johnson opposes the insistence that boys be allowed into all-girls' groups and vice-versa. A major goal for this age range, he suggests, is having girls feel comfortable with and accepted by girls, and boys by boys—a purpose not served by having boys become members of Pony Tail Softball teams, or girls of Little League teams.

Such reservations deserve careful consideration. It is critical that we overcome unfair discrimination, but at the same time preserve the right of males and females to be different, in areas where such differences are logical and justified.

Equality of Opportunity for Racial and Ethnic Minorities

A closely related issue is the need for public and voluntary recreation and park agencies to provide more adequate facilities and programs for racial and ethnic minority groups. Earlier sections of this text have shown how blacks in particular were historically confined to racially segregated recreation programs, and how, more recently, recreation was provided as a key element in antipoverty and "crash" recreation programs provided with Federal assistance, in inner city areas where there were threats of racial violence.

What has happened since this time? The militance of the 1960s has largely died away, and an increasing number of capable black, and to a lesser degree, Spanish-speaking persons have moved into all ranks of the recreation and park profession. On the other hand, there are few special efforts today to provide enriched or compensatory recreation programs in inner city communities, apart from a number of bussing programs or summer job-related programs.

396

The real question, as far as administrative policy is concerned, is whether racial and ethnic minority groups today do receive adequate and equal recreation opportunities, or whether they are in effect being deprived of such programs by the severe budgetary cutbacks which have affected many central city recreation and park departments, and by the steady growth of fees and charges which many departments have adopted to supplement their operational budgets. The obvious economic base of leisure in modern society suggests that a high proportion of racial and ethnic minority group members today have a more limited range of recreation opportunities than the rest of the population.

What of deliberate forms of discrimination and exclusion? Title VI of the Civil Rights Act of 1964 prohibited racial discrimination in Federally assisted programs, which includes large numbers of state and municipal outdoor recreation programs that have received Federal grants. In 1970 and again in 1974, the U. S. Civil Rights Commission made extensive evaluations of the government's efforts to end discrimination against American minorities and women, finding that

> "Dedicated staff in a number of federal agencies have tried hard to establish viable equal opportunity programs, but, largely because of inadequate government-wide leadership, these efforts have often been futile." While there have been many small efforts, there has been little action. Departments and agencies have been slow to identify actual cases of discrimination, even though many exist, and are almost totally unwilling to do anything about those cases which are identified.[29]

Grants from the Bureau of Outdoor Recreation for acquisition and development of state and local recreation and park areas are subject to the nondiscriminatory clauses in Title VI. All resulting facilities must be open to all, and not limited to special groups. However, the Bureau has not required that civil rights information, priorities, or concerns be included in statewide outdoor recreation plans, and has not acted to determine whether facilities are distributed to serve all income groups and sections of the funded governmental unit.

What about other levels of compliance with civil rights equality of opportunity practices? As indicated earlier, municipal recreation and park departments in Southern states took several different courses of action in response to legislation and court orders forbidding racial discrimination in publicly owned facilities during the mid-1960s. The Supreme Court in 1971 ruled that city officials might close swimming pools and other recreational facilities, rather than open them to racially integrated participation. Some cities did so, and then sold the facilities to "private" clubs to avoid interracial swimming in particular.

The Civil Rights Act of 1964, although it prohibited discrimination in public accommodations, made exceptions for "a private club or other establishment not in fact open to the public." In a series of decisions from 1969 to 1973, the Supreme Court ruled that neighborhood swimming clubs in predominantly white suburbs might not exclude from membership blacks who lived within close geographical proximity and who should, according to the nonprofit organization's charter, receive membership preference. In one decision, the Court ruled against privately owned recreation businesses that sought to masquerade as "clubs" to avoid racial integration, when in fact they were really serving the general public.

In many cities, both North and South, widespread desegregation of public recreation and park facilities and programs has been accomplished—without negative incidents or resistance by either white or black residents. It seems probable that interracial attitudes have been favorably affected by the large-scale integration of college and professional sports, and that this in turn has made it possible for recreation and park authorities to operate integrated programs on all levels. Voluntary organizations have also made strenuous efforts to integrate their programs, and to provide enriched programs for inner city minority group populations.

On the other hand, a number of national organizations, like the Moose and Elks, continued to maintain racially discriminatory membership policies through the early 1970s. Courts and tax commissions have used such devices as withdrawal of property tax exemptions or state liquor licenses as a way of breaking down racial barriers in these large and powerful organizations. The extent of racial discrimination in private membership organizations was illustrated in 1977, when some of newly inaugurated President Carter's cabinet appointees, including Attorney General Griffin Bell, were revealed to be active members of racially and religiously exclusive social clubs.

A final important aspect of this question lies in the growing trend throughout metropolitan areas in the United States for each government jurisdiction to limit participation in its recreation facilities and programs to its own residents. Restrictions usually are enforced by bumper stickers, windshield emblems, and other forms of seasonal passes, usually given out at minimal charge, to bona fide residents only. Although a logical argument can be made that the residents who paid for constructing a swimming pool or building a golf course should be permitted exclusive use of it, particularly when it tends to be overcrowded, such policies may also be seen as reflecting racial prejudice.

The issue is more complicated when a suburban community restricts the use of an ocean beachfront to its own residents. A state court decision against Avon, New Jersey ruled that residents of a neighboring municipality might not be barred or required to pay a higher fee.

> In the Avon case . . . the challengers were able to point out that money from Federal and state taxpayers had gone to construct and maintain the beach jetties. . . . along the whole New Jersey coast, more money for anti-erosion projects came from the state . . . than from all the towns combined.[30]

The court also invoked the principle of English law known as "public trust," which holds that land covered by tidal water belongs to the sovereign but is for the common use of all the people. However, many suburban communities continue to restrict beach access by prohibiting nonresident automobile parking within walking distance of the waterfront. Such practices are part of an overall policy described by an American Civil Liberties Union official as "a pattern by which white suburbs manage to erect barriers to inner-city residents, thereby cementing residential segregation."[31]

Since such practices appear likely to continue, the efforts by both Federal and state governments to develop new outdoor recreation resources in and near large urban centers is of major importance. Because these facilities are for use by all residents, they are available to the poor and to minority group members alike, without restriction.

398

Serving the Disabled

The problem of meeting the leisure needs of mentally or physically disabled persons was discussed at length in chapter 14. In both institutional and community settings, strenuous efforts have been made to provide specially designed facilities and programs to meet the needs of populations with impairment. It must be stressed, however, that despite the progress that has been made, only a small percentage of the mentally retarded, physically handicapped, mentally ill, or dependent aging persons in society are actually being served in high quality recreation programs.

Although much emphasis has been given to "leisure counseling" to equip individuals to use their free time in constructive and creative ways, little real support has been given to the process of deinstitutionalization, described in the following terms:

> Deinstitutionalization encompasses three interrelated processes: (a) prevention of admission by finding and developing alternative community methods of care and training; (b) return to the community of all residents who have been prepared through programs of habilitation and training to function adequately in appropriate local settings; and (c) establishment and maintenance of a responsive residential environment which protects human and civil rights and which contributes to the expeditious return of the individual to normal community living, whenever possible.[32]

Community-based programs for the disabled are generally believed to be preferable to institutional settings. For this reason, radical changes have been made in recent years to facilitate the return of the physically or emotionally disabled to the community. However, we are beginning to understand that unless positive programs are provided within the community, this practice may actually be less desirable than sound institutional arrangements.

In many states where large-scale hospital care for the mentally ill has been deemphasized and replaced by the establishment of small, local mental health centers, large numbers of mentally ill persons have been placed in residential settings in the community itself. Often they live in run-down "welfare hotels," or single-room accommodations in shabby tenements, preyed upon by muggers and drug addicts. Often, too, the back-up services required to make the community living experience successful are lacking; often, no recreation or activity therapy programs at all are provided for such individuals. *Time* magazine described such experiences in California:

> Chronically ill patients have been returned to communities poorly equipped to provide adequate treatment. With no one to care for them, former patients have ended up on welfare rolls, in boarding houses, cheap hotels, and even jail.[33]

Similarly, in New York,

> since New York State started emptying its mental hospitals of thousands of inmates six years ago, many of them have been jammed into

399

tiny rooms, basements, and garages, and fed a semi-starvation diet. . . . they are taken from the steps of mental institutions by operators who jam them into what can only be described as a private jail and confiscate their monthly welfare checks.[34]

Studies have also shown that foster homes or group homes for disturbed or retarded children and youth may also be inferior to traditional institutional care. For example, Murphy, Pennee, and Luchins studied foster home programs for the mentally retarded in Canada, and found a striking lack of interaction, or indeed of any meaningful activity, involving residents and their foster families or members of the outside community. Luchins summarized the study's findings:

> It is my opinion that those who think foster home placement enables a patient to escape the disadvantages of an institutional life are mistaken. Foster homes can be as institutionalized as hospitals are, while lacking the compensatory advantages that some hospitals might possess.[35]

The point is that there is a tremendous range of quality in the care and overall range of services provided for the disabled in the United States and Canada today. There continue to be many recreation and park facilities which they cannot use because of steps, narrow doorways, lack of proper toilet facilities, or other problems. Although some penal institutions provide enlightened and varied programs, by far the majority have extremely limited recreation activities. Too often, nursing homes or extended-care facilities provide only a modicum of activity, and the disoriented, deaf, or otherwise seriously disabled patient is hardly served at all.

The mission of both therapeutic recreation specialists and community recreation and park administrators in the decades ahead must be to extend a higher level of recreational opportunity to all disabled persons. For those in residential or treatment programs, the effort must be to use recreation as a therapeutic medium, to minimize the effects of disability, and to help equip patients for independent community living. For those already in the community, recreation's role must be to enrich the total quality of their life experience to the fullest extent possible.

Often, disabled individuals receive care in traditional "service" organizations that are paternalistic and insensitive. More and more, they are militantly demanding their rights as human beings. At a recent Cerebral Palsy Telethon, a delegation of wheelchair-users demonstrated; one woman with cerebral palsy explained, "They portray us as poor helpless cripples. But people with cerebral palsy grow up, and a lot of us work, keep house and make love." Schultz points out:

> How much longer it will be before the disabled are allowed to live up to their full potential depends on Congress, the courts, and, most important, on the persistence of the handicapped themselves in insisting on their civil rights from a society that has, until now, presumed it would never have to give them any.[36]

It is critical that recreation professionals recognize that their role with the disabled must not be that of the provider alone; they must also be advocates for the rights of the disabled, as well as enablers and facilitators, and when appropriate, simply onlookers.

Problems of Fiscal Support for Recreation and Parks

Although the amount of money spent annually by government on recreation and parks has grown steadily since World War II, the need for additional budgetary support is one of the field's most pressing problems today. *Newsweek* magazine commented in 1966 that

> meeting recreation needs in goods and services, in fact, is now one of the nation's largest industries. . . . And yet, from Congress to county boards of supervisors, recreation is still puritanically regarded as a luxury. Despite all the oratory about natural beauty, physical fitness and mental health, when it comes to trimming the budget, most legislators put the shears first to parks.[37]

On all levels, financial problems began to affect rapidly expanding recreation and park systems during the late 1960s and early 1970s. Sharp reductions in the appropriated funding of national and state parks compelled reduced operations, including the closing of some parks and campgrounds, the linking of small park areas for joint administration, shortened seasons and visiting hours, and raised fees.

But the most severe fiscal difficulties were in the cities. In 1972, based on a survey of recreation and park departments in many of the largest cities in the United States, the author reported that 60 percent of the departments studied had been severely hampered in the staffing of programs or the development of badly needed facilities by budget freezes and cutbacks.

> Cities throughout the nation reported massive cuts in service, ranging from the closing of park restrooms to reducing the hours of operation of ice rinks or pools, shortening the seasons of summer day camps, or reducing maintenance operations. . . . budget problems tended to be most severe among the larger cities, particularly those on the West and East coasts.[38]

Recreation and park departments were particularly hard hit for several reasons: (a) they tend, more than other municipal agencies, to be heavily dependent on part-time and seasonal personnel, who are more easily slashed from austerity budgets than full-time, union-protected employees; (b) in many cities, extensive facilities were acquired or built during the 1960s without adding adequate new staff, resulting in a severe shortage of personnel even before the budget cuts; and (c) many of the federally supported recreation programs of the 1960s ended, but municipal administrators were expected to continue their services—without adequate funding.

Despite these factors, the increased costs created by inflation, severe problems of vandalism, and the need to rehabilitate older facilities, many urban recreation and park departments were expected to face new challenges. Often these difficulties stemmed from changing lifestyles and behaviors and demands for new forms of leisure behavior; a classic example, described by Gold, is the trend toward public nudity on many Federal and state beaches, as well as in several California city and county areas. In addition, such park uses as rock music festivals, social protest meetings, and similar events pose new demands on administrators, as well as the need to control gambling, drug use, and a host of other antisocial activities or unaccustomed uses of parks.[39]

It is apparent that the image of the urban or wilderness park as an island of tranquil peace is no longer valid. In parks of every type, there is a growing need to safeguard cyclists, campers, mothers, their children, and other recreation participants against muggers, sneak thieves, and rapists—as well as to protect the physical surroundings against vandalism, littering, or other destructive acts. The problem of safe park use is closely related to the entire matter of program development and fiscal management. Connors summarized findings of the American Park and Recreation Society's national survey of crime, violence, and vandalism in park and recreation areas:

> Important social effects resulted from criminal activity in park and recreation areas. It was found that inadequate public safety may be a significant factor in the user's choice to seek alternative sites. Specifically, more than 35 percent of the APRS survey respondents reported an underutilization of facilities due to increased criminal activity. Another important finding is that a vast majority of park and recreation managers indicated that visitors are more willing to pay use fees if they are provided adequate safety and security.[40]

The relationship is twofold: (a) many facilities are underutilized because of unsafe conditions, which tends to undercut the public's interest in public recreation and support for it; and (b) the ability to provide better supervision and more carefully protected recreation programs is obviously dependent on adequate recreation and park budgets.

The financial plight of urban leisure opportunity systems is illustrated not only by cuts that have affected recreation and park departments, but the fact that many public school systems, municipal museums, libraries, and cultural arts programs have been forced to reduce their services for fiscal reasons. Many large orchestras and other major music, dance, theater, and opera companies throughout the United States have reduced their performing schedules because of financial deficits in recent years.

Within this framework, many departments have turned to the obvious solution of sharply increasing fees and charges and relying on these funds for the support of current operations and for the capital development of recreation areas and facilities.

Fees and Charges as Sources of Revenue

Traditionally, the major source of support for public recreation and park agencies has been general tax funds. Secondary sources have included special taxes, grants-in-aid from Federal or state agencies, and donations of land or program subsidies from private sources. As indicated, however, there has been increasing reliance on fees and charges to provide operating income for recreation and park agencies. Among the types of charges to recreation and park users are entrance fees, rental fees, user fees, sales revenues, license and permit fees, instructional, registration, and special service fees. In addition, many departments have introduced season permits for entire families, permitting them to use swimming pools, tennis courts, or other department facilities. Some municipal departments today operate large-scale golf, tennis, and swimming clubs which are comparable to private clubs; often, the annual membership fees for such clubs are several hundred dollars a year. As recreation and park facilities became increasingly complex and expensive to build and pressure by the taxpaying public for budgetary economy in municipal agencies grew, the imposition of fees and charges became a widespread practice. Many public departments now rely on fees and charges to supply 10 to 15 percent of their annual budgets, and some cities obtain as much as 30 to 40 percent of their funds from such revenue sources.

For many years, opponents of this trend suggested that imposing fees and charges constituted double taxation, since residents are taxed to construct and operate public facilities, and then taxed again to be permitted to use them. Others argued that recreation has been widely accepted as an important government function, like education or law enforcement, and should not have to depend on fees for support. Many fear that if revenue and park development becomes heavily dependent on such revenue sources, ultimately government will initiate only programs that are self-sustained by fees and charges.

Chase presents an illustration of the paradoxical public demand for increased recreational service and lower taxation in Abington Township, Pennsylvania.

> While maintaining [their] progressive posture in terms of providing tax money for capital improvements to township park facilities, elected officials have all but mandated that additional major park facility requests, such as swimming pools, golf courses, indoor ice rinks, and indoor tennis courts, will not be publicly financed unless funding can be provided through user fees over preestablished periods of time.[41]

This approach has led Abington Township public recreation officials and their counterparts in many other communities to follow the policy of establishing special leisure facilities only when there is a sound basis for anticipating sufficient income to help finance construction costs and offset maintenance and operating costs as well. More and more local recreation and park departments are also turning to concession arrangements to operate golf courses, restaurants, skating rinks, and similar types of facilities; it is widely agreed that private management is better able to guarantee a substantial profit in operating many facilities than government. In Los Angeles, for example, where an intensive effort was made to maximize income from concessions, the annual income derived from such sources rose over a three-year period from about $350,000 to over $850,000. In addition, the city department of recreation and parks was authorized to use 20 percent of the revenue from concessions for new facilities, rather than return it all to general tax funds.

The major criticism of the growing use of fees and charges is that it tends to discourage recreational participation by economically disadvantaged groups. As more and more facilities and services charge admission or registration fees, it may well be that in time the only free opportunity for poor people will consist of the limited use of neighborhood parks or playgrounds. Even when charges are moderate, they tend to be far too high for many families on public welfare, particularly when the cost of transportation must be added.

What solutions are there for this problem? Some facilities that normally charge admission may be opened for certain sessions without charge. Facilities in poorer neighborhoods may be free, while those in more affluent areas charge fees. Arrangements may be made for sliding scales of charges for participation, or to have members of families in financial need admitted free, while others pay. Such a procedure could not be implemented, however, without determining extent of need, which tends to be an embarrassing or humiliating process.[42]

Although it seems clear that the implementation of revenue-supported recreation will continue to grow, strenuous efforts must be made to educate the public to the need to support recreation and parks as a public function through specific taxes rather than permit it to become a governmentally sponsored counterpart of commercial recreation operations.

In addition to identifying new potential sources of revenue, productivity, cost cutting, and "zero-budgeting" must all become important priorities of recreation and park administrators dealing with the critical financial problems they face today. Innovative recreation and park administrators like Richard Trudeau, director of the East Bay Regional Park District in California (see page 243), have developed a number of effective techniques for stretching the tax dollar. Some of these are:

1. Construction management—a new technique of having outside management firms supervise departmental construction projects, as a proven means of carrying out faster and more economical capital projects.

2. Contracting with outside companies to do such jobs as sanitary pickup, when they can do the work as well with less cost than through public employees.

3. Investing temporarily idle funds at the highest going rate of interest, and leasing out open space parklands for grazing purposes which brings in revenue and reduces potential forest fire problems.

4. Intensive use of volunteers to do public relations jobs, facilities rehabilitation, or even negotiation of real estate deals, when qualified and available.

5. Using a modified zero-base budget approach, as a means of focusing more sharply on key departmental priorities, improving internal communication, and saving substantial sums.

6. Expanding cooperative arrangements with private and voluntary organizations which, in many cases, have helped to develop needed recreational facilities in major parks.

7. Joint development and management programs with other governmental units, to create new parks, waterfront areas, or busing services.

8. Aggressive pursuit of funds from gifts, wills, bequests and grants, as well as strong legislative efforts, either to support specialized programs and needs, or to expand the district's total tax base.[43]

In Trudeau's view, it is essential to be able to demonstrate the boosts a given park provides to the local economy through employment, construction spending, and money spent for transportation, equipment, food for picnics, and similar expenditures.

Some Chamber of Commerce groups have developed such "economic impact statements." One said a new shoreline park was the equivalent of a new industry for the city. But nobody has done this really well. If the Mayor of San Francisco figures the Giants are worth $3.3 billion to San Francisco, with an annual attendance of 600,000, what must a Regional Park system of 32 parks and 9 million visitors annually be worth to the East Bay? If we can develop such an . . . assessment, this will help keep the public with us.[44]

Clearly, recreation and park administrators must apply such innovative approaches if they are to gain and hold badly needed public support.

Changing Role of Government

A major trend of the last several years has been the shifting roles of Federal and state governments, with respect to the support of local recreation and park services.

Although there has been a decline in direct assistance to urban programs for the economically and socially disadvantaged, the Federal government has provided new outdoor recreation and park areas in or close to the major cities of the nation. The effect of the shift of Federal funding approaches to block-grant, rather than categorical-grant funding, meant that in the mid- and late 1970s, much fuller assistance was being given to small towns, suburbs, and Southern and Western cities, rather than the heavily impacted central cities of the North and East. This shift in policy was in direct contrast to the Federal government's own conclusions, published in *The Recreation Imperative,* that there was a critical need to upgrade recreation resources and programs in the major metropolitan areas where the greatest inequities and problems exist. The report called for stronger cooperative Federal-state efforts to identify and develop resources for outdoor education, construct or lease facilities, contract with other agencies for operating facilities or programs, train leadership, provide technical assistance, and provide facilities for those urban populations most seriously underserved.[45]

The greatest need is for the Federal government to develop a coordinated plan for planning and monitoring its functions in the nation's recreational system. As pointed out in earlier chapters, varied Federal agencies sponsor a tremendous range of programs, resources, and other forms of assistance—with only a limited level of joint planning, and with a major focus on outdoor recreation, rather than the full range of leisure needs and services required by the public at large.

Beyond this, there is an increasing need to develop a more effective policy for the management of the National Parks and other large-scale wilderness areas owned by the Federal government. Fuller assistance must be provided, to remedy the deterioration caused during the past several years by the establishment of additional parks and recreation areas without adequate funding for staff and operational budgets.

The Federal government has begun to move into other important leisure-related areas. Recognizing the crisis situation in the arts, the government has steadily increased Federal funding for the National Endowment for the Arts over the past decade, although on a per capita basis, the funding remains less than that given by other national governments to the arts and humanities. Proponents of sports activities have urged the Federal government to assume a much stronger role. In 1976, the President's Commission on Olympic Sports warned that amateur sports in the United States were "fragmented, ill-defined, nondirected," and torn by feuds for public support. The commission pointed out that the general level of active participation in the United States was far below that in other countries:

> It is not unusual to find one-third to one-half of the population of European countries engaged in regular sporting activity of one type or another. Political leaders are personally involved in amateur sport and fitness concerns.
>
> Almost every country in the world supports its athletes and athletic programs out of the governmental treasury. In West Germany, the figures have risen from $34 million in 1970 to nearly twice that amount in 1975, with state governments contributing a similar sum. . . . The Canadian Government spent close to $24 million in 1975 for sports and recreation [and] some Canadian provinces are spending even more than the national Government for their own sports programs.[46]

The report suggested that the highest sports authority be placed within either the State Department, the Interior Department, or the Department of Health, Education, and Welfare, with coordination of high-level competitive sports assigned to an agency like the U. S. Olympic Committee or the Amateur Athletic Union. The Federal government was strongly urged to provide Olympic training centers, and to support a stronger national focus on the development of highly accomplished athletes. While legislation based on such recommendations has not yet been enacted, it seems probable that the Federal government will be assuming more support of sports programs on all levels throughout the United States.

Numerous other critics have challenged present national policies in sport, which give by far the greatest amount of support to the high-level athlete and do little to encourage mass participation on a recreational level. In Canada, for example, there was sharp criticism of the extremely expensive sponsorship of the 1976 Montreal Olympics. Representatives of the Confederation des Loisirs de Quebec stated that the Olympics gave priority to a major series of competitive events

> offered by the sports elite to the social elite. The price of admissions to the events alone draws the line that reserves participation for the privileged few . . . the common people participate by way of the media . . . By building fantastic sports installations, in which the audience is more important than the participants, we have opted for the consumption of events rather than participation in sports for all.[47]

The critics pointed out that had government officials wanted to facilitate mass involvement in sports by the people of Quebec, the Olympic budget alone could have provided thousands of smaller arenas, indoor-outdoor swimming pools, and operational subsidies to municipalities and sports organizations. In the years ahead, this kind of critical scrutiny will be applied to all government programs designed to assist recreation and leisure throughout the United States and Canada.

State governments have also expanded their roles in recreation and parks. The California park and recreation system is an excellent example of how states operate today. In a presentation before the 1975 National Recreation and Park Congress, Russell W. Porter, Chief of Grants and Statewide Studies of the California

406

Department of Parks and Recreation, described the two important roles of his agency: (a) to serve the general public through the state's million-acre park system; and (b) to assist cities, counties, and park and recreation districts through financial and technical assistance programs. He describes how, through the state park system,

> we preserve our diminishing natural landscapes, preserve important segments of California's history, and provide recreation. In the aggregate, our 240 units offer an extraordinary array of leisure pursuits. At your choice you may wish to picnic at the site of gold discovery in California or in a redwood grove; or tour a Spanish Mission, a gold rush ghost town or Hearst's "castle"; or lie on an ocean beach or water-ski at a reservoir; or motorcycle in a 1,700-acre motorcycle park or careen your dune buggy over miles of sand dunes.[48]

But it is in the other area of responsibility that the California State Department of Parks and Recreation has changed its functions drastically. In the past, it provided rather limited, remedial forms of assistance to local recreation administrators; as they grew more resourceful and sophisticated, however, the state agency altered its approach. It became more concerned with major social problems arising from population growth, building expansion, and shortages of tax revenues. To resolve these conditions, the State Department of Parks and Recreation undertook the following actions.

First, it helped establish a California State Parks Foundation, to encourage and administer gifts and legacies for the California park system. This nonprofit organization with extremely influential advisors and directors has been immensely successful in raising funds and adding thousands of acres and other valuable properties to the state's parkland. Legislation created an Off-Highway Vehicle Fund to establish a wide range of trails for dirt bikes, dunebuggies, four-wheel drive, and other vehicles, and to help both the state and local governments develop riding, hiking, and biking trails and hostels.

A $250 million bond issue provided substantial sums to cities, counties, and districts as 100 percent grants; another $60 million issue provided for recreational development at water reservoirs. Vigorous efforts were made to obtain matching land gifts from numerous individuals, organizations, and corporations, to be matched with Land and Water Conservation Fund dollars. Finally, the state solicited and achieved extensive citizen involvement through advisory committees, surveys and other public relations efforts—including a state park film, a radio public information release program, and numerous publications printed in Spanish, German, Japanese and Chinese. Park opportunities have also been enhanced, through the use of a computerized reservation system to maximize use of campsites and eliminate user delays, and an electronic tour guide system at historic units of the park system. The State Park and Recreation Department has also experimented with special transportation programs using Amtrak to take family groups from inner city areas to state beaches, and with environmental living programs to use camp grounds. It also offers "mobile park experiences," which tour urban centers throughout the state with environmental and historical exhibits.

Many other state governments are developing new program approaches similar to those of California. The undertaking of expanded responsibilities by state governments is essential to meet the critical challenges facing the leisure-services field today.

407

National Awareness of Recreation and Leisure

Probably the most critical problem is the need to elicit more public concern about recreation, leisure, and problems of conservation and open-space development. Although organized recreation service has grown tremendously over the past four decades, a strong case could be made that in our individual understanding of the meaning of leisure in our lives and our willingness as a society to support recreation as a vital public function, we have made no significant progress since the 1930s and 1940s.

From an historical perspective, recreation was a vital tool of the Federal government's effort to combat the Depression during the 1930s; it was seen not only as a way to create jobs and spur the economy, but also as an important means of restoring community morale and meeting significant human needs. The use of recreation during the 1960s and 1970s has been far more limited, and public figures have rarely spoken out on leisure issues, as they did in the earlier period. When budget cuts were mandated on various levels of government, recreation and parks were generally among the most sharply reduced in many cities.

Even today, many individuals have an extremely narrow view of the meaning of leisure; they are content to take part in a limited range of activities that do not begin to challenge their capabilities or contribute to the total quality of their life experience. The widespread reliance on television to "kill" great bulks of time (as a universal convenient baby sitter for the young, or as mind-duller for the middle-aged and elderly) is probably the best example of this. While certainly no individual or professional body should tell others what they must do with their time, it seems clear that we need to be able to make more intelligent and rewarding use of our growing leisure. The facts that so many strive for material success and then do not know what to do with it—particularly after retirement from business—and that so many of our social pathologies stem from boredom and the search for "kicks" suggest that more attention should be given to understanding the relative roles of leisure, work, and play in our lives.

Considering the growing number of persons who are likely to become unemployed or underemployed as a result of increased mechanization and automation, it will be increasingly necessary for us to develop a national policy that comes to grips with the needs of a leisure-oriented society that values rather than scorns free time, and that sees importance in human experiences other than work.

Since its inception, the National Recreation and Park Association has taken a vigorous lead in interpreting the field to the public. Although the association has been successful in achieving much desirable legislation and in mobilizing professional efforts for more effective action, it is obvious that much remains to be accomplished among the public at large to create a vital and enthusiastic constituency for recreation and parks.

Education for Leisure, Past and Present

The need to prepare young people for leisure was first identified as an important educational concern in the 1918 report, "Cardinal Principles of Secondary Education," which stressed that education for the "worthy use of leisure" was one of the seven major goals of American education. In successive statements of the Educational Policies Commission, the position was taken that the "unworthy" use of leisure impaired health, disrupted home life, lessened vocational efficiency, and destroyed civic-mindedness. American schools were urged to move vigorously to guide and direct the use of leisure in constructive recreation by children and youth.[49]

In part, this mandate was carried out by school systems that assumed direct responsibility for community recreation. During the period between the 1920s and the 1940s, the community school concept first became popular; the school served as a center for much community activity, including forums, vocational projects, cultural programs, and recreation.

Following World War II, however, as recreation and park departments merged to provide a full range of community recreation facilities and programs, schools began to renounce their recreation responsibilities. The critical examination of American education during the late 1950s and early 1960s forced many schools to focus on their academic functions—particularly science and mathematics—and relinquish, at least in part, other concerns. By the mid-1960s, only about 5 percent of the public recreation programs in the United States were operated by school systems.

Although some educational authorities made a genuine attempt during this period to continue education for leisure, the majority of schools gave this effort little more than lip service. A study by the National Education Association in 1967 reported that a high proportion of modern schoolteachers still regarded education for leisure as an important function of the schools, but one toward which little was being accomplished.[50] Assuming that leisure *is* a valid concern of education, how is it to be approached?

Present-Day Approaches

Most authorities agree that the schools should strive to teach skills and implant habits and attitudes to ensure that individuals will use their leisure time in creative, active, and self-enriching pursuits. This goal is best met by offering classes in sports and games, music, dance, the theater, literature, and other subjects with obvious potential for continuing interest. Other subjects like natural sciences and social studies may provide important knowledge or affect attitudes toward leisure. Some schools approach problems of leisure—such as gambling, alcohol use, or drug experimentation—as part of instruction intended to create healthy and informed attitudes about these activities. Still others, although all too few, approach problems of leisure as a topic in economics, government, and other social studies courses.

What is important is that leisure be presented to children and youth not simply as a set of skills or activities, but as a rewarding experience that will enrich their lives. Far from being peripheral to education, such a focus must be at the central core of education in the years ahead. This point is affirmed by Robert Maynard Hutchins, president of the Center for the Study of Democratic Institutions, who urges that we begin the transition from a "working" to a "learning" society:

> The man who is truly educated, rather than narrowly trained, is ready for anything. He has developed his human powers and is able to use them and his understanding of the world to meet any new problem he has to face. He is prepared by his education to go on learning. Hence he is prepared for the human use of his free time. This is, in fact, the purpose of education in childhood and youth. . . . If work is our salvation, we are

409

lost indeed, and we are on the way from full employment to full unemployment. But if we will only recognize it, the great opportunity that men have always yearned for is ours at last.

Other nations have had affluence and leisure, or their ruling classes have had them. They have been destroyed, usually from within, and usually from causes associated with affluence and leisure.[51]

It should be stressed that education for leisure involves far more than recreational activities alone. Gardner states that serving as class officers, working on school projects or public service activities, planning school events, and similar activities are also important growth experiences which may help students learn to assume and enjoy such responsibilities. He stresses that in a variety of ways, the school

must serve as a laboratory situation. Schools need not add new subject matter to their already crowded schedule. Rather, leisure is built into the existing curriculum.

Our society is full of dynamic change. Leisure pursuits of today may not be the same as those twenty years from now, but by establishing good attitudes toward leisure in our youth, teachers will have laid a groundwork that can be built upon. Children will have developed a sense of individual identity and self-worth and will be in a much better position to adapt themselves to an ever changing lifestyle.[52]

In many ways, it will be necessary for us to broaden our concept of leisure to meet future needs. Twardzik points out that we will have to think of recreation itself as being far broader than outdoor pastimes or traditional games and sports, and that work itself must be seen as potentially fulfilling and creative. Students must understand that unless it is used well, "leisure time can be boring, frightening, and the most lonely and insecure of all times."[53] If youth understand the choices that lie before them, they will recognize the value of education for leisure in helping them to meet life's challenges.

As stated in chapter 12, the National Recreation and Park Association received a major grant to carry out a study and develop action proposals for promoting leisure education in American schools. The major purpose of LEAP (Leisure Education Advancement Project) is to develop a model which will help students appreciate the potential of leisure, understand the various kinds of uses to which it may be put, recognize its significance in society, and learn other important appreciations and skills.

Leisure education must also be expanded beyond schools and colleges; education is a continuous, lifetime concern, and people should be encouraged to continue to learn creative use of leisure in their middle decades and even after retirement. Thus it is essential that a wide variety of agencies—schools and colleges, public recreation and park departments, museums, libraries, and other institutions— join in a concerted effort to enrich the public's understanding and effective use of leisure at *all* ages. The growth of interest in "leisure counseling," which is, after all, simply an individualized and intensive form of education for leisure for those with

410

emotional or physical disability, illustrates this point vividly. Neulinger points out that leisure counseling need not deal only with special populations, but may be used as a form of leisure resource guidance, or lifestyle counseling.

> Leisure counseling is not a service only for a "leisure class," or the affluent middle and upper classes. Leisure counseling must serve all of our society, particularly those most in need of it. . . . to serve all of our society [it] must be as varied as the conditions of our society in fact are.[54]

In Milwaukee, Wilson and Overs developed a leisure counseling model, including a leisure interest rating scale and profile sheet and a specific inventory of nine hundred categories of activity provided by varied public and private agencies in the metropolitan area. It was used not only with the general population, through the Milwaukee Public Schools' Division of Municipal Recreation and Community Education, but also through special contracts with alcoholism treatment units, and psychiatric and physical rehabilitation hospitals.[55]

Citizen Support of Community Recreation and Parks

A second important means of improving national awareness of leisure needs and promoting support for government recreation programs is to encourage direct participation of citizens in planning and operating recreation programs. Howard writes:

> In every community there are influential individuals or groups of individuals who play a dominant role in the making of public decisions. Support from these "power elites" or "economic notables," as they are sometimes called, can significantly enhance the development of the community recreation system. . . . research has concluded that: (1) persons not elected to office, operating behind the scenes, play very significant parts in the making of many important decisions, and (2) that there are some persons, groups, or combinations of the two that wield a disproportionate share of influence in the community decision-making process.[56]

Input from private citizens is a major source of power for recreation and park departments in modern communities. Citizens serving on boards and commissions represent the diverse views of individuals and interest groups and provide a two-way bridge for communication. In many cities, citizens form district councils or committees which raise funds, provide volunteer leadership, advise on policy, and, when necessary, bring out the votes to support bond issues or other needed legislation. Organizations like Little League and other youth sports programs usually depend heavily on adult volunteers to coach and manage teams. Neighborhood volunteers in some cities have cleaned up small parks and playgrounds, rehabilitated other facilities, or even raised funds regularly to meet critical needs. New York has over ten thousand block associations, which reduce the anonymity and frustrations of urban living by providing neighborhood contacts and friendliness and working to improve security on the city streets:

411

They have fought massage parlors and pornographic bookstores in the neighborhood, sponsored field trips for the children, organized babysitting pools and food co-ops, published newsletters and purchased bicycle racks. They have planted trees, purchased fences, flowers, sodium vapor lamps, covered potholes, curbed (literally) dog litter, created vest pocket parks from vacant lots, painted benches and repaired sidewalks.[57]

Block associations often use recreation as a means of unifying the neighborhood or raising money, through block parties, carnivals, bazaars, covered-dish suppers, holiday celebrations, raffles, and similar events. Municipal recreation and park departments have learned to work closely with such citizen groups, and to seek their support to testify for needed programs or facilities, or to assist citywide projects.

Only through effective programs of education for leisure and through cultivation of strong community groups with a stake in recreation and park programs can the fullest level of support for recreation and leisure be achieved.

Upgrading Professionalism in Recreation and Parks

As chapter 12 has indicated, there has been substantial growth in the numbers and status of recreation and park professionals. Nevertheless, there is a strong continuing need to strengthen their public image, improve the process of professional development, and create more effective research programs in recreation and parks.

A number of factors have clouded the public's understanding of the role and identity of practitioners in recreation and parks. Those in the field itself have sometimes contributed to the confusion by labeling every person working on any level and in any position related to recreation and parks as a professional in this field. Clearly, such a designation should be extended only to those who have a primary concern for the planning, development, and maintenance of areas and facilities, or for leadership, supervision, administration, consultation, research, or teaching directly related to the delivery of recreation services. These are the persons who should be identified by job titles and Civil Service personnel codes, and by training and organizational affiliations, as recreation professionals. Others in the field should be recognized as nonprofessional or support personnel, or as professionals in other disciplines who happen to be employed in leisure-related agencies.

A second major problem is the need to strengthen the recruitment, selection, training, and certification or licensing of those working as professionals in recreation. Vigorous recruitment efforts should identify talented young people and encourage them to gain early job experience in recreation and to enter college curricula for professional training in recreation and parks. A successful recruiting campaign will require career days, sophisticated recruitment literature and films, and the combined efforts of colleges and universities, school guidance counselors, professional organizations, and local recreation agencies.

Every effort must be made to apply higher standards of selection to those who seek admission to the field and to upgrade recreation and park curricula in colleges and universities. Accreditation of qualified institutions will be necessary to eliminate substandard programs and to enable the recreation field to compete with other professions for highly qualified entrants and for foundation and government research grants or other forms of support. Certification, licensing, and registration must become part of the process of upgrading professional selection throughout the nation, and the politically motivated hiring that is common in many communities must be strongly resisted.

A closely related problem is the need to fit the professional qualifications of those entering the field to the demands of the jobs they will perform. Some workers in recreation and parks today are overqualified for their positions in terms of academic background; larger numbers are underqualified in that they hold responsible positions without having had formal training in the field. A systematic effort to suit job requirements to the actual demands of the position could help to remedy these inequities. Higher education in recreation and parks seems likely to become more specialized. Although some have criticized this trend, suggesting that specialization should only come on the graduate degree level, specialization appears to be a realistic accommodation to existing personnel needs and a legitimate way to extend the scope of the recreation and park profession.

Another important need is to employ greater numbers of minority group individuals in recreation and park positions with real opportunity for advancement. To provide job mobility for such individuals, some municipal agencies have initiated work-study programs which permit promising candidates to hold jobs while earning degrees at nearby colleges. Such career-ladder programs are essential to a successful opportunity program for underrepresented population groups.

Need for Improved Research Programs

A final problem is the need for more effective programs of research in recreation and park service. If the field is to justify its claims for support, it will be necessary to document its values and outcomes with convincing research evidence. Even though it is extremely difficult to measure the effects of any form of social service or social welfare program, it is important that attempts be made. Sherwood has written:

> Why isn't there greater demand from various segments of our society—public officials, the public itself, program administrators—for hard evaluations of action programs that attack one or more of the social ills of our . . . system? . . . More and better evaluation studies of social action programs are needed if our society is going to be able to make increasingly more rational allocations of resources to the solution of social problems.[58]

Improved programs of research within recreation and parks will have the dual effect of achieving greater public understanding of recreation as a significant public service and of helping recreation administrators determine needs and user preferences, as well as program methods and outcomes, more intelligently. The U. S. Forest Service was one of the first major government agencies to develop an extensive list of problems in its field which requires careful research. It includes the need to: (1) obtain better understanding of visitor preferences and attitudes regarding forest recreation opportunities; (2) develop better procedures for measuring current recreation uses in terms of numbers, duration, and type of activity; (3) determine the factors that influence recreation demand and reliable procedures for predicting trends and estimating future needs; (4) develop guidelines for recreation resource planning and allocation; (5) determine the compatibility of various types of recreation uses with each other and with other forest uses; (6) develop methods for improving visitors' understanding and appreciation of natural areas through visitor information services; (7) determine direct and indirect monetary costs and returns associated with recreation development and uses; and (8) determine nonmonetary individual and social values accruing from recreation development and use.[59]

Far more sophisticated ways of assessing benefits and costs, determining appropriate activities for different populations and agencies, and achieving a realistic order of priorities need to be developed. Unkel, Smith, and Van Doren have pointed out that despite the widespread acceptance of computers, the systems approach, and management information systems methods in the field of public administration, relatively few recreation and park departments are using such tools as an integral part of administration.

> An MIS (management information system) for a parks and recreation department should have the potential to provide significant economic, administrative, and social benefits. It should provide information about the operations of the department, about the recreation needs of the community, and about the implications of various decisions.[60]

There is also a critical need for more effective programs of scientific evaluation of all elements of the agency's operation. McLean and Spears point out that in the past too many programs have been judged by the number of complaints received or by the lack of complaints, with many administrators and program directors "flying by the seat of their pants." Program budgeting, revenue sharing, and other factors today demand that we reexamine our traditional modes of operation and evaluative procedures:

> Few local governments have well-developed program evaluation depart-ments. One reason is the difficulty of measuring the effectiveness of . . . programs. To measure effectiveness requires that the output of a particular service delivery activity or program be specified and prefera-bly quantified. Once objectives for programs have been specified and output measures developed, it is possible to evaluate performance.[61]

The field of therapeutic recreation has developed this approach, using systems planning, careful evaluation of patient outcomes, and other measures of effectiveness.[62] It is important to recognize that interest in recreation-related research is relatively new. The first national conference in this field was held in the fall of 1965 at Pennsylvania State University, cosponsored by the National Recrea-tion and Park Association and the American Association for Health, Physical Education, and Recreation. Several other research conferences have been held at this university, due in large measure to the efforts of Dr. Betty van der Smissen, a strong force in recreation research. The National Recreation and Park Association has conducted several major studies related to recreation manpower, curriculum de-velopment, and community practices, under contract with Federal agencies. The Society of Park and Recreation Educators publishes the *Journal of Leisure Research,* a quarterly journal which reports and reviews major studies in this field. In Canada, a similar publication, *Recreation Review,* is issued by the Ontario

Research Council on Leisure, and the federal government and provinces have sponsored numerous recent research projects, several of which are reported in this text.

Outdoor Recreation and Urban Needs

The bulk of funded research has been in the area of outdoor recreation, resource development, and environmental and economic concerns. A comprehensive statement of research objectives and priorities in outdoor recreation was developed by a special conference convened in 1968 by the Bureau of Outdoor Recreation and the National Academy of Sciences.[63] The Outdoor Recreation Research Needs Workshop in 1974, sponsored by the Bureau of Outdoor Recreation in cooperation with other Federal agencies, at Harpers Ferry, West Virginia was extremely influential in directing the course of much recent leisure research.[64]

However, comparatively little research has been concerned with the urban setting. Although Dunn and others have done some important surveys of current needs and practices, the consensus, as expressed in a report on urban recreation needs by the U. S. Department of Housing and Urban Development, is that

> there is a serious lack of research and evaluation in urban recreation. The Federal data base is useless for policy formulation. We do not know who uses municipal recreation lands, facilities, or programs, or why others do not use them.[65]

Information of this kind is critical to the successful operation of urban recreation and park departments. The report of the Outdoor Recreation Resources Review Commission pointed out a "need for problem-solving research to establish general principles and techniques essential for efficient management"; a later planning report issued by the New York State Office of Parks and Recreation clarified the need.

> Sound policy and program formulation requires that basic recreation research be expanded [to provide] a strong foundation for the immediate issues around which policy decisions revolve.[66]

The promotion of more effective research in recreation and parks will require the collaboration of four types of agencies: *professional organizations,* which sponsor national studies, hold conferences and symposiums, and public research findings; *colleges and universities,* which contribute to scholarship in this field, both through graduate theses and the work of faculty members who are capable of staffing sophisticated interdisciplinary studies; *state and Federal agencies,* which provide funding for significant research projects related to their areas of concern; and *recreation and park agencies* of all types, which can carry on much direct research themselves, as well as provide settings and populations through which other agencies can conduct meaningful studies.

What will be the direction of future research related to recreation and leisure? An extensive study of practitioners, educators, and scholars in related disciplines reported in 1976 by Crandall and Lewko indicated a wide range of

415

concerns and perceived needs.[67] When asked what they considered priorities for future research, respondents indicated the following subjects (Table 16-1).

It is critical that theoretical research be coupled with more practical or applied studies, to provide a solid base of knowledge for both practice and professional preparation in recreation and leisure in the decades that lie ahead.

Table 16-1.

Proposed Areas for Future Research

Subjects Listed as First Choices	*Frequency of Citation*
Antecedents and consequences of leisure behavior	63
Resource planning, management, and the provision of leisure services	27
Methodology, measurement, analysis	24
Sociology of leisure (including groups and family)	19
Theory building	17
Environment, ecology, energy	15
Leisure and the elderly	14
The work-leisure relationship	14
Special populations	13
Reinforcement and/or modification of behavior patterns	13
Future demands, trends, and changes in leisure	13
Ethnic and minority groups, including women	10

Recognition of this need was evidenced in the late 1970s when Congress authorized the Bureau of Outdoor Recreation to study urban recreation throughout the United States. Field studies were initiated in forty-four standard metropolitan statistical areas to provide detailed information on urban recreation needs to help guide Federal policy in this area in the years ahead.

In reviewing this national study, Maguire warned that the study should not be permitted to deal solely with problems of land acquisition and preservation, although Congress has traditionally viewed these as the major areas of need. She pointed out strong evidence that the real need of cities was for assistance in the areas of operation and maintenance, as well as the rehabilitation or redevelopment of physical resources. It was essential, in her view, that the BOR study examine the total leisure delivery system in cities, linked as it is to social service functions and to cooperative programs with many other government and voluntary agencies. She concluded that

> the urban recreation study mandated by Congress . . . if well done, could set in motion a set of new policies and revised priorities . . . It could educate Congress about the crucial importance of recreation in human growth, in shaping cities, in combatting our social and physical ills.[68]

Clearly, studies of this nature will be of critical importance in solving many of the problems and issues described in this chapter, in both the United States and Canada.

Chapter Sixteen

1. David Gray, "The Case for Compensatory Recreation," *Parks and Recreation,* April 1969, p. 23.

2. David Gray and Seymour Greben, "Future Perspectives," *Parks and Recreation,* July 1974, p. 53.

3. "Leisure in Canada," Report of Montmorency Conference on Leisure, Montmorency, Quebec, 1969.

4. Jack Foley, cited in Donald Henkel, "NRPA Position Statements," *Parks and Recreation,* January 1976, p. 59.

5. James F. Murphy, *Recreation and Leisure Service: A Humanistic Perspective* (Dubuque, Iowa: Wm. C. Brown, 1975), p. 50.

6. "Anything Goes: Taboos in the Twilight," *Time,* 13 November 1967, p. 74.

7. Bertram M. Beck, "A Role for Recreation," in *Juvenile Delinquency and Youth Crime,* Task Force Report of the President's Commission on Law Enforcement and Administration of Justice (Washington, D. C.: U. S. Government Printing Office, 1967), p. 400.

8. "Modern Living: Manners and Morals," *Time,* 27 June 1969, p. 54.

9. Gray and Greben, "Future Perspectives," p. 48.

10. Gordon J. Dahl, "Work, Play and Worship—Toward a New Moral Economy," *Leisure Today: Selected Readings* (Washington, D. C.: American Association for Leisure and Recreation, 1975), p. 23.

11. See Erich Fromm, *The Anatomy of Human Destructiveness* (New York: Holt, Reinhart and Winston, 1973).

12. Stewart Udall, quoted in "Man . . . An Endangered Species?" Conservation Yearbook No. 4 (Washington, D. C.: U. S. Department of the Interior, 1968), p. 3.

13. See "The Big Cleanup, A Special Issue on Water Quality," *Parks and Recreation,* February 1977, pp. 1a–35a.

14. Bayard Webster, "The Lasting, but Partial, Influence of 'Silent Spring'," New York *Times,* 9 January 1977.

15. Russell E. Train, "Editorial: Clean Rivers for the People," *Parks and Recreation,* August 1976, p. 11.

16. Gladwin Hill, "The Great Lakes Have a New Enemy: The Air," New York *Times,* 10 October 1976.

17. "Protection of Rare Plant Could Block Dam Project," New York *Times,* 29 March 1976.

18. Gladwin Hill, "Consultants Debate the Recreational and Preservation Roles of National Park System," New York *Times,* 18 April 1972.

19. Robert J. Badaracco, "ORV's: Often Rough on Visitors," *Parks and Recreation,* September 1976, p. 34.

20. Gladwin Hill, "Environmentalists Propose Switching Expenditures from Narrow Interests to Entire Natural Groupings," New York *Times,* 2 October 1976.

21. William F. Theobald, *The Female in Public Recreation: A Study of Participation and Administrative Attitudes* (Waterloo, Ontario: Waterloo Research Institute and Ontario Ministry of Culture and Recreation, 1976), pp. 9–10.

22. Michael J. Heit and Don Malpass, *Do Women Have Equal Play?* (Ontario, Canada: Ministry of Culture and Recreation, 1975).

23. Foster Rhea Dulles, *A History of Recreation: America Learns to Play* (New York: Appleton-Century-Crofts, 1965), p. 96.

24. Helen M. Dauncey, *Planning for Girls in the Community Recreation Program* (New York: National Recreation Association, 1953), pp. 8, 16, 20.

25. Bill Gilbert and Nancy Williamson, "Sport Is Unfair to Women," *Sports Illustrated,* 28 May 1973, p. 85.

26. Dorothy V. Harris, "The Female Athlete—Psycho-Social Considerations," *Journal of Physical Education and Recreation,* January 1975, p. 32.

27. Barbara J. Drinkwater, "Aerobic Power in Females," p. 36, and Jack H. Wilmore, "Body Composition and Strength Development," p. 38, in *Journal of Physical Education and Recreation,* January 1975.

28. Thomas Johnson, "Boys and Girls Together?" New York *Times,* 5 January 1974.

29. "Washington Scene," *Parks and Recreation,* January 1976, p. 14.

30. "Shore Rights: Do the Beaches Belong to the People?" New York *Times,* 30 July 1972.

31. Ibid.

32. R. C. Scheerenberger, "A Model for Deinstitutionalization," *Mental Retardation*, December 1974, p. 3.

33. Quoted in Scheerenberger, p. 4.

34. Ibid., p. 4.

35. Cited in Scheerenberger, "Model for Deinstitutionalization," p. 4.

36. Terri Schultz, "The Handicapped, a Minority Demanding Its Rights," New York *Times*, 13 February 1977.

37. "Race for Recreation Space," *Newsweek*, 20 June 1966, p. 99.

38. Richard Kraus, *Urban Parks and Recreation: Challenge of the 1970's* (New York: Community Council of Greater New York, 1972), p. 23.

39. Seymour M. Gold, "Deviant Behavior in Urban Parks." *Leisure Today, Selected Readings* (Washington, D. C.: American Association for Leisure and Recreation, 1975), p. 17.

40. Edward F. Connors III, "Public Safety in Park and Recreation Settings," *Parks and Recreation*, January 1976, p. 21.

41. Ronald W. Chase, "Commercial Approaches to Public Recreation," *Parks and Recreation*, May 1973, p. 26.

42. See, for example, case study of fees and charges in Richard G. Kraus and Barbara J. Bates, *Recreation Leadership and Supervision* (Philadelphia: W. B. Saunders, 1975), pp. 373–75.

43. Richard C. Trudeau. "Ways and Means to Stretch Tax Dollars." (Washington, D. C.: NRPA Seminar on Finance, May 1976), pp. 1–9.

44. Ibid., p. 12.

45. *The Recreation Imperative: A Nationwide Outdoor Recreation Plan* (Washington, D.C.: Senate Committee on Interior and Insular Affairs, Senator Henry Jackson, Chairman, June 1974).

46. Joseph Durso, "Report to Ford Calls for Amateur Reform," New York *Times*, 8 February 1976.

47. "The Olympic Mania," *Recreation Canada*, 34 (March 1976): pp. 45, 47.

48. Russell Porter (Address to National Recreation and Park Congress. Dallas, Texas, October 1975).

49. *Policies for Education in American Democracy: Report of the Educational Policies Commission of the National Education Association and the American Association of School Administrators* (Washington, D.C.: National Education Association, 1946), pp. 65, 192, 203, 206.

50. National Education Association Research Division, "A New Look at the Seven Cardinal Principles of Education," *NEA Journal*, January 1967, pp. 53–54.

51. Robert Maynard Hutchins, "Are We Educating Our Children for the Wrong Future?" *Saturday Review*, 11 September 1965, p. 83.

52. C. Hugh Gardner, "Education for Leisure in the Elementary School Curriculum," *Journal of Physical Education and Recreation*, March 1976, p. 46.

53. Louis F. Twardzik, "Beyond Leisure Time: Expanding the Recreation Concept," *Parks and Recreation*, August 1975, p. 37.

54. John Neulinger, "Leisure Counseling: A Plea for Complexity," *Journal of Physical Education and Recreation*, April 1977, p. 27.

55. Cited in Michael Magulski, Virginia H. Faull, and Barbara Rutkowski, "The Milwaukee Leisure Counseling Model," *Journal of Physical Education and Recreation*, April 1977, pp. 25–26.

56. Dennis Howard, "Tapping Community Power," *Parks and Recreation*, March 1976, p. 31.

57. Ruth Rejnis, "Power on the Block," New York *Times*, 16 January 1977.

58. Clarence C. Sherwood, "Issues in Measuring Results of Action Programs," *The Research Letter*, October 1967, p. 1.

59. For report of first major national conference on recreation, see *Recreation Research* (Washington, D.C.: American Association for Health, Physical Education and Recreation, and National Recreation and Park Association, 1966).

60. M. B. Unkel, A. W. Smith, and C. S. Van Doren, "Putting Computers to Good Use," *Parks and Recreation*, November 1975, p. 20.

61. Christine McLean and Charles R. Spears, "Leisure Programs: Quandary or Quality," *Parks and Recreation*, July 1975, p. 21.

62. See, for example, Carol A. Peterson, "Application of Systems Analysis Procedures in Program Planning in Therapeutic Recreation Service," in Elliott M. Avedon, *Therapeutic Recreation Service: An Applied Behavioral Science Approach* (Englewood Cliffs, N. J.: Prentice-Hall, 1974), pp. 128–55.

63. National Academy of Sciences, *A Program for Outdoor Recreation Research* (Washington, D.C.: Bureau of Outdoor Recreation, 1969).

64. *Proceedings of the Outdoor Recreation Research Needs Workshop, Harpers Ferry, West Virginia, September 1974* (Washington, D.C.: Bureau of Outdoor Recreation, 1974).

65. *Urban Recreation: A Report Prepared for the Nationwide Outdoor Recreation Plan by the Interdepartmental Work Group on Urban Recreation* (Washington, D.C.: U. S. Department of Housing and Urban Development, 1974), pp. 6, 12.

66. *New York State Parks and Recreation: People, Resources, Recreation* (Albany, New York: State Office of Parks and Recreation, Outdoor Recreation Plan, 1972), p. 22.

67. Rick Crandall and John Lewko, "Leisure Research, Present and Future: Who, What, Where," *Journal of Leisure Research,* 3rd Quarter, (1976):150–59.

68. Margaret Maguire, "The Urban Recreation Study: Doing It Right," *Parks and Recreation,* April 1977, pp. 28–31, 56–57.

Suggested Topics for Examination Questions, Student Papers, or Panel Reports

PART ONE: CONCEPTS OF RECREATION, PLAY, AND LEISURE

1. What major social factors have been responsible for the growth of the recreation movement in the United States and Canada during the past several decades? Identify and discuss these in detail.

2. Why is it essential that those who work in the field of leisure service delivery have an in-depth understanding of the social and behavioral sciences, as they affect recreational participation?

3. Define *recreation, play,* and *leisure,* both in terms of their treatment in the text, and your understanding of their meaning.

4. Which of the traditional and contemporary theories of play described in the text are most significant, in your view? How may they be used in shaping the content of community recreation programs?

5. Select one major theme in recent or contemporary sociological research in leisure, such as the influence of social class or occupational status on leisure attitudes and behavior, or shifting work-vs.-leisure attitudes and values. Summarize the major findings in this area, and their implications for the field of organized recreation service.

6. Describe the overall impact of recreation on the national economy, in the United States or Canada. Then present in fuller detail a single major area of participation (such as the cultural arts, sports, or travel and tourism), including trends in participation, problem areas, and economic outcomes.

PART TWO: THE HISTORY OF RECREATION AND LEISURE

7. Contrast the attitudes toward work and leisure, and the functions of recreation in primitive society, with the same elements in modern, industrial society.

8. Select three periods of world history, such as the pre-Christian or Renaissance eras. Show how organized religion sought to influence or control leisure attitudes and behavior in these periods. To what extent does religion play a similar role today, and what is the key significance of recreation, from a religious point of view?

9. It is widely believed that the early American colonists condemned and repressed most forms of recreation and leisure. To what extent was this true? How did Puritan values influence later attitudes toward recreation in the United States?

10. Trace the development of parks and other outdoor recreation facilities in the

421

United States or Canada, on several levels of governmental sponsorship. How has the philosophy of park use changed over the past several decades?

11. Select one of the following periods or events during the twentieth century, and show its influence on the developing recreation movement: (a) growth of urban centers; (b) the Great Depression; (c) World War II; (d) the Civil Rights movement and the War on Poverty of the 1960s.

12. Some authors have asserted that leisure was not widely available to all social classes until the present era. How true is this? What class had the bulk of leisure in past centuries—and what class or population groups have it today?

PART THREE: THE RECREATION MOVEMENT TODAY

13. Outline the major recreation and park functions in the United States or Canada today, showing how specific responsibilities are shared or distributed among various types of agencies. How might this system of sponsorship and assistance be improved, in your judgment?

14. Identify and summarize the most important comprehensive planning studies that have been carried out in recent years on the national level, in the United States or Canada. What types of recommendations have they made? How might planning on this level be improved?

15. Select a specific important area of governmental concern such as the cultural arts, recreation for the disabled, or travel and tourism. Show how this is sponsored or assisted on the state or provincial level, and what linkages there are to other levels of government.

16. What are the major arguments supporting the assumption of recreation and park responsibilities by municipal government agencies? Show how, in large metropolitan settings, different government agencies, including the schools, may cooperate, along with voluntary, private, commercial or other sponsors, in the total leisure service delivery system.

17. It has been said that the role of the recreation professional has grown increasingly complex and varied in recent years. Discuss this statement, and point out its implications for professional education.

18. During the past two decades, professional organizations have sought to develop registration, licensing, and certification procedures, along with accreditation of recreation and park curricula, in order to upgrade the status of this field and improve professional practices. Discuss the need for such procedures, and their present level of development.

PART FOUR: GOALS, PROBLEMS AND ISSUES IN RECREATION SERVICE

19. Develop a carefully documented statement of the important contributions of recreational experience in human growth and development. Select a single age group, such as adolescence or the elderly, and analyze its special needs for recreation and how they may best be met.

20. The prevention or reduction of juvenile delinquency has often been cited as an important goal of community recreation. How significant is this goal, and how may it best be achieved?

21. The text suggests that rapidly changing moral values in areas such as sex, alcohol or drug use, and gambling pose serious problems for recreation practitioners today.

Discuss the nature of this challenge, and outline a number of key issues which must be resolved in order to develop appropriate leadership or administrative policies.

22. Another important challenge facing the recreation movement is to provide fuller opportunity (both in terms of participation and employment) to such special populations as the disabled, the aging, women and girls, and racial and ethnic minority groups. Discuss this problem, describe what has been done in recent years, and suggest appropriate strategies for the years ahead.

23. Programs of energy and environmental conservation and protection have gained widespread impetus lately; ecology has become an important national concern. What are the shared goals that unite environmentalists and recreation and park professionals? At what points may they come into conflict? Suggest ways in which the two fields may work together for their mutual benefit.

24. The text concludes that it is necessary to develop national awareness of leisure as a societal concern, as well as greater personal understanding of recreation as an aspect of healthy living. Two recent trends to achieve these outcomes have been the emergence of *leisure counseling,* and the development of *leisure education curricula.* Describe appropriate goals and strategies in one of these two areas.

BIBLIOGRAPHY

Avedon, Elliott M., *Therapeutic Recreation Service: An Applied Behavioral Science Approach* (Englewood Cliffs, N.J.: Prentice-Hall, 1974).

Bannon, Joseph J., ed., *Outreach: Extending Community Service in Urban Areas* (Springfield, Ill.: Charles C. Thomas, 1973).

Bannon, Joseph J., *Leisure Resources: Its Comprehensive Planning* (Englewood Cliffs, N.J.: Prentice-Hall, 1976).

Brightbill, Charles K., *Man and Leisure: A Philosophy of Recreation* (Englewood Cliffs, N.J.: Prentice-Hall, 1961).

Butler, George D., *Introduction to Community Recreation* (New York: McGraw-Hill, 1976).

Caillois, Roger, *Man, Play and Games* (London: Thames and Hudson, 1961).

Carlson, Reynold; Deppe, Theodore; and MacLean, Janet, *Recreation in American Life* (Belmont, Calif.: Wadsworth, 1972).

Cheek, Neil H., Jr., and Burch, William R., Jr., *The Social Organization of Leisure in Human Society* (New York: Harper and Row, 1976).

Clawson, Marion, and Knetsch, Jack, *Economics of Outdoor Recreation* (Baltimore: Johns Hopkins Press, 1960).

Corbin, H. Dan, and Tait, William, *Education for Leisure* (Englewood Cliffs, N.J.: Prentice-Hall, 1973).

Cosgrove, Isobel, and Jackson, Richard, *The Geography of Recreation and Leisure* (London: Hutchinson University Library, 1972).

Craig, Timothy, ed., *The Humanistic and Mental Health Aspects of Sports, Exercise and Recreation* (Chicago: American Medical Association, 1975).

Dahl, Gordon, *Work, Play and Worship in a Leisure-Oriented Society* (Minneapolis: Augsburg Publishers, 1972).

Doell, Charles E., and Fitzgerald, Charles B., *A Brief History of Parks and Recreation in the United States* (Chicago: The Athletic Institute, 1954).

Dulles, Foster R., *A History of Recreation: America Learns to Play* (New York: Appleton-Century-Crofts, 1965).

Dumazedier, Joffre, *Toward a Society of Leisure* (New York: Free Press, 1967).

Dumazedier, Joffre, *Sociology of Leisure* (Amsterdam: Elsevier, 1974).

Ellis, M. J., *Why People Play* (Englewood Cliffs, N.J.: Prentice-Hall, 1973).

Fisher, A. Craig, ed., *Psychology of Sport: Issues and Insights* (Palo Alto, Calif.: Mayfield, 1976).

Frye, Virginia, and Peters, Martha, *Therapeutic Recreation* (Harrisburg, Pa.: Stackpole, 1972).

Godbey, Geoffrey, and Parker, Stanley, *Leisure Studies and Services: An Overview* (Philadelphia: W.B. Saunders, 1976).

Gold, Seymour M., *Urban Recreation Planning* (Philadelphia: Lea and Febiger, 1973).

Gray, David E., and Pelegrino, Donald A., *Reflections on the Recreation and Park Movement* (Dubuque: Wm. C. Brown, 1973).

Haun, Paul, *Recreation: A Medical Viewpoint* (New York: Teachers College, Columbia, Bureau of Publications, 1965).

Hjelte, George, and Shivers, Jay, *Public Administration of Recreational Services* (Philadelphia: Lea and Febiger, 1972).

Hormachea, Marion N., and Hormachea, Carroll R., *Recreation in Modern Society* (Boston: Holbrook, 1972).

Huizinga, Johan, *Homo Ludens: A Study of the Play Element in Culture* (Boston: Beacon Pr., 1950).

Jensen, Clayne R., *Outdoor Recreation in America* (Minneapolis: Burgess, 1973).

Jubenville, Alan, *Outdoor Recreation Planning* (Philadelphia: W. B. Saunders, 1976).

Kando, Thomas M., *Leisure and Popular Culture in Transition* (St. Louis: Mosby, 1975).

Kaplan, Max, *Leisure in America: A Social Inquiry* (New York: Wiley, 1960).

Kaplan, Max, *Leisure: Theory and Policy* (New York: Wiley, 1975).

Kelley, Jerry D., ed., *Expanding Horizons in Therapeutic Recreation II* (Urbana-Champaign, Ill.: University of Illinois, Office of Recreation and Park Resources, 1974).

Kraus, Richard, *Recreation and the Schools* (New York: Macmillan, 1964).

Kraus, Richard, *Recreation Today: Program Planning and Leadership* (Santa Monica, Calif.: Goodyear, 1977).

Kraus, Richard, *Therapeutic Recreation Service: Principles and Practices* (Philadelphia: W. B. Saunders, 1978).

Kraus, Richard, and Bates, Barbara, *Recreation Leadership and Supervision* (Philadelphia: W. B. Saunders, 1975).

Kraus, Richard, and Curtis, Joseph, *Creative Administration in Recreation and Parks* (St. Louis: C. V. Mosby, 1977).

Larrabee, Eric, and Meyersohn, Rolf, *Mass Leisure* (Glencoe, Ill.: Free Press, 1958).

Lee, Robert, *Religion and Leisure in America* (Nashville: Abingdon, 1964).

Lutzin, Sidney, and Storey, Edward, eds., *Managing Municipal Leisure Services* (Washington, D.C.: International City Management Association, 1973).

McFarland, Elsie M., *The Development of Public Recreation in Canada* (Vanier City, Ontario: Canadian Parks/Recreation Association, 1970).

McIntosh, Peter C., *Sport in Society* (London: C. A. Watts, 1963).

Millar, Susanna, *The Psychology of Play* (Baltimore: Penguin, 1968).

Miller, Norman, and Robinson, Duane, *The Leisure Age* (Belmont, Calif.: Wadsworth Pub., 1963).

Murphy, James F., *Recreation and Leisure Service: A Humanistic Perspective* (Dubuque: Wm. C. Brown, 1975).

Murphy, James F., and Howard, Dennis R., *Delivery of Community Leisure Services: An Holistic Approach* (Philadelphia: Lea and Febiger, 1977).

Murphy, James F.; Williams, John G.; Niepoth, E. William; and Brown, Paul D., *Leisure Service Delivery System: A Modern Perspective* (Philadelphia: Lea and Febiger, 1973).

Nash, Jay B., *Philosophy of Recreation and Leisure* (Dubuque: Brown, 1960).

Neal, Larry L., ed., *Leisure Today: Selected Readings* (Washington, D.C.: American Association for Leisure and Recreation, 1975).

Neale, Robert E., *In Praise of Play* (New York: Harper and Row, 1969).

Nesbitt, John A.; Brown, Paul D.; and Murphy, James F., eds., *Recreation and Leisure Service for the Disadvantaged* (Philadelphia: Lea and Febiger, 1970).

O'Morrow, Gerald S., *Therapeutic Recreation: A Helping Profession* (Reston, Va.: Reston, 1976).

Pieper, Josef, *Leisure: The Basis of Culture* (New York: Mentor-Omega, 1963).

Sapora, Allen V., and Mitchell, Elmer D., *The Theory of Play and Recreation* (New York: Ronald, 1961).

BIBLIOGRAPHY

Shivers, Jay S., and Fait, Hollis F., *Therapeutic and Adapted Recreation Services* (Philadelphia: Lea and Febiger, 1975).

Sessoms, H. Douglas; Meyer, Harold D.; and Brightbill, Charles K., *Leisure Services: The Organized Recreation and Park System* (Englewood Cliffs, N.J.: Prentice-Hall, 1975).

Smigel, Erwin O., ed., *Work and Leisure: A Contemporary Social Problem* (New Haven: College and University Press, 1963).

Stein, Thomas A., and Sessoms, H. Douglas, *Recreation and Special Populations* (Boston: Holbrook, 1977).

Weiskopf, Donald, *A Guide to Recreation and Leisure* (Boston: Allyn and Bacon, 1975).

OTHER REPORTS AND SPECIAL PUBLICATIONS

Anderson, Nancy, *Senior Centers: Information from a National Survey* (Minneapolis: American Rehabilitation Foundation, June, 1969).

Berryman, Doris L.; Logan, Annette; and Lander, Dorothy, *Enhancement of Recreation Service to Disabled Children* (New York: New York University, Report of Children's Bureau Project, 1971).

Burton, Thomas L., and Kyllo, Leo T., *"Federal-Provincial Responsibilities for Leisure Services in Alberta and Ontario,"* (Report funded by provincial governments of Alberta and Ontario, 1974).

Dunn, Diana R., *Open Space and Recreation Opportunity in America's Inner Cities* (Washington, D.C.: U. S. Department of Housing and Urban Development, July 1974).

Dunn, Diana R., *Modernizing Urban Park and Recreation Systems* (Arlington, Va.: National Recreation and Park Association, 1972).

Employee Physical Fitness in Canada (Ottawa: Proceedings of National Conference on Employee Physical Fitness, Ministry of National Health and Welfare, 1975).

Jarrell, Temple R., *Directory of National Organizations Related to Recreation, Parks and Leisure* (Arlington, Va.: National Recreation and Park Association, 1974).

Kraus, Richard, *Urban Parks and Recreation: Challenge of the 1970's* (New York: Community Council of Greater New York, 1972).

National Academy of Sciences, *A Program for Outdoor Recreation Research* (Washington, D.C.: Bureau of Outdoor Recreation, 1969).

Ontario Recreation Survey: Tourism and Outdoor Recreation Planning Study (Toronto: Ministry of Resources Development, 1973).

Outdoor Recreation: A Legacy for America (Washington, D.C.: Bureau of Outdoor Recreation, 1973).

Proceedings of the Outdoor Recreation Research Needs Workshop, Harpers Ferry, West Virginia, September, 1974 (Washington, D.C.: Bureau of Outdoor Recreation, 1974).

The Recreation Imperative: A Nationwide Outdoor Recreation Plan (Washington, D.C.: Senate Committee on Interior and Insular Affairs, Senator Henry Jackson, Chairman, June, 1974).

Stein, Thomas A., *SPRE Report on the State of Recreation and Park Education in Canada and the United States* (Arlington, Va.: Society of Park and Recreation Educators, 1975).

Theobald, William F., *The Female in Public Recreation: A Study of Participation and Administrative Attitudes* (Waterloo, Ontario: Waterloo Research Institute and Ontario Ministry of Culture and Recreation, 1976).

Urban Recreation: Report Prepared for Nationwide Outdoor Recreation Plan (Washington, D.C.: Department of Housing and Urban Development, 1974).

BIBLIOGRAPHY

van der Smissen, Betty, ed., *Recreation Research: Collected Papers from National Conference on Recreation Research* (Washington, D.C.: American Association for Health, Physical Education, and Recreation and National Recreation and Park Association, 1966).

van der Smissen, Betty, ed., *Indicators of Change in the Recreation Environment—A National Research Symposium* (State College, Pa.: Penn State HPER Series, 1975).

Van Doren, Carlton S., and Hodges, Louis, *America's Park and Recreation Heritage: A Chronology* (Washington, D.C.: Bureau of Outdoor Recreation, 1975).

Verhoven, Peter J., and Vinton, Dennis A., *Career Education for Leisure Occupations, Curriculum Guidelines for Recreation, Hospitality, and Tourism* (Lexington, Ky.: University of Kentucky and U. S. Dept. of Health, Education and Welfare, 1972).

Picture Credits

Plate 1

All pictures from Robert Gardner and Karl G. Heider, *Gardens of War* (Random House, New York), and used courtesy of Film Study Center, Harvard University. They also appear in the film *Dead Birds* available from Image Resources, Inc., New York. Photographs: boys playing "spear the hoop," Samuel Putnam; battle scene, Karl G. Heider; warriors dancing, Michael C. Rockefeller.

Plate 2

Maya, the Ball Player, c. 750 A.D., from Irene Nicholson, *Mexico and Central American Mythology* (Hamlyn, England). Photograph: Eugene Kusch. King Shamba from Geoffrey Parrinder, *African Mythology* (Hamlyn, England), courtesy of the Trustees of the British Museum. Kalapalo Indian wrestlers, Stan Wayman, *Life* Magazine, © Time Inc.

Plate 3

Polo Game, School of Bokhara, Persia, c. 1522 A.D., Hewitt Fund Collection, Metropolitan Museum of Art. Achilles and Ajax, detail of vase by Exekias, c. 550 B.C., Vatican Museum, from Gisela M.A. Richter, *Greek Art: A Handbook* (Phaidon Press, London). Wall painting, Tutankhamen Hunting Lions, c. 1357 B.C., Cairo Museum.

Plate 4

Jousting scene from 15th Century miniature in Bibliotheque Royale, Brussels. Frank Scherschel, *Life* Magazine, © Time Inc. King and Queen's Bath at Bath, by Thomas Johnson, 1672, courtesy of the Trustees of the British Museum. Peasant Dance, by Pieter Breughel, c. 1567, Kunsthistorische Museum, Vienna.

Plate 5

Plan of the Parc de Monceau, executed in 1718 by Carmontelle for the Duc d'Orleans. Walk upon the ramparts of Paris, rendering, after St. Aubin. Fireworks on the Pont-Neuf, old print, Paris, 1745.

Plate 6

The Columbia College Regatta, from *Harper's Weekly,* June 1, 1878. Artist: W.P. Snyder. Skating in Central Park, from *Harper's Weekly,* Feb. 24, 1877. Artists: Schell and Hogan. A Ten-Strike, from *Harper's Weekly,* Aug. 28, 1869. Artist: C.G. Bush.

Plate 7

Formal college prom, in 1950's. Photograph: Francis Miller, *Life* Magazine, © Time Inc. Beer bust in singles apartment in California. Photograph: Arthur Schatz, *Life* Magazine, © Time Inc. Youths cool off in mud at rock concert. Photograph: John Robaton.

Plate 8

Teenagers take joyride. No hands on wheel. Photograph: Ralph Crane, *Life* Magazine, © Time Inc. Crowding into a Volkswagen. Photograph: Bill Bridges, *Life* Magazine, © Time Inc. Bed pushing contest. Photograph: Bill Bridges, *Life* Magazine, © Time Inc.

Plate 9

Civic Opera House and Seattle Sports Arena, courtesy Seattle Visitors Bureau. Rugby playfield on Hackney Marsh, copyrighted Associated Newspapers Limited, London.

Plate 10

Simulated environments: leisure pool. Courtesy Oasis Leisure Centre, Swindon, England; Gillinson Barnett & Partners. Old Bethpage village restoration, and the *Bicentennial Belle,* courtesy Nassau County Department of Parks and Recreation.

Plate 11

National bridge tournament, *The Washington Post*. Hula-hoop contest. Photograph: Ralph Morse, *Life* Magazine, © Time Inc. Motorcycle racing. Photograph: Bill Eppridge, *Life* Magazine, © Time Inc.

Plate 12

Swimming pool, courtesy of *Parks and Recreation Magazine.* Photograph: Levittown Public Recreation Association, N.Y. Water skiing on Guntersville Lake and camping on Land Between the Lakes, courtesy of Tennessee Valley Authority.

Plate 13

Street marked with games, *New York Times*. Photograph: Jack Manning, Children playing in gutter, courtesy of *Parks and Recreation Magazine.* Men playing cards, *New York Times*. Photograph: G. Gerald Frazer.

Plate 14

Wheelchair basketball at Quonset Naval Air Station, U.S. Navy photograph by Frazier. Nature trail for blind at National Arboretum, U.S. Dept. of Agriculture photograph by Rana. Party for handicapped children, from Aurora, Ill., Playground Department, courtesy of *Recreation* Magazine. Photograph: Spring Studio.

Plate 15

High risk activities—mountain climbing, Bureau of Outdoor Recreation. Surfing off Florida coast, Florida News Bureau, Department of Commerce. Snow skiing, Mt. Hood National Forest, U.S. Forest Service.

Plate 16

Art exhibit in penitentiary, Kerby C. Smith/Lu News Service. Older man doing wood sculpture, *Parks and Recreation Magazine.* Folk dancing fun for young and old, Country Dance and Song Society.

INDEX